CONFLICT ANALYSIS AND PRACTICAL CONFLICT MANAGEMENT PROCEDURES

The Peace Science Studies Series
edited by Walter Isard

CONFLICT ANALYSIS AND PRACTICAL CONFLICT MANAGEMENT PROCEDURES
An Introduction to Peace Science

WALTER ISARD
and
CHRISTINE SMITH

Fields of Peace Science, Regional Science
and Economics
Cornell University

BALLINGER PUBLISHING COMPANY
Cambridge, Massachusetts
A Subsidiary of Harper & Row, Publishers, Inc.

International Standard Book Number: 0-88410-899-6

Library of Congress Catalog Card Number: 82-11626

Printed in the United States of America

Library of Congress Cataloging in Publication Data

Isard, Walter.
  Conflict analysis and practical conflict management procedures.

  Includes bibliographical references and index.
  1. Peace—Research. I. Smith, Christine, 1956- II. Title.
JX1904.5.I8   1982   327.1'7   82-11626
ISBN 0-88410-899-6

CONTENTS

        Conceptual Framework   490

        14.2.1   Begin with a Basic Production
                  Subsystem with Simple Conflict among
                  Two Participants over the Joint Action   490
        14.2.2   Add on the Decisionmaking Subsystem.
                  Identify each Nation (Community) in a
                  System as a Production Subsystem Plus
                  a Decisionmaking Subsystem   493
        14.2.3   Add the Information Subsystem,
                  Information Flows, and their Perception   495
        14.2.4   Next, Make Explicit the Subsystem
                  Coupling Function *Regarding Real
                  Interactions*, and System Filtering of
                  Information   496
        14.2.5   Finally, Introduce the Subsystem
                  Coupling Function *Regarding Cognitive
                  Interaction* and View the Framework as
                  a Historic Process in Macrotime   498

14.3   The Detail of the P^K Box, the Production
        Subsystem of K   500

        14.3.1   Production Models: Economic and
                  Ecologic Inputs and Outputs   500
        14.3.2   Industry Location, Development,
                  Programming, and Policy   503
        14.3.3   Noneconomic Commodities: Production
                  and Exchange   504
        14.3.4   A General Equilibrium Framework   505
        14.3.5   Macromodels of Social Group
                  Production and Behavior   509
        14.3.6   Emergence of Leaders   509
        14.3.7   The Hierarchical Structure of Regional
                  Production within the National System   510

14.4   The Detail of the R Box, the Real Interaction
        Subsystem   511

        14.4.1   Different Kinds of Interface Inputs   511
        14.4.2   Econometric (LINK), Input-Output,
                  Central Place Theory, and Linear
                  Programming Methods of Analysis   513

LIST OF FIGURES

LIST OF TABLES

PREFACE

A turn-on of a signal; and the result was 70,000 dead, another 70,000 mangled and maimed, with Hiroshima smoking and covered with debris.

This unprecedented act of horror and destruction imposed by one civilized society upon another was not a simple act. It was exceedingly complex—as complex as any taken by man up to August 6, 1945. Its roots go far back into history, even, some may say, before the advent of man. Its augur for the future was ominous, and today, less than half a century later, we have destructive capability that dwarfs that of August 6, 1945.

It would be presumptous to attempt to date the first conflict of man with man, but a very early conflict must have been over the share of prey that two or more prehistoric men cooperatively killed— a type of conflict still prevalent today; witness the bitter conflict of nations over shares of the God-given ocean resources. To this early type of conflict, history has seen the addition of many more types. Territorial conflict between one pair-bonded male and female and another must have evolved early. Then conflict pitting one kin group against another, one clan against another, one tribe against another must have arisen. Today we see all sorts of conflict involving interest groups, communities, institutions, organizations, regions, nations, and individuals of all imaginable characteristics. Moreover, conflict ranges from the very simple to the mind-bogglingly complex, the Middle East conflict being a prominent case of the latter. One thing is certain: the complexity of the most complex will increase with the more intricately interconnected complex of technology, communication, organizational structures, and motivated behavior.

Against the background of all this complexity, one might wonder why we attempt this book, as the impact from the ruminations of two minds can be at most infinitesimal. We would make this rejoinder: while the specific contributions of these two minds have been infinitesimal, the contribution of the book lies in our having compiled from the careful analysis of a multitude of concerned thinkers, the wisdom accumulated over time from before the days of Solomon to the present. In our little way, we have tried to record this wisdom in a manner that makes it more quickly and easily accessible to potential users—users who may be involved in a small conflict (say over sharing the use of a computer) or an infinitely more significant conflict (say over appropriate arms control policy). Also, we attempt to make a comprehensive and systematic survey and analysis of conflict management procedures, to stimulate their further development by both scholars and practitioners, and to make them more commensurate with the size of the problem in its various configurations. In doing so, however, we have deliberately not covered the most sophisticated of approaches at one extreme (because they are not practical for general use) or some obvious or trivial rules of thumb at the other.

In considering the phenomena of conflict in this book, we do not take the "utopian" position that all conflict can be completely resolved and should be eliminated. Rather, we take the view that conflict is part of the competition process that is basic to the survival and successful evolution of the species *homo sapiens* and to his search for new and better ways to cope with limited resources and stress from environmental change. Conflict in a sense will and must always be with us. On the other hand, we insist that conflict and competition of the intense order now existing among the two major powers in the world—a competition that threatens the extinction of our species—is not in any way essential or necessary.

But let us make some cautionary remarks. In one sense, it may be said that there is no one who is not involved in some way with a conflict that is perceived by him to be major. But that in itself does not mean that he should expect to find a directly usable conflict management procedure in this book. If he has little or no knowledge about the conflict situation within which he is involved, he certainly will not know how to select from among the conflict management procedures one of potential use. However, he may find it useful to read parts of the book, especially Chapter 9, to identify characteristics of that conflict situation about which he should become informed.

For the individual who does have considerable knowledge about the particular conflict situation in which he is involved, we must warn him of dangers in the unqualified use of conflict management procedures discussed in this book. While we have tried to present as comprehensively and systematically as possible the diverse approaches, techniques, and methods of conflict management that have evolved over the centuries in different disciplines, we do not wish to imply that these procedures are able to handle all aspects of conflicts of the real world. Bluntly speaking, we know relatively little about the interplay of the numerous forces that give rise to conflict and resist management and resolution. For example, we are all keenly aware of the factor *personality* and the major role it plays in both conflict generation and management. But why do personalities of certain types arise? How are they related to culture? Exactly how does one type of personality mesh with different types in bargaining and negotiation? These are just a few of many important questions that relate to the personality factor, and they are questions for which we have most inadequate answers. Ideally, conflict management procedures should be tailored to the set of personalities directly and indirectly involved in a conflict. Actually, we are able to do so only to a minor extent. We sorely need more research in this area and many others, such as macroanalysis of social systems, coalition analysis, individual and group learning processes, and the dynamics of social conflicts. A discussion of future research needed in these and other areas is contained in Chapters 13 through 15.

With all the above and other inadequacies in mind, different readers may find it desirable to read the materials of this book in different ways. The busy administrator, mediator, or other third party confronting an actual conflict situation should read Chapter 2 first. This chapter is specifically designed for his use. If he finds it useful, he should then proceed to read Chapter 12 and then those pages of the book that develop the specific conflict management procedures listed in Chapter 12 as relevant for his conflict situation.

The serious student and scholar, on the other hand, need not go through Chapter 2. However, it is such easy reading that he may wish to cover it to obtain an appreciation of the needs of a busy administrator or mediator. He may find in it and Chapter 12 motivation for intensive research. The material that is directly relevant for him begins with Chapter 3 and proceeds in order through the book. In general, he should also read the appendixes to each chapter to obtain deeper understanding of the shortcomings of different approaches and a clearer picture of needed research directions. We hope that this book will serve to spark his development of innovative ideas, tools, and techniques—ranging anywhere from abstract mathematical game theory to practical procedures for immediate use.

This book is also designed to be used as a textbook for graduate and advanced undergraduate courses in political science, international relations, labor relations, operations research, sociology, law, city and regional planning, and economics. For such use, the chapters may be read in order.

Finally, there may be laymen interested in the state of the art, or busy administrators, mediators, or other third parties who might take this book along for vacation or other leisurely reading. While they should read the chapters in order, they should avoid the appendixes, where they may get bogged down by technical materials not relevant for today's use. They also might find interesting Chapters 14 and 15, which point out needed visionary-type research for the long run.

This book does not present a balanced coverage of the field of Peace Science and its needs for development. Hence, it is not a true "Introduction to Peace Science," as indicated in the title. Rather, it is an introduction to a restricted but critically important part of the field of immediate practical application. In Chapters 14 and 15 we indicate a number of other critical parts of the field that require development and make an attempt at a broad definition of it. In an attempt to chip away at this development, a sequel to this book is currently being written digging more deeply into (1) the memory, beliefs, perceptions, attention capabilities, aspirations, expectations and perspectives of participants in a conflict situation, (2) changes in these basic elements, particularly as they are related to the level of stress and degree of crisis, (3) the historical data base and information requirements of a social system, and (4) the relationship of information and learning to decisionmaking in the presence of diverse interest groups and to policy formulation when several conflicting and interdependent policy areas are at issue. The impatient reader may glean some insight into the contents of this volume from Isard and C. Smith (1982, 1982c), Isard and Liossatos (1978), Anselin and Isard (1979), and as yet unpublished papers by Isard presented at peace science conferences at Cincinnati, Ohio (March 1982), Binghamton, N.Y. (May 1982) and Reading, England (August 1982) and by Isard and Smith at College Park, Md. (November 1982). Other books must follow if the field is to see balanced development.

We thank the editors of *Scientific American* and *Conflict Management and Peace Science,* Harper and Row, and Roger Fisher for permission to reproduce materials appropriately cited in the text.

In the writing of this book we have had over a number of years generous support from the National Science Foundation. The Peace Studies Program of Cornell University, the University of Queensland, and the Australian government have also helped with scholarship and other financial assistance. Frank Moulaert contributed significantly to the development of the broad conceptual framework of Chapters 14 and 15; and in indirect ways these chapters draw heavily from his ideas. Over the years we have gained considerable insight from Phyllis Kaniss on hierarchical and evolutionary theory. Others who have provided helpful comments and constructive criticisms include James P. Bennett, Roger Fisher, Thomas M. Fogarty, Stephen Gale, Ralph B. Gentile, Nancy Meiners, Tony E. Smith, Leonard Starobin, and Stephen Weiss-Wik. Of course, these individuals are in no way responsible for any of the inadequacies of our analysis and statements. We are also indebted to Karen M. Westcott and Sarah L. Marcus for their cheerful perseverance in typing many drafts of the chapters, to Bruce Burton and Ralph B. Gentile for diligently constructing the index, and to Nancy Nosewicz for her careful artwork. The senior author continues to be indebted to his wife and children for their unending devotion and patience. The junior author is extremely grateful to her parents for their constant support and encouragement.

Though the difference in the age of the authors is large, there was no difference in their contribution to the development of this book. Work on it began in 1977. We have tried to cover all relevant published materials as of July 1980. Since then, we have covered relevant published materials that, as they appeared, could easily be incorporated in the framework that had been constructed.

Before bringing this preface to a close, it might be of interest to the reader to set down some information regarding the past development of the field of Peace Science. In a very real way, this field is centuries old. The scientific, objective-type study of how to achieve conflict resolution, peace, and world order has long been undertaken by motivated scholars, leaders, and others. Since the termination of World War II, and particularly since the Cold War years of the 1950s, there has been a renewed major effort in the development of the field. This effort was reinforced by the worldwide reaction to the Vietnam conflict in the 1960s. One response was the formation in August 1963 in Malmo, Sweden of the Peace Science Society (International), originally designated the Peace Research Society (International). Its first conference was held in November 1963 in Chicago. In the issue of its annual *Papers* and at its conferences it aims to apply directly to the conflict problem new mathematical and quantitative approaches developed in economics, applied mathematics, operations research, engineering, business management, regional science, government, and other social sciences.

The student uprisings in the 1960s generated by the Vietnam war led to the establishment at the University of Pennsylvania of the first Ph.D. program in Peace Science and the publication there of the *Journal of Peace Science,* recently renamed *Conflict Management and Peace Science.* Among other journals in the field are the *Journal of Conflict Resolution* and the *Journal of Peace Research.* Most recently, there have developed Ph.D. concentrations in Peace Science at Cornell University. Elsewhere, there has been a concomitant emergence of a large variety of undergraduate and graduate programs in peace studies and related areas, research centers, and publications. In addition, commencing with this book a Peace Science Studies Series is being initiated by Ballinger Publishing Company.

Walter Isard
Christine Smith
1982

1 INTRODUCTION

In this chapter we present in succinct form the contents of each subsequent chapter and the rationale for their sequence. As indicated in the Preface, Chapter 2 is developed primarily for the busy practitioner and other readers who may need a hurried introduction. There we present a nontechnical discussion of how the busy administrator, mediator, arbiter, counselor, or other third party forced to cope with or serving to manage a conflict may efficiently use the knowledge, insights, and other materials contained in this book. Specifically, we suggest a number of questions that may help him to categorize his conflict situation and thus identify relevant conflict management procedures. We also suggest a number of properties that will help him narrow these relevant conflict management procedures down to a manageable number.

We begin analysis in Chapter 3. There we first define our basic concepts: actions and joint actions, states of the environment, outcomes, preferences and utility, and level and nature of information. Then we consider the most frequent type of conflict situation, namely, that where participants can only rank outcomes (i.e. order their preference for outcomes) and where there exists, or they perceive, only a small number of options (joint actions). We develop some simple compromise procedures but also touch on the more sophisticated ones deliberated upon by leaders with sophisticated analysts behind them such as in Big Power conflicts.

Chapter 4 takes the analysis of Chapter 3 into situations less frequent but still very relevant, namely, those where participants face many options. Because there are many options, we can often represent them by continuous variables (such as the level of military expenditures) and this makes available additional new concepts. These new concepts include indifference curves, the efficiency frontier, best reply lines, improvement sets, and limited commitment sets. With the continuous action space and these new concepts, we are able to develop a whole new set of procedures that are both reasonable and practical. These also comprise simple procedures such as equidistant improvement (or concession) and split-the-difference, as well as more involved procedures for more sophisticated analysts, such as incremax and decremax procedures. Again some of the properties of these procedures, such as the veto power, will have most appeal to unsophisticated participants while others, such as limited commitment and guaranteed improvement within the efficiency set, will appeal only to more sophisticated analysts.

In a number of important although less frequent situations, participants can state outcomes of alternative options in relative terms. That is, they can say that they prefer o_a twice as much as outcome o_b and three times as much as o_c and so on. Accordingly, concepts such as percents of improvement or concession become relevant. In the first part of Chapter 5 we consider procedures for situations where parties to a conflict confront or perceive only a small number of options. In the second part, we consider procedures for those still less frequent situations where participants confront many options and where these options can be represented as varying continuously. Here we start to use some simple mathematics, which, however, is largely confined to the notes.

In Chapters 6 and 7 we make the strong assumption that the conflict situation involves parties who can assign precise values to outcomes that they can define comparably among themselves, and as a result we can carry the analysis to an even higher level of sophistication. While the contents of these chapters are the least applicable to the real world, they will often be the most interesting to the abstract analyst. But it should also be borne in mind that the probing of abstract analysts in the situations of Chapters 6 and 7 may provide new insights on conflict management procedures in general, and these may in turn suggest new conflict management procedures for the more realistic situations covered in Chapters 3 through 5. Chapter

6 takes up situations of a small number of options while Chapter 7 takes up those of many options (that is where joint actions vary continuously). These two chapters also attack the distribution problem that is only implicitly treated in the preceding chapters. Specifically, they consider the use of weights, constraints, and changes in the objective function, singly and in combination, to achieve a more equitable distribution. They also examine different ways of dividing a pie of fixed size.

Chapter 8 shifts the focus. There has recently been developing a voluminous literature pertaining to the analysis of the different conflicting objectives that a single decisionmaking unit may confront. In Chapter 8 we carry this analysis into a much less researched area—but one of critical importance to us—namely, that where several participants, each with a different set of objectives, need to reach agreement on a joint policy to be adopted. Here, we first examine procedures that can handle situations where achievements on objectives can be measured along a precise (cardinal) scale and made comparable through the use of weights, constraints, or both. We focus primarily on recursive interaction in a programming framework. Then we examine procedures that can handle the many important situations of reality where achievements on objectives cannot be made comparable. We do so for situations where achievements on each objective can be: (1) precisely valued, (2) relatively valued, and (3) only ranked in order of preference.

While each of the previous chapters has suggested practical and reasonable procedures for each of several types of conflict situations, none has attempted to provide a means for evaluating the relative desirability of these procedures. In line with the scientific tradition of finding a best or optimal action—in our case the suggestion of a best procedure—we develop in Chapter 9 the notion of an index of inadequacy to be constructed for each of several procedures for a given targeted conflict situation. While this attempt has not been too successful, its way of probing into the problem does provide new insights into the difficulties of matching a conflict situation with one or more appropriate procedures.

Having pushed the development of quantitative-type procedures as far as we can without immersing ourselves too deeply in unrealistic abstraction, we turn in Chapter 10 to an examination of the traditional wisdom of qualitative approaches to conflict management. There we try to summarize, through concentration upon the writings of three leading scholars, the important elements of knowledge accumulated over the years. Specifically, we bring into the discussion much of the best thinking from psychology, sociology, and international law—areas not drawn upon in previous chapters. This thinking (1) searches for and emphasizes common basic values often ignored in conflict analysis, (2) points up the fruitfulness of workshop interaction and like activity among participants to develop understanding of their own and their opponents' perceptions and to explore the political viability of proposed solutions, and (3) suggests a legal benefit-cost, nonquantitative type of accounting for evaluating alternative proposals embodying such real-world elements as offers, threats, and promises.

In Chapters 3 to 9, as already intimated, we primarily focus on quantitative approaches, in Chapter 8 even forcing a quantitative mold onto situations involving objectives and criteria that are not strictly comparable. In developing these approaches we draw heavily upon the fields of applied mathematics, economics, operations research, regional science, and related disciplines. By contrast, Chapter 10 sets down the conventional wisdom and newer thinking on qualitative approaches, drawing heavily upon the fields of sociology, anthropology, psychology, international relations, and law. Surely, these approaches should be synthesized so as to improve the state of the art regarding conflict management and resolution. This we do in Chapter 11, first conducting some synthesis for the qualitative approaches, then for the quantitative approaches, and finally for the combination of both types. While we are able to achieve some fruitful synthesis, we do not expose all that is possible or indeed desirable. Many readers may find this chapter useful as a jumping-off point for more basic research, while many practitioners may, from their experience, add new elements and come up with improved practical-type procedures.

Chapter 11 in effect completes our basic analysis. But, having in mind the needs of the practitioner who does not have time to read Chapters 3 to 11 and who has only enough time to consider the procedures relevant for the particular pressing conflict situation confronting him, we have written Chapter 12. If after reading Chapter 2 the busy practitioner considers further reading worthwhile, we suggest that he proceed to Chapter 12 and read that part of it that is relevant to him. If he finds there certain procedures pertinent for his further consideration, he can obtain from the tables in Chapter 12 the pages in the main text to which he should refer for a more detailed discussion.

In Chapter 13 we make a few concluding remarks, in particular pointing up areas of neglect and directions for further research. Chapters 14 and 15 point up long-run research directions that may interest the seasoned scholar, the graduate student emerging as a scholar, and others who would like to do unhurried reading about Peace Science as a social science field; and learn how our book on practical conflict management procedures relates to this field.

2 A PREVIEW FOR THE BUSY PRACTITIONER

In this chapter, we aim to illustrate how the busy administrator, mediator, arbiter, counselor, or other third party forced to cope with, or serving to manage a conflict may efficiently use the knowledge, insights, and other materials contained in this book. If we are to be effective, this chapter must necessarily be succinct. We explicitly avoid presenting technical refinements; therefore, the scholar concerned primarily with analysis should proceed immediately to Chapter 3.

If a third party is to be effective regarding a conflict situation, and if he is to know which tool to use, he must clearly know much about that conflict situation. In Tables 9-1 through 9-3, we have indicated a long list of characteristics of conflict situations that could possibly be relevant, and the inexperienced third party may find it useful to refer to these tables. The experienced third party knows what information he needs and will take the steps necessary to obtain it. He may have secret or nonsecret discussions with each participant; he may have preworkshop sessions with several representatives of each relevant interest group in a participant's constituency (see pp. 339-343); he may hold workshops for the participants (see pp. 332-338); he may hold brainstorming sessions (see pp. 359-361); or he may gather together a set of experts to pick their brains for key information. In any case, until the third party knows the forces —e.g., cultural or psychological—driving participants, the issues involved, and other important dimensions of the conflict, he will not be in a position to select a procedure intelligently. We therefore assume in what follows that the third party has or acquires the information that is requisite for the use of any procedure we may suggest.

In Table 12-1 on page 436 we list the many conflict management procedures that can be used singly or in combination for difficult types of conflict situations. This list is too long for effective use by a busy third party. To quickly narrow down the range of useful procedures for a particular conflict situation, we would suggest that he answer the following clear-cut questions:

1. How many actions (options, alternatives, plans, etc.) are possible—a *small* number or *many*?
2. What kinds of information do participants have concerning their preferences. Can they only *rank* possible outcomes in order of preference, or can they do more by stating preferences in *relative terms* (e.g., state that outcome o_a is preferred twice as much as outcome o_b), or can they do still more by attaching *precise numbers* that indicate the values of different outcomes (e.g., $o_a = 200$, $o_b = 100$, etc.)?
3. Are the participants concerned with *improvement* over the current state of affairs; or must they make *concessions* from stated (fixed) positions that differ, the position of each being that which he considers best?
4. Can the participants deal with procedures that relate directly to the *outcomes* participants will receive? Or will a direct focus on outcomes make it impossible for participants to reach agreement on a compromise? In the latter case it becomes necessary to use procedures that focus on *actions* and only indirectly on the resulting outcomes.

The answers to each of these questions can be set down in Table 2-1 to yield twenty-four general categories of conflict situations defined by these answers. (In Chapter 12 we indicate how the third party might proceed when he can answer three or only two of the four questions.) Column 1 of Table 2-1 records the two kinds of answers possible in response to the first question; Column 2 records the three kinds of answers possible in response to the second question; Column 3, the two kinds of answers possible to the third question; and Column 4, the two kinds of answers possible to the fourth question. Column 5

Table 2-1. General Categories of Conflict Situations.

Category	(1) Number of Options is	(2) Participants Can	(3) Participants Need to Focus On	(4) Participants Can Focus On	(5) Relevant Chapter 12 Table	(6) On Page Number
1	Small	Rank Outcomes	Improvement	Only Actions	12-2	441
2	"	"	"	Outcomes	12-3	442
3	"	"	Concession	Only Actions	12-4	443
4	"	"	"	Outcomes	12-5	444
5	"	Assign Relative Values	Improvement	Only Actions	12-6	445
6	"	"	"	Outcomes	12-7	446
7	"	"	Concession	Only Actions	12-8	447
8	"	"	"	Outcomes	12-9	448
9	"	Assign Precise Values	Improvement	Only Actions	12-10	449
10	"	"	"	Outcomes	12-11	450
11	"	"	Concession	Only Actions	12-12	452
12	"	"	"	Outcomes	12-13	453
13	Many	Rank Outcomes	Improvement	Only Actions	12-14	455
14	"	"	"	Outcomes	12-15	456
15	"	"	Concession	Only Actions	12-16	457
16	"	"	"	Outcomes	12-17	458
17	"	Assign Relative Values	Improvement	Only Actions	12-18	459
18	"	"	"	Outcomes	12-19	460
19	"	"	Concession	Only Actions	12-20	461
20	"	"	"	Outcomes	12-21	462
21	"	Assign Precise Values	Improvement	Only Actions	12-22	463
22	"	"	"	Outcomes	12-23	464
23	"	"	Concession	Only Actions	12-24	466
24	"	"	"	Outcomes	12-25	467

indicates the relevant Chapter 12 table number; and Column 6, the page on which it can be found.

To illustrate our method, suppose that with respect to a given conflict situation the answers are that a *small* number of options exist, that participants can only *rank* outcomes in order of preference, that they need to focus on *improvements,* and that they can focus on *outcomes.* These answers identify the conflict situation confronting the third party as one falling in the category defined by Row 2 in Table 2-1. The relevant Chapter 12 table, namely Table 12-3 on page 442, is reproduced as Table 2-2. That table indicates that there are twelve conflict management procedures that a third party may now wish to consider suggesting for use by participants. However, before considering any of them he may wish to employ further criteria to narrow down the number. For example, everything else being the same, he may like to avoid any procedure that may be *high cost*—i.e., procedures involving many rounds, much shuttling back and forth, and extensive data collection. Those procedures that may be high cost have an oval over their number in Table 2-2. Thus in that table, two procedures, namely (1) changing actions to "if . . . , then . . . " policies and (2) method of determining group priorities (Saaty) are eliminated. Further, the third party may perceive that the conflict over issues may become a conflict over which procedure to employ when relatively sophisticated participants can determine beforehand what the outcome of each procedure will be. One participant may prefer a given procedure because it yields him a better outcome than a second procedure, while another participant may prefer the second procedure to the first because it yields him a better outcome than the first. Hence, to avoid such conflict over which procedure to use, it may be desirable for the outcome of a procedure to be *preindeterminate*—that is, for it to be impossible to determine beforehand what the outcome will be. Procedures whose outcomes are preindeterminate have been shaded over. In Table 2-2 there are four of these, but one is high cost, leaving three. Still more, the conflict situation may be such that each participant has *little or no information about the preferences of other participants.* Therefore, if there is no possibility for participants to engage in an activity, such as a workshop, whereby they can easily become informed of each other's preferences, the third party must eliminate all procedures that require such information. Procedures that can be used when participants have little or no information about each other's preferences are outlined by a

Table 2-2. A *SMALL* Number of Options, Participants Can Only *RANK* Outcomes in Order of Preference, Participants Need to Focus on *IMPROVE-MENTS*, Participants Can Focus on *OUTCOMES.*

---

5. min total of ranks[a] (highest rank = 1), pp. 39–40 and 273–77
   (weighted or unweighted)

6. min difference in ranks, pp. 64 and 39–40
   (weighted or unweighted)

7. max total of rank improvements[a], pp. 39–40 and 275–77
   (weighted or unweighted)

9. max the min in rank improvements, pp. 64 and 39–40

11. min difference in rank improvement, pp. 39–40
    (weighted or unweighted)

12. max equal rank improvement, pp. 39–40 and 271–75
    (weighted or unweighted)

15. changing actions to "if . . . , then . . . " policies, pp. 42–48, 53–57

16. max good-cause payment, pp. 107–13 and 212–13

17. apportionment principles, pp. 114–19

20. achievement of minimum requirements (satisficing), pp. 206–07

41. last-offer arbitration (with incentive to think of others), pp. 102–06

75. method of determining group priorities (Saaty), pp. 147–55, 165–68

---

[a] Side payments may be required. See Table 12-28, on p. 472.

▓▓▓ Techniques that have preindeterminate outcomes

◻ Techniques that may be high cost

▭ Techniques that require of a participant little or no information about other participants' preferences

Other more technical and presumably less practical procedures are those in Table 12-1 numbered 98, 99, 100, 101, and 102.

rectangle. There are five of these in Table 2–2, however only two may not involve high cost and at the same time have preindeterminate outcomes. Thus these two: (1) achievement of minimum requirements (satisficing) and (2) last-offer arbitration (with incentive to think of others)[1] may be ones the third party suggests participants use.

To give a second illustration,   suppose the answers to the questions are: there exist *many* options,[2] participants can only *rank* outcomes, participants need to focus on *improvement*, and can only focus on *actions*.

These answers identify the conflict situation confronting the third party as falling in the category defined by Row 13 in Table 2-1. The relevant Chapter 12 table, namely Table 12-14 on page 455, is reproduced as Table 2-3. That table indicates that there are nine conflict management procedures a third party may now wish to consider suggesting for use. Seven of these can immediately be eliminated because they may be high cost (depicted by an oval over their number). Each of the two remaining procedures requires little or no information about other participants' preferences, but only one has a preindeterminate outcome. This procedure, namely last-offer arbitration (with incentive to think of others), may then be the one that the third party thinks about employing first. However, he should pursue further checks. He may wish to see whether or not this procedure can yield an *efficient outcome* or if, to do so, it must be constrained. He should then refer to Table 12-27, on p. 469 which lists those procedures that are not efficient or cannot be constrained to be efficient. He may also want to check whether a procedure has the desirable property of providing a mechanism capable of *building up trust*. Again, see Table 12-27. In the case of the one procedure that was not eliminated from Table 2-3, the possibilities for trust building are limited. The third party may attach so much significance to this property that he is willing to forego a low-cost operation in order to achieve trust building. He should therefore reconsider all the procedures that were initially eliminated due to the likelihood of their being high cost. He might, for example, want to select for initial suggestion to participants either: (1) GRIT (reciprocated tension-reducing actions, a sequence of) or (2) minimum information incremax (involving maximizing in each of a series of steps, each of which ensures improvement for each participant). Both procedures may indeed be high cost, and the first of these requires that one participant take, or be persuaded to take, an initial unilateral action for the benefit of the other. Nonetheless, either of these may be more likely to help resolve the conflict in the mind of the third party than last-offer arbitration.

In the above manner then, the busy third party may find this book useful. If he is interested in going beyond this chapter, we suggest that he proceed directly to Chapter 12. There, the use of tables such

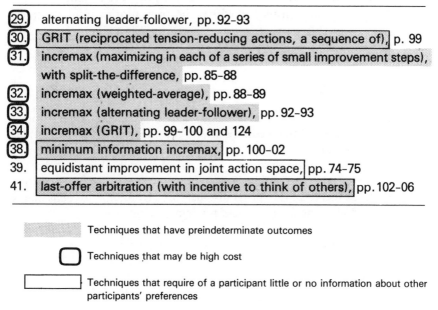

Table 2-3. *MANY* Options, Participants Can Only *RANK* Outcomes in Order of Preference, Participants Need to Focus on *IMPROVEMENTS*, Participants Can Focus Only on *ACTIONS*.

29. alternating leader-follower, pp. 92–93
30. GRIT (reciprocated tension-reducing actions, a sequence of), p. 99
31. incremax (maximizing in each of a series of small improvement steps), with split-the-difference, pp. 85–88
32. incremax (weighted-average), pp. 88–89
33. incremax (alternating leader-follower), pp. 92–93
34. incremax (GRIT), pp. 99–100 and 124
38. minimum information incremax, pp. 100–02
39. equidistant improvement in joint action space, pp. 74–75
41. last-offer arbitration (with incentive to think of others), pp. 102–06

Techniques that have preindeterminate outcomes

Techniques that may be high cost

Techniques that require of a participant little or no information about other participants' preferences

as 2–2 and 2–3 is further discussed. Finally, if he wishes to study carefully the way in which any specific conflict management procedure operates, and the assumptions that lie behind it, then he must read carefully the section of the book where that procedure is discussed. He may also need to read other sections where concepts relevant to that procedure are defined and the behavior underlying it is analyzed. These sections can be quickly identified by the use of the index.

A few cautionary statements are in order. Clearly, the specifics of a given conflict situation are as important as the characteristics it may have in common with other conflict situations in its general category. These specifics in large part must determine the choice of a conflict management procedure that a third party might propose for use (or that participants themselves may agree to use). Moreover, there are many conflict situations for which no useable procedure has been devised. There are others that change so rapidly that a procedure initially chosen for use may set in motion forces that make it inapplicable. Moreover, the scientific approach to conflict analysis, management, and resolution, and the related field of Peace Science are in their infancy. More telling concepts, tools, hypotheses, and theories must be invented and developed, and existing ones must be reformulated to be more effective. Nevertheless, there are a number of important conflict situations for which the presentation and rudimentary analysis in this book can be of considerable value.

NOTES

1. In last-offer arbitration, each participant proposes a compromise joint action and the mediator selects for adoption what he considers to be the fairest.
2. This may be so because, say, we are dealing with objectives that can be varied almost continuously—e.g., number of armed forces and tanks or social welfare programs measured by number of beds in hospitals and number of teachers for retarded children.

3 PROCEDURES FOR SITUATIONS WITH A SMALL NUMBER OF OPTIONS WHERE PARTICIPANTS CAN ONLY RANK OUTCOMES

3.1 INTRODUCTION

With this chapter we begin our analysis of conflict situations and conflict management procedures applicable to them. Our ultimate objective is to develop the set of currently available or potentially developable procedures for diverse conflict situations in an orderly and comprehensive fashion. However, before we can focus on any kind of conflict situation and relevant conflict management procedures we first must treat (as we do in Section 3.2) certain elementary concepts basic to conflict analysis, specifically: actions and joint actions, states of the environment, outcomes, preferences and utility, guiding principles, attitudes, objectives and objective functions, and the level and nature of information. In Section 3.3 we examine the first and perhaps the most frequent type of conflict situation, namely, where each participant has available or can perceive only a small (finite) number of actions (options) and can only rank outcomes in order of preference. We identify conflict management procedures, both simple and sophisticated, that we consider relevant for these situations. Other sets of conflict situations and their relevant conflict management procedures are examined in subsequent chapters.

Before we begin analysis, however, it is useful to sketch briefly two conflict situations to help us study the workings of conflict management procedures. The first conflict situation is a zero-sum war situation where no relevant property of an outcome other than control of a disputed piece of territory is relevant. What territory one nation acquires (wins) is territory that the other nation does not acquire (loses). Each is motivated to maximize the amount of territory it acquires. Variants of this situation would permit not only the division of this territory, but also compensation (in dollars) for lost territory and other relevant outcome elements.

Another conflict situation involves two participants: the developed nations and the developing ones. These two sets of nations are, for instance, in major conflict over the extent and allocation of funds to be made available by advanced industrialized countries for assisting development in developing countries. Other relevant considerations might include control by developing countries of domestic violence and unrest, transfer of technology and sales of advanced equipment, tariff levels, military expenditures, respect from the world community, power, and support in the United Nations. We shall focus many of the conflict management procedures discussed in subsequent text on this latter situation and its variants.

3.2 SOME ELEMENTARY CONCEPTS FOR SIMPLE CONFLICT SITUATIONS

3.2.1 Actions and Joint Actions

The first basic notion is that of an action a^J by the leader(s) of nation J.[1] An action may be either simple or complex. At one extreme, it may consist of a single elementary act (like pulling a trigger), which we may define for J to be any single identifiable event involving an intentional change by J of his relation to his environment. At the other extreme, an action taken at a particular point of time by J may consist of a sequence of performances and nonperformances of elementary acts that he currently perceives to be a meaningful alternative (like a decision to mobilize for war).[2] Of course, there exists a tremendous range of possible types of actions. In the analysis that follows, we shall most of the time be dealing with situations in which each participant makes a *proposal*. A proposal involves the specification of a direct action to be taken by each participant (including the participant who makes the proposal). Occasionally we shall be dealing with a situation where each participant independently selects a *direct action* from his set of possible actions (which may or may not be restricted by various constraints) without proposing the direct actions to be taken by other participants.[3]

If there are U-1 active participants (nations) other than J, then a set of simultaneous actions $(a^A, a^B, ..., a^J, ..., a^U)$, where each participant $K = A, B, ..., U$ including J selects one action a^K from his own action set, is called a *joint action a*.[4]

3.2.2 States of the Environment

Aside from the actions of participants, there are many other factors that operate to determine outcomes. We define those that are *independent* of the participants' joint actions (presumed to be beyond their control) as the *environment*. Each environmental factor (such as weather or the level of international tension when it is not affected by the actions of the participants) can occur (be realized) in many different ways. Any combination consisting of one and only one realization of each factor is designated as a state z of the environment. Obviously, many states of the environment are realizable, and it is usually posited that the outcome of a joint action a cannot be identified without knowledge of the state z of the environment.[5]

3.2.3 Outcomes

The combination of a realized state z of the environment and joint action a produces an outcome o. This outcome can be both simple and complex. However, even a simple one can consist of many different properties p which may be numbered from 1 to $\bar{p}$ (i.e., $p = 1, ..., \bar{p}$). While many of these properties may be able to be "objectively" described (such as GNP, balance of payments, number of men killed in battle, profits, number of divorces, church attendance, unrest among minorities, and votes in primary elections), each behaving unit may perceive only a limited number of them and consider only some of them relevant. Each property may range over many magnitudes, and any two behaving units J and L may perceive differently the magnitude of any given realization of a property.

Formally, the outcome o may be described by a set of realized magnitudes, $o_1, o_2, \ldots, o_{\bar{p}}$, one for each property.[6] Typically, the outcome o is taken to be a function of the joint action a and the state of the environment z realized at the time the joint action is taken. That is, it may be written

$$o = f(a,z) . \qquad (3\text{--}1)$$

However, any joint action a may take place over a sequence of points of time, during which the state of the environment may change in an unpredictable manner. Hence, whatever complete information with regard to the state of the environment may exist at the point of time the decision on an action is taken, such information does not exist during the subsequent points of time. Consequently, to the extent that an outcome is realized over a sequence of points of time, it cannot be projected with full certainty. To circumvent this difficulty, economists and others often assume that the joint action and outcome take place instantaneously at the time of decision or that, over a sequence of points of time, conditions of "statics" obtain such that nothing changes over that sequence; hence Equation (3–1) remains appropriate.

With regard to the behaving unit (say nation J) who does not perceive all the properties p of an outcome as objectively described and who may consider some of the perceived properties as irrelevant, the outcome function becomes

$$o^{J} = f^{J}(a,z) \qquad J = A, \ldots, U \qquad (3\text{--}2)$$

where o^{J} may have components less than $\bar{p}$ in number.[7]

The outcome functions represented by Equations (3–1) and (3–2) assume that the analyst or behaving unit is able to say with absolute certainty that action a in environment z will result in outcome o or o^{J}. This will not be so when chance elements are present and uncertainty obtains. Later, we will to some extent allow for these factors by associating with every pair (a,z) a set of possible outcomes, each with some nonzero probability—i.e., a probability distribution over outcomes.

3.2.4 Preferences and Utility

Given the actions of all other participants and z, the state of the environment, the outcome function (3–2) associates an outcome o^{J} with each action a^J that J may take. The unit J is now taken to be able to state preferences among the outcomes associated with all his possible actions. For our purposes, we assume that the behaving unit is able to state, for every pair of outcomes o_a and o_b, whether he prefers o_a to o_b, whether he prefers o_b to o_a, or whether he is indifferent between the two. Also, for any three outcomes o_a, o_b, and o_c, we assume that if he prefers o_a to o_b and o_b to o_c, then he prefers o_a to o_c.[8]

In considering preferences for different outcomes, it is often desirable to use numbers to represent these preferences.[9] When these numbers indicate exactly how much utility (including zero) a behaving unit derives from each outcome, then he can be said to have a cardinal preference function,[10] frequently designated a *cardinal utility function*. Often, however, if he can use numbers, they only tell him whether he prefers one outcome to another. That is, the numbers associated with outcomes indicate nothing more than a set of rankings, where the highest number is associated with the most preferred outcome. The ratios of these numbers, for example, have no meaning; nor do their absolute differences. In this case, he may be said to have an ordinal preference function,[11] often designated an *ordinal utility function*.

Between these two extremes are situations where the ratios of the numbers associated with outcomes are meaningful but the numbers themselves are not. For example, a participant may be able to say that he values (prefers) one outcome twice as much as another but that it does not matter to him whether the first outcome has a number 200 and the second 100, or the first 150 and the second 75. In this case, he may be said to have a relative preference function,[12] which we shall designate a *relative utility function*.

At this point we shall not consider other possible types of preference and utility functions.[13] We note, however, that often when the relevant properties of an outcome are all quantitatively measurable, representing achievements on objectives such as dollar profits, number of votes, and level of environmental quality, we can speak of payoff functions rather than utility functions.[14]

3.2.5 Guiding Principles

Once the outcome function is known or specified, the behaving unit in a conflict situation must consider his objectives as well as the "guiding principles" that he and other behaving units may singly or in unison use to manage their conflict. We define guiding principles as moral codes, religious scruples, cultural practices, procedural rules, standards of fairness, rules-of-thumb, or any other norms or standards of conduct adopted by behaving units to reach acceptable solutions or steps toward solutions to conflict. At times, the behaving unit in a conflict may first consider his objective (for example, to minimize expected costs) and then guiding principles. At other times, he may first consider the specific guiding principle that will govern the situation (for example, a split-the-difference principle) and then his objective.

The use of a guiding principle implies that the behaving unit relates his actions (conduct) to that of other behaving units. Often (as suggested above) such use is associated with an expectation by the behaving unit that other participants are also aware of the relationship among the actions of participants and are motivated to adopt the same or some reasonably similar guiding principle. If this expectation is not realized, then a new conflict may arise concerning the choice of a guiding principle to be employed, and this conflict may then motivate participants to seek another standard to manage their problem. Frequently in reality, such standards cannot be found and, consequently, no steps can be taken toward resolution of the initial conflict.

When a common guiding principle is adopted, its role is to constrain the set of possible outcomes (and underlying joint actions) to a fewer number of elements. (For example, since the joint action of the United States and the Soviet Union to engage in all-out nuclear war would allow no participant to survive—at least in the light of accepted objective information—the guiding principle of survival excludes such a joint action from consideration.) By reducing this set of outcomes, the range of conflict over joint actions is reduced and the probability of agreeing on steps toward its resolution will tend to be increased.[15]

3.2.6 Attitudes, Objectives, and Objective Functions

If for each action a behaving unit takes the outcome is unique—that is, is independent of whatever actions other participants may take or of the state of environment that may be realized—then the choice of an action by the unit is automatically implied. He chooses the action that yields the most preferred outcome.[16] Conflicts by definition lie beyond this type of simple situation. The behaving unit, say nation J, may not know what state of the environment will be realized or what the actions of at least some other behaving units are or will be. The unit J *does* make decisions when confronted with these uncertainties; these decisions depend on his *motivations* and *attitudes* toward such uncertainties. These motivations and attitudes lie behind what we shall call *objectives.*

Within the framework of any guiding principles that may be adopted, the objectives of the behaving unit are the "driving mechanism" that directs his behavior. They embody the concept of the "optimal state of affairs" he considers attainable, and they define the nature of his optimizing behavior, which usually takes one of the following forms:

1. to maximize the level of some index reflecting the desirable properties of different sets of possible outcomes; or
2. to minimize the level of some index reflecting the undesirable properties of different sets of possible outcomes.

By focusing on a single index of different sets of possible outcomes, the behaving unit's objectives effectively "reduce" or "transform" these sets into readily comparable simple elements.

To illustrate, we consider a "once-for-all" decision situation—that is, a situation where each behaving unit (say nations J and L) makes one and only one decision and where there is no possibility for reconsideration and reaction. Let the conflict be over a piece of territory. Let it be a simple win-or-lose situation with no relevant properties except the amount of territory won or lost.

Let the payoff matrix be two by three as in Table 3-1. Nation J perceives two possible actions: (a) conduct a sudden all-out attack and (b) conduct a cautious staged attack. The actions of nation L are ($\propto$) set a trap for an all-out attack by opponent and (β) conduct a cautious staged attack. Recognizing that the weather is unpredictable, nation J distinguishes between the possibility of a (β) action by nation L under conditions of both bad weather (β_1) and good weather (β_2). A set of outcomes that J may perceive for each of the six relevant combinations of a joint action and weather is given in Table 3-1.

Table 3-1. A Payoff Matrix of Territorial Gains: J's Perception.

J's Actions	L's Actions	Set a Trap For All-Out Attack (α)	Cautious Staged Attack	
			Bad Weather Conditions (β_1)	Good Weather Conditions (β_2)
All-Out Attack (a)		0 , 1	0.6 , 0.4	1 , 0
Cautious Staged Attack (b)		0.8 , 0.2	0.3 , 0.7	0.5 , 0.5

The first element in each cell refers to the fractional share of the territory that nation J wins, the second to what nation L wins. If nation L sets a trap and J chooses to conduct an all-out attack, J perceives that he will lose the entire territory. On the other hand, if L chooses to conduct a cautious staged attack and good weather prevails, J anticipates that by adopting an all-out attack he will score a complete victory (and gain all the territory). However, J recognizes that if bad weather prevails the impact of his all-out attack would be reduced and consequently he would be able to gain only six-tenths of the territory. In addition, J considers possible outcomes when he conducts a cautious staged attack. If L were also to conduct such an attack, J estimates that he would gain half the territory if good weather prevails but only three-tenths under conditions of bad weather. That is, he considers both nations to have equal capabilities under good weather conditions but recognizes that nation L has superior bad weather capabilities. Finally, if L were to set a trap, J estimates that he could acquire eight-tenths of the territory.

At this point we shall not consider L's perception of the problem or the issue of solutions to the conflict. We merely wish to illustrate different attitudes and associated objectives that a participant might have. We concentrate on nation J, who has options (a) and (b).

Suppose J has the attitude of an extreme optimist or a religious fanatic motivated to conquer the territory to spread the holy doctrine. He is 100 percent certain that nature or God is working for him. Hence, he looks at the payoffs he associates with each of his actions and identifies the best possible (max) payoff as the sure value to be associated with that action. For actions (a) and (b), they are 1.0 and 0.8, respectively. He then compares these max values and chooses that action—namely (a), the all-out attack—with the highest max value. This is a max-max strategy.

At the other extreme, J might be an extreme pessimist, 100 percent certain that nature or the devil is out to get him. Hence, he looks at the payoffs he associates with each of his actions and identifies the worst possible (min) payoff as the sure value to be associated with that action. For actions (a) and (b) they are 0.0 and 0.3, respectively. He then compares these min values and chooses that action—namely (b), the cautious staged attack—with the highest min value. This is a max-min strategy.

J might have yet another attitude—that of the extreme conservative motivated to consider sure things only. Again he considers the worst payoff that can be associated with each action. He then values each action accordingly and chooses that action, (b), associated with the maximum of these worst payoffs—again a max-min strategy.

All the above attitudes are extreme. Take a realistic one that is not: J identifies the best and worst possible outcomes that could result from the adoption of any action and weights the payoffs associated with these outcomes equally to get the value for that given action. Thus, in our example, he values action (a) at $1/2(0) + 1/2(1) = 0.5$ and (b) at $1/2(.8) + 1/2(.3) = 0.55$. He then compares these values for all possible actions and chooses (b) the action yielding him the maximum value.

Finally, let us consider the expected-payoff calculator. He attaches a probability to each of the three perceived payoffs associated with any of his actions (in accord with his attitude as to the possible realization of these payoffs), say .5, .3, and .2 for the conditions designated (α), (β_1), and (β_2), respectively, in Table 3–1. The expected payoffs for his actions (a) and (b) are then $.5(0) + .3(.6) + .2(1) = .38$ and $.5(.8) + .3(.3) + .2(.5) = .59$, respectively. He then compares these values and chooses that action, (b), which maximizes his expected payoff.

There are many other possible attitudes that can be considered.[17] However, in each case, the behaving unit either implicitly or explicitly employs an objective function that assigns weights to each outcome in the set of possible outcomes perceived to result from an action. Summing weighted outcomes yields the value (or an index level of the value) of the action. The behaving unit is then interested in choosing the action that has the optimal value given his attitude. By summing the weighted outcomes (payoffs), we have employed a linear objective function in each case dealt with so far. In later cases, we will consider the use of nonlinear objective functions. In all cases, the attitude of the party will be involved as an extremely important decisionmaking variable.

3.2.7 Level and Nature of Information

In the diverse conflict management procedures to be examined, the information variable plays a key role. Frequently this variable is not treated explicitly because of its subjective nature as well as the many possible different states of information that can obtain. For example, in Isard, T. Smith, *et al.* (1969:188–99) there is the definition of a statement of knowledge, the distinction between objective and subjective knowledge, the consideration of the degree of belief associated with any piece of knowledge, the distinction between being fully informed of a piece of knowledge and being positive of that knowledge, the distinction between knowing a relationship and assuming it, the distinction between certain, probabilistic, and uncertain knowledge of the state of the environment and outcomes, and recognition of the need to specify the different amounts and kinds of knowledge that participants have regarding other participants' preferences and perceptions.

All these elements are important for specifying the state of information characterizing a conflict situation. So also is the possession of knowledge by each participant, say J, of the knowledge that each other participant, say L, possesses concerning others, A, . . . , L − 1, L + 1, . . . , U. As J is included in this latter set, J's knowledge of L is dependent upon L's knowledge of J, which in turn is dependent upon J's knowledge of L, and so on ad infinitum. Moreover, knowledge of other participants' preferences, perceptions, psychological propensities (hang-ups, etc.), and actions, as well as states of the environment, may range continuously between "full knowledge" and "no knowledge."

Understandably, it has been difficult for analysts to specify the state of information that may exist for any general category of conflict situation. We too will be unable to do so. However, we will attempt to specify wherever possible key elements of the information state that are required for the use of a conflict management procedure.

3.3 ANALYSIS OF RELEVANT CONFLICT MANAGEMENT PROCEDURES[18]

The first set of cases we examine are those where each of two participants has only a small (finite) number of possible actions and can only order preferences over outcomes. To handle these cases we construct a payoff matrix for two participants, each having five possible actions. See Table 3-2. One of the two participants is the leader of a group of developed (industrialized) nations. The second is a leader of a group of nations in the process of development, which we will call developing nations. The actions of the developed nations' leader relate to the type of development programs that he (acting for the developed nations) will fund and otherwise support for the benefit of the developing nations. These programs are:

1. *No Program.*
2. *Food.* This program covers the supply and distribution of food to the needy in the developing nations at zero or low cost to the developing nations.[19]
3. *Agricultural Development and Food.* This program incorporates the elements of program (2), but in addition covers (a) the supply of agricultural equipment to the developing nations and (b) provision of know-how and training programs regarding the use of such equipment.
4. *Industrial and Agricultural Development and Food.* This program incorporates the elements of program (3), but in addition covers (a) the supply of capital for plant construction and equipment purchase by enterprises having a sound economic base in the developing nations and (b) the provision of know-how and training programs for those to be employed in these enterprises.
5. *Infrastructure, Industrial and Agricultural Development, and Food.* This program incorporates the elements of program (4), but in addition covers (a) the supply of capital for constructing and equipping infrastructure facilities in the developing nations and (b) provision of know-how and training programs for personnel to operate these facilities.

To aid exposition, we shall designate these five programs and their corresponding symbols as: No Program (NP), Food (F), Agricultural Development (AG), Industrial Development (IND), and Infrastructure (INF).

Table 3-2. Joint Outcome (Utility, Action) Matrix.

a^L Level of J's Program	(1) L	(2) J	(3) L	(4) J	(5) L	(6) J	(7) L	(8) J	(9) L	(10) J
Infrastructure Development (INF)	160	40	208	50	216	60	184	70	122	80
Industrial Development (IND)	120	90	176	110	192	130	168	150	114	170
Agricultural Development (AG)	80	95	144	125	168	155	152	185	106	215
Food (F)	40	70	112	110	144	150	136	190	98	230
No Program (NP)	0	0	80	50	120	100	120	150	90	200
a^L	No Control (C_0)		Limited Control (C_1)		Moderate Control (C_2)		Extensive Control (C_3)		Full Control (C_4)	

Level of L's Control

The actions of the developing nations' leader relate to different levels of control of unrest, violence, and other destabilizing elements in the societies he represents. These levels and their corresponding symbols are:

1. *No Control* (C_0). Riots, civil war, assassinations, strikes, and demonstrations are not or cannot be controlled.
2. *Limited Control* (C_1). Riots and civil warfare can be and are controlled; strikes, demonstrations and assassinations cannot be or are not controlled.
3. *Moderate Control* (C_2). Assassinations as well as riots and civil war can be and are controlled; strikes and demonstrations cannot be or are not controlled.
4. *Extensive Control* (C_3). Strikes and all other forms of unrest except demonstrations can be and are controlled.
5. *Full Control* (C_4).

With the actions of the two participants well defined, Table 3-2 represents a payoff matrix of numbers that might depict their preferences over the perceived outcomes. While in this chapter the numbers are only required to indicate order of preference among outcomes, we shall find it useful in later chapters to let the numbers be relative and cardinal magnitudes, representing respectively the relative and precise payoffs as perceived by participants. Therefore, it is useful at this stage to provide a rationale for these numbers as absolute magnitudes—a rationale that can also pertain when these numbers are used to indicate order of preference only.

Consider first the leader of the developing nations. Were she to choose the action *no control* (C_0) and were the leader of the developed nations to choose the action *no program* (NP), then both participants would realize zero payoff. However, were the developed nations to undertake a *food program* (F), then the developing nations would perceive their own payoff to be 40. (See the first column of Table 3-2.) Moreover, were the developed nations to choose the *agricultural development program* (AG), the *industrial development program* (IND), or the *infrastructure program* (INF), the developing nations would perceive their payoffs to be 80, 120, or 160, respectively. When they undertake a program of *no control* (C_0),[20] the shift by the developed nations from any level of program to the next higher is perceived by the developing nations to yield them (the developing nations) an increase in payoff of 40. (Again, see Column 1 of Table 3-2.)

However, if the developing nations were to choose a program of *limited control* (C_1), then the economies of these nations would in general be much better off than if riots and civil warfare were permitted. Thus they perceive a payoff of 80 when the developed nations choose *no program* (NP). But, if the developed nations were to move by steps from any level of program to the next higher, the developing nations would perceive the increase in their payoff to be only 32 at each step. (See Column 3 of Table 3-2). This would be a smaller increase than if the developing nations were to have chosen *no control* (C_0), since their internal economies would be less disorganized, operating at a higher level and, hence, in less need of outside assistance.

Were the developing nations to choose an action *moderate control* (C_2), then they perceive their payoff to be 120 were the developed nations to choose *no program* (NP). This would be so since their internal economies would be operating at a still higher level than if they had chosen the action (C_1). Additional payoff of only 24 would be estimated for each step by the developed nations J from a given level of program to the next higher. (See Column 5 of Table 3-2.) Once again, the change in payoff to the developing nations L is perceived to be smaller than if they had chosen the action (C_1) since the programs of J would be adopted within the framework of a still better internal situation for L.

Were the developing nations to choose the action *extensive control* (C_3), their internal economies would be operating still more effectively, given *no program* (NP) by the developed nations. However, at this point, the developing nations would not perceive their payoff to increase. This is so because another factor becomes an increasingly important element within their payoff function, namely, the desire to be "mean" and take revenge on the developed nations for perceived "injustices" of the past. So, given the action (NP) of the developed nations, going from an action of *moderate control* (C_2), to one of *extensive control* (C_3) means that the developing nations must forego much satisfaction in "getting back" at the developed nations—in fact, so much so that it offsets the internal economic gains that developing nations obtain from exercising greater control. The payoff remains at 120. (See Column 7 of Table 3-2.) For reasons already cited, the increment of payoff to the developing nations for any step by the developed nations from any level of program to the next higher is only 16.

Finally, were the developing nations to choose the action *full control* (C_4), the gains from increase in levels of operation of their internal economies would be much more than offset by the decrease in the payoff element associated with the desire to be mean and to get back at the developed nations. The payoff that they perceive, given an (NP) action by the developed nations, is therefore 90, and the increments in the level of their payoff are reduced to 8. (See Column 9 of Table 3-2.)

While this rationale for the payoff numbers to the developing nations is subject to considerable questioning, these numbers do facilitate analysis. They are only one possible set that can be employed. The reader is free to develop his own set. By and large, the analysis will remain unaffected. We now turn to a possible rationale for the payoffs in Table 3-2 perceived by developed nations.

Were they to choose an action of *no program* (NP), and were there *no control* (C_0) in the developing nations, the developed nations would perceive their resultant payoff as 0. But given their action (NP), for every step from a given control situation to a higher control situation, the developed nations would perceive their payoff to increase by 50. They would perceive this to be so because every such step would increase the level of operation of the economies of the developing nations and thereby accessibility to them as markets.

Were the developed nations to choose the *food program* (F) and the developing nations *no control* (C_0), the payoff would be perceived by the developed nations to be 70. This would be so because the food program would help to preserve some order in the internal economies of the developing nations and perhaps bolster them somewhat, thus allowing limited markets to exist and some limited accessibility to them. Also we may imagine another type of payoff element, namely satisfaction derived from being a "big brother" or "good Christian" to the developing nations or at least to the interest groups in the developing nations with whom the developed nations side and who represent elements of law and order. Then, given the food program (F), were the developing nations to take a step from any given level of control to the next higher level, the increment in payoff that would be perceived by the developed nations would be 40. This increment is lower than that which would exist were the developed nations to have chosen the action (NP). This is so because action (F) would have allowed the potential market in the developing economies to have already grown even though the developing nations chose (C_0).

Were the developed nations to choose the program of *agricultural development* (AG) and were the developing nations to choose *no control* (C_0), the payoff perceived by the developed nations would be 95—again an increase, but not as great as the increase of 70 were the developed nations to choose the food program rather than no program given the action (C_0). One may argue that this would be so because the payoff elements associated with (1) being a big brother, (2) the growth of markets within the developing economies, and (3) having increased accessibility to these markets would, singly or in combination, be subject to diminishing returns. This diminishing returns phenomenon is assumed to set in strongly were the developed nations to consider the action *industrial development* (IND) and even more so with the adoption of the action *infrastructure development* (INF), where the payoffs would fall to 90 and 40, respectively. (See Column 2 of Table 3-2). Such falloff may be claimed to reflect exponentially increasing costs to the developed nations as they undertake higher level programs, as well as the generation of negative attitudes toward the developed nations by the developing nations because the increased aid is perceived as involving too much interference and too much indirect control by the former over the economies of the latter.[21] Note that with each of the programs *agricultural development* (AG), *industrial development* (IND), and *infrastructure* (INF), there are associated increments of payoff when the developing nations shift from any given control level to the next higher. These increments are 30, 20, and 10, respectively, and reflect the fact that the market base and accessibility to markets are subject to decreasing returns from additional increases in development assistance; there also may be diminishing returns in the exercise of brotherly love.[22,23]

We are now prepared to do analysis with this matrix. To help define our notion of conflict, consider the case where the mediator anticipates that given the payoff matrix of Table 3-2, the conflict could be irresolvable because of historical, psychological, or rigid religious beliefs. He might tell the participants: "Look here. Let's consider only sensible actions. We are currently at the (0,0) point, the (NP, C_0) joint action. The most that developed nations can consider at this stage is a program of agricultural development (AG). Higher level programs such as industrial development (IND) and infrastructure development (INF) are inconceivable. So why confuse the issue by including actions (IND) and (INF) of the developed nations in the payoff table. Exclude them and concentrate attention on the three feasible actions (NP), (F), and (AG). Also, let's be sensible with respect to actions by developing nations. Full control (C_4) is an idealist's dream, and there does not exist sufficient organization within developing nations to enable control of demonstrations (C_3). The most the developing nations can be expected to do is to control assassinations, riots, and civil warfare. So, let's concentrate on their three feasible actions: (C_0), (C_1), and (C_2). Now, put down your preferences over this realistically reduced joint action set. (Reader: Use 1 to rank your most preferred joint action; 2, your next most preferred joint action, etc. Recall that the numbers in Table 3-2 are used here simply to represent order of preference.) We obtain Table 3-3.[24] Lo and behold, each of you most prefers the same joint action, (AG,C_2). We don't have conflict after all. Let's adopt that joint action.''

The above discussion illustrates how the skillful setting of the agenda (in this case defining the set of reasonable actions) can be influential in determining the nature of the solution. However, to ensure that the agenda adopted acts to narrow down rather than highlight the extent of conflict between participants, the mediator does require knowledge of the preferences of the participants.

This simple conflict situation allows us to distinguish effectively between conflict and two levels of harmony. *Pure harmony* exists when the participants have exactly the same preferences over all joint actions. *Harmony* exists if the most preferred joint actions are the

Table 3-3. Order of Preferences over a First Set of Joint Actions.[a,b]

Level of J's Program	(1) L	(2) J	(3) L	(4) J	(5) L	(6) J
(AG)	6^+ ,	⑥	2^+ ,	③	1 ,	①
(F)	8 ,	⑦	5 ,	④	2^+ ,	②
(NP)	9 ,	⑨	6^+ ,	⑧	4 ,	⑤
a^J a^L	(C_0)		(C_1)		(C_2)	

Level of L's Control

[a]For ties regarding preferences on outcomes, we use highest possible rank with a + superscript.

[b]Circled numbers relate to preferences of developed nations; uncircled numbers relate to preferences of developing nations.

same. (In the situation just examined we have a harmony game and (AG,C_2) is the harmony joint action or point.) A *conflict* exists when there is no harmony joint action or point, that is, where there is conflict regarding the most preferred joint action. *Pure conflict* exists when, as in a win-lose, zero-sum game, whatever one acquires the other loses. This was the case in the territory war game discussed on pages 21–23.[25]

3.3.1 Compromise over Proposed Outcomes (Outcome Compromise Principle)

We now proceed to a first procedure that participants might adopt for managing (resolving) a conflict. Assume that the wise mediator in the case just cited is not able to rule out the action *extensive control* (C_3) by developing nations. They can control strikes, assassinations, riots, and civil war, but not demonstrations. Let the participants state their preferences. Then construct Table 3–4. The developing nations most prefer joint action (AG,C_2) while the developed nations most prefer (F,C_3). Hence, we have a conflict game. We do not have dollar (or equivalent) payoffs in this game, hence we cannot have side payments. To resolve the conflict the wise mediator can then point to and suggest the adoption of a joint action (AG,C_3), which yields a compromise outcome to each participant, namely, an outcome in between that which would result from her most preferred action and that which would result from the most preferred action of her opponent. When participants do take a joint action that yields a compromise outcome in a conflict situation, we shall say that they adopt an *outcome compromise principle*.

The mediator can also point out that in the above case there is only one such joint action that yields a compromise outcome to each; hence, if they follow the mediator's suggestion, they will have no further conflict. Furthermore, the wise mediator can also point out that they are better off opting for such a joint action yielding a unique compromise outcome than if they act independently, with each choosing an action corresponding to his most preferred joint action. For then the developing nations would choose (C_2) and the developed nations (F), and they would end up with outcomes that are 3^+ and 4^+ in their preference listings, respectively. (See Table 3–4.) Each would be better off if both adopt the joint action (AG,C_3) consistent with

Table 3-4. Order of Preferences over a Second Set of Joint Actions.[a]

Level of J's Program	(1) L	(2) J	(3) L	(4) J	(5) L	(6) J	(7) L	(8) J
(AG)	9^+	⑨	3^+	⑥	1	③	2	②
(F)	11	⑩	8	⑦	3^+	④⁺	5	①
(NP)	12	⑫	9^+	⑪	6^+	⑧	6^+	④⁺
	(C_0)		(C_1)		(C_2)		(C_3)	

Level of L's Control

a^L a^J

[a]For ties regarding preferences on outcomes, we use highest possible rank with a + superscript.

the compromise outcome principle; each could then achieve the outcome that is the second most preferred in his listing.

Unfortunately, as already noted, there may be several joint actions consistent with the use of this compromise outcome principle.[26] This is the case for Table 3-5, and also Table 3-6, which will be examined later. In Table 3-5, of all joint actions consistent with the compromise outcome principle, the developed nations most prefer the joint action (AG, C_3) while the developing nations most prefer (IND, C_2).[27]

3.3.2 Compromise over Proposed Actions (Action Compromise Principle)

We can move on to consider another compromise principle. Assume that the wise mediator is not able to rule out *industrial development* (IND) as a feasible action on the part of developed nations, but that he can rule out *infrastructure development* (INF). Likewise, for the developing nations he cannot rule out *extensive control* (C_3), but he can rule out *full control* (C_4). Then he may ask the participants to order their perceived preferences. A conflict appears, as seen in Table 3-5. The developed nations most prefer (F, C_3), the developing nations, (IND, C_1). To resolve the conflict the wise mediator may try to invoke the principle of a compromise over proposed joint actions. He can ask each participant to concede a step. He can ask developed nations to step up the level of their program from (F), which is in their most preferred joint action, to (AG) while requesting (demanding) from developing nations not (C_3) but only (C_2). He can ask the developing nations to step up the level of their control from (C_1), which is in their most preferred joint action, to (C_2) while requesting (demanding) from developed nations not (IND) but only (AG). The joint action (AG, C_2) is a compromise joint action. Each participant's outcome, while not the most preferred, is still better than what it would be if his opponent's most preferred action were chosen. Moreover, there is only one such compromise joint action possible, so there cannot be conflict over which compromise joint action to choose. Use of a compromise joint action to resolve a conflict may then be said to involve an *action compromise principle*. By eliciting concessions it achieves a unique harmony point.[28]

Table 3-5. Order of Preferences when Unconstrained Payoff Table is Constrained to Reasonable Actions.[a, b]

Level of J's Program	(1) L	(2) J	(3) L	(4) J	(5) L	(6) J	(7) L	(8) J
(IND)	9^+ ,	(13)	1^c ,	(9^+)	2^c ,	(7)	3^+ ,	(4^+)
(AG)	13^+ ,	(12)	6^+ ,	(8)	3^+ ,	(3)	5 ,	(2)
(F)	15 ,	(14)	12 ,	(9^+)	6^+ ,	(4^+)	8 ,	(1)
(NP)	16 ,	(16)	13^+ ,	(15)	9^+ ,	(11)	9^+ ,	(4^+)
a^J / a^L	(C_0)		(C_1)		(C_2)		(C_3)	

Level of L's Control

[a]For ties regarding preferences on outcomes, we use highest possible rank with a + superscript.

[b]Developing nations are not circled; developed nations are circled.

[c]For illustrative purposes, this table was constructed from Table 3-2 with 172 instead of 192 in the (IND, C_2) cell; hence these two rankings.

Table 3-6. Order of Preferences regarding Joint Actions.[a,b]

Level of J's Program	(1) L	(2) J	(3) L	(4) J	(5) L	(6) J	(7) L	(8) J	(9) L	(10) J
(INF)	8	(24)	2	(22^+)	1	(21)	4	(19^+)	13	(18)
(IND)	14^+	(17)	5	(13^+)	3	(11)	6^+	(8^+)	17	(6)
(AG)	22^+	(16)	10^+	(12)	6^+	(7)	9	(5)	19	(2)
(F)	24	(19^+)	18	(13^+)	10^+	(8^+)	12	(4)	20	(1)
(NP)	25	(25)	22^+	(22^+)	14^+	(15)	14^+	(8^+)	21	(3)
a^J	(C_0)		(C_1)		(C_2)		(C_3)		(C_4)	

a^L

Level of L's Control

[a] For ties regarding preferences on outcomes, we use highest possible rank with a + superscript.

[b] Developing nations are not circled; developed nations are circled.

3.3.3 A Sequence of Compromises over Proposed Outcomes/Actions (A Sequential Outcome/Action Compromise Principle)

If the full payoff matrix were considered relevant, we would have the order of preferences as listed in Table 3-6. There we are not able to define a compromise joint action involving a one-step concession by each.

In certain situations, the particulars might be such that a second try or even further tries are suggested.[29] We give three of many possible illustrations. For example, take the case of Table 3-5 when a first try at reaching a compromise solution has not worked. The mediator might say: "Let's try again. Let's not focus on the most preferred joint actions, because that does not work. Rather let's focus on each one's second most preferred joint action and see if this works." From Table 3-5 we can see that the developing nations will propose (IND,C_2) and the developed nations will propose (AG,C_3). Again, the two proposed joint actions are incompatible. However, the mediator can then suggest that they employ a compromise outcome principle. Only two joint actions are consistent with the use of this principle—(AG,C_2) and (IND,C_3). However, (AG,C_2) dominates (IND,C_3); it is more efficient, being better for developed nations and just as good for developing nations. (The concept of efficiency is rigorously defined on pages 71–72 below.) Hence the mediator may recommend that they use this principle: that is, an outcome compromise principle with reference to their second most preferred joint actions. He may also point out that they will realize the same outcome if they each narrow-mindedly choose an action consistent with attaining their second most preferred outcome.

Another case where a second try might work would occur if in Table 3-6 the payoffs in the cells at the top of the third and fifth columns were interchanged so that the most preferred joint action of the developing nations is at the top of Columns 3 and 4. After the first try fails, the mediator suggests a second try. He asks each participant to state the joint action corresponding to his second most preferred outcome. This would be (AG,C_4) for the developed and (INF,C_2) for the developing nations. These two proposals are incompatible. The mediator then suggests the use of an action compromise principle—namely, that each participant concede by one step (level). This then yields the unique joint action (IND,C_3). This joint action yields an outcome that each prefers to the outcome that would be yielded if each were to choose an action consistent with the joint action that yields him his most preferred outcome. For if such conduct were pursued, joint action (F,C_1) would be realized. (IND,C_3) is clearly preferred to (F,C_1) by each. Hence, a procedure involving an action compromise principle with reference to their second most preferred joint actions may both have appeal to participants and work. Note that the outcome (IND,C_3) is not efficient. It is weakly dominated by (AG,C_2), since (AG,C_2) yields the developed nations a more desirable outcome without yielding a less desirable outcome for the developing nations. However, it does not follow that the mediator should propose that the joint action (AG,C_2) replace joint action (IND,C_3). Such would destroy the symmetry of action concession and as a consequence would be less likely to attain agreement.

As a final case, consider the situation depicted in Table 3–13 (p. 52) to be discussed later. Here, there are many compromise outcomes with reference to the L's and J's most preferred joint actions (INF, C_2) and (AG,C_4) respectively. There are also two compromise joint actions—one, (AG,C_2), involving a two-step concession by each participant and the other, (IND,C_3), involving a one-step concession. Hence, without an additional rule like "consider concessions one step at a time and stop when a unique compromise joint action is found," there is no unique compromise joint action to serve as a solution to the conflict. A variety of other particular cases where more than one step is employed can be imagined.[30,31]

When the mediator has not been successful in inducing participants to resolve their conflict, he might also suggest the adoption of a *last-offer arbitration (incentive to think of others)* type of technique. This technique involves the choice by participants of a wise, neutral, respected party by whose judgment they are willing to abide. Such a party might be the mediator himself. His role is to select as the joint action to be put into effect the fairest or most equitable of the two proposed by the two participants. As discussed more extensively on pages 102–106, this criteria would then motivate each participant to consider the needs and demands (welfare) of the other. Such might lead each to propose the same joint action, such as (AG, C_2) in Table 3–5.

As should be implied already, the conflict depicted by a payoff matrix may not be resolvable, as a unique compromise outcome or action may not exist, or the participants may not be willing to be guided by either a compromise outcome or action principle. Further, a sequential outcome/action compromise principle may not work either. Frequently, then, the mediator or the concerned third party may suggest changing the finite action space into either a partially or wholly continuous action space as another avenue to be explored in the search for a solution. We will examine this question in the next chapter, where we treat cases of continuous action spaces and ordinal utility. But first we must examine several other possibilities.

3.3.4 Principles Focusing on Rankings of Outcomes

With Respect to Improvements from a Current Standpoint.   While some participants may be optimistic and attach a high probability to reaching their most preferred outcome, others may be more realistic. In particular, after protracted discussion and interaction in which participants come to recognize that each cannot have his most preferred joint action and that they are unable to agree on consistent concessions from their most preferred joint actions, they may agree on a change of focus. They may agree to focus on the current standpoint and then seek improvements from it.

In Table 3–4, let the present situation be (NP,C_0). After examining the joint rankings of the possible outcomes, the participants might agree on a move from (NP,C_0) to (AG,C_3). This move might be justified in one of several different ways:

1. The move (change in joint action) would correspond to equal "upping" or improvement in the ranking of joint actions by participants—a procedure using a max *equi-rank improvement principle.*[32]
2. The move would result in a joint outcome that minimizes the total of ranks—a *min total rank principle.*[33]
3. The move would correspond to a maximum total of rank improvements—a *max total rank improvements principle.*

In effect, each of these three principles is available as a basic element of reasonable compromise procedures, and the mediator may suggest their possible use in conflict situations in the general categories being discussed in this section.[34]

The three principles just mentioned may also be initially considered for breaking a deadlock at a current situation (NP,C_0) depicted by Table 3–5. Upon further examination, however, it is seen that the equi-rank improvement principle cannot be employed since there exists no possible move from (NP,C_0), ranked sixteenth by each, to another joint action having the same ranking by both participants. Hence, the mediator can only suggest that they adopt a procedure using a principle that comes closest to equal rank improvements—that is, a procedure using a *min the difference in rank improvements principle.*[35] If participants were to adopt this procedure, they would take joint action (AG,C_2) yielding outcomes with ranks 3^+ and 3 for L and J, respectively.

Use of a min the difference in rank improvements principle can also be depicted with Table 3-7, which ranks the outcomes of Table 3-13. There we see that if the current standpoint is (NP,C_0), a joint action that minimizes the difference in rank improvements is (AG,C_3) since its outcome corresponds to an improvement of 12 or almost 12 (from 22 to 10^+) in ranks for L and more or less 13 (from 17^+ to 4^+) for J. This joint action would also be consistent with the use of either a min total of ranks or a max total of rank improvements principle.

With respect to Concessions from an Ideal Point.   The use of ranks as a concept also suggests other types of approaches in conflict situations where participants feel comfortable with a focus on their best possible outcome, or simply cannot cease from making comparisons with the outcome of their most preferred joint action and seek to concede as little as possible from this outcome. In Table 3-4, the most preferred joint actions are (AG,C_2) and (F,C_3) for L and J, respectively. After examining the joint rankings of the possible outcomes, the participants would be able to see a very desirable joint action, (AG,C_3), which would involve minimal concessions—namely, a change in each one's demand for her most preferred joint action to a demand for her second most preferred joint action. This concession in demand on the part of each (which also would result from the use of an outcome compromise principle) might be justified in one of several different ways:

1. The resulting joint action (AG,C_3) would correspond to an equal concession (decrement in the ranking of joint actions) by participants—a procedure using a min *equi-rank concession principle.*[36]

2. The resulting joint action would yield a joint outcome that minimizes the total of ranks—the *min total of ranks principle* already noted above.

Table 3-7. Rankings of Outcomes from Joint Action.[a,b]

Level of J's Program	(1) L	(2) ⌣	(3) L	(4) ⌣	(5) L	(6) ⌣	(7) L	(8) ⌣	(9) L	(10) ⌣
(INF)	10^+	25	3	22	1	24	2	20^+	5	15^+
(IND)	13^+	23	7	20^+	4	17^+	6	10	10^+	4^+
(AG)	16	19	9	13^+	8	8^+	10^+	4^+	21	1
(F)	18^+	15^+	13^+	11^+	13^+	7	18^+	3	24	2
(NP)	22	17^+	17	13^+	20	11^+	23	8^+	25	6
a^J	(C_0)		(C_1)		(C_2)		(C_3)		(C_4)	

a^L

Level of L's Control

[a]For ties regarding preferences on outcomes, we use highest possible rank with a + superscript.
[b]Developing nations are not circled; developed nations are circled.

3. The resulting joint action would correspond to a minimum total of rank concessions—a procedure using a *min total of rank concessions principle.*

In effect, each of these three principles are available as basic elements of reasonable compromise procedures and the mediator may suggest their possible use to cut through the impasse resulting from incompatible demands for joint actions.[37]

The procedures just mentioned may also be considered in the case of Table 3-5. However, in the situation depicted in that table, the equi-rank concession principle cannot be employed because there exists no joint action whose adoption would involve an equal concession in ranks by participants. Hence, the mediator can only suggest that they adopt a procedure using a principle that comes closest to equal rank concessions—that is, a procedure using a *min the difference in rank concessions principle.* If participants were to adopt this procedure, they would take joint action (AG, C_2), involving concessions of 2^+ and 2 for L and J respectively.

Starting from an existing situation and concentrating on improvements or starting from an infeasible ideal point (where each person fictitiously receives his most preferred outcome) and considering concessions yields the same compromise joint action (outcomes) in the cases of Tables 3-4 and 3-5. In general, however, this will not be the case. For example, in Table 3-7, the use of a min the difference in rank concessions principle yields the compromise joint action (AG, C_2), while the use of a min the difference in rank improvements principle would result in the adoption of either (AG, C_3) or (IND, C_4)[38] were (NP, C_0) the current position.

3.3.5 Changing Actions to "If . . . , then . . . " Policies: A Principle of the Metagame Approach

A particular type of conflict situation that has claimed much attention in the literature is the Prisoner's Dilemma game. It has claimed much attention because it is prevalent in many facets of life and pertains to particularly important situations such as Big Power nations in conflict. Recently, significant progress has been achieved in handling this type of situation.

The basic elements of a Prisoner's Dilemma game can be illustrated by Table 3-8, a two by two table. There are two participants: J and L. Each participant may choose one of the two actions c and d. (c stands for cooperation; d stands for defection from cooperation.) J's actions correspond to Rows c and d. L's actions correspond to Columns c and d. The numbers in the cells of the table represent the payoffs to each participant when J chooses the action corresponding to the row of that cell, and L the action corresponding to the column of that cell. The first number in each cell is the payoff to J, while the second number is the payoff to L.

Assume that each participant is strictly self-interested and is motivated to maximize his payoff (or achieve his most preferred outcome). In such a case, given the action of the other participant, it would always be the best strategy for a given participant to choose d. For example, suppose J has chosen action c. Then L finds it better to choose d than c, for if she chooses d she gets a payoff of 10; if the choice were c, she would get a payoff of only 2. Or suppose J has chosen action d. Then L still finds it better to choose d than c, for if she chooses c her payoff is -12, whereas if she chooses d her payoff is -5. Since this payoff matrix is symmetrical, it also always pays J to choose d for any given action that L may take. Hence, in this game, each chooses d, and the equilibrium payoff to each is -5. It does not pay for either to change his or her action unilaterally.

It may also be argued that if by chance both participants had started off by choosing action c, so that their payoffs were (2,2), this outcome would not be an equilibrium outcome, for, where actions are independent and retractable and where this game is played only once, each participant would, out of pure self-interest, find it profitable to switch to action d. Thus, the joint action dd results. It is a stable equilibrium, yet undesirable. In addition to the set of specific payoffs of Table 3-8, there are innumerable other sets of payoffs that would lead to the same undesirable joint action dd. The set of

Table 3-8. A Payoff Matrix in a Prisoner's Dilemma Game.

		L's Actions	
		c	d
J's	c	2 , 2	-12, 10
Actions	d	10 , -12	-5, -5

payoffs in Table 3-9 would do so, as would any set of payoffs for which each participant's preference ordering for outcomes in the cells are such that the most preferred occurs where 4 is in this table, the least preferred occurs where 1 is, and the second most preferred and second least preferred occur where 3 and 2 are, respectively. More generally, we need not use payoff numbers for the cells of the payoff table, but only numbers to indicate the order of preferences for outcomes.[39] That is, we need information from participants requiring only that they be able to state their order of preferences for outcomes.

In this situation Howard's work (1968, 1971a) suggests an approach that a wise mediator or the participants themselves might employ. The approach involves changing the view (more formally, the structure) of the "game." In particular, Howard suggests that participants should focus on policy options rather than actions, or that the mediator ask the participants to select policies rather than actions. For example, from Table 3-8, L's two actions may be replaced by four policies:

1.   always choose c (cooperate)
2.   always choose the same action as J's (tit-for-tat)
3.   always choose the action opposite to J's (tat-for-tit)
4.   always choose d (do not cooperate, or defect)

Constructing a table to reflect L's new options, we obtain Table 3-10. Studying this table reveals, however, that the participants will either sooner or later end up in the cell at the extreme lower right with payoff (− 5, − 5) or constantly move in a cycle. For example, if they were initially at the cell corresponding to Row 1 and Column 1, L might change her policy to "choose the opposite of J,"[40] since by so doing she perceives her payoff to increase from 2 to 10. In that case

Table 3-9.   Participants' Preference Orderings for Outcomes.[a]

| | | L's Actions | |
		c	d
J's	c	3 , ③	1 , ④
Actions	d	4 , ①	2 , ②

[a] J's preferences are not circled; L's preferences are circled.

they move to the cell at Row 1, Column 3. There, J is motivated to change his action from c to d, since by so doing he perceives his loss of 12 to become a gain of 10. They reach the cell corresponding to Row 2, Column 3. At this point L is motivated to change her policy to either "choose the same action as J," or "always choose d." If she chooses the former, they move to Row 2, Column 2, where J is motivated to change his action to c and so they move to Row 1, Column 2 and then to Row 1, Column 3, then perhaps to Row 2 and Column 3, to Row 2 and Column 2, to Row 1 and Column 2, and so forth until perhaps L chooses the policy "always choose d," which moves them to Row 1 and Column 4, at which point J changes his action to d so that they finally end up at the Row 2 and Column 4, a dd joint action that is a stable equilibrium point.

Also, studying the table carefully reveals that L's policy "choose the opposite of J," while sensible if J were to choose c, is foolish and stupid if J were to choose d; it surely would encourage J to select d, leaving L with the highly undesirable payoff of -12. As a mediator, we could not suggest that L consider it as a meaningful policy option. We therefore drop it and suggest that L retain only the other three policy options.

Since we have not been able to avoid the undesirable dd outcome with payoffs of $(-5, -5)$ for the participants, we may suggest to J that he also choose from among policies rather than actions. If he were to follow a specific set of policies, we can show that there exists a stable joint policy that in effect leads the two participants to be taking the cooperative joint action cc with payoff $(2,2)$. Here J's policies, in reaction to the three policies of L, can be: (1) always choose c (this involves the response of c, c, c, respectively, to the three policies of L in the order listed at the head of the columns in Table 3-11); (2) always choose d (this involves the response of d, d, d, respectively, to the same three policies of L); and (3) always choose c except if L chooses the policy "always choose d," in which case J's response to L's three policies is c, c, d, respectively; and so forth. Thus we obtain Table 3-11. Studying this table reveals that two more stable equilibrium points have emerged. In addition to that one resulting from the joint policy d, d, d by J and "always choose d" by L, the joint policy c, c, d by J and "choose the same action as J" by L leads to a stable equilibrium point as does the joint policy d, c, d by J and "choose the same action as J" by L. Both these equilibrium points yield payoffs of $(2,2)$ to the participants, the outcome corresponding to a joint cooperative action c, c—the desired result.

Table 3-10. A Payoff Matrix, with Participant L Choosing Policies.

		L's Policies		
		Always Choose c	Choose the Same Action as J	Choose the Opposite of J	Always Choose d
J's Actions	c	2 , 2	2 , 2	-12 , 10	-12 , 10
	d	10 , -12	-5 , -5	10 , -12	-5 , -5

Table 3-11.   A Payoff Matrix Regarding Joint Policies.[a]

J's Policies	L's Policies		
	Always Choose c	Choose the Same Action as J	Always Choose d
c, c, c	2,2	2,2	−12,10
c, c, d	2,2	2,2	−5, −5
c, d, d	2,2	−5, −5	−5, −5
c, d, c	2,2	−5, −5	−12,10
d, c, c	10, −12	2,2	−12,10
d, c, d	10, −12	2,2	−5, −5
d, d, c	10, −12	−5, −5	−12,10
d, d, d	10, −12	−5, −5	−5, −5

[a] Payoffs corresponding to stable joint policies are blocked in.

In developing his ideas, Howard (1968, 1971a) uses the concept of an inescapable sanction. To understand this concept, reexamine Table 3-8. Assume the participants have chosen the cooperative joint action c,c, each obtaining payoff 2. L could defect by choosing d to obtain a more preferred outcome, namely 10, but then she potentially confronts an inescapable sanction, namely, a change of action from c to d by J, which then would result in an outcome, namely −5, less preferred to the initial outcome of 2. In this sense, J is able to impose an inescapable sanction on L to deter her from defection from the cooperative joint action c,c. What the transformation of the game based on a choice of actions (as in Table 3-8) to one based on a choice of policies (as in Table 3-11) does is to embed the inescapable sanction in the choice of a policy so that L knows that it will be applied if she defects—that is, if she were to defect from a policy choice consistent with the realization of some desirable joint action, say the cooperative joint action c,c, yielding payoff (2,2).[41] That is, an inescapable sanction has been embedded in J's policy c,c,d, or d,c,d, since either of these policies prespecifies the action d by J should L switch to the third of his policies (namely, "always choose d"). Hence, L is not motivated to change from his policy "choose the same action as J," which yields him an outcome 2, since he knows that he would surely receive −5 if he allowed himself to be tempted to the policy "always choose d."[42]

The Howard approach represents a major advance in analysis. However, it leaves unresolved the problem of how to move from the d,d in the typical Prisoner's Dilemma game to any of the stable equilibrium joint policies in Table 3-11 that yield the participants the cooperative payoff. For example, in pointing up potential applications of his approach, Howard (1968) used the U.S. - Vietnam war as an example. In one of the many possible ways to depict the key elements of this situation, he considers a game between two coalitions: the United States plus South Vietnam as one, and the National Liberation Front plus North Vietnam as another. If we were to consider the payoffs of Table 3-8 as relevant, or any other set of payoffs consistent with the preference orderings in Table 3-9, then a negotiated settlement (as Howard has described it) might be said to correspond to a joint policy c,c,d (or d,c,d) by J and "choose the same action as J" by L. The adoption of such a negotiated settlement policy leads to the realization of the joint action c,c with payoffs 2,2. But the problem is how to reach this policy when the current joint policy is d,d,d by J and "always choose d" by L, or any other that results in the joint action d,d. In later chapters we shall be discussing approaches that the mediator may suggest to participants in order to effect the desired movement.

The Howard approach is clearly applicable to situations other than two by two games. With the use of computers, he has established effective ways to examine a multitude of conflict situations defined as relevant by participants and to display relevant equilibrium joint policies. The basic idea is to translate actions into policy alternatives and then to identify all policy alternatives that are stable, leaving it up to the participants or the mediator or both to identify the more desirable of the stable joint policies and, of these, the ones that are attainable with the use of other procedures. In the appendix to this chapter we give an additional illustration to point up the rationale of the Howard approach. We also discuss a related analytic approach that yields a cooperative solution to the Prisoner's Dilemma game, namely, the Brams approach involving a rationale for nonmyopic behavior on the part of participants.

3.3.6 Multicriteria/Objective Conflict Situations

It is useful to point up the conflict problem in another way—a way in which political leaders might actually perceive it. Specifically, political leaders might view an outcome not in terms of a utility number as in Table 3-2, or in terms of a rank in a preference ordering, but in terms of a set of relevant properties—for example, dollars of aid to developing nations, dependency of developing nations on the developed, and international stability. Consider the case to which Table 3-5 relates, namely, the situation where infrastructure development (INF) and full control (C_4) are ruled out as inconceivable at the time of conflict. Examining Table 3-5, one sees that there are only five efficient joint actions. We have accordingly listed these five at the top of the columns of Table 3-12. Along the left-hand tab of this table we indicate the relevant properties. Along each row (say Row 1, which refers to property #1, namely dollar aid) we list the preferences associated with the outcome of each joint action regarding this property. Thus, the developing nations, whose rankings are indicated by uncircled numbers, most prefer $\overline{a}_1$ and $\overline{a}_2$ regarding dollar aid, and least prefer $\overline{a}_5$. In contrast, the developed nations, whose rankings are indicated by circled numbers, most prefer $\overline{a}_5$ and least prefer $\overline{a}_1$ and $\overline{a}_2$. Likewise, with regard to property i (dependency of developing nations on the developed) and most other properties, there may be differences in the preference orderings of developed and developing nations.[43]

With the information provided by Table 3-12, we are in no better position to suggest or identify a reasonable solution. However, the difficulties of doing so may be more easily appreciated. In one sense, we have a multicriteria, or multiobjective decisionmaking problem where the participants can only rank outcomes regarding each objective. Without information from participants on the relative importance of the several objectives (criteria or relevant properties) or on their valuations in cardinal numbers, we are not able to proceed further at this point. It would be meaningless, for example, to add the numbers indicating preferences. However, in Sections 8.2 and 8.3, we will suggest types of additional information that can be introduced to assist in identifying solutions.

3.3.7 Some Categories of Response Patterns

The example depicted by Table 3-2 is based on a particular type of response pattern by participants. This pattern is one in which a participant tends to respond to a change in the action of his opponent that makes him (the participant) worse off with a change in his action

Table 3-12.   Preferences by Outcome Properties for Selected Joint Actions.[a]

Properties (Criteria, Objectives)	Joint Actions				
	$\bar{a}_1$ (IND,C_1)	$\bar{a}_2$ (IND,C_2)	$\bar{a}_3$ (AG,C_2)	$\bar{a}_4$ (AG,C_3)	$\bar{a}_5$ (F,C_3)
1. $ Aid	1 , ③	1 , ③	2 , ②	2 , ②	3 , ①
i. Dependence	4 , ②	5 , ②	2 , ①	3 , ①	1 , ③
p. Stability	neg.[b] , ③	neg., ②	neg., ②	neg., ①	neg., ①

[a]Developing nations are not circled; developed nations are circled.

[b]neg. = negligible

that makes the opponent better off. This is a response consistent with appeasement or a sense of inadequate previous consideration or exercise of goodwill/brotherly love toward one's opponent. This is clear in Table 3-2 for the developed nations. Were the developing nations to decrease their level of control from (C_4) to (C_0) the change in the best response by the developed nations would involve an increase in their level of assistance from (F) to (AG). This type of response is also implied in Figure 4-6. Such a response pattern is one that is often met in reality. There are two others that also occur frequently.

The first involves a situation where each participant responds to more meanness with more meanness. This retaliatory type of response is clearly seen in Table 3-13 (and Figure 4-5). For example, if the developed nations were to change their action from (INF) to (NP)—that is, become more mean—the change in the best response by developing nations would involve a decrease in the level of control from (C_2) to (C_1)—in effect, an increase in meanness. Or if the developing nations were to change their action from (C_4) to (C_0)—that is, become more mean—the change in the best response by the developed nations would involve a decrease in the level of assistance from (AG) to (F).[44]

Another important response pattern occurs when one party reacts to a less favorable action of his opponent by a change in his best response that involves appeasement or increase in brotherly love while the opponent responds to a less favorable action by the first participant by a change in his best response that involves increase in meanness. This case often occurs where the participants are "have" and "have-not" nations, or "in-power" and "out-of-power" groups. Generally, the "haves" or those "in-power" tend to be the appeasers, while the "have-nots" and those "out-of-power" tend to retaliate meanness with meanness.[45]

3.4 CONCLUDING REMARKS

In this chapter we have begun analysis of procedures for managing conflicts including the attainment of compromise solutions. We first set down and discussed basic concepts such as actions, states of the environment, outcomes, preferences and utility, guiding principles, attitudes, objectives and objective functions, and level and nature of information. We then examined specific procedures for treating con-

Table 3–13. Another Joint Outcome (Utility, Action) Matrix.

Level of J's Program	(1) L	(2) J	(3) L	(4) J	(5) L	(6) J	(7) L	(8) J	(9) L	(10) J
(INF)	42 ,	0	54 ,	18	60 ,	16	59 ,	24	52 ,	32
(IND)	39 ,	17	49 ,	24	53 ,	30	50 ,	37	42 ,	44
(AG)	36 ,	28	44 ,	33	46 ,	39	42 ,	44	31 ,	50
(F)	33 ,	32	39 ,	36	39 ,	40	33 ,	45	21 ,	49
(NP)	30 ,	30	34 ,	33	32 ,	36	24 ,	39	10 ,	42
a^J	(C_0)		(C_1)		(C_2)		(C_3)		(C_4)	

a^L Level of L's Control

flict situations where each participant has or perceives only a few actions as available and where he can only order his preferences for outcomes. Some of the more relevant principles that underly procedures involve outcome compromise, action compromise, sequential outcome/action compromise, equi-rank improvements, equi-rank concessions, and others based on rankings. The Howard metagame approach also has significant potential.

In treating these situations, we introduced additional concepts and ideas as required, for example, the concept of response patterns and transformation of actions to "If . . . , then . . . " policies. We shall follow this procedure of introducing new concepts and ideas, as required when we treat other categories of conflict situations in subsequent chapters.[46]

APPENDIX TO CHAPTER 3

3A.1 Additional Notes on the Howard Metagame Approach

To illustrate in another way the metagame approach developed by Howard, we use one of the more complex situations he has examined. Consider his oversimplified description of the Vietnam War situation of the 1960s. There he identified four participants: United States (U.S.), North Vietnam (N.V.N.), South Vietnam (S.V.N.), and the Vietcong (N.L.F.). Among the main issues he listed are:

1. U.S. bombing in North Vietnam;
2. N.V.N. infiltration into the South;
3. S.V.N. and Vietcong acceptance of some peaceful governmental arrangement in the South (e.g., a coalition or an election);
4. U.S. withdrawal from South Vietnam;
5. N.V.N. military withdrawal from South Vietnam; and
6. Continuation of warfare in the South by the U.S., S.V.N., N.L.F., and N.V.N.

From the above list of issues, Howard derives meaningful options in the form of "yes" or "no" decisions that the participants might take. For example, the United States had the option to Bomb in the North. If it chooses this option, that is says "Yes" to it, such is designated by 1; if it chooses not to take that action, that is says "No" to the option Bomb in the North, such is designated by 0. Similarly, N.V.N. has the option to Infiltrate in the South. If it takes that option, such is designated by 1; if it chooses not to infiltrate, such is designated by 0. The main options for the participants are listed in the left-hand tab of Table 3A-1, where Fight means "continue war in South" and Settle means "be willing to accept peaceful settlement in South." To repeat, 1 indicates that the player takes the option of that row, and 0 indicates that he does not. Further, when an asterisk appears as a superscript, it means that the value of that option was implied by the Yes/No response to another option. For example, if the United States decides to withdraw, that is, set the value of 1 for the option Withdraw (the third row of the table), then it means that United States has chosen the value 0 for both Bomb and Fight as indicated by 0* for each of these options in the column headed "The Joint Action: Settlement."[47]

Now Table 3A-1 is set up to make one of four tests of the stability of the Joint Action: Settlement,[48] where the definition of stability will become evident from the discussion. This joint action is specifically defined by the set of options taken by the four participants as indicated in the middle column of the table headed "The Joint Action: Settlement." Such a joint action corresponds to both U.S. and N.V.N. choosing the option Withdraw (as indicated by 1 in the appropriate rows), to S.V.N. and N.L.F. choosing the option Settle (as indicated by 1 in the appropriate rows), and so on. Specifically, Table 3A-1 helps to answer the question: "Would it pay S.V.N. to take a unilateral action different from its action Settle (1) and do not Fight (0) in the column of The Joint Action: Settlement?" It helps by listing some of the joint actions more preferred by S.V.N. to the left of the column The Joint Action: Settlement and some of the joint actions less preferred to the right. To see how this table helps, note that the only unilateral change in joint action that S.V.N. can make to improve its outcome is for it to choose to Fight (1) and not to Settle (0). This is indicated in Column 149. Note that the joint action of Column 149 is preferred by S.V.N. to the Joint Action: Settlement since, if every other participant does not fight, S.V.N. will gain a victory, which Howard claims S.V.N would prefer to Settlement. Likewise, the joint actions corresponding to Columns 147 and 148 are, according to Howard, preferred by S.V.N. to Settlement. But does it make sense for S.V.N. to make a unilateral change in the joint action Set-

Table 3A-1. Sanctions Against a S.V.N. Unilateral Defection from a Settlement.

	Joint Actions ... Preferred by S.V.N.			The Joint Action: Settlement	Joint Actions Not Preferred by S.V.N. ...		
	147	148	149	150	151	152	153
U.S. options							
1. Bomb	... 0	0*	0*	0*	0*	0*	0*
2. Fight	... 1	0*	0*	0*	0*	0*	0*
3. Withdraw	... 0*	1	1	1	1	1	1
S.V.N. options							
4. Fight	... 1	1	1	0	0	0	1
5. Settle	... 0	0	0	1	1	1	0
N.L.F. options							
6. Fight	... 1	1	0	0	1	1	0
7. Settle	... 0	0	1	1	0	0	1
N.V.N. options							
8. Infiltrate	... 0*	0*	0*	0*	0*	1	1
9. Fight	... 0*	0*	0*	0*	0*	1	1
10. Withdraw	... 1	1	1	1	1	0*	0*

Note: When an asterisk appears as a superscript, it means that the value of that option was implied by the Yes/No response to another option.

tlement to achieve the more preferred joint action of, say, Column 149? In the metagame approach, the answer is no. For if S.V.N. unilaterally changes the joint action to be that of Column 149, N.V.N. can impose an *inescapable sanction*. That is, N.V.N. can change its action from (Withdraw (1), not to Fight (0*), and not to Infiltrate (0*)) to (Infiltrate (1), Fight (1), and not to Withdraw (0*)) so that the joint action of Column 149 no longer obtains but rather the joint action 153 does. The joint action 153 is much less preferred by S.V.N. to Settlement. If this unilateral change in N.V.N.'s action is credible as a reaction, then N.V.N. has an inescapable sanction against S.V.N.'s defection from the joint action Settlement. Hence, S.V.N. will not defect; it will abide by the joint action Settlement. As a result, Settlement is a stable joint action, according to this one test.

In similar manner, a table like 3A–1 can be drawn up for each of the other three participants. If it turns out in each case that there is a credible inescapable sanction against a unilateral change of (defection from) the joint action Settlement by each of these three participants, then that joint action may be defined as *stable* for situations in which coalitions are not possible. Further, should further analysis demonstrate that there are also credible inescapable sanctions against a unilateral change in that joint action by every possible coalition that might be formed, then that joint action meets all tests of local stability.

Note that Howard views his approach as a tool to help participants analyze their assumptions about a situation. His method does not give any guidance to participants as to what assumptions to make or how their preferences arise. Ideally, a metagame analyst stands before a task force of persons with expert knowledge of the conflict problem being considered. Ideally, these persons should be involved in the problem as the actual decisionmakers. The analyst obtains from them various assumptions about the problem. From these assumptions a game theoretic model is constructed and conclusions are deduced. The conclusions are of the form: For this outcome to be stable, such-and-such policies would have to be pursued by the different parties involved.

As Howard (1970:35) states:

The whole exercise is carried out in the mode of a discussion. It may take several days or weeks. The "experts" really build and analyze their own model, guided by the analyst. The procedure is designed to be simple to understand, so that persons with no knowledge of mathematics or game theory can participate. The end product is a report on the political situation that may be used as a guide to decision-making.

Essentially, the procedure is a refinement of the usual methods of discussing and analyzing a political situation. Much the same ground is covered as in an ordinary discussion; but the procedure enables the task force to see more different aspects of the problem while avoiding value judgments, repetition, self-contradiction and irrelevancy. The task force need not avoid these things, but at least it can do so if it wants to. This is the advantage of a more formal approach.

Continuing, Howard (1973:61) says:

We hope ultimately to store on computers all relevant judgments about a country's foreign policy. When a foreign policy decision has to be made, it would be possible instantly to call up an analysis of that policy area and its linkages to other areas. The analysis called up would be a meta-game analysis, with options in metagame form . . . so that the decision-maker could review the assumptions on which the analysis is based, and alter them if he desires by means of an interactive program. In addition to calling up the metagame tableaux that displays these assumptions, the decision-maker would be able to call up supplementary documents stating why the assumptions were made.

3A.2 POTENTIAL FOR GAIN FROM NONMYOPIC BEHAVIOR: THE BRAMS ANALYTIC APPROACH

Another approach that is analytic and aims to provide a rationale for the cooperative solution as a stable equilibrium solution to the Prisoner's Dilemma game has been developed by Brams (1977, 1980). Brams claims that in realistic Prisoner's Dilemma game situations participants are not likely to be as shortsighted as is generally assumed. Rather, they have at least some ability to recognize that (1) their opponents will react to whatever action they take and (2) several rounds of actions and reactions may occur. In effect, Brams would insist that participants' behavior is generally not myopic. It is nonmyopic in that a sequence of actions and reactions is anticipated. When this is the case, Brams would contend that in the typical Prisoner's Dilemma situation, such as that presented in Table 3–8, there are two nonmyopic equilibrium joint actions.

One is the joint action (c,c), for if the participants have sometime or other reached the joint action (c,c), each would reason as follows: "At first blush, it appears desirable for me to change my action from c to d; to do so would immediately increase my payoff from 2 to 10. But surely my opponent, who would receive an outcome of -12, would not be happy with this outcome and would change his action from c to d, thereby reducing his loss from 12 to 5. But that means that I, too, would incur a loss of 5, and any subsequent change in action on my part would increase that loss to 12. Hence, I would not consider a subsequent change in action, nor would my opponent consider a subsequent change in action, because doing so would bring his loss again to 12. Hence, we would come to rest at the (d,d) cell. My outcome would be -5 and I would be worse off than I was at our initial position (c,c) where my payoff is 2. Hence, why change from our initial position?" Given this nonmyopic reasoning, both participants will remain at (c,c) and that joint action then becomes a stable equilibrium point.[49]

Also, according to Brams, nonmyopic participants would find the (d,d) joint action to be a stable equilibrium point. If the participants are initially at the (d,d) cell each receiving -5, neither is motivated to change since to do so would make him worse off while his opponent would receive the largest possible payoff that he can realize.

Another familiar game in the literature is that of "Chicken," which takes the form shown in Table 3A-2.

The myopic equilibriums in this game are (4,2) and (2,4). To see this, suppose the players are initially at (3,3). J has incentive to change his action from c to d, thereby increasing his payoff to 4. L has an incentive to change her action from c to d, thereby increasing her payoff to 4. However, if both were to simultaneously change from c to d they would both receive their worst outcome (1,1). Whichever one of the

Table 3A-2. The "Chicken" Game.

		L's actions	
		c	d
J's actions	c	(3,3)	(2,4)
	d	(4,2)	(1,1)

participants is the more aggressive, say L, changes her action first and gets her most preferred outcome. The other, J, must then be content to accept a reduction in his payoff, for once (2,4) is reached, neither L nor J has an incentive to change her or his action. J, the less aggressive, is in effect a "chicken" since, although at the start he could have done better by changing his action from c to d, provided he changed before L did, he hesitated to do so for fear that his opponent would do the same simultaneously and that consequently they would end up at (d,d) with a payoff of $(1,1)$.

The recent development of the nonmyopic equilibrium concept by Brams promises to yield significant contributions to game theory. It has appeal in the sense that it does introduce some of the dynamics embodied in a sequence of actions and reactions. When compared to the metagame approach in this regard, it is superior. On the other hand, it does make the strong implicit assumption that the participants are fully informed, have equal capabilities and, more important, perceive themselves to be equal in bargaining ability. These assumptions are indeed strong and therefore, the potential of this approach must be qualified. See Isard and C. Smith (1982b:98–100).

NOTES

1. Formally $a^J \epsilon A^J$, where A^J is the set of actions perceived by the leader of nation J at the point of time t when he makes an action choice.
2. See Isard, T. Smith, et al. (1969:162–63) for a more extensive presentation of the notion of action.
3. We shall also consider (very infrequently) the adoption of either a straightforward policy on a single issue or a complex policy involving several issues.
4. Formally $a \epsilon A,$ where A is the set of all possible actions, that is the joint action space.

    Strictly speaking, we should use vector notation. However, in what follows it will be clear by the text whether or not a symbol represents a vector; and oftentimes a specific symbol can be used both as a scalar or vector depending upon how the reader interprets a situation. Hence, we shall refrain from the use of vector notation and, for similar reasons, from matrix notation.
5. It follows that $z \epsilon Z$, the set of all possible (realizable) states of the environment.
6. Thus the set of outcomes may be defined as a vector with $\overline{p}$ components. Formally, $o \epsilon O$ where O is the set of all possible outcomes,

each element of which is associated with a pair (a,z) where $a \in A$ and $z \in Z$. Thus, the outcome function is a mapping $f: A \times Z \to O$ which associates each pair (a,z) with an outcome o.

7. Thus, $o^J \in O^J$, the set of all possible outcomes perceived as relevant by J. Formally, the outcome function is a mapping $f^J: A \times Z \to O^J$, which associates each pair (a,z) with a relevant outcome o^J, as perceived by participant J for each participant $J = A, \ldots , U$.

8. These two assumptions correspond to "completeness" and "transitivity" respectively. Where the symbol $>$ indicates "is preferred to" and the symbol $\geq$ indicates "is either preferred or indifferent to," these assumptions can be more precisely stated as (1) for any pair o_a and o_b, either $o_a \geq o_b$ or $o_b \geq o_a$ and (2) for any three o_a, o_b and o_c, if $o_a \geq o_b$ and $o_b \geq o_c$, then $o_a \geq o_c$. However, we must bear in mind that the assumption of complete and transitive preferences is strong. Transitivity may not prevail when participants are considering various joint actions in sequence. The order in which they consider joint actions and their outcomes might well influence their preference ordering of outcomes. Also, the mediator must constantly recognize that, for many leaders, a time sequence of comparisons also involves learning and changing aspirations. For many situations we too often fail to recall the unreality of these assumptions.

9. Formally the function $r^J(o)$, which assigns a numerical representation to each o^J, is called a preference function for the behaving unit J.

10. Strictly speaking, both the origin and unit of measure are fixed in a cardinal preference function, and the behaving unit's preferences can be represented by only one such function. The function is then said to be unique up to an identity transformation.

11. Strictly speaking, in this case his preferences can be represented by any of a set of preference functions such that each function in the set represents an order-preserving (i.e., a positive monotone) transformation of any other.

12. See pp. 170-172 for a strict definition of this function.

13. See Isard, T. Smith, et al. (1969:170-185, 892-895) for further discussion of some of these other types.

14. See Isard, T. Smith, et al. (1969:183-185, 895-897) for further discussion. Formally, if we order these quantitatively measurable state properties relevant for J as $(o_1^J, o_2^J, \ldots , o_{p'}^J)$, then J's payoff function is any (real-valued) function $\pi^J(o_1^J, o_2^J, \ldots, o_{p'}^J)$ that is instrumental in the determination of his preferences among outcomes.

15. When a joint action a is reached by application of some rule (principle) to the joint actions proposed by participants, we may write $a = f (p^A, p^B, \ldots , p^U)$ where f is a rule that in one simple form, for example, may be a simple or weighted average of the proposals. The

proposal p^J by J of a joint action namely $p^J = (a^A, a^B, \ldots a^U)$ may be said to be chosen from a proposal set P^J where $p^J \epsilon P^J$, and where P^J is a subset of A and may or may not be restricted by various constraints.

16. This may be considered a simplistic notion of an objective. Also, here and in what follows, we consider the problem of breaking "ties" among two or more actions yielding outcomes "equally" preferred to be trivial and able to be solved, for example, by the toss of a coin. See also pp. 113–114.

17. Some that have been explicitly considered in Isard, T. Smith, et al. (1969), are those of the equiprobable expected-payoff calculator, the 100 percent pessimistic regretter, the 100 percent conservative regretter, the equiprobable expected-regret calculator, the simple utility maximizer, the 100 percent conservative utility maximizer, the certainty-equivalent payoff calculator, the expected payoff utility maximizer, the certainty-equivalent payoff utility maximizer, the ūlity maximizer, the rulity minimizer, the simple satisficer, the lazy-ish satisficer, and the satisficer as a constrained maximizer.

18. Unless otherwise stated, we assume for each case examined in this book that each participant assumes that only one state of the environment will materialize, that they all agree on the same single state, and in some cases where necessary, that this state is realized. We also assume that to know his preference structure in any given situation, the participant must also know the outcomes to him of each relevant action or joint action that might be taken.

19. While in a highly technical sense, one may argue that this program and the others to follow involve, within certain ranges at least, continuous actions because there can be different levels of expenditures on each, we wish to focus in this example on the qualitative jump, both in levels of expenditures and provision of know-how. Given the limited capabilities of the human mind, frequently leaders do focus on the major differences among programs, and neglect or consider as relatively unimportant the possible variation of expenditures and effort on any given program.

20. We may imagine that in reaching their perceptions of payoff the developing nations employ input-output and programming procedures in establishing employment, outputs of economic sectors, and the like. Discussion of the use of such procedures will be presented in Chapters 6 through 8.

21. Of course there can be numerous other reasons suggested to explain this falling off. For example, these higher level programs may increase significantly the ability of the developing nations to compete effectively against the developed and invade the latter's markets.

22. See Isard, T. Smith, et al. (1969:227-30) for a rationale where the payoff table is taken to refer to a family (the husband being J and the wife L) wherein there is a conflict over how to spend a vacation—whether at the mountains or seashore. Also see *ibid* pp. 278-88 for a rationale where the payoff table refers to a two-region situation wherein there are gains from cooperative action regarding industrial investment programs.

23. The payoff matrix of course has the same structure as a joint action matrix where in each cell the joint action (a_g^J, a_h^L), g = (NP), (F), (AG), (IND), (INF), and h = (C_0), (C_1), (C_2), (C_3), (C_4) replace the pair of numbers therein.

24. In doing so we face the problem of ranking ties. When any two outcomes are tied, we adopt the convention of assigning the highest of the two possible ranks with a + superscript on that rank. For example, in Table 3-3 joint actions (AG,C_1) and (F,C_2) are tied for second place in L's preference structure. We assign each a rank of $2+$, rather than a $3-$ or a 2.5.

Whenever three or more joint actions are tied for a position we follow the same convention. For example, in Table 3-5 the three joint actions (IND,C_3), (NP,C_3), and (F,C_2) are tied for fourth place in J's preference structure. We assign each a rank of 4^+. This might be thought to be an incorrect assignment of ranks since the joint actions represent at the same time the fourth, fifth, and sixth most preferred joint actions and the appropriate rank from a mathematical standpoint is 5 for each. However, we consider that most decisionmakers would not adopt the reasoning of the mathematician but rather would follow the convention we use.

25. From a classification standpoint we can of course recognize that there may be situations (for example, a set of regions each isolated from the others) in which the utility outcome to any participant is completely independent of any action except the one she takes, that is, $u^J = u^J(a^J)$, $J = A, \ldots, U$. When this is the case, there is in effect no conflict situation, and this situation is therefore of little interest to us in this book.

26. There are of course a number of other kinds of possible outcome compromises, some of which are noted in Section 3.3.4.

27. In the above procedure, both participants must be able to specify their preferences over outcomes. Without a mediator, each must also know the other participant's preference ordering. When a mediator is present, it is sufficient that the mediator knows the preference orderings of all participants. Also see note 18.

28. While in the use of this principle each participant must know his entire preference ordering over joint actions, he need know only the

most preferred joint action of the other participant. If it turns out that the unique compromise joint action is preferred by each participant to the most preferred joint action of the other, then the principle may be acceptable.

29. Because "tries" are involved, the sequential outcome-action compromise principle might alternatively be designated the *successive tries principle.*

30. In the use of this principle, each participant must know his preference orderings over outcomes/joint actions, and the mediator must know the preference orderings of all participants. Provided participants are willing to accept the neutrality of the mediator, they do not need to be aware of each other's preference orderings.

31. For example, we can conceive of a case wherein the most preferred joint action of L occurs in the upper most cell at the extreme left in Table 3-6, and that of J occurs at the bottom most cell at the extreme right. Two successive one-step concessions by each participant would lead them to the middle cell of Table 3-6, where outcomes might be found acceptable to both participants.

A variant of the sequential outcome/action compromise principle might be applicable where each participant is, or approaches being, a 100 percent pessimist or conservative. In this case, each chooses his "sure thing" action—i.e., an action consistent with a max-min strategy, which, in Table 3-13 (p. 52) (to be discussed later), is (F) for participant J and (C_1) for participant L. This yields outcome (39,36). Assuming only ordinal preferences on the part of participants, a mediator might then propose that each restrict his action space by one step—in the case of J, by choosing actions that involve more development aid than (F), and in the case of L, by exercising a level of control greater than (C_1). This would eliminate the bottom two rows and first two columns of Table 3-13. Within the restricted joint action space that results, each participant may again adopt his max-min strategy, leading to the outcome (46,39)—an improvement for each. In Table 3-13, no further joint improvement would be possible were each to restrict his action space by still another step. But in other situations, further joint improvement may be possible. This variant might be designated a principle of *successive tries in a successively contracted joint action space.*

32. In a situation where moves to several different joint actions would each satisfy the equi-rank improvement principle, obviously, all else being equal, the one resulting in the max improvement should be adopted.

33. Since we use the numbers 1,2,3 . . . to rank the best (most preferred), second best, third best, . . . outcomes (joint actions), improvement

for both participants corresponds to decreasing the value of the ranks assigned to outcomes of a joint action. Hence, when the focus is on the total of ranks, the appropriate principle is to min rather than max the total of ranks.

Strictly speaking, as with ordinal utilities, it is improper to perform mathematical operations such as addition, subtraction, division, and multiplication with ranks. On the other hand, just as equal distance concessions in the joint action space may have appeal to participants, so too with the principles (just discussed) that perform mathematical operations on ranks. What is important in the use of conflict management procedures is not what is logical or mathematically rigorous but what can lead participants with limited knowledge and ability for abstract thinking to adopt joint actions involving less conflict and an improved state of affairs for all.

34. In Chapter 8, we recognize that weights can or may need to be attached to different participants. Thus, weighted ranks or rank improvements may become relevant in the various operations associated with compromise procedures discussed in this section.

35. In situations where participants cannot agree on a common reference point from which to measure rank improvements, an alternative principle that may be used is *min the difference in ranks*.

Also, participants may consider more involved procedures such as one that maximizes the minimum improvement (weighted or unweighted) in the ranks of any participant. Such a procedure would involve a *max the min rank improvement principle*.

Even more complicated procedures would require that the compromise joint action adopted meet an efficiency condition and others that will be discussed in later chapters.

36. In a situation where adoption of several different joint actions would each satisfy the equi-rank concession principle, obviously, all else being equal, the one resulting in the min concession would be the most acceptable to participants.

37. Also, participants may consider more involved procedures; such as one that minimizes the maximum concession (weighted or unweighted) in the ranks of any participant. Such a procedure would involve the use of a *min the max rank concession principle*.

Even more complicated procedures would require that the compromise joint action adopted meet an efficiency condition or other conditions to be discussed in subsequent chapters. Also in Chapter 8, we recognize that participants may wish to focus on weighted rank concessions should their differences in power, needs, etc. require this.

38. Also, use of a *max the min rank concession principle* would yield a different joint action than would use of a *min the max rank improvement principle*.

39. Rapoport and Chammah (1965) have designated the numbers as follows:

1 = Sucker's Payoff (S) 3 = Reward (R)
2 = Punishment (P) 4 = Temptation (T)

40. If L were to choose the policy "always choose *d*," then J would change his action from *c* to *d* and they would end up in the stable *dd* position almost immediately.

41. Of course, the threat that an inescapable sanction will be applied, that is, that J will take action *d*, must be *credible*; otherwise, this sanction loses its potential effect.

42. In this approach, each participant knows the preference structure of all participants, at least with reference to outcomes from joint actions proposed as solutions, and knows that each other participant also knows the same.

Note also that Howard's approach, unlike the compromise over proposed actions or proposed outcomes and many other procedures to be discussed in subsequent chapters, involves a direct action and not a proposal by each participant.

43. Note that property *p* (stability) is taken to be of negligible importance to the developing nations. The reader may assume otherwise; the method of analysis remains unaffected.

44. The equations underlying this case are presented in note 1 of Chapter 4.

45. For some further relevant discussion, see Section 6.4.1. Note also that there can be cases where, in some regions of the response pattern, one type of response (say brotherly love) predominates while in others, another type (say meanness) predominates.

46. Here as well as in subsequent chapters we should recognize the conflict situations that result when the outcome to any participant is independent of his own action and fully dependent on the actions taken by others. This may be the case, for example, when sometime in the future a world-environmental (or species-protection or resource-conservation) authority is established and where within a set of agreed-upon constraints, the regulatory policy it imposes on any nation is the result of a joint action of all nations excluding that nation. Also, this would be the case in Table 3–2 if L's outcome (the first number in each cell) were fully dependent on the foreign aid program selected by J, and J's outcome were fully dependent on the level of control selected by L.

We do not treat this important set of cases, which may require the development of new concepts; however, it is evident that a number of the procedures that will be developed in this book may be useful as starting points.

47. Note also that if N.V.N. chooses to Withdraw as indicated by the value of 1 for that option in column 150 of Table 3A.1, the values 0* are implied for both Infiltrate and Fight. Or if N.V.N. chooses the option Fight, as is indicated by the value of 1 for that option in column 153 of that same table, then by implication the value of Withdraw is 0, as indicated by 0*.

48. A similar table can be constructed to make any one of the four tests of the stability of any joint action—one for each participant. To facilitate exposition, we do not present the more efficient and complete table that Howard develops, which lists all preferred joint actions to the right of column 150, and all not preferred to the left. For this table, see Howard (1968:135).

49. Brams and Wittman (1980) have shown that nonmyopic equilibriums exist in many other two by two games of the sort described by Table 3-8, but in which the ranking of payoffs in the cells differ. In the seventy-eight possible two by two games, thirty-seven have nonmyopic equilibriums. Of these, twenty-one are no-conflict games in which the nonmyopic equilibrium gives both players their single best outcomes; and nine yield a nonmyopic equilibrium in which one player receives his best outcome but not the other. In the other seven games with nonmyopic equilibriums, neither player obtains his best outcome.

4 PROCEDURES FOR SITUATIONS WITH MANY OPTIONS WHERE PARTICIPANTS CAN ONLY RANK OUTCOMES

4.1 INTRODUCTION

While the typical leader and decisionmaker can think only about a small number of actions (alternatives, options) in conflict situations, increasingly, through the use of computers and mathematical operations by his staff of analysts, he is able to consider many (often a continuous) set of actions, such as in the choice of a specific dollar level of military expenditures. Sometimes there are upper bounds on his actions, such as may be set by the maximum amount of national debt that has been legislated. Sometimes, there are lower bounds, as the minimum amount of food he must obtain for his constituents in order for them to survive. Sometimes there are both. Therefore, we now wish to consider conflict management procedures where there are many joint actions, in effect continuous joint action spaces, but where participants still can only rank outcomes in order of preference, that is, state their preferences ordinally.

To do so, we first develop in this section the notion of a continuous joint action space. We then proceed to Section 4.2 to represent a participant's preference structure by a set of indifference curves. There then follows a number of sections wherein we intersperse the presentation of relevant procedures and development of new concepts as the discussion requires. For example, Sections 4.3

and 4.4 consider efficiency and programming to identify the efficiency frontier, respectively, while Section 4.5 presents the procedure of equidistant improvement (concession). Some of the procedures are simple, such as the one using a one-step split-the-difference or alternating leader-follower principle. Others, such as the incremax and decremax procedures, are more complex but still practical.

Before proceeding to our analysis, we develop here the notion of a continuous joint action space. To do so, measure within upper and lower bounds along the vertical axis of Figure 4-1 actions of the developed nations in terms of dollars of foreign aid—a continuous variable. Along the horizontal axis measure actions of the developing nations, in terms of police expenditures, standardized man hours of effort devoted to the control of disorder, or the like—another continuous variable. Doing so in effect changes (smooths out) the finite joint

Figure 4-1.   Selected Indifference Curves for J.

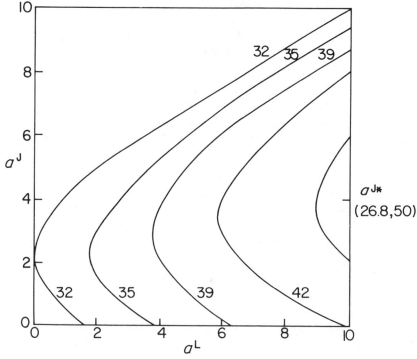

action spaces of Tables 3-2 and 3-13 that pertain to actions of the developed and developing nations. When smoothed out, the finite joint action space of Table 3-13 becomes the continuous joint action space A depicted by the box of Figure 4-1 for the participants J and L.[1]

Just as we associated a unique outcome with every joint action in Table 3-13, so we associate a unique outcome with every point in the box of Figure 4-1. Moreover, as before, the developing nations and the developed nations each order their preferences over these outcomes, each one's preference ordering being, as defined in Section 3.2.4, an ordinal utility function. Hence, the numbers in the cells of Table 3-13 representing the preferences of the developing nations for outcomes are now replaced by a utility function u^L defined on the joint action space A, and those representing the preferences of the developed nations are replaced by the utility function u^J defined on the same space. Further, since joint actions that are infinitesimally close to each other in A can be arbitrarily assigned utility numbers that are also infinitesimally close, we take these utility functions to be continuous.[2]

4.2 PREFERENCE STRUCTURES AS REPRESENTED BY INDIFFERENCE CURVES

Before considering the first case, we find it convenient to represent the preference structure of each participant by a set of indifference curves. An indifference curve for a participant is defined as the set (locus) of all those joint actions whose outcomes are considered to be equally desirable to him. For example, in Table 3-13 the outcomes to J of the two joint actions (INF, C_4) and (F, C_0) both yield J a similar value, to which we have arbitrarily assigned a value 32 both in Table 3-13 and Figure 4-1 (in keeping with the assumption that participants can only state their preference structures ordinally). We then say that, from the standpoint of outcomes, participant J is indifferent among these two joint actions and every other that is equally valued as these two and thus necessarily assigned a value of 32. All such joint actions can then be said to lie on the indifference curve representing the ordinal utility value 32. For each other ordinal utility value, higher or lower than 32, we can likewise construct an indifference curve that is the locus of all those joint actions to whose outcomes the participant assigns that value. We thus can obtain a set of indifference curves such as those in Figure 4–1, which represent the preference structure, that is, the ordinal utility function, of participant J for the situation depicted in Table 3–13. In practice, the participant is asked to make a sufficient number of pairwise comparisons of outcomes so that the analyst can approximate his set of indifference curves in the relevant region of conflict over joint actions.

For the developing nations L too, we can construct a set of indifference curves that represent their preference structure, that is, their ordinal utility function, for any situation in which they are involved. We do so for the situation depicted in Table 3–13 and, overlaying this set of indifference curves for L (dashed lines) on J's, we obtain Figure 4–2. (For the moment ignore the straight lines and the RR′

Figure 4-2.   Selected Indifference Curves for J and L and the Efficiency Frontier.

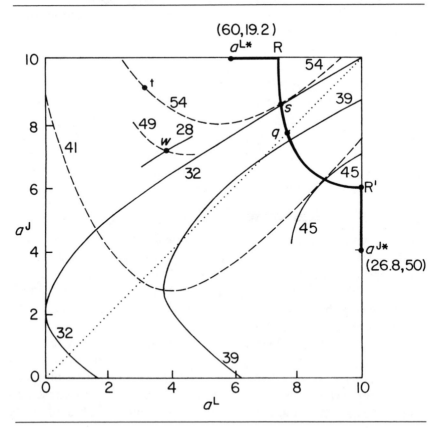

curve.) In effect, Figure 4-2 is the complete continuous analogue of the matrix of Table 3-13. Note that J most prefers the joint action a^{J*}; it lies on his highest indifference curve (which reduces to a point), while L most prefers the joint action a^{L*}. Thus Figure 4-2 depicts a conflict situation in a continuous action space.

4.3 EFFICIENCY AS A DESIRABLE FEATURE

There are several ways to start to consider procedures to eliminate this conflict. A natural scientist or biologist might suggest that those joint actions that would not allow one or more participants to survive be eliminated. A moralist would suggest that those that are grossly unfair to either participant be eliminated. (It would of course be desirable if he could define grossly unfair.) A political scientist might suggest that those that would give rise to major unrest be eliminated. A sociologist might suggest those that would lead to destruction of the family or other key social institutions be eliminated, and, finally, an economist would suggest that those that would give rise to an inefficient outcome should be eliminated. Since the economist's criterion can be more precisely defined than any other, and is for that reason frequently employed, we begin with it.

An *inefficient* joint action, from the standpoint of both parties, can be defined as one whose outcome is less preferred by both participants than some other joint action—that is, an action that is *strongly dominated* by another. Thus, joint action w in Figure 4-2 is inefficient since both participants prefer joint action s (s lies on a higher indifference curve for each).[3] Also, a joint action is taken to be *inefficient* if there exists another joint action whose outcome is less preferred by one participant but only equally desired by the second. For example, t is inefficient because while it is equally valued to s by L (it lies on the same indifference curve for L as does point s), it is less preferred by J (it lies on a lower indifference curve for J than does s). In this case t is *weakly dominated* by s. Thus, it follows that efficient actions are those that are neither strongly nor weakly dominated by some other joint action.

With the concept of an efficient joint action defined, we can immediately eliminate from consideration most of the joint actions in Figure 4-2. Just as it was shown for the joint action corresponding to point w, so it can be shown for every joint action corresponding to a point lying between L's 54 and J's 32 indifference curves that it is less preferred by each participant than the joint action corresponding to point s. (That is, it lies on lower indifference curves.) In fact, the only points in Figure 4-2 that are noninferior, that is, undominated and efficient, are those that either (1) represent points of tangency of a pair of indifference curves—one from the set of each participant—and so lie on the curve RR' or (2) lie on the horizontal stretch a^{L*}R or vertical stretch R'a^{J*}. These two stretches represent bounds on the joint action space. The points on them are efficient even though they are not points of tangency of indifference curves. They are efficient because every point vertically below the horizontal stretch a^{L*}R can be shown to be an intersection point of two indifference curves each of which is lower in value than the respective curve of a pair touching a point on that stretch. Likewise for every point directly to the left of the vertical stretch R'a^{J*}. Moreover, the points on the stretches themselves are undominated and therefore efficient because points that could dominate them lie outside the joint action space (the box of Figure 4-2). Thus, only points of tangency of indifference curves that lie within the joint action space and points on the two stretches a^{L*}R and R'a^{J*} are undominated. The locus of these points, curve a^{L*}RR'a^{J*} in Figure 4-2, can then be said to be the efficient (noninferior) set of joint actions, or to constitute the *efficiency frontier.*

4.4 PROGRAMMING TO DEFINE THE SET OF EFFICIENT JOINT ACTIONS (THE EFFICIENCY FRONTIER)

The identification of the set of efficient joint actions, the *efficiency frontier,* has been of major interest to scholars in applied mathematics, operations research, economics, regional science, engineering, planning, and other disciplines. In their concern for programming development (whether urban, regional, national, or system), they often confront conflict because of the scarcity of resources. Hence, wherever possible they suggest development plans that are in keeping with an efficient rather than inefficient use of resources.

We now illustrate how programming can be used to define the set of efficient joint actions. To keep the illustration as simple as possible, we assume that each participant derives satisfaction from only a single good or objective and that he prefers more rather than less of a good or objective. (In Chapter 8 we drop this assumption and allow participants to be concerned with more than one good or objective.)

Consider a developing region granted a fixed sum of money K to use as capital for investment purposes. One interest group within this region demands the use of capital for construction of housing, health, and related social welfare facilities, which we designate activity h, whose level is represented by y_h. A second interest group demands the use of capital for industrial and related development, which we designate activity i, whose level is y_i. The amount of capital required per unit of activity h is a_{kh} and that amount required per unit of activity i is a_{ki}. Hence, the conflict problem is to find weights w_h and w_i (where $w_h + w_i = 1$) to apply to the level of activities h and i respectively so as to:

$$\max \ w_h y_h + w_i y_i \qquad (4\text{-}1)$$

subject to:

$$a_{kh} y_h + a_{ki} y_i \leq K \qquad (4\text{-}2)$$

Here $a_{kh} y_h$ is the capital to be assigned to housing and related activities, and $a_{ki} y_i$ is the capital to be assigned to industry and related development.[4] Not knowing at the start what weights to apply, we consider all possible combinations of w_h and w_i subject to the constraint $w_h + w_i = 1$; and for each set we determine the maximum value of the objective function (4-1). More specifically, we can set up a computer program and instruct the computer to begin with weights $w_h = 1$, $w_i = 0$ and vary them continuously (subject to the constraint $w_h + w_i = 1$) until the set $w_h = 0$ and $w_i = 1$ is reached. While doing so, we ask it to plot the maximum outcome regarding y_h and y_i for every given set of w_h and w_i, thereby yielding a curve that is the efficiency frontier.[5] Of course, for the extremely simple example presented above, one does not need a computer. Equation (4-2) defines an efficiency frontier that is a straight line. However, in general, for a set of constraints (linear or nonlinear) of the form:

$$g(y_h, y_i) \leq K, \qquad (4\text{-}3)$$

a computer would be required. The efficiency frontier that it would identify might be like the $a^{L^*} a^{J^*}$ curve on Figure 4-3 on page 76.

4.5 EQUIDISTANT IMPROVEMENT
(OR CONCESSION)
IN THE JOINT ACTION SPACE

Having identified the efficient set of joint actions (the efficiency frontier), and eliminating inefficient joint actions from the set to be considered as a possible solution to the conflict, we look for other criteria to help identify the most reasonable, fairest, or best joint action in the efficient set, that is, on an efficiency frontier, such as $a^{L^*}RR'a^{J^*}$ in Figure 4-2.

An extremely simple, but not necessarily acceptable, procedure is to construct a 45° line from the (0,0) point through the efficiency frontier. (See the dotted line of Figure 4-2.) The point of intersection q with the frontier defines a compromise joint action that may have appeal since the 45° line is the locus of all points *equidistant* from the two axes. (Recall that each axis represents the action space of one of the participants.) For the sophisticated, observant participant, however, this procedure is not acceptable. The unit of measurement of each axis is arbitrary and the variables being measured along the two axes are therefore not comparable. Thus, when considering successive points along the 45° line, the amount of improvement in the position of each participant can only be stated arbitrarily.[6] Yet there may exist standard generally accepted units (like degrees of temperature, millions of dollars of foreign aid, billions of dollars of GNP, miles) that unsophisticated participants may find acceptable for use in marking off equal increments along the vertical and horizontal axes of a figure.[7]

Yet another serious drawback in the use of a 45° line is that movement from the (0,0) point along this line to the efficiency frontier does not guarantee steady improvement for both participants. This is easily seen to be the case for J in the stretch immediately before the intersection point q is reached.

At this stage, in order to point up another usable procedure, we wish to refer back to conflict situations for which the number of options is small. In such situations we cannot hope, except by chance, to find a joint action that would fall on the equidistant line that we have defined in the above paragraph simply because there exists only a *small* number of joint actions. However, the participants or mediator may be able to locate the joint action that lies closest to that line and find it acceptable as a compromise solution. If so, they would be in effect employing the principle *min the distance to the equidistant improvement line.*

Parallel to this notion of equidistant improvement is that of *equidistant concession.* We may imagine that participants are willing to concede from some unrealistic ideal reference point, but only along a 45° line from that point. This possibility is examined on pages 228–235. In the finite joint action space, it leads to the principle *min the distance to the equidistant concession line.*

4.6 MEDIAN EFFICIENT JOINT ACTION PRINCIPLE

Recognizing that the magnitudes being measured along the two axes are noncomparable and that the units used for measurement of each are arbitrary, the participants may find it reasonable to focus immediately on the set of efficient joint actions (i.e. the efficiency frontier). They may find acceptable the suggestion that a fair joint action is that one in the efficient set that is the median in the ordering of both participants. Since the efficiency frontier is a continuous arc, we may take the midpoint of the arc as the median and characterize this method as involving the use of the *median efficient joint action principle.* Note, though, that this method breaks down when more than two participants are involved, since the midpoint is not then identifiable.

This principle has appeal because of its simplicity. However, it does require that each participant know the preference structure of the other, and the outcome is not preindeterminate from the standpoint of the participants.[8] Other things being equal, it is generally desirable for the outcome of a procedure to be preindeterminate. This is so because when outcomes from the use of conflict management procedures are unable to be "predicted," then it is often possible to avoid the conflict situation that arises when one participant is able to determine that one procedure yields him a better outcome than a second procedure, but his opponent is also able to determine that the second procedure yields him (the opponent) a better outcome than the first procedure.

4.7 CONCESSION ALONG THE EFFICIENCY FRONTIER PRINCIPLE

Another way to reach a solution while focusing on the efficiency frontier involves successive contraction of the efficiency frontier. After participants have been deadlocked, each insisting that his most preferred joint action be the solution, a mediator may suggest the following procedure:

Step 1.   Each participant proposes his most preferred joint action. In Figure 4–3 these are a^{J*} and a^{L*} for leaders J and L, respectively.

Figure 4–3.   Concession along the Efficiency Frontier.

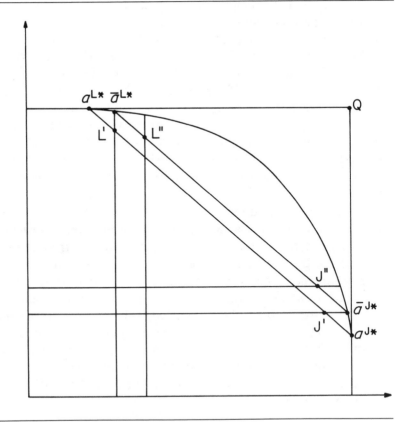

Step 2.   The mediator constructs a straight line connecting these two joint actions.

Step 3.   On a first round of concession, each participant indicates the maximum distance along this line that he is willing to consider in defining a "reduced" efficiency frontier for a second round proposal. (This reduced efficiency frontier is to be defined by the stretch cut off by a horizontal line through J' —the point that corresponds to J's actual concession—and a vertical through L' —the point which corresponds to L's actual concession.)

Step 4.   The mediator selects the lesser of the two maximums as the actual concession required from each participant and thus defines points J' and L' on the straight line $a^{J*}a^{L*}$ for J and L, respectively. He then demarcates the reduced efficiency frontier.

Step 5.   J and L each select their most preferred joint action on the restricted efficiency frontier. In Figure 4–3 these are $\bar{a}^{J*}$ and $\bar{a}^{L*}$, respectively.

Step 6.   The mediator constructs a straight line connecting these two new proposals, namely, line $\bar{a}^{J*}\bar{a}^{L*}$.

Step 7.   On the second round of concession, each participant indicates the maximum distance . . .

and so forth. This round-by-round procedure continues until the reduced efficiency frontier becomes too small for another round, at which time the participants employ some simple averaging to reach a solution. We might characterize this method as involving the use of a *concession along the efficiency frontier principle.*[9]

4.8 GUARANTEED IMPROVEMENT AS A DESIRABLE FEATURE

While the "median efficient joint action" and the "concession along the efficiency frontier" principles have certain desirable features, the use of either may not guarantee an improvement to each participant from their *current* position in the joint action space. There are any number of joint actions that might characterize their *current* position. One is the (30, 30) point corresponding to the (NP, C_0) joint action. If we focus on the indifference curve of each that passes through this point (as we do in Figure 4-4),[10] we can then define a set comprising all joint actions more preferred by both participants to the (30, 30) point—that is, lying on a higher indifference curve for each. These points are included in the lightly shaded area of Figure 4-4, which we designate the *improvement set*.[11] Note that only part of the efficiency set is included in this improvement set. Hence, participant J, whose most preferred joint action does not lie in the improvement set, might object to the use of the median efficient joint action principle for resolving the conflict. However, he might not object if the median efficient joint action principle were applied to only that part of the efficiency frontier included in the improvement set, namely $GR'G'$.

Figure 4-4.   Improvement Sets Regarding Reference Points.

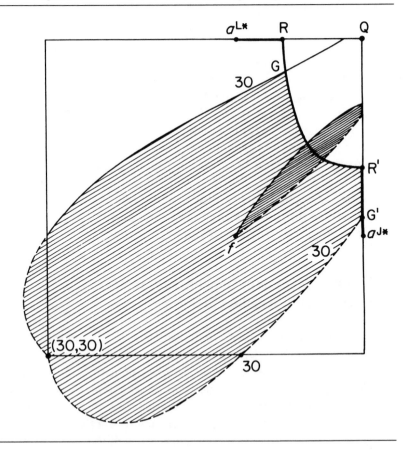

Such an application may be said to involve the use of a *median efficient joint action principle with guaranteed improvement.*

This can be seen even better when their current position is that which results when each chooses his direct action corresponding to his most preferred joint action. (This might happen when each party is uneducated and is completely unaware of interdependence, or when each is an unbounded, unfounded optimist.) This is point *f* in Figure 4–4. Once again we define the improvement set (this time the heavily shaded area), and again only part of the efficiency set is included in the improvement set. As in the previous case, a reasonable procedure for reaching a compromise joint action might involve the use of the median efficient joint action principle with guaranteed improvement. Note that where programming is employed to define the efficiency frontier, additional constraints can be introduced into the programming operation to restrict the set of joint actions considered to the improvement set, and so, to yield the relevant reduced efficiency frontier.

4.9 THE BEST REPLY LINE AND THE SEQUENTIAL BEST REPLY PATH

Finally, consider another joint action that may represent the participants' current standpoint. This action may have been reached through a series of direct actions and reactions by participants who have not been educated to or are not aware of the fact of interdependence, or who are simply shortsighted, narrow-minded, and self-interested. To understand the nature of this action/reaction process, we first define a best reply.

Take any point, say *t* in Figure 4–5, and any participant, say J. Out of pure self-interest J will consider whether he can obtain a better outcome than what he receives at *t*, given the level of control chosen by L. Clearly he can do so. By decreasing the level of his assistance—that is, by moving down vertically from point *t*—he can reach higher levels of utility—that is, a higher indifference curve—until he reaches point *t'*, which lies on the highest of his indifference curves that he can reach. Hence, the reply consistent with joint action *t'* is his *best reply*. Likewise, for any other point in Figure 4–5 that might be his initial position, J can find a best reply. If we connect all these best replies in the continuous joint action space, we obtain J's *best* *reply line* (given by Ja^{J*} in Figure 4-5). Note that this line passes through all of J's indifference curves where they turn—that is, where they are tangent to a vertical.[12]

Participant L may behave in a similar manner. If the initial position is *t* and if L is the first participant to move, she will decrease the level of her control—that is, move horizontally, until she reaches point *t''* which lies on her highest possible indifference curve given the level of assistance chosen by J. The reply consistent with the joint action *t''* is her *best reply* in this situation. Likewise, for every other current standpoint we can identify L's best reply and thus construct her *best reply line* given by La^{L*} in Figure 4-5. This line also passes through all of L's indifference curves where they turn—that is, where they are tangent to a horizontal.[13]

With these two best reply lines defined, we now can determine another point likely to be a current standpoint. If J were at *t* we saw how he would move to *t'* (if he were the first to react). But were *t'* reached, sooner or later we may expect L to react and change her level of control so that joint action *t'''* is realized. J then reacts by decreasing his level of assistance to *t*^{iv}, and so on. This process continues until they converge to point *e*, the intersection point of their best reply lines. In Figure 4-5, *e* is a stable equilibrium point. Once it is reached there is no incentive for either party, given their shortsightedness, to take an independent action to improve his situation. Thus *e* is a "natural" current standpoint that is often reached unknowingly by both participants in real life situations.[14]

If we now take *e* as the current standpoint, then, as in Figure 4-5, only part of the efficiency frontier, namely HH', is included in the improvement set with respect to *e*. Hence, the relevant median efficient joint action principle is applicable only to the HH' stretch.

4.10 SPLIT-THE-DIFFERENCE PRINCIPLE— ONE-STEP AND SEQUENTIAL

Another procedure relying only on ordinal utility and continuous action spaces involves the use of a simple fifty-fifty or *split-the-difference principle*. Take participants J and L in Figure 4-5. Each proposes as the joint action to be adopted his most preferred joint action, namely a^{J*} and a^{L*}, respectively. Construct a straight line connecting these two joint actions. Application of the split-the-

Figure 4-5.   Best Reply Line and a Sequential Best Reply Path.

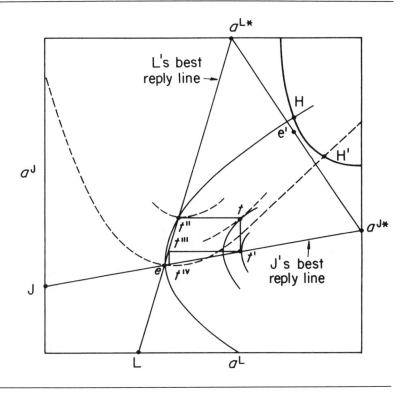

difference principle then identifies the midpoint *e'* of this line as the compromise joint action.

Note that the compromise joint action that results from a single application of the split-the-difference principle yields an inefficient outcome. However, in the case of Figure 4-5, point *e'* is so close to the efficiency frontier that the participants may prefer to stop their negotiations at that point rather than face additional haggling over how to reach the efficiency frontier from point *e'*. In other situations, such as that depicted in Figure 4-6 (which represents the smoothing of the data of Table 3-2), the compromise joint action *e'* resulting from a single application of the split-the-difference principle lies a significant distance away from the efficiency frontier. Consequently, participants may be motivated to seek further improve-

Figure 4–6.   A Sequential Split-the-Difference Procedure.

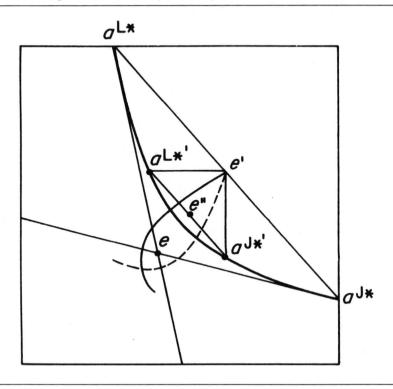

ment by a second application of the split-the-difference compromise principle. In doing so they may be motivated to consider only those joint actions lying within the area bounded by (1) a vertical from point e'_l (2) a horizontal from point e'_l and (3) the efficiency set. Each then proposes his most preferred joint action in this restricted joint action space. In Figure 4–6, these proposals are $a^{J*'}$ and $a^{L*'}$. Once again, a straight line is constructed connecting these two proposals and the application of the split-the-difference principle yields the midpoint e'' as the new compromise joint action. This procedure can be repeated until participants become tired or reach a compromise joint action sufficiently close to the efficiency frontier that it does not pay them to proceed further.[15]

While in practice the precise working of this principle as just outlined is not strictly followed, it is often approximated, either knowingly or unknowingly. This approach does not require that a participant have any information about the preference structure of the other except the other's most preferred joint action at the start of each round. On the other hand, it does not guarantee improvement for both on each step. In fact, in the situation depicted by Figure 4–6, the application of the split-the-difference principle in the first round leads to a worsening of each participant's position.

An important case for which the simple split-the-difference principle is often used is when the efficiency frontier is or approximates a straight line, as in Figure 4–7. For example, this might occur if leaders L and J chose joint policies that most accurately reflect the wishes of their constituents—particularly when most of their constituents' wishes cluster around positions a^{L*} and a^{J*}, respectively. Each leader judges that the more distant the joint action that he proposes

Figure 4-7.   A Split-the-Difference Procedure for a Straight Line Efficiency Frontier.

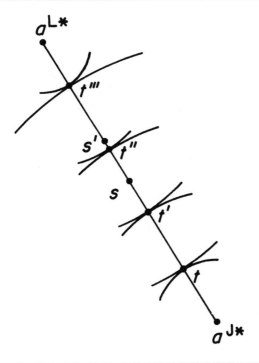

from that around which his constituency clusters, the more costly it will be to him in terms of loss of support of his constituency, additional favors and patronage that he must offer to hold that support, or both. But he is unable to identify how costly. For example, leader J knows that movement to position t involves cost to him, to t' more cost, to t'' still more cost, and so forth. Not knowing the precise function that defines these costs, he takes all positions on a circle with fixed radius from a^{J*} to involve approximately the same cost to him. Accordingly, we can assign ordinal numbers to J's circles, which now are his indifference curves, as in Figure 4-7. Likewise for L, with reference to a^{L*}, the position around which her constituents cluster. As a consequence, the points of tangency defining the efficiency frontier fall on the straight line connecting the two most preferred joint actions. A single application of the split-the-difference yields the midpoint s as the solution. This in essence involves equal concessions by the two leaders in the joint action space. Such a situation often occurs when two political leaders can form a winning coalition and when, to them, being members of the winning coalition more than offsets the costs involved in movement to s.

Consider another situation. Take a key figure, such as the secretary-general of the United Nations who knows the most preferred position of the leader of each of two blocs of nations. He has no information other than that each leader prefers to be less distant rather than more distant from his most preferred position. He then may approximate their preference structures in terms of indifference curves that are circles around these two most preferred positions. To break the impasse, he then may propose the application of a split-the-difference principle in the joint action space that, if adopted, would yield the midpoint s as the solution—a position involving equal concessions in the joint action space.[16,17]

4.11 THE WEIGHTED-AVERAGE PRINCIPLE

The split-the-difference principle implicitly attaches equal importance to each participant—that is, each participant's proposal is equally weighted in determining a solution on any round. However, when the participants are not equal in a key aspect of the conflict situation—for example, one may bring to the conflict more resources than the other, have more power or greater need, or be more inflexible or historically more committed to a position—then "fairness" suggests that the compromise joint action be taken as an appropriately weighted average of the two proposed joint actions. That is, use of a *weighted-average principle* is required and can become applicable when participants agree on the weights.[18] In practically all, if not all, cases for which the one-step (or sequential) split-the-difference principle is relevant, it can be replaced by a one-step (or sequential) weighted-average principle. For example, in the situation depicted in Figure 4–7, a mediator, say an important official of the United Nations, may consider the developing nations L to have needs or to represent constituencies twice as important as those of the developed nations J. He then might propose the use of a weighted-average principle that would yield point s' as the solution. This point is one third of the straight-line distance from a^{L*} to a^{J*}; it corresponds to a joint action involving equal concessions (after weighting) in the joint action space.

4.12 GUARANTEED IMPROVEMENT AND SEQUENTIAL SPLIT-THE-DIFFERENCE PRINCIPLE

A variant of the sequential split-the-difference principle may be suggested when political leaders (or other behaving units) are surrounded by their own research and development teams or brain trusts and insist upon improvement on each step in the use of the split-the-difference or weighted-average principles. For example, if point e in Figure 4–8 has already been reached at the end of a best reply action-reaction path and is taken as an initial point of reference, then the improvement set associated with e is first identified; and for the first round the participants' joint action proposals are constrained to fall within this improvement set.[19] In Figure 4–8, then, the first round proposals by J and L would be $a^{J*'}$ and $a^{L*'}$, respectively. Next, the midpoint e' of the straight line connecting $a^{J*'}$ and $a^{L*'}$ is found and taken to be the compromise joint action associated with the first round; also the midpoint e' serves as the reference point for the next round. The improvement set with reference to point e' is then constructed, and so forth. Note, however, that the use of this variant assumes each participant knows the preference structure of the other (or can be told what the improvement set is on any round). This is necessary in order for each participant to know the restricted joint action space

Figure 4-8.   Guaranteed Improvement and Sequential Split-the-Difference.

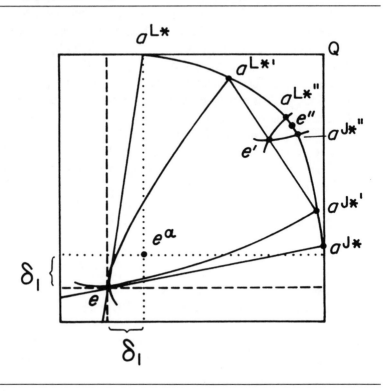

within which he can make proposals. Hence, from a practical standpoint, the desirable property of guaranteed improvement on each step may need to be sacrificed when the required information cannot be (or is not) made available.

4.13 LIMITED COMMITMENT
AS AN ADDITIONAL DESIRABLE FEATURE

Still another variant of the split-the-difference or weighted-average principle may be suggested when uncertainty and/or conservatism makes one or more participants set a limit on the maximum amount of change he will consider on any move from the current standpoint or any other reference point. In this variant, each participant specifies the maximum change along both the vertical and horizontal axes (his action and that of his opponent) that he is willing to consider. Then, by taking the lesser of these maximums, first along the vertical and then along the horizontal, a box can be defined around the reference point. We designate this box a *limited commitment set*, which helps define the relevant restricted action space on the first move. See Figure 4-9, where, in addition to this box (the limited commitment set), we show the improvement set based on e and the overlap of these two sets. Within this overlap (restricted joint action space) J and L may go on to specify their most preferred joint actions ($a^{J*'}$ for J and $a^{L*'}$ for L) and then to identify a split-the-difference compromise joint action e'. This joint action then represents a solution to the first round of compromise and serves as the new reference point. Then, in a series of rounds (where the maximum level of commitment may or may not be allowed to change), participants may proceed *toward the efficiency frontier*—with or without the guaranteed improvement constraint on each round. See Figure 4-10, wherein is shown the limited commitment set (box) for a second round and the compromise

Figure 4-9. The Limited Commitment Set on the First Round and Its Overlap with the Improvement Set.

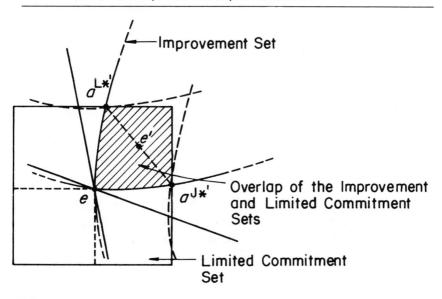

Figure 4-10. A Sequence of Split-the-Difference Compromises.

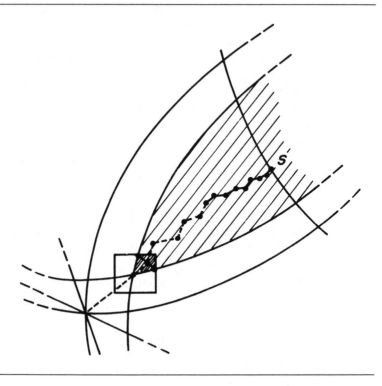

joint action reached in each of a series of rounds—there being guaranteed improvement on each round.

Note we say "toward the efficiency frontier" because in practice participants may perceive the time, haggling, and other costs of a next move to be greater than the gains from a more preferred joint action, or they may reach a level where they are satisficed.[20]

4.14 EFFICIENCY, GUARANTEED IMPROVEMENT, LIMITED COMMITMENT, AND SEQUENTIAL-WEIGHTED-AVERAGE AS FEATURES OF AN INCREMAX PROCEDURE

The above discussion has indicated several of many possible ways in which a step-by-step compromise procedure may be devised wherein one or more participants are optimizing on each round. Such procedures may be designated *incremax procedures*. Of course, not all desirable features need be included in an incremax procedure. Participants may wish to stop short of the efficiency frontier. They may define a step, and the sequence of steps comprising the procedure, in many different ways. They may not insist that there be guaranteed improvement to each party on all rounds. They may replace one or more of the above features with others. The important point is that simple step-by-step procedures involving combinations of desirable features define a large *set* of compromise procedures that can be considered for use in a specific conflict situation.

4.15 DECREMAX PROCEDURES

Another reference point that for diverse reasons participants might find acceptable for use in an incremax procedure is that defined by the joint action corresponding to the upper bound of each participant's action space—for example, Q in Figure 4-4, page 78. Sometimes this point may have appeal, for, as in Figure 4-4, it may correspond to a joint action in which each participant chooses an action consistent with the other participant's most preferred joint action. Whatever the rationale for its use as a reference point, it clearly is inefficient. We can construct the indifference curve of each participant passing through this point and employ incremax or other procedures already discussed to lead participants toward a solution on the efficiency frontier.

There are, however, situations often encountered for which the term "incremax" is inappropriate and should be replaced by the term "decremax." Suppose, for example, we measure along one axis of Figure 4-8 an objective, such as environmental quality (reflecting the primary interest of a citizen's group), and along the other, growth in terms of industrial output (reflecting the primary interest of a business group). Suppose, also, that there is limited capital available for the achievement of any combination of these two objectives. Using programming techniques discussed on pages 72–73, we can identify the efficiency frontier in the joint action space.[21] In such a case, point Q represents an *infeasible* joint action. The combination of environmental quality and growth that it represents cannot be attained given the capital constraint. Thus we cannot use incremax, in the sense of achieving a series of realizable improvements from point Q.

However, the participants may be able to define equidistance or other distance concessions in the joint action space to serve as a basis for moving toward a feasible and efficient joint action as a compromise. Perhaps, more significantly, they may be motivated to employ a decremax procedure that parallels the incremax procedure already discussed. To illustrate one possible type of decremax procedure, we construct Figure 4-11. Along one axis, we measure environmental quality (or actions contributing to environmental quality) in standard units; along the other, we measure growth (or actions contributing to growth) in terms of increase in dollar value of industrial output. With the use of an appropriate programming model, we identify the efficiency frontier and points a^{L*} and a^{J*} as the most preferred joint actions of L and J, respectively.

Figure 4-11. A Concession Procedure from an Ideal but Infeasible Joint Action.

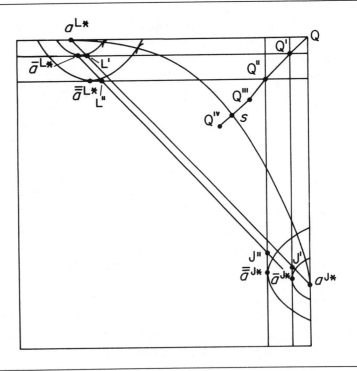

Suppose now that each has insisted in previous interactions on taking that action consistent with the joint action he most prefers—demands that correspond to the infeasible point Q—and that accordingly there has developed a deadlock in agreeing upon a feasible way to employ the available capital to achieve some combination of the two objectives. After some time, a mediator might propose a distance-type concession procedure as follows:

Step 1. Each participant proposes his most preferred joint action. In Figure 4-11 these are a^{J*} and a^{L*} for leaders J and L, respectively.

Step 2. The mediator constructs a straight line connecting these two joint actions.

Step 3. On a first round of concession, each participant indicates the maximum distance along this straight line that he is willing to consider in defining a "reduced" joint action space within which second round proposals may be made. (The reduced joint action space is to be defined by the area bounded by and below a horizontal line through the point corresponding to L's concession and bounded by and to the left of a vertical through the point corresponding to J's concession.)

Step 4. The mediator selects the lesser of the two maximums to determine concession points L' and J' on straight line $a^{J*}a^{L*}$ for L and J, respectively. He then constructs the reduced joint action space, and Q becomes Q'.

Step 5. J and L each select their most preferred joint action in the reduced joint action space. In Figure 4-11, these are given by points $\bar{a}^{J*}$ and $\bar{a}^{L*}$, respectively.

Step 6. The mediator constructs a straight line connecting these two new proposals, namely, line $\bar{a}^{J*}\bar{a}^{L*}$.

Step 7. On the second round of concession, each participant indicates the maximum distance . . . and so forth. This round-by-round procedure continues until the joint action space is so reduced that the series of straight line stretches QQ', Q'Q'', Q''Q''' . . . intersects the efficiency frontier. The point of intersection s is then the appropriate compromise.[22] There are of course many possible variants of this procedure, and each may need to be supplemented by additional rules to avoid excessive complication in certain situations.

Note that this procedure has several desirable properties, namely, a series of rounds, limited commitment and the use of maximizing proposals on each round, and the guarantee of a solution on the efficiency frontier. In contrast to an incremax procedure which involves for each participant increments from a series of inefficient points, this procedure involves for each participant decrements from a series of "ideal" but infeasible points. So on these grounds, it may have more appeal in certain situations than the incremax procedure.[23]

While the above discussion centered on point Q, the decremax procedure can also be used to move participants from some other apparently rational, ideal, or intuitively appealing but infeasible point to the efficiency frontier.

4.16 THE ALTERNATING LEADER-FOLLOWER PRINCIPLE: A SUBSTITUTE FOR SPLIT-THE-DIFFERENCE OR WEIGHTED-AVERAGE

Another procedure that may be employed in conflict situations is the simple alternating leader-follower procedure. As in a football game or in deliberations, a coin may be tossed to determine who goes first. The winner of the toss is the one who selects the compromise joint action to serve as both the solution of the first round and the reference point for the second round. The loser then becomes the leader on the second round, and his compromise proposal is adopted as both the solution of the second round and the reference point for the third round. The winner then becomes the leader on the third round, and so on.

We illustrate this procedure for the case when guaranteed improvement is required on each round. In Figure 4–9, a box is constructed on the basis of the lesser of the maximum change that each participant is willing to consider in either direction from e on a first round. This box then defines the limited commitment set for the first round, and its overlap with the improvement set based on point e defines the restricted set of joint actions (the shaded area of Figure 4–9) from which the participants may choose in the first round. Let L be the winner of the toss of the coin. As leader on the first round, she proposes as the solution of the first round her most preferred joint action, $a^{L*'}$, in the restricted joint action space. As shown in Figure 4-12, $a^{L*'}$ then comes to serve as the reference point on the second round. Around this point a box is constructed on the basis of the lesser of the maximum change in either direction from $a^{L*'}$ that each participant is willing to consider on the second round. Also, the overlap of the box with the new improvement set based on $a^{L*'}$ is identified as the new restricted joint action space. This is the heavier shaded area of Figure 4-12. Then J, as leader on the second round, proposes as the solution for this round his most preferred joint action, $a^{J*''}$, in the new restricted joint action space, and so forth. Figure 4-12 illustrates the sequence of steps toward the efficiency frontier that may result.[24]

Figure 4-12.   A Sequence of Alternating Leader-Follower Proposals.

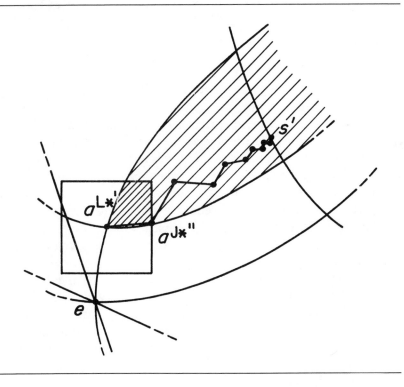

4.17 THE BEST REPLY PRINCIPLE IN A SUCCESSIVELY CONTRACTED JOINT ACTION SPACE AND RELATED PRINCIPLES

Another possible procedure that recognizes that participants often have little, if any, information concerning the preference structures of other participants and that they are often inflexible, myopic, and self-interested is the *best reply principle* in a series of rounds on each of which the relevant joint action space has been appropriately contracted.

For example, assume as in Figure 4-8, that the best reply point e has been reached by participants after a series of actions and reactions. At this point the mediator can suggest that each allow a restriction to be applied to his action space. This restriction is to be defined by the use of a magnitude, say δ_1, which is the minimum of the maximum change from e that each one is willing to consider. Specifically, L should restrict her actions to those that involve a level of control greater than that corresponding to the joint action e by at least a δ_1 amount; and J should restrict his actions to those that involve a level of foreign aid program greater than that corresponding to the joint action e by at least a δ_1 amount. As a result, the joint action space is contracted to the space above and to the right of the dotted line in Figure 4-8, and e^α becomes the joint best reply equilibrium point in this restricted joint action space. With a series of such contractions in the joint action space, a sequence of mutual improvements for participants may be generated.[25] Hence, the participants may find such a procedure acceptable, even though it does not guarantee that an efficient solution will be reached. In fact they may only be able to reach an inefficient joint action at a considerable distance from the efficiency frontier. Also, this procedure assumes unsophisticated participants who do not attempt to compare the significance of a δ_1 change from e in one's action space with that same change in the other's action space.[26]

Additionally, in certain situations where each participant is or approaches being a 100 percent pessimist or conservative and pursues only a max-min strategy, a principle of max-min strategy in a successively contracted joint action space may be applicable. So may a principle of max-max strategy in a successively contracted joint action space when each participant is an unfounded, unbounded 100 percent optimist or a religious fanatic or the like.

4.18 SIMPLE HIERARCHICAL PROGRAMMING: A SEQUENTIAL EXERCISE OF LEADERSHIP

Programming has at times focused on situations wherein interest groups in conflict are each primarily concerned with a single but different objective[27] and the participants or some respected outsider has ranked these objectives in order of importance. Under these circumstances, a very simple (but often highly unrealistic) procedure is to run a program to maximize achievement on the most important objective. Then, if resources are still available, the program is operated further to maximize achievement on the second most important objective, subject to a constraint ensuring (at least) the optimal value on the first objective. If some resources are still unused, the program is once again operated to maximize achievement on the third most important objective, and so forth.[28,29]

In the context of a leadership procedure, however, the simple hierarchical programming approach can be made much more realistic by incorporating constraints restricting actions to both improvement and limited commitment sets. To be more specific, each interest group (in order of importance of their primary objectives) takes its turn in maximizing the achievement on its objective subject to both limited commitment and improvement set constraints, until the efficiency frontier is reached—or until all participants have had a chance to be leader. In the latter case, a second series of rounds can be instituted and so on until the efficiency frontier is reached.

The improvement set constraint could, for example, guarantee that on each round no participant's objective achievement fall below that level attained on the previous round. The limited commitment constraints, typically prespecified before a set of rounds is initiated, might limit the first participant to the use of, say, no more than 8 percent of the resources available, the second participant to no more than 12 percent, and so on.

A more sophisticated version of the hierarchical programming approach would allow for relaxation of achievements on objectives. That is, where dissatisfaction is expressed by a participant regarding the final achievement on his objective, each participant concerned with a higher priority objective may be asked to yield some of the achievement on his objective (say 5 percent of it), in order that additional achievement can be attained on the lower priority objective.

This version of the approach is discussed in more detail in pages 162–164.

4.19 THE LEADERSHIP POINT AS A PREFERRED JOINT OUTCOME AND THE LEADERSHIP PRINCIPLE

At this point we should recognize the great diversity of personalities in the world of reality. We therefore consider several types of leaders and followers. Leaders may include those motivated to take a first step because of impatience, wisdom, religious fervor, desire for world respect, or other psychological factors. Followers may include those who, whether passive or aggressive, like to sit back and let the opponent go first, are infinitely patient, are hesitant because of an exaggerated fear of making a mistake, are wise enough to know that there are several reasonable solutions and that their opponent psychologically needs to appear as the leader, or are convinced that regardless of what action anyone takes, the complexities and uncertainties of the situation are such as to ensure that the action will be a wrong one.

As a first case, take a wise leader and a passive type of follower who is, however, an optimizer. If both have reached the joint best reply equilibrium action e in Figure 4–5 (or in Figure 4–13), the wise leader, knowing his opponent's nature and his opponent's best reply line, may choose his (the leader's) leadership point. This point is that one on the best reply line of the follower,[30] which is optimal for the leader (i.e., lies on the leader's highest indifference curve). For illustrative purposes consider the situation depicted in Figure 4–13. If L is the leader, then she identifies her leadership point ℓ^L and accordingly chooses action $\tilde{a}^L$ anticipating that J will select an action on his best reply line so that in effect, joint action ℓ^L will be realized. On the other hand, if J is the leader, he identifies his leadership point ℓ^J and accordingly chooses action $\tilde{a}^J$, expecting that the joint action ℓ^J will be realized. When a leader does adopt such a procedure, we say that he is guided by a *leadership principle*.[31]

A second case involves a leader who recognizes that he faces an aggressive follower. This type of follower, say L, knowing that the leader J desires (psychologically needs) world acclaim or some equivalent for assuming leadership, simply states that she will respond in accord with her best reply line for any action taken by the leader

Figure 4-13. The Leadership Points ℓ^L and ℓ^J.

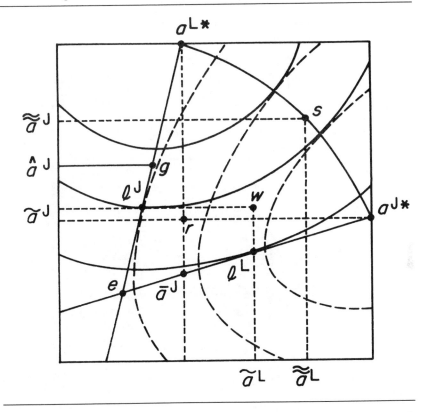

equal to or greater than $\hat{a}^J$. For all smaller actions, she, the aggressive follower, will choose zero control (C_0). Thus her reply line is given by the vertical axis up to $\hat{a}^J$, jumps to point g at $\hat{a}^J$, and then becomes ga^{L*}. The leader, who must act because of psychological need, can do no better than to choose level $\hat{a}^J$, thus leading to the joint action g.[32]

Another case is the *conditional obliging follower*, who does not want to be bothered with haggling and who is willing to oblige the leader provided that he, the follower, is made at least somewhat better off (say by some factor ε) than at e. See Figure 4-14, where J is taken to be the follower. The leader L then estimates this ε factor, however small, and accordingly chooses that joint action s′ on the efficiency frontier that is best for her given this condition.[33]

Figure 4-14.   The Solution in the Case of a Conditional Obliging Follower.

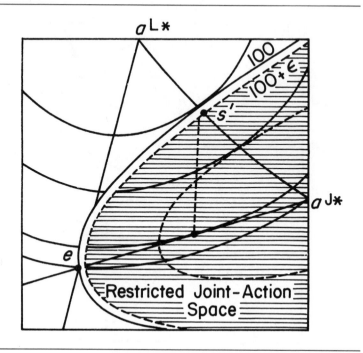

There are innumerable other types of followers that the reader may introduce into the analysis,[34] as well as many types of leaders. For example, there is the leader who is a religious fanatic. She demands that the solution be her most preferred joint action. For example, if she is L in Figure 4-13, she demands a^{L*} and acts accordingly. The follower, being wise and rational and recognizing he faces a fanatic, can do no better than choose an action yielding $\bar{a}^J$ on his best reply line. He knows that even if he were to suggest to the fanatic the benefits that may be derived from a joint action corresponding to her leadership point, the fanatic would not listen.[35]

There are other interesting cases. Suppose in the situation depicted by Figure 4-13 that both participants strongly demand (psychologically need) to be a leader. If they are both fanatics (or unbounded, unfounded optimists), they end up at point r, an outcome that is inefficient but represents an improvement for both. If both were to follow the leadership principle, they would both end up at point w. Finally, if both participants are aggressive followers, they may even end up on the efficiency frontier at s where L and J choose actions $\tilde{a}^L$ and $\tilde{a}^J$, respectively.

The above are just a few of the innumerable cases and outcomes that are possible. Depending on the situation, each case can improve or worsen the position of one or both participants. The above graphic and associated analysis may help clarify the nature of any particular conflict and so help narrow down the range of procedures that may be found acceptable.

4.20 THE GRIT (GRADUATED AND RECIPROCATED INITIATIVES IN TENSION-REDUCTION) PROCEDURE

At this point we may comment upon another procedure—*Graduated and Reciprocated Initiatives in Tension-Reduction*, or GRIT, developed by Osgood (1966, 1980).[36] In many ways, Osgood's scheme resembles a leader-follower type of situation wherein the leader initiates the procedure by making a small unilateral concession. In doing so he may be impatient for world acclaim or merely frustrated with endless attempts at negotiations that always end up at a stalemate, or he may simply want to get on with the game. Alternatively, he may be a bit "godly," or sincerely believe that this is the only way to build up confidence and trust. Specifically, he makes a small ε concession to his opponent's demands that improves his opponent's position noticeably while improving his own only negligibly.[37] He hopes that his opponent will reciprocate—that is, that his opponent will take an action that will improve his (the leader's) position significantly while improving her (the opponent's) position only negligibly. If not, and if the opponent tries to take advantage of his unilateral initiative, the leader has the capacity to restore the status quo that existed before the concession was made. If, on the other hand, the opponent does reciprocate, then the leader will make a second unilateral concession, and so on, thereby generating an alternating leader-follower sequence of actions and reactions. This sequence may be mapped as a zig-zag path from the initial current standpoint toward the efficiency frontier somewhat similar to the path depicted in Figure 4–12.

If for one reason or another a unilateral initiative is not reciprocated, let alone advanced, the introduction of a mediator is suggested. He would ideally be a highly respected person sensitive to the personalities of participants, skilled in discerning which dimensions of a conflict situation are most important to which participants, and able to ask for and achieve agreement from each participant for a concession in an area of lesser importance to him but of significance to others.[38, 39] Also, see Isard and C. Smith (1982b:95–98).

4.21 A MINIMUM
INFORMATION INCREMAX PROCEDURE

We now return to the subject of incremax procedures wherein no participant is required to or has the inclination to take on the role of leader. We wish to discuss a variant wherein the participants' preference structures are such that each prefers more of any of two or more elements of "outcomes" than less.[40] Going back to the developed-developing nations case discussed on pages 25–30, suppose the developed nations are deeply concerned with the welfare of the developing nations and always prefer (within limits) to give them more assistance rather than less. They may of course more intensely desire a greater amount rather than a lesser amount of control by the developing nations. Suppose also the developing nations always prefer more control to less, whatever the level of assistance rendered by the developed nations. They may of course desire more intensely a greater amount rather than a lesser amount of assistance.[41] It follows that on any round in the use of the sequential split-the-difference principle the compromise joint action will always lie in an improvement set defined by the upper right quadrant formed by axes passing through a relevant (0,0) reference point. See Figure 4–15. In that figure, the vertical stretch OM for any round would be the lesser of the maximum changes in assistance that the participants find acceptable, and the horizontal stretch ON would be the lesser of the acceptable maximum changes in control. To randomize the entire procedure, a third party may be asked to connect the two points M and N with an elliptical-type arc concave to the origin, using, for example, a French curve.[42]

This then defines the limited commitment set in the upper right quadrant and thus the intersection (overlap) with the improvement set, this intersection being the shaded area of Figure 4–15. The par-

Figure 4-15. First Round in an Incremax Procedure with Minimum Information.

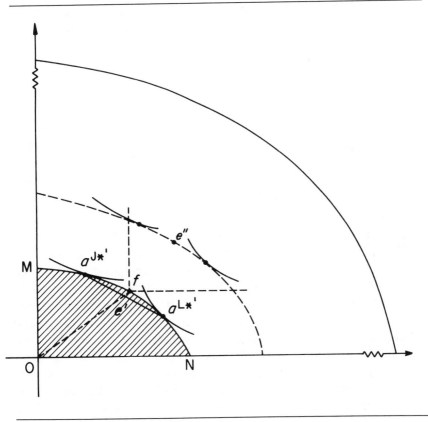

ticipants then identify their most preferred joint actions within this intersection, namely $a^{J*'}$ and $a^{L*'}$, which yields the split-the-difference compromise e'.[43] From there on, the participants may proceed toward the efficiency frontier in a series of rounds wherein the compromise solution on any round becomes the reference point for the following round.

Hence, given the assumptions that each participant always prefers more of each element of an outcome, we have a procedure that (1) requires each participant to know only his own preference structure, (2) guarantees each improvement, (3) meets maximum commitment requirements on each round, (4) achieves efficiency (even when satisficing replaces optimizing), (5) generally satisfies the desirable property of preindeterminacy, (6) is simple, and (7) has appeal as being fair. It thus stands out as the best procedure that may be adopted when the required assumptions are satisfied. We designate it as the *minimum information incremax procedure.*

4.22 THE VETO POWER AS ANOTHER DESIRABLE FEATURE

To the above approaches to conflict resolution we can add another element. To those procedures involving a series of rounds and preindeterminacy of both the path taken to reach the final solution and the nature of the final solution itself, we can add the property of veto power on any one round, on any subset of rounds, or on the entire set of rounds. Adding such a property to a procedure may increase significantly its acceptability, especially for insecure participants. In procedures guaranteeing improvements on each round, it might be expected that no participant would want to exercise the veto. However, there is no assurance that this will be the case when the participants to the conflict are human and hence are not necessarily 100 percent rational. Indeed, the participants may continue to veto for a large (and theoretically an infinitely large) number of times, since each participant may argue that it involves zero cost and he has nothing to lose by holding out for something better. When such is the case, the introduction of the veto power as a property may preclude the reaching of a compromise joint action as a solution. In many other cases, however, the introduction of the veto power can make sense, especially when there is some cost for undertaking one or more rounds one or more times, and when there are initial psychological blocks. If the veto power is introduced into an incremax procedure, we can speak of a *veto-incremax procedure.*

4.23 LAST-OFFER ARBITRATION (WITH INCENTIVES TO THINK OF OTHERS)

Now we move to another set of approaches that cannot be as formally stated as the procedures discussed previously. However, these techniques may work in a setting where participants are less than 100 percent rational in their ways of reaching compromise. These techniques have been put forth forcefully in seminars by Roger Fisher, and are discussed at length in Farber (1980) and Stern et al. (1975).

To facilitate the development of the last-offer arbitration approach, consider a situation that approximates one that might have existed in 1976. Suppose as a result of successful negotiations between NATO and Warsaw Pact countries regarding mutual force reductions, the problem of sharing the military cost savings among NATO countries had arisen. To simplify the discussion, we confine our attention to the three major NATO participants—the United States, West Germany, and Britain. To West Germany an *equal* sharing of cost savings might have seemed most reasonable at first, although after further thought West Germany might have been inclined to propose a sharing somewhat in favor of Britain because of Britain's past economic troubles. West Germany therefore might have proposed a 30-30-40 percent division, with West Germany receiving 30 (the first percentage figure), the United States receiving 30 (the second percentage figure), and Britain receiving 40 (the third figure). Britain, very much concerned with its own internal economic problems and aware of the high prosperity of West Germany and the affluence of the United States, might have proposed a division strongly reflecting *its* perception of relative economic needs. It might have proposed a 15-15-70 split, with it receiving 70 percent of the savings. The United States, being sensitive to the feelings of its populace that it should not be spending money and basing troops in Europe and yet sensitive to Britain's economic needs and aware of the high prosperity of West Germany and the excessive strength of the mark, might have proposed a 10-60-30 percent division.

To aid understanding of the situation, we construct a very simple figure, namely Figure 4-16. Along its vertical axis we measure possible percentages (from 0 to 100) of United States' share of the cost reduction. Along the horizontal axis we measure possible percentages (from 0 to 100) of West Germany's share. We do not need to specify an axis measuring Britain's percentage share since that share will always be 100 minus the sum of the shares of the United States and West Germany. We can then plot in Figure 4-16 the three proposals. The West German proposal, for example, corresponds to the 30 percent mark along the vertical United States axis, the 30 percent mark along the horizontal West German axis, and the remaining 40 percent in Britain's share. As noted on pp. 80–84, one standard approach

Figure 4-16.   Proposals for Sharing a Cost Saving.

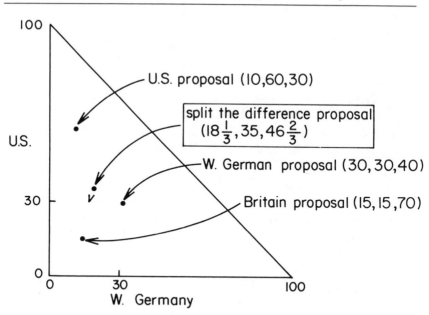

to resolving the difference among the three proposals is to split the difference. If we were to split the difference we would obtain a division (18⅓, 35, 46⅔), which corresponds to point v in Figure 4-16.[44]

It is clear that this split-the-difference procedure can work only if the three participants are responsible in the sense of stating proposals that truly reflect what they consider fair. In some situations this can be expected. But in other situations the participants may seek to gain advantage by not doing so and, specifically, by bluffing. For example, if Britain had bluffed and proposed 90 instead of 70 as its percentage share, and the others had not bluffed, then Britain would have come out with a higher percentage than the 46⅔ percent that comes from splitting the difference.

The split-the-difference procedure does not require a mediator. In some situations, however, it may be useful to use a procedure involving a mediator. One such procedure, which also does away with bluffing, is last-offer arbitration. In this procedure, a mediator or third person is chosen by the participants because he is well informed, judicious, and highly respected. His role is to choose the fairest of the three joint action proposals that might be made. He may be motivated to do so because it is his job, because he is paid to do so, because he receives respect (acclaim) from the world community, or because he gains self-respect. By introducing this fourth participant with his implicit (or explicit) payoff function, an incentive has been created for each of the remaining participants to take into account the needs (desires, demands) of other participants and even attempt to see that the needs of others are met. Each participant knows that if he proposes a joint action based on his own self-interest, then it is less likely to be selected than is one that considers the welfare of the other participants. Thus, each comes to propose a "compromise" joint action more distant from his own most preferred and closer to the most preferred of the others than would otherwise be the case. For example, West Germany might have recognized Britain's economic woes and thus been willing to suggest that Britain receive 44 (not 40) percent of the cost savings. Thus, it might have proposed a 28-28-44 division. The U.S. and British proposals might have also been less self-interested. (See Figure 4–17.) From these three proposals, the mediator then chooses the one he considers fairest.[45]

There are, however, some shortcomings in the use of last-offer arbitration. For example, when the mediator selects the fairest of three proposed joint actions, he in effect assigns a weight of either unity or zero to each. Such might not be acceptable to the two participants whose proposals receive weights of zero; they may feel that their proposals should be given at least some weight even if judged not to be the fairest. Hence a modified version of last-offer arbitration might be suggested. In this version, the mediator weights each proposed joint action by a factor ranging between zero and unity that (in his opinion) represents the degree of its fairness.[46] Summing the weighted proposals and dividing by the sum of the weights yields the compromise solution.

Last-offer arbitration can take on different characteristics for different situations. For example, when there are only two participants involved, as in the cases relating to developed and developing nations, it may turn out that the compromise solution reached after weighting is not efficient. In view of this possibility, or to allow the mediator to specify another joint action that is still more efficient and desirable than the above compromise solution, the mediator may be given the authority to change up to some factor, say 10 percent, any dimension of the proposed joint action he selects as fairest.

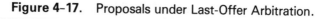

Figure 4-17.   Proposals under Last-Offer Arbitration.

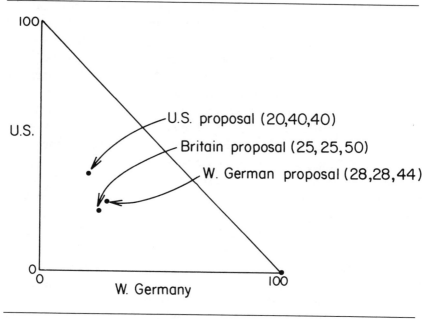

Where a limited commitment feature must be introduced because of the psychological needs of one or both participants, the unmodified or modified last-offer arbitration procedure can be used on each of a number of rounds. Moreover, for situations where information exists that allows the improvement set on each round to be identified and where proposed joint actions are restricted to this set, last-offer arbitration can also be used.[47,48]

4.24 CONCLUDING REMARKS

This chapter concludes our examination of procedures wherein we use the very realistic assumption that participants only be able to order their preferences over outcomes. While we require that these preferences be consistent (for example, we do not allow indifference curves to intersect), this is not unreasonable.

Because there are many options, this motivated the development of new concepts. These related to the representation of preference structures by indifference curves, the identification of the efficiency frontier, the construction of best reply lines, the use of guaranteed improvement and limited commitment sets and the option of a veto power. With the continuous joint action space and these new concepts we were able to develop a whole new set of procedures: split-the-difference and weighted-average (one-step and sequential), alternating leader-follower, GRIT, last-offer arbitration, various incremax and decremax procedures, and others.

As already noted, ordinal preference structures are very realistic. On the other hand, assuming them restricts the range of techniques that can be employed to manage conflicts. Therefore, whenever participants can make more precise statements about their preference structures, such as state the ratio of the utilities they would receive from any pair of outcomes or even assign precise values to them, we are in a position to suggest to participants a broader range of procedures to consider for use. Hence, in Chapters 5 through 8 we shall examine the methods of conflict management when participants can be more precise in stating their preferences and do more than simply rank outcomes.

APPENDIX TO CHAPTER 4

4A.1 A "Good-Cause" Payment Procedure (with or without the Bearhug Principle)

While a number of conflict situations of reality involve finite action spaces, a mediator or third party may be able to introduce another variable into a finite action situation to extend the range of possible actions and acceptable procedures. In particular, he may be able to introduce some finely divisible variable like money, territory, number of beads, number of postage stamps, or square feet of territory that participants value, do or can possess, and are able to transfer among themselves.[49] To motivate the discussion, consider two developing nations (or regions) trying to decide among themselves who gets what share of the components of an assistance program proffered by a group of developed nations. To keep the analysis as simple as possible we shall consider only two components: a petrochemical complex and a food processing complex, which each of the two developing nations prefers in that order. Each component is accompanied by the skilled labor, management, and other know-how required for its effective operation, so that a dollar value (based on world prices) cannot be established for it. A wise political leader representing the developed nations immediately recognizes the potential conflict that will be generated among the two developing nations—a conflict whose negative aspects could even nullify the advantages expected to accrue from the assistance program. He therefore adds another, finely divisible, component (such as a fixed amount of dollars) to ease the allocation problem.

In Figure 4A-1 we depict the problem with the use of indifference curves. In the middle of the figure is a vertical axis along which we order the preferences of the two participants regarding all possible allocations, excluding the money component. For participant L, the order of preference goes from the top down; L most prefers that she obtains both components—the petrochemicals complex, p, and the food production complex, f—while M receives nothing, namely 0. This allocation is $(pf,0)$, the first item in the parentheses being the allocation to L and the second element being that to M. L least prefers the allocation $(0,pf)$ where she receives nothing. For participant M, the order of preference is the same. His most preferred outcome is therefore $(0,pf)$ and his least preferred $(pf,0)$.

If we now introduce a sufficiently large pot of money, which at the start is considered to be equally divided among the two participants, we can construct for each a set of four indifference "curves" one passing through each of the four points on the vertical axis. (Strictly speaking, each such indifference curve is not a curve, as it connects only four points; but we find it convenient to use the word.) The procedure for constructing these curves is simple. We start off with any allocation, say (f,p), which gives f to L and p to M. Measuring money to be received by L in the positive direction from the central vertical line, and money to be paid out by L in the negative direction, we then ask L to specify how much money she would require to compensate for her giving up f (this amount is given by QV in Figure 4A-1). Further, we ask L how much money she would be willing to give up, when she has f, to have p instead of f (this would be KJ) or to have pf (this would be EF). Thus we obtain four points to plot and connect by line segments. When we smooth these segments we obtain the indifference curve EKAV.[50] We also construct for L three other indifference curves, each starting with one of the three other allocations that L might receive as indicated along the central vertical line. In similar

Figure 4A-1.   Indifference Curves for Mixed Finite/Continuous Action Spaces.

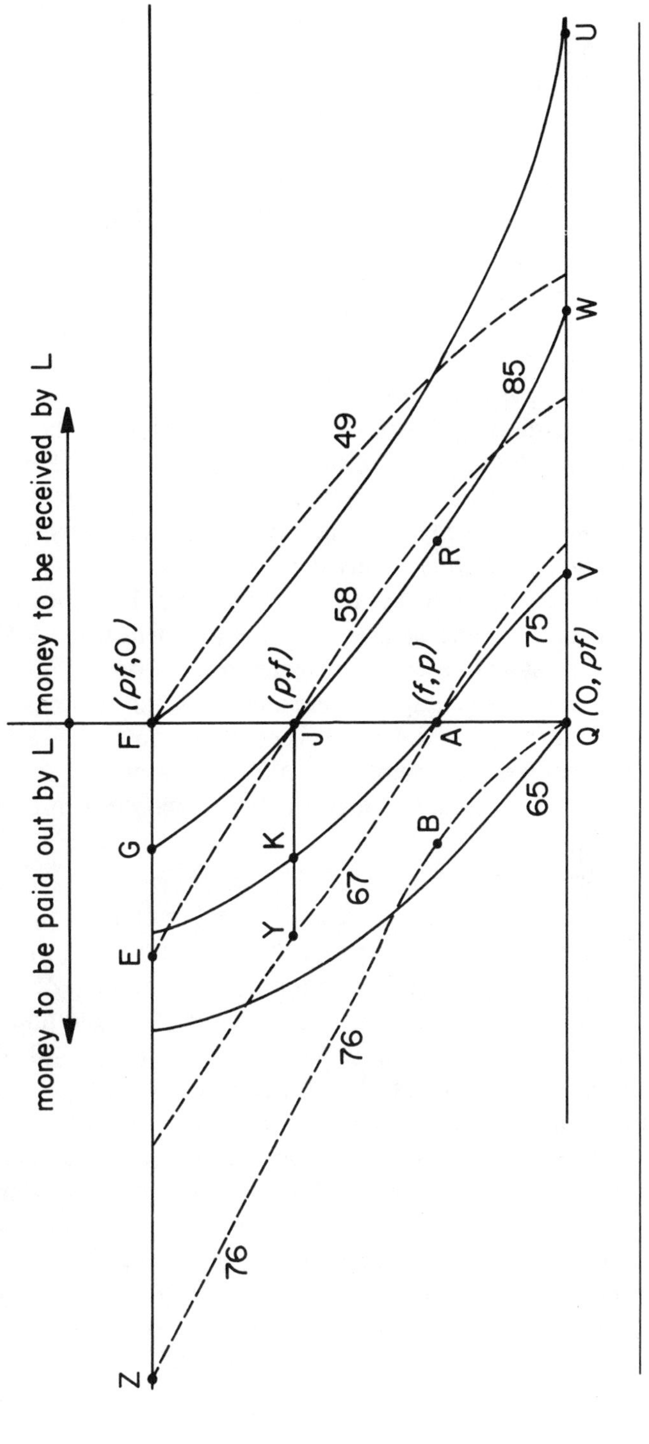

manner we construct M's four indifference curves (as dashed lines) in Figure 4A-1.

Next, the mediator proposes and obtains agreement by participants to the following set of rules:

Rule 1. Each participant is to take a turn in serving as leader, the one who serves first being determined by a toss of a coin. So long as a leader is willing to make a money payment, the leader can choose an allocation to propose as optimal. However, he cannot propose an allocation if it involves a money payment by the follower.

Rule 2. In proposing any allocation, the leader must make a money payment (to some good cause) equal to the amount that would make the follower as happy with his share of the allocation if he were to receive the money as he would be if he were to receive just the leader's share. We shall designate this a "good-cause" payment (or tax).

Rule 3. If it turns out that the two participants cannot reach a common acceptable proposal, the payment that each is required to make to a good cause under his proposal is to increase by small percentage increments until one participant finds the other's proposal more acceptable than his under the required increased payment. When the mediator puts this rule into effect, we shall speak of the use of the "bearhug" principle.[51]

To illustrate using Figure 4A-1, start off with the allocation where L receives all, that is $(pf,0)$. We identify the point Z on M's 76 indifference curve, which passes through the point representing the allocation $(0,pf)$. Point Z indicates that amount of money ZF which, given his receipt of nothing in the allocation $(pf,0)$, would make M as well off as if he had received pf (from the allocation $(0,pf)$) and no amount of money. We ask L if that amount of money, a good-cause payment, in addition to pf (in the allocation $(pf,0)$ proposed by L) would be satisfactory. L states "no" since it would put her on a very low indifference curve, much lower than her 85 indifference curve coursing through her next most preferred allocation depicted by the (p,f) point. The allocation $(pf,0)$ is then rejected and L is permitted to propose her next most preferred allocation, namely (p,f). Again we identify the sum of money YJ that M would need to receive to leave him as content with f plus that money as he would be under an allocation (f,p), where he receives p. Again we ask L if she finds that a good-cause payment of that amount of money is acceptable to supplement her share p in the proposed allocation (p,f). Again L would want to reject, since she would come to be on an indifference curve lower than her 75 indifference curve, which courses through her next most preferred point (f,p). But here, by Rule 2, L cannot reject since there is no other allocation she can propose that does not require M to make a payment. To see this, note that up to this point L was obtaining a share of the allocation that both L and M preferred to the share M was obtaining. Thus, L had to make the payment—that is, give up something because she was getting the more preferred share. However, once L chooses the allocation (f,p), L receives a share f. Both L and M prefer f less than p, the share that M receives under this allocation. Therefore, L cannot reject (p,f) and make her next most preferred proposal (f,p) since that would involve a payment by M, for M too prefers (f,p) to (p,f). By Rule 2, a proposal by L of (f,p) is disallowed. L must stop at (p,f). L can only hope that M, in his role of leader, will suggest this allocation that she (L) prefers to the allocation (p,f) with the required payment of YJ, equal say to $450, from L.

Next we consider M as leader. He first considers the allocation $(0,pf)$, which he most prefers. But that would involve a payment of QU, the amount of money that L would require to keep her as happy with the allocation $(0,pf)$ as she would be if she were to receive pf in the allocation $(pf,0)$. But to make a money payment of QU, even if he were to receive pf, would leave M most unhappy. He then considers his next most preferred allocation, (f,p). That, too, would involve money payment by M of AR, say $400. But M finds that this money payment plus his receipt of p in the allocation (f,p) would make him more happy (on a higher indifference curve) than the receipt of f in the allocation (p,f), which would put him on his 58 indifference curve. So M is satisfied with the proposal of an allocation (f,p) plus a money payment by him of AR. But also L prefers this allocation (f,p) to the allocation (p,f) where, in addition, she must make a money payment of YJ to a good cause. So then the allocation (f,p) together with a good-cause payment of $400 by M may be considered a stable (equilibrium) allocation.

Of course, both L and M would be still better off if they could somehow divide the $400 between themselves. But to allow them to do this would destroy the ability of the procedure to lead them to an acceptable and stable allocation.[52] In this procedure, it is essential that neither participant know the intensity of the preferences of the other. It is also essential that the mediator keep the participants apart or in other ways preclude collusion to avoid the payment to a good cause, since this would be a destabilizing element.

However, it may turn out that under Rules 1 and 2 the two participants do not come to prefer the same allocation. If the curves are as in Figure 4A–2, then L prefers to stop at allocation (p,f) even though she must make a payment of WJ,[53] and M prefers to stop at (f,p), even though he must make a payment of AB.[54] At this point, the mediator applies Rule 3, the bearhug principle, increasing the payments until one finds it preferable to accept the allocation proposed by the other, and the other makes the good-cause payment.

Figure 4A-2.   A Solution in a Mixed/Finite Continuous Action Space.

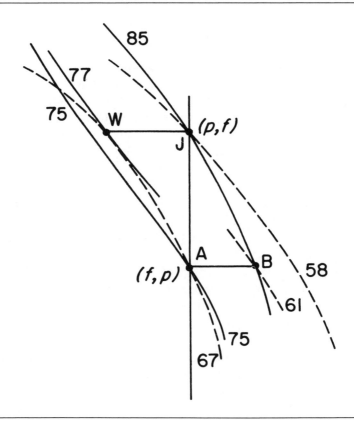

The above analysis can easily be generalized to more than two objects. However, it pertains to a situation where both participants have the same preference ordering for all allocations of two components (objects), excluding the variable money. This is so for many situations of reality. However, if they do not have the same preference orderings, then the process of finding an acceptable allocation becomes more complicated. Research on this problem is beyond the scope of this book; so too is analysis when the indifference curves are not relatively well behaved. An extension of this type of approach that involves money as side payments to reluctant participants is examined in Chapter 8 on pages 275–278.

Still another method for making finite action spaces continuous is to introduce probabilities with regard to the several possible allocations. Since probabilities can be varied continuously, a small change in the probability of any allocation can be associated with small changes in utility or satisfaction derived by a participant. Thus we can establish continuous indifference maps to take the place of maps with a discrete number of indifference curves, such as in Figure 4A-1. However, realistic situations involving participants who construct such continuous indifference curves by varying probabilities are few and far between.

4A.2 The Use of Procedures in Situations with Many (Continuous) Actions and a Limited Number of Utility Outcomes

While traditionally economists and applied mathematicians associate a continuous utility function with a participant whose actions can be represented continuously in a Euclidean space, there are nonetheless a number of important situations of reality for which this is not the case. For example, in considering military budgets a preference ordering may be strictly in terms of a finite set of ranks wherein all possible actions (military budgets) lead to outcomes classified as either (1) increased national security, (2) unchanged national security, or (3) decreased national security. For example, it could be perceived that military budgets less than $120 billion lead to the outcome *decreased national security*, while those above $180 billion lead to the outcome *increased national security*. If this is the case for both participants, then the continuous joint action space maps onto a finite joint utility (outcome) space with the joint actions ranked in terms of each participant's preferences. Accordingly, the participants can consider the use of several procedures already discussed in Chapter 3 (and to be developed further in Chapter 8) for finite outcome spaces. For example, one might be an action compromise principle, another, an equirank improvement principle. There is, however, one problem that is evident from studying the continuous joint action space of Table 4A-1, wherein we have mapped the utility outcomes of L and J with regard to two continuous action variables (say military expenditures and social welfare expenditures). The problem is that an infinite number of joint actions correspond to each set of ordinal utility outcomes. However, where participants are satisficers, they may be able to agree to the choice of the first joint action that meets, say, an equirank concession principle. If not, they may be able to employ a *lexicographic* approach once the compromise joint outcome is identified. Here the participants would need to introduce another criterion (say, inflationary impact), formerly infinitely dwarfed by both the security and welfare criteria, to select among joint actions.[55]

4A.3 Apportionment Procedures

Frequently there are situations in which a fixed number of indivisible objects is to be divided among a set of competing participants. The

Table 4A-1.   A Finite Joint Outcome Matrix for a Continuous Joint Action Space.

Social Welfare Program Expenditures (billions of dollars)	a^J		20 , 7	16 , 7	12 , 10
		60			
			17 , 6	13 ,11	9 , 14
		30			
			12 ,10	8 ,15	4 , 18
		0			
			0 120 180 a^L		

Military Expenditures (billions of dollars)

apportionment of these objects may be made on the basis of many criteria—e.g., in accord with number of constituents that participants represent, their wealth, the resources they command, their "power," their need, or any combination of these and other factors. Conflict over criteria to be used, often a problem of reaching a compromise on weights to be attached to each criteria, can be viewed as falling within the category of conflict over objectives (discussed on pages 48–49 and pages 95–96 and to be treated further in Chapter 8). The particular new element of conflict that enters in the apportionment problem occurs when the fixed number of indivisible objects cannot be exactly distributed among participants by some accepted and fair criteria. This situation arises frequently in the classic case of the number of seats in the legislature to be distributed among states in proportion to their populations or, in the hypothetical case now to be discussed, of eleven U.N. fellowships to be distributed among four developing regions in proportion to their college populations.

To keep the example simple, assume the regions' proportions of a relevant population are as given in Column 1 of Table 4A-2, where p^J ($J = 1,2,3,4$) is the relevant population of region J and p is the total population of all regions. In Column 2 we calculate the fractional numbers (exact quotas) q^J to which they are theoretically entitled where $q^J = (p^J/p)h$. Here h is the number of fellowships (objects) to be allocated. Since fellowships come only in nonfractional form, the problem is to choose a method for converting the fractional numbers q^J into whole numbers (integers) that sum to the total number of fellowships available.

Table 4A-2.   A Problem of Allocation.

	p^J/p	$q^J = (p^J/p)/h$	$\lfloor q^J \rfloor$	a^J	$\lceil q^J \rceil$
	(1)	(2)	(3)	(4)	(5)
Region 1	.35	3.83	3	4	4
Region 2	.30	3.30	3	3	4
Region 3	.20	2.20	2	2	3
Region 4	.15	1.65	1	2	2
Total	1.00	11	9	11	13

If we define the *lower quota*, designated $\lfloor q^J \rfloor$, for each participant J to be the quota obtained by rounding q^J *down* to the nearest integer, then not all objects are allocated. See Column 3 of Table 4A-2. In line with the general approach of an incremax procedure, the $\lfloor q^J \rfloor$ may be gradually increased by small but equal amounts until one or more of the adjusted $\lfloor q^J \rfloor$ experience a unit increase making the total of the adjusted $\lfloor q^J \rfloor$ equal to the total number of objects. At that point, the adjusted $\lfloor q^J \rfloor$ yield a full allocation, designated a^J (as at the head of Column 4 in Table 4A-2). For example, as the $\lfloor q^J \rfloor$ in Column 3 are gradually increased, first Region 1 obtains another unit for its quota, and then Region 4, at which point all eleven of the objects are allocated. This assignment on the basis of the finally adjusted $\lfloor q^J \rfloor$ may be said to correspond to a type of minimum distance procedure—a minimum "distance" from a feasible (inefficient) allocation to a complete (efficient) one, a^J.[56]

In parallel fashion, each participant may be assigned his *upper quota*, designated $\lceil q^J \rceil$, obtained by rounding q^J *up* to the nearest integer. When this is done, more than the available number of objects are allocated. See Column 5. In line with the general approach of a decremax procedure, the $\lceil q^J \rceil$ may be gradually decreased by small but equal amounts until one or more of the adjusted $\lceil q^J \rceil$ experience a unit decrease, making the total of the adjusted bounds equal to the total number of objects. At that point, the adjusted $\lceil q^J \rceil$ yield a full feasible allocation a^J. For example, with reference to Table 4A-2, as the $\lceil q^J \rceil$ in Column 5 are gradually decreased, first Region 3 suffers a unit decrease in its quota and then Region 2 does, at which point no more than eleven objects are allocated. See Column 4. Apportionment on the basis of these adjusted $\lceil q^J \rceil$ may then be said to correspond to a type of minimum distance procedure—a minimum distance from an infeasible allocation (more objects are allocated than exist) to a feasible (efficient) one.[57]

The above procedures involve equal absolute increments or decrements for all participants. It may be, however, that participants are able to agree not on absolute but only on percentage increments or decrements. Hence, two alternative approaches become possible. One is to assign objects according to the lower quota method and to increase all $\lfloor q^J \rfloor$ gradually by the same small percentage amounts until all objects are allocated (that is, until the efficiency frontier is reached). This corresponds to a minimum distance along a straight line from the origin (the zero allocation point for all participants) through the exact quotas q^J in the upward direction from the q^J. Thus it represents one way of moving from an inefficient allocation (based on lower quotas) to an efficient allocation where weak improvement is guaranteed for each participant.[58]

Another approach assigns objects according to the upper quota $\lceil q^J \rceil$ (an infeasible quasi-utopian assignment), and then decreases all $\lceil q^J \rceil$ gradually by the same small percentage amounts until no more objects than available are allocated, that is, until a point that represents a feasible (and in this case efficient) allocation has been reached. This corresponds to a minimum distance from the exact quota q^J in the downward direction along the above straight line. Thus it represents one way of moving from an infeasible allocation (based on upper quota) to a feasible and efficient one that involves a series of weak concessions.[59]

The methods of both equal absolute increments to the $\lfloor q^J \rfloor$ and equal absolute decrements from $\lceil q^J \rceil$ reach one and the same allocation. In contrast, the methods of equal percentage increases of the $\lfloor q^J \rfloor$ and of equal percentage decreases of the $\lceil q^J \rceil$ do not in general reach the same allocation; hence, an additional principle must be employed to select from among the latter two methods.

The above procedures may be found unacceptable on several grounds. For example, the one involving equal percentage increases tends to be more favorable to the developing regions having the larger quotas and less favorable to those having the smaller quotas. To avoid this objection, another procedure may be suggested. In this next procedure, the aim is to switch objects around among participants such that when we compare all possible pairs of participants, $(J, L = A, ... U, J \neq L)$, the absolute difference $(p^L/a^L) - (p^J/a^J) > 0$ is minimized (where J is the more favored participant).[60]

Still another method starts with the zero allocation $(0,0,0,...,0)$ and involves the allocation of only one object on each of a series of rounds. On any round, regions eligible to receive this object are those whose upper quota $\lceil q^J \rceil$ would not be exceeded if they were to receive it. Among eligible regions, the object is allocated to that region which has the largest "index of justification." For any eligible region J and any round e, this index is given by $p^J/(a^J_{e-1} + 1)$, where a^J_{e-1} is the allocation to region J at the close of the previous round. The series of rounds comes to an end when all objects have been allocated. Note that this procedure is identical to a leader-follower incremax procedure, where (1) the limited commitment space on any round is defined by that set of points each element of which represents a change in one object for one eligible region, this region being different for each element; (2) the improvement space on any round is a weak improvement set, since only one region realizes an improvement; and (3) the leader on any move is the one with the highest index of justification.[61] Thus a series of moves from an inefficient $(0,0,0,...0)$ allocation toward the efficiency frontier ensues, and on the last move an allocation on that frontier is attained.[62]

In contrast, a decremax procedure might be employed. This procedure starts from an ideal-type allocation, for example an allocation $(h,h,h,...h)$, or any other infeasible point considered relevant. On each round one object is to be taken away from one and only one region. Regions eligible for such a loss are those whose lower quota $\lfloor q^J \rfloor$ would not be violated were they to lose one object. Among eligible regions, the object is taken away from that region which has the smallest "index of justification." For any region J and any round e, the index is given by $p^J/(a^J_{e-1} - 1)$. Note that this procedure has properties similar to a decremax procedure where (1) the limited commitment space on any round is defined by that set of points each element of which represents a loss of one object by one eligible region, this region being different for each element and (2) the conceder on any round is the one with the least index of justification. Thus a series of moves from an infeasible allocation toward the efficiency frontier takes place, and on the last move an allocation on that frontier is attained.[63]

The above procedures can be subject to reasonable constraints. For example, the allocation might be required to guarantee that each participant acquires a minimum number of the objects, or that no participant can acquire more than some maximum number.[64]

With so many possible apportionment procedures available for use, it may be asked: "Does any one provide a better solution to the problem than the others?" In attempting to answer this question, Balinski and Young (1975) have adopted an axiomatic approach and identified a set of desirable properties that they claim any reasonable apportionment scheme should satisfy.

The "static" properties that are generally considered most desirable include:

1.   The allocation of objects received by each participant should not fall outside the upper and lower bounds of his exact quota (as defined earlier).[65] (This property is equivalent to (2) and (3) below.)

2. The allocation of objects received by each particpant should be at least equal to his lower quota (as defined earlier).[66]

3. The allocation of objects received by each participant should be no greater than his upper quota (as defined earlier).[67]

The "nonstatic" properties that are generally considered most desirable include:

1. If the (exact) quota of any participant increases and the number of objects to be allocated remains constant, he should not receive a reduced allocation of objects using the same apportionment procedure.[68]

2. If the population of just one participant increases and all else remains constant, he should not receive a reduced allocation of objects using the same apportionment procedure.[69]

3. If the number of objects to be allocated (house size) increases and all else remains constant, no participant should receive a reduced allocation of objects using the same apportionment procedure.[70]

In examining the apportionment procedures discussed in this section, Lucas (1978) has found that none of them satisfies all the above-mentioned properties.[71] Therefore, in making recommendations as to which apportionment procedure should be used in any given situation, the best approach might be to identify which of the properties outlined above could most reasonably be violated and then to suggest for use that procedure which meets all properties except one (or more) that can be most reasonably violated.[72]

Notes

1. In smoothing out Table 3–13 the action space of each participant is taken to lie within the range of 0 to 10. To facilitate understanding of the transformation, the reader may take the points corresponding to 0,2.5,5.0,7.5, and 10.0 on each scale to correspond in order to the five finite actions of each participant noted in Table 3–13. However, because of smoothing, the most preferred joint action of each participant in the continuous joint action space of Figure 4–1 and of Figure 4–2 (to be discussed later) corresponds only approximately to the preferred joint action in the finite joint action space of Table 3–13. For example, a^{J*}, J's most preferred joint action in Figure 4–1, is now

associated with the outcome (26.8,50) whereas in Table 3-13 J's most preferred joint action (AG,C$_4$) is associated with outcome (31,50).

The equations underlying the ordinal utility values assigned to the participants are:

$u^J = 2a^J + 0.2a^Ja^L - (a^J)^2/2 + 1.2a^L + 30$ for participant J, and $u^L = 3a^L - 0.3a^Ja^L - (a^L)^2/2 + 1.2a^J + 30$ for participant L.

2. However, see Isard, T. Smith et al. (1969:237n).

3. We may imagine that through point w passes J's indifference curve, assigned a value of 28, and L's indifference curve, assigned a value 49. Through point s passes J's indifference curve, valued at 32, and L's, valued at 54. Hence, both participants prefer s to w.

4. We may assume in this illustration that none of the output of activity i is required for the output of activity h, and vice versa.

5. This is so since any point not on this curve is dominated by at least one point on the curve. That is, the level of at least one of the activities can be increased without reducing the level of the other activity.

6. For example, if in Figure 4-2 the unit of foreign aid were to be redefined to be twice as large (say $2 million instead of $1 million), the intersection point q in the new figure would in general be more favorable to L and less favorable to J.

7. To be meaningful to sophisticated participants, the solution in the joint action space should correspond to an outcome on the efficiency frontier.

8. Where a respected and trusted third party is present and is able to estimate each participant's preference structure (and thus identify the median efficient joint action) it is only necessary that participants know their own preference structure.

9. This procedure requires that each participant knows his own preference structure and that the mediator knows the preference structure of all participants. Note that this procedure could conceivably be adopted in the absence of a mediator if each participant were aware of all other participants' preference structures.

10. Figure 4-4 is constructed on the basis of Table 3-13 smoothed out to be a continuous joint action space.

11. The set *interior to* the indifference curves is the *strong improvement set;* the set including these indifference curves is the *weak improvement set.*

12. Since a^J is the variable J controls, and since his utility outcome u^J is a function of both a^J and a^L, that is, $u^J = f(a^J, a^L)$, the best reply is defined as $\partial u^J/\partial a^J = 0$ for all values of a^L.

13. Since a^L is the variable L controls, and since her utility outcome u^L is

a function of both a^J and a^L—that is, $u^L = g(a^J, a^L)$—her best reply curve is defined as $\partial u^L / \partial a^L = 0$ for all values of a^J.

14. As with the metagame approach and unlike most approaches discussed in this book, the best reply process involves a direct action (and not a proposal) by each participant. Here, as elsewhere, it is clear from the context of the discussion whether each participant takes a direct action or makes a proposal. Hence, we shall no longer indicate explicitly when the situation involves direct actions by participants.

15. In a one-step procedure, the use of this principle requires that each participant know his own preference structure and the other participant's most preferred joint action. When applied sequentially, it is required that each participant know his own preference structure and the other participant's most preferred joint action on each round. Where there are many rounds, this amounts to complete knowledge of the other's preference structure. When it is meaningful for a respected and trusted mediator to be present, and when the mediator knows all participants' most preferred joint actions on each round, it is only necessary that each participant know his own preference structure.

16. In a more complicated situation, where there was a dispute among the Committee on the Biological Effects of Ionizing Radiation of the U.S. National Academy of Sciences, a bitter internal dispute (among outstanding scholars) over assessing the health risks of low-level radiation was resolved by the use of a split-the-difference principle. As reported by the *New York Times* (July 30, 1980:A12):

> The dispute focused on the best way to estimate cancer risk from radiation at levels so low that no human epidemiological data are available. Dr. Radford argued for a *linear dose-response model,* meaning that the same proportional risk seen at high levels should be extrapolated directly to low levels. Dr. Rossi and others contended that experiments on animals had suggested that the risk was proportionately lower at low levels and that a *quadratic* model was needed to make statistical estimates.
>
> The subcommittee's resolution, in a diplomatic and political compromise, adopted both arguments, using a *linear quadratic model* that gave an estimate roughly between the two extremes, describing Dr. Radford's linear model as defining the *upper limit* of risk and Dr. Rossi's quadratic model as the *lower limit* of risk.

17. For situations involving three or more political leaders or blocs, see the discussion on pages 228–235.

18. For a discussion of procedures that may be employed in the determination of appropriate weights, see pages 190–192.

19. Note that the use of an improvement set by a participant who is in-

itially myopic and 100 percent self-interested does imply a change in psychology, namely, that he is willing to be cooperative enough to consider a guarantee of improvement for all other participants. To posit such a change in psychology may not be realistic in certain conflict situations.

20. A satisficer may be considered to be an optimizer since he in effect maximizes leisure or some other factor subject to the constraint that he reach some satisfactory level regarding the outcome as defined in the problem being studied. For further discussion, see pages 206–207.

21. This is so here because more of both environmental quality and growth is preferred to less.

22. In this situation, the successive points Q, Q', Q'', each being an infeasible joint action, correspond to (0,0) points in the joint utility space of the two participants. On the move in which point s is reached, the corresponding point in the joint utility space jumps from (0,0) to a point on the efficiency frontier in that space. Here we continue to assume that each participant prefers more rather than less of any objective (or action contributing to that objective), given the level of the other objective (or action contributing to that objective).

23. This procedure requires that each participant know his own preference structure, and the mediator know the preference structure of all participants. This procedure could conceivably be adopted in the absence of a mediator if each participant were aware of the other participant's preference structure.

24. Corresponding to this alternating leader-follower incremax procedure, we can develop an alternating leader-follower decremax procedure. See Isard, T. Smith, et al. (1969:447–48).

25. For this procedure to be applicable, each participant need only know his own preference structure.

26. If they were to make such comparison, then one or more of them might be motivated to change the unit of measurement of his action space.

27. The utility of each interest group is assumed to be a monotonically increasing function of achievement on its primary objective. The function may involve either ordinal, relative, or cardinal preferences.

28. Assuming that objectives E^A, E^B . . . E^U are ranked in order of importance and considering the joint action a to be the only relevant variable, the simple hierarchical programming model can be formalized as:

Step 1.   max $E^A(a)$

s.t. $a \in K$

where $a\epsilon K$ stands for resource, technological, and other constraints that may be imposed on the choice of joint action a. Such constraints are discussed further on pages 191-196 and 235-237.

Step 2.   max $E^B(a)$

s.t. $a \in K$

$E^A(a) \geq E^A(a)^*$

where an asterisk designates an optimal solution to the previous program.

Step 3.   max $E^C(a)$

s.t. $a \in K$

$E^A(a) \geq E^A(a)^*$

$E^B(a) \geq E^B(a)^*$

and so on.

29.   In the above application, we have assumed that no interest group reaches a satiation level of achievement on its single objective. When the procedure is modified to include the possibility of satiation, we need to add an additional constraint $E^J(a) \leq E^J(a)^S$ for all objectives J ($J = A, B, \ldots ,U$) at each round, where $E^J(a)^S$ represents the satiation level on objective J.

30.   Given the follower's psychology, once e has been reached, the follower's best reply line is in effect his restricted action space.

31.   In this case the leader must know his own preference structure as well as that of the follower; however, the follower need only know his own preference structure.

32.   In this case the leader must know his own preference structure as well as that of the follower; however, the follower need only know his own preference structure and enough information about the leader's preference structure to know that her demand is technically feasible.

33.   The same information is required here as in the general leader-follower case except that the follower may only need to have information on his preference structure in a limited area around e.

34.   Corresponding to each type of follower, we can identify specific cases. For example, for conditional-reply or aggressive-reply followers we can have cases: "the Ordinal Utility Maximizer as a Leader Constrained by a Conditional-Reply Follower" and "the Ordinal Utility Maximizer as a Leader Constrained by an Aggressive-Reply Follower," respectively. See Isard, T. Smith, et al. (1969: 295-97).

35.   In this case the leader not only needs no information on the follower's preference structure, but might even attribute a nuisance

value to such information. The follower needs to know his own preference structure, but not that of the leader.

36. Isard and Kaniss (1976) show how the veto-incremax procedure can be made part of the GRIT approach and how the notion of unilateral initiatives can be incorporated into the veto-incremax procedure. They also indicate how the GRIT approach can accommodate various personality types within its framework—for example, the perceptive leader, the rational leader opposed by the aggressive follower, and the imaginative leader opposed by an unimaginative follower.

37. In making his concession, the leader may think of a commitment set for himself. He knows that there is a maximum amount of change his opponent would be willing to undertake in any reciprocating action. This maximum represents one possible limit on what a leader may think of as his (the leader's) commitment set. In addition, when making his concession, the leader does not want to stand to lose too much should his opponent not reciprocate. Therefore, he sets a maximum change he is willing to undertake in any initiating action. This maximum represents a second possible limit on what the leader may think of as his commitment set. With the lesser of these two possible limits, the leader may mentally construct his commitment set.

38. Generally speaking, this technique requires that on each round each participant have some limited knowledge of the preference structures of all in the area surrounding the current standpoint for that round. See Note 15 above.

39. Theoretically, the GRIT approach may also be applied in a finite joint action space when there exists a moderately large number of joint actions and small enough steps between joint actions. However, such a situation is not likely to exist frequently; hence, we have assigned the GRIT procedure to the continuous joint action space category.

40. For example, in water resource development where the three major variables are (1) water supply, (2) reliability of supply, and (3) cost, generally all participants always prefer more water, more reliability, and less cost—each, however, with a different set of intensities.

41. More precisely, the assumption is that

$$\frac{\partial u^J}{\partial a^J} , \frac{\partial u^J}{\partial a^L}$$

and

$$\frac{\partial u^L}{\partial a^J} , \frac{\partial u^L}{\partial a^L}$$

are each positive but it may be that

$$\frac{\partial u^J}{\partial a^L} > \frac{\partial u^J}{\partial a^J}$$

and

$$\frac{\partial u^L}{\partial a^J} > \frac{\partial u^L}{\partial a^L}.$$

42.   Note that one might normalize the action spaces of each participant so that they both range from 0 to 1. Doing so then permits the construction of a circle with radius equal to the lesser of the maximum percent changes along either axis that the participants find acceptable. Such a normalization, however, requires the assumption that each participant has at the minimum a lineal utility function. See Isard, T. Smith, et al. (1969:242–44.) Where such an assumption is realistic, this circle technique can be used.

43.   Note that e' does not lie on the arc $a^{J*'}a^{L*'}$ and therefore is inefficient. Hence, participants may find desirable, or insist upon, a variant of this procedure that would require that any compromise joint action such as e' not representable by a point on the relevant efficiency frontier for a given round be replaced by another. It should be replaced by that joint action (such as f in Figure 4–15) defined by the intersection with the frontier of a radial from the reference point for the given round through the point corresponding to the compromise joint action.

44.   We obtain the split-the-difference outcome for West Germany by summing 10, 30, and 15 (the three percentage shares proposed for West Germany) and dividing by 3 to yield 18⅓, and so forth.

45.   To be able to make what he considers to be a fair proposal, each participant must have at least some information about the preference structures of others as well as his own. The mediator too does not require a large amount of information on participants' preferences, but having complete information would enhance his ability to select the fairest of the proposals.

46.   Where the mediator judges that a participant is bluffing or allowing other "inconsiderate" elements to enter into his proposal, he tends to assign a low weight to that participant's proposal.

47.   Note that when the exercise of veto power is permitted on each round and last-offer arbitration is employed, then the participants may be able to reveal the underlying social welfare function of the mediator through the exercise of a sufficient number of vetoes. This occurs because each time a round is reconsidered, a preference statement

between two proposals is made by the mediator. Hence, the greater the number of vetoes exercised on each round, the greater the number of pairwise preference statements revealed pertaining to that round. Over many rounds, participants may then be able to approximate the continuous social welfare function of the mediator.

48.   Also, last-offer arbitration can be used without a mediator. To take a simple example, the participants may agree beforehand that each will rank the three proposals 1, 2, and 3 in order of desirability, and that the one to be selected shall be the one for which the sum of the ranks is lowest. This, however, then is equivalent to the min the total of ranks procedure discussed on pages 39–42.

49.   In technical language, we have a situation with a *modified* finite joint action space continuous in one dimension.

50.   With regard to this indifference curve, the allocations including money to which L is indifferent are: (pf less EF money), (p less JK money), (f), and (nothing plus QV money). In constructing each indifference curve, we assume for each participant that he has positive but diminishing marginal utility for money. However, because the points along the vertical axis in the center of the figure can be arbitrarily located except that their order must be preserved, no significance should be attached to the particular shape of the indifference curves.

51.   In this procedure, each participant must know at least his own preference structure and, in order to tell the participants what money payments would be required with any proposed allocation, the mediator must know the preference structure of all participants.

52.   Rigorously speaking, this procedure requires (as with the Clarke-Vickrey method to be discussed on pages 184–188) that the money payment to a good cause have no perceivable effect on any participant's welfare.

53.   If L were to receive p and make a payment WJ, she would be on a higher indifference curve (say 77) than if she were to accept f in the allocation (f,p), through which her 75 indifference curve passes.

54.   If M were to receive p and make a payment AB, he would be on a higher indifference curve (say 61) than if he were to accept f in the allocation (p,f), through which his 58 indifference curve passes.

55.   This approach implies a lexicographic utility function for each participant. Here a participant first states preferences over joint actions with reference to the property (or criterion) of utmost importance. Then for all joint actions yielding an optimal value for that most important property (he discards all others as nondesirable), he states his preferences with regard to the second most important property. Then, for all joint actions yielding optimal values for both the first and sec-

ond properties, he states preferences with regard to a third most important property, and so on.

56. This procedure has been designated the *Method of Largest Fractions.* See Lucas (1978:17–23).

57. Although the gradual increase of the $\lfloor q^J \rfloor$ or decrease of the $\lceil q^J \rceil$ may be viewed as employing a standard acceptable social practice or rule-of-thumb, it also may be viewed as involving intercardinal utility functions on the part of participants, and thus, as falling within the categories of procedures to be discussed in Chapters 6 and 7.

58. This procedure has been designated the *Method of Greatest Divisors.* It can be shown to be equivalent to minimizing the absolute difference $(a^J p^L / p^J - a^L > 0)$ between pairs of participants J and L, where J is the more favored participant. See Lucas (1978:23–28).

59. This procedure has been designated the *Method of Smallest Divisors.* It is equivalent to minimizing the absolute difference $a^J - (p^J / p^L)\, a^L > 0$ between pairs of participants J and L, where J is the more favored participant. Still another method, called the *Method of Major Fractions,* adjusts each q^J by adding to it the amount 0.5. The adjusted quota is then rounded down to the nearest integer and summed over all J. If the sum is less than the number of objects to be allocated, the adjusted $\lfloor q^J \rfloor$ are increased percentagewise (as noted in the text) until all objects have been allocated. If the sum is more than the number of objects, the adjusted $\lceil q^J \rceil$ are decreased percentagewise (as noted in the text) until no more objects have been allocated than are available. It can be shown that this latter method is eqivalent to minimizing the absolute difference $(a^J / p^J) - (a^L / p^L) > 0$ between pairs of participants J and L, where J is the more favored participant. See Lucas (1978:28–30, 39).

60. This method has been designated the *Method of the Harmonic Mean.* An alternative procedure is to take as the measure of inequity between any two participants the ratio:

$$\left| \frac{p^J}{a^J} - \frac{p^L}{a^L} \right| \bigg/ \ \min \left\{ \frac{p^J}{a^J}, \frac{p^L}{a^L} \right\} \qquad (\text{J,L} = \text{A}, \ldots, \text{U}; \ \text{J} \neq \text{L})$$

and to switch objects around among participants until this measure of inequity between all possible pairs of participants is minimized. This method has been designated the *Method of Equal Proportions.* See Lucas (1978:33–39).

61. Problems of ties can arise. When they do, some ad hoc rule, like toss a coin, may be employed. When this is done some technical analysts may claim that in effect the procedure implies participants with comparable identical cardinal utility functions that are strictly linear

(monotonically increasing) functions of the "index of justification" employed.

62. This corresponds to the *Quota Method* developed by Balinski and Young (1974). Also, see Isard and C. Smith (1982b:94–95).

63. This corresponds to the *Dual Quota Method* developed by Mayberry (1978).

64. In the literature, these have been termed *Generalized Quota Methods.* See Lucas (1978:52–57). In an apportionment procedure each participant in effect demands a certain number of objects (fellowships, beads, seats in a House of Representatives, number of delegates to the United Nations Assembly), that is a certain portion of a pie to be allocated. When these demands are inconsistent, that is, add up to a total that exceeds the supply, there is conflict. An effective conflict management procedure then is one that arrives at an allocation where total demand equals total supply.

65. This has been termed the property of *(Exact) Quota* and can be expressed mathematically as $\lfloor q^J \rfloor \le a^J \le \lceil q^J \rceil$ for all $J = A, \ldots, U$.

66. This has been termed the property of *Lower Quota* and can be expressed mathematically as $\lfloor q^J \rfloor \le a^J$ for all $J = A, \ldots, U$.

67. This has been termed the property of *Upper Quota* and can be expressed mathematically as $a^J \le \lceil q^J \rceil$ for all $J = A, \ldots, U$.

68. This has been termed the property of *Quota Monotonicity* and can be expressed mathematically as: if $q^{J'} > q^J$ for any $J = A, \ldots, U$, then $a^J = f^J(q^J, h) \le a^{J'} = f^J(q^{J'}, h)$.

69. This has been termed the property of *Population Monotonicity* and can be expressed mathematically as: if $p^{J'} > p^J$ and $p^L = p^{L'}$ for all $L = A, \ldots, U, L \ne J$, then $a^J = f^J(p, h) \le a^J = f^J(p', h)$.

70. This has been termed the property of *House Monotonicity* and can be expressed mathematically as: if $h' > h$, then for all $J = A, \ldots, U$, $a^J = f^J(p, h) \le a^{J'} = f^J(p, h')$.

71. For example, the *Method of Largest Fractions* fails to satisfy both Quota Monotonicity and House Monotonicity; the *Methods of Greatest and Smallest Divisors* fail to satisfy Upper and Lower Quota, respectively; and the *Quota and Dual Quota Methods* both fail to satisfy Population Monotonicity.

72. For example, if the apportionment problem is a one-time rather than a recurring problem, then violation of the property of population monotonicity may be considered to be of negligible importance. Or, if the number of objects to be allocated is not subject to change for technical or legal reasons, then violation of the property of house monotonicity may not cause much concern. Finally, when the number of participants is large (e.g., ≥ 10) then the probability that the property of (exact) quota would be violated by such techniques as the *Method of Major Fractions* becomes negligible.

5 PROCEDURES FOR SITUATIONS WHERE PARTICIPANTS CAN VALUE OUTCOMES IN RELATIVE TERMS

5.1 Introduction

In the previous two chapters we examined procedures for situations where participants could not attach precise (absolute) or relative values to outcomes or compare alternative improvements and deteriorations from a given position. They could only list outcomes in the order in which they prefer them—that is, they had ordinal preference structures or utility functions. We also mentioned that, at the other extreme, there are situations where participants can attach precise absolute values to outcomes; in these cases, participants have cardinal preference structures or utility functions. However, there are many situations where participants may not be able to attach precise absolute values to outcomes but yet can do more than order outcomes. They may be able to attach *relative* values to outcomes. More precisely, each participant may be able to state with regard to any two outcomes o_a and o_b that o_a is k times as valuable to him as o_b. For example, if k is 2, then the value of o_b is 100 if o_a is arbitrarily set at 200, and is 16 if o_a is arbitrarily set at 32. In general, the k factor will vary among individuals for any pair of given outcomes. Of course, this factor will vary among pairs for any given individual. However, we do require that the individual be consistent in the sense that for any three outcomes o_a, o_b, and o_c if $o_a = k_{ab}o_b$ and $o_b = k_{bc}o_c$, then $o_a = k_{ab}k_{bc}o_c$ (that is, if $k_{ab} = 2$ and $k_{bc} = 3$, then $o_a = 6o_c$).[1]

When participants are able to value outcomes in relative terms, we shall say that they possess a *relative preference structure,* or have a *relative utility function.* Also, in the discussion that follows we shall assume, unless otherwise stated, that each participant knows his own relative preference structure and that of all other participants. However, when it is meaningful for a respected and trusted mediator to be present and when the mediator knows all participants' preference structures, it is only necessary that each participant know his own preference structure.

In Section 5.2 we treat procedures applicable to situations wherein participants have available or perceive only a small number of options, percent improvements and percent concessions being key concepts. In Section 5.3 we examine a relatively new method useful for determining group priorities in a wide range of situations. In Section 5.4 we present procedures for situations wherein participants confront many options that we handle as situations with continuous joint action spaces. Some of these procedures involve modifications of those previously discussed; others plough new ground.

5.2 Procedures for Situations with a Small (Finite) Number of Options

At first thought it would seem reasonable to expect that all the procedures applicable for conflict situations involving a small (finite) number of options where participants can only rank outcomes in order of preferences (discussed on pages 25–51) would also be applicable to situations involving a small (finite) number of options where participants can value outcomes in relative terms (i.e., have relative utility functions). This is so since participants who can value outcomes in relative terms can provide more information about the situation than if they cannot do so. Therefore, this should not preclude the use of procedures requiring less than the full amount of information that is available. Thus, one would expect that both the compromise over proposed outcomes principle and the compromise over proposed actions principle discussed on pages 32–36 might be found acceptable by participants in the conflict situations now being considered. This may turn out to be so for a number of them. On the other hand, this expectation may not be so for other situations simply because the new information may generate additional standards. These standards may then lead one or more participants to consider such principles unacceptable because they are "unfair" or for other reasons. To see this, reexamine Table 3-5 on p. 35. L most prefers (IND,C_1); J most prefers (F,C_3). A unique compromise joint action, namely (AG,C_2), exists when each concedes one step, and hence the use of a principle of compromise over proposed actions may be acceptable to participants. Now construct Table 5-1, where we insert the utility values for each participant in Table 3-2 on p. 26 as a fraction of the highest attainable by him for the restricted set of actions to which Table 3-5 pertains. We have blocked in the compromise joint action. Whether or not participants consider their relative utilities comparable (that is, that 10 percent of the way from J's worst outcome toward his most preferred is comparable to 10 percent of the way from L's worst outcome toward her most preferred), an element of unequal concession (loss) appears when we contrast (.955,.816), the outcome of the compromise joint action (AG,C_2), with the ideal (1,1) point as a benchmark. (At this ideal point, each attains 100 percent of the utility that he would derive from his most preferred joint action.) L concedes only .045 of the utility associated with her most preferred joint action, while J concedes .184. An equal percent decrement (loss) principle is implicitly introduced. Hence the compromise joint action might turn out to be unacceptable to J, and the wise mediator knowing that a unique compromise joint action does exist may in fact find it useful to repress information on relative utilities in this case. He may ask participants to state their ordinal preferences only.

This point is also clear if we consider the procedures using the principle of compromise over proposed outcomes. Take Table 3-4 on p. 33, where there exists a unique undominated compromise outcome (AG,C_3). Construct Table 5-2 based on the same restricted joint action space as Table 3-4, wherein utility values relative to the maximum attainable by each participant are inserted into the cells. The (AG,C_3) joint action yields relative utility outcomes of .905 and .974 to L and J, respectively. Clearly, with reference to an ideal (1,1) point, L may find this joint outcome unacceptable since L would concede .095 while J concedes only .026. So once again, the mediator may find it desirable to (1) ask for information regarding ordinal preferences only and (2) avoid any statement of relative preferences.

5.2.1 Min the Percent Difference Principle

In the first case we examine, let there be a finite joint action space with both participants having relative utility functions. While each can

Table 5-1. Percentage Improvements for a Set of Reference (0,0) and (1,1) Points.

a^J Level of J's Program	(1) L	(2) J	(3) L	(4) J	(5) L	(6) J	(7) L	(8) J
(IND)	(.682,	.474)	(1,	.579)	(.977,	.684)	(.955,	.789)
(AG)	(.455,	.500)	(.818,	.658)	(.955,	.816)	(.864,	.974)
(F)	(.277,	.368)	(.636,	.579)	(.818,	.789)	(.773,	1)
(NP)	(.000,	.000)	(.455,	.263)	(.682,	.526)	(.682,	.789)
a^L	(C_0)		(C_1)		(C_2)		(C_3)	

Level of L's Control

Table 5-2. Percentage Improvements for a Set of Reference (0,0) and (1,1) Points.

Level of J's Program	(1) L	(2) J	(3) L	(4) J	(5) L	(6) J	(7) L	(8) J
(AG)	(.476,	.500)	(.857,	.658)	(1,	.816)	(.905,	.974)
(F)	(.238,	.368)	(.667,	.579)	(.857,	.789)	(.810,	1)
(NP)	(.000,	.000)	(.476,	.263)	(.714,	.526)	(.714,	.789)
	(C_0)		(C_1)		(C_2)		(C_3)	

a^J

a^L

Level of L's Control

identify her worst and best outcomes, they are not able to compare their worst or best outcomes. But then participants may be willing to agree that if each could go from his worst to his best, such improvements would be comparable and would constitute a fair solution. They might also agree that if they could go one half or two thirds, or any other fraction of the way to their best, that also would be a fair change. Since participants with relative utility functions are able to identify how much of the way from their worst to their best any joint action goes, they may agree to the principle that they should adopt the joint action that yields each the same percent distance from their worst to their best outcome and that also maximizes this same percent distance. In terms of Figure 5–1 (where we measure percent of the way from L's worst to her best along the horizontal and percent of the way from J's worst to his best along the vertical), the participants in effect seek that joint action which lies on the 45° line from the (0,0) point (the line of equal percent distance from each one's zero point), and which at the same time is farthest along it.

Observe that any percent of the way from the worst to the best for a given participant is also a percent improvement over the worst, the worst corresponding to zero percent improvement. That is, 15 percent of the way from the worst to the best corresponds to 15 percent improvement over the worst. Hence, we shall frequently use the term "percent improvement" for the longer term "percent of the way from the worst to the best." Also we shall speak of the line of equal percent improvements in place of the line of equal percent distance from each one's zero point.

When a finite joint action space exists, however, it is unlikely that any joint action will take the participants the same percent of the way from their worst to their best—that is, yield them the same percent improvement. For example, if in Table 3–2 on p. 26, we let outcome 0 be L's worst and 216 be her best, and 0 be J's worst and 230 his best, and if both J and L have relative utility, we obtain Table 5–3 as indicating their relative utilities. If we then plot these utility outcomes on Figure 5–1, we observe that none of the outcomes for the joint actions of Table 5–3 fall on the equal percent improvement line. For example, joint action (F, C_1) represents 51.8 percent improvement for L and 47.9 percent improvement for J. Hence, if no joint action maps onto the equal percent improvement line, the participants may be motivated to adopt a principle: choose that joint action whose pair of relative utilities maps closest to this reference line.[2] This action is

Figure 5-1. Equi-Percent Improvement Line from Worst Outcomes in a Relative Utility Space.

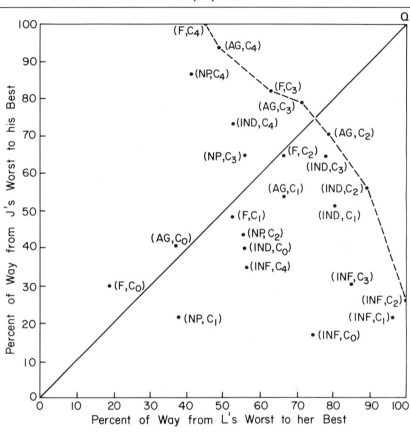

(F,C_2), which, as indicated in Figure 5-1, is 66.7 and 65.2 percent improvement for L and J, respectively. Since this principle involves selection of the joint action that minimizes the difference between the participants' percent improvements, this principle may be designated the *min the percent difference in improvements principle.* If more than one pair of outcomes are at the same distance from this line, the joint action yielding the pair with the higher percent for both should be chosen.[3]

Note also that in a situation where there is a mediator, he may suggest to participants that they focus on the "ideal" but nonrealizable

Table 5-3. Relative Improvements from Worst to Best (in Fractional Terms).

Level of J's Program	(1) L	(2) J	(3) L	(4) J	(5) L	(6) J	(7) L	(8) J	(9) L	(10) J
(INF)	(.741,	.174)	(.962,	.217)	(1.000,	.261)	(.852,	.304)	(.565,	.348)
(IND)	(.556,	.391)	(.814,	.479)	(.889,	.565)	(.778,	.652)	(.528,	.739)
(AG)	(.370,	.413)	(.667,	.544)	(.778,	.674)	(.704,	.804)	(.491,	.935)
(F)	(.185,	.304)	(.518,	.479)	(.667,	.652)	(.630,	.826)	(.454,	1.000)
(NP)	(0,	0)	(.370,	.217)	(.556,	.434)	(.556,	.652)	(.417,	.869)
	(C_0)		(C_1)		(C_2)		(C_3)		(C_4)	

a^J a^L

Level of L's Control

point Q in Figure 5-1 where each would receive the outcome associated with his most preferred joint action. If participants are able and willing to consider as fair and equal percents of distance from their best outcome toward their worst—that is of concessions from the ideal point—one can construct a line that is the focus of all equal percent concessions. (Actually, such a line will coincide with the line of equal percent distances from worst to best outcomes—that is, the equal percent improvement line.) They may regard the equal percent concession line as a set of fair compromise points; and if any joint action yields relative utility outcomes that fall on this line, then that joint action may be regarded as an acceptable compromise joint action. If two or more joint actions fall on that line, the one involving the lowest percent concession should be recognized as the best of the acceptable compromises.

Again, the probability is small that the relative utilities of any joint action will map on to the equal percent concession line. Consequently, participants may be willing to adopt a principle: choose that joint action whose pair of relative utilities maps closest to this fair compromise line. Again, this action is (F,C_2), which, as indicated in Figure 5-1, represents percent concessions of 33.3 and 34.8 for L and J, respectively. Since this principle involves selection of the joint action that minimizes the difference between the participants' percent utility concessions, this principle may be designated the *min the percent difference in concessions principle.*

Obviously, the application of a min the percent difference principle with regard to improvements—i.e., distances from the worst to the best—will always yield the same compromise joint action as the application of a min the percent difference principle with regard to concessions—i.e., distances from the best to the worst.

5.2.2 The Constrained
Min the Percent Difference Principle

Upon further thought, the participants may not be willing to consider the unqualified use either of the min the percent difference principles discussed in the previous section. For example, if such were to result in 1.1 and 1.2 percent improvement, while another possibility was 94 and 95 percent improvement, respectively, clearly most participants would prefer the latter even though it does not minimize the percent difference in improvements. This suggests the introduction of constraints. One possible constraint would set a lower bound (say 60 percent) on the level of percent improvement for each participant that must be achieved by any joint action for it to be eligible as a compromise joint action.[4] When this constraint is enforced, the compromise joint action in Figure 5-1 becomes (F, C_2), which represents 66.7 percent improvement for L and 65.2 percent improvement for J.

Another constraint that might appeal to participants would require a joint action to be efficient if it is to be eligible as a compromise action. Thus, in Figure 5-1, only points lying on the dashed line (the efficiency frontier) are efficient and thus eligible.[5] Other points are dominated by one or more of the efficient points, and (AG, C_3), representing improvements of 70.4 and 80.4 percent for J and L, respectively, becomes the compromise joint action. Still other constraints that have appeal may be introduced. (See pages 192-196 for discussion of other relevant constraints.)

Similarly, where the min the percent difference principle is used regarding concessions, participants may prefer to adopt a joint action yielding a larger difference in percent concessions if this involves a much smaller level of concession by both. This then suggests the introduction of an upper bound (say 40 percent) on the level of percent concession required by each participant that must not be violated if any joint action is to be eligible as a compromise joint action.

5.2.3 Max the Min
Percent Improvement Principle

Another approach that may be used in searching for a compromise joint action employs a *max the min percent improvement principle*. For two-participant cases, it focuses on the lower percent improvement in the pairs of outcomes achievable by all possible joint actions and selects that joint action whose pair of outcomes involves the highest percent improvement for the less-favored participant.

Hence, in examining a table of relative utilities such as Table 5-1, 5-2, or 5-3, we look for that joint action whose lower relative utility (ratio) is higher than the lower relative utility (ratio) in any other cell. In Table 5-3, this would be (AG, C_3), whose ratios of .704 and .804 represent improvements of 70.4 and 80.4 percent for L and J, respectively. This procedure has an appeal in the sense that it is concerned with, that is, maximizes, the welfare of that one who turns out to be less favored in a compromise—an element of equity or justice.

Observe that use of this principle guarantees that the compromise joint action will be efficient (because there exists no other joint action that can make the less-favored participant better off without making the other participant worse off). Hence, this principle is equivalent to a principle that might be designated *max the min percent improvement in the efficiency set*. However, it suffers from the fact that it may yield great discrepancies in the percent improvement of the several participants. For example, we may obtain an outcome 55 and 95 where at the same time there might be an outcome 54.5 and 54.5, which, although inefficient, may be much more intensely preferred by the first participant for obvious reasons. Hence, a constraint might be imposed that restricts the size of the difference in percent improvements—say to not greater than 20 percent. This then defines a restricted set of feasible efficient joint actions.

5.2.4 Min the Max
Percent Concession Principle

In some situations, an alternative approach: the *min the max percent concession principle* may have appeal to participants. It would focus on the higher of the two participants' percent concessions from the ideal outcome, and select as the compromise solution that joint action whose pair of outcomes involves the lowest percent concession for the less-favored participant.

When adopting this principle, the outcome of each possible joint action is converted to a percent of concession from the ideal, as in Table 5-4 (which is based on the joint action matrix of Table 3-4). Then the compromise joint action namely (AG, C_3), is selected as that cell whose higher percent of the two is the lowest of all. This procedure has appeal in the sense that it is concerned with and minimizes the concession of that one who turns out to be less favored (i.e., makes the larger concession).

Observe that the use of this principle also guarantees that the compromise joint action will be efficient (because there exists no other joint action which would involve a smaller concession by the less-favored participant without requiring that the other participant make a larger concession). However, it too suffers from the fact that it may

Table 5-4. Percentage Concessions for a Set of Reference (0,0) and (1,1) Points.

Level of J's Program	(1) L	(2) J	(3) L	(4) J	(5) L	(6) J	(7) L	(8) J
(AG)	(.524,	.500)	(.143,	.342)	(0.000,	.184)	(.095,	.026)
(F)	(.762,	.632)	(.333,	.421)	(.143,	.211)	(.190,	0.000)
(NP)	(1.000,	1.000)	(.524,	.737)	(.286,	.474)	(.286,	.211)

a^J (C_0) (C_1) (C_2) (C_3)

a^L Level of L's Control

yield great discrepancies in the percent concessions of the several participants. Hence a constraint that restricts the size of the difference in percent concessions may be imposed.

5.2.5 Max Total of Percent Improvements (Min Total of Percent Concessions)

Another principle that might be used focuses on the total of the percent improvements and selects that joint action which maximizes this total. This would correspond to joint action (AG, C_3) in Figure 5-1. A related principle is that of *minimizing the total of percent concessions* (penalties or losses) measured from the ideal (100,100) point when both participants are equally weighted.

When participants are not equally weighted, then the above principles may be modified to be *max the total of weighted percent improvements* or *min the total of weighted percent concessions*. Moreover, in all these cases, with equal or unequal weights, meaningful constraints may be imposed. For example, when focusing on improvements, one such constraint might set an upper bound on the difference in percent improvements between any pair of participants. Another might set a lower bound on the percent improvement for any participant.[6]

Note also that, as with a number of other procedures discussed in this chapter, money may be used as side payments to participants reluctant to agree to the use of a max total of percent improvements principle. For some analysis of side payments see pages 275–278.

5.2.6 Principle of Min the Difference in Percent Improvement from Current Standpoint

While at times participants with relative utility functions may agree that the difference between the worst and best for each are equivalent, at other times they may not. The differences may be perceived by at least one participant as being too "unequal" and that, even as an ideal, equal percent improvement would be greatly in his disfavor. Under such circumstances it may be possible to find another prominent point to replace either the worst outcome or best outcome in order to reach agreement on equivalent differences. For example, the current standpoint, or the security level outcome, or the threat point, or a number of others may be used to replace the worst or best or both outcomes to reach such agreement.

Suppose participants are focused on the current outcome and are able to agree that the difference between each one's worst and the current outcome are equivalent, so that the current standpoint can be viewed as a fair reference point from which improvements can be explored. To be explicit, suppose participants are in a situation where in Table 3-2 on p. 26, the action "no program-no control" (NP, C_0) is considered unrealistic. It may be unimaginable that developed countries would ever propose, let alone carry through, a "no program" (NP) action given the condition of starvation of such a large fraction of the world's population. Also, it may be inconceivable that any political leader of a developing nation, no matter how stupid or vengeful, would advocate and exercise "no control" (C_0) over the constituency he represents. Hence, if we eliminate these two actions, we obtain a table like Table 3-2 without its first column and last row. Given that table, participants could still use the joint action (NP, C_0) as a $(0,0)$ point in the joint utility space from which to measure relative utility, and the numbers in the table might be taken to reflect relative and only relative utility. For example, in the first row of the table, J's utilities listed as the second number in the cells, namely 50, 60, 70, and 80 would simply mean that the outcome in the second cell of that row has $6/5$ times more utility to J than the outcome in the first cell, that the outcome in the third cell has $7/5$ times more utility to J than that in the first cell, and so forth.

Suppose participants do agree that the difference for each between the outcome of the joint action "no program, no control" (NP, C_0) and his current standpoint are equivalent and taken to be equal to unity. Suppose further that the joint action (F, C_1) is currently in effect. If the utility outcomes derived from any other joint action are recorded relative to (i.e., as a ratio of) the utility outcomes derived from this joint action, the utility numbers of Table 3-2 may be transformed into relative utilities of Table 5-5. Next, consider these relative utilities as expressing percent changes of utilities for participants when any joint action is compared with the reference joint action (F, C_1). We then plot the percentage changes associated with each joint action in Figure 5-2. Along the horizontal axis we measure percent change in L's utility and along the vertical, percent change in J's utility. For example, joint action (AG, C_2) represents 50 and 41 per-

Table 5-5. Relative Utilities of Participants with Reference to the Difference between Zero and the Current Standpoint.[a]

Level of J's Program	(1) L	(2) J	(3) L	(4) J	(5) L	(6) J	(7) L	(8) J	(9) L	(10) J
(INF)	1.43,	0.36)	1.86,	0.45)	1.93,	0.55)	1.64,	0.64)	1.09,	0.73)
(IND)	1.07,	0.82)	1.57,	1.00)	1.71,	1.18)	1.50,	1.36)	1.02,	1.55)
(AG)	0.71,	0.86)	1.29,	1.14)	1.50,	1.41)	1.36,	1.68)	0.95,	1.95)
(F)	0.36,	0.64)	1.00,	1.00)	1.29,	1.36)	1.21,	1.73)	0.88,	2.09)
(NP)	0,	0)	0.71,	0.45)	1.07,	0.91)	1.07,	1.36)	0.80,	1.82)
a^J / a^L	C_0		C_1		C_2		C_3		C_4	

Level of L's Control

[a] Joint actions shaded are considered as unrealistic and hence not eligible for selection.

Figure 5-2. Equi-Percent Improvement Line from Current Standpoint in a Relative Utility Space.

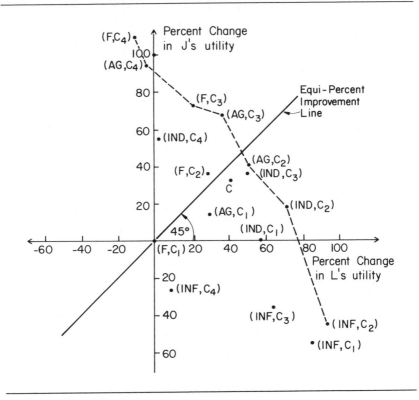

cent improvement in L's and J's utility, respectively, when compared with the existing joint action (F, C_1). In essence, we make a complete mapping of the joint actions of Table 5-5 onto Figure 5-2. However, it is important to bear in mind that the action "no program, no control" (NP, C_0) has been excluded as a meaningful joint action.

If participants are able and willing to think in terms of equal percents of improvements from the current standpoint, one can construct a line that is the locus of all equal percent improvements. They again may regard the equal percent improvement line as a set of fair compromise points and agree to adopt a variant of the *min the percent difference in improvements principle* discussed earlier.

5.2.7 Principles of Min the Percent Difference in Improvement from Other Prominent Points

In the case just examined, participants may not agree to consider the difference between the outcome of the (NP,C_0) joint action and that of the current standpoint (F,C_1) as equivalent for each participant. This might be the case if the percents in a table, such as Table 5-5, were in general much higher for one participant than the other. Participants may then seek to use another "prominent" or other points in place of the current standpoint to reach agreement on equivalent differences. For example, in war and in games similar to war involving punitive actions, a reasonable substitute $(1,1)$ point may be viewed as the participants' security level utility outcomes—that is, the maximum utility outcome each participant can obtain with 100 percent certainty regardless of the action of the other. With reference to Table 3-2 (without the first row and first column), these are 144 and 125 for L and J, respectively.

However, often in international and other situations involving negotiations, before sitting down to interact, the political powers or other participants may use the actions consistent with their security level utility to establish their (relative) initial positions of strength. For example, in Table 3-2 (without the first row and the first column), L takes (C_2) as his security-level action because he is certain to achieve 144 no matter how mean, blind, or inconsiderate J may be—that is, no matter what action J takes. In turn, J takes (AG) as his security-level action because he is certain to achieve at least 125. The resulting joint action (AG,C_2) yields outcomes $(168,155)$. These may be taken to replace the security level outcomes as the $(1,1)$ point and, together with the outcomes of the (NP,C_0) joint action, might be considered by participants in reaching agreement on equivalent differences. Still another set of outcomes that may serve as a $(1,1)$ point are those of a "threat" point—for example, a set to which either participant can force them both, independent of the action of the other.

When the participants do agree on equivalent differences using one of these points or any other together with the "agreed-upon" $(0,0)$ point, they can then specify their relative utilities in a table like Table 5-5, construct a figure like Figure 5-2, use the equal percent improvement line as an ideal, and employ the various principles already enunciated in this chapter to reach agreement on a compromise joint action.

However, the (0,0) point that thus far we have taken to be the "no program, no control" joint action (NP,C_0) may also be replaced by another prominent point. One such point may be defined by the security level outcomes of each participant. In such a situation, participants may choose to regard the difference between their security level outcome and their best outcome for each as equivalent. Accordingly, from a table such as Table 3-2 we can construct another table like Table 5-4, and another figure like Figure 5-1 and proceed to use all the principles enunciated in Sections 5.2.1 through 5.2.5.

But also, participants may wish to consider the threat point as a zero point or any other deadlock or stalemate point. In many situations, suggesting relevant (0,0) and (1,1) points or their equivalent may require the highest level of skill from the mediator.[7]

5.2.8 Max the Total of the Percents of Goal Achievement

A principle closely related to the max total of percent improvements principle (discussed above on page 141) focuses on goals (targets). Let each participant have a clearly defined goal. Since he may be a realistic individual, his goal need not be his most preferred outcome. When participants agree on the relevance and comparability of goals, they may then choose to focus specifically on the percent of each one's goal that is achieved, and adopt a compromise that employs the principle *max the total of the percents of goal achievements*. For example, in Table 5-5 where J's outcome from the joint action (F,C_4) is his goal and where L's outcome from the joint action (INF,C_2) is her goal, use of this principle would result in the compromise joint action (AG,C_3), yielding 70.4 percent of L's goal and 80.4 percent of J's for a total of 150.8. Note that use of the max total of percent improvements principle yields the same result; however, it may be more psychologically appealing for participants to focus on goal achievements.[8] In a simple extension of this procedure, participants agree on different weights to be applied to their percent achievements. In such a case, participants use the principle *max the total of the weighted percents of goal achievements*.

In the above, the (0,0) outcome point was implicitly used as a natural base from which to determine the percent of each participant's goals achieved by each joint action. As noted in the previous section, other bases can be used in a weighted or unweighted version of this principle. For example, where strategic potential is taken into account, percent achievements from the (0,0) reference point toward the "optimal outcome" goal may be replaced by percent achievements from the security-level reference point. In Table 3-2 where the security-level outcomes of 95 and 120 for J and L, respectively, are taken as the base from which to determine the percents of goal achievement, and where the goals are once again the "optimal outcomes" of 230 and 216, the use of the principle max the total of the percents of goal achievement would then result in the compromise joint action (IND,C_2), yielding 75 percent of J's goal and 26 percent of L's goal for a total of 101.[9]

5.3 METHOD OF DETERMINING GROUP PRIORITIES (SAATY)

We now come to a class of procedures that require only crude relative utility evaluations, implicitly or explicitly, and are applied most frequently in situations with a small (finite) number of joint actions. When the goal is to identify the compromise joint action, strategy, or set of policies that is best—or alternatively, that joint action which best reflects the forces at play and is most likely to be taken. In these procedures (sometimes designated prioritization or eigenvector procedures) participants employ a finite number of values to scale the importance of objectives, outcomes, influence, and so on. See Saaty (1979, 1981). To motivate the discussion, consider a set of joint actions each of which might correspond to a plan, development alternative, policy, legislative bill, or other type of option.

First, we construct a typical example, oversimplified for presentation purposes. Consider the developed countries J, and the developing countries L. Let each attach different importance to several objectives—economic growth, environmental quality, international stability, etc.—and be concerned with appropriate energy and pollution control policies (actions). Three of the policies of the developed countries might be:

1. an all-out effort at development of solar energy (S)
2. an all-out effort at development of coal with state-of-the-art pollution control technology (C)
3. concentration on more efficient use of oil resources with state-of-the-art pollution control technology (O)

Two of the politically feasible policies of the developing countries might be:

1.   partial pollution control (P)
2.   no pollution control (Z)

We thus have six possible joint policies (actions): (S,P), all-out solar by the developed and partial pollution control by the developing nations; (S,Z), all-out solar by the developed and no pollution control by the developing; (C,P), all-out coal by the developed and partial pollution control by the developing; (C,Z); (O,P); and (O,Z). We then can construct a six by six matrix as in Table 5-6. At this point, the simplest application of the Saaty approach could be made if the leader of each set of countries were (1) fully cognizant of the implications of each joint policy for each relevant objective and (2) able to combine these implications into a comparison of the relative desirability of each pair of joint actions for a given objective. Then taking into account the weight they internally attach to the several objectives, they could make overall comparisons of the relative desirability of each pair of joint actions for all objectives. To make comparisons, a scale is required. Saaty suggests the one given in Table 5-7. However, there is nothing sacred about Saaty's suggestions. The partici-

Table 5-6.   Relative Value of Joint Policies for Developed Countries J over All Objectives.

Joint Policies	(S,P)	(S,Z)	(C,P)	(C,Z)	(O,P)	(O,Z)
(S,P)	1	2	7	6	5	4
(S,Z)	1/2	1	7/2	6/2	5/2	4/2
(C,P)	1/7	2/7	1	6/7	5/7	4/7
(C,Z)	1/6	2/6	7/6	1	5/6	4/6
(O,P)	1/5	2/5	7/5	6/5	1	4/5
(O,Z)	1/4	2/4	7/4	6/4	5/4	1

Table 5–7.   The Saaty Scale and Its Description.

Intensity of Importance	Definition	Explanation
1[a]	Equal importance	Two policies contribute equally to the objective
3	Weak importance of one over another	Experience and judgment slightly favor one activity over another
5	Essential or strong importance	Experience and judgment strongly favor one policy over another
7	Demonstrated importance	A policy is strongly favored and its dominance is demonstrated in practice
9	Absolute importance	The evidence favoring one policy over another is of the highest possible order of affirmation
2, 4, 6, 8	Intermediate values between the two adjacent judgments	When compromise is needed
Reciprocals of above nonzero numbers	If policy i has one of the above nonzero numbers assigned to it when compared with policy j, then j has the reciprocal value when compared with i	
Rationals	Ratios arising from the scale	If consistency were to be forced by obtaining n numerical values to span the matrix

[a]On occasion in 2 by 2 problems, Saaty has used $1 + \epsilon$, $0 < \epsilon < 1/2$ to indicate very slight dominance between two nearly equal activities.

Source: adapted from Saaty and Khouja (1976:34).

pants or the mediator or both may, and usually could be expected to, choose another scale for evaluation—a scale that might be tailored to the views of the participants and needs of the situation.

Once the scale is decided upon, the leaders may proceed with pairwise comparisons. For example, the leader of the developed countries J might value a joint policy (C,P) as having "demonstrated importance" compared to joint policy (S,P) and thus assign 7 to the ratio of (C,P) to (S,P). He may make this assignment simply because the extremely high dollar savings of an all-out effort at coal development compared to all-out effort at solar development dominates the significant environmental benefits of the latter. Hence in Table 5-6 we place 7 in the cell of the first row, third column and, to be consistent, we place 1/7 in the cell of the third row, first column, since the latter cell gives the ratio of the importance of the joint policy (S,P) to that of the joint policy (C,P). Also, the leader of J might consider a joint policy (O,P) as only 5/6 as important as joint policy (C,Z), indicating that to him that the gains in environmental quality achieved when the developing nations undertake partial pollution control (P) is not quite as important as the gains in growth that come when they invest all their capital in industrial plant and equipment and none in pollution control (Z). Hence, we place 5/6 in the cell of the fourth row of the fifth column and the reciprocal value 6/5 in the cell of the fifth row of the fourth column. Likewise the leader of J makes all other pairwise comparisons to fill in the cells of Table 5-6.[10]

In similar manner the leader of the developing nations L makes pairwise comparisons and records them. See Table 5-8, in which the number 9 in the cell in the first row, fourth column indicates that a joint policy (C,Z) is of "absolute importance" relative to joint policy (S,P), reflecting the critical significance that developing nations attach to growth.

Note that in Table 5-6, we have recorded pairwise comparisons that are consistent. That is, going along the first row of Table 5-6 we have ratios 1, 2, 7, 6, 5, and 4; these ratios hold likewise for every other row and for every column. They truly reflect the relative importance to J of the several joint policies. We then can convert (normalize) these ratios (weights) so that they add up to unity, deriving $(1/25, 2/25, 7/25, 6/25, 5/25, 4/25)$ or w_j^J, $j = 1, \ldots, 6$, where $\sum_{j=1}^{6} w_j^J = 1$. However, when we normalize (as Saaty frequently does in his steps), we are in effect taking the importance ratios to reflect relative utility.

Table 5-8. Relative Value of Joint Policies for Developing Countries L over All Objectives.

Joint Policies	(S,P)	(S,Z)	(C,P)	(C,Z)	(O,P)	(O,Z)
(S,P)	1	2	7	9	6	7
(S,Z)	1/2	1	8/2	10/2	6/2	7/2
(C,P)	1/7	2/8	1	9/7	6/7	1
(C,Z)	1/9	2/10	7/9	1	6/9	7/9
(O,P)	1/6	2/6	7/6	9/6	1	7/6
(O,Z)	1/7	2/7	1	9/7	6/7	1

In contrast, in Table 5-8 we have introduced some inconsistency, which we would expect in the *normal* case. For example, the ratios of 1, 2, 7, 9, 6, 7 of the first row are not the same as the ratios 1, 2, 8, 10, 6, 7 of the second row, or 1, 7/4, 7, 9, 6, 7 of the third row. Saaty then employs a procedure to derive a set of ratios that best reflects the relative importance of joint policies inherent in these pairwise comparisons. These are likely to involve small adjustments so that they can be written 1^-, 2^-, 7^+, 9^+, 6^-, 7^-, where a number with a minus (plus) superscript means a little less (more) than that number; or symbolically after normalization as w_j^L, $j = 1, \ldots, 6$, $\sum_{j=1}^{6} w_j^L = 1$. (This procedure is presented in technical form in Appendix 5A.1.)

Suppose the two sets of countries are considered of equal importance. Then one may take a simple average of J's ratios 1, 2, 7, 6, 5, 4 (now to be interpreted as relative utilities) and L's ratios 1^-, 2^-, 7^+, 9^+, 6^-, 7^-. That joint policy whose average is highest, namely (C,Z), may then be taken as the best compromise to be put into effect.

The above case, when generalized to more than two participants, however, is not likely to be typical. Usually, political leaders, no matter how astute and capable, cannot work out the implications of different joint actions for the several objectives as a whole. Hence, a more involved procedure must be employed. In the first step, the political leaders can be asked to make not pairwise comparisons of the relative importance of joint actions but rather pairwise comparisons of the relative importance of several relevant objectives—say, economic growth (G), environmental quality (EQ), and energy independence (IND). Then, as in Table 5-9, we may construct for leader J a matrix of pairwise comparisons of the importance of the several objectives. Since this table involves inconsistency, we employ Saaty's method and derive relative importance weights, which, after being normalized, are .691, .160, and .149 for the three objectives in the order listed above. Similarly, we can do the same for leader L.

Having determined for each set of nations the normalized relative weights they attach to the several objectives, and considering J and L to be of equal importance, we take the simple average of the two sets as the one to be used in further analyses. Let the three average weights be λ^G, λ^{EQ}, and λ^{IND}.

The next step is to determine the relative importance of each joint policy for the realization of each objective. When formal programming-type procedures are available and adequate to this task, they may be employed. For the moment, being realistic, we may judge that adequate programming techniques are not available. Hence, a team of experts, knowledgeable in all relevant aspects of the situation, is assembled. On the basis of both subjective and objective knowledge, each member is asked to make pairwise comparisons—in particular, comparisons of the relative importance of all pairs of joint policies for the realization of each objective. Averaging in an unweighted or weighted fashion over all judgments,[11] the derived pairwise com-

Table 5-9.   A Matrix of Inconsistent Pairwise Comparisons of Objectives.

	(G)	(EQ)	(IND)
(G)	1	4	5
(EQ)	1/4	1	1
(IND)	1/5	1	1

parison matrix for the economic growth objective might be as in Table 5-10. From this matrix, the normalized weights w^G_1, w^G_2, w^G_3, w^G_4, w^G_5, and w^G_1 are derived. For the objective "environmental quality," a similar pairwise matrix is constructed, from which normalized weights w^{EQ}_1, w^{EQ}_2, w^{EQ}_3, w^{EQ}_4, w^{EQ}_5, and w^{EQ}_6 are derived. Likewise for the objective "energy independence," for which the normalized weights w^{IND}_1, w^{IND}_2, w^{IND}_3, w^{IND}_4, w^{IND}_5, and w^{IND}_6 are derived. Multiplying each of these sets of weights by the relative importance of the corresponding objective derived above and summing the products for each joint action yields:

$$\lambda^G w^G_1 + \lambda^{EQ} w^{EQ}_1 + \lambda^{IND} w^{IND}_1 = \overline{w}_l$$

$$\lambda^G w^G_2 + \lambda^{EQ} w^{EQ}_2 + \lambda^{IND} w^{IND}_2 = \overline{w}_2$$

$$\cdot \qquad \cdot \qquad \cdot \qquad \cdot \qquad \qquad (5\text{-}1)$$

$$\cdot \qquad \cdot \qquad \cdot \qquad \cdot$$

$$\cdot \qquad \cdot \qquad \cdot \qquad \cdot$$

$$\lambda^G w^G_6 + \lambda^{EQ} w^{EQ}_6 + \lambda^{IND} w^{IND}_6 = \overline{w}_6$$

Table 5-10.   Relative Importance of Joint Policies to the Economic Growth (G) Objective.

Joint Policies	(S,P)	(S,Z)	(C,P)	(C,Z)	(O,P)	(O,Z)
(S,P)	1	2/3	2/7	2/9	2/6	2/8
(S,Z)	3/2	1	3/7	3/9	3/6	3/8
(C,P)	7/2	7/3	1	7/9	7/6	7/8
(C,Z)	9/2	9/3	9/7	1	9/6	9/8
(O,P)	6/2	6/3	6/7	6/9	1	6/8
(O,Z)	8/2	8/3	8/7	8/9	8/6	1

Normalizing the $\overline{w}_j$, $j = 1, \ldots, 6$ so that they add to unity, we derive the relative weights w_j, $j = 1, \ldots, 6$ of the six joint actions. The joint action with highest weight may then be considered the best compromise joint action, the one that reflects best the full interplay of forces, or the one that is most likely to be implemented.

The above presentation of the Saaty approach can be even further extended to take into account the fact that the participants themselves may have different importance, power, or influence in the choice of a joint compromise policy. For example, in considering the selection of a policy by NATO or the Warsaw Pact, at the present time the preferences of the United States and the Soviet Union, respectively, would have to be given greater weights than the preferences of Belgium or Bulgaria, respectively. But what weights? Here again, a team of experts may be called in and each member asked to make pairwise comparisons of the influence of these nations. After appropriate averaging, weighted or unweighted, of the importance ratios of nation J to nation L over all experts, an average importance ratio is obtained to be put into the appropriate cells of the matrix. From this derived matrix, using the Saaty method and after normalizing, a set of weights γ^J, $\gamma^L \ldots$ can be derived for the several nations.

Next, for each nation J, the set of weights to be attached to the several objectives can be derived as above. We then obtain $^J\lambda^G$, $^J\lambda^{EQ}$, $^J\lambda^{IND}$. When we multiply these weights by the importance of nation J, we obtain $\gamma^J\,^J\lambda^G$, $\gamma^J\,^J\lambda^{EQ}$ and $\gamma^J\,^J\lambda^{IND}$. Summing these products for each objective over all nations, we derive:

$$\gamma^J\,^J\lambda^G + \gamma^L\,^L\lambda^G + \ldots = \overline{\lambda}^G$$

$$\gamma^J\,^J\lambda^{EQ} + \gamma^L\,^L\lambda^{EQ} + \ldots = \overline{\lambda}^{EQ} \qquad (5\text{-}2)$$

$$\gamma^J\,^J\lambda^{IND} + \gamma^L\,^L\lambda^{IND} + \ldots = \overline{\lambda}^{IND}$$

The gross weights $\overline{\lambda}^G$, $\overline{\lambda}^{EQ}$, $\overline{\lambda}^{IND}$ can then be normalized to yield the weights $\tilde{\lambda}^G$, $\tilde{\lambda}^{EQ}$, $\tilde{\lambda}^{IND}$ of the three objectives based on the views of all nations properly weighted, to be employed in subsequent steps.

The above discussion is an oversimplification of the Saaty method of determining group priorities. There are many variants to treat more effectively specific situations. The great value of this approach is that through the use of pairwise comparisons, involving implicitly approximations to relative utility once arithmetic operations of addition and division are employed, the approach can more satisfactorily involve participants with the help of analysts and experts in the choice of a compromise action (policy). See Isard and C. Smith (1982b:110–12).

5.4 PROCEDURES FOR SITUATIONS WITH MANY (CONTINUOUS) OPTIONS

We now consider situations involving relative utility in which the actions of each participant, and thus the joint actions, are many and can vary continuously (as discussed in Chapter 4, pages 67–69). As in Section 5.2, unless otherwise stated, for procedures in this section to be applicable each participant must know both his own preference structure and that of all other participants. However when it is meaningful for a mediator who is respected and trusted to be present and when he knows all participants' preference structures, it is only necessary that each participant know his own preference structure.

5.4.1 Max Equal Percent Improvement (Min Equal Percent Concession) Principle

When actions can be varied continuously, every point on an equal percent improvement line corresponds to a possible joint action, as does every point on an equal percent concession line. Consequently, consider the cases of this chapter, where participants are taken to be able to specify preferences only in terms of relative utilities and where, therefore, comparisons are made in terms of percents of improvement from a relevant (0,0) or other relevant reference point or in terms of percents of concession from an "ideal" (1,1) or other relevant reference point. For these cases, participants may adopt a *max equal percent improvement* or *min equal percent concession* principle.[12] If so, the identification of a compromise joint action is simple. It is that joint action which corresponds to the maximum of the equal percent improvements technically possible or the minimum of the feasible equal percent concessions. Since the efficiency frontier is the set of all efficient (nondominated) joint actions, the intersection point of the equal percent improvement or percent concession line and the efficiency frontier defines the natural compromise joint action. In a figure such as Figure 5–3, where e is taken to be the relevant (0,0) point, this solution would be point s.[13] Note that when (1) the efficiency frontier is a straight line in the joint action space (as for cases examined with regard to Figure 4–7 on p. 83) and (2) information exists on relative utilities for different distances in the joint action space from a participant's most preferred joint action, the adoption of an equal percent concession principle yields point s in Figure 5–4 as a solution. This compromise joint action represents a point of tangency of two indifference curves involving equal percentage concessions in utility outcomes from those corresponding to each one's most preferred joint action.[14]

5.4.2 Sequential Split-the-Difference Principle (in Outcomes)

A similar, but not identical, procedure may have appeal to participants. It is one that derives a reference line for comparison in terms of a connected series of split-the-difference points designated a *split-the-difference line.* In this procedure, the continuous joint utility space is constructed as in Figure 5–5. Then the relative utilities of J and L are measured along the horizontal and vertical axes respectively, assuming that participants have agreed say that differences between worst and best outcomes are equivalent. Next we plot the utility outcomes to L and J, namely $^Lu^{J*}$ and $^Ju^{J*}$, which they would receive if J's most preferred joint action a^{J*} were realized. We also plot the utility outcomes to L and J, namely $^Lu^{L*}$ and $^Ju^{L*}$, respectively, which they would receive if L's most preferred joint action a^{L*} were realized. We then suggest as a fair approach that each participant (1) identify the utility outcome she receives when her most preferred joint action is adopted, (2) identify the utility outcome she receives when the other participant's most preferred joint action is adopted, and (3) be content with a joint action yielding her an outcome midway between these two utility outcomes.[15] This compromise joint outcome corresponds to point c in Figure 5–5. Since c is inefficient, in the sense that both participants could receive higher utilities as outcomes, the mediator may suggest, as in Section 4.10, that they take another step to realize joint improvement. Define the improvement set relative to c. Again he may suggest as the compromise joint action that one yielding for each participant an outcome midway between the outcome to her associated with her best proposal in this set and the outcome to her associated with the other's best proposal. Such a joint action maps as point

Figure 5-3. A Sequence of Alternating Leader-Follower Outcomes.

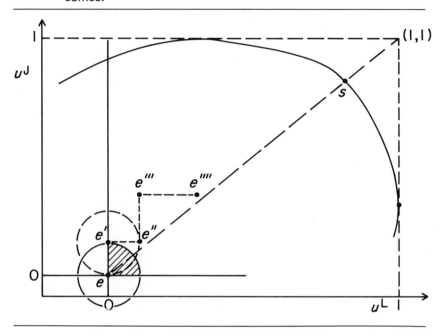

Figure 5-4. A Joint Action Involving Equal Concessions in Relative Utilities.

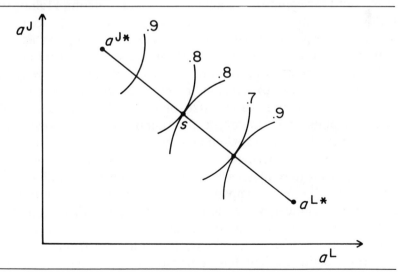

Figure 5-5.   A Sequence of Split-the-Difference Outcomes.

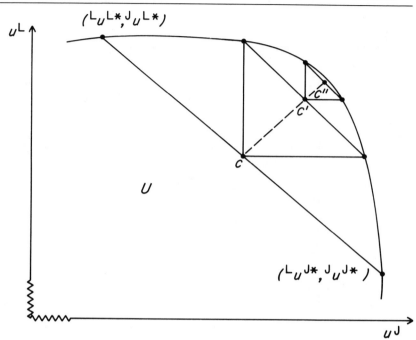

c' in Figure 5-5. Since c' is also inefficient, additional steps may be taken until the compromise joint action yields outcomes falling within some small distance from the efficiency frontier in the joint utility space. At this point the participants may decide to stop and adopt the compromise joint action reached at the end of the last round.[16]

Note that the above procedure uses each participant's worst outcome to define a (0,0) reference point when she proposes her most preferred joint action on the first round. In many situations, other reference points will be relevant, for example the fixed threat point in very hostile situations. This point would then serve to define for the first round the improvement set in the joint utility space. Hence, only joint actions with outcomes in this improvement set would be eligible for selection by the participants in the first round. This restricted set might well exclude a joint action that is a participant's most preferred in the unrestricted set.[17] In other situations, for example highly competitive price-warfare cases, the equilibrium point from shortsighted best reply actions might be the appropriate reference point. (This would be e in Figure 4–13 on p. 97.) In still other situations where both participants insist on being leaders or are fanatics (or unbounded unfounded optimists), other points become the relevant reference points. (In these cases, points w and r, respectively, in Figure 4–13 would serve as relevant reference points.) Finally, from a psychological standpoint and in the words of Schelling (1963), there may be any one of a number of prominent (half-way, subsistence, base year, etc.) points that may appeal to participants as relevant reference points.[18]

5.4.3 The Alternating Leader-Follower Principle (with Regard to Outcomes)

As in Chapter 4, participants may find an alternating leader-follower principle more appealing than that of sequential split-the-difference for reaching a compromise solution that is efficient. In an application of the former, one of the relevant reference points cited in the previous section may be used to define the improvement set of the first round. For example, in Figure 5–3 the reference point may be point e which may correspond to the current situation. Once the improvement set with reference to e is identified, this set can be normalized, that is, the reference point may be taken to be the new (0,0) point, and the ideal (1,1) but infeasible point may be taken to be the most preferred outcome for each. The next step requires that each participant specify the maximum percent improvement in his opponent's utility position (or his own) that he finds acceptable; the lesser of these two maximums may then be taken to define the radius of a circle to be constructed around point e. This circle represents the limited commitment set. The lesser of these two maximums is also taken to serve as the minimum allowable radius for circles to be constructed in subsequent rounds.[19] Next, a coin is tossed to determine who shall be leader on the first round. Assume it is J. J then specifies that joint action e', which yields him his maximum utility outcome in the shaded area common to both the improvement and the limited commitment sets. Point e' then serves as the reference point to determine the improvement set for the second round. On the second round each participant again specifies the maximum percent improvement in his opponent's utility position (or his own) that he finds acceptable, where such must not be less than the lesser of the two maximums in the first round. The lesser of these two maximums is used to define a second circle—the limited commitment set for this round. The second participant L then proposes that joint action e'' common to both the improvement and the limited commitment sets for this round, which yields her maximum utility outcome. And so the process continues through points e''', e'''', and so on, until the compromise outcome is within a negligible distance from the efficiency frontier, or until it reaches a level where both participants agree to call the procedure to a halt.

The sequence of compromise actions in Figure 5-3 suggests that acceptance of this procedure by the participants in this situation may require that each participant be assured that he be a leader the same number of times that he is a follower.

5.4.4 The Zeuthen Concession (Least to Lose Goes First) Procedure

Let us turn to another procedure—one that involves a way of proceeding that may have much more appeal to participants than ones we have already discussed. Assume the efficiency frontier in the joint action space to be well behaved as in the Figure 4-3 on p. 76. In the corresponding joint utility space (where for ease of exposition we set, as we are free to do, each participant's worst outcome at 0, and each one's best outcome at 1), plot the joint utilities $(^Lu^{L*}, {}^Ju^{L*})$ and $(^Lu^{J*}, {}^Ju^{J*})$ associated with the most preferred actions a^{L*} and a^{J*}, respectively. (See Figure 5-6.) Clearly, if L were to demand the relative utility $^Lu^{L*}$ associated with her most preferred joint action, and J were to demand the relative utility $^Ju^{J*}$ associated with his most preferred joint action, such demands could not be met. No joint action exists that could yield these two utilities. The two participants must be willing to concede if they are to get anything.

When considering concession, L may reason as follows: "If I concede completely to J's present demand a^{J*} then I will realize a utility outcome $^Lu^{J*}$; while if J concedes completely to my present demand a^{L*}, then I will receive a utility outcome $^Lu^{L*}$. Therefore, if I were to concede completely to J, my loss would be $^Lu^{L*} - {}^Lu^{J*}$; while if the present stalemate were to continue (with neither of us reducing our demands) my loss would be the maximum possible, that is, $^Lu^{L*}$. As a fraction of my maximum possible loss, the loss in utility that I would incur were I to concede completely to J is given by ratio $\ell_{LJ} = (^Lu^{L*} - {}^Lu^{J*})/^Lu^{L*}$. This

Figure 5-6. A Sequence of Concessions along the Efficiency Frontier.

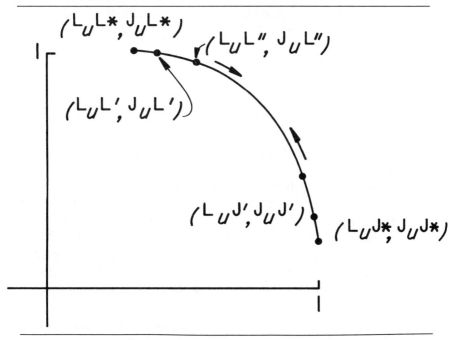

ratio may be designated my *potential loss ratio*. On the other hand, if J were to concede completely to my demand, the relevant fraction (or his potential loss ratio) would be $\ell_{JL} = ({}^{J}u^{J*} - {}^{J}u^{L*})/{}^{J}u^{J*}$." From Table 5–3 these two ratios are $1 - .454/1$ and $1 - .261/1$ or .546 and .739 for L and J, respectively.[20]

If both J and L are willing to engage in comparisons of these potential loss ratios, a procedure that a mediator may suggest is as follows:

Step 1.   The participant who stands to lose the least fractional amount concedes a little (no matter how little) along the efficiency frontier on the first round. Since in the case discussed above L has the least to lose (i.e., her potential loss ratio is the lesser of the two), she concedes first.

Step 2.   The utility outcomes associated with the conceder's reduced demand $a^{L'}$ say, are used to recalculate the potential loss ratios for J and L. That is, ${}^{L}u^{L'}$ and ${}^{J}u^{L'}$ replace ${}^{L}u^{L*}$ and ${}^{J}u^{L*}$ respectively. (See Figure 5–6.)

Step 3.   New potential loss ratios are calculated and compared, and again the participant who stands to lose the least (i.e., has the lower potential loss ratio) concedes a little. While L may be required to concede again on the second round and the third and fourth, sooner or later J will be required to concede from a^{J*} to $a^{J'}$.

This series of concessions continues until they reach a unique point on the efficiency frontier where the two loss ratios are identical and, in particular, equal to zero.[21] If participants adopt this procedure, we shall say that they are each guided by the *Zeuthen concession principle*.[22]

In situations in which participants are not willing (or able) to consider potential loss ratios as comparable, they may be willing to consider an alternative concession procedure that also yields the same compromise solution as the Zeuthen procedure. Again, participants consider two of their utility outcomes, namely, that corresponding to their own most preferred joint action ($^{L}u^{L*}$ and $^{J}u^{J*}$ for L and J, respectively) and that corresponding to the other participant's most preferred joint action ($^{L}u^{J*}$ and $^{J}u^{L*}$ for L and J, respectively). However, in deciding which participant should make the concession on any round they compare the ratios $\phi_{LJ} = {}^{L}u^{J*}/{}^{L}u^{L*}$ and $\phi_{JL} = {}^{J}u^{L*}/{}^{J}u^{J*}$, where ϕ_{LJ} is the ratio of (1) the utility outcome to L from conceding completely to J's demand and (2) the utility outcome to L from having her own demand completely met. Thus ϕ_{LJ} may be interpreted as a measure of the relative value to L of J's demand in relation to L's own demand. The rule that may be adopted on each round is, then, that the participant who has the greater relative value for the other's demand in relation to her own should concede on that round. The relative value ratios are recalculated after each concession has been made, and the series of concessions continues until both relative values are identical and equal to one.

5.4.5 Relaxed Hierarchical Programming

In a situation where we have several interest groups, each concerned primarily with a single objective[23]—say, J with environmental quality (EQ), K with growth (G), L with recreation (R), and so on—and technical analysts have been able to specify in at least relative units the levels of objective achievement associated with each joint action, then we may adopt a relaxed hierarchical programming approach. We let the participants or some respected outsider determine the order of importance of the objectives—as, for example, in the Saaty method of determining group priorities. Say that (EQ) is first, (G) second, (R) third, and so forth. The basic approach of relaxed hierarchical programming is then to run a program maximizing achievement on each objective in order of priority, subject to constraints ensuring achievement of (at least) some fraction of the optimal level of higher priority objectives, until all available resources are utilized. These constraints are based upon relaxation (or concession) factors which specify the fraction of each objective's optimal achievement to be guaranteed at the minimum on any round of the program.[24]

One of several ways to determine relaxation factors is through recursive interaction of participants. The steps may be as follows: First, a program is run that maximizes achievement of the first objective (EQ) subject to the availability of resources. This yields (EQ*), an optimal value for the first objective. Next, a program is run that maximizes achievement on the second objective (G) subject to the availability of resources, and the achievement of (at least) the optimal value (EQ*) of the first objective. This yields optimal values (EQ*) and (G*) for the first and second objectives, respectively. Participants are then asked whether they approve of these outcomes, or whether they would be willing to relax a little (say 5 percent of the achievement on the first objective in order to be able to attain a little more achievement on the second). If they request that such a relaxation factor be adopted, the second program is run subject to the achievement of (at least) 95 percent of the optimal value (EQ*) of the first objective. This modified program yields new optimal values (EQ**) and (G**) for the first two objectives, respectively. Again participants are asked if they approve of the outcomes. If not, the 5 percent relaxation factor is changed and continues to be changed until they do approve the outcomes.

Next, a program is run that maximizes achievement on the third objective (R) subject to (1) resource availability, (2) achievement of (at least) the fraction of the optimal value of the first objective agreed upon in the final version of the previous program, and (3) achievement of (at least) the optimal value of the second objective achieved in that previous program. This step yields optimal values ($\overline{EQ}$*), ($\overline{G}$*) and ($\overline{R}$*) for all three objectives, respectively. Again participants are asked to suggest relaxation factors if they disapprove of the implied tradeoff between these three objectives, and the appropriate modifications are made to the program's constraints. So the process continues, constantly changing relaxation factors and taking up objectives in order of importance until both all available resources are utilized and satisfactory relaxation factors have been reached with regard to all objectives.[25]

The recursive interaction approach will be discussed more extensively in Section 8.1. Note that even with the presence of a mediator it is necessary for participants to come to know each other's preference structures in order to interact effectively.

5.5 CONCLUDING REMARKS

In this chapter we have examined procedures for a class of realistic conflict situations wherein participants can state their preferences in relative terms. In general, this is a fairly strong requirement. We pointed out that it is more likely that participants can only order their preferences, and, as we shall point out in the next chapter, there are only very few situations wherein participants can assign *precise* values to outcomes, using common units to measure utility, satisfaction, or the equivalent.

When only a small (finite) number of joint actions exist or can be considered, a variety of procedures has been suggested. They are relevant for conflict situations where participants (1) have reached a stalemate, deadlock, or equivalent position including their worst possible outcomes and are willing or eager to consider improvements from this position; (2) in contrast, have each taken a fixed position that tends to be optimal (ideal) for them and upon which they have insisted but are now willing to consider reasonable concessions; or (3) are intensely concerned with their security and sensitive to their strategic potential. Some of these procedures are max the total of percent improvements (concessions), min the percent difference in improvements (concessions), and max the min percent improvement.

In addition, we have examined a recent development, the Saaty method of determining group priorities, requiring of participants only an ability to scale things roughly. They do not need to make precise statements on relative utilities. However, this procedure does need to translate the rough scaling of participants into average relative utilities or the equivalent, which, while involving certain short-comings and questionable assumptions, may have considerable appeal to participants in many situations.

For cases where the actions of participants are many and can be viewed as continuous, we also examined the three general categories of situations listed in the second paragraph above. Here we were better able to treat the need of some participants to move slowly and reach a compromise solution through a sequence of rounds of improvements or concessions—for example, by employing either the sequential split-the-difference principle in the outcome space or the Zeuthen concession procedure. We also were able to introduce programming approaches and associate the objective functions with particular goals and utilities of specific individuals. Such approaches can be extremely helpful to analysts in enabling them to evaluate for participants the impacts and distribution effects of alternative policies upon them and their objectives. This will be discussed more extensively in Chapter 8.

APPENDIX TO CHAPTER 5

5A.1 The Derivation of Relative Weights (The Components of the Eigenvector) in the Saaty Procedure

Consider a case as in Saaty and Khouja (1976) where there are three objectives whose weights (relative importance) w_1, w_2, w_3 are to be determined. Also consider a pairwise comparison table (such as Table 5–6) to be matrix A with the same number of rows and columns where the element a_{ij} of the matrix A represents the number in the ith row and jth column of the pairwise comparison table. Assume for the moment that the judgments are of one or more experts and consistent, so that for each $a_{ij} \times a_{jk} = a_{ik}$. Since $a_{11} = 1$, $a_{12} = w_1/w_2$, and $a_{13} = w_1/w_3$, it follows that:

$$a_{11}w_1 + a_{12}w_2 + a_{13}w_3 = 3w_1 \qquad (5A\text{-}1)$$

Likewise it follows that:

$$a_{21}w_1 + a_{22}w_2 + a_{23}w_3 = 3w_2, \text{ and}$$

$$a_{31}w_1 + a_{32}w_2 + a_{33}w_3 = 3w_3 \qquad (5A\text{-}2)$$

Putting these three equations in matrix form, we have

$$\begin{bmatrix} a_{11} & a_{12} & a_{13} \\ a_{21} & a_{22} & a_{23} \\ a_{31} & a_{32} & a_{33} \end{bmatrix} \begin{bmatrix} w_1 \\ w_2 \\ w_3 \end{bmatrix} = 3 \begin{bmatrix} w_1 \\ w_2 \\ w_3 \end{bmatrix} \qquad (5A\text{-}3)$$

or

$$Aw = 3w \qquad (5A\text{-}4)$$

In general, when there are n objectives (n columns and rows) we obtain $Aw = nw$ or

$$\begin{bmatrix} A - In \end{bmatrix} w = 0 \qquad (5A\text{-}5)$$

Suppose we obtain as a set of consistent a_{ij}:

$$\begin{bmatrix} 1 & 2 & 4 \\ 1/2 & 1 & 2 \\ 1/4 & 1/2 & 1 \end{bmatrix} = A \qquad (5A\text{-}6)$$

We can proceed to determine the weights implicit in this matrix by explicitly stating the equations involved and solving them. By (5A-5) and (5A-6), the equations involved are:

$$(1-n)w_1 + 2w_2 + 4w_3 = 0$$
$$1/2w_1 + (1 - n)w_2 + 2w_3 = 0$$
$$1/4w_1 + 1/2w_2 + (1 - n)w_3 = 0 \qquad (5A\text{-}7)$$

But since $n = 3$, (5A-7) becomes

$$-2w_1 + 2w_2 + 4w_3 = 0$$
$$1/2w_1 - 2w_2 + 2w_3 = 0$$
$$1/4w_1 + 1/2w_2 - 2w_3 = 0 \qquad (5A\text{-}8)$$

Of these three equations, only two are independent. To obtain a unique solution, we add the natural constraint that the set of weights add to unity, for example,

$$w_1 + w_2 + w_3 = 1 \qquad (5A\text{-}9)$$

Solving, we derive

$$w_1 = .5714 = 4/7$$

$$w_2 = .2857 = 2/7$$

$$w_3 = .1429 = 1/7 \qquad \text{(5A-10)}$$

(The observant reader could have anticipated this solution by considering the values in one row or one column only.)

In general, however, judgments will be inconsistent, at least to a certain extent, because only rare minds, if any, can develop consistent pairwise judgments when many objectives are involved. (Also bear in mind that the limited scale permitted by Saaty rules out the possibility, for example, of $a_{12} = 3$ and $a_{23} = 4$ so that $a_{13} = 12$.) Then from spelling out (5A-5) and substituting the symbol r for n, for reasons to be seen below:

$$(1 - r)w_1 + a_{12}w_2 + a_{13}w_3 = 0$$

$$a_{21}w_1 + (1 - r)w_2 + a_{23}w_3 = 0$$

$$a_{31}w_1 + a_{32}w_2 + (1 - r)w_3 = 0 \qquad \text{(5A-11)}$$

If we require that $w_1, w_2, w_3 > 0$, then by (5A-5), the determinant value of $[A - Ir]$ must be zero—that is,

$$|A - Ir| = \begin{vmatrix} 1 - r & a_{12} & a_{13} \\ a_{21} & 1 - r & a_{23} \\ a_{31} & a_{32} & 1 - r \end{vmatrix} = 0 \qquad \text{(5A-12)}$$

which is generally called the *characteristic equation* of matrix A. Since the only unknown in the determinant is r, and since in determining the value of the above determinant, r is generally involved to the third power (i.e., a cubic equation is involved), there will be three values of r that will solve the equation. These three values are generally called the *characteristic roots or eigenvalues*.

Substituting each value of r in (5A-11) and introducing the additional meaningful constraint

$$w_1 + w_2 + w_3 = 1 \qquad \text{(5A-13)}$$

yields a different set of w_1, w_2 and w_3, each $\begin{bmatrix} w_1 \\ w_2 \\ w_3 \end{bmatrix}$ being generally called an eigenvector

For example, if we take the initial pairwise (inconsistent) matrix to be

$$\begin{bmatrix} 1 & 4 & 5 \\ 1/4 & 1 & 1 \\ 1/5 & 1 & 1 \end{bmatrix} \tag{5A-14}$$

we obtain the characteristic equation

$$|A - Ir| = \begin{vmatrix} 1-r & 4 & 5 \\ 1/4 & 1-r & 1 \\ 1/5 & 1 & 1-r \end{vmatrix} = 0 \tag{5A-15}$$

We solve and obtain the three values of r

$$r = 3.0125$$
$$\left. \begin{array}{l} r = \\ r = \end{array} \right\} \quad \text{complex (i.e. nonreal)} \tag{5A-16}$$

If we take the maximum value of r, namely $r = 3.0125$, and employ constraint (5A-13), we obtain

$$w_1 = .691$$
$$w_2 = .161$$
$$w_3 = .149 \tag{5A-17}$$

or the eigenvector $\begin{bmatrix} .691 \\ .161 \\ .149 \end{bmatrix}$.

As already indicated, we can obtain three eigenvectors, one for each root (value of r). Which should we use?

According to Saaty, inconsistency appears because of perturbations or inability of the human mind to make precise computations when many variables are involved. Hence, the value of r that comes closest to the natural meaningful value that would be obtained if there were 100 percent consistency is to be used. The other two values of r represent the effect of perturbations on the two natural roots, namely $r = 0$, which are always obtained from a consistent pairwise matrix but which are meaningless in our context.

5A.2 Equal Role Opportunities Principle

Another procedure which, while not applicable to very many cases, may nevertheless be quite effective in managing conflict involves the use of an equal role opportunities principle. The application of this principle is best illustrated in connection with a Prisoner's Dilemma game in which payoff elements are relative (or cardinal) utilities. Also, while it typically does not yield equal improvements to participants, it may do so.

Suppose there are two participants with two tasks to perform jointly. There are only two ways in which any given task can be performed, and each participant is assigned the problem of selecting the way in which only one of the tasks is to be completed. Let the time spent at tasks be that shown in Table 5A-1, where the first number in each cell represents time spent at Task A, and the second number, time spent at Task B.

If it were known that J would in fact perform Task A, and that L could perform Task B, then J out of self-interest would choose Way 2 for Task A, and L would choose Way 2 for Task B. The results would be 20 minutes at each task, and, all told 40 minutes would be spent performing the joint task. This is the standard Nash solution to the Prisoners Dilemma Game. The cooperative solution, however, would be (15, 15), that is, 15 minutes at each task.

Change the structure of the game such that it is not known beforehand which of the two tasks a participant will be required to perform. Rather, let the assignment of tasks to participants be chosen randomly, say by a toss of a coin. Then the payoff matrix becomes that shown in Table 5A-2. Now, out of self-interest, each participant is motivated to choose Way 1, and the cooperative solution results.

Table 5A-1.   Time Spent at Tasks.

		Task B (L selects the way to perform Task B)	
		Way 1	Way 2
Task A (J selects the way to perform Task A)	Way 1	15, 15	25, 10
	Way 2	10, 25	20, 20

Table 5A-2.   Payoff Matrix for Tasks chosen Randomly.

	Way 1	Way 2
Way 1	$[15(.5) + 15(.5)]$, $[15(.5) + 15(.5)]$	$[25(.5) + 10(.5)]$, $[25(.5) + 10(.5)]$
Way 2	$[10(.5) + 25(.5)]$, $[10(.5) + 25(.5)]$	$[20(.5) + 20(.5)]$, $[25(.5) + 20(.5)]$

or in effect

15, 15	17½, 17½
17½, 17½	20, 20

In a sense the equal role opportunities procedure as outlined above can be used as a device to convert a conflict situation into a harmony game. However, it does require that the probabilities of assignments to tasks and the relative or cardinal payoff values be such as to yield a harmony game.

NOTES

1. Using the word "relative" in the term relative utility, means that there is some relevant base against which a participant makes comparisons. One obtains different utility numbers then according to what the base is. In the cases we now examine, we often take the participant's base to be the difference between the satisfaction or utility derived from his worst outcome and that derived from his best outcome. We may represent this difference by the number 1, and thus conveniently attach a 0 value to the worse possible outcome and a 1 to the best possible outcome. (Alternatively, in terms of percents we may attach a 0 and 100 to these two outcomes, respectively.) This then produces a utility scale that we can employ. However, as we shall observe below, a participant may attach the zero value to another outcome and not to his worst outcome in a conflict situation.

   We assume that each participant is able to state the ratio of (1) the difference between the satisfaction (utility) derived from any given outcome and that derived from his worst, to (2) the difference between the satisfaction (or utility) derived from his worst outcome and that derived from his best outcome. This ratio then can be measured as a fraction along the scale from 0 (corresponding to worst outcome) to 1 (corresponding to best outcome). (Alternatively, it can be stated in terms of a percentage along a scale from 0 to 100.) Since this assumption makes it possible for him to compare the distances of any two intervals along his utility scale, it is equivalent to the assumption of a lineal utility function in Isard, T. Smith, et al. (1969), or an interval utility function in the game theory literature stemming from von Neumann and Morgenstern (1953). That is, when a lineal (interval) utility function characterizes a participant's preference structure, then any linear transformation $t(u(o)) = ru(o) + s$ of the participant's utility function $u(o)$ is also permissible. To show this, let $u'(o) = ru(o) + s$ or $u' = ru + s$, when we omit the argument o. Then from the fact that $(u'_a - u'_b)/(u'_b - u'_c) = [(ru_a + s) - (ru_b + s)]/[(ru_b + s) - (ru_c + s)] = [r(u_a - u_b) + (s - s)]/[r(u_b - u_c) + (s - s)] = (u_a - u_b)/u_b - u_c$ it clearly follows that $u'_a - u'_b = k(u'_b - u'_c)$ whenever $(u_a - u_b) = k(u_b - u_c)$. If a participant's utility function is unique up to a linear transformation, he is free to select values for both r and s. If then he identifies his worst as well as his best outcome and arbitrarily assigns them numbers, we know that if he sets min $u(o) = -s/r$ and max $u(o) = (1 - s)/r$, or equivalently $r = -s/\min u(o)$ and $s = 1 - r \max u(o)$, he obtains from any linear transformation,

$$u' = ru(o) + s$$

$$= \frac{-s}{\min u(o)} u(o) + s = ru(o) + (1 - r \max u(o))$$

$$= 0 \text{ when } u(o) = \min u(o)$$

$$= 1 \text{ when } u(o) = \max u(o)$$

Since there is always such a transformation that can convert a participant's utilities (when he has a lineal or interval utility function) to a range from 0 to 1, and more important, since this is the simplest framework in which to think of relative utility, *as well as the framework by far most frequently used by the mass of decisionmakers and leaders*, we use it in what follows.

To give a numerical example, one participant J, may say "Hell" is worst and "Heaven" is best and arbitrarily assign a value of -100 MM (million) utility units to Hell and $+1$MMM (billion) utility units to

Heaven. Choosing $r = -s/-100\text{MM}$ and $s = 1 - r(1\text{MMM})$, which we are free to do if we have lineal utility, and solving these two equations yields $r = 1/1100\text{MM}$ and $s = 1/11$. Hence $u' = (1/1100\text{MM}) \times u(o) + 1/11$, and thus we come up with Hell $= 0$ and Heaven $= 1$ when we recall that min $u = -(s/r)$ and max $u = (1-s)/r$. A second participant may set her worst, an "all-out nuclear war," at -100 and her best, the "good life," at 150. Again, since the second participant has lineal utility, we can set $r = -s/-100$ and $s = 1 - 150r$ to get all-out nuclear war $= 0$ and the good life $= 1$. (Solving these two equations yields $r = 1/250$ and $s = 0.4$. Hence $u' = (1/250) \times u(o) + 0.4$.)

Formally, we shall say that participants have *interrelative* utility when they agree to view the difference between the worst (or some other relevant reference outcome) and the best (or some other relevant reference outcome) for each as unity. However in order to avoid the awkward term "interrelative" in the discussion that follows, we shall speak of participants having relative utility when it is clear from the context that we mean interrelative utility.

It is also very important to note that in some contexts there naturally exists or is given a fixed reference point—a zero point, a half-way point, the current standpoint, or some other—in terms of which participants are able to state relative values over all possible pairs of utility outcomes. In these contexts, participants have in effect one less degree of freedom, and are free to determine only a scale factor when assigning utility numbers to outcomes. Here, too, we shall say that participants have interrelative utility sometimes designated *interscalinal* utility (see Isard, T. Smith et al. 1969:174–75) when they are able to agree on what are comparable percent changes.

Of course, when participants cannot reach agreement on comparable relative units—that is, on the percent changes that are comparable—they may need and at times be agreeable to use of a conflict management procedure to resolve this difference.

2. In the case of two participants, the measure of closeness can be in terms of distance along the horizontal, distance along the vertical, or perpendicular distance to the line. They all yield the same result. In the case of more than two participants, the perpendicular to the reference line is one reasonable measure of distance the participants may be willing to accept.

3. If there happened to be a prominent kink in the set of efficient joint actions when plotted on a graph—for example, as would be the case in Figure 5-1 if the point indicating outcome (77.8,67.4) were replaced by a point indicating outcome (88,80)—unsophisticated participants might seize upon this point as representing a natural compromise solution, be happy, and not proceed with any further interaction.

4. Even with a lower bound constraint, use of this principle may not be acceptable. For example, if a joint action yielding 60.00 and 60.01 as percent improvements satisfies the lower bound on percent improvement, participants may still prefer a joint action yielding 94 and 95 percent improvements. This example points up the fact that a fundamental problem of tradeoff between equity and joint improvement becomes involved. Another principle would need to be introduced to handle this problem.

5. Even with an efficiency constraint, any given efficient joint action may not be acceptable if another nonefficient joint action greatly diminishes the percent difference. Again, a fundamental problem of tradeoff between efficiency and equity becomes involved.

6. Still another related principle is the *max the max percent improvement principle*. This principle might be put to use where there is a "winner-loser" or a "have and have-not" situation involving a group *in* and a group *out* of power. This principle, while frequently employed, obviously pays no attention to either the difference between or the smaller of the percent improvements. That is, it gives zero weight to the latter. Correspondingly, when we consider concessions, we can suggest the principle of *min the min percent concession*.

7. The problem of establishing the (0,0) and (1,1) reference points is essentially the basic problem of selecting the initial and terminal conditions from which improvements and concessions should be measured. It is also related to the question of identifying relevant joint actions.

8. For the same reason one may suggest the use of a principle of *min the difference in percent goal achievements* to replace the principle of *min the difference in percent improvements* (discussed on pages 131–137) in an appropriate situation.

9. Parallel to the max the total of percents of goal achievements (weighted or unweighted) principle can be a *min the total of percents of goal shortfalls* (weighted or unweighted) principle. Use of this principle would yield the same results as the min total of percent concessions (weighted or unweighted) principle when the joint goal and ideal points coincide. Also, when the goal shortfall is viewed as a penalty (cost), we may speak of one type of a *min the total penalty principle*.

10. Note that all the cells along the principal diagonal have a value of unity indicating that the importance of a joint policy relative to itself is unity.

11. In an unweighted case, the averaging process would simply sum the ratio of, say, the importance of joint action (S,P) to the importance of joint action (C,P) over all members of the team, and divide by the number of members. The resulting fraction would represent the average ratio of the importance of (S,P) to that of (C,P).

12. When goal achievements or shortfalls are the pertinent criteria, then we may speak of the principles *max equal percent goal achievements* or *min equal percent goal shortfalls*.

13. Where the equal percentage improvement line is drawn from a point that is not a (0,0) point, such as in Figure 5–2, then this line will usually not coincide with the equal percentage concession line drawn from a relevant ideal point or other point from which concession is considered reasonable.

14. See Figure 7–4 on page 229 for the case of three participants.

15. For example, if 1.00 were L's relative utility corresponding to $^{L}u^{L*}$ and 0.34 to $^{L}u^{J*}$, then she should be content with 0.67. This step also assumes that a joint action does exist that could yield the midpoint utilities as outcomes. Such will not always be the case when the utility space is nonconvex.

16. The participants may adopt a variant of this procedure when only a finite number of joint actions is possible. In this case, the outcome of each joint action is plotted in the joint utility space. On the first round, each participant proposes her most preferred joint action. In the joint utility space, the outcomes of the two proposed joint actions are connected by a straight line and the midpoint c is identified. This point serves as the reference point for the second round. In the second round, the improvement set in the joint utility set relative to c is constructed. Each participant then proposes a joint action whose outcomes fall in this improvement set. Once again the outcomes of the two proposed joint actions are connected by a straight line, and the midpoint c' is identified. This point serves as the reference point for the third round, and so on, until only one or two joint actions remain yielding outcomes within the last improvement set. If only one remains, then it is the compromise solution. If two remain, then the outcomes of both are by definition equally distant from their midpoint, and some additional procedure (like toss a coin) must be adopted to break the tie.

     However, this variant may not be acceptable should the outcome of the compromise joint action represent a large difference in relative utilities to be received by the participants. Under these circumstances, participants may be willing to adopt a compromise joint action yielding an inefficient outcome that, however, results in much more equal relative utilities.

17. Note that the fixed threat point can also serve as a reference point for use in a split-the-difference procedure (simple or sequential) when participants can state their preference in an ordinal manner only.

18. For further discussion see Isard, T. Smith, et al. (1969:chap. 7, particularly Table 7–2).

19. Other conventions are also possible to insure that the participants reach the efficiency frontier within a reasonable number of rounds and in a fair manner.

20. Using Table 3-2, they could be calculated as $(216 - 98)/216$ and $(230 - 60)/230$, which yield the same ratios.

21. If the two potential loss ratios happen to be identical and not equal to zero, then an ad hoc tie-breaking rule, such as tossing a coin, must go into effect.

22. Formally, it has been shown that the compromise solution that results is the same as that which maximizes the product of the percent improvements in the utilities of the participants, that is $u^J u^L$, for L and J, respectively. See Harsanyi (1953:272) and Isard, T. Smith, et al. (1969:264–67).

23. That is where each interest group's utility is a monotonically increasing function of the achievement on its primary objective. The utility functions may be either ordinal, relative, or cardinal.

24. Assuming objectives are ranked E^A, E^B, . . . , E^U in order of importance, the relaxed hierarchical programming model is the same as that in note 28 of Chapter 4 except that: $E^A(a) \geq E^A(a)^*$ is replaced by $E^A(a) \geq \beta^A E^A(a)^*$, and $E^B(a) \geq E^B(a)^*$ is replaced by $E^B(a) \geq \beta^B E^B(a)^*$ and so on, where β^A and β^B are relaxation factors and where $0 \leq \beta^A$, $\beta^B \leq 1$.

25. In the above application, we assumed no satiation, that is, we assumed that no interest group reaches a satiation level of achievement for its objective (i.e., a level beyond which utility decreases rather than increases). To avoid "oversatiation," upper bound constraints on objective achievement can be employed. See note 29 of chapter 4.

In certain extreme situations, participants may not agree to permit (or often other factors may preclude) any relaxation at all in optimization of objectives taken in order of importance. Such would imply that (within the realm of the action space being considered) a unit of achievement of a higher priority objective is always infinitely more valuable than any unit of achievement on a lower priority objective. Under these circumstances, hierarchical programming may be designated *lexicographic programming* in conformity with the concept of *lexicographic utility*.

6 PROCEDURES FOR SITUATIONS WITH A SMALL NUMBER OF OPTIONS WHERE PARTICIPANTS CAN ASSIGN PRECISE VALUES TO OUTCOMES

6.1 INTRODUCTION

While in general participants to conflict situations are not able to assign precise values to outcomes (even though social scientists frequently assume they can), there may be some situations when participants are able to do so. For these situations, an extensive set of procedures has been developed. This is to be expected since when participants can assign precise values to outcomes, that is, when in the words of the technical analyst they possess cardinal utility functions, it becomes possible to make many more precise numerical comparisons.

Recall that when an individual has a cardinal utility function, it means that he can state both the relative strengths of his preferences for any pair of outcomes and the absolute difference (in utility units) between them. Thus, the assumption that an individual does have a cardinal utility function is a strong one. Moreover, when theoretical analysts compare the cardinal utilities of participants in a conflict situation, they are using an even stronger set of assumptions. They are making the further assumption that the participants are using the same unit in measuring or stating their cardinal preferences (utilities) —something that is hard to imagine—as well as employing the same *zero* point from which to measure their cardinal utilities. Hence, many procedures they suggest to resolve conflict (some of which we examine for use below) are primarily of academic interest only, though they may be helpful to the analyst in giving him insight into complex conflict situations.[1]

We begin in Section 6.2 by assuming situations in which participants have comparable cardinal utility functions. We extend a number of the procedures of the preceding chapters so that they now become applicable to absolute improvements and concessions. We also develop a new, demand-revealing procedure. In Section 6.3 we delve deeper into the distribution problem, specifically exploring the use of weights, constraints, and changes in the objective function to achieve greater equity. More complex utility functions are touched upon in Section 6.4.

6.2 PROCEDURES WHEN PARTICIPANTS' UTILITIES ARE COMPARABLE

Before we discuss procedures for situations where participants have comparable cardinal utility, that is, have *intercardinal utility*,[2] we repeat that procedures applicable for conflict situations involving less information concerning preference structures (specifically those involving ordinal or relative utility) may not be applicable here. As before, the possibility to compare absolute changes may lead participants to consider one or more of these procedures unfair.[3] See the discussion on pages 130–131.

6.2.1 Max Total Utility Principle

When comparable cardinal utility pertains, a first obvious procedure is to select the joint action that maximizes the sum of the utilities received by participants. Accordingly, for a situation for which the numbers of Table 3-2 on page 26 are cardinal utilities, joint action (AG, C_3) yielding the total utility 337 should be selected.[4] An obvious shortcoming of this procedure is that it ignores the distribution factor, which we will discuss in Section 6.3.

6.2.2 Max Total of Utility Improvements Principle

In the max total utility principle, the (0,0) point is implicitly used as a natural reference point for determining a total. However, other reference points can be employed. For example, where strategic potential is taken into account (as on pages 145–146), increments from the (0,0) point may need to be replaced by increments from the security-level reference point. In Table 3–2 *cardinalized*, that is, where the values in the cells are taken to be comparable cardinal utilities, the security level outcomes are 95 and 120 for J and L, respectively. Under this circumstance, the max total utility principle may be replaced by a *max total of utility improvements principle*, where any utility above the corresponding utility of the security-level reference point is defined as an improvement. However, the optimal joint action in Table 3–2 remains unchanged since the joint action that maximizes total utility will maximize total improvement over any sum of outcomes associated with a reference point.

Frequently, the needs of the several participants, the contributions they make, their strategic potentials, or other relevant elements in a conflict situation differ. Accordingly, there may exist a rationale for applying different weights w^J and w^L to the utilities of participants J and L, respectively. Hence, a second compromise procedure is to *max total of weighted utilities* ($w^J u^J + w^L u^L$)—another procedure that inadequately handles the distribution problem to be discussed in Section 6.3. Correspondingly, where the focus is on improvement from some reference point other than the (0,0) point, still another compromise procedure is to *max total of weighted utility improvements*. Note also that when participants view ideal outcomes (with regard to some relevant reference point) as goals or targets, and choose to focus on the extent of achievement toward each one's goal, then they may wish to adopt a principle of *max total of achievements toward goals* (weighted or unweighted). This principle is equivalent, however, to that of *max total of utility improvements*. The procedures discussed in this section can obviously be extended to *percent improvements* (or *percent achievements*).

6.2.3 Min the Difference of Improvements Principle

One compromise procedure that takes into account the distribution factor involves the selection of that joint action which *minimizes the difference in absolute improvements* in utilities from the (0,0) point. In Table 3–2 cardinalized, this joint action is (F, C_1) yielding the outcome (112,110). This outcome is grossly inefficient. As a consequence, participants may be motivated to restrict the application of this principle to some meaningful subset of the joint actions, for example, the subset of efficient joint actions. Here, the joint action (AG, C_2) is selected, yielding the outcome (168,155). Another useful constraint might involve a lower bound for any participant's improvement.

Reference points other than the (0,0) point can be used. For example, the joint action (F, C_2), with outcome (144,150), which results from each participant behaving as an unbounded, unfounded optimist (see page 79) may serve as the base from which improvements are measured. The joint action that minimizes the difference of improvements from this reference point is, once again, (AG, C_2), yielding the outcome (168,155).

Where participants differ in terms of their needs, contributions, power, and other relevant elements, as on pages 84–85, they may agree on applying different weights to their absolute improvements. As a consequence, they may adopt a compromise procedure based on the principle *min the difference of weighted absolute improvements* from some relevant reference point.

Note also that where participants set goals or targets in utility terms and choose to focus on the extent of achievement toward each one's goal, then they may apply the principle *min the difference of absolute goal achievements* in either a weighted or unweighted fashion.[5]

6.2.4 Max the Min Improvement Principle

Another related procedure is to select that joint action which maximizes the lesser of the two absolute improvements, that is, to employ the principle *max the min improvement*. In Table 3-2 cardinalized, this corresponds to joint action (AG, C_2) where the outcome 155 is the largest of the lower outcomes in any cell. Once again, the participants may agree that different weights should be applied to their respective improvements and that a reference point other than the (0,0) point of Table 3-2 should be used.[6]

6.2.5 Min Total Concessions
(Penalty or Cost) Principle

Another set of compromise procedures focuses on concessions from an *ideal point*, often defined as that infeasible point corresponding to the pair of maximum possible cardinal utilities for the two participants. In Figure 5-1, Q is such a point, and in Table 3-2 corresponds to the outcomes 216 and 230 for L and J, respectively. One procedure selects that feasible joint action which *minimizes the sum of concessions* from the ideal point. In Table 3-2 cardinalized, this joint action is (AG,C_3), whose outcome is $(152,185)$, involving concessions of 64 and 45 for L and J, respectively, for a total of 109. Note that this procedure always yields the same joint action as the procedure that maximizes the total utility. This result follows since the total of ideal outcomes will always exceed the largest realizable total from any joint action, and so the joint action that minimizes the sum of concessions from the ideal point is the joint action that maximizes the realizable totals.[7] In some contexts, a concession may be viewed as a penalty or cost. In such contexts, we may speak of a *min total penalty principle*, or a *min total cost principle*.[a] Again the distribution factor is ignored in this procedure.

[a]Mathematically, this principle is

$$\min_J \sum (u^{J*} - u^J(a_k)) \qquad J = A, \ldots, U \qquad (6\text{-}1)$$

where u^{J*} is J's utility associated with his ideal point and $u^J(a_k)$ is J's utility that would result from joint action a_k. Where participants associate a higher cost (penalty) per utility unit with a larger concession (deviation) than a smaller, an alternative procedure would be to min the sum of the squares of concessions, that is:

$$\min_J \sum (u^{J*} - u^J(a_k))^2 \qquad J = A, \ldots, U \qquad (6\text{-}2)$$

A somewhat more sophisticated, but not necessarily realistic procedure identifies for each participant both the joint action a^{J*} that yields him the highest utility u^{J*} and the joint action $\bar{a}^J$ that gives him the lowest utility $\bar{u}^J$. Then taking the difference between the best and worst outcome as a reference magnitude, for each participant J it considers any joint action a_k yielding utility $u^J(a_k)$ and calculates a percent improvement as

$$v^J = \frac{u^J(a_k) - \bar{u}^J}{u^{J*} - \bar{u}^J} \qquad (6\text{-}3)$$

(continued on next page)

Once again, the participants may agree that the absolute concession that each makes should be given a different importance. They may also agree on the weights to be applied. Also, infeasible points other than an ideal point, such as Q, may be employed from which to measure concessions, weighted or unweighted. (See the discussion on pages 227–228.) Also, they may prefer to focus on percentage concessions rather than absolute concessions, and adopt a procedure that *minimizes the total of percentage concessions*, weighted or unweighted.[8]

6.2.6 Min the Difference of Concessions Principle

A compromise procedure that takes into account the distribution factor regarding concessions (penalties) is to select that joint action which *minimizes the difference in absolute concessions* in utilities

The procedure then selects that joint action which maximizes the total of percent improvements, that is:

$$\max_J \sum v^J \qquad\qquad J = A, \ldots, U \qquad\qquad (6\text{-}4)$$

This joint action will necessarily be efficient.

A variation of this procedure emphasizes losses, costs, or penalties associated with deviations of each participant from his maximum obtainable utility u^{J*} and so would correspond to $\min \sum (1 - v^J)$. Where participants associate a higher cost (penalty) per utility unit with a larger deviation (concession) than a smaller, an alternative procedure would be to $\min \sum (1 - v^J)$.[2]

Still other variants are possible when participants do not agree that the quantity $(u^{J*} - \bar{u}^J)$ is acceptable as a reference magnitude. For example, if they agree that the utility u^{J*} for any participant J associated with the ideal point is an acceptable reference magnitude, they might adopt a variant of the above procedure, which defines the improvement factor $\tilde{v}^J = (u^J(a_k)/u^{J*})$ and either minimizes $\sum_J (1 - \tilde{v}^J)$ or $\sum_J (1 - \tilde{v}^J)^2$. Additionally it should be noted that technical analysts often use a general measure such as $\sum_J (1 - \tilde{v}^J)^p$, p being some positive integer, associated with which is the distance measure $(\sum_J (1 - \tilde{v}^J)^p)^{1/p}$, designated the Minkowski metric. However, the only values for p that we find generally useful for practical conflict management are 1 and 2.

Finally, penalty functions may take a more general form. For example, the penalty function (6–2) may be viewed as a special case of

$$\sum_J \ell^J (u^{J*} - u^J)^2 + \sum_J \sum_L m^{JL} (u^{J*} - u^J)(u^{L*} - u^L) \qquad J,L = A, \ldots, U$$
$$J \neq L$$

or of still more general functions.

from the ideal point—resembling in part a *min the range principle*. In Table 3-2 cardinalized, this joint action is (AG,C_0), yielding the outcome (80,95) and involving concessions of 136 and 135 for L and J, respectively. The difference in concessions (penalties) is thus only 1. However, the joint action (AG,C_0) is grossly inefficient; it involves large concessions by both participants. Hence, they may be motivated to restrict the application of this principle to some meaningful subset of joint actions, that is, the subset of efficient joint actions. In this case, the joint action (AG,C_3) is selected, yielding the outcome (152,185) involving concessions of 64 and 45 for L and J, respectively. Another simple appealing constraint might involve an upper bound on any participant's concession (penalty).

As before, it is possible for participants to take into account different needs, contributions, power, and other elements relating to the participants and accordingly attach different weights to the absolute concessions (penalties). As a consequence, participants may wish to use a principle *min the difference of weighted absolute concessions* (penalties) from the ideal point. Also points other than the ideal may be employed from which to measure concessions, and participants may agree to make comparisons in terms of *percents*.[9]

6.2.7 Min the Max Concession Principle

Still another related procedure is to select that joint action which minimizes the larger of the two absolute concessions from the ideal point. In Table 3-2 cardinalized, this corresponds to joint action (AG,C_3) where the outcome (152,185) involves a concession of 64 by L (which is the least of the larger concessions associated with any joint action for any participant). In this case, participants may be said to be using the principle *min the max concession*.[10]

6.2.8 Max the Difference of Improvements Principle

In a few highly significant situations, the problem is to avoid the diseconomies of scale (or failure to capture the full externalities, or other disadvantages) that would result from an even division of a total of an object for which all participants have positive marginal utility. Yet, at the same time, certain forces at play may make it unacceptable for any of the participants to return to their constituencies with none of the total or a zero level of improvement. In these situations, the rational objective (not only of society but also of the participants) may be to select that joint action which maximizes the difference in shares—that is consistent with a principle *max the difference of improvements*—subject to a lower bound on the share each participant is to receive. This lower bound may differ for the several participants since they confront different sets of forces in their constituencies.

To take a specific example, there may exist limited funds for the development of an industrial complex within the region of East Africa. Each nation constituting that region naturally desires to have the complex located within its borders. At the same time, the situation may be such that each of the several nations has much to gain (via trade and exchange) from the efficient operation of the industrial complex—and much to lose if that industrial complex cannot effectively compete in world markets because of diseconomies of scale. Under these circumstances, the participants may agree to a procedure that, subject to the lower bounds on projected development spinoffs (benefits) set by each participant as constraints,[11] maximizes the difference in the allocation, thereby maximizing the overall gain to the region.

6.2.9 Demand-Revealing (No Bluffing) Method (Clarke-Vickrey)

In the max total utility principle discussed on page 178, there is the basic problem of obtaining accurate and true estimates of the utility of an outcome to each participant. Often participants make such a calculation impossible because they find it advantageous to be a free rider, misrepresent the true value to them of an outcome, or, in short, bluff. As with the last-offer arbitration and max good-cause payment procedures already discussed, the Clarke-Vickrey procedure is devised to make it pay each participant to state (as best he can) the true value to him (in terms of units of some standard commodity) of the outcome of each joint action or alternative. If we assume that the values stated by participants can be taken to represent their cardinal utilities for these joint actions and that society considers their cardinal utilities to be comparable in the sense that equivalent values in the standard commodity represent equivalent cardinal utilities to participants, then these values may be recorded in a table such as Table 3–2 (cardinalized) extended to cover more than two participants.[12]

By imposing a tax on him, the Clarke-Vickrey procedure makes it disadvantageous (costly) for a participant to misrepresent or bluff. The determination of this tax can be simply illustrated by means of a graph. Let there be five possible joint actions, alternative plans for regional development, or alternative settlements to an international conflict, and let them be designated a_1, a_2, a_3, a_4, and a_5. Let there be three participants J, L, and M, each representing a well-defined interest group. Focus on how the procedure operates for any one, say J. First, each participant states the value to him of each alternative. The participants may or may not bluff in stating these values; at this point, there is no control that precludes them from bluffing. Plot M's values as " + " marks on Figure 6-1. Next, for each alternative add to M's value the value reported by L, yielding a cumulative value that is indicated by the "o" marks. Finally, for each alternative, add to its cumulative value the value reported by J. This then gives its total value and is indicated by the "•" marks. To ease graphic analysis we

Figure 6-1.   Total and Participant Valuations of Selected Alternatives.

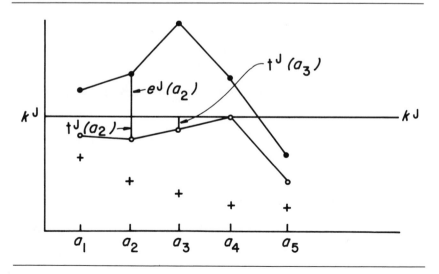

connect the "•" marks by straight line segments; we do the same to the "o" marks.

Next, we draw a horizontal at the maximum point of the line segments connecting the "o" marks. The level of this horizontal, namely k^J, indicates the maximum cumulative value achieved by any alternative when J's value is entirely ignored. It would be the total value realized by participants if J were not included and if other participants as a whole were to adopt maximizing actions. In Figure 6-1, the alternative having the largest cumulative value is a_4. If J were to prefer some other alternative, such as a_3, then clearly the cost to all other participants (*a social cost*) would be given by the *difference* between (1) the highest total of the values to all other participants that would be realized if J were ignored and their best joint action a_4 chosen and (2) the total of the values to all participants realized if the joint action most preferred by J, namely a_3, were chosen. Accordingly, J should be taxed to the extent of this social cost. In Figure 6-1, this tax would be of the level indicated by $t^J(a_3)$ were J's most preferred alternative a_3 chosen.

It is exactly this procedure that the Clarke-Vickrey principle involves. Further, we now can show that if J is self-interested and motivated to maximize his gains less the tax he must pay, then he will in fact opt for that alternative which yields the maximum total value for all participants. Using Figure 6-1, we can see that the value $v^J(a_k)$, $k = 1, \ldots,$ 5 of any alternative to J, say a_2, is composed of two parts, namely, the part above the horizontal, $e^J(a_2)$, and the part below the horizontal, $t^J(a_2)$, that is,

$$v^J(a_2) = e^J(a_2) + t^J(a_2) \qquad (6\text{-}5)$$

But J's net gain from alternative a_2 is its value to him less taxes, that is,

$$v^J(a_2) - t^J(a_2) \qquad (6\text{-}6)$$

which by (6-5) is

$$e^J(a_2) + t^J(a_2) - t^J(a_2), \text{ or} \qquad (6\text{-}7)$$

$e^J(a_2)$, the stretch above the horizontal k^J.

Therefore J searches for the alternative k associated with the maximum value of $e^J(a_k)$. This alternative must be the one with the highest total value to all participants.[b]

We now extend the analysis to apply to each participant. We thereby reach the conclusion that each participant will, out of self-interest, opt for the alternative that achieves the maximum total value, irrespective of whether the other participants initially misrepresented or bluffed. For example, if initially L and M misrepresented the values of different alternatives to them, this would simply mean that the k^J line in Figure 6-1 would have been higher or lower. It would not have affected the choice by J since the alternative with largest total value has the largest vertical stretch above any horizontal, regardless of its level.[13]

There is a major problem associated with this demand-revealing (no bluffing) method, namely, what to do with the taxes collected. If the taxes collected were to be used for some purpose that would have beneficial or detrimental effects on any of the participants, another term would need to be added to the definition of his gains, which is $(v^J(a_k) - t^J(a_k))$, and this could easily destroy the effectiveness of the procedure. Hence, it must be made clear to the participants that the taxes collected will go to some good cause or other unspecified

---

[b]To show this using simple algebra, let $V(a_k)$ be the total value of any alternative k. Then $V(a_k) - v^J(a_k)$ is the value of that alternative to all participants excluding J. From Figure 6-1

$$t^J(a_k) = k^J - [V(a_k) - v^J(a_k)] \qquad k = 1, \ldots, 5 \qquad (6\text{-}8)$$

and J out of self-interest wishes to

$$\max \ v^J(a_k) - t^J(a_k) \ , \qquad (6\text{-}9)$$

or replacing $t^J(a_k)$ by its value in (6-8), to

$$\max \ v^J(a_k) - (k^J - [V(a_k) - v^J(a_k)]) \qquad (6\text{-}10)$$

or

$$\max \ v^J(a_k) - k^J + V(a_k) - v^J(a_k) \qquad (6\text{-}11)$$

which after cancellation is

$$\max \ V(a_k) - k^J \ . \qquad (6\text{-}12)$$

But k^J is a constant. Hence, to max (6-12) out of self-interest is to choose the alternative a_k that maximizes $V(a_k)$, namely the total value to all participants.

"sink" (e.g., shipment via rocket to Jupiter) that would leave all participants unaffected.[c] See Isard and C. Smith (1982b:95).

6.3 PROCEDURES FOR MANAGING THE DISTRIBUTION PROBLEM

As suggested above, the distribution problem often becomes major when participants have comparable cardinal utility. This problem is obviously affected by the set of weights that may be associated with the utilities of the participants. For example, in Section 6.2.1 where the utilities of participants were weighted to obtain a total of weighted utilities that was to be maximized, the outcomes to participants would be directly affected by the weights employed. *Everything else being the same,* weighting tends to lead to a higher outcome to the participant whose utility is weighted more heavily. To this extent, then, weighting does involve consideration of distribution effects. However, where a compromise joint action has to be selected from only a finite set, there is no guarantee that the joint action that maximizes the sum of weighted utilities will not be one that gives a lion's

---

[c]Vickrey has noted other problems in the use of this procedure. One is a problem that generally arises with the use of any procedure when more than two participants are involved. This is the familiar problem of *collusion* among participants. Another is the problem of *agenda,* namely, which alternatives (settlements) are to be considered. The latter problem does not exist when the set of alternatives (settlements) is given and the question is how to choose among them. Finally, there is the general problem of determining the *relevant interest groups,* not only those affected directly, but also those affected indirectly. Again this problem does not come up when the set of participants is indicated beforehand, as in many conflict situations.

Note that the Clarke-Vickrey principle can also be applied to total weighted values (or payoffs) of alternatives. This is an important extension of the procedure—since then many of the ways of calculating weights, either explicitly or implicitly (to be discussed on pages 190–197), can be applied. Hence, the Clarke-Vickrey principle can also eliminate bluffing while handling the distribution problem.

To indicate the application of this principle to total weighted values, let the weight of the single participant on whose behavior we focus at any point in time, say J as in Figure 6-1, be set at unity. This can be done by dividing any set of weights w, $J = A, \ldots , U$, by w^J which also converts the weights of all other participants into ratios relative to w^J, yielding $\widetilde{w}$. Plot the weighted valuations of all participants other than J in cumulative fashion as we did for M and L in Figure 6-1 to obtain for each alternative the summation

$$\sum_L \widetilde{w}^L \, v^L(a_k) - v^J(a_k) \qquad L = A, \ldots , U; \qquad L \neq J \qquad (6\text{-}13)$$

and set k^J equal to the max of these cumulative values over all alternatives. Then we proceed as before.

share of the sum to one participant and little to a second. Hence, determining appropriate weights to apply to participants' utilities does not mean that the distribution problem is adequately treated. We may need to consider using constraints and other modifications in order to tackle the problem more satisfactorily.

The distribution problem appears in other forms too. In one category of situations, participants may derive utility from possessing (consuming) a set of objects (e.g., beads, shells, or money) that are finely divisible. While the participants may agree that the total of their payoffs as defined by the number of objects should be maximized, they frequently fail to agree on the distribution of that total. When there exist laws, cultural practices, institutional rules, and the like that specify the weights (fractions) for dividing that total, no problem exists. There is no conflict. Participants are effectively involved in a harmony game. This is not so when such laws, practices, and rules do not exist, which too often is the case.

In another category of situations, such as those treated in Section 6.2.2, outcomes are directly derived utilities and hence nontransferable. Here, however, side payments in terms of utilities may be possible through the transfer of relatively finely divisible utility-yielding objects from one participant to another. Again, in these situations participants may frequently agree that the total of their utilities is to be maximized, but fail to agree on the size of the transfer of objects from the participant receiving the larger directly derived utility to the other. We thus must look into the question of how to establish weights in a total weighted utility function and use constraints and other modifications, and also consider appropriate ways to divide up a total.[14]

Before proceeding, however, we need to make an important point to facilitate our analysis. This is that cases where the total of weighted utilities is to be maximized directly cover many of the interesting problems in multiobjective programming or multicriteria analysis. Recall our discussion on pages 48–49. Suppose it is so that developing nations perceive only one of the several relevant properties of outcomes, namely "$ foreign aid from developed countries," and therefore that all numbers indicating their utilities in a table such as Table 3–2 (when cardinalized) are simply the utilities directly derived from a simple utility function that is linearly related to dollar aid and only dollar aid. Suppose that the developed nations, too, perceive only one of the several relevant properties of outcomes, namely "international stability," and therefore, that all numbers indicating their utilities in a table such as Table 3-2 (when cardinalized) are simply the utilities directly derived from a simple linear function of international stability. Then when we attach weights w^L and w^J to the utilities u^L and u^J of developing and developed nations, respectively, we are in essence attaching a related set of weights to the objectives: "$ foreign aid from developed nations," and "international stability." That is

$$u^L = k^L E^L \tag{6-14}$$
$$u^J = k^J E^J$$

where E^L and E^J correspond to the level of objectives (criteria), "$ foreign aid," and "international stability," respectively, and where k^L and k^J are conversion constants. Thus, the problem of maximizing the sum of weighted utilities, that is,

$$\max (w^L u^L + w^J u^J) \tag{6-15}$$

(given the joint actions of Table 3-2) becomes a problem of multiple objective programming, namely to:

$$\max (\overline{w}^L E^L + \overline{w}^J E^J) \tag{6-16}$$

where $\overline{w}^L = w^L k^L$ and $\overline{w}^J = w^J k^J$.

6.3.1 The Choice of Weights in Calculating Total Utility

The first aspect of the distribution problem is the selection of weights for determining the total of weighted utilities that is to be maximized.[15] The simplest procedure is, of course, to strike an average of the weights proposed by the several participants. Another simple procedure would involve equidistant type of concessions by participants on their proposed weights. With intense conflicts, these two simple procedures will frequently not work. One effective procedure for determining these weights in difficult situations, namely the Saaty method of determining group priorities, has already been extensively discussed on pages 147–155. This procedure involved obtaining from a team of experts pairwise comparisons of the relative importance of different individuals (behaving units), objectives, production sectors, or other relevant elements in a decisionmaking situation. Also, the method of determining group priorities can be used in an iterative fashion in a search for the most acceptable set of weights. After a first set of weights has been determined, participants may be permitted to redefine the relevant set of joint actions, options, alternatives, plans, and so forth and eliminate those that turn out at the end of the first round to be trivial or clearly dominated. Likewise with objectives, interest groups, production sectors, and so forth. When unimportant items are eliminated, a second application of the Saaty procedure can be pursued to yield new, more appropriate weights (or probabilities of realization) to be attached to the different joint actions, policies, or the like. Successive iterations can be pursued until participants are no longer motivated to search for an improved set of weights.[16]

Still another set of approaches which involve recursive interaction of the analyst with one or a group of individuals (behaving units) are sequentially evaluated programming procedures (hierarchical or non-hierarchical, linear or nonlinear). To illustrate these procedures, which can take innumerable forms, assume there are several individuals or interest groups, each concerned with maximizing achievement with regard to a single but different objective. We could have a situation such as that discussed at the beginning of this section where, however, there are more than two individuals and two objectives. Further, let there be a natural leader, mediator, or analyst who estimates what he considers to be a fair, best, wise, or otherwise acceptable set of weights w^J regarding the importance of the several objectives. The analyst then sets the problem up as a programming problem where the objective is:

$$\max (w^A u^A + w^B u^B + \ldots + w^U u^U), \text{ or} \qquad (6\text{--}17)$$

$$\max \sum_J w^J u^J \qquad J = A, \ldots, U$$

subject to the constraint that any joint action a_k is selected from the finite set A of possible joint actions, namely,

$$a_k \in A \qquad k = 1,2,3, \ldots, n \qquad (6\text{--}18)$$

and the constraint that the sum of the requirements of any scarce resource h to achieve the several objectives may not exceed the available supply g_h of that resource. That is, if E^J is the objective J (as in (6--14) given by $E^J = u^J/k^J$) and r_h^J is the required amount of resource h to achieve one unit of objective J, so that $r_h^J E^J$ is the total amount of resource h required to achieve the level E^J of the objective J, then the total requirement (demand) for h is $\sum_J r_h^J E^J$. This total must not exceed the available supply g_h, that is

$$\sum_J r_h^J E^J \leq g_h \qquad (6\text{-}19)$$

The significance of such a constraint will be discussed more fully on pages 201–202. This program then yields the optimal value E^{Jo} for the objectives (and indirectly u^{Jo} for the corresponding utilities). (For example, where weights $w^L = 1$ and $w^J = 2$ are agreed upon and where the utilities in a cardinalized Table 3-2 pertain for a two-participant conflict situation, the optimal joint action is (F,C_4), yielding outcomes to L and J of 98 and 230, respectively.) If one or more participants find the outcomes E^{Jo} and u^{Jo} of this program unsatisfactory, the analyst assembles the participants; suggests, urges, or stimulates them to engage in frank, open discussion; asks them to perhaps consider the interests of each other; and otherwise encourages them to come up with a revised set of weights $\tilde{w}^J$. The program is run again with the new weights $\tilde{w}^J$ replacing the old in Equation (6-17). This process is continued until the resulting outcomes are deemed acceptable by all participants. Note that this recursive interactive programming resembles the relaxed hierarchical programming discussed on pages 162–164 and is less formal than the method of determining group priorities. It also has close affinity to the Delphi method discussed in Appendix 10A.1.[17]

An alternative to recursive interaction is the use of a last-offer arbitration type procedure. Here, instead of proposing a joint action, each participant proposes a set of weights, and the mediator selects what he considers to be the fairest set. Alternatively, the mediator may himself attach a weight to each participant's proposed set and suggest a compromise set. The weight the mediator establishes for any participant's proposed set may reflect the mediator's opinion on the degree of its fairness. Other variants of the last-offer arbitration procedure may also be employed. See the discussion on pages 102–106.[18]

6.3.2 The Use of Constraints to Supplement Weights

Alternatively, the participants may wish to abide by a set of weights initially set by a wise person or a respected analyst or mediator, and consider the use of additional constraints to ensure a satisfactory outcome for each participant.

At the start of the mediation process the participants may have in mind a level of utility achievement for any objective J, namely $\tilde{u}^J$ (say 100), which should at the minimum be achieved by the program. Hence, into the program given by Equations (6–17) through (6–19) we may add additional *lower bound constraints* (sometimes called *minimum standards*)

$$u^{Jo} \geq \tilde{u}^J = 100 \qquad J = A, \ldots, U \qquad (6\text{–}20)$$

In such a case, the outcome (98,230) of the previous example (where $w^L = 1$ and $w^J = 2$) violates constraint (6–20); since J receives an outcome less than 100, it must be ruled out as a possibility. Rerunning the program leads to joint action (AG, C_4) and outcome (106,215). If on the second round the set of outcomes is still unsatisfactory—for example, there may be large differences among achievements on the several objectives of concern to interest groups—the participants may establish new lower bounds, or change the weights w^J in the objective function, or both, and continue to do so until a satisfactory set of outcomes is realized.

The participants have still another tool via which to eliminate excessive disparity or otherwise control the set of resulting outcomes, especially when they cannot agree on changes in lower bounds or weights to be employed in further runs of the program when unsatisfactory results have been yielded on some round. This tool is to set upper limits $\tilde{\tilde{u}}^J$ on the achievement with respect to any objective J. Doing so adds still another set of constraints (*upper bound constraints,* sometimes called *maximum standards* or *satiation levels*) to the program (6–17) through (6–20), namely[d]

$$u^{Jo} \leq \tilde{\tilde{u}}^J \qquad J = A, \ldots, U \qquad (6\text{–}21)$$

The addition of these upper bound constraints increases the number of places at which participants can give and take in their negotiations. Still, agreement may not be forthcoming, in which case the skillful analyst or mediator must introduce additional avenues via which participants may engage in give and take. He may suggest con-

---

[d]Constraints (6–20) and (6–21) can then be consolidated into

$$\tilde{\tilde{u}}^J \geq u^{Jo} \geq \tilde{u}^J \qquad J = A, \ldots, U \qquad (6\text{–}22)$$

straints that set a maximum allowable difference between achievement on the objective whose realized utility value is highest and achievement on the objective whose realized utility value is lowest.[e] Or the mediator may be able to shift the focus of participants on to the average of the realized utility values for the objectives, and suggest constraints that set a maximum allowable deviation of the utility value for any objective *above* the average,[f] or *below* the average, or both.

This avenue, too, may not turn out to be one along which participants are able to give and take. Still another to be explored shifts the focus from absolute deviation to ratios and percentages. A first procedure that may have appeal to participants sets an upper bound on the ratio of realized utility values derived from any two objectives.[g] A

---

[e]As a consequence, some of the previously binding constraints may no longer be effective. This new constraint may be written as:

$$u^{Jo} - u^{Lo} \le d_1 \qquad J,L = A, \ldots ,U; \qquad J \ne L \qquad (6\text{--}23)$$

where d_1 is the maximum allowable difference. Note that the maximum allowable difference must be meaningful, for if it is too low, none of the joint actions may be able to satisfy this constraint.

Another alternative might focus on some or all possible pairs of utilities and set a different maximum allowable difference for each.

[f]Defining

$$u^o_{av} = \sum_{J=A}^{U} u^{Jo}/U,$$

this constraint may be written as:

$$(u^{Jo} - u^o_{av}) \le d_2 \qquad J = A, \ldots ,U \qquad (6\text{--}24)$$

where d_2 is the maximum allowable deviation from the average for any participant.

[g]That is,

$$\left(\frac{u^{Jo}}{u^{Lo}}\right) \le s_1 \qquad J,L = A, \ldots ,U; J \ne L \qquad (6\text{--}25)$$

where typically the constant $s_1 > 1$. Alternatively, this procedure might be written as

$$\left(\frac{u^{Lo}}{u^{Jo}}\right) \ge \frac{1}{s_1} \qquad (6\text{--}26)$$

which corresponds to formulating the same constraint as a lower bound (i.e., minimum ratio).

second sets a maximum permissible value on the ratio of any realized utility value of an objective to the average.[h] A third sets a minimum permissible value on this ratio; and a fourth sets both maximum and minimum permissible values.[i] Still other constraints involving ratios and percentages may have appeal.

Additional points of give and take can exist with regard to the use of resource constraints when they are binding. In place of a single overall constraint on any given resource h

$$\sum_J r'_h E^J \leq g_h \qquad (6\text{-}19)$$

there may be employed several constraints. For example, the participants may wish to use a procedure with the constraint that the use of resource h (say capital) in the achievement of any objective E^J (say environmental quality) should not exceed some magnitude $g_h^{J;j}$ or that at least $g_h^{J'}$ *amount of resource* h shall be available for the achievement of objective E^J.[k]

[h]That is,

$$\left(\frac{u^{Jo}}{u^o_{av}} \right) \leq s_2 \qquad J = A, \ldots, U \qquad (6\text{-}27)$$

where typically the constant $s_2 > 1$.

[i]That is,

$$s_2 \geq \left(\frac{u^{Jo}}{u^o_{av}} \right) \geq s_3 \qquad J = A, \ldots, U \qquad (6\text{-}28)$$

where $s_2 > 1$ and $s_3 < 1$.

[j]That is,

$$r_h^J E^J \leq g_h^J \qquad J = A, \ldots, U \qquad (6\text{-}29)$$

where $\sum_J g_h^J \geq g_h$. While technically speaking, this kind of constraint is only meaningful when the achievement of any one objective is independent of the achievement of any second objective (that is, objectives are not joint products), nonetheless participants may choose (irrationally?) to use such a constraint in situations when objectives are jointly produced.

[k]That is,

$$r_h^J E^J \geq g_h^{J'} \qquad \text{where } \sum_J g_h^{J'} \leq g_h \qquad (6\text{-}30)$$

Still other resource constraints can be devised that may have appeal to participants. As a last resort, the binding magnitude g_h may be increased, but this increase in g_h must come from elsewhere and be at the expense of other interest groups. Hence these groups and their objectives must be introduced, and as a consequence a broader problem results.[19]

6.3.3 Changing the Objective Function and Constraints

It is well recognized in linear programming literature that there exists considerable flexibility in setting up a program. Such flexibility enables a mediator to consider several ways of formulating a conflict problem in programming format. He may select that way which he judges will have most appeal to the participants; or he can try out these several ways on the participants to determine which is the most acceptable.

Consider the program as we have so far formulated it without resource constraints. Let there be two objectives yielding the utility values u^L and u^J to participants L and J as discussed on pages 189–190. Then the problem is

$$\max (w^L u^L + w^J u^J) \tag{6-15}$$

subject to

$$a_k \in A \qquad k = 1,2,3, \ldots ,n \tag{6-18}$$

Suppose $w^L = 2$ and $w^J = 1$. Then, using Table 3–2 cardinalized, the joint action that maximizes total utility (IND,C_2) which yields the outcome (192,130). Clearly we can obtain the same result if we redefine the program to maximize achievement on the objective E^L (from which participant L derives utility $u^L = k^L E^L$ where k^L is constant), namely

$$\max E^L \tag{6-36}$$

subject to (6–18) and the additional constraint

$$u^J \geq 130. \tag{6-37}$$

The optimal joint action (the one that participant L would select) is once again (IND,C_2). Alternatively, we can obtain the same result if we redefine the program to maximize the achievement on the objective E^J (from which participant J derives utility $u^J = k^J E^J$ where k^J is a constant), namely

$$\max E^J \tag{6-38}$$

subject to (6–18) and the additional constraint

$$u^L \geq 192. \tag{6-39}$$

Thus, it does not matter whether we put both objectives in the objective function or only one with an appropriate lower bound constraint on the other. In Chapter 7, when we treat continuous action spaces, we will generalize to more than two objectives and show that the objective function can be reduced so that it contains only one objective in a program that has lower bound constraints on all others. Hence, if the participants cannot agree on the appropriate weights regarding one or more of the objectives, the mediator may consider reformulating the problem as either (1) maximizing just one objective with all others introduced in a program via lower bound constraints, *without explicit reference to weights* or (2) maximizing a weighted combination of the several objectives where there is agreement on the weights to be attached to them, with appropriate lower bound constraints on the objectives for which there is no agreement on weights.[20]

6.3.4 Concessions and the Use of Penalty, Cost, and Related Functions

Suppose the mediator is unsuccessful in having participants agree on any of the procedures thus far discussed. There exists another set of procedures, similar in many respects to those already presented, but involving the use of different words, terms, concepts, and reference points (orientations). These are the procedures that focus on the ideal (1,1) points or the equivalent.

To begin, recall that in Section 6.2.5 we discussed the use of the principle *min the total of concessions* from the ideal point, or in equivalent form *min total penalty or total cost*. In the discussion of this and related principles in the footnote on pages 181–182, we implicitly assumed weights of unity for all participants. We now relax this assumption and raise the question of appropriate weights.

Once again, as in the discussion of the previous section, we may start with a set of weights suggested, say, by a mediator considered by the participants to be wise and just, and then propose the use of a principle *min the total of weighted concessions,* namely[21]

$$\min \sum_J w^J(u^{J*} - u^J) \qquad J = A, \ldots, U \qquad (6\text{-}40)$$

subject to:

$$a_k \in A \qquad (6\text{-}18)$$

$$\sum_J r^J_h E^J \leq g_h \qquad h = 1, 2, 3, \ldots \qquad (6\text{-}19)$$

where u^{J*} is J's highest possible utility and is associated with the ideal point. For example, take a case where there is no resource constraint (6-19). If the weights suggested by a wise mediator are $w^L = 1$ and $w^J = 1$, and if Table 3-2 (cardinalized) is used where u^{L*} is 216 and u^{J*} is 230, the joint action $a_k \in A$ that satisfies (6-40) is (AG, C_3) with outcome (152, 185).

Or the participants may wish to use one of the following procedures:

1.   they may use simple averaging or equidistant concessions on proposed weights;
2.   they may use the method of determining group priorities (Saaty) to determine the weights;
3.   they may recursively interact with an analyst using programming procedures to determine a new set of weights w^J;
4.   they may use a last-offer arbitration procedure to determine a fair set of weights;
5.   they may supplement weights with upper bound constraints on concessions; or
6.   they may additionally impose lower bound constraints on concessions. Recalling that the utility of J may be directly related to achievement on the single objective E^J, and for simplicity taking $u^J = k^J E^J$ as in (6-14), we may also suggest to participants the use of one of the following procedures.
7.   they may set a meaningful maximum allowable difference between the concession on the objective whose realized utility

value is highest and the concession on the objective whose realized utility value is lowest, that is, set a maximum range;[22]

8.   they may set a maximum allowable deviation of the concession
      on any objective below or above the average or both;

9.   they may restate the problem when they cannot agree on ap-
      propriate weights on some concessions, say on objectives E^L
      and E^M—that is, they may set up a problem: min the weighted
      sum of concessions on objectives for which agreement on
      weights is obtained subject to upper bounds on concessions on
      those objectives for which there is no agreement on weights;[l] or

10.   when they cannot agree on any weights, they may restate the
      problem so as to avoid explicit reference to weights. The problem
      then is to minimize the concession on one objective, say L,
      with all other concessions introduced via upper bound con-
      straints.[m]

There is still another class of situations in real life that must be ad-
dressed. In these situations a cost is not only placed on *underachievement with regard to a goal or target* set for an objective, say a level of
growth (industrial development), but also on *overachievement* with
respect to that objective (for example, when excessive growth leads to
congestion and resulting mental-health costs). In such situations, a
simple penalty function takes the form:

[l]That is,

$$\min \sum_J w^J(u^{J*} - u^J) \qquad J = A, \ldots, U; \qquad J \neq L,M \qquad (6\text{–}42)$$

subject to (6–18), (6–19) and

$$(E^{L*} - E^L) \leq d_3 \qquad\qquad (6\text{–}43)$$

$$(E^{M*} - E^M) \leq d_4 \qquad\qquad (6\text{–}44)$$

where the asterisk indicates the highest possible level of achievement, and d_3 and d_4 are the upper bounds on concessions with regard to objectives L and M, respectively.

[m]That is,

$$\min (E^{L*} - E^L) \qquad\qquad (6\text{–}45)$$

subject to (6–18), (6–19), and

$$(E^{J*} - E^J) \leq d^J \qquad J \neq L; \qquad J = A, \ldots, U \qquad (6\text{–}46)$$

where d^J is the upper bound on concession with regard to objective J.

$$\min \sum_J w^J \mid z^{J+} + z^{J-} \mid \qquad J = A, \ldots, U \qquad (6\text{-}47)$$

where z^{J+} or z^{J-} are respectively, the amount of overachievement or underachievement with respect to the goal (target) set on objective J.[23] This penalty function then plays the role of (6–40) and is subject to constraints (6–18) and (6–19) and any others (a number of which have been previously discussed) that participants may wish to impose.

Alternatively, participants may wish to focus on percentage rather than absolute concessions. If so, it becomes necessary to normalize, that is, set each participant's most preferred outcome equal to 1 and least preferred to 0. In effect we obtain from a table such as cardinalized Table 3–2 a table like Table 5–3 on p. 136. The (0,0) point is the common (0,0) point in their joint utility space. The (1,1) point corresponds to an ideal point such as Q in Figure 5–1 (p. 135).[24]

Under these circumstances, the participants may agree on a wise and just person to set weights for use with a principle *min the total of weighted percent concessions,* as in Section 5.2.5. The program then becomes

$$\min \sum_J w^J \left(1 - \frac{u^J}{u^{J*}}\right) \qquad J = A, \ldots, U \qquad (6\text{-}48)$$

another form of a penalty or cost function, subject to (6–18) and (6–19). Or they may adopt alternative procedures that tend to parallel closely the ten alternative procedures listed on pages 198–199, with reference to absolute concessions. For example, the first four alternative procedures are, without change in wording, applicable to percent concessions, while the fifth alternative procedure must read "they may supplement weights with upper bound constraints on percent concessions." Some of these parallel procedures have already been discussed in unweighted form in Section 5.2, to which the reader is referred.[25]

6.3.5 Procedures for Distributing a Total Payoff

As indicated on page 189, the distribution problem arises in a different form when a total payoff that all participants agree should be maximized is to be distributed among a set of participants (or a set of activities, or, in general, a set of categories that can be variously defined) and where the total is independent of such distribution.[26] The total may be beads or money and each member of a team (assumed to be a maximizer) is interested in seeing that the total is maximized, since, whatever the fraction to which he is entitled, he will receive more when the total is larger rather than smaller. Also, the total may be exogenously given, for example, the surface of the earth, ocean resources, a World Bank fund to be allocated among developing nations, a federal surplus to be divided among regions, or a prize.

How should the total be distributed? One effective way to attack this problem is to relate it to the programming problem of the previous section. Let the total correspond to the total available quantity of a single commodity h. In the first case, let that total be distributed directly to participants (categories) for consumption purposes where g_h^J is the amount that participant J receives. The constraint (6–19) then simplifies to

$$\sum_J g_h^J \leq g_h \qquad J = A, \ldots, U \qquad (6\text{-}49)$$

It then becomes necessary to identify a relevant utility function for each participant J, as we did in Equation (6–14) when we discussed the relationship between utility and objectives. Here the utility function states the amount of utility J receives from consuming any given amount g_h^J of commodity h. Let it be

$$u^J = u^J (g_h^J) \qquad (6\text{-}50)$$

Accordingly, the problem is to define a set of weights w^J, as before, to apply to J's utility, J = A, $\ldots$, U, to yield the objective function

$$\max \sum_J w^J u^J \qquad J = A, \ldots, U \qquad (6\text{-}17)$$

Thus all the procedures already discussed in Section 6.3.1 become applicable to determine an acceptable allocation of the total among participants.

In a second case, let the total fixed amount of commodity (resource) h be allocated for the achievement of a set of objectives E^J, J = A, $\ldots$, U. For example, let there be available ten U.N. fellowships for training administrators to be allocated to a developing region for achievement of the three objectives: growth, environmental quality, and political stability—each promoted to the exclusion of others by an interest group within that region. Let e_h^G, e_h^Q, e_h^S, be the number of fellowships awarded to train business administrators (to achieve the objective growth G), environmental engineers (to achieve the objective environmental quality Q), and public administrators (to achieve the objective political stability S), respectively. If then E^G, E^Q, and E^S represent the resulting number of units of achievement for these three objectives, respectively, then $(e_h^G/E^G) = r_h^G$, the man years of trained business administrators required to achieve one unit of the growth objective; and $(e_h^Q/E^Q) = r_h^Q$ and $(e_h^S/E^S) = r_h^S$ have corresponding meanings. Thus the constraint that the (integer) number of fellow-ships awarded for all objectives not exceed 10, namely[n]

$$e_h^G + e_h^Q + e_h^S \leq 10 \qquad (6\text{-}51)$$

becomes, by substitution,

$$r_h^G E^G + r_h^Q E^Q + r_h^S E^S \leq 10 \qquad (6\text{-}53)$$

See Figure 6-2. Further, the achievements on the three objectives E^G, E^Q, and E^S lead to utilities u^G, u^Q, and u^S for the corresponding three interest groups, respectively, via the utility functions

$$u^G = u^G(E^G)$$

$$u^Q = u^Q(E^Q) \qquad (6\text{-}54)$$

$$u^S = u^S(E^S)$$

Thus the distribution problem becomes, as in Section 6.3.1, to find weights to apply to the several utilities in order to identify the objective function

$$\sum_J w^J u^J \qquad J = G, Q, S \qquad (6\text{-}55)$$

which is to be maximized, with or without the use of constraints and other modifications. Once again, all the discussion on procedures on pages 191–197 applies.

In a third case, which is more involved, let the total fixed amount of resource h be allocated to production sectors j, $j = 1, \ldots, n$, such as food production and iron and steel production, as noted in Figure 6-3. Here, $x_{h1}, x_{h2}, \ldots x_{hj}, \ldots, x_{hn}$ represent the number of

[n]Observe that technically speaking we have an integer programming problem, and that we should also specify the integer number constraint

$$e_h^G, e_h^Q, e_h^S = 1, 2, 3, \ldots, 10 \qquad (6\text{-}52)$$

The interested reader is referred to Bradley, Hax, and Magnanti (1977) and other standard texts for algorithms to reach solutions.

Figure 6-2. An Allocation of a Total Resource (Payoff) Governed by a Program with Objectives as Intermediate Variables.

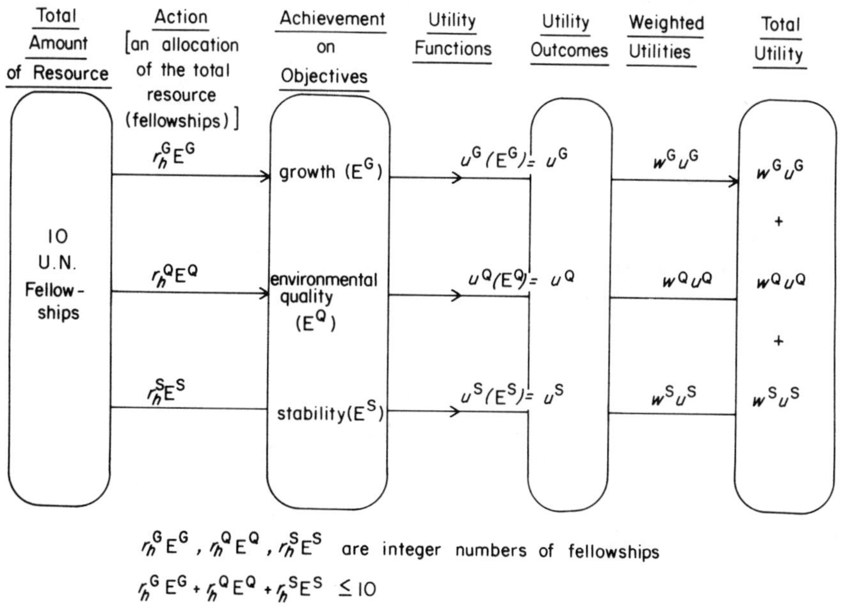

Total Amount of Resource	Action [an allocation of the total resource (fellowships)]	Achievement on Objectives	Utility Functions	Utility Outcomes	Weighted Utilities	Total Utility
10 U.N. Fellow-ships	$r_h^G E^G$	growth (E^G)	$u^G(E^G) \doteq u^G$		$w^G u^G$	$w^G u^G$
						+
	$r_h^Q E^Q$	environmental quality (E^Q)	$u^Q(E^Q) \doteq u^Q$		$w^Q u^Q$	$w^Q u^Q$
						+
	$r_h^S E^S$	stability(E^S)	$u^S(E^S) \doteq u^S$		$w^S u^S$	$w^S u^S$

$r_h^G E^G$, $r_h^Q E^Q$, $r_h^S E^S$ are integer numbers of fellowships

$r_h^G E^G + r_h^Q E^Q + r_h^S E^S \leq 10$

fellowships awarded to train scientists, engineers, and business administrators in the food production sector (sector #1), the textile production sector (sector #2), . . . , the iron and steel production sector (sector j), and so forth, respectively. If $X_1, X_2, \ldots, X_n$ represent the resulting increase in outputs of these sectors respectively, then $x_{h1}/X_1 = a_{h1}$, the man years of trained fellows required to achieve an increase in one unit of output in the food production sector, and $x_{h2}/X_2 = a_{h2}, \ldots, x_{hj}/X_j = a_{hj}, \ldots, x_{hn}/X_n = a_{hn}$ have corresponding meanings. The constraint that the (integer) number of fellowships awarded to all production sectors not exceed 10, namely,

$$x_{h1} + x_{h2} + \ldots + x_{hj} + \ldots + x_{hn} \leq 10 \qquad (6\text{--}56)$$

becomes by substitution

$$a_{h1}X_1 + a_{h2}X_2 + \ldots + a_{hj}X_j + \ldots + a_{hn}X_n \leq 10 \qquad (6\text{--}57)$$

Figure 6-3. An Allocation of a Total Resource (Payoff) Governed by a Program with Sector Outputs and Objectives as Intermediate Variables.

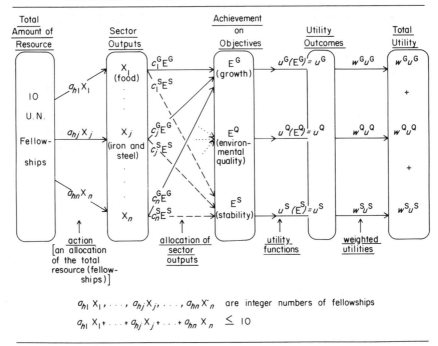

$a_{h1}X_1, \ldots, a_{hj}X_j, \ldots, a_{hn}X_n$ are integer numbers of fellowships

$a_{h1}X_1 + \ldots + a_{hj}X_j + \ldots + a_{hn}X_n \leq 10$

See Figure 6-3. The outputs of the production sectors are then used to yield achievements on the three objectives: growth E^G, environmental quality E^Q, and stability E^S. To achieve one unit of the objective growth requires c_1^G units of output from the food production sector, c_2^G units of output from the textile production sector, . . . ,c_j^G units of output from the iron and steel production sector, and so forth. If E^G represents the number of units of achievement for the growth objective, then $c_1^G E^G$ is the number of units of output from the textile production sector required to achieve this level of growth, . . . ,$c_j^G E^G$ is the number of units of output from the iron and steel sector required to achieve this level of growth, and so forth. See the solid arrows in Figure 6-3 going from the sector outputs box to the box labelled achievement on objectives. Interpretation of $c_1^Q E^Q$, . . . ,$c_j^Q E^Q$, . . . $c_n^Q E^Q$ and $c_1^S E^S$, . . .,$c_n^S E^S$ can be made in a parallel way with respect to the environmental quality and stability objectives, respectively. However, the requirements for the output of any sector, say food production, cannot exceed the actual production (supply) X_1. So, summing the requirements for food over all objectives, namely $c_1^G E^G + c_1^Q E^Q + c_1^S E^S$ or $\sum_J c_1^J E^J$, we obtain the additional constraint

$$\sum_J c_1^J E^J \leq X_1 \qquad J = G,Q,S \qquad (6\text{--}58)$$

or when we generalize to any production sector j, $j = 1, \ldots, n$, we have the additional constraints

$$\sum_J c_j^J E^J \leq X_j \qquad j = 1, \ldots, n; \qquad J = G,Q,S \qquad (6\text{--}59)$$

As with Figure 6–2, the achievement E^G, E^Q, and E^S on objectives lead in Figure 6–3 via utility functions (given by (6–50) above) to the utilities u^G, u^Q, and u^S for the corresponding interest groups. To derive the objective function (6–54) we then have the same distribution problem as we had before—that of determining appropriate weights, with or without lower and upper bound constraints and reformulation of the objective function or the equivalent. Once again all the discussion of Sections 6.3.1 through 6.3.3 pertains, and appropriate compromises must be reached before the allocation in this third case can be determined. [27]

Note that in certain conflict situations it may be possible to introduce money payments to a good cause and thereby consider a broader range of procedures for conflict management. When it is possible to do so, we have situations that we discuss in the Appendix 6A.2 and which parallel those situations already discussed in Appendix 4A.1.

Finally, we should note the many important cases where the money payment is not to a good cause that has no perceivable effect on the welfare of participants. Rather the money payment takes the form of a side payment from one participant to other participants when the latter are reluctant to accept a joint action desired by the former. These important cases will be examined in Section 8.3 and the analysis there of side payments is directly applicable to many of the cases of finite action situations with comparable cardinal utilities. One of these cases involves a procedure based on a principle of *max total utility improvements* wherein side payments are required to get the least favored participants to "go along" with this principle.

6.3.6 Achievement of Minimum Requirements (Satisficing) and
Other Nonoptimizing Procedures

In a number of important situations of reality, it is impossible to get participants to agree on weights, lower bounds, upper bounds, alternative forms of an objective function, and thus to achieve an optimal compromise (or to agree on how to divide up a total with or without side payments) once the problem has been set up as a program. At this point, the skillful and experienced mediator may say, "Let's forget about the objective function. Let's agree on a set of lower bounds and get out of here." In essence, the mediator is appealing to the participants to adopt satisficing behavior. In such behavior, an outcome equal to or greater than some critical magnitude—for example, the lower bound in the above situation—is placed in the category of "satisfactory" as opposed to the category of "unsatisfactory" outcomes.[28] Further, the first alternative examined that meets these lower bounds on all participants' outcomes is taken as the solution, since by definition there can be no more preferred solution. For example, if this lower bound on both u^L and u^J is set at 125, then if by chance the participants happened to choose to go from left to right along the middle row of a cardinalized Table 3-2, they would reject joint action (AG,C_0) and stop at joint action (AG,C_1), which yields the satificing outcome (144,125).[29]

However, satisficing behavior can also be viewed as optimizing behavior since it may be interpreted as implicitly assuming the existence of an objective such as *minimize time spent in search, costs of computation, or some other element or combination of these elements* subject to the lower bound constraints. Thus the utility (satisfaction) that might be derived from a second satisfactory alternative that might be found must be less because of the disutility associated with the time and costs involved in searching for this alternative. However, where participants behave in this manner, it becomes impossible to predict the joint action that will be selected unless we have additional information on the sequence in which alternatives are to be examined. All we can predict is that the joint action chosen will be one of the set of satisfactory joint actions, if such is not a null set.[30]

Another "last-resort type" of procedure often becomes appropriate when the main elements of a conflict have been resolved but compromise remains to be achieved on fine, trivial matters or issues. In such cases, the mediator suggests a final compromise solution. If participants do not find this acceptable, the mediator imposes a dollar or equivalent cost on participants for each additional round of debate and discussion—this dollar amount corresponding to the cost to be donated to some good cause that has no direct or indirect feedback effect on participants' utility functions.

6.4 MORE COMPLEX UTILITY FUNCTIONS

In many realistic situations, individual utility functions are not as simple as we have assumed, nor are the total welfare (utility) functions implied in the sums of unweighted or weighted utilities of participants. Rather, they are more complex and lead to conflict management procedures that are too complex for development in this book dealing with general procedures of practical use. Nonetheless, it is useful to discuss briefly some of the implications of these more complex functions.

6.4.1 Simple Interdependent Utility Functions

On many occasions, participants (e.g., political leaders) are motivated not simply to maximize payoff (gains) or utility. They frequently compare their outcome with the average outcome of others—a traditional rival or one or more other participants whose outcomes have significance to them. There are many ways in which such comparisons are made, the simplest involving absolute differences. For example, take the case where all participants but one, say J, are self-interested and are motivated to maximize their utility (or payoff). In contrast, J may be interested in maximizing the difference between his payoff and the average. If participants can then agree on a lower bound for the outcome for each except J, a program can be run to maximize the difference between J's outcome and the average. (Here lower bounds would need to be set high enough to induce all participants except J to give him in effect the final decisionmaking power.)

If there are two or relatively few participants like J, an objective function may need to be set up that is a weighted sum of several differences from the average, one for each of these participants. All the problems of obtaining a weighted or substitute objective function that were discussed in Section 6.3 appear here, often in more complex form.

Often a participant, again say J, may make comparisons of his outcome with that of a historical rival or competitor (a business firm, region, or nation), say L. Then a program may be run when there is agreement on the lower bound constraint for each participant except J with the objective function to maximize $(u^J - u^L)$. In this formulation, the lower bound on L's outcome may need to be carefully (and generously?) established since the program, consistent with J's motivation, tends to minimize L's utility and, within the constraints set, always shifts from one joint action to another when the reduction in L's utility is greater than that in J's. Such an objective function may tend to lead to better outcomes for participants other than J and L.

It also may be the case that some participant, again say J, is interested in both his utility outcome and the difference between his and a reference participant's outcome, say L. He therefore may be guided in his choice of an action by an objective function such as max $(u^J - 0.5u^L)$, which signifies that he is willing to take a reduction in his own utility, but only if the reduction in L's utility is at least somewhat more than twice his.

In other instances, J may intensely desire to be mean to L, in the sense that he is willing to suffer a loss greater than one unit of utility for every unit that J loses. His objective function may be max $(u^J - 1.5u^L)$. In contrast, J may be concerned with how well L is doing because L is his kin, friend, or a person for whom he has brotherly love. In these instances, his objective function might be $(u^J + u^L)$, which indicates that L's utility is just as important to J as his own. He is willing to take a loss of one unit of utility every time L's utility thereby increases by at least one.

To generalize we may restate J's driving mechanism as an aggregate utility function

$$\hat{u}^J = \tilde{u}^J + b_{JL}\tilde{u}^L \tag{6-60}$$

where, to avoid confusion we use the symbol $\hat{u}^J$ to indicate a special type of utility, namely *aggregate utility,* and where we use the symbol $\tilde{u}^J$ to indicate that part of the utility that results only from the outcome to J.[31] When $b_{JL} < 0$, J is mean (hostile) to L; when $b_{JL} = 0$, J is strictly self-interested; when $0 < b_{JL} \leq 1$, J is friendly to (concerned with) L's welfare; and when $b_{JL} > 1$, J is "altruistic" towards L.

There are of course, other possibilities involving more participants and other factors that may be involved in J's aggregate utility function in a specific conflict situation, to which a wise mediator might be sensitive.° They are too numerous to present here.

6.4.2 Nonlinear Utility Functions

When we consider the utility function of each participant as a function of several objectives, and not one and only one, then of course complexities are introduced. In subsequent chapters, we will generally use a linear function of the objectives to derive the corresponding utilities. This is admittedly not a good representation of realistic utility functions, but there is no other that can be claimed to be generally better. It is the simplest. One may even argue that since this is the simplest it will pervade the thinking of simple-minded people more than any other function.

Another utility function that might be used would involve the product of two or more objectives with appropriate units for a constant. Abstract economic theorists do of course use homothetic, Cobb-Douglas, or Constant Elasticity of Substitution (CES) utility functions[32] to derive "interesting" results; however, we know of no general basis to justify the use of these functions in place of the two we have mentioned. They must clearly be considered as more unrealistic, simply because of the intellectual effort needed when thinking in the manner required by them. Only the best of minds are likely to consider utility in a way that would correspond either explicitly or implicitly to these functions, and only in high-powered decisionmak-

---

°One particular form involves ratios and percentages. For example, J's aggregate utility function might be

$$\hat{u}^J = \frac{u^J}{u^J/U} \; ; \; \text{or } \hat{u}^J = b_{JL} \left(\frac{u^J}{u^L} \right) \; ; \; \text{or } \hat{u}^J = b'_{JL} \left(\frac{u^J - u^L}{u^J} \right) \; ; \text{ and so forth.} \tag{6-61}$$

For further relevant discussion, see Bishop (1963).

Generally speaking, the aggregate utility function takes the form

$$\hat{u}^J = \hat{u}^J (u^J, u^L, \ldots) \tag{6-62}$$

and an overall objective function involving such aggregate utility functions would be

$$\hat{U} = \hat{U}(\hat{u}^J, \hat{u}^L, \ldots) \tag{6-63}$$

ing activity within major business firms and organizations (where variables are well defined and can be controlled) are they likely to be used.[33]

6.5 CONCLUDING REMARKS

In this chapter, we recognize that it is more likely than not that participants to a conflict situation will not be able to assign precise values to outcomes. Nonetheless, we do examine compromise procedures for conflict situations when they can make such valuations. The analysis of these situations may provide useful insights to analysts even when they confront situations in which participants do not have comparable cardinal utilities.

In general, the procedures we treat involve maximizing the total of utilities or percentage improvements, minimizing the total of concessions or percentage concessions, minimizing or maximizing differences in improvements or concessions, and so forth. These procedures may or may not involve the use of different weights for the utilities of the different participants. Each of these procedures, because of its wording or the concepts upon which it focuses, has its own particular appeal to participants who may have different psychologies or psychological blocks and hangups. The Clarke-Vickrey tax principle to eliminate the effects of bluffing was discussed as a useful procedure—and one that has not been given sufficient attention in the past.

Most of the procedures in the first part of the chapter ignore or inadequately treat the distribution problem. We attempted to attack this problem explicitly by the use of a programming format and by exploring different ways in which constraints can be added to a program in order to reach a compromise solution. Such constraints can be used to (1) supplement weights in the objective function, (2) alter the objective function, (3) minimize disagreement on weights, or (4) eliminate entirely the explicit use of weights.

We also discuss satisficing and other last-resort procedures, and recognize the possibility that one or more participants may possess a simple interdependent utility function and behave accordingly. Finally, some participants may have more complex utility functions that may be exceedingly difficult to incorporate in practical procedures.

While we have made extensive use of a programming approach in this chapter, its fuller development will be the province of the next chapter, where the assumption of continuous action spaces facilitates such development.

APPENDIX TO CHAPTER 6

6A.1 DERIVATION OF A SET OF WEIGHTS YIELDING EQUIVALENT SOCIAL VALUES FOR MOST PREFERRED JOINT ACTIONS

A last-resort type of technique to determine a set of weights to be used in the objective function of a program that may have appeal to sophisticated participants is as follows: Construct the payoff Table 6A-1. Each column relates to the utility of a participant J, J = A,B, . . . ,U. (It may also relate to a single objective in the case where each participant is concerned with one and only one objective $E^J(J = A,B, . . . ,U.)$ The corresponding row represents the joint action a^{J*} that J most prefers—that is that maximizes his utility.

Table 6A-1. A Utility/Outcome Table for Participants Selecting Optimal Joint Actions.

Joint Actions / Utilities	u^A	u^B	...	u^J	...	u^U
a^{A*}	$u^{A,A}$	$u^{B,A}$	.	$u^{J,A}$	.	$u^{U,A}$
a^{B*}	$u^{A,B}$	$u^{B,B}$	.	$u^{J,B}$	.	$u^{U,B}$
.	.	.	.	.	.	.
.	.	.	.	.	.	.
:	.	.	.	.	.	.
a^{J*}	$u^{A,J}$	$u^{B,J}$	...	$u^{J,J}$	...	$u^{U,J}$
.	.	.	.	.	.	.
.	.	.	.	.	.	.
.	.	.	.	.	.	.
a^{U*}	$u^{A,U}$	$u^{B,U}$	...	$u^{J,U}$	...	$u^{U,U}$

Record in each cell of a row the utility each participant receives when the joint action of that row is taken. By definition, the largest value in any column is recorded in the cell of that column falling along the main diagonal, these being, in order, $u^{A,A}$, $u^{B,B}$, . . . ,$u^{U,U}$. The main diagonal is thus the locus of optimal utility values by columns. Next, normalize the columns by dividing each entry of a given column by the maximum value in that column. (Thus, entries along the main diagonal all become unity.) Finally, find a set of weights that, when used in proper order to multiply the entries along each row, yield the same total value for each row.[34] In a technical sense, these weights make all joint actions (each being the most preferred joint action a^{J*} of a single participant J (J = A,B, . . .U)) equivalent in terms of what might be loosely designated "total utility" (or "social value"). These weights may then be used as the weights for the objective function in the multiobjective program.[35]

6A.2 A GOOD-CAUSE PAYMENT PROCEDURE (WITH OR WITHOUT THE BEARHUG PRINCIPLE)

As discussed in Appendix 4A.1, in certain conflict situations it may be possible to introduce money payments and thereby consider a broader range of procedures for conflict management. When it is possible to do so, we have situations that may be characterized as involving modified finite action spaces. The reader should reread pages 107-113. In those pages, utilities were assumed to be ordinal; here they are cardinal. Hence we may take the numbers used for exposition purposes only in pages 107-113 (and in Figure 4A-1) to represent actual cardinal utilities. Accordingly, we can proceed to identify immediately the allocation that would maximize the sum of the utilities of L and M when we take the weights of L and M to be unity. This allocation would be (p,f) given by point J on Figure 4A-1 where L receives a utility of 85 and M a utility of 58. But such a principle, namely, to choose the joint action (an allocation) that maximizes the total of utilities, is not acceptable to M. He would prefer the allocation (f,p) to (p,f) and, of course, most prefers $(0,pf)$. If we were then to use a procedure involving a money payment to a good cause by that participant who receives the better of the two proposed allocations, we reach the same conclusion as in Appendix 4A.1. Having cardinal rather than ordinal utilities in this situation does not improve or lessen the usefulness of the procedure that is postulated. In Figure 4A-1, for example, both participants come to agree on allocation (f,p) as the most desirable given the rules of the game, even though L receives a utility of 75 and M one of approximately 60 (that is, 67 less the utility value of AR money which we approximate to be 7).[36]

NOTES

1. When participants can make precise valuations of outcomes, we must distinguish between two possibilities. One is where the precise valuations of the several participants are not comparable. For example, J and L may be able to state their utilities from any outcome as a precise number, but their units of measurement may be different. J may use as his unit of utility that which he derives from a standard gold coin, while L uses as her unit that which she derives from a cow. If then they do not have in common a rate at which gold coins and cows are considered equivalent in utility terms, or exchangeable— that is, if J values twenty gold coins as he does one cow, while L values one cow as she does ten gold coins—then their scales are not convertible one into the other. Thus, their cardinal utilities are noncomparable. On the other hand, they may agree that fifteen gold coins are equivalent to one cow in utility terms. Then their utility scales are convertible one into the other, and their cardinal utility valuations are comparable. Since the latter case is much less realistic than the former and thus requires stronger assumptions for analysis, it would seem logical that we should treat first the procedures requiring noncomparable cardinal utility.

    Probing more deeply into this issue, we find that a situation wherein participants are not able to compare their cardinal utilities in essence is a situation wherein only information regarding relative values can be used in devising a conflict management procedure. That is, when participants do not have comparable cardinal utilities, and in particular when they cannot agree on a common unit in which they are able to express their utilities—for example, that a gold coin, a cow, or a U.S. dollar bill represents a unit of utility to each—then we can speak meaningfully of their relative utilities only. (When they can agree on a common unit but not on a common zero point, they may be said to have common utility functions only in the sense that they are intertransinal.) See Isard, T. Smith, et al. (1969:175-76). In this situation, all of the procedures discussed in Chapter 5 may be found useful, but we are not able to develop any new conflict management procedures.

2.   In the discussion that follows, however, we shall speak of participants having cardinal utility functions when it is clear from the context that we mean comparable utility functions.

3.   As in Section 5.2, unless otherwise stated, for procedures in this section to be applicable, each participant must know his own preference structure and that of all others. However when it is meaningful for a mediator who is respected and trusted to be present and when the mediator knows all participants' preference structures, it is only necessary that each participant know his own preference structure.

4.   Observe that here as well as in previous and subsequent discussion we assume only one state of the environment and no risk and uncertainty regarding outcomes and thus utilities derived from such outcomes. However, when in reality the numbers such as those in Table 3–2 are expected outcomes or expected utilities, we might logically consider the principle *max total expected utility.* When the participants attach a cost (benefit) to risk, then an appropriate amount ought to be subtracted from (added to) the total, where the cost (benefit) may be associated with the second moment or other measure of the distribution of each participant's outcomes around her expected. The problem becomes more complicated when the several participants have different attitudes toward risk or employ different measures of risk. To facilitate the discussion and to avoid complications in the analysis, we, like many others, unrealistically abstract from risk and uncertainty.

5.   The two procedures discussed in this section can obviously be extended to percent improvements and achievements, respectively. Still another related principle would involve selection of that joint action which *minimizes the largest absolute deviation (above or below) the average improvement,* or *min deviation from average absolute improvement.*

6.   Note that the procedures discussed in this section can be extended to percent improvements.

7.   Further, it can be observed that the *min total concession* principle automatically restricts the choice of a compromise joint action to the efficiency set.

8.   Another related principle that may have appeal to participants who think in terms of goals and wish to focus on the extent of shortfalls from each one's goal is that of *min the total of goal shortfalls* (absolute or percent, weighted or unweighted).

9.   Another related principle that participants may find more psychologically appealing is that of *min the difference of goal shortfalls.* These shortfalls may be weighted or unweighted and measured in either absolute or percentage terms.

10. Still another related principle would involve the choice of that joint action as the compromise solution which *minimizes the largest absolute deviation (above or below) the average concession.* This principle could be applied in either weighted or unweighted fashion. Also, participants may prefer to make comparisons in percentage terms, and adopt a *min the max percent concession principle* (weighted or unweighted) or focus on the extent of shortfalls from each one's goal, and adopt a *min the max goal shortfall principle* (weighted or unweighted, absolute or percent).

11. There may, however, be bluffing regarding lower bounds. In such a case the participants may agree to the use of a last-offer arbitration procedure, with a mediator and his team of experts determining the most reasonable of the set of lower bounds proposed. See pages 102–106 for a discussion of the procedure, which may be stated in *percentage* terms if this is found more appealing.

    An obvious parallel to the max the difference of improvements principle is the *max the difference of concessions principle* which would have a similar rationale.

12. Also, if we assume that the participants' cardinal utilities are comparable in the sense that the same value in the standard commodity represents the same cardinal utility to all participants, then the Clarke-Vickrey procedure (which aims to determine which joint action yields the maximum total value) also identifies that joint action which maximizes the total of their utilities.

13. With regard to information, at the minimum when an analyst or tax administrator is present each participant needs to know the value that he would receive from each joint action and the tax that would be imposed on him if that joint action were chosen. Practically speaking, it is very likely that at least some of the participants would insist upon having more information concerning the values that other participants attribute to one or more of the joint actions.

14. Generally speaking and unless otherwise indicated, the procedures in this section involve, in one form or another, interaction among participants. When this is the case, they must come to know each other's preferences as well as their own if the interaction is to be effective in resolving the distribution problem. When, however, they accept the weights, lower bounds, upper bounds, and objective functions suggested by a trusted mediator without questioning them, each needs to know only his own preference structure. Generally speaking, in order to be able to specify acceptable parameters, the mediator must know the preference structures (or a relevant region of them) of all participants.

15. We should keep in mind that when we spoke about the max total utility principle in Section 6.2.1 we implicitly assumed that weights of unity

were given. Likewise when we spoke of *min the difference in improvements, min the total of concessions from ideal point, min the difference of concessions,* and other principles discussed in Section 6.2.

16.   See Saaty and Alexander (1977, 1977a).

17.   While the use of the GRIT approach (reciprocated tension-reducing actions, a sequence of), discussed on pages 99–100, has not been extensively discussed with regard to the determination of weights in a difficult conflict situation, it is easily seen that a unilateral concession from a fixed position that an individual has taken on weights can spark reciprocal actions by others, in GRIT-like fashion, ultimately leading to a compromise set of weights on which all participants agree. In this regard, GRIT may be viewed as a recursive interaction procedure when that category is broadly viewed.

18.   Another more technical approach that may appeal to sophisticated participants is to derive that set of weights which, when applied appropriately to the utility outcomes derived from considering in turn the most preferred joint action of each participant, yields the same total of weighted utility outcomes. This total may be regarded as some kind of "social value." See Appendix 6A.1.

19.   Note that when there are many alternatives (joint actions) to be considered, and when the participants desire to use the demand-revealing (no bluffing) procedure based on the Clarke-Vickrey tax principle, they may set up a program to calculate quickly (through the use of a computer) the gains any participant J can expect to receive from each alternative. The program for any participant J is:

$$\max \; v^J(a_k) - t^J(a_k) \qquad k = 1, 2, \ldots, n \qquad (6\text{-}31)$$

$$\text{s.t.} \quad t^J(a_k) = k^J - (V(a_k) - v^J(a_k)) \qquad (6\text{-}32)$$

$$k^J = \max \, (V(a_k) - v^J(a_k)) \qquad (6\text{-}33)$$

where

$$V(a_k) = \sum_J v^J(a_k) \qquad J = A, \ldots, U \qquad (6\text{-}34)$$

when all participants are weighted equally and where

$$V(a_k) = \sum_J \widetilde{w}^J \, v^J \, (a_k) \qquad J = A, \ldots, U \qquad (6\text{-}35)$$

when participants are weighted as on page 188.

20.   It should also be recognized that among relatively sophisticated participants there may be conflict over not only weights and constraints but also over the objective function of a mathematical program—for example, whether it should be linear, quadratic, or of another form. See the discussion in Chapter 11.

21. Another frequently used penalty or cost function is

$$\min_{J} \sum w^J(u^{J^*} - u^J)^2 \qquad J = A, \ldots, U \qquad (6\text{-}41)$$

which then may require the use of a quadratic programming algorithm in order to derive a solution. Others might be associated with the general distance measure discussed in the footnote on pages 181–182. Still another version may be associated with the min discrepancy from ideal (using rank correlation) procedure discussed in Appendix 8A.2.

22. Where the maximum allowable difference is set too low, none of the joint actions may be able to meet this condition. An alternative might focus on some or all possible pairs and set a different maximum allowable difference for each.

23. In effect, where E^{J^*} is the goal (target), $z^{J+} = (E^J - E^{J^*})$ and $z^{J-} = (E^{J^*} - E^J)$ when E^J exceeds or falls short of E^{J^*}, respectively. Clearly, for each objective J either $z^{J+} = 0$, $z^{J-} = 0$, or both are zero.

Formally there has developed a set of procedures that are generally designated "goal programming" procedures. Such procedures may: (1) assign different weights to overachievement and underachievement with respect to any objective; (2) consider overachievement and underachievement in percentage rather than absolute terms; and (3) employ various types of nonlinear functions (a subset of those functions being the Minkowski distance functions). Here a frequent nonlinear function is

$$\min_{J} \sum [w^{J+}(z^{J+})^2 + w^{J-}(z^{J-})^2]$$

which penalizes overachievement and underachievement differently and penalizes larger discrepancies more than smaller.

24. Note that when participants do desire to use the ideal point as a reference point, the technical analyst would say that they are losing information, in particular, information on the absolute values of their utilities. In reality, they may not be aware or sensitive to such loss, or perhaps they do not wish to know the information that is not used.

25. Also, still other possible alternatives involve alternative formulations of resource constraints. See pages 196–197. Additionally, a penalty function can be developed for situations where costs are generated by both underachievement and overachievement in percentage terms, the (1,1) point then being defined by prespecified targets.

26. In these cases, we assume that there exists no possibility for redistributing to any participant a part or the total of an allocation made to another.

27.   In the above paragraphs we assume comparable cardinal utility on the part of participants. However, whenever a programming operation involving a resource (or equivalent) constraint can be used to obtain results when relative utility is involved, so too can the problem of dividing a total be effectively treated.

28.   See Hill and Lomovasky (1980) for a recent application.

29.   Here each participant is required to be able to specify which joint actions yield outcomes satisfactory to him—that is, achieve at least the lower bound on this relevant magnitude—and to give this knowledge to the mediator.

30.   Note that participants may desire to use a more general satisficing procedure—that is, one involving more than two categories of outcomes (such as unsatisfactory, just satisfactory, and highly satisfactory). When they do so, they are in effect employing ranks on a utility scale. For relevant discussion, see pages 39–42.

31.   Theoretically, a rigorous definition of $\bar{u}^j$ would be complicated because of the interdependence from joint actions. From a practical standpoint, the definition in (6-60) is adequate for many situations.

32.   In their analysis, economists frequently employ the concept of a *homogenous utility function*. A utility function is said to be homogeneous of degree k if

$$u(tx_1, tx_2) = t^k u(x_1, x_2)$$

where k is a constant, and t is any positive real number. That is, if both arguments x_1, x_2 (which are typically commodities but can be objectives in our context) are increased by a factor t, utility is increased by a factor t^k. Any utility function that can be expressed as a monotonically increasing function of a homogenous utility function is called a *homothetic utility function*. It has the same indifference curves as its underlying homogeneous function although the numbers associated with each indifference curve are generally different. Hence, if a utility function is homothetic, rates of commodity (or objective) substitution will depend upon relative rather than absolute commodity (objective) quantities.

Economists have also frequently used a *Cobb-Douglas utility function*. For two commodities (objectives) that function takes the form

$$u(x_1, x_2) = Ax_1^a x_2^{1-a}$$

and since any monotonic transformation of this function represents the same preferences, it is often expressed as

$$u(x_1, x_2) = \ln A + a \ln x_1 + (1 - a) \ln x_2$$

For n commodities (objectives) it takes the form

$$u(x_1, x_2, \ldots, x_n) = A x_1^{a_1} x_2^{a_2} \ldots x_n^{a_n}$$

or

$$u(x_1, x_2, \ldots, x_n) = \ln A + a_1 \ln x_1 + a_2 \ln x_2 + \ldots + a_n \ln x_n$$

where A is a constant, $a_i > 0$ $(i = 1, \ldots, n)$, $\sum a_i = 1$.

Still another function used by economists is the *constant elasticity of substitution (CES) utility function*. For two commodities (objectives) it takes the form

$$u(x_1, x_2) = (a_0 + a_1 x_1^p + a_2 x_2^p)^{1/p}$$

and since any monotonic transformation of this function represents the same preferences it is often expressed as

$$u(x_1, x_2) = a_0 + a_1 x_1^p + a_2 x_2^p$$

which the reader can easily generalize to n commodities (objectives).

33. It should be noted that we have already dealt with some nonlinear total utility (social welfare) and total penalty functions when we discussed goal programming, procedures to minimize the unweighted or weighted sum of the square of concessions, and procedures such as Zeuthen's (least to lose goes first) involving concessions. See footnotes on pages 181–182, Note 20 of this chapter, and pages 160–165

34. These weights should be nonnegative fractions which add to unity. However under certain conditions, it may not be possible to find such a set of weights and thus to use this method. See Rietveld (1980:95, 160).

35. In order to employ this procedure participants need to know their own preference structure and that of all other participants regarding each proposed joint action.

36. If the allocation (p,f) were chosen, L would receive 68 (that is, 85 less the utility value of YJ money which we take to be 17) and M would receive 58. Both would then be worse off than with the allocation (f,p).

7 PROCEDURES FOR SITUATIONS WITH MANY OPTIONS WHERE PARTICIPANTS CAN ASSIGN PRECISE VALUES TO OUTCOMES

7.1 INTRODUCTION

As we have already indicated, most decisionmaking of reality is concerned with situations of a small (finite) number of options (joint actions) or, if many options (a continuous joint action space) exist, with only a small number of options upon which a decisionmaker focuses in that space. For example, when the problem is to decide upon a budget involving billions of dollars, the joint action involving for a given participant a budget corresponding to $1,000,000,000.01 is not considered, nor is $1,000,000,001.00 or innumberable other sizes of budgets. Rather, the participant may focus on budgets of $1.0, $1.2, $1.4, $1.7, $2, $2.3 billion, or some other limited set. Nonetheless, the analyst who must advise a decisionmaker or policymaker may find it helpful to assume a continuous action space in order to employ some powerful analytical tools that require this assumption.

In what follows, much of what has been said in the previous chapter with regard to a small (finite) number of options is directly applicable, bearing in mind that the possibility of taking innumerably more options may make certain of these procedures no longer acceptable to participants.[1] Sections 7.2 and 7.3 simply present the logical extensions of procedures already discussed in Chapter 6 and elsewhere, with some more sophistication where the continuous action space permits. Concluding remarks are made in Section 7.4.

Again note that the assumption of comparable cardinal utility is a strong one and one not generally characteristic of reality. Still, we examine situations involving such an assumption. Doing so provides considerable insight to analysts for unraveling complex conflict situations and enables them to furnish useful information to participants on tradeoffs and the like.

7.2 PROCEDURES WHEN THE DISTRIBUTION PROBLEM IS IGNORED OR NOT RELEVANT[2]

7.2.1 Max Total Utility Principle

As with finite joint action cases, a first obvious procedure to consider when comparable cardinal utility pertains is to select that joint action which maximizes the sum of the utilities to participants. To illustrate, consider Figure 7-1, where we measure along the horizontal axis the magnitude associated with a continuous joint action space such as expenditures in dollars on foreign aid (the percent contributions or formula for absolute contributions of participants being prespecified). There we graph the utility outcome for each of three participants and the sum of these outcomes. The solution using the *max total utility principle* is the joint action $a*$, which yields the maximum sum of the utilities.[a] Again, as with finite actions, this procedure ignores the distribution problem.

In the above case, the outcomes to the participants are unweighted. If the participants agree to apply different weights to outcomes, we then can say that they employ a *max total weighted utility principle*, and the solution is easily determined.[b]

7.2.2 Max Total of Utility Improvements Principle

The max total utility principle just discussed clearly can also be stated as max the total of utility improvements by participants where the current or reference position corresponds to the (0,0) utility point. How-

---

[a]The objective function is simply

$$\max_{J} \sum u^J \qquad J = A, \ldots, U \tag{7-1}$$

[b]The objection function becomes

$$\max_{J} \sum w^J u^J \qquad J = A, \ldots, U \tag{7-2}$$

where w^J is the weight to be applied to J's utility.

Figure 7-1. Utility to J, M, and L and Total Utility.

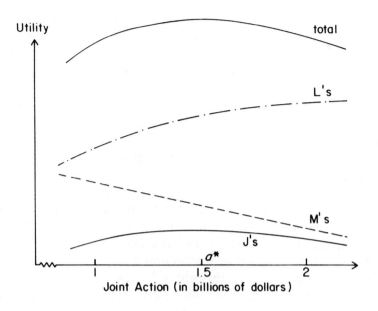

ever, as indicated in previous chapters, participants may wish to use other reference points—for example, the security-level point, the threat point (which may involve different negative utilities for participants), and the current standpoint. When such is the case, the max total utility principle must be replaced by a *max total of utility improvements principle.*[c]

[c]The objective function becomes

$$\max \sum_{J} (u^J - \bar{u}^J) \qquad J = A, \ldots, U \qquad (7\text{--}3)$$

where $\bar{u}^J$ is the utility outcome to J at the relevant reference point, and weights of unity are employed. Additionally, such a principle may be modified to relate to weighted absolute improvements, or alternatively to percent improvements (weighted or unweighted). When the *max total of weighted improvements principle* is adopted, the objective function becomes

$$\max \sum_{J} w^J(u^J - \bar{u}^J) \qquad J = A, \ldots, U \qquad (7\text{--}4)$$

When the *max total of percent utility improvement principles,* unweighted and weighted, are employed, the objective functions become, respectively

$$\max \sum_{J} \left(\frac{(u^J - \bar{u}^J)}{(u^{J*} - \bar{u}^J)} \right) \qquad J = A, \ldots, U \qquad (7\text{--}5)$$

and

$$\max \sum_{J} w^J \left(\frac{(u^J - \bar{u}^J)}{(u^{J*} - \bar{u}^J)} \right) \qquad J = A, \ldots, U \qquad (7\text{--}6)$$

where u^{J*} is the utility J associates with his most preferred joint action.

7.2.3 Max Equal Improvements Principle

Another very simple procedure that many participants may wish to employ is one that involves equal improvements in utility for each. In a joint utility space, this would restrict eligible joint actions to those that yield outcomes that fall on a 45° straight line drawn from the origin. While each point along this line would satisfy the *equal improvements principle*, the optimal compromise solution would be given by the intersection of this line with the efficiency frontier.[d] This corresponds to point s_1 in Figure 7-2, which is a mapping onto the joint utility space U of Table 3-2 (when cardinalized and smoothed into a continuous action space).

While the origin is a natural (0,0) point from which to measure equal improvements, there can be other reference points that participants may find more acceptable. One might be the current standpoint, or the best reply point such as e in Figure 4-5. Another might be the security-level point as discussed in Section 5.2.7. Still another might be the threat point or one of the others discussed on pages 158–159.

Again, participants may focus on percent improvements in utility rather than absolute increments. The relevant principle would then be that of *max equal percent improvements*.[e] In a normalized

[d]The objective function is

$$\max \sum_J u^J \tag{7-1}$$

subject to

$$u^J = u^L \qquad J,L = A, \ldots, U \tag{7-7}$$

When the utilities are weighted, the objective function is

$$\max \sum_J w^J u^J \tag{7-2}$$

subject to

$$w^J u^J = w^L u^L \qquad J,L = A, \ldots, U \tag{7-8}$$

Note that when a unit of improvement is twice as important to L as to J, then $w^L = \frac{1}{2}$ when $w^J = 1$. Also see note 9 on pages 244–45.

[e]The objective function would be

$$\max \sum_J \left(\frac{u^J}{u^{J*}}\right) \tag{7-9}$$

subject to

$$\left(\frac{u^J}{u^{J*}}\right) = \left(\frac{u^L}{u^{L*}}\right) \qquad J,L = A, \ldots, U \tag{7-10}$$

When utilities are weighted, the objective function would be

$$\max \sum_J \left(\frac{w^J u^J}{u^{J*}}\right) \tag{7-11}$$

subject to

$$\left(\frac{w^J u^J}{u^{J*}}\right) = \left(\frac{w^L u^L}{u^{L*}}\right) \qquad J,L = A, \ldots, U \tag{7-12}$$

Figure 7-2.   The Continuous Utility Space for the Developed (J) and Developing (L) Nations.

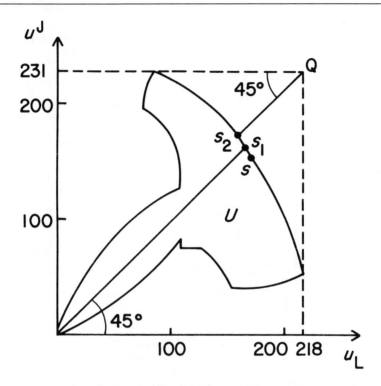

joint utility space such as depicted in Figure 7-3, where unity (100%) corresponds to the maximum of each participant's possible utility outcomes and zero corresponds to the absolute utility to him of the base reference point (here taken to be the (0,0) point in the joint utility space), this would restrict eligible joint actions to the 45° line drawn from the (0,0) point to the (1,1) point. While each point along the line would satisfy the equal percent improvements principle, the optimal compromise solution would be given by the intersection of this line with the efficiency frontier, namely point $\bar{s}$.

Paralleling the principles of max equal improvements and max equal percent improvements are the principles *max equal goal achievements* and *max equal percent of goal achievements*, respectively, when participants focus on goal achievements.

Figure 7-3. An Equal Percent Improvement Solution in Normalized Utility Space.

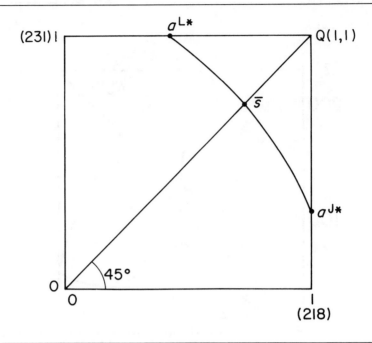

7.2.4 Min Total of Concessions Principle

While some participants may be inclined to start with the (0,0) point when considering compromises, others may find it easier to start from an ideal (1,1) point. In the latter case, participants would be concerned with concessions since the (1,1) point is, by definition, infeasible. In doing so, they may agree on a compromise procedure based on the principle *min the total of concessions.*[f] If they do so, the solution would be point s in Figure 7-2.

If, however, participants can only agree on percent concessions as a relevant measure, then they might consider a compromise procedure

---

[f]The objective function would be

$$\min_{J} \Sigma \ (u^{J*} - u^{J}) \qquad J = A, \ldots, U \qquad (7\text{-}13)$$

When concessions are weighted, this function becomes

$$\min_{J} \Sigma \ w^{J} \ (u^{J*} - u^{J}) \qquad J = A, \ldots, U \qquad (7\text{-}14)$$

that uses the principle *min the total of percent concessions.*[g] If they do so in the situation depicted in Figure 7–2, it turns out that the solution would remain close to point *s*.

7.2.5 Min Equal Concessions Principle

When considering relaxation of their demands represented by an infeasible ideal (1,1) point, participants may only be able to agree on a procedure involving a principle of *min equal absolute concessions* from this point.[h] Use of this principle would restrict eligible, but not necessarily feasible, joint actions to those that yield outcomes falling on a 45° straight line drawn from the ideal point in the joint utility space toward the efficiency frontier. See Figure 7–2. Those falling on the equal concessions line before it reaches the efficiency frontier are obviously infeasible. The optimal compromise solution is then given by that joint action corresponding to the intersection of this line and the efficiency frontier. In Figure 7–2 this corresponds to point s_2.

While the above discussion centers on the ideal point Q, equal concessions can also be measured from other infeasible points that may be apparently rational, ideal, appealing, or relevant on some other score. A classic point is a current standpoint (a status quo position) which is no longer feasible because of changed conditions—e.g., a

[g]The objective function would be

$$\min_{J} \Sigma \left(\frac{(u^{J*} - u^J)}{u^{J*}} \right) \qquad J = A, \ldots, U \qquad (7\text{-}15)$$

When concessions are weighted, this function becomes

$$\min_{J} \Sigma \left(\frac{w^J(u^{J*} - u^J)}{u^{J*}} \right) \qquad J = A, \ldots, U \qquad (7\text{-}16)$$

[h]The objective function would then be

$$\min_{J} \Sigma (u^{J*} - u^J) \qquad (7\text{-}13)$$

subject to

$$(u^{J*} - u^J) = (u^{L*} - u^L) \qquad J,L = A, \ldots, U \qquad (7\text{-}17)$$

When weights are applied to concessions to reflect differences in need or the equivalent, this function would become

$$\min_{J} \Sigma \ w^J (u^{J*} - u^J) \qquad (7\text{-}14)$$

subject to

$$w^J (u^{J*} - u^J) = w^L (u^{L*} - u^L) \qquad J,L = A, \ldots, U \qquad (7\text{-}18)$$

point that corresponds to (1) the current labor wage and fringe benefits package that can no longer be paid by a firm because of sudden contraction of the economy, (2) the current level of revenue sharing among regions when federal taxes have precipitously declined, or (3) a level of funding of development projects by the World Bank because contributions to it from the industrialized nations have suddenly diminished. Another might be a level of world consumption of a commodity (say energy) expected on the basis of existing or projected growth rates in consumption—a level that exceeds the projected world supply.

On the other hand, the principle of min equal concessions (weighted or unweighted) from an infeasible point may fail to appeal to participants but a principle of min equal percent concessions might.[i] In this case the participants might agree on a compromise procedure based on the use of this principle; and for the situation depicted in Figure 7-3 the solution would be given by $\bar{s}$, the intersection with the efficiency frontier of the 45° line connecting the (0,0) and (1,1) points.[3]

Paralleling the principle of min equal concessions (absolute or percent) could be the principle of *min equal goal shortfalls* (absolute or percent) when participants prefer to focus on goals.

7.2.6 The Principle of Equidistant Concession in the Joint Action (Policy) Space

For various psychological reasons, participants may not be able to agree on improvements or concessions (absolute or percent) in the joint utility space. On the other hand, participants may be able to

[i]In this case, the objective function would be

$$\min_{j} \Sigma \left(\frac{(u^{j*} - u^j)}{u^{j*}} \right) \tag{7-15}$$

subject to

$$\left(\frac{(u^{j*} - u^j)}{u^{j*}} \right) = \left(\frac{(u^{L*} - u^L)}{u^{L*}} \right) \qquad J,L = A, \ldots ,U \tag{7-19}$$

When weights are employed to reflect, for example, the relative needs or power of the participants, the function becomes

$$\min_{j} \Sigma \left(\frac{w^j (u^{j*} - u^j)}{u^{j*}} \right) \tag{7-16}$$

subject to

$$\frac{w^j (u^{j*} - u^j)}{u^{j*}} = \frac{w^L (u^{L*} - u^L)}{u^{L*}} \qquad J,L = A, \ldots ,U \tag{7-20}$$

consider compromise solutions when the focus is shifted from the utility directly received to the joint action adopted—that is when no explicit reference is made to utility but only to nonutility factors. One natural procedure would involve equal distance concessions from the joint action that each most prefers,[4] employing some form of an action compromise principle. In connection with the discussion on pages 74–75 and Figure 4–2, we illustrated an equidistant set of compromise solutions with a 45° line drawn from the (0,0) point on a two-dimensional figure. We suggested as the compromise solution the joint action corresponding to the intersection of this line with the efficiency frontier. Such would achieve both efficiency and equal improvements in terms of distance.

We can illustrate this type of procedure in another way that is enlightening. Let there be two policy issues. One concerns dollars of foreign aid measured along the horizontal in Figure 7–4. A second

Figure 7-4. Compromise Solutions in the Joint Action (Policy) Space.

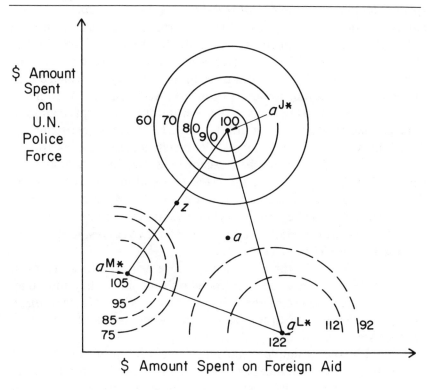

concerns level of U.N. Police Force, either in man hours or expenditures, measured along the vertical axis in Figure 7-4. Let there be two participants, J and M, whose most preferred joint policies are a^{J*} and a^{M*}, respectively. Connect these two points by a straight line. See Figure 7-4, and ignore everything but this straight line. The midpoint z of this line then represents a compromise position based on the use of the *equidistant concession principle*. Note that this conflict situation is a somewhat different type than the one discussed up to now. In the latter type each participant takes an action regarding one and only one policy issue, the joint action then being a combination of actions, one by each participant. In the type discussed here, each participant states his preference or votes for a combination of policies, that is, a joint policy; and the compromise is with regard to the most preferred joint policies. However, most of the analysis relevant for one type of conflict situation also pertains to the other.

Now let there be three participants, J, L, and M, to the conflict over a joint policy (action) in the above two-dimensional policy space. Identify each one's most preferred joint policy, namely a^{J*}, a^{L*}, and a^{M*}, respectively. Connect them by straight lines to form a joint policy triangle. We then construct on this figure a set of indifference curves for each participant to reflect the basic structure of her cardinal utility (payoff) function. For example, around a^{J*}, which J estimates would yield him 100 units of utility, we construct J's 90 indifference curve, which connects in this continuous action space all joint policies that would yield J a utility of 90. Likewise we construct J's 80, 70, and 60 indifference curves. We construct these curves around a^{J*} just as we did in Figure 4-2, except here the numbers associated with each indifference curve represent cardinal utilities while there, they indicated ordinal utilities. Also around a^{M*}, M's most preferred joint action, which she estimates would yield her a cardinal utility of 105, we construct her 95, 85, and 75 indifference curves, and around a^{L*}, L's 112 and 92 indifference curves.

Assuming that the three participants are not able to agree on a compromise solution when they focus on outcomes, they then may find acceptable the use of the principle of *equidistant concession in the joint action space*.[5] In that case, joint policy a would be the compromise solution.

It could be that a simple equidistant concession procedure yields a joint action whose outcomes are too easily perceived by participants, and therefore, again fails to lead to agreement on a compromise solution. In this situation, a procedure involving a series of pairwise equidistance concessions in policy space may be found to be acceptable, primarily because it makes it more difficult for the participants to visualize (or calculate quickly) the compromise joint action that will be achieved, and thus the utility outcomes associated with it. We illustrate this procedure with the use of Figure 7–5. First, each participant states his most preferred joint policy, yielding the points a^{J*}, a^{L*}, and a^{M*}. Second, each pair of these points is connected by a straight line, and the midpoints of each line q^{JM}, q^{JL}, and q^{ML} are identified. Third, each pair of midpoints—q^{JL} and q^{JM}, q^{JL} and q^{ML}, and q^{JM} and q^{ML}—is connected by a straight line to yield midpoints $\bar{a}^J$, $\bar{a}^L$, and $\bar{a}^M$, which may be interpreted as indicating the first round concessions for J, L, and M, respectively. The procedure is continued until the new concession points are within a negligible distance from each other such that the point toward which they are converging can be approximated, with agreement by all, and then taken to be the compromise solution.[6,7]

The conflict situation depicted above may, however, be more complex than indicated. Each of the three participants may have his own

Figure 7–5.   A Series of Pairwise Equidistant Concessions.

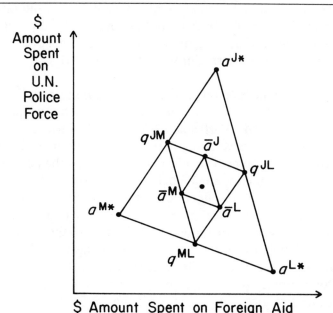

pet goal, assigning relatively small importance to the pet goals of the other two. In that situation, where three dimensions are required to represent achievement on the three goals, simple graphic analysis by mediators or participants themselves would not be possible. However, when participants agree to consider either percent improvement or concessions regarding their pet goals, then graphic analysis can still be employed.

Let us now restructure the problem. Consider a conflict over level of programs of the United Nations (or some world system government of the future) and the size of contributions of nations to this governmental organization. Let there develop three relevant objectives, each one primary to one and only one of three groups of nations. Let these objectives be:

1.   large U.N. Police Force, the primary goal of the highly industrialized-urbanized nations of the world (participant J) who are very much concerned with coping effectively with international terrorism;
2.   large aid program to developing regions, an obvious primary goal of developing regions (participant L); and
3.   large internal development implying small contributions to the United Nations for both its police force and aid program, the primary goal of a group of nations such as some of the Socialist economies of Eastern Europe (participant M).

Also we can imagine that there is some maximum total dollar support that is set as feasible—to be contributed in prespecified proportions by participants J and M. (Participant L does not contribute an amount since she represents developing nations.) Now consider the percents of this total to be devoted to all three objectives—the percent to objective "internal development" being the percent of the total that is returned to contributors—in effect, the amount that is not levied and so is not available for either or both of the other two programs. Let us measure along the horizontal axis in Figure 7-6 the percent of that total to be devoted to the aid program, ranging from 0 to 100 percent, and along the vertical, the percent of that total to be devoted to U.N. Police Force. If we connect the 100 percent points along these two axes by a straight line to mark off the shaded triangle of Figure 7-6, then the shaded triangle together with its legs contains all possible percentage allocations of the total to the three programs.

Figure 7-6.   The Budget Allocation Policy Space.

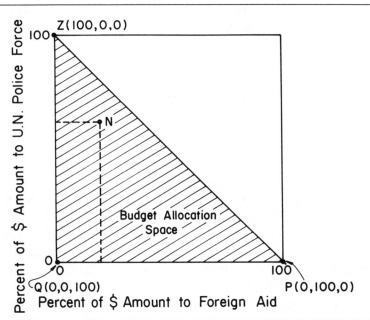

To show this, consider the three end points in Figure 7–6. Point Z represents a situation where 100 percent of the budget goes for U.N. Police Force, 0 percent for Foreign Aid, and 0 percent for Internal Development. We may associate with this point the three percentages (100,0,0). Point P corresponds to the budget allocation of 0 percent for U.N. Police Force, 100 percent for Foreign Aid and 0 percent for Internal Development. We may associate with it the three percentages (0,100,0). Point Q corresponds to 0 percent for U.N. Police Force, 0 percent for Foreign Aid, and 100 percent for Internal Development. We may associate with it the three percentages (0,0,100). Any other point within the figure, such as N, corresponds to a percentage allocation to each of the three sets of programs, which together add up to 100 percent. For N, we have 60 percent for U.N. Police Force, 20 percent for Foreign Aid, and 20 percent for Internal Development. Note that in this figure it is not necessary to measure the percent to be allocated to Internal Development along a third axis. It must necessarily equal 100 percent less the sum of the percentages allocated to U.N. Police Force and to Foreign Aid. To make this point clearer, consider the most preferred allocations of the three participants (sets of nations), with reference to Figure 7-7. J most prefers the allocation (60,30,10). We determine the point a^{J*} in the figure that corresponds to 60 percent along the vertical axis and 30 percent along the horizontal axis. Then the portion not allocated to these two goals, namely 10 percent, must be allocated to the third goal, Internal Development, which, as explained above, we do not need to measure along any axis. Likewise, M most prefers the allocation (10,20,70). Hence, to represent it we need only plot the two percents 10 and 20 along the vertical and horizontal axes, respectively, to identify the point a^{M*}—the remaining 70 percent is automatically assigned to the third goal, Internal Development. So, too, with L's most preferred allocation of (20,70,10). Plotting the point (20,70) on the figure, namely a^{L*}, automatically implies the allocations (20,70,10).

We have plotted in Figure 7-7 the most preferred allocations of the three parties J, L, and M. Because they are not identical, there exists conflict. Again, a compromise procedure that may have appeal to participants in this situation is one that involves the principle of equal distance concessions from the joint policies (actions) that each

Figure 7-7.   Most Preferred Allocation in Budget Allocation Space.

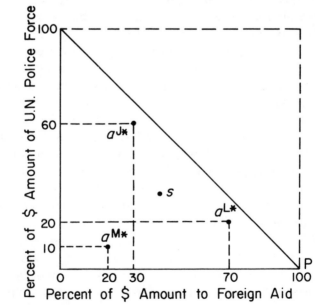

most prefers in the joint policy (action) space of Figure 7-7. The use of such a principle would yield the joint policies represented by point s as the compromise solution. As with the equidistant solution a in Figure 7-4, the outcomes associated with point s may be too easily perceived by participants to enable them to agree on the use of an equidistant concession principle. They then might find appealing the use of a series of pairwise equidistant concessions paralleling the procedure discussed in connection with Figure 7-5, or some other procedure that has an element of fairness in terms of the joint policy space of Figure 7-7 but which does not allow the participants to identify beforehand the compromise solution that will be reached and its associated utilities.

7.2.7 Constraints on Procedures

As discussed in preceding chapters, participants may agree to impose several different kinds of constraints in order to remove feelings of insecurity and fears of being outwitted or cheated or of receiving a sucker's outcome. The setting of constraints may be encouraged by a mediator in order to provide an atmosphere for positive discussions, deliberations, and negotiations. We now discuss several types of constraints in a general way.

Lower and Upper Bound Constraints. We have already suggested on several occasions that participants may be motivated to insure at least some minimum improvement for each. Consequently, they may set a *lower bound* constraint on the absolute utility increment when they use (1) a max total utility principle (with utilities weighted or unweighted)[j]

---

[j]Accordingly, in a program with the objective function

$$\max \sum_{J} u^J \qquad (7\text{-}1)$$

we add the constraint

$$u^J \geq k_1 \qquad J = A, \ldots, U \qquad (7\text{-}21)$$

where k_1 represents the minimum acceptable absolute utility improvement. Or to a program with the objective function

$$\max \sum_{J} w^J u^J \qquad (7\text{-}2)$$

we add the constraint

$$w^J u^J \geq k_2 \qquad J = A, \ldots, U \qquad (7\text{-}22)$$

where k_2 represents the minimum acceptable absolute utility improvement when J's utility is weighted by the factor w^J. Note that lower bound constraints (and upper bound constraints) do not have any real meaning when there are also imposed constraints that require equal improvements, absolute or percent.

or (2) a max total of utility improvements principle (with improvements weighted or unweighted). Alternatively, they may set the constraint on the percent utility increment when they use a max total of percents of utility improvements principle (with improvements weighted) or unweighted).[k] Or participants may be motivated to ensure that no one will be required to make a concession that exceeds some maximum amount. Consequently, they may set an *upper bound* constraint on this absolute utility concession when they use a *min total concession principle* (with absolute utility decrements weighted or unweighted)[l] or on the percent concession when they use a *min total*

---

[k]Thus, in a program with the objective function

$$\max_{J} \Sigma \left(\frac{u^J}{u^{J*}} \right) \tag{7-9}$$

we add the constraint

$$\left(\frac{u^J}{u^{J*}} \right) \geq k_3 \qquad J = A, \ldots, U \tag{7-23}$$

where k_3 represents the minimum acceptable percent improvement. Or to a program with the objective function

$$\max_{J} \Sigma \left(\frac{w^J u^J}{u^{J*}} \right) \tag{7-11}$$

we add the constraint

$$\left(\frac{w^J u^J}{u^{J*}} \right) \geq k_4 \qquad J = A, \ldots, U \tag{7-24}$$

where k_4 represents the minimum acceptable percent improvement in weighted utility.

[l]Thus in a program with the objective function

$$\min_{J} \Sigma \left(u^{J*} - u^J \right) \tag{7-13}$$

we add the constraint

$$\left(u^{J*} - u^J \right) \leq k_5 \qquad J = A, \ldots, U \tag{7-25}$$

where k_5 represents the maximum acceptable absolute concession. Or to a program with the objective function

$$\min_{J} \Sigma \, w^J \left(u^{J*} - u^J \right) \tag{7-14}$$

we add the constraint

$$w^J \left(u^{J*} - u^J \right) \leq k_6 \qquad J = A, \ldots, U \tag{7-26}$$

where k_6 represents the maximum acceptable absolute concession in weighted utility.

of percent concessions principle (with percent concessions weighted or unweighted).[m]

In some instances, they may even wish to impose both upper and lower bounds. In all these cases, however, the restrictions that such constraints impose on proposals may be considered clearcut; and the analysis is easily developed.[8]

Discrepancy Constraints. A somewhat more complicated situation occurs when participants focus on the difference in their outcomes and can only agree to compromise procedures that ensure this difference does not exceed some maximum amount. Such constraints might be imposed when the participants employ (1) a max total utility principle, (2) a max total weighted utility principle, (3) a max total of percent improvements principle, (4) a min total concessions principle, (5) a min total weighted concessions principle, (6) a min total of percent concessions principle[9] or some other related principle.

7.2.8 Other Procedures

As already mentioned, when additional information on preferences becomes available, and when finite action spaces are replaced by continuous ones, the usefulness of a number of procedures changes. Let us discuss how for selected procedures.[10]

[m]Thus, in a program with the objection function

$$\min_{J} \Sigma \left(\frac{(u^{J^*} - u^J)}{u^{J^*}} \right) \qquad J = A, \ldots, U \qquad (7\text{-}15)$$

we add the constraint

$$\left(\frac{(u^{J^*} - u^J)}{u^{J^*}} \right) \leq k_7 \qquad J = A, \ldots, U \qquad (7\text{-}27)$$

where k_7 represents the maximum acceptable percent concession; or, to a program with objective function

$$\min_{J} \Sigma \left(\frac{w^J(u^{J^*} - u^J)}{u^{J^*}} \right) \qquad J = A, \ldots, U \qquad (7\text{-}16)$$

we add the constraint

$$\left(\frac{w^J(u^{J^*} - u^J)}{u^{J^*}} \right) \leq k_8 \qquad J = A, \ldots, U \qquad (7\text{-}28)$$

where k_8 represents the maximum acceptable percent concession in weighted utility.

Sequential Split-the-Difference and Related Procedures.   We have already noted the usefulness of a sequential split-the-difference procedure in a continuous action space when participants cannot agree on a compromise procedure related directly to their outcomes in the joint utility space. If they were to use a sequential split-the-difference procedure in the joint utility space, they would be employing in each of a series of rounds an equal percent improvement principle. In each round, the relevant reference points for each participant would be (1) the outcome he would receive were his opponent's most preferred joint action realized and (2) the outcome he would receive were his most preferred joint action realized. (See the discussion on pages 156–159). The procedure can be modified to consider limited commitment on each round and other features of an incremax procedure. In some cases, participants may prefer the term "sequential split-the-difference with limited commitment on each round," or "veto-incremax," but clearly the outcome would be no different than equal percent improvement on each round with limited commitment and other features.

The above comments also pertain to the minimum information incremax procedure. (See pages 100–102). In this procedure, the split-the-difference principle in each round is once again an appropriately defined equal percent improvements principle.

Alternating Leader-Follower Procedure.   The alternating leader-follower procedure is most useful when participants can only order their preferences (see pages 92–94), since when participants are able to state cardinal utilities that are comparable, many more kinds of comparisons can be made on each round and new difficulties may arise. For example, in defining the limited commitment set or equivalent for each round, there may be more difficulty in obtaining agreement on the use of a commitment set defined by the lesser of the maximum amount of change each participant is willing to consider on any round. The participants know that effective comparisons of utility gains are now possible and that perhaps they may be outwitted. In general they may feel less confident that their interest will be protected, especially since beforehand they do not know who will be the leader on the first round. Nonetheless, the alternating leader-follower procedure can and should be used if it has psychological appeal to participants—particularly so when they prespecify for each round the maximum change for defining the limited commitment set.

GRIT (Graduated and Reciprocated Initiatives in Tension-Reduction) Procedure.   Just as additional information regarding cardinal utility may lead to new difficulties for participants in agreeing on an appropriate limited commitment set for each round, so too in employing elements of the GRIT procedure. (See pages 99–100.) For example, additional information may lead to constant bickering among participants as to whether or not a response to a unilateral concession at any stage was sufficiently large to be considered an appropriate reciprocating concession. Nonetheless, participants may be able to agree on and proceed effectively with the GRIT procedure.

Last-Offer Arbitration Procedures.   Here also, having additional information on cardinal utiities that are comparable may make it more difficult to apply last-offer arbitration. (See pages 102–106.) Whatever proposal the wise, respected, and judicious mediator selects as the fairest, it becomes possible for one or more participants to claim foul play since there can now be more comparisons and, in particular, direct comparisons of absolute improvements in utility, percent improvements in utility, absolute concessions, percent concessions, and so on. In short, there can be many more objections to whatever criteria the mediator may have used in selecting the proposal he judged to be fairest.

The Demand-Revealing (No Bluffing) Method (Clarke-Vickrey).   As indicated on pages 184–188, the Clarke-Vickrey demand-revealing (no bluffing) method requires participants to provide cardinal estimates of the value to them of any action. We now inquire whether the validity and appeal of this procedure are affected when participants are able to consider a continuous action space. (In effect, the horizontal axis in Figure 6–1 comes to represent the continuous joint action space—a continuous range, say, of the size of a joint project.) Theoretically, for every possible joint action, each participant can be asked to state the value to him of its outcome, and all such points can be connected to yield a continuous curve. This curve then replaces the series of points connected by straight line segments in Figure 6–1. In practice, this could not be done, as it would require each participant to state his valuation of an infinite number of joint actions. At best, participants may be asked to state values for a fairly large number of joint actions; then the value for other joint actions would need to be approximated by the analyst on the basis of this information. Once again, participant J is taxed by the amount that selection of his most preferred joint action would reduce the total value realized by all other participants were he ignored. Again this tax motivates each participant, out of self-interest, to state as best he can the true value to him of the outcome of each possible joint action, thereby leading to selection of a joint action with the maximum total utility. In short, the existence of a continuous action space has little effect on the validity and appeal of the procedure.

Zeuthen Concession (Least to Lose Goes First) Procedure. Although the Zeuthen concession procedure only requires participants to have relative utility, it is just as useful when participants have comparable cardinal utility. As discussed in more detail on pages 160–162, this procedure requires each participant to state his most desired joint action (policy). It then requires that for each participant the potential loss ratio be computed, in this situation, on the basis of his absolute (cardinal) utility values as

$$\ell_{LJ} = (^L u^{L*} - {}^L u^{J*})/^L u^{L*}$$

and

$$\ell_{JL} = (^J u^{J*} - {}^J u^{L*})/^J u^{J*}$$

for L and J, respectively. The participant whose potential loss ratio is lower then concedes on each round, after which new potential loss ratios are computed. This procedure continues until the participants reach a unique point on the efficiency frontier where the two loss ratios are identical and, in particular, equal to zero.

7.3 PROCEDURES FOR MANAGING THE DISTRIBUTION PROBLEM[11]

As already discussed on pages 188–189 in connection with finite action situations, employing procedures based on weighted utilities does not mean that the distribution problem is adequately treated. So, too, with continuous action situations. Hence, we must consider different ways of handling the distribution problem. All the ways found useful for finite action cases are also applicable here. Among these are:

1. simple averaging of proposed weights and/or constraints
2. equidistant concessions on proposed weights and/or constraints

3.   method of determining group priorities (Saaty) (see pages 147–155)
4.   Delphi methods (see pages 372–376)
5.   last-offer arbitration (see pages 102–106)
6.   recursive interactive programming (see pages 188–192)
7.   to supplement programming, the use of constraints (lower bounds, upper bounds, both lower and upper bounds, maximum allowable differences between participants, maximum allowable deviation above or below average or both, maximum ratio of realized utility values for any pair of participants, maximum percent above or below average or both, maximum or minimum use of resources for any single objective or both—see pages 192–200[12])

In addition, the availability of a continuous action space allows relaxed hierarchical programming to take on greater significance as a procedure for managing the distribution problem. Recall from pages 162–164 that this procedure involves a ranking of objectives at the start and then, until all available resources are exhausted, the running of successive programs to maximize the achievement on each objective in order of priority, subject to constraints ensuring achievement of at least some fraction of the optimal value of higher order objectives.

When only a finite number of joint actions are available, it is not possible to conduct such hierarchical programming in an effective way. This is especially so when, through recursive interaction of participants, the fraction of each objective's optimal value to be guaranteed in subsequent runs has to be determined and frequently reexamined and reset. To do so, one generally requires a large number of possible joint actions and most desirably a set of continuous joint actions.

When the above procedures do not work, the mediator can suggest to participants alternative views (conceptions) of the problem that do not fundamentally change the results but have greater psychological appeal because they add positive elements to the situation or eliminate negative ones. Typically, they involve shifting the focus of negotiations and deliberations by changing the objective functions and constraints. For example, the objective function may be reduced to maximizing only one participant's utility subject to lower bound constraints on all others—a formulation that has no explicit reference to weights. (See the discussion in Section 6.3.3.) Alternatively, participants may focus on ideal points or other points that are infeasible;

then they may consider procedures involving concessions and reformulate the objective function so as to minimize penalty, cost, and shortfalls in goal achievement. They may (1) use principles such as min total of concessions from the ideal or other infeasible point, and min total penalty or total costs (with or without the use of weights); (2) set constraints such as upper bounds or lower bounds on any concession, maximum allowable differences between concessions on any pair of objectives (utilities), maximum allowable deviation of any concession above or below the average or both; and (3) focus on percent rather than absolute concessions; and accordingly devise comparable principles to the above. (For full discussion of these options see Section 6.3.4.)

Also, when there is a fixed total to be distributed and when the allocation of this total can be specified by a set of nonnegative fractions as weights that add to unity, all the procedures discussed in Section 6.3.5 are relevant. And in particular, the problem can be redefined as a programming problem.

Again, a type of procedure involving achievement of minimum requirements (satisficing)—discussed in Section 6.3.6—may be applicable when participants cannot agree on the adoption of any of the above procedures. For example, they may be able to reach agreement to select the first joint action or policy that meets some feasible set of lower bounds, upper bounds, or some other nonoptimizing criteria.

7.4 CONCLUDING REMARKS

This chapter has dealt with situations characterized by continuous action spaces and intercardinal utility. While continuous action spaces frequently exist, decisionmakers often consider only a small set of actions. Nonetheless, for the analyst, the existence of continuous action spaces allows him to employ a wider range of techniques and, in some cases, more powerful techniques. The assumption of comparable cardinal utility, however, is a strong one, and can be found to be realistic only for a very limited number of situations. But it does allow the analyst to play around with sophisticated models and, at times, to derive insights directly relevant to the real world.

In this chapter we have gone through numerous techniques that have already been examined in Chapters 5 and 6, such as max the total of utility, max the total of utility improvements, min the total of concessions, and the use of upper bound, lower bound, and discrepancy constraints. Because of the continuous joint action spaces, we are able to develop further the max equal improvements, min equal concessions, and equidistant concessions princples. We have also examined necessary changes in the statements and applications of still other procedures. The procedures for managing the distribution problem are essentially the same, except that relaxed hierarchical programming and recursive interactive programming take on added significance. The distribution problem, major as it is, can still be said not to be adequately treated.

In the next chapter, we make more explicit some of the useful dimensions of multiobjective programming in a recursive interactive setting. Clearly, this as well as many other conflict management procedures must be used in a most flexible manner to take into account (1) the limited level of sophistication possible in real life discussion and interaction among political leaders and (2) its doubtful relevance to many cultural settings.

NOTES

1.   See the discussion on pages 130–131. For reasons discussed in Section 6.1, we will be dealing with cases involving comparable cardinal utility only. When participants can state cardinal utilities, but only in noncomparable units, they in effect can only employ procedures requiring at most comparable relative utility.

2.   As in Section 6.2, unless otherwise stated, for procedures in this section to be applicable each participant must know his own preference structure and that of all others. However, when it is meaningful for a mediator who is respected and trusted to be present and when this mediator knows all participants' preference structures, then it is only necessary that each participant know his own preference structure.

3.   Note that the principles: (1) min the deviation of any participant's improvement from the average improvement, (2) min the deviation of any participant's percent improvement from the average percent improvement, (3) max the min percent improvement (or achievement of a goal), (4) min the deviation of any participant's concession from the average concession, (5) min the deviation of any participant's percent concession (or goal shortfall) from the average percent concession, (6) min the max percent concession (or goal shortfall) are respectively equivalent to the principles: (1) max equal improvements, (2) max equal percent improvements, (3) max equal percent improvements (or

achievements of a goal), (4) min equal concessions, (5) min equal percent concessions (or goal shortfalls), (6) min equal percent concessions (or goal shortfalls), when the latter principle yields a solution. Otherwise, participants may use the former principle; and in some cases when they are simple-minded they might find the former principle acceptable and not the latter because the wording of the former is appealing.

4. This distance would normally be Euclidean distance, the distance with which most participants are familiar. Theoretically, however, participants with brilliant minds or with a willingness to be guided by sophisticated analysts might agree on the use of Minkowski-type distance. See the discussion in the footnote on pages 181–182.

5. Observe that this principle can also be employed when the three participants have only ordinal utility or relative utility functions and where, accordingly, the numbers associated with the indifference curves indicate the order of preferences or relative values, respectively. The principle also works when participants have different kinds of utility functions. It may appear strange that we are not able to suggest here additional compromise procedures in situations with additional information regarding preference structures. However, this follows from the fact that when participants retain complete freedom to exercise a "direct" action (and do not make proposals), they are only able to play around in their action spaces in their effort to reach a solution to the conflict.

6. Many other procedures are possible here using only the joint action space or both the joint action space and the sets of indifference curves that can be taken to represent the joint utility space. For example, see Isard, T. Smith, et al. (1969:440–48), where a distance-decrement concession procedure, a generalized split-the-difference procedure, and an alternating leader-conceder concession procedure are discussed.

7. In this section, each participant must know his own preference structure. When a mediator is not present, each participant must also have limited knowledge of the other participants' preference structures, such as their most preferred positions on one or a sequence of moves. When a mediator is present, it is sufficient that he (the mediator) have the above information for each participant.

8. Recall from Section 6.2.8 that when scale economies or equivalent factors suggest that development funds, resources, or activities be concentrated at one location or allocated to one participant, lower bound constraints play a key role in defining politically feasible joint actions (policies).

9. The constraints to be added are, respectively, for all $J, L = A, \ldots, U$; $J \neq L$:

(1) $$(u^J - u^L) \leq k_9;$$

(2) $$(w^J u^J - w^L u^L) \leq k_{10};$$

(3) $$\left(\frac{u^J}{u^{J*}}\right) - \left(\frac{u^L}{u^{L*}}\right) \leq k_{11}; \text{ or } w^J\left(\frac{u^J}{u^{J*}}\right) - w^L\left(\frac{u^L}{u^{L*}}\right) \leq k_{12}$$

when utilities are weighted and (0,0) is the relevant reference point;

(4) $$(u^{J*} - u^J) - (u^{L*} - u^L) \leq k_{13};$$

(5) $$w^J(u^{J*} - u^J) - w^L(u^{L*} - u^L) \leq k_{14}; \text{ and}$$

(6) $$\left(\frac{(u^{J*} - u^J)}{u^{J*}}\right) - \left(\frac{(u^{L*} - u^L)}{u^{L*}}\right) \leq k_{15}$$

$$\text{or } w^J\left(\frac{(u^{J*} - u^J)}{u^{J*}}\right) - w^L\left(\frac{(u^{L*} - u^L)}{u^{L*}}\right) \leq k_{16} \text{ when}$$

percent concessions are weighted. Note also that participants may wish to apply an unweighted discrepancy constraint, as in (1) above, when using a principle focussing on weighted utilities, improvements, or concessions. In such a case when a unit of improvement is judged twice as 'important' for L as for J, then $w^L = 2$ when $w^J = 1$, and so forth.

10. By and large, the information requirements for all of the procedures mentioned in this section have been stated when each was first discussed.

11. Generally speaking and unless otherwise indicated, the procedures in this section involve, in one form or another, interaction among participants. When this is the case, they must come to know each others' preferences as well as their own if the interaction is to be effective in resolving the distribution problem. When, however, they accept the weights, lower bounds, upper bounds, objective functions, and so on suggested by a trusted mediator without questioning them, each needs to know only his own preference structure. Generally speaking, in order to be able to specify acceptable parameters the mediator must know the preference structures of all participants, or a relevant region of them.

12. Because the availability of a continuous joint action space makes the last two types of options more useful, they will be discussed in more detail in Chapter 8.

8 MULTIOBJECTIVE PROGRAMMING, MULTICRITERIA (ATTRIBUTE) ANALYSIS

8.1 INTRODUCTION

In the preceding chapters, we have concentrated directly on preference structures and compromise procedures. However, as mentioned on pages 48–49, preference structures may be based on outcomes that involve many properties (or attributes) of different significance to participants. Frequently, these properties or attributes correspond to objectives or goals (full employment, 100 percent literacy, zero pollution, etc.) that are sought after by participants, and the extent of achievement on these objectives that is realized in an outcome is what determines the preference structures of participants. Often these objectives are not easily quantified and, as a consequence, criteria are employed in the place of objectives. Thus, we may speak of *control of violence and unrest* as a criteria where we can only classify outcomes as involving a large, satisfactory, or low amount of control; or classify outcomes regarding the criteria on *quality of environment* as very good, good, acceptable, poor, or very poor.

In this chapter, we first pay attention to conflict situations wherein achievements with regard to different objectives, goals, attributes and/or criteria explicitly enter into the preference structures of participants. We then proceed to examine conflict situations that focus primarily on objective achievements when participants are unable or unwilling to use procedures focusing explicitly on preference structures and utilities.[1]

The literature on *multiobjective* programming (examined in Section 8.2), and *multicriteria (attribute) analysis* (examined in Section 8.3) is voluminous; however, we will touch on only some of the main points and possibilities for use by nontechnical decisionmakers and policy formulators.

8.2 MULTIOBJECTIVE PROGRAMMING

The multiobjective programming approach is most relevant when participants can consider objectives in common quantitative terms and where a continuous joint action space is available. This approach is particularly useful for *analytic* purposes and also for situations where a decisionmaking body can go beyond simplistic methods when searching for a solution to a conflict involving several different objectives. We shall develop the basic elements of this approach, reviewing and extending materials we have already covered in previous chapters.

8.2.1 The Problem of a Single Decisionmaker

The Statement of Relevant Objectives.   A first step in multiobjective programming is to define the relevant objectives. These objectives may be those of a single decisionmaker, say the secretary-general of the United Nations, and reflect his own desires and personality traits, or they may be those of the decisionmaking body (covering diverse interest groups) that he represents. In the case of the latter, imagine for example, that there are three blocs of nations in the United Nations, each with a single key objective. As discussed on pages 232–235, these objectives are:

1.   a large U.N. Police Force, the primary desire (goal) of the highly industrialized nations of the world (designated participant J) who are very much concerned with coping effectively with international terrorism;

2.   a large aid program to developing regions, an obvious primary desire (goal) of developing regions (designated participant L); and

3. a large intranational development program implying small contributions to the United Nations for both its police force and aid program, the primary desire (goal) of a group of nations (designated participant M), which would include some of the Socialist economies of Eastern Europe.

For the moment, ignore other objectives and assume that the United Nations, through the actions of the secretary-general, behaves as a single decisionmaking body.

The Statement of Constraints.   With objectives defined, the next step is the identification of (1) the amount of scarce resources available to accommodate these objectives and (2) the exact manner in which these resources are used up. As on page 201, let g_h represent the amount of scarce resource $h(h = 1,2,3, \ldots)$ available for use. Also let e_h^J be the amount of that resource used up in the achievement of any given objective J, J = A, . . . ,U. Thus for each resource h we can state

$$e_h^J + e_h^L + e_h^M \leq g_h \tag{8-1}$$

or

$$\sum_J e_h^J \leq g_h \tag{8-2}$$

Recall that when a *constant* amount r_h^J of resource h is required per unit of achievement of objective J, then $e_h^J = r_h^J E^J$ where E^J is the number of units of objective J achieved. Equations (8–1) and (8–2) can then be stated respectively, as

$$r_h^J E^J + r_h^L E^L + r_h^M E^M \leq g_h \tag{8-3}$$

or

$$\sum_J r_h^J E^J \leq g_h \tag{8-4}$$

Identifying Efficient Combinations of Objective Achievements.   Given resources and technology, the next step is to identify efficient combinations of objective achievements. To do so, take as given some level of achievement on the third objective say $\overline{E}^M$, and thus the amount of resource h, namely $\overline{e}_h^M$ that is to be used up in achieving that level. Now consider the different combinations of the other two objectives E^J and E^L that can be produced with the remaining resources, namely $g_h - \bar{e}_h^M$. In the general case, where there is diminishing returns in the use of resource h for realizing (producing) any objective[2] and where we assume that production is efficient,[3] these different combinations would be given by a curve such as RR' in Figure 8–1. For the given $\overline{E}^M$, this curve corresponds to an efficiency frontier in terms of objective achievements. It therefore defines a *tradeoff function* between one objective and the other. For any given combination of objectives, say that given by point v, the curve shows how much of one objective must be given up in order to achieve one additional unit of the second. (For example, in the blowup of the immediate area around v on Figure 8–1, uv amount of achievement on the United Nations Police Force objective must be given up to obtain one more unit of achievement on the Foreign Aid objective.) We can derive such a tradeoff function for any other given feasible level of the third objective, say $\overline{\overline{E}}^M$. Also we can derive tradeoff functions between the first and third objectives for every feasible level of the second, and tradeoff functions for the second and third objectives for every feasible level of the first.[4]

Specifying Weights and Deriving An Optimal Combination of Objective Achievements. Assuming that $\overline{E}^M$ is given, which one of the efficient combinations depicted by the curve RR' in Figure 8–1 will be

Figure 8-1. Efficient Combinations of Objectives E^J and E^L.

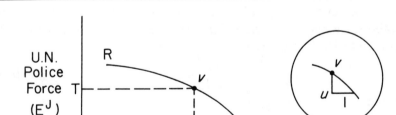

attained? The answer to this question depends upon the weights that are employed in the objective function. Recall from the discussion in connection with Equation (6-16) that one form of the objective function may be

$$\max \overline{w}^J E^J + \overline{w}^L E^L + \overline{w}^M E^M \qquad (8\text{-}5)$$

or, more conveniently

$$\max z \qquad (8\text{-}6)$$

$$\text{where } z = \overline{w}^J E^J + \overline{w}^L E^L + \overline{w}^M E^M$$

Suppose we are given the weights

$$\overline{w}^J = 2; \ \overline{w}^L = 1; \ \overline{w}^M = 0.5 \qquad (8\text{-}7)$$

Then if we are also given $\overline{E}^M$ so that $w^M \overline{E}^M = 0.5 \, \overline{E}^M$ is a constant k, we want to maximize

$$z = \overline{w}^J E^J + \overline{w}^L E^L + \overline{w}^M E^M = 2E^J + E^L + k \qquad (8\text{-}8)$$

Since k is a constant this is equivalent to

$$\max \hat{z} = 2E^J + E^L \qquad (8\text{-}9)$$

subject of course to

$$r_h^J E^J + r_h^L E^L \leq g_h - \overline{e}_h^M \qquad (8\text{-}10)$$

To show graphically how the solution to this maximization problem can be identified, we construct in Figure 8-2 the line for which $\hat{z} = 200$. This line is the locus of all *combinations* of achievements on the two objectives E^J and E^L for which the value of $\hat{z}$ is 200. For example, the combination given by point D yields a value of 200 for $\hat{z}$ (since there $E^J = 100$ and $E^L = 0$); so does point F (since $E^J = 0$ and $E^L = 200$); and so also does every point on the straight line connecting D and F. Similarly, we can construct lines that are the locus of all points representing combinations of achievements on the two objectives, E^J and E^L, which yield other prespecified values for $\hat{z}$. We have plotted the lines, which we designate *isovalue* lines, for the values 400, 600, and 800 in Figure 8-2. Clearly, the point of tangency, namely v, of one of these isovalue lines with the efficiency frontier RR' represents the combination of objective achievements that is both feasible and optimal. That is, it yields the maximum possible value of $\hat{z}$ and thus

Figure 8-2. Identification of the Optimal Combination of Objectives E^J and E^L.

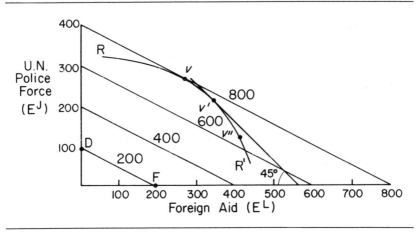

represents the best of the efficient combinations on RR'. However, v is the optimal combination only for the given level of achievement E^M. We can also identify the optimal combination, say $\bar{v}$, for any other prespecified value of E^M. Taking into account that $\bar{w}^M E^M = 0.5$ E^M for any prespecified value of E^M, it then follows that the best overall combination is that one of these optimal combinations which lies on the highest of all isovalue lines. It is the one that maximizes the overall objective function

$$z = \hat{z} + \bar{w}^M E^M = \bar{w}^J E^J + \bar{w}^L E^L + \bar{w}^M E^M \qquad (8\text{-}11)$$

subject to the resource constraint (8-3).

In essence, the above depicts in a simple manner the multiobjective programming approach when there is a single individual representing himself or some decisionmaking body, when the levels of achievement on the several objectives are the only decision variables, and when the objective function is a simple addition of the levels of these achievements when weights are applied to them. But what should these weights be? This is the key question, for clearly the weights determine the slope of the isovalue lines in Figure 8-2. In that figure, the slopes of those lines are -2, which is the negative of the ratio $\bar{w}^J / \bar{w}^L$. However, if we were to let $\bar{w}^J = \bar{w}^L$, then the slopes of the isovalue lines would cut off 45° angles with the two axes and have slopes of -1. Under those circumstances, v' would replace v as the optimal combination, that is v' would now lie on the highest isovalue line, given $\bar{E}^M$. This question of determining appropriate weights for an *individual decisionmaker* has been discussed extensively in the multiobjective literature; however, not much progress has been scored beyond what has already been discussed on pages 190–197. See, for example, Rietveld (1980).

We now ask: Why should the objective function be the simple addition of the levels of achievements when appropriate weights have been applied to them? In some cases of reality this is the way decisionmakers think, but there are many other cases of reality when such a simple linear type of objective function is not how decisionmakers see the world. This is particularly so where the level of achievement on one objective influences the level of any achievement on another objective. Put in another way, this is the problem of (1) defining an appropriate objective function, which is closely allied to the problem of defining an appropriate utility function for an individual—a problem which has plagued psychologists and economists for many decades—and (2) defining an appropriate social welfare function that has similarly challenged welfare economists, sociologists, and political scientists for so many decades. We have already alluded to these unresolved problems.

8.2.2 The Problem of Many Decisionmakers

The above framework applies to a single decisionmaker or to a political leader who must reach a decision after he has heard and considered the arguments put forth regarding the relative importance of the different objectives.[5] This is an extremely important area of study. In this book, however, we are primarily concerned with conflict management where more than one decisionmaker, political leader, community, region, nation, or interest group is actively involved. More specifically, in Equations (8-5) and (8-6) we are concerned not with how an individual internally decides on the weights for himself—a problem belonging primarily to psychology; or how a political leader or judge, after hearing the arguments for and against different proposals by different interest groups, determines on the basis of his experience and wisdom what these weights should be—a problem belonging primarily to political science and adjudication. Rather, we are concerned with the explicit determination of these weights through the use of various procedures wherein the different interest groups interact (engage in a process of give and take) either with or without the presence of other parties (analysts, mediators, arbitrators, scholars, etc.).

Programming with a Focus on Utilities. To help illustrate the role that multiobjective programming can play in such multigroup conflict management cases, we take up the conflict situation of the blocs of nations J, L, and M referred to on pages 248–249.

There, each bloc has in mind a single objective. The decisionmaking problem for them is to reach an acceptable policy on both the total of resources to be contributed by them and the allocation of these resources.[6] In such a case, we must introduce outcome (utility) functions. As on pages 200–205, we initially make the simplest possible assumption, namely that each interest group's utility function is related to one and only one objective, namely its primary objective. Accordingly, the utility functions for participants (blocs of nations) J, L, and M can be specified, respectively as

$$u^J = u^J(E^J); \; u^L = u^L(E^L); \text{ and } u^M = u^M(E^M) \qquad (8\text{-}12)$$

In such an oversimplified situation, the objective function to be maximized becomes

$$z = w^J u^J + w^L u^L + w^M u^M \qquad (8\text{-}13)$$

Now when we prespecify the level of achievement on the third objective, let us say it is $\overline{E}^M_3$, and so also $\overline{e}^M_h$ the amount of resources required to attain that level (defined by a production function or estimated by technicians), we can again identify the efficiency frontier (the tradeoff function) regarding the other two objectives such as in Figure 8–2. But now, the $\hat{z}$ function, namely

$$\hat{z} = w^J u^J + w^L u^L \qquad (8\text{-}14)$$

relates to weighted utilities of J and L. If we assume that these utilities are cardinal and comparable, to repeat a very strong assumption, we can once again construct isovalue lines for $\hat{z}$ and derive the overall best combination of objectives.[7]

To see this, we map the joint objective achievement space of Figure 8–2 onto the joint utility space depicted in Figure 8–3. Since $u^J = 1.5E^J$, the points corresponding to 100, 200, and 300 on the E^J axis of Figure 8–2 now correspond to points 150, 300, and 450 on the u^J axis

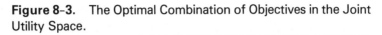

Figure 8-3.   The Optimal Combination of Objectives in the Joint Utility Space.

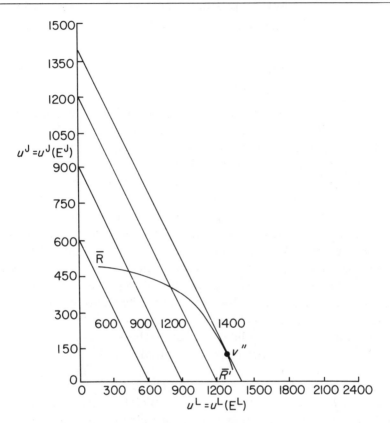

of Figure 8-3; while, since $u^L = 3E^L$, the points corresponding to 100, 200, and 300 on the E^L axis of Figure 8-2 now correspond to points 300, 600, and 900 on the u^L axis of Figure 8-3. Mapping the efficiency frontier (tradeoff function) RR′ in Figure 8-2 onto the joint utility space, we obtain an appropriately modified curve $\overline{R}\overline{R}'$,[8] which is now the joint utility frontier. Constructing constant isovalue lines 600, 900, and so forth, shows that the highest isovalue attainable in the joint utility space is 1400 and that the optimal combination of utility outcomes is that given by point v''. This point v'' in Figure 8-3 can then be mapped back onto Figure 8-2 to determine the corresponding optimal levels of objective achievements.

While in many important situations participants may choose to focus on their primary objective when stating their cardinal utilities and treat as negligible the levels of other objectives, in other important situations they may not. Then the utility functions in (8–12) must be replaced by

$$u^J = u^J(E_1, E_2, E_3); u^L = u^L(E_1, E_2, E_3); \text{ and} \qquad (8\text{–}15)$$
$$u^M = u^M(E_1, E_2, E_3)$$

The axes on Figure 8–3 should be relabelled accordingly, and participants J and L, if they are well informed and properly interviewed, could provide the corresponding utility numbers, because this is what we mean when we assume cardinal utility.

Having posed an important class of situations, where either $u^J = u^J(E^J)$ or the more complex function $u^J = u^J(E_1, E_2, E_3)$ are the appropriate utility functions of participants, we now return to the key problem of how to determine (either directly or indirectly) the weights w^J, w^L, and w^M. As noted on pages 190–197 there are several procedures that participants might employ to derive the required weights. One way of particular relevance in multiobjective situations involves recursive interaction, and this procedure is best developed when the focus is on objective achievements per se and only indirectly, if at all, on the more subjective utilities. Hence, in the next section we shall illustrate the approach with respect to objective achievements.

Recursive Interaction with a Focus on Objective Achievements

A First Example: Compromise over Weights. To illustrate how multiobjective programming can be used effectively when the focus is on objective achievement in a multiparticipant conflict situation, particularly when there is recursive interaction among participants, we first develop a hypothetical case; later we will refer to a more realistic case. Let there be assembled in some future year the leaders of three blocs of nations J, L, and M concerned with three sets of objectives (policies). Let the blocs be: (1) J, the developed regions; (2) L, the resource-poor, less-developed regions; and (3) M, the resource-rich, less-developed regions.[9] The objectives or policies initially proposed by blocs J, L, and M are, respectively: (1) *preservation of old economic order,* thereby maintaining the dominant power position of the J nations; (2) *establishment of the new economic order*, defined as reduction of the per capita income discrepancy between the developed and the resource-poor, less-developed regions by 50 percent by the year 2000, with developed regions financing the balance of payments deficits of the developing regions; and (3) *arms limitation scenario,* where (a) the United States and the U.S.S.R. reduce military expenditures to a level that would be two thirds of the level that would be reached in the year 2000, if they were to devote the same fraction of their incomes to military expenditures as they did in 1970, and (b) all other regions cut their military expenditures by 40 percent by the year 2000. Additionally, the developed nations are assumed to allocate 25 percent of the cuts in military expenditures to development aid.

After discussion it should become clear to the leaders of J, L, and M that these three policies (objectives) are inconsistent. A mediator may then point up the implicit weights that J, L, and M attach to these three programs, namely (1,0,0), (0,1,0), and (0,0,1), respectively (where the first number in any triplet times 100 represents the percentage of the first objective to be realized; the second times 100, the percentage of the second objective to be realized; and the third times 100, the percentage of the third objective to be realized). He suggests that these weights be revised in order to reach a consistent joint policy. He might suggest that they simply average their implicit weights, yielding the set of weights (0.33, 0.33, 0.33)—an equidistant concession for each participant. But suppose, as is likely to be the case, such is not acceptable. The resource-poor developing nations might be most unhappy with this arrangement since it would not come even close to their aspirations. The resource-rich developing nations would perhaps be the next most unhappy. The mediator then may suggest a leader-follower arrangement whereby there is a series of rounds wherein each of the participants takes a turn at being the leader. The task of the leader on any round is to propose what he considers to be a fair set of weights taking into account the other participants' needs and aspirations. The series of rounds is to continue until a mutually acceptable set of weights has been established. The mediator may, for example, suggest that L be the leader on the first round, M on the second, and J on the third, and that this order be preserved in subsequent sets of rounds.

On the first round, L makes a proposal regarding weights. Let it be (0.10, 0.80, 0.10). There follows discussion concerning the implications and fairness of adopting this set of weights (based on crude off-the-cuff estimates of what this would mean for growth rates, unemployment, balance of power, etc., in the several regions). We may imagine that clearly M and J are unhappy with these weights. On the second round, M proposes a different set of weights, namely (0.15, 0.20, 0.65), in which the arms limitation program is given the major weight. Again, extensive discussion follows with both L and J objecting strongly to M's proposal on the grounds that it gives too little weight to establishment of the new economic order and too much weight to arms limitation. It is then J's turn to make a proposal. Let it be (0.60, 0.20, 0.15). Again there occurs extensive discussion, perhaps followed on the fourth round with a proposal of (0.15, 0.70, 0.15) by L, and so the recursive interaction would proceed. It may be that the pressures for reaching an agreement are so great—pressures from the increasing number of crises, unstable regimes, and threats of war—that an agreement will be attained after a reasonable number of rounds of proposal and counter-proposal have been engaged in. On the other hand, the pressures may not be that intense and the number of rounds required to reach agreement might appear to be so large as to be impractical. At that point, the mediator may suggest that in order to speed up the deliberations they each make a proposal, but that there be a lower bound on any proposal regarding the weight to be attached to each one's objective. He suggests lower bounds of 0.25 for preservation of old economic order, 0.30 for arms limitation, and 0.35 for establishment of a new economic order. He also suggests that, after each has made a proposal within these lower bounds that they consider fair, they allow him to choose the fairest of the three proposals.

Participants might agree in principle to this last-offer arbitration type of suggestion, but disagree with the use of the suggested lower bounds. In particular, J may find his lower bound much too low, and M may find hers somewhat low. There may ensue much heated discussion from which emerges a set of lower bounds on weights on which there is agreement, namely an increase of 0.03 (from 0.25 to 0.28) for the lower bound on the weight of J's objective, an increase of 0.01 (from 0.30 to 0.31) for the lower bound on the weight of M's objective, and a consolation increase of 0.01 (from 0.35 to 0.36) for the lower bound on the weight of L's objective. Thus the set of acceptable lower bounds are assumed to be (0.28, 0.31, 0.36) whose total is 0.95, then leaving some leeway for variation in proposals. We then may imagine that the three do make proposals, namely (0.30, 0.32, 0.38) by J, (0.29, 0.34, 0.37) by M, and (0.29, 0.32, 0.39) by L, and the mediator chooses the proposal that he considers fairest. It could, for example, be J's.[10] The mediator then gives these weights to the analyst and instructs him to set up the appropriate objective function involving these weights and proceed to construct a programming model to maximize this function subject to resource limitations, production technologies, and so forth. The solution to this program then represents the compromise outcome expressed in terms of objective achievements.

Although it is unlikely, it may be that participants have well-defined utility functions in this conflict situation. For example, they might be:

$$u^J = k^J(E^J/E^{J*}) \tag{8-16}$$

$$u^L = k^L(E^L/E^{L*}) \tag{8-17}$$

$$u^M = k^M(E^M/E^{M*}) \tag{8-18}$$

where k^J, k^L, and k^M are constants with appropriate units to transform objective achievements into utilities, where E^{J*}, E^{L*}, and E^{M*} are the goals regarding objectives (policies),[11] and where (E^J/E^{J*}), (E^L/E^{L*}), and (E^M/E^{M*}) are the percentage achievements realized on these objectives. Once the program is run for a given set of compromise weights, we can derive estimates of (E^J/E^{J*}), (E^L/E^{L*}), (E^M/E^{M*}) directly from the program's output. By substituting these estimates into (8-16), (8-17) and (8-18) we can derive the corresponding utility outcomes to J, L, and M, respectively. We can then add these utilities (since we have assumed them to be cardinal and comparable) to derive the total utility that can be associated with the compromise solution.[12]

A More Realistic Example: Compromise over Constraints. Having presented some idea of recursive interaction, we now proceed to an illustration of the recursive interactive multiobjective programming approach in a more realistic situation.[13] Let us assume that when the mediator assembled the participants J, L, and M at the start he asked them what set of techniques they would find acceptable in measuring the impacts of their different objectives (policies) upon each region. He tells them that his analyst suggests a technique combining a world input-output model (of the Leontief type) and a multiregional econometric model (of the LINK type)[14] somewhat modified by a linear programming model (of the Novosibirsk type).[15] He asks his analyst to explain why, giving the strengths and weaknesses of each technique. However, given the participants' limited knowledge of the more recent developments in econometrics and linear programming and their skepticism of economic models in general, let them find acceptable only the relatively simple and straightforward world input-output model. Accordingly, the mediator asks the team of input-output experts associated with Leontief at the United Nations to estimate the impacts of each of the participants' different objectives (policies) for year 1990.

The input-output experts run three different programs.[16] One is consistent with the preservation of the old economic order, that is to maximize u^J, the utility (welfare) of the developed regions as they perceive their utility (welfare), subject to constraints incorporating best estimates of available world resources and technology under the scenario. A second is consistent with the establishment of the new economic order, that is to maximize u^L subject to best estimates of resource and technology constraints. A third is consistent with the arms limitation scenario, that is to maximize u^M, again subject to estimated resources and technology.[17]

The input-output experts present their findings on per capita income in tabular and/or graphic form. See Figure 8–4 for a realistic set of findings. The participants observe that per capita income of the resource-poor regions would increase from approximately $185 in 1970 to $235 by 1990 were the old economic order preserved, to $260 by 1990 under the arms limitation scenario, and almost double by 1990 under the new economic order. Over the same period (1970 to 1990) the per capita income of the resource-rich, less-developed regions increases by three to four times, regardless of which scenario is adopted (or objective achieved). For the developed regions, per capita income increases most under the arms limitations scenario and is about $200 to $300 greater under the old economic order than under the new. Economic factors, however, are not the only elements affecting preferences and perceived utility or welfare. Clearly the developed regions want to maintain their dominant power base, and the slight increase in per capita income achievable under an arms limitation scenario in no way compensates for the loss of power that would be incurred were an arms limitation objective to replace the objective of preserving the old economic order. On the other hand, under each scenario the resource-rich, less-developed regions achieve tremendous increases in per capita income—some would say exacerbating the problems of these regions, who are already experiencing growth too large to maintain internal political stability. They themselves strongly prefer the arms limitation scenario because it somewhat alleviates their fears of takeover by one or more of the Big Powers.

Figure 8-4. Projected Economic Development of the Developed Regions of the World, the Resource-Poor, Less-Developed Regions and the Resource-Rich, Less-Developed Regions to the Year 2000.[a]

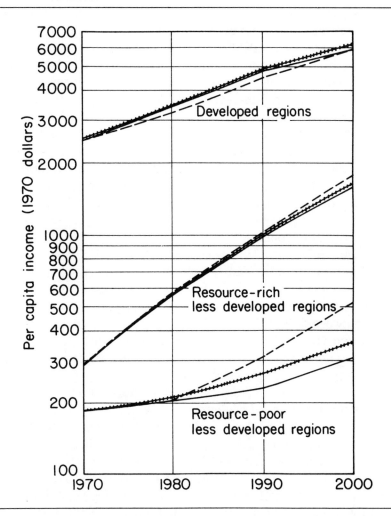

[a]Under the old-economic-order scenario (solid black lines), the new-economic-order scenario (broken black lines), and the arms-limitation scenario (hatched lines). For the resource-poor less developed regions the levels of per capita income and consumption (not shown) grow much faster under the arms-limitations scenario than under the old-economic-order scenario, but not so fast as under new-economic-order scenario, where income targets are prespecified.

Source: Leontief (1980:231).

The mediator lets the participants study the graphs and discuss their various interpretations of the significance of the per capita income projections (given the shaky quality of the data, the questionable relevance of the world regional input-output model, and other shortcomings of the model output). Then recognizing that they will never reach any agreement on weights that might be applied to these three objectives (policies), the mediator makes a suggestion. He suggests that since the adoption of one scenario rather than another makes a major difference in terms of the impact on per capita income of the resource-poor, less-developed regions, it seems fair and reasonable to modify the program designed to preserve the old economic order so that by the year 2000 the income gap between the developed and the resource-poor would be reduced by at least 25 percent—a lower bound constraint. He concomitantly suggests that after the impacts on the three blocs of this constrained program are obtained, a further modification be considered to meet the desires of the resource-rich, less-developed regions, and so on. Accordingly, the program to preserve the old economic order is run subject to the above lower bound constraint. The outcome for each participant is examined carefully, and there is again much discussion over what the data mean, and how valid the estimates are. It is clear from Figure 8–4 that while the per capita income of the developed regions might decrease between $50 to $100 under this modified scenario, the projected change in per capita income of the resource-rich, less-developed regions would not be perceived as significantly different from that projected under the original scenario (particularly so given the great uncertainty about the validity of the estimates). In any case, under the rules suggested by the mediator, and agreed on by participants, it is the resource-rich, less-developed regions' turn to propose a further modification of the program just run. After much discussion and give-and-take, it is agreed to examine the resulting estimates of the program under an additional lower bound constraint requiring the achievement of one half of the specific targets lying behind the arms limitation scenario. Again the projected impacts of this revised scenario are derived and presented to the participants for evaluation. After much interaction, the developed regions are given an opportunity to suggest certain modifications of the two lower bound constraints or to suggest a third constraint (either a lower or upper bound) that would yield them what they perceive to be a fairer outcome. And so the discussion—and programming operations—continue through a number of rounds. Hopefully, the suggested changes converge to a program (or scenario) with an objective function, a set of constraints, and a set of outcomes that they each find acceptable.[18,19] If so, the output of the program constitutes the compromise solution.

Should it be that the participants have cardinal utility functions that are known (which is unlikely), then we could calculate the utility each participant derives under each scenario being considered.[20] Further, if these cardinal utilities are comparable, as we have been assuming in this chapter, then we can add their utilities to obtain the total utility resulting from the compromise solution.[21]

However, perhaps more important is the fact that the compromise solution is independent of whether or not participants have comparable cardinal utility. All that is required to reach such a solution is the ability of participants to order their own preferences (i.e., ordinal utility) and to come to know the ordering of other participants' preferences through the interaction process.

In sum, multiobjective programming, with its many simplifying assumptions, can nonetheless provide a useful framework for participants and the mediator in their discussions. It does, however, require much data, systematically collected, processed and organized. Such information is often of dubious quality, if available at all. Moreover, its use involves a set of concepts, assumptions about behavior, identification of relevant variables and relationships, and so forth that have been developed by the culture of the highly industrialized societies. These concepts, behavioral assumptions, and relevant variables and relationships may indeed not be very relevant for other cultures in the world system. Hence, the enthusiasm for using this approach, which characterizes industrialized societies, must be severely tempered when other cultures are involved.

8.3 MULTICRITERIA (ATTRIBUTE) ANALYSIS

The cases examined in Section 8.2 all involved specifying an objective function (or the equivalent) to be either maximized or minimized, wherein conflicts over the parameters and variables in such a function are resolved by compromise procedures (whether simple, as in equidistant concessions, or complex, as in recursive interaction). That is, once the objective function and all the constraints of the program are specified, the conflict is over. In contrast, we now examine cases wherein the characteristics of the conflict situation are such that a traditional multiobjective program cannot be operated, even after all conflicts over weights and other magnitudes may have been resolved. This is the consequence of an inability to make comparable, except in a backhanded way, the various properties and/or attributes of outcomes of joint actions, or the criteria used in evaluating outcomes.

Again, we do not plan to cover systematically multicriteria analysis, but rather to examine conflict management procedures for several of the more important sets of cases. Some of the more technical approaches are discussed in the appendix to this chapter.

8.3.1 Situations of Many Options where Precise Values Can Be Assigned to Objective Achievements but Participants Can Only Rank Outcomes in Order of Preference

One of the most important sets of cases is where: (1) there are many options (a continuous joint action space); (2) achievements on objectives can be precisely valued (cardinally measured); and (3) participants can only order their preferences regarding combinations of achievements on objectives. If we are dealing with just two objectives, for example *growth in developing nations,* designated E_G, and *control of unrest, violence, and destabilizing elements,* designated E_c, and if we use the numbers of Table 3-2 on p. 26 wherein each of two participants, J and L, are concerned with both objectives, we may take the first number in any cell to record the achievement on E_G, the growth objective, and the second number the achievement on E_C, the control of unrest objective. (These numbers may result from programming or other analyses conducted by experts.) Then by transforming (smoothing) the joint action matrix represented by Table 3-2 into a continuous joint action space, we derive the box of Figure 8-5. Just as we associated unique outcomes regarding the two objectives with cells in the joint action matrix of Table 3-2, we now associate unique outcomes with every point in this box. Further, just as we constructed indifference curves (in effect, isoutility curves) for J and L in the joint action space of Figure 4-1 (derived by smoothing the finite joint action matrix of Table 3-13), we may now construct iso-achievement curves for E_G and E_C in Figure 8-5. For example, the

Table 8-5.   Selected Isoachievement Curves in a Continuous Joint Action Space.

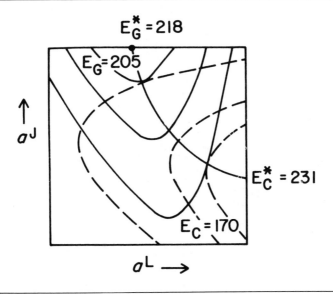

curve labelled $E_G = 205$ (which courses around point E_G^*) is the locus of joint actions that yield 205 units of achievement on objective E_G; and the dashed curve $E_C = 170$ (which courses around point E_C^*) is the locus of joint actions that yield 170 units of achievement on objective E_C. Thus, we obtain for objective E_G a set of isoachievement curves (non-dashed) that converge upon E_G^*, the highest level of achievement possible on objective E_G, and, similarly, a set of isoachievement curves (dashed) that converge upon E_C^*, the highest level of achievement possible on objective E_C.[22] In effect, Figure 8-5 represents the complete continuous analogue of the matrix in Table 3-2.

Because each point in Figure 8-5 specifies two cardinal values, one for each objective, we can proceed to map each point of the joint action space onto an objective achievement space depicted by Figure 8-6. Along the vertical axis we measure achievement on the control of violence objective E_C, and along the horizontal, achievement on the growth objective E_G. We then obtain the *joint objective achievement space E* (lightly shaded),[23] which is the set of all possible combinations of objectives that are achievable by the joint actions at the

Figure 8-6. The Joint Objective Achievement Space.

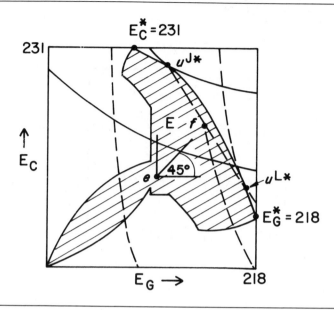

disposal of the participants. Note that the efficiency frontier in E is given by points on the arc $E_C^* E_G^*$. Every other point of the objective achievement space E not on this arc is dominated by some point on this arc, in the sense that the latter corresponds to a larger achievement on at least one objective and no smaller on any other objective when compared to the former. Given the joint objective achievement space E in a figure such as Figure 8-6, each participant may be asked to order her preferences for every combination of objectives represented by a point in E. We thus may derive, and map onto Figure 8-6, a set of indifference curves for each participant representing her ordinal utility function over objective achievements. (Recall from pages 69–71 that these indifference curves are approximations developed by an analyst based upon a finite number of comparisons made by each participant.) The solid curves represent J's indifference curves. We see that the point u^{J*} corresponds to J's most preferred combination of objective achievements; it is that combination on the efficiency frontier (in the joint objective achievement space) that lies on the highest of J's indifference curves. The dashed curves represent L's indifference curves. We see that the point u^{L*} corresponds to L's most preferred combination of objective achievements.

Note that in the case of Figure 8-6, the *joint utility frontier* is given by the arc $u^{J*}u^{L*}$. Any combination of objective achievements represented by a point within the feasible space E that is not on this arc is dominated by some point on that arc, in the sense that, when compared to the former point, the latter yields at least one participant a greater utility and no less utility to the other. In the situation depicted by Figure 8-6, the joint utility frontier is a subset (subarc) of the joint objective efficiency frontier $E_C^* E_G^*$.[24] In other situations, however, they may coincide.[25]

We are now in a position to suggest meaningful compromise procedures when a conflict exists in this type of situation. We know that J most prefers the combination of objectives and the corresponding joint action associated with point u^{J*}, and L most prefers that associated with u^{L*}. Immediately it is seen that this case parallels the situation in Figure 4-2 on p. 70 (or Figure 4-13) where the point u^{J*} takes the place of the point a^{J*} and the point u^{L*} takes the place of the point a^{L*}. There are, however, two differences. First, the part of the efficiency frontier that maps onto the joint utility frontier (which is defined by $u^{J*}u^{L*}$ in Figure 8-6) does not extend to the bounds of the figure as does the efficiency frontier $a^{*J}a^{*L}$ in the joint action space in Figure 4-2. (In Figure 4-2, each point on the efficiency frontier maps on to the relevant joint utility frontier.) Second, the joint action space in Figure 4-2 (or 4-8, 4-11, or 4-13) was unrestricted; it was the entire box. Here the joint objective achievement space is restricted.

In general, where the joint objective achievement space replaces the joint action space, all the utility-focused and rule-of-thumb techniques considered applicable in Chapter 4 are applicable here with minor modifications. With modifications, these techniques become:

1. the unsophisticated equidistant improvement in the joint objective achievement space. For example, if e in Figure 8-6 is the current standpoint, then there could be equidistant improvement along the 45° line from e to the efficiency frontier, a procedure that may not be acceptable were participants to try to compare units of objective achievement;

2. the selection of the median combination of objective achievements among those defined by the joint utility frontier ($u^{J*}u^{L*}$ in Figure 8-6);

3. concession along the joint utility frontier principle in the objective achievement space;

4. split-the-difference (and weighted-average) principle in the joint objective achievement space.[26] For example, the use of a one-step, split-the-difference principle would yield point f in Figure 8-6;

5. incremax (decremax) procedures in the joint objective achievement space—modified to avoid consideration of points not in the feasible joint objective achievement space;[27]

6. alternating leader-follower principle—modified to avoid consideration of points not in the feasible joint objective achievement space;[28] and

7. GRIT, minimum information incremax, last-offer arbitration, and other procedures when applicable in the joint objective achievement space.

In addition, when none of these techniques or others discussed in Chapter 4 are acceptable, a number of objective-focused techniques may be found applicable. For example:

1. max total of weighted objective achievements
2. max total of weighted improvements in objective achievements
3. min total of weighted concessions in objective achievements
4. max equal improvements in weighted objective achievements
5. min equal concessions in weighted objective achievements

8.3.2 Situations of Many Options where Relative Values Only Can be Assigned to Objective Achievements and Participants Can Only Rank Outcomes in Order of Preference

The second set of cases that are of importance also pertain to situations that involve: (1) continuous joint action spaces and (2) participants who can only order their preferences over combinations of objectives. Here, however, the information on objective achievements is not as complete as in the previous set. In this set, objective achievements can only be measured in relative terms since all that experts are able to say regarding any given objective is that the achievement of one joint action on that objective is, for example, twice that of another joint action. For instance, when reference is made to regions where illiteracy rates range from 55 percent to 90 percent, one plan may be able to reduce the illiteracy rate of a given region by 10 percent and another by only 5 percent. The former plan is twice as effective as the latter. Or, when we are concerned with disarmament, one joint action (scheme) may be estimated by experts to lead to twice as much security against attack as another joint action (scheme) when there is no precise definition of "full," "zero," or any other level of security.

In such situations, when we have smoothed a finite joint action matrix (as Table 5-3 on p. 136), into a continuous action space (such as the box of Figure 8-5), we are not able to construct on the latter a set of isoachievement curves regarding each objective.[29] However, we can identify the joint action that yields the maximum achievement on any objective and set that equal to 100 percent. Then we can construct isopercent achievement curves for each objective. For example, we can connect with a curve all those joint actions that yield 90 percent of that maximum achievement and designate it the 90 percent curve. And so forth. Thus, on Figure 8-7, we construct the 90 percent, 75 percent, and other percent achievement curves for E_G, and the 85 percent, 65 percent, and other percent achievement curves for E_C.

Figure 8-7. Selected Isopercent Achievement Curves in a Continuous Joint Action Space.

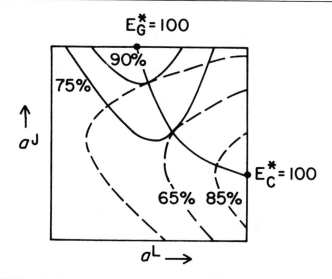

Because each point in Figure 8–7 represents two percentage values, one for each objective, we can proceed to map each point of the joint action space onto a figure depicting the *joint "percentage objective achievement" space.* Along the vertical axis we would measure percentage achievement on the control of violence objective E_C, and along the horizontal, percentage achievement on the growth objective E_G. Such a figure is not constructed but would resemble Figure 8–6, where E_C^* would correspond to 100 percent achievement on objective E_C, and E_G^* would correspond to 100 percent on objective E_G, and an efficiency frontier would connect these two points. On such a figure we could also construct ordinal indifference curves for each participant, identify each participant's most preferred combination of objectives (the u^{L^*} and u^{J^*} points for L and J, respectively), and the associated joint utility frontier. Then in general all the utility-focused and rule-of-thumb techniques just indicated as applicable in the joint objective achievement space are also applicable for the joint "percentage objective achievement" space. When the term "objective achievement" appears in their statement, it needs to be replaced by the term "percentage objective achievement." However, when none of these techniques are acceptable to participants, a number of percentage objective-achievement-based techniques may be found applicable. For example:

1. max total of percent improvements in objective achievements after weighting
2. min total of percent concessions in objective achievements after weighting
3. max equal percent improvements in objective achievements after weighting
4. min equal percent concessions in objective achievements after weighting[30]

8.3.3 Situations with a Small Number of Options where Achievements on Objectives Can Only be Ranked and where Participants Can Only Rank Outcomes in Order of Preference

A third set of cases relate to situations where participants can state only ordinal utilities and where the most information that is available regarding objectives is also information of an ordinal character—that is, information that can be ranked and only ranked. Since ordinal information on objective achievement is all that can be provided, such cases are realistic only when a finite number of joint actions are considered.[31] Note that these cases are very important in reality and are often associated with multicriteria analysis. Consider for example the following situation. There are five plans for redevelopment of a major metropolitan region. Associated with the choice of a plan are as many criteria as are considered relevant by the decisionmakers. With regard to each objective or criterion, an expert or his equivalent is brought in and asked to *rank* each plan in terms of its achievement on that objective or criteria. This information is then provided in an appropriate table. For example, if there are two relevant criteria, then the five plans α, β, γ, δ, and ϵ and the existing situation Z may be evaluated as indicated in Table 8-1. Each row of this table refers to a plan or the existing situation; each of the first two columns refers to a criteria. Going down either of these columns indicates the rankings of the plans and the existing situation with regard to the criterion at the head of the column.

Next, the leader of each interest group is asked, because he cannot do any better, to state his ordinal preferences with regard to each plan (and the existing situation Z) given the ranks of each plan on each criterion. Recording these ordinal utilities in Columns 3 and 4 of these tables as rankings (which is permissible for ordinal utilities) it is seen that interest group J most prefers plan β and interest group L most prefers plan δ; hence, conflict exists. (For the moment ignore Columns 5 and 6 of Table 8-1.)

The conflict in the situation depicted by Table 8-1 is comparable to conflict situations with finite joint action spaces and ordinal utilities discussed in Chapter 3. Thus the available compromise procedures include equal rank improvements or concessions, either in the joint objective achievement space or in utility outcomes.

For example, consider the ordinal rankings of J and L in Columns 3 and 4, respectively, of Table 8-1. If Z represents the existing situation, the interest groups may adopt an equal rank improvement procedure and proceed from the existing situation Z to the situation that would result from joint action β, which involves going up three steps for each participant in their ordinal rankings. Note however, that this involves moving to J's most preferred joint action and L's second most preferred. This may not be acceptable to L. On the other hand,

Table 8-1. The Ranking of Plans and the Existing Situation on Two Criteria.

	Criteria		Interest Group J's Ordinal Utility	Interest Group L's Ordinal Utility	Values of Plans over Existing Situation for J	Values of Plans over Existing Situation for L
	Growth	Control of Unrest				
	(1)	(2)	(3)	(4)	(5)	(6)
Plan α	6	6	6	6	$ − 1000	$ − 800
Plan β	3	1	1	2	+ 1700	+ 1600
Plan γ	2	3	3	3	+ 700	+ 900
Plan δ	1	2	2	1	+ 1200	+ 2000
Plan ε	4	5	5	4	− 500	+ 400
Existing Situation Z	5	4	4	5	0	0

adoption of an equal rank concessions procedure with each interest group conceding two steps in their ordinal rankings from their most preferred situation yields joint action γ. Because γ is the third most preferred joint action for each participant, it may be considered as being much more "fair," a property whose desirability outweighs its inefficiency (since each is worse off in terms of their utility rankings by agreeing to γ rather than β).

Where there are more than two criteria—say five—for the several plans including the existing situation, we may once again construct a table like Table 8-1. See Table 8-2, where each row refers to a plan or the existing situation and where each of the first five columns refers to the rankings of each plan on a given criteria. Each of the five plans and existing situations are ranked by experts or the like on each of the five criteria, yielding an outcome matrix with six rows and five columns. Because five or more criteria make the choice problem more complex, for these cases we present three additional columns for use by participants in reaching their ordinal utilities. One is on the simple sum of ranks across criteria (Column 6). The other two (Columns 7 and 8) are the order of plans after each participant, J and L, has weighted the criteria and then summed the weighted ranks; their derivation will be discussed below. We also indicate in Columns 9 and 10 the ordinal utility ranking of each plan by J and L, respectively, assuming they are able to state such rankings. Again, J and L may consider equal rank concession or improvement procedures, using the orderings recorded in Columns 9 and 10. On the other hand, simple-minded participants may not be able to state ordinal utilities in a complex situation such as that of Table 8-2. Conceivably, before knowing the experts' rankings of the five plans and existing situation on each criteria, they may have agreed to adopt the plan whose sum of ranks over all criteria is least, in essence establishing a harmony game with plan δ as a solution. (See Column 6.) Hence, a min total of ranks principle is used as a rule of thumb.[32]

On the other hand, participants may be alert enough to recognize that the several criteria differ in their importance or significance to them. While they may not be able to specify a finely tuned set of weights for the criteria, they may be able to apply a few simple weights—for example, a weight of one to the ranks of the more important criteria and a weight of two to the ranks of the less important criteria.[33] (Bear in mind that when the best plan on a criteria is given a rank of 1, the second best a rank of 2, and the third best a

Table 8-2. The Ranking of Plans and the Existing Situation on Five Criteria.

		Criteria				Sum of Ranks	Order of Sum of Weighted Ranks		Ordinal Utility Ranking of J	Ordinal Utility Ranking of L
	#1	#2	#3	#4	#5					
	(1)	(2)	(3)	(4)	(5)	(6)	(7)	(8)	(9)	(10)
α	6	6	3	3	5	23	5	5	6	6
β	5	1	6	6	4	22	6	6	5	3
Plans γ	2	3	1	4	1	11	2	1	2	1
δ	1	2	4	1	2	10	1	2	1	2
ε	4	5	2	5	3	19	3	3	3	4
Existing Situation Z	3	4	5	2	6	20	4	4	4	5
Weights w^J	1	1	1	2	2					
w^L	2	1	2	1	1					

rank of 3, and so forth, the weight of "2" for the rank of any criteria is equivalent to specifying that that criteria is half as important as a criteria whose rank is given a weight of "1.")[34] When, as in Table 8–2, J assigns weights of 1,1,1,2, and 2, respectively, to the five criteria listed at the head of Columns 1 through 5 and sums the weighted ranks, he can order these sums over all plans and the existing situation. His ordering is indicated in Column 7.[35] Plan δ has the lowest sum of weighted ranks, and plan β has the highest. When L assigns weights of 2,1,2,1, and 1 to the same five criteria and sums the weighted ranks for each plan and the existing situation, she obtains an ordering of these sums as indicated in Column 8. For her, plan γ has the lowest sum of weighted ranks, and plan β has the highest. Clearly, with J most preferring plan δ and L most preferring plan γ, a conflict situation exists. The mediator may suggest to the participants the use of a number of compromise procedures. Some of these procedures have been discussed for participants who are able to specify ordinal utilities over plans in less complicated situations such as that depicted in Table 8–1. Others are also possible. For example, they may consider equi-rank improvement from the existing situation, leading to the adoption of plan ε; or equi-rank concession from their most preferred plan, which again would lead to the adoption of plan ε. On the other hand, they may strongly desire to use the principle of max total rank improvement or min total rank concession—in which case a tie results with a new conflict as to whether plan γ or δ should be adopted.

8.3.4 Situations with a Small Number of Options and Continuous Side Payments

The conflict resulting from a tie situation, such as the one just noted as well as many others, leads to a fourth set of significant cases. This set can be characterized as involving (1) a finite joint action space with continuous side payments, (2) at least ordinally measured objective achievements, and (3) at least ordinal utilities. The most important of these cases are those where side payments can be made in money or the equivalent to induce an otherwise reluctant participant to accept a compromise plan or proposal. Consider again the simple situation of Table 8–1. Now let us take the existing situation as a reference state of affairs and list in each cell of Column 5 the dollar value to J of going to plan k (k = α, β, γ, δ, ε) from existing situation Z. (These dollar values may be positive or negative.)[36] Do likewise for participant L in Column 6.

Suppose participants are simple-minded and straightforward and have no inclination to think of strategy and bluffing, so that the money values specified in Columns 5 and 6 do represent the true value to the participants of any movement from the existing situation. Accordingly, J might propose that plan β (his most preferred) be put into effect, while L might propose that plan δ (her most preferred) be adopted. For J, plan β has a worth of $500 more than plan δ. For L, plan δ has a worth of $400 more than plan β. Hence plan β might be considered more appropriate for adoption since the difference between β and δ is more significant in dollar terms for J than for L—that is, J is willing to pay $500 to go from his rank of 2 to 1 (i.e., from δ to β), whereas L is only willing to pay $400 to go from her rank of 2 to 1 (from β to δ). Plan β might then be adopted with a fifty-fifty split on the $500 payment that J is willing to make in order to have plan β rather than δ. If this rule of thumb is adopted, J keeps one half of the $500 for himself and makes a side payment of $250 to L.

As already indicated, for more complicated situations, as in Table 8-2, where five criteria are involved, participants may be unable to specify ordinal utilities such as those recorded in Columns 9 and 10 of that table. Were this to be the case, simple-minded as well as more sophisticated participants can be asked to state the worth (in dollar value) of each plan over and above the existing situation. If they were able to do so, we would obtain two additional columns with dollar figures in them just as we obtained Columns 5 and 6 in Table 8-1.[37] Then, participants may adopt some kind of procedure involving side payments to induce one or more reluctant participants to accept a compromise plan or proposal. For example, as mentioned on page 275, where a max total of rank improvements procedure is adopted in the situation depicted in Table 8-2, a tie arises since both plan δ and γ have the same total. J most prefers plan δ whereas L most prefers plan γ. Accordingly, whoever is willing to make the greater money payment in order to have his most preferred rather than his second most preferred plan adopted makes a side payment to the other of, say, half the money payment he (the first participant) is willing to make.

The most general case arises, however, when max the total of rank improvements yields a unique plan, but where each of the participants for whom this unique plan does not represent her most preferred must be given a side payment in order to make that unique plan acceptable to her—the side payment being made by the participant who finds the plan optimal. Once again, a procedure involving an equal or some other prespecified split considered fair may be used to determine the amount(s) of the side payment(s). This point holds not only for a max total of rank improvements but also for min total of ranks or min total of rank concessions procedure. However, it should be fully recognized that the difficulties are major in reaching a compromise solution on how much side payment one (or more) participants who most prefer the joint action that maximizes (or minimizes) a total should make to each participant who most prefers another joint action. The analysis in the literature dealing with this problem of side payments is most inadequate. The problem of appropriate side payments is still more complex for the many situations where participants are disposed to bluffing. For example, J may realize that if he misrepresents the value of a plan, say plan β in Table 8-1, by stating that its worth over the existing situation is not $1700 but only $1620, he would come out better off since a fifty-fifty split would require that he make a side payment of only $210 to L. But also, L may not be indisposed to bluffing and J may be aware of this, which then will affect the bluffing strategy adopted by J. As a consequence, all kinds of complicated situations involving bluff, counter-bluff, and other strategic behavior can arise for which there are no compromise procedures that may be considered to be generally applicable.

There is, however, one principle (already discussed) which, when fully understood by participants, can in certain situations act to eliminate bluffing and misrepresentation. This is the Clarke-Vickrey demand-revealing (no bluffing) method. (See pages 184–188 and 239–240.) The usefulness of this principle can be clearly seen by referring to the dollar figures in Columns 5 and 6 of Table 8-1. There we may suppose that L represents either the single participant L or a set of participants other than J. The dollar values in L's column represent the values to L of the different plans compared to the existing situation Z. Clearly, plan δ having a $2000 excess value is most preferred by L (or the set of participants other than J). Clearly, also, from Column 5, J prefers plan β to plan δ. But, according to the Clarke-Vickrey method, J cannot have β unless he pays a tax of $400 or, in our thinking, a money payment to a good cause of at least $400. (Note that $400 would be the loss to L (or the set of participants other than J) were plan β to be adopted.) A shift from δ to β, however, provides an increase of more than $400 worth to J, and so plan β might be proposed as the one to be adopted; it does represent that plan which has the maximum total value over all participants compared to the existing situation. Note that plan β yields a total of $3300 excess value to all participants, while plan δ yields only $3200.[38]

In brief, while the Clarke-Vickrey method has potential use for certain situations, in general there are no practical procedures for handling the side payments problem.

8.4 CONCLUDING REMARKS

Focusing on a single decisionmaker, we presented in this chapter the straightforward application of optimization in a multiobjective programming framework when weights and constraints were specified. The analysis was then extended to the problem of many decisionmakers, each with different objectives. Recognizing that a direct focus on utilities is generally not feasible with many participants, the objective function was reformulated to focus on objective achievements and the recursive interaction approach suggested as a means by which to reach compromise over weights, constraints, or both.

A traditional programming approach, however, cannot be used where achievements on different objectives cannot be made comparable, even when achievements on each objective can be measured in a precise or relative way. Then multicriteria analysis must be pursued. Using the concept of a joint objective achievement space we were able to extend multicriteria analysis employing many of the conflict management procedures developed in previous chapters.

For example, the "max total of weighted utility" principle becomes "max total of weighted objective achievements," and the "max total of percent improvements in utility" principle becomes "max total of percent improvements in objective achievements" after weighting.

When achievements on each objective can only be ranked, we illustrate how many of the ranked-based procedures in previous chapters can be extended to cover these cases. For example, the principle of "max equi-rank improvement in utility outcomes" becomes "max equi-rank improvement in objective achievements" and so on.

This chapter completes our treatment of quantitative-type conflict management procedures per se. It would now seem useful to develop some way of evaluating the relative desirability of different procedures for any given conflict situation. To this we turn in the next chapter.

APPENDIX TO CHAPTER 8
SOME TECHNICAL PROCEDURES APPLICABLE TO MULTICRITERIA SITUATIONS

8A.1 The Concordance-Discordance Procedure[39]

Concordance-discordance analysis can conceivably be used in a multiparticipant situation to select an optimum plan (or joint action) from a series of conflicting alternatives that have been proposed. The fundamental feature of the method is that it attempts first to eliminate a subset of less desirable plans (or joint actions) from the complete set of alternatives, after which a complementary analysis is used to select the best plan from this reduced set. To the authors' knowledge (1980) this analysis has been used excusively in situations where there is a single decisionmaker confronting conflicting criteria for evaluating plans. We consider here its possible extension to a utility-focused situation where there are U participants ($J = A, \ldots, U$) and consideration of n alternative plans ($j = 1, \ldots, n$).

Step 1. Construction of an Outcome Matrix.   The first step is to construct an *outcome* or *utility matrix U* in which the utility outcomes to all participants from each alternative plan are specified. A typical element u_j^J of *U* represents the utility outcome to participant J from plan j. (See Table 8A-1.)

Step 2. Specification of a Set of Weights.   The second step is to specify a *set of weights* to be applied to the utility outcomes of the different participants:

$$w = (w^A, \ldots, w^U)$$

A typical element w^J represents the relative weight attached to participant J, ($J = A, \ldots, U$) and may reflect his importance, power, need, or supporting population. These weights may be derived using one of the procedures listed in Table 12–28.

Table 8A-1. A Joint Utility/Outcome Matrix U.

Participants

| | | A | $\ldots,$ | J $\ldots,$ | | U |

$$
\text{Plans}
\begin{array}{c}
1 \\ \\ \\ \\ j \\ \\ \\ \\ n
\end{array}
\left[
\begin{array}{ccccccc}
u_1^A & . & . & . u_1^J & . & . & . u_1^U \\
. & & & . & & & . \\
. & & & . & & & . \\
u_j^A & . & . & . u_j^J & . & . & . u_j^U \\
. & & & . & & & . \\
. & & & . & & & . \\
u_n^A & . & . & . u_n^J & . & . & . u_n^U
\end{array}
\right]
$$

Step 3. Identification of Concordance Set. The third step is to identify a *concordance set* $C_{jj'}$ of participants for each pair j,j' of plans (j,j' $= 1, \ldots,$ n):

$$C_{jj'} = \{J \mid u_j^J \geq u_{j'}^J\}$$

That is, the concordance set comprises the subset of all participants for whom a certain plan j is not less preferred by them to a compromise plan j'. Since there are n(n − 1) pairs of plans to be considered, this step identifies n(n − 1) such concordance sets.

Step 4. Calculation of Concordance Index. The fourth step is to calculate a *concordance index* for each pair of plans. The concordance index $c_{jj'}$ between plans j and j' is equal to the sum of the weights associated with those participants placed in the concordance set $C_{jj'}$, divided by the sum of all participants' weights:

$$c_{jj'} = \sum_{J \epsilon C_{jj'}} w^J \Big/ \sum_{J=A}^{U} w^J$$

This index gives a measure of the relative importance, power, needs, and so forth of the participants for whom plan j (weakly) dominates plan j'. The values of the index range between 0 and 1. If $c_{jj'} = 1$, there exists a complete (weak) dominance of plan j relative to plan j' — that is, no participant (strongly) prefers plan j' to j. On the other hand, if $c_{jj'} = 0$, there exists a complete (strong) dominance of plan j' relative to plan j—that is, all participants (strongly) prefer plan j' to j.

Step 5. Construction of Concordance Matrix. The fifth step is to construct a *concordance matrix C* by recording the succcessive values of the concordance indices $c_{jj'}$ (j,j' = 1, . . . , n; j ≠ j') in a matrix of order of n by n. See Table 8A-2.[40]

Step 6. Identification of Discordance Set. The sixth step is to identify a *discordance set $D_{jj'}$* of participants for each pair j,j' of plans (j,j' = 1, . . . , n):

$$D_{jj'} = \{J | u_j^J < u_{j'}^J\}$$

That is, the discordance set comprises the subset of all participants for whom a certain plan j is less preferred by them to a competing plan j'. Clearly, this step identifies n(n − 1) such discordance sets.

Step 7. Calculation of Discordance Index. While the calculation of the concordance index does not make comparisons (in either percent or absolute terms) of the outcomes of different plans, a second index, called a *discordance index,* does. To calculate the latter for a pair of plans j,j', each participant J in the discordance set $D_{jj'}$ is considered separately. Her absolute difference, namely $|u_j^J - u_{j'}^J|$, in utility outcomes from the two plans j and j', is divided by the largest absolute

Table 8A-2. A Concordance Matrix C.

$$C = \begin{bmatrix} - & c_{12} & c_{13} \cdots & c_{1n} \\ c_{21} & - & c_{23} \cdots & c_{2n} \\ c_{31} & c_{32} & - \cdots & c_{3n} \\ \cdot & \cdot & \cdot & \cdot \\ \cdot & \cdot & \cdot & \cdot \\ c_{n1} & c_{n2} & c_{n3} \cdots & - \end{bmatrix}$$

difference, namely, q^{Jmax}, in utility outcomes that she would realize from any possible pair of plans. That is, for each J, we consider the ratio

$$\frac{|u^J_j - u^J_{j'}|}{q^{Jmax}} \quad \text{where} \quad q^{Jmax} = \max_{j,j'} |u^J_j - u^J_{j'}| \quad j,j'=1,\ldots,n$$

and define the level of the discordance index $d_{jj'}$ as the maximum of these ratios over all participants J in the discordance set, namely

$$d_{jj'} = \max_{J \epsilon D_{jj'}} \frac{|u^J_j - u^J_{j'}|}{q^{Jmax}}$$

The values of $d_{jj'}$ range between 0 and 1; the lower the value, the less acceptable the outcomes of plan j compared to those of plan j', at least as far as the most disadvantaged participant in the discordance set is concerned.

Step 8. Construction of Discordance Matrix.   The eighth step is to construct a *discordance matrix D* by recording the successive values of the discordance indices $d_{jj'}(j,j' = 1, \ldots, n)$ in a matrix of order n by n. See Table 8A–3.[41]

Step 9. Evaluation of Alternative Plans.   The final step uses the information contained in the concordance and discordance matrices to evaluate the alternative plans. An ideal plan would be one yielding a concordance index with respect to all other plans of approximately 1,

Table 8A-3.   A Discordance Matrix *D*.

$$D = \begin{bmatrix} - & d_{12} & d_{13} \cdots & d_{1n} \\ d_{21} & - & d_{23} \cdots & d_{2n} \\ d_{31} & d_{32} & - \cdots & d_{3n} \\ \cdot & \cdot & \cdot & \cdot \\ \cdot & \cdot & \cdot & \cdot \\ d_{n1} & d_{n2} & d_{n3} \cdots & - \end{bmatrix}$$

and a discordance index with respect to all other plans of approximately 0. In a conflict situation, such an ideal plan rarely exists—if it did there would be little or no conflict. However, based on the hypothesis that a compromise plan (joint action) is more likely to be acceptable to participants the higher its concordance indices relative to alternative plans (joint actions) and the lower its discordance indices, a "second best" selection procedure is adopted. This procedure involves the specification of certain (critical) threshold values $\bar{c}$ and $\bar{d}$ for the concordance index and discordance index respectively, and the elimination of all plans (joint actions) that do not satisfy the conditions $c_{jj'} \geq \bar{c}$ and $d_{jj'} \leq \bar{d}$ for every possible j', (j' = 1, . . . , n; j' ≠ j).[42]

If it is reasonable to assume that plan j will be more acceptable than (i.e., dominate) plan j' if both (1) its concordance index $c_{jj'}$ exceeds the (overall) *average* concordance index and (2) its discordance index $d_{jj'}$ does not exceed the (overall) *average* discordance index, then the threshold levels c and d are defined, respectively, as

$$\bar{c} = \sum_{\substack{j=1 \\ j \neq j'}}^{n} \sum_{\substack{j'=1 \\ j' \neq j}}^{n} c_{jj'} / n(n-1)$$

and

$$\bar{d} = \sum_{\substack{j=1 \\ j \neq j'}}^{n} \sum_{\substack{j'=1 \\ j' \neq j}}^{n} d_{jj'} / n(n-1)$$

Clearly, other reasonable threshold values can be used instead of these averages.

Note that there is no guarantee that there is only one plan satisfying the two threshold conditions specified above. If this is the case, then complementary analysis is required to select from among these nondominated plans. One approach that has been suggested is to arbitrarily increase the threshold value $\bar{c}$ by some amount and lower the threshold value $\bar{d}$ by some second amount until only one nondominated plan remains.

Concluding Remarks.   Regardless of whether the utility-focused or an objective-focused variant is adopted, the flexibility in the setting of the initial threshold values ($\bar{c}$ and $\bar{d}$) and then in changing these values to arrive at the final nondominated plan (joint action) may be considered an attractive feature of the technique when it is used inter- actively with a single decisionmaker. However, in a multiparticipant situation this flexibility introduces another element of conflict, for one needs to attain agreement on which pair of initial threshold values will be used, and then, on each round of plan elimination, on which threshold values will be changed and by how much they will be changed. Such agreement may be difficult to attain, especially once the choice has been narrowed down to only a few plans and the final nondomi- nated plan is sensitive to the relative changes of the two threshold values.

Because of this arbitrariness, the concordance-discordance ap- proach cannot be generally advocated as a useful procedure. How- ever, when we recognize the numerous occasions on which partici- pants are unable to employ a compromise procedure because they are reluctant to make the necessary concessions from their optimal or desired outcomes (targets, etc.), and thus when a mediator may need to suggest a last-resort technique, it may well be that the concordance- discordance method has more appeal to participants than a simpler procedure like split-the-difference in the joint action space. This is because the concordance-discordance approach may turn out to be sufficiently complex for participants that they are unable to *predeter- mine outcomes* as they can with split-the-difference or other simple last-resort techniques.

8A.2 Minimize Discrepancy from Ideal (Using Rank Correlation Analysis)[43]

This approach, sometimes designated *discrepancy analysis*, may be employed as an alternative to procedures based on the total sum of ranks and differences among ranks. It focuses on the ideal plan—that is, the hypothetical plan yielding each participant J the ordinal utility outcome (or level of objective achievement) he would derive from his most preferred plan. It then uses a statistical correlation technique[44] to derive a measure of the degree of closeness between the jth plan and the ideal plan. When this measure has been calculated for each of the j plans separately, the plans can be ranked according to their degree of closeness to the ideal. The alternative that may be designated the most desirable is that one which is closest in terms of the measure used.

Since this technique is based on ordinal data only, it is unable to discriminate effectively among the several discrepancies between a given plan's outcomes and the ideal—a major shortcoming.

8A.3 Maximum Correspondence to Underlying Pattern of Outcomes[45]

This approach, sometimes designated *correspondence analysis,* involves a pattern-recognition method aimed at providing metric information on differences among subjects (e.g., alternative plans or joint actions) and their attributes (e.g., objective achievements, utility outcomes) such that the basic features in the information pattern are revealed. An outcome matrix O is constructed with the alternative plans along one dimension and the attribute values along the other, such that a typical element o_{ij} is the standardized value of attribute i in plan j. The relationships between the attributes and the alternative plans are then examined on the basis of a separate principal components analysis of the rows and then the columns of the outcome matrix. In other words, through the use of existing procedures, the two sets of data (plans and attributes) are analyzed in order to identify simultaneous correspondence between either the plans or attributes or both.[46] Once these relationships (correspondences) have been identified, the plan with the maximum correspondence to the derived pattern of clusters is identified and may be suggested as an acceptable compromise plan.

A drawback of this procedure is that the clusters derived are mainly based on the statistical pattern of the outcome matrix and less on the relative importance of the attributes (objective achievements, or utility outcomes). Further, many of the problems inherent in the use of principal components analysis arise here too. In particular, the derived clusters are not easy to interpret, nor is their meaning intuitively clear. Thus, the concept of maximum correspondence is, by and large, of statistical significance only.[47]

8A.4 Max Total of Ranks Weighted by Outcome "Importance"

This method, sometimes designated the *expected value* method, is similar to the max total of weighted ranks method first discussed on pages 273–275.[48] Using the example on these pages, the outcomes of all five alternative plans proposed by participants *and* the existing situation are ranked by outside experts on each objective (decision criteria) separately, being assigned the values of 1,2,3,4,5,6 in ascending rank order from the best to the worst. All objectives (decision criteria), which are five in number, are then ranked in order of importance and assigned a value of 1,2,3,4,5 in ascending rank order from the most to the least important. These latter ranks are treated as weights, and the expected value of a plan is then calculated as the weighted sum of ranks over all objectives. The optimal plan is that one which has the lowest expected value. (Note that when plans are ranked in descending order 6,5,4,3,2,1 from the best to the worst on a criteria, and when weights are also ranked in descending order 5,4,3,2,1 from best to worst, then the optimal plan is the one with the highest expected value.) The name *expected value* is misleading and results from considering the importance rankings (i.e. weights) as "semiprobabilities."

8A.5 Max Correspondence to Outcomes Weighted by Relative Importance

This approach, sometimes designated the *permutation method*,[49] is a highly technical extension of the *max total of ranks weighted by outcome "importance"* or *expected value* approach. Given information (in payoff matrix form) on the rankings of each plan (joint action) on a number of objectives, and information on the relative importance of objectives, this method uses correlation analysis to determine that permutation of weights and rankings of the alternatives which is most in accordance with such information. Its application to a *multiparticipant situation* as a possible last-resort technique can only be of significance to the highly sophisticated analyst.

8A.6 Frequency above Threshold Value (Using Weighted Ranks) Method

This method, sometimes designated the *frequency method,* places the criteria (objectives) in a number of importance categories. It uses these placements to "weight" the ranks recorded in Table 8-2—a questionable step from a scientific standpoint. In this way, a new table of "weighted" ranks is obtained and the frequency with which each plan exceeds some threshold value on these weighted ranks might be used in evaluating the several plans. See van Delft and Nijkamp (1977:58–60).

8A.7 Stochastic Methods

As indicated several times in the text, uncertainty is omnipresent, and hence the numbers in any payoff table (and even weights) must be considered to be at least partially affected by noise and other random factors. This then suggests that *stochastic methods* be employed that formally admit such influences, and thus recognize that any payoff element must be viewed as a probability distribution (i.e., a prospect)[50] over a set of relevant values. Frequently a mean or, more generally, an expected value may be used in place of that distribution, so that analysis can proceed as in the text. However, the notion of a 100 percent certain best compromise joint action (implicit in the discussion of the text) must then be replaced by the notion of the most probable "best" compromise joint action (i.e. the one most likely to be best). While for engineering-type problems that can be precisely defined and for which parameters of frequency distributions are known this more advanced approach is desirable, in the *multiparticipant situations* we wish to confront in this book, such a sophisticated approach is of little practical use.

In one development of this approach where the preference structures of participants permit only ordinal values, these values are approximated by cardinal values selected at random from a prespecified probability distribution, usually the normal. Once this is done, a stochastic optimization approach may be pursued. See Rietveld (1980: 169–71).

8A.8 Second-Round (Half-Compromise) Procedures

In suggesting the notion of half-compromise solutions, which essentially are second-round compromises applied to first-round compromises that are not found to be acceptable, Rietveld (1980:102–4) provides important suggestive insights for procedures that might be developed in multiparticipant situations when agreements have not been reached in the first round of discussions. Each half-compromise solution proposed can be related to (1) one (or more) of the compromise solutions put forth as the best on the first round; and (2) the optimal joint actions of each participant before the first round of compromise was considered. Rietveld, however, does not suggest any specific conflict management procedure per se to employ in the second round or even a third round if such is required. Hence, his procedure is not recorded in the master list of Table 12-1.

8A.9 Reduction Method to Identify the "Most Relevant" Outcome Components (Objectives)

This method, sometimes designated *interdependence analysis,* pertains to situations involving many participants, say U, each concerned with one and only one objective. This method may then be employed to identify a small number of "most relevant" objectives, say four. In this method, a selection of a specific set of four objectives is made. Next, for each of the U − 4 remaining objectives as a dependent variable, a correlation coefficient is computed from the regression employing the four selected objectives as the independent variables. The minimum value of this series of correlation coefficients is retained, and the procedure is repeated for all possible combinations of four independent objectives. One appropriate selection can then be made by using the max-min principle—application of this principle selects that set of four objectives which yields the highest value of the minimums of the correlation coefficients. See Boyce et al. (1974) and Rietveld (1980:178). This method, while useful in reducing the number of objectives to a manageable size for compromise solutions, does not yield a specific compromise solution and hence is not listed in the master list in Table 12-1.

8A.10 Fuzzy Set Analysis

Often the outcomes of alternative plans (joint actions) can only be placed in a set of fuzzy categories for any given objective, that is, categories that may have clear-cut center points but no clear-cut boundaries. For example, one set of such categories might be "high environmental quality," "medium environmental quality," and "low environmental quality." Similarly, the relative importances of objectives may only be able to be stated fuzzily for each participant— e.g., "great importance," "negligible importance," and so on. In these situations, the use of fuzzy set analysis, which recognizes the imprecision associated with the transition between membership and nonmembership in such categories, may be suggested. However, except for some very simple applications, this type of analysis is not operational, so that for the time being its application to multiparticipant conflict situations is necessarily limited. See Nijkamp et al. (1979:247–91) for some further discussion and simple applications.

NOTES

1. In what follows we shall often need to distinguish between *cardinal, relative,* and *ordinal measures of objective achievement.* By cardinal objective achievement we mean that any given achievement on an objective can be measured along a ratio and interval scale. By relative objective achievement we mean that any given achievement on an objective can be measured on a ratio scale only—that is, stated as a ratio to every other level that is obtainable. By ordinal objective achievement we mean that any given achievement on an objective can be measured on an ordinal scale only—that is, stated as being more, less, or equal to any other level that is attainable. Frequently, analysis of situations involving ordinal objective achievements is associated with multicriteria analysis.

2. That is, where increasing amounts of the resource h are required to produce a unit of achievement as the level of achievement on any objective increases.

3. Specifically, we assume that given any feasible level of achievement on one objective, the maximum level of the other objective will be achieved (produced), subject, of course, to the resource constraint $e_h^J + e_h^L \leq g_h - \bar{e}_h^M$. For example, in Figure 8-1 if OT is the level of achievement on the U.N. Police Force objective, then we assume that at least OS level of achievement on the Foreign Aid objective will be attained, and nothing less.

4. The entire set of all these tradeoff functions combine to yield the efficiency surface in a three-dimensional figure, where each objective is measured along one of the axes. This entire set is easily obtainable by continuously varying the weights for the three objectives (subject to the constraint that they add to unity) over all possible combinations

of weights. This method for generating the efficiency surface has been designated *parametric programming.*

5. In practice, a decisionmaker may not go about identifying his best combination of objectives in the way just presented. When he lacks adequate computational facilities he may instead consider only a finite number of possible combinations of objective achievements, and consider in successive pairwise fashion substitution of one objective for a second. That is, holding constant achievement levels on all objectives but two, he may opt for more achievement on one at the expense of achievement on the second until he has the best combination of achievements on both. Then he considers in succession substitution with regard to other possible pairs of objective achievements until he can do no better on any pair. In the technical literature, this successive pairwise tradeoff analysis has been termed the *surrogate worth tradeoff method.* See Cohen (1978:191–200). Observe that the surrogate worth tradeoff method relates to objectives that can be cardinally measured. However, as already noted, achievement on certain objectives can only be stated in relative terms or just ordered or noted just in terms of presence or absence of achievement. On these occasions, the decisionmaker has no way of developing a surrogate worth tradeoff function. He may be able to weight relative achievements (or even ranked achievements) and use some last-resort quantitative calculations, or he may refrain from so doing. In any case, if he must choose with care a plan covering objectives that can only be measured on different scales, implicitly he must conduct pairwise tradeoff analysis of the type indicated above.

6. Another type of conflict situation is where there is no constraint on the individuals that requires them to reach a common policy, but where the policy or joint action is the result of each bloc (or participant) independently selecting its own action that, taken together with the actions of others, yields the joint action or policy.

7. Note that this combination need not be the same as in Figure 8–2. This important point can be clearly seen if we assume participants are agreeable to an equal weighting of their utilities (i.e. $w^J = w^L$) and that $u^J = 1.5E^J$, while $u^L = 3E^L$ (reflecting the fact that one unit of achievement on the Foreign Aid objective yields twice as much "group" utility as one unit of achievement on the U.N. Police Force objective, even though they accrue primarily to different participants).

8. We obtain the similar shaped curve because of the particular way in which we have constructed the utility scales along the two axes.

9. These may be taken to correspond to the set defined by Leontief in his pathbreaking multiregion input-output study for the United Nations, *The Future of the World Economy* (1977), summarized in *Sci-*

entific American (1980). The J nations constitute those in North America, Oceania (mainly Australia and New Zealand), Western Europe, Japan, the U.S.S.R., Eastern Europe (other than the U.S.S.R.), South Africa, and Mediterranean Europe. The L nations include arid Africa, medium-income Latin America, the centrally-planned nations of Asia, and low-income Asia. The M nations include tropical Africa, the oil-producing states of the Middle East, and low-income Latin America.

10.   Since the multiobjective programming procedure discussed in this section involves recursive interaction by participants, it is essential that each participant knows or comes to know much about all other participants' preference structures for this interaction to be effective, especially if each is to make a fair proposal of weights.

11.   In this hypothetical example, the E^{J*}, E^{L*}, and E^{M*} levels might be determined by operating a model with weights in the objective function of $(1,0,0)$, $(0,1,0)$, and $(0,0,1)$, respectively.

12.   Such a total might be considered a surrogate social welfare for the three blocs of nations.

Also, the utility functions may be more complex. For example, they may involve the sum of levels of goal achievement on all three objectives—in which case we have $u^J = k^{JJ}(E^J/E^{J*}) + k^{LJ}(E^L/E^{L*}) + k^{MJ}(E^M/E^{M*})$ for J and similar functions for L and M. Once again, it would be possible to calculate the resulting total utility.

13.   We say more realistic because it is based on a study authorized and supported by the United Nations. We recognize, however, that the United Nations may not acquire the necessary strength in the future to effect any implementation of proposals based on this study.

14.   See Klein (1977) and Isard and C. Smith (1982a:42–64).

15.   See Granberg and Rubinshtein (1979).

16.   In the eyes of some scholars, input-output analysis is not a programming model, since it involves constant production coefficients, constant trade or inter-regional flow coefficients, and the like, and because no factor and process substitutions are allowed in the pure technical sense. In the eyes of other scholars, input-output is a special case of programming models. Whatever the view, *in practice,* as any experienced input-output analyst knows, input-output involves much programming analysis. Any analyst skilled in input-output work knows that in defining a meaningful set of sectors, regions, and trade flows that incorporate the cross-hauling of reality (there has never been a system that meets the theorist's first-order conditions of no cross-hauling), and even in developing from the limited imperfect data available constant production and trade coefficients and the like, he constantly must introduce scale economies, factor substitu-

tion, and process substitution. In a very real sense then, input-output is programming analysis. When used appropriately for projection purposes, its strictly linear system form embodies optimization processes in the very specification of relevant relations and coefficients.

17.   Technically speaking, the input-output model does not optimize the value associated with an objective function (or the utility that might be associated with the arguments of that function). However, it does so indirectly. For, in practice, the analyst tries out alternative final demand vectors (bills of goods) to ensure not only that they are feasible (i.e., do not require more resources than are available) but also that they are efficient (i.e., do not leave unused any resources that can be effectively employed for the assumed state of affairs, including, for example, the stage of the business cycle at the year of projection). In effect, the setting up of alternative final demand vectors (alternative levels of goal achievements) and testing for both feasibility and efficiency serves the same purpose as optimizing the value associated with an objective function.

18.   In certain situations where there exists an "institutional" rule (such as a majority rule), the requirement that a joint policy (action) be acceptable to all participants reduces to the requirement that it be acceptable to a majority of participants. There are of course problems with such procedures. For example, where there are more than two participants, the solutions arrived at by use of a majority voting rule are not independent of the order in which joint policies (actions) are presented to participants—as is clear in the well-known Arrow paradox. In this book, however, application of such a rule raises the whole complex of problems dealing with coalition analysis and so we do not refer to the use of such rules in the discussion that follows.

19.   To reiterate, this book aims to present techniques for consideration for use by mediators and participants in a conflict situation. As a result, we are less concerned with the property of efficiency, upon which technical analysts often focus. Further, we are much less concerned with and thus do not discuss the property of convergence, especially within a recursive interaction process, to which some analysts give much attention.

20.   These utilities would be functions of objectives such as per capita incomes, and the level and pattern of military expenditures by region.

21.   This of course would not normally be the total utility that would be obtained were a beneficent dictator to determine an optimal solution after specification of the weights to be given to the participants' utilities, their utility functions being known, as discussed earlier.

22.   Note that because the data of Table 3-2 are smoothed, the optimal value of each objective in the continuous joint action space of Figure 8-5 corresponds only approximately to the optimal value in the finite joint action space of Table 3-2. For example, the optimal value for E_G is 218 in Figure 8-5, while only 216 in Table 3-2.

   With appropriate replacement of variables, the equations underlying the values of the curves of Figure 8-5 are identical, except for scale, to those of Footnotes 6 and 8 on pages 281–82 in Isard, T. Smith, et al. (1969).

23.   This space E has the same geometric form as the joint utility space U of Figure 7-2, since both are derived directly from smoothing the data of Table 3-2.

24.   This means that points along the subarc $E_C^* u^{J*}$ (but not including u^{J*}) and along the subarc $u^{L*} E_G^*$ (but not including u^{L*}) are inefficient. Any movement from a point on the subarc $E_C^* u^{J*}$ toward u^{J*} leads to higher ordinal utility for both participants, as does any movement from a point on the stretch $u^{L*} E_G^*$ toward u^{L*}.

25.   So long as the marginal utility of an objective remains positive for each participant, independent of the level of the other objective, the joint utility frontier will never be a strict subarc of the joint objective efficiency frontier, assuming regular conditions.

26.   If the resulting compromise in joint objective achievements is not efficient, then there may be more than one joint action that could yield this outcome, and some procedure needs to be devised to select among them.

27.   In particular, if the current standpoint lies in the lower left-hand segment of the joint objective achievement space E, the intersection of the limited commitment and improvement sets may include actions not in E. Such actions would need to be excluded from consideration by the adoption of some convention or rule. See also Note 26.

28.   See Notes 26 and 27.

29.   When objective achievements can be measured in relative terms only, numbers representing achievements on each objective (such as might be indicated by the first set of numbers in the cells of Table 3-2) are unique up to a scale factor only. Ratios, such as improvements relative to the improvement from worst to best in Table 5-3 on p. 136, are unique.

30.   The analysis in this and the previous section can easily be extended to cover more than two objectives, where the achievements on these objectives are noncomparable. The two-dimensional figures then become three dimensional, four dimensional, or in general n-dimensional, and the indifference curves become indifference surfaces. However, for practical purposes, analysis covering more than three objectives is not likely to be useful.

31. Were an infinite number of joint actions possible, information consisting of an infinite number of combinations of ordinal rankings of objectives would not in general be of use in a utility-focused conflict situation.

32. But also highly sophisticated analysts may be willing to use the min total of ranks principle as a last-resort procedure after many unsuccessful attempts to resolve their conflict in a rational or reasonable manner.

33. When weights are applied to rankings of objective achievements, this in essence converts the rankings into standard units that can then be added to yield a meaningful total index.

34. In general, the importance of a criteria is given by the reciprocal of the factor (weight) that is used to multiply its rank.

35. This computation needs to be modified when participants disagree on whether a particular criterion is a benefit or a cost and when, therefore, both positive *and* negative weights must be involved.

36. A positive value indicates the amount of money J is willing to pay to have plan k adopted rather than stay at Z, while a negative value indicates that amount of money J needs to receive in order to agree to plan k's adoption.

37. Recall that in Note 33 of Chapter 3 we indicated that summing of ranks is an improper mathematical operation but still of significance for simple-minded participants (and even sophisticated participants when nothing else works). The objections to summing ranks over criteria become less valid when participants can state (roughly estimate) the dollar value to them of one plan when compared to another. In a sense, the continuous variable dollar money payments adjusts for the crudity (imperfections) of summing ranks. The same holds when the Clarke-Vickrey demand-revealing (no bluffing) method is employed in a situation such as depicted by Table 8-2 in order to provide an incentive for J and L to state their true valuations.

38. Were we to begin with Column 5 representing J's values (or the sum of the values of the participants other than L) of the different plans when compared to the existing situation Z, then the tax or money payment to a good cause that L would need to make to change the joint action from plan β, which J most prefers, to plan δ would be $500. But L only values δ over β by $400. Hence she will not propose δ rather than β and will find β acceptable when the Clarke-Vickrey demand-revealing method is used.

39. An alternative name for this procedure is the Electre (Elimination et Choice Translating Reality) Method. See van Delft and Nijkamp (1977).

40. Note that the diagonal elements c_{11}, c_{22}, . . . , c_{nn} are omitted since they are meaningless, and that in general the matrix is nonsymmetrical, that is, $c_{jj'} \neq c_{j'j}$. This latter point follows from the fact that the participants in the concordance set $C_{jj'}$ are in general different from the participants in the concordance set $C_{j'j}$.

41. Note that, as with the concordance matrix, the diagonal elements d_{11}, d_{22}, . . . , d_{nn} are omitted since they are meaningless, and in general the matrix is nonsymmetrical, that is, $d_{jj'} \neq d_{j'j}$. This latter point follows from the fact that the participants in the discordance sets $D_{jj'}$ and $D_{j'j}$ are different.

42. The elimination procedure is complex and involves several steps. First we construct two dominance matrices. One is called the *concordance dominance matrix A* with typical elements $a_{jj'}$, defined as:

$$a_{jj'} = 1 \text{ if } c_{jj'} \geq \overline{c}$$

$$a_{jj'} = 0 \text{ if } c_{jj'} < \overline{c}$$

(The meaning of $a_{jj'} = 1$ is that plan j is more acceptable than plan j' with respect to concordance.) The other matrix is called the *discordance dominance matrix B* with typical elements $b_{jj'}$ defined as:

$$b_{jj'} = 1 \text{ if } d_{jj'} \leq \overline{d}$$

$$b_{jj'} = 0 \text{ if } d_{jj'} > \overline{d}$$

(The meaning of $b_{jj'} = 1$ is that plan j is more acceptable than plan j' with respect to discordance.)

Then we derive an *aggregate dominance matrix F* (as the intersection of A and B) with typical elements $f_{jj'}$ defined as

$$f_{jj'} = 1 \text{ if both } a_{jj'} = 1 \text{ and } b_{jj'} = 1$$

$$f_{jj'} = 0 \text{ otherwise}$$

If element $f_{jj'} = 1$, then plan j is more acceptable than plan j' on both the concordance and discordance criteria. But $f_{jj'} = 1$ only implies a relative dominance of plan j to j'. There may concomitantly be an alternative plan j" such that it dominates j (i.e., $f_{j''j} = 1$).

So for j to be a nondominated plan (that is for j not to be eliminated),

$$f_{jj'} = 1 \text{ for at least one j', j'} = 1, \ldots ,n \qquad j \neq j'$$

$$f_{j''j} = 0 \text{ for all j''} = 1, \ldots ,n \qquad j'' \neq j \qquad j'' \neq j'$$

43. See Nijkamp et al. (1979:257–58) for further details and references.

44. Such as the Spearman rank correlation coefficient or the Kendall rank correlation coefficient.

45. See Nijkamp et al. (1979:82–86) for further details and references.

46. This requires the description of the plans and attributes in the same metric space such that the positions of the plan outcomes and the attribute outcomes reflect the actual differences between these outcomes. In other words, where there are n plans and m attributes, a data transformation is carried out. In this transformation, the points from the n-dimensional and the m-dimensional spaces are positioned in a joint k-dimensional space ($k < \min(n, m,)$) such that the loss of information is as small as possible.

47. Van Delft and Nijkamp (1977) have suggested the possibility of the use of *entropy analysis* in the selection of a best compromise plan (joint action). Their suggestion is made since entropy is a measure for the expected information content of a message, and since the outcomes of a plan may be interpreted as a message. By means of a diversification factor for weighted plan outcomes, they would then identify, with the entropy measure, the most probable plan—with the implication that this would be the one to be put into effect.

48. See Nijkamp et al. (1979:252–53).

49. See Paelinck (1976) and Nijkamp et al. (1979:277) for further details and references.

50. See Isard, T. Smith, et al. (1969:166–68).

9 MATCHING CONFLICT SITUATIONS AND CONFLICT MANAGEMENT PROCEDURES—A STATIC FRAMEWORK[1]

9.1 INTRODUCTION

In Chapters 3 through 8, we completed a fairly comprehensive and systematic presentation of conflict management procedures in terms of certain key properties that may be relevant in a conflict situation. Such properties are, for example, type of action space, nature of participants' preference structures, and the focus (on utility or objectives) of participants. We now proceed to take another important step to deepen the analysis and the process for identifying relevant conflict management procedures. This step involves the recognition that each conflict situation itself can be said to have an important set of characteristics, some common to many situations, others unique to that situation. In Section 9.2 we discuss key characteristics of conflict situations. This step in effect sets up the specific conflict situation as the target in the use of any conflict management procedure.

With key characteristics of conflict situations identified and having in mind the need to match the unique as well as nonunique elements of any given conflict situation with one or more useful conflict management procedures, we discuss key properties of conflict management procedures in Section 9.3.

Once these key properties of conflict management procedures are set down, we are in a position to consider the process of matching a

297

specific conflict situation (a target) with one or more useful conflict management procedures. We do this in Section 9.4, where we discuss steps in the matching process. For the moment we assume that the target is a nonchanging one, although in reality this is not the case. Moreover, the properties of a conflict management procedure may also change, but such change is generally of a smaller magnitude. Here, too, we must assume that such change does not occur.

The matching process suggests that ideally there is one and only one conflict management procedure suitable to a specific conflict situation and that this procedure should be adopted once the specific conflict situation is adequately defined. Such an ideal, implying an assumption of complete information concerning relevant items, is far from attainable. Rather, fully recognizing the extremely high probability that each conflict situation will be in one way or another unique, we are nonetheless motivated to search for a large but not unmanageable number of procedures that can, on one occasion or another, be generally useful in view of what history and experience tell us. We seek to match a given conflict situation not with an ideal conflict management procedure, but with one or more admittedly imperfect ones that are, nonetheless, adequate in certain important respects and are among the best available for that conflict situation.

To make possible this matching process, we develop the concept of an index of inadequacy. As discussed in Section 9.5, this index can be computed for each actual conflict management procedure for any specific conflict situation.

In Section 9.6, we present the method in a more rigorous mathematical manner. The nontechnical reader need only glance through this section. Finally, we discuss in Section 9.7 the overwhelming number of shortcomings of the matching and evaluation processes. However, we suggest in the concluding remarks of Section 9.8 that these shortcomings are no more severe than those for all social science operational models, except those that attack the most simple problems.

9.2 KEY CHARACTERISTICS OF CONFLICT SITUATIONS

Although each conflict situation is unique, there are important general characteristics whose presence or absence may be noted in many, if not every situation. The purpose of this section is to identify such general characteristics so that any important conflict situation that does arise can be easily classified with respect to them.

Our classification of general characteristics is presented in Tables 9-1 through 9-3. Table 9-1 pertains to *structural characteristics of the underlying systems* from which the participants come. These are distinct from the nonsystemic structural characteristics of a particular conflict situation, which are listed in Table 9-2, and from the characteristics of participants (behavioral units), which we take to be nonstructural and which are listed in Table 9-3.

In Table 9-1 we have constructed a tentative list of characteristics under the headings: cultural, social psychology, social groups and social organizations, economic system, political system, and system information. To illustrate, under the cultural heading, we have: (1) need to have (exercise) power, (2) need to have identity, (3) need to achieve, and so on. We consider neither these subclasses nor the characteristics listed under them as final. They simply represent what we consider for the moment to be a reasonable set to be subsequently modified.

Obviously, system characteristics are important in considering the use of any conflict management procedure. For example, a procedure that involves a step at variance with the legal system, religious principles, or underlying driving force of a participant's system (nation) is not likely to be a relevant procedure.

In Table 9-2 we list the *nonsystemic structural characteristics* of a conflict situation by the following categories: nature of disagreement (issues and stakes); participants involved; coalition-related characteristics; nature of reference point; and so forth. Obviously we need to know the nature of disagreement, the number of participants involved, and various other characteristics listed in Table 9-2 before we can proceed to identify a possible relevant conflict management procedure.

In Table 9-3 we list relevant *participants' characteristics*. They are psychological, level of education (sophistication), control of resources, and so forth.

9.3 KEY PROPERTIES OF CONFLICT MANAGEMENT PROCEDURES

To effect a matching we need to know the properties of relevant conflict management procedures that can meet the requirements of a con-

Table 9-1. Systemic Structural Characteristics.

I *Cultural*

1 Need to have (exercise) power
2 Need to have identity
3 Need to achieve
4 Type of legal system (e.g., Roman, Common, Islamic, Old Testament)
5 Language and communication capabilities

II *Social Psychology*

10 Conservative (e.g., a Have nation)
11 Bold and Daring (e.g., a Have-not nation)
12 Intermediate between 10 and 11
13 Solutions sought via group action (or bureaucratic means)
14 Solutions sought via individualistic action
15 Calculating (methodical) approach
16 Abstract (logical) approach
17 Intuitive (religio-mystic) approach
18 Experimental approach
19 Precedent (tradition) oriented

III *Social Groups and Social Organizations*

20 Division within society with regard to public purpose

21 Division within society as reflected in socioeconomic and political inequalities
22 Division within society as reflected in the history and time period (duration of protracted social conflict)
23 Division within society as reflected in the probability of imminent revolution
24 Division within society as reflected in absence of major conflict in recent past
25 Significant experience with conflict management

IV *Economic System*

30 Developed
31 Developing
32 Significant dependence on foreign aid, trade, and/or investment
33 Largely small individual entrepreneurship
34 Dominated by large domestic corporations
35 Significant presence of foreign multinationals
36 In takeoff period
37 High rate of growth
38 Low to modest rate of growth
39 No growth
40 Recently declining
41 Long-run declining and stagnation

V *Political System*

50 Military dictatorship (authoritarian)

Table 9-1. Systemic Structural Characteristics. *(cont'd)*

Political System (cont'd)		
51 Socialistic-Communistic, independent	59	Stability (electoral standing) of incumbent government
52 Socialistic-Communistic, dependent	60	Nature of hierarchical decisionmaking structure
53 "Western" democracy, 2 party	61	Functional centralization (decentralization)
54 "Western" democracy, many party	VI	*System Information*
55⎫ 56⎬ other types 57⎭	70	Low (e.g., some fourth world nations)
58 "Big Power" nation	71	Medium
	72	High

flict situation. Again, based on our existing knowledge of the literature on conflict management and resolution, we set down in Table 9-4 a listing of these properties in a format that seems most useful for the matching process. Our set of categories and listing of properties is only tentative and is subject to significant change. The categories are: structural properties, time-related properties, motivating properties, psychological properties, solution properties, and implementability of solutions.

9.4 STEPS IN THE MATCHING PROCESS

To discuss effectively the steps in the matching process, it is best to begin with a particular illustration involving a specific conflict situation (designated a CS) and a specific conflict management procedure (designated a CMP). In this illustration we will want to evaluate the relevance of the specific procedure for the specific situation. To do so, we construct Table 9-5. In Column 3 of this table we list all the important characteristics that any conflict situation (CS) may possess. These characteristics have been detailed in Tables 9-1 through 9-3. The first is "need to have (exercise) power," the second is "need to

Table 9-2.   Nonsystemic Structural Characteristics.

I *Nature of Disagreement (Issues and Stakes)*

100   Qualitative—Major
101   Qualitative—Minor
102   Quantitative—Major
103   Quantitative—Minor

II *Participants Involved*

110   Two
111   Several
112   Representing themselves
113   Representing larger constituency
114   Technical support team available
115   Technical support team not available
116   Mediator present
117   Mediator not present

III *Coalition-related Characteristics*

120   Presence of coalitions by type
121   Stability of coalitions by type
122   Potential for new coalitions by type

IV *Nature of Reference Point*

130   Current standpoint
131   Nature of current demand
132   Nature of current offers
133   Threat points possible
134   Ideal points possible

V *Time-related Characteristics*

150   Historical factors to be considered
151   Static or slowly changing
152   Dynamic
153   Highly dynamic (explosive)
154   Multiple applications of procedure envisaged
155   Single application of procedure envisaged

VI *Policy Options (Joint Actions) Available*

160   Number (small, large, continuous)
161   Number (fixed or variable)
162   Agenda (fixed or variable)

VII *Fractionation Possibilities (Decomposability)*

170   Re: issues (including logrolling)
171   Re: participants
172   Re: actions and policies
173   Re: outcomes

VIII *Information Available*

180   Available "objective" knowledge of conflict situation
181   Participants' knowledge of conflict situation
182   Participants' knowledge of others' knowledge and preference structures

Table 9-3.   Participants' Characteristics.

I *Psychological*

200   Conservative
201   Mixed conservative-
        wild
202   Wild (bold)
203   Pessimist
204   Mixed pessimist-
        optimist
205   Optimist
206   Regretter
207   Risk-averse
208   Risk-lover
209   Optimizer
210   Expected payoff
        calculator
211   Satisficer
212   Altruist
213   Retaliatory
214   Obstinacy
215   Cooperative
216   Competitive
217   Passive
218   Aggressive
219   Myopic
220   Nonmyopic
221   Strategy-oriented
222   Outcome-oriented
223   Action-oriented

II *Level of Education
(Sophistication)*

230   Low
231   Medium
232   High
233   Extent and type of
        misperception

III *Control of Resources*

240   Economic (money, jobs,
        patronage)
241   Political (c-power, etc.)
242   Social (c-respect, etc.)
243   External support

IV *Perceptive*

250   Sees many joint actions
251   Sees few joint actions
252   Recognizes interdependence
        of actions
253   Recognizes interdependence
        of outcomes
254   Sees many outcome prop-
        erties
255   Sees few outcome properties

V *Receptive*

260   Ability to learn
261   Willingness to learn (explore
        new ideas and thinking)
        — about situation
        — about other participants
262   Ability to change focus
263   Extent of commitment to a
        position

VI *Preference Structure and Statement
Capability*

270   Ordinal
271   Relative
272   Cardinal
273   Independent
274   Interdependent

Table 9-4. Properties of Conflict Management Procedures.

A *Structural Properties*

Information Requirements Regarding Preferences

1 Ordinal
2 Relative
3 Cardinal
4 Interdependent or in-dependent
5 Other
6 No knowledge of others
7 Full knowledge of others
8 Partial knowledge of others

Other Information Require-ments

9 Full
10 Relatively large
11 Relatively small

Number of Joint Actions Considered

12 Small
13 Large
14 Continuous

Nature of Interaction

15 Participatory
16 Nonparticipatory
17 Face-to-face
18 Non-face-to-face

Cost

19 High in initial phases
20 Low in initial phases
21 High in later phases
22 Low in later phases

Coalition Formation

23 Encouraged
24 Discouraged
25 Changes in allowed

Other

26 Requires weights
27 Does not require weights
28 Objective achievement focused
29 Utility outcome focused
30 Last resort capability
31 Usable in a workshop setting
32 Statable in balance-sheet form
33 Statable mathematically
34 Statable without mathematics
35 Presence of mediator required
36 Pairwise comparisons possible

B *Time-related Properties*

37 Single application-oriented
38 Multiple application-oriented
39 Able to be coupled with others in a fractionated conflict

Number of Rounds

40 One
41 Many
42 Either one or many

Size of Steps Involved

43 Small (Limited commitment)
44 Large
45 Either small or large

Interactive (feedback effects)

46 With search processes
— for efficient solutions

Table 9-4. *(cont.'d)*

Interactive (feedback effects) (cont'd)

— for better satisficing solutions
47 With knowledge accumulation
48 With learning by participants
49 Encourages invention of new tools and creative thinking by participants
50 Removes misperceptions
51 Develops common language and communication channels

C *Motivating Properties*

Guaranteed Improvement

52 Overall strong
53 Overall weak
54 On each round strong
55 On each round weak
56 Guaranteed nondeterioration

Concessions

57 From ideal point
58 From overly optimistic point
59 From status quo point (in contraction)

Limited Commitment

60 Overall
61 On each round

Fairness

62 Fairness (weighted equity) over microtime
63 Fairness over macrotime
64 Equitable over microtime
65 Equitable over macrotime

Other

66 Can accommodate improvements or concessions
67 Shifts focus from fixed positions
68 Permits reconstruction (reformulation) of a game-type conflict
— from zero to nonzero sum
— from action to policy-oriented
69 Eliminates bluffing
70 Reveals preferences

D *Psychological Properties*

71 Security preserving
72 Confidence building overall
73 Confidence building on early rounds
74 Trust building in first step(s)
75 Allows leader-follower arrangement
76 Conflict-reducing (escalating) potential
77 Induces positive reciprocal action
78 Induces negative reciprocal action
79 Provides an incentive to think of others

Table 9-4. *(Cont'd)*

Psychological Properties (cont'd)			
80	Recognizes strategic potential	93	Efficient outcome guaranteed
81	Involves strategy-oriented behavior	94	Nonefficient outcome possible
82	Involves outcome-oriented behavior	95	Certain outcome
83	Involves action-oriented behavior	96	Uncertain, risky outcomes
		97	Probabilistic outcomes

E *Solution Properties*

F *Implementability of Solutions*

84 Steps to solution defined
85 Inescapable sanctions possible
86 Veto power possible
87 Unstable
88 Stable in both microtime and macrotime
89 Stable in microtime only
90 Unique outcome
91 Nonunique outcomes
92 Preindeterminate outcome

98 Is the solution consistent with international law
99 Is the solution simple enough for the minds of existing administrators (legislators)
100 Is the solution implementable with existing tools, policy instruments
101 Does the solution require development of new tools, policy instruments for implementation

---

have identity," and so forth. In Column 5, we list possible "corresponding" properties of a conflict management procedure (CMP). That is, given a characteristic of a CS, we set down by its side the one or more properties that it is desirable for a CMP to have to match this characteristic. For example, the first characteristic of conflict situations, "need to have (exercise) power," can be said to be matched by, that is, can be met by, a conflict management procedure if that procedure possesses the properties "inescapable sanctions possible," "veto power possible," "leader-follower arrangement possible," and perhaps others. These latter properties are listed in Column 5 to

Table 9-5.   Worksheet to Calculate Index of Inadequacy.

Presence of Characteristic in Conflict X	Weight for Conflict X $\overline{w}_j$	Characteristics of Conflict Situation (CS)	Relative Importance ρ_{jj}	Corresponding Properties of Conflict Management Procedure (CMP)	Presence of Property in CMP Y	Calculation of Inadequacy Score of CMP Y
(1)	(2)	(3)	(4)	(5)	(6)	(7)
1	9	Cultural 1. Need to have (exercise) power	0.45	85 inescapable sanctions possible	0	$(1-0)9(.45)=4.05$
			0.45	86 veto power possible	1	$(1-1)9(.45)=0$
			0.10	75 leader-follower arrangement possible	1	$(1-1)9(.10)=0$
0	0	2. Need to have identity	1	17 face-to-face interaction	1	$(0-1)0(1)=0$ (whenever <0, set equal to zero)
1	6	Social Psychology 15. Calculating	.50	93 efficiency	1	$(1-1)6(0.5)=0$
			.03	33 statable mathematically	1	$(1-1)6(0.03)=0$
			.47	52 guaranteed improvement	1	$(1-1)6(0.47)=0$
1	3	Political System 58. Big Power involvement	1	81 involves strategic behavior	1	$(1-1)3(1)=0$
1	0.2	Economic System 31. Developing	.30	82 involves outcome oriented behavior	0	$(1-0)(.2)(.3)=.06$
			.40	44 large size of steps	0	$(1-0)(.2)(.4)=.08$
			.30	96 uncertain risky outcomes	0	$(1-0)(.2)(.3)=.06$
1	6	Social Group 22. Division over history	.30	62 fairness (weighted)	1	$(1-1)6(.3)=0$
			.02	79 provides incentive to think of others	0	$(1-0)6(.02)=.12$
			.58	74 trust building in first steps	.2	$(1-.2)6(.58)=2.78$

the right of the "need to have (exercise) power" characteristic in Column 3. Or, to take another illustration, the general characteristic #15 of conflict situations, namely a "calculating social psychology" may be said to be matched by a conflict management procedure if that procedure possesses the properties "efficiency," (that is, can lead to an efficient outcome) "statable mathematically," and "guaranteed improvement." These properties are listed in Column 5 of Table 9–5 to the right of the "calculating social psychology" characteristic in Column 3.

Just listing characteristics of a CS and corresponding properties of a CMP is not enough. We need to indicate the relative importance of each of the CMP properties for a given CS characteristic. We do this in Column 4 of Table 9–5. For example, with regard to the CS characteristic "need to have (exercise) power," we have judged the relative importance of CMP properties "inescapable sanctions possible," "veto power possible," and "leader-follower arrangement possible" to be 0.45, 0.45, and 0.10, respectively.

Having completed this part of the table—namely Columns 3, 4, and 5, which we will later indicate can be computerized—we take the next step. This is to fill in Column 1 of Table 9–5. To do this, however, we must have a given conflict situation in mind. It may be, for example, the current (April 1982) Iraq-Iran conflict or the U.S.-Vietnam conflict of the 1960s. We need to specify in Column 1 whether or not each characteristic listed in Column 3 is relevant for the specific conflict being examined. In the relevant row we place a 1 if the answer is yes, and 0 if the answer is no. For example, the "need to have (exercise) power" was a relevant characteristic of the Vietnam conflict, so we have placed a 1 in the first column of Table 9–5.

Having filled in Column 1, we proceed to Column 2. In this column we specify the relative importance of each CS characteristic present (i.e., those characteristics that have a 1 in Column 1) in the particular conflict situation we are studying. Here we will need a ranking system or the like, such as the Saaty scale which we have discussed on pages 148–150.[2] If we do so, then we might, for the Vietnam conflict, set down the number 9 for the "need to have (exercise) power," indicating that we judge this characteristic to be of paramount (overwhelming) importance in this conflict situation. In contrast, we may judge the characteristic "need to have identity," the second listed in Column 3, to be of negligible importance; so we simply transfer the 0 in Column 1 to Column 2. We may judge characteristic #15 in Column 3, "calculating social psychology," to be rather significant, so we give it a weight of 6.[3]

We next proceed to fill in Column 6. We first identify the specific CMP to be examined for possible use for the given CS. The CMP might be a sequence of split-the-differences over utility outcomes, or a veto-incremax procedure, or the metagame approach. In each row of the column we indicate whether the corresponding property of a CMP listed in Column 5 is present or absent in the specific CMP being examined. If present, we record a 1; if not, a 0. For example, the property "inescapable sanctions possible" at the top of Column 5 is not present in a sequential split-the-difference or veto-incremax procedure. So, for each of these specific procedures we would record a 0 at the top of Column 6. (Note a possible modification of our method, which uses a fraction between 0 and 1 to indicate the degree of presence of a CMP property in Column 6 or of a CS characteristic in Column 1, or both. We do not pursue this here.)

Once the first six columns have been filled in we can proceed to evaluate the specific CMP for use for the given CS. We do this in a very simple, admittedly inadequate, way in Column 7. In particular, we evaluate a CMP in terms of its ability to match each of the CS characteristics properly weighted by its importance to the specific situation being examined. For example, with regard to the characteristic "need to have (exercise) power," we make three calculations, as indicated in the first three rows of Column 7. Specifically, in Row 1 of Column 1 there is a 1, which indicates that the CS characteristic the "need to have (exercise) power" is present in the specific CS being examined. In Row 1 Column 6 there is a 0, which indicates that the property "inescapable sanctions possible" is not present in the specific CMP being examined. Hence the term $(1-0)$ in Row 1 Column 7 represents a first rough index of inadequacy. The significance of this inadequacy is in part determined by the importance of the CS characteristic the "need to have (exercise) power" for the specific CS. This importance, as given in Row 1, Column 2, is 9; so we must multiply the term $(1-0)$ by 9, obtaining $(1-0)9$. Finally, as indicated in Rows 1 to 3 of Column 5, "inescapable sanctions possible" is only one of three CMP properties relevant for the "need to have (exercise) power" characteristic and, among the three properties, its relative normalized weight, as indicated in Column 4, is 0.45. So the inadequacy score on the "inescapable sanctions possible" dimension is $(1-0)9(0.45) = 4.05$, as noted in Row 1 of Column 7. In like manner, we calculate inadequacy scores for the CMP properties "veto power possible" and "leader-follower arrangement possible" with regard to CS characteristic "need to have (exercise) power." See Rows 2 and 3 of Column 7. Note that these two properties are fully present in the CMP—say veto-incremax—being considered; so the first term for each is $(1 - 1)$ and in their respective rows we have $(1 - 1)9(.45) = 0$ and $(1 - 1)9(.10) = 0$. That is, the veto-incremax procedure has zero inadequacy on both these counts. Thus, in terms of matching the characteristic "need to have (exercise) power," the inadequacy of the specified procedure is in total 4.05 for the given CS.

In this manner, we proceed with respect to all characteristics of the given CS. We then sum the inadequacy scores in Column 7 to obtain a measure of total inadequacy of the given CMP, say veto-incremax. We can do likewise for every other CMP. Note that the information in Columns 3, 4, and 5 is common for all procedures and so may be stored in a computer. Further, for every possible CMP we can develop the information in Column 6, and store that, too, in a computer. Hence, when an analyst (mediator) does face a specific CS, all he needs to do is to fill in Columns 1 and 2. The computer can then print out in order of magnitude the inadequacy score for each processed CMP.

One further point to understand the calculations in Table 9–5. Often, the first term in Column 7 is negative. This will always be the case if (1) the particular CS does not require a characteristic so that the entry in the row corresponding to that characteristic in Column 1 is 0 and (2) the CMP being studied has a property that could match that characteristic so that the entry in the row corresponding to that characteristic in Column 6 is 1. When this occurs, we set the first term equal to 0 so that an actual CMP with more of a given property than is needed is not penalized. We discuss this convention later.

9.5 EVALUATING ACTUAL CONFLICT MANAGEMENT PROCEDURES

In Section 9.4 we illustrated how with Table 9–5 we can carry through a set of calculations to derive an index of inadequacy for each CMP. To describe the method efficiently and in more general terms we need to employ simple algebra. First we let j, $j = 1, \ldots, n$ represent an important characteristic of any possible CS, there being n such characteristics (as listed in Tables 9–1 through 9–3) when we consider all possible conflict situations. We also let i, $i = 1, \ldots, m$ represent a possible relevant property of any CMP that may be adopted (as listed in Table 9–4), there being m such properties over all possible conflict management procedures.

We next let ρ_{ii} indicate the relative importance of property i of a CMP in matching the characteristic j of CS. Typical ρ_{ji} are listed in Column 4 of Table 9–5. Thus, if all characteristics j of a CS had the same weight, namely one, then the weight of property i of a CMP would be given by $\tilde{w}_i$ where $\tilde{w}_i = \sum_{j=1}^{n} \rho_{ji}$ for all i, indicating that the weight of property i is simply the sum of its "importances" over all characteristics j. However, not all characteristics j of a CS are of equal importance. Rather, each characteristic j must be given a relative weight $\overline{w}_j$, as recorded in Column 2 of Table 9–5. Hence the weight of any property i becomes the sum of its "importances" over all characteristics j after each of these characteristics has been multiplied by its relative weight $\overline{w}_j$. Accordingly, we obtain

$$w_i = \sum_{j=1}^{n} \overline{w}_j \, \rho_{ji}, \, i = 1, \ldots, m. \tag{9-1}$$

With these derived weights for i, we then can calculate for each actual CMP its index of inadequacy π.

To do so, conceive of an "ideal" CMP to match a given CS. It has all the properties required by that CS. We designate an ideal CMP for the given CS by the symbol (or vector) p with properties $p_1, p_2, \ldots, p_i, \ldots, p_m$. If p is an ideal procedure, then by definition the property p_i of this procedure is always equal to 1 whenever property i is required by any characteristic of a given CS, and for reasons to be discussed later, equal to 0 otherwise.

In practice, we know of no actual conflict management procedure that is "ideal," except perhaps for a very simple CS. Hence, we want to contrast an actual CMP with an ideal to see how far short the actual falls from the ideal. For the purpose of this section, we shall designate any actual CMP by $\overline{p}$ with properties $\overline{p}_1, \overline{p}_2, \ldots, \overline{p}_i, \ldots, \overline{p}_m$ with $\overline{p}_i = 1$ or 0, according to whether property i is present or absent in the actual CMP being examined. Thus, $(p_i - \overline{p}_i)$ represents a first crude index of inadequacy with regard to property i. In evaluating any actual CMP on a total basis, we must multiply $(p_i - \overline{p}_i)$ by the weight of property i to obtain $w_i(p_i - \overline{p}_i)$. Hence, over all properties i, the index of inadequacy of the actual CMP might seem to be

$$\pi = \sum_{i=1}^{m} w_i(p_i - \bar{p}_i) \tag{9-2}$$

However, recall that we set $(p_i - \bar{p}_i) = 0$ whenever $p_i < \bar{p}_i$ indicating that in calculating an index of inadequacy for an actual CMP with more of any property i than is required, this surplus is not allowed to be used to reduce the CMP's inadequacy on other scores. Thus, (9–2) must be rewritten as:

$$\pi = \sum_{i=1}^{m} w_i(p_i - \bar{p}_i) \quad | \quad \text{for } (p_i - \bar{p}_i) \geq 0 \tag{9-3}$$

In this way, given any CS with relative weights $\bar{w}_j$, one can immediately calculate the index of inadequacy π for each CMP that exists or is to be considered. This implies that the best CMP is the one with the lowest index π.

9.6 THE MATHEMATICAL FORMULATION OF THE METHOD

The use of the index of inadequacy derived above involves a set of most serious shortcomings. However, before we discuss these shortcomings, we need to outline in more rigorous mathematical language the steps in the matching and evaluation processes discussed in Sections 9.4 and 9.5. The nontechnical reader need only glance over this section.

Recall our first task, namely to list the n important characteristics, $j = 1, \ldots, n$, of all possible conflict situations (theoretical and actual). See Tables 9–1 through 9–3. Taking all possible combinations of these characteristics yields theoretically the set S of all possible conflict situations. See the upper left of Figure 9–1. Hence, any particular conflict situation s that we examine is contained in this set, that is, $s \in S$ where $S \subset R^n$.

The next task is to list all possible properties, $i = 1, \ldots, m$, of conflict management procedures. See Table 9–4. Taking all possible combinations of these properties yields the set P of all possible CMPs. See the right of Figure 9–1. We designate any procedure, theoretical or actual, as p, with $p \in P$ and $P \subset R^m$.

Now any actual CMP we have discussed is contained in this set as well as many still to be developed, and presumably still more that are purely theoretical. We designate the subset of actual CMPs as $\overline{P}$ where $\overline{P} \subset P$, and any actual CMP as $\overline{p}$ where $\overline{p} \in \overline{P}$. See Figure 9-1.

Next we map each characteristic $s_j (j = 1, \ldots, n)$ of a conflict situation s into one or more properties $p_i (i = 1, \ldots, m)$ of a CMP required (or, more weakly, desirable) to match that characteristic s_j. The set of p_i $(i = 1, \ldots, m)$ defines a point $p \in P$. The mapping Θ of s into p is shown in the upper part of Figure 9-1. The point p may be said to describe for s the properties of an ideal CMP. As will be discussed below, this CMP is taken to be the "minimal property-containing ideal CMP." In reality, however, we know of no actual procedure $\overline{p}$ that meets or historically has met all the requirements of the characteristics s_j of an actual conflict situation s, except perhaps

Figure 9-1.   Mappings for Determining a "Best" Practical Conflict Management Procedure.

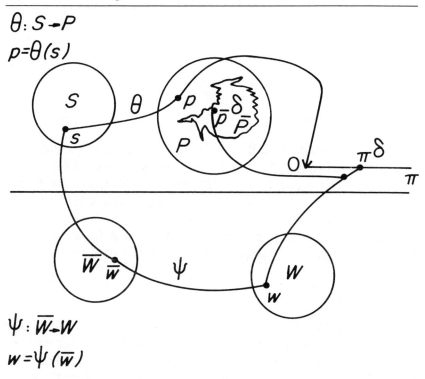

$$\theta: S \to P$$
$$p = \theta(s)$$

$$\psi: \overline{W} \to W$$
$$w = \psi(\overline{w})$$

for some highly simplified situations. Invariably, each existing procedure $\bar{p} \in \bar{P}$ is "inadequate" (imperfect) for a given s with regard to one or more of the required properties p_i. Therefore, we need to distinguish among existing procedures on the basis of their adequacy to match the characteristics s_j of the given s. As discussed in Section 9.5, we need to develop an index of inadequacy for each $\bar{p} \in \bar{P}$. To do so, we define (establish) relative weights $\bar{w}_j (j = 1, \ldots, n)$ for each s_j of the given s. This yields $\bar{w}$, which is a point in the general space $\bar{W}$ of all possible sets of relative weights, that is, $\bar{w} \in \bar{W}$ where $\bar{W} \subset R^n$. See the lower left of Figure 9-1. The mapping of s into $\bar{w}$ is a perceptual mapping—that is, is the importance of characteristics as perceived by one or more participants, the mediator, or both.

As discussed in Section 9.5, the relative importance ρ_{ji} of every property $i(i = 1, \ldots, m)$ for each given characteristic $j(j = 1, \ldots, n)$, and hence the matrix

$$
\begin{bmatrix}
\rho_{11} & \rho_{12} & . & . & . & \rho_{1m} \\
\rho_{21} & \rho_{22} & . & . & . & \rho_{2m} \\
. & . & . & . & . & \\
. & . & . & \rho_{ji} & . & . \\
. & . & . & . & . & \\
\rho_{n1} & \rho_{n2} & . & . & . & \rho_{nm}
\end{bmatrix}
= \begin{bmatrix} \rho_{ji} \end{bmatrix} \quad (9\text{-}4)
$$

must be specified. Typically, the ρ_{ji} are not technologically determined. Rather, they reflect the perceptions of relevant participants, the mediator, or both. Theoretically, they should be independent of the particular CS being studied and the particular CMP being investigated for relevance.

Given the matrix $[\rho_{ji}]$ and the relative weights $\bar{w}$ for a given s, we derive the weights w_i to apply to the properties of CMPs.[4] That is

$$
w_i = \sum_{j=1}^{n} \bar{w}_j \rho_{ji} \qquad i = 1, \ldots, m
$$

which defines the point $w \in W$. The mapping ψ of $\bar{w}$ into w is shown in the lower part of Figure 9-1. The w_i then allow us to map each actual CMP namely $\bar{p}^\delta$ ($\delta = \alpha, \beta, \ldots, \zeta$) into a single dimension along which π, the index of inadequacy, is measured. (See the upper part of Figure 9-1.) That is[5]

$$\pi^\delta = \sum_{i=1}^{m} w_i(p_i - \bar{p}_i^\delta) \quad | \quad \text{for } (p_i - \bar{p}_i^\delta) \geq 0 \quad \delta = \alpha, \beta, \ldots, \zeta$$
(9–5)

Finally, at this point we may set up the trivial program

$$\min_{\bar{p}^\delta \epsilon \bar{P}} \quad \pi^\delta$$
(9–6)

which will not be trivial when relevant constraints are introduced.

9.7 SHORTCOMINGS OF THE MATCHING AND EVALUATION PROCESSES

We now turn to an evaluation of the method developed in Sections 9.2 through 9.6. We shall consider the validity and reasonableness of each step. First, however, note a serious general shortcoming. This shortcoming relates to the fact that our thinking follows that of a rational economist or applied mathematician. It is heavily oriented to traditional natural science methods. For example, it does not meet the challenge of neo-Marxists when they claim, and rightly so, that ideology plays a central role in conflict of human societies as history records these conflicts. However, along one direction we do try to indicate how the natural science and neo-Marxist approaches must and can be complementary in actual conflict management. In effect, what we attempt to do is to cull from the natural sciences a systematic and comprehensive framework for studying conflicts in general and then when we study any particular conflict we start with value judgments (ideology) at the core, and continue to consider explicitly the different values and perceptions of the diverse participants at all stages, in ways that will be detailed later.

In the method presented in the previous sections, the first step is to specify the set of all important characteristics j that any conflict situation may have. We recognize that what one writes down as important today may become rapidly obsolete tomorrow, when we may try to employ our method to some degree. Nonetheless, given our social science and related knowledge, we may be able to do a credible job here—credible in the sense of loosely identifying many, if not all, relevant characteristics. On the other hand, given our different language systems and their different capacities at communications, we may not be able to state precisely and without confusion these characteristics in all languages, let alone in any one language. Further, characteristics relevant for one cultural system may be of zero consequence for another. On the other hand, our list of characteristics can be extended at little or no cost until we do include all those that are relevant to any culture.

While we list characteristics in keeping with our social science and related knowledge, it must be recognized that any analyst comes to this task with certain disciplinary biases. He sees most clearly those elements (variables) central to his own discipline, and less clearly and in less disaggregated fashion elements central to other disciplines—especially those disciplines far from his own. We, therefore, look to significant enrichment of Tables 9-1 through 9-3 from scholars, particularly those from disciplines other than regional science and economics. For instance, a cultural anthropologist would clearly extend Category I (cultural) in Table 9-1, and a cognitive psychologist would surely extend Category IV of Table 9-3.[6]

The second step in our method is to specify the set of all properties i that any conflict management procedure (theoretical or actual) may possess. We have listed in Table 9-4 what we presently consider relevant properties. This listing reflects not only our limited knowledge and perceptions of basic aspects of other cultures, but also a major bias in that it focuses on properties that have tended to be present in CMPs written about and proposed for actual use—such as GRIT and the metagame approach. New concepts, new theories, new operational frameworks—all of which are sorely needed—would undoubtedly result in major changes in the list of Table 9-4.

The third step in our method is to carry through the matching of all properties i with each of the characteristics j that might be present in a specific conflict situation s. This task is required for the identification of p, an ideal CMP.[7] It is extremely difficult and needs the cumulative wisdom of experienced negotiators in each of the several major conflict areas of society. In a utopian world, of course, one may assume that all participants and the mediator may be able to agree fully on the matchings for each j.

Note that an s may map into more than one point in p. This is so since more than one CMP may have all the desirable properties required by an s, and still other desirable properties. For example, the "veto power" may not be required for a given s, yet one CMP may have all the properties i required by an s and the veto power, while a second CMP has all the properties but not the veto power. Both are ideal in the sense of having all required properties i. Yet, strictly speaking, we treat only the second CMP (without the veto power) as "ideal" since in subsequent calculations with actual CMPs, those CMPs which do not have the veto power would be wrongly penalized for not having it, were the first CMP used as the benchmark for the ideal. Thus we map every s into a unique p, the minimally ideal CMP.[8]

The fourth step is taken when it is appreciated that every $\bar{p}$ currently in our tool kit is inadequate for handling any conflict situation s. Such recognition then requires that the relative importance, ρ_{ji}, of all properties i that are matched with a given characteristic j, be specified (with $\Sigma_i \rho_{ji} = 1$, and $0 \leq \rho_{ji} \leq 1$). Difficulties arise not only because of differences in perceptions among participants (to be discussed below), but also because a given property i of a CMP may be required to simultaneously serve (match) several characteristics j of a given s. Our method assumes that the matching of a property i with a characteristic j of any s does not affect its ability to match any other characteristic j' of that s.

Once the ρ_{ji} are determined, we confront in the fifth step the problem that the simple addition of ρ_{ji} over all j is not meaningful in interpreting the role of a property i. To give significance to the ρ_{ji} we must have in mind a particular target, that is a particular conflict situation s. This then poses the next problem, namely what characteristics j of the given s are important. This again is a highly subjective matter about which there may be differences among analysts. In addition, at least some characteristics may be present (absent) to different degrees— another issue involving subjective perceptions. For the simplest case possible, we can assume that the characteristic j is either wholly present (1) or completely absent (0) in a conflict situation.

Moreover, once the degree of presence or absence of a characteristic j is identified or estimated, we need in the sixth step to state the relative importance $\bar{w}_j$ of each characteristic j for the given conflict situation s. This, as well as the degree of presence, is required if we are to add meaningfully the several inadequacies (contributions) of any i (via the different j) for the resolution of the conflict s. How to obtain the $\bar{w}_j$? A first problem is to settle on an appropriate scale. From a technical standpoint, there is no commonly accepted scale by which to measure the $\bar{w}_j$. At one extreme, each property j may be placed into one of two categories, say of *major* importance and given a weight of 9, or of *minor* importance and given a weight of 1. If a more discriminating weighting is possible, the weight may be given by one of the odd integer numbers 1, 3, 5, 7, and 9.[9] But why place characteristics in only five categories of relative importance? Why not more? Or less? This question needs to be decided by participants and the mediator. Note that where a characteristic j is overwhelmingly dominant (or close to indispensable), it might be given a weight of 9 and all others given a weight of 1 or close to 1. If such relative weights do not adequately portray j's dominance, the upper limit to the scale, namely 9, can be increased to be sufficiently large, or the lower limit sufficiently decreased, or both, so that an adequate portrayal of dominance is achieved. Note that all characteristics of conflict situations that are not important for the actual conflict situation s are not involved in the assignment of relative weights. In effect, their relative weights are zero.

Whatever the difficulties in establishing the $\overline{w}_j$ for the calculations to follow, it is essential that precise relative weights be derived—that is, relative weights that are measurable on a ratio scale.

With the j, i, ρ_{ji}, and $\overline{w}_j$ defined, we can now proceed in the seventh step to examine actual CMPs for potential use in managing the given conflict s. But before an analyst or others can effectively do so, he must establish what properties are present in any actual conflict management procedure $\overline{p}^{\delta}$ ($\delta = \alpha, \beta, \ldots, \zeta$). This has difficulties similar to those in identifying the j that are important to any given conflict situation s. Once again, this is a subjective matter, but here the subjective perceptions of an experienced mediator may be of greater importance, relatively speaking, than the participants' perceptions. At one extreme, all that can be observed or envisaged is the presence (1) or absence (0) of a property i in any given $\overline{p}^{\delta}$. Consequently, only a nominal scale is possible—that is $\overline{p}_i^{\delta} = 1$ or 0. A somewhat better situation may exist if it becomes possible through the use of participants, experts, or both to establish the precise degree of presence $\overline{p}_i^{\delta}$ of a property i in the given $\overline{p}^{\delta}$ (e.g. using Saaty-type procedures). Hence, we would have $0 \leq \overline{p}_i^{\delta} \leq 1$. Or, it may be possible to use scaling techniques such as Thurstone's to establish a seemingly more precise measure along a ratio and interval scale of the degree of presence (or absence).

Having established the degree of presence $\overline{p}_i^{\delta}$ of property i in a given $\overline{p}^{\delta}$ ($\delta = \alpha, \beta, \ldots, \zeta$), we then may proceed in the next step to the measure of inadequacy. The measure (9-5) employed in the previous section is[10]

$$\pi^\delta = \sum_{i=1}^{m} w_i(p_i - \bar{p}_i^\delta) \mid \text{for } (p_i - \bar{p}_i^\delta) \geq 0 \qquad \delta = \alpha, \beta, \ldots, \zeta$$

where

$$w_i = \sum_{j=1}^{n} \bar{w}_j \rho_{ji}, \qquad\qquad i = 1, \ldots, m.$$

We have all the necessary elements to do so, namely $\bar{w}_j$, the ρ_{ji}, the $\bar{p}_i^\delta$ and the p_i.[11] However, there are many problems involved in the use of (9–5) as a measure of inadequacy of $\bar{p}^\delta$.

First recall that, whenever $\bar{p}_i^\delta > p_i$, by (9–5) we in effect set $(p_i - \bar{p}_i^\delta)$ equal to zero. That is, we do not allow an excess of an actual CMP on one property i over what is required by a given s to reduce the inadequacy of that CMP with regard to other properties i'. We can imagine that for certain s, such reduction might be permissible.

Second, π^δ as defined by (9–5) employs a specific way, a specific "distance," for measuring inadequacy (namely, the city-block distance). Many other possible ones could be used, one frequent alternative being[a]

$$\pi^\delta = \left(\sum_{i=1}^{m} w_i(p_i - \bar{p}_i^\delta)^2 \right)^{1/2} \mid \text{for } (p_i - \bar{p}_i^\delta) \geq 0 \qquad (9\text{–}7)$$

which has the effect of penalizing larger inadequacies more than smaller ones. But then why should the inadequacies be evaluated in the particular way suggested by (9–7) or (9–5)? Again this is an issue that must be confronted by participants and the mediator.

The problem of measuring the inadequacy of $\bar{p}^\delta$ is still more complex. The formulae of (9–5) and (9–7) simply add inadequacies over each property and, importantly, assume that an inadequacy of a CMP on one count does not influence its inadequacy on any other

[a]Equations (9–5) and (9–7) are special cases of the general Minkowski metric:

$$\pi^\delta = \left(\sum_{i=1}^{m} w_i(p_i - \bar{p}_i^\delta)^q \right)^{1/q} \mid \text{for } (p_i - \bar{p}_i^\delta) \geq 0 \qquad (9\text{–}8)$$

where q is a parameter taking any positive value.

count. But frequently such is not the case in reality. One possibility is to add to (9-5) an interaction term:

$$\pi_{\substack{i \ i' \\ i \ne i'}} a_{ii'} \, (p_i - \bar{p}_i^\delta)(p_{i'} - \bar{p}_{i'}^\delta), \text{ again for } (p_k - \bar{p}_k^\delta) \ge 0, \, k = i, i' \tag{9-9}$$

where $a_{ii'}$, can be either positive or negative to indicate more or less inadequacy as a result of interaction between properties i and i', and where the above term can be restricted to selected pairs of properties rather than cover all pairs.

There are obviously many other possible formulas for measuring inadequacy. One that is difficult to set down mathematically would state that a CMP be rejected if it fails to achieve for any given s a critical mass, complex, or bundle of required (matching) properties. What we are unable to define is the nebulous concept of a critical mass, complex, or bundle. However, an operational way to attack the problem of achieving a critical mass, complex, or bundle, as well as to ensure that an "indispensable" property i is present, is to introduce constraints into the trivial program (9-6) which now becomes the nontrivial program

$$\min_{\{\bar{p}^\delta \, \epsilon \, P\}} \pi^\delta \tag{9-10}$$

subject to $\bar{p}_h^\delta \ge c_h$

where $h \, \epsilon \, H$, H being a set of selected properties, and where c_h equals 1 for any "indispensable" property. Still other kinds of constraints are possible.

Additionally, if there are interdependencies among the properties i, are there not likely to be interdependencies among the characteristics j? If so, as is frequently the case in reality, such would need to be taken into account in at least the specification of the $\bar{w}_j$. For example, if one characteristic j implies the existence of another characteristic j', then perhaps the $\bar{w}_j$ and the $\bar{w}_{j'}$ need to be adjusted to avoid overcounting or undercounting. This in turn would lead to a new value for some of the w_i.

Hitherto, we have assumed that all participants and the mediator have the same language, concepts, perceptions, and cultural background and, in all other respects, are identical so as to permit the problem to be symmetric. However, in actuality we know that this is not so and that major asymmetries exist in most if not all situations. We now address the problems that arise because of asymmetries. These problems involve a sequence of secondary conflicts that must be managed before attacking the main problem of selecting an actual CMP to resolve the primary conflict. We shall stress that the diverse participants with their different values and perceptions, and not the analyst or mediator, should in the main determine relevant variables and magnitudes.

The first problem is the language problem—that is, the problem of developing a common language among the participants so that they come to agree, at least to some extent, on the meaning of words, terms, and sentences. However, associated with this problem is also the problem of differences among participants in relevant concepts, theories, and ideas—a problem that is not as easily managed. This latter problem leads participants to have differences in perceptions concerning what are the relevant characteristics of the given conflict situation.

The secondary conflict at this point, like a number of others to be noted below, needs to be resolved before the analyst can move on to the next step. In this secondary conflict, as well as the others to follow, there is the problem of attaching different weights to the views, opinions, suggestions, and the like of the several participants. This problem itself generates more conflict to be resolved, and so on. Moreover, debate and discussion that may be undertaken to resolve these secondary conflicts may often be required to eliminate differences in perceptions; but at the same time, such starts to introduce interdependence of perceptions, which will then affect the ease with which subsequent conflicts are resolved.

Once the first secondary conflict is resolved, a next one that may arise concerns the relevant scale to use in measuring the degree of presence or absence of a relevant characteristic j in the given conflict situation. This issue and many others mentioned below may become so involved that the participants and mediator may reach the conclusion to forget it (put it aside), that is, assign either a 1 (relevant and present) or 0 (irrelevant or absent) to any characteristic j. If this is not the case, one participant might be sold on an extension of one approach, say the Saaty approach, a second on another approach, say the Thurstone single-dimensional scaling approach, and a third on still another approach, say a simple hunch or a Delphi method. A skillful mediator, here and in other places noted below, may be able to get the participants to use simple procedures to resolve their differences quickly—for example, a simple *action compromise* procedure involving not the most sophisticated, nor the most simple, but an approach falling in between these extremes.

A third secondary conflict arises when the participants and mediator, again because of differences in language or perception, try to settle on relevant properties i for each given characteristic j.[12]

A fourth secondary conflict concerns the problem of determining for any given j of s the relative importance of the i, that is the ρ_{ji}. As with the previous problem, each participant's notions may be fuzzy and he may need much assistance from the analyst or mediator. The participants may also follow a suggestion by the mediator that they engage in a give and take discussion—that is, that they interact recursively, perhaps relying heavily on the mediator's or analyst's knowledge, experience, perceptions, and the like.

A fifth secondary conflict arises when it is necessary for the participants to agree on what properties any given actual CMP has. Again, they may recursively interact, and rely heavily on the knowledge and experience of the mediator and experts to resolve this problem.

A sixth secondary conflict concerns the degree of presence or absence of any property i in an actual CMP being examined. Again the participants may choose to avoid this problem by employing a nominal 1 (presence) -0 (absence) scale. Here, however, the participants may be more receptive to statements by the mediator and experts concerning the degree of presence or absence of a property i than they would be to statements on the degree of presence or absence of a characteristic j.

A seventh secondary conflict arises over the need to set up criteria for selecting a best CMP. For some participants, this may be a problem of finding a simple formula for determining an index of inadequacy π, which must also involve a choice of values for the several relevant coefficients and exponents. For more technically minded participants, this may be a problem of choosing an objective function. In the case of the latter, one participant may wish to employ the ideal p as a target and select that actual CMP which minimizes the sum of weighted deviations (distances) from this ideal. A second may want to identify what he considers to be the two chief properties of the ideal CMP—say efficiency and security—and then to min the max deviation over these two criteria in selecting a best actual CMP. A third, perhaps a Nash convert, may be enamoured with the multiplication process and want to maximize the product of efficiency and security after each has been standardized. Finally, another may simply want to minimize search time, subject to satisficing on each relevant property i of a CMP. After recursive interaction and suggestions from the analyst or mediator, or both, or by the use of some last-resort compromise procedure, the participants may reach agreement on a relevant objective function.

If, however, the objective function agreed to is of the type given in Equation (9–5) then it becomes necessary to establish relative weights $\overline{w}_j$ for those characteristics j which the participants and mediator have agreed on as important for conflict situation s. Inevitably, a conflict will arise here since participants will have different perceptions on the relative importance of the characteristics. Again, recursive interaction may be employed in resolving these differences. However, in practice there may need to be several occasions for discussion among participants to avoid inconsistency. For example, in the first round of discussions they may agree to set a high relative weight $(\overline{w}_j)$ on the characteristic "calculating social psychology," but later discover that the score of the "information available" characteristic is extremely low. When this is the case, they will need to enter another round of discussions in order to adjust (lower) the $\overline{w}_j$ attached to the characteristic "calculating social psychology," since this characteristic demands that a high level of information be available.

Additionally, in the use of any objective function, there is the problem of establishing values for the parameters and relevant constraints to which all participants are agreeable. For example, consider the simplest objective function—namely, that of the satisficer which aims to minimize the search time in finding a $\overline{p} \ \epsilon \ \overline{P}$ whose properties i exceed a set of binding magnitudes (constraints). The conflict here concerns the relevant i on which to set constraints. Moreover, there is the problem earlier noted on how the i should be measured, which is presumably solved so that the participants can confront the question: What should the level be for each of these i?

When all the above secondary conflicts are managed, we come to the problem of selecting an actual CMP to resolve the primary conflict.[13] We employ, say, the formula or objective function agreed upon in the above processes, and lo and behold the computer churns out a ranking of actual CMPs from best to worst. But does it?

As is obvious in the workshop approaches of Burton (1972) and Kelman (1976), and the "yesable proposition-fractionation" approach of Fisher (1979), to be discussed in Chapter 10, the actual conflict resolution process, successful or unsuccessful, is a dynamic process. It almost invariably involves learning, especially during the recursive interaction and related activity of the participants. The static framework presented in this chapter ignores completely this basic aspect. Even more fundamental is the recognition that the conflict situation itself is constantly changing, and hence, too, the set of relevant characteristics *j* against which a conflict management procedure needs to be matched.[14]

9.8 CONCLUDING REMARKS

We have just noted a major deficiency of our framework—its static character. It is possible to remove this deficiency to a small extent—to the extent that all economic, regional science, and other social science models are able to when they attack other than the most simple problems. Like those who put forth these models, we can claim that until better models are constructed that incorporate the dynamic aspects of reality more effectively, we must make do with the anemically dynamic models that we have, or we must merely rely on intuition in attacking problems. But at least for some practitioners, as for us, intuition plus anemic dynamic models is better than intuition alone.

A more telling ground on which the reader may be inclined to reject our model is that it involves so many factors (variables) that it cannot be made operational. But we would claim otherwise. To support our claim, we can illustrate with a parallel situation which pertains to an industrial location decision involving just as many factors (variables) and which in a real sense is operational and leads to clearcut recommendations. This situation pertains to a decision on the location of an integrated iron and steel works. In considering such a situation we would construct a table almost identical to Table 9–1. For example, all the items listed under "Economic System" in Table 9–1 pertain. Instead of Table 9–3 on participants' characteristics we would have a table on structural properties of labour force and associated institutions. Many of the items would be similar, such as those under the headings "Psychological" and "Level of Education." Others would be dissimilar, such as those relating to the "Productivity of Existing Labour Force," "Wage Rates," and "Institutions." The latter we list in Table 9–6. The number of items in the table substituting for Table 9–3, and which would include Table 9–6 as a part, would be at least as many as in Table 9–3. Further, in place of Table 9–2 and 9–4 there would be tables on:

Table 9-6.   Structural Properties of Labor Force and Associated Institutions.

I   *Skills (Training and Education) of Existing Labor Force with Regard to:*

— entrepreneurship
— business administration
— financial and accounting personnel
— advanced engineering and technical (Ph.D level) personnel
— foremanship
— manual labor

II *Productivity of Existing Labor Force*

— receptivity of new production methods
— capability of retraining
— absenteeism
— attitude toward work
— morale
— participation in routine decisionmaking

III *Wage Rates*

— money wages
— work week
— fringe benefits
    — social security
    — unemployment compensation
    — vacation
    — sick days

IV *Institutions*

— extent of unionism
— quality of union leadership
— labor laws and practices
— unemployment compensation
— social security taxes and provisions
— overtime rates and practices
— tenure
— paternalism
— diverse work incentives
— local, state, and federal tax system
    — progressiveness
    — regressiveness

- Structural Properties of the Transportation System
- Structural Properties of the Market
- Structural Properties of Raw Material Supply
- Structural Properties of the Energy System
- Structural Properties of Production
- Structural Properties of the Capital Market
- Structural Properties of Impacts on External System

The items listed in these tables are even more numerous than those in Tables 9-2 and 9-4. To illustrate the contents of one of these tables, we present Table 9-7 on structural properties of the market.

All the factors in the tables just mentioned that could be constructed are considered by a wise industrial-location practitioner when he is hired as a consultant to identify the best location for an integrated iron and steel works. Despite the fact that there are so many factors—as numerous as those that a skilled international mediator must consider when he is assigned the task of identifying the best conflict management procedure(s) to handle a given situation—the skillful and wise industrial-location practitioner is able to proceed. He looks for what he would designate the *major locational cost differentials* among alternative sites for the integrated iron and steel works (including existing locations of works and those outside the region or nation that are likely to go into operation in the future because of their efficiency characteristics). For the situation in the United States, these major cost differentials would comprise transport costs on coal, transport costs on ore, transport costs on scrap, and transport costs on finished product to the market. Although labor costs constitute by far the largest cost in U.S. iron and steel production, labor costs do not differ from site to site (existing or potential) because of national unionization of steel labor. On the other hand, labor costs do differ markedly from nation to nation. For the United States, a fifth major cost differential would arise from scale economies, wherein competition from small, nonintegrated electric steel operations would be taken into account.

With a half-dozen or so major cost differentials in mind, the skilled industrial-location practitioner constructs a core framework by which to evaluate alternative locations. Onto this framework he grafts many adjustments and qualifications which come to be additional costs and benefits at each location, often at best only crudely estimated. This he does when his mind, sometimes unknowingly, races through the

Table 9-7. Structural Properties of The Market and Production.

I *Spatial Distribution of Demand for Finished Product*
  — by world region
  — by national region
  — by metropolitan area
  — by type product
    — structural shapes
    — plate
    — sheet
    — wire rod
    — pipe, etc.

II *Cyclical Character (Stability) of Demand*
  — by world region
  — by national region
  — by type product
    — structural shapes
    — plates
    — sheet
    — wire rod
    — pipe, etc.

III *Presence of Competitors and Competitive Strategies*
  — foreign
    — old established countries
    — new industralizing countries
    — developing nations
  — domestic
    — by integrated producers
    — by electric and other small mills
  — extent of cartelization
    — international
    — domestic

IV *International Situation (Penetrability of Foreign Markets)*
  — exchange rates
  — import quotas, duties
  — pricing discrimination (dumping)
  — other legal and nonlegal constraints
  — foreign policy constraints

V *Multiplier Effects (Impact)*
  — directly via steel fabrication relocation
  — indirectly via general economic growth

many factors already mentioned and more. Ultimately he comes up with a recommendation as scientific as any that can be achieved for complex problems. For example, see Isard and Cumberland (1950).

In the same manner we conceive the future international conflict mediator identifying the half-dozen or so major factors in a conflict situation as, for example, Fisher (1979) does in his balance sheet analysis to be discussed in the next chapter. Focusing first on these major factors, he then can select among conflict management procedures that can effectively address them. Better yet, as we shall discuss in Chapter 11, he may even be able to tailor conflict management procedures to focus upon them. Subsequently, he then may be able to both trim and attach frills and lace to effectively handle a number of less important factors as his mind races through the innumerable possible factors at play. Ultimately, he reaches a conclusion on the procedure (tailored or not) he recommends or uses, at least at the start, along with a number of back-up ones.

NOTES

1. This chapter draws heavily upon Isard and C. Smith (1980a).
2. See Glugiewiez and Isard (forthcoming) for further discussion.
3. In order to keep our presentation as simple as possible, we do not consider in Table 9–5 the possibility that the presence of certain CMP properties may have a negative influence in the use of a given CMP; they may escalate a conflict. Such influence may be incorporated in a straightforward manner in the construction of an index and hence is left to the reader.
4. In matrix form we have: $w = \overline{w} [\rho_{ji}]$ where w and $\overline{w}$ are 1 x m and 1 x n row vectors, respectively.
5. In matrix form we have: $\pi = w [p - \overline{p}]$ where π is a $1 \times \zeta$ row vector and where the elements in the δ column of the $m \times \zeta$ matrix $[p - \overline{p}]$ are $(p_1 - \overline{p}_1^\delta)$, $(p_2 - \overline{p}_2^\delta)$, $\ldots$, $(p_m - \overline{p}_m^\delta)$.
6. Note that the problem of elimination of characteristics (errors of commission as opposed to errors of omission) is not a critical one. For example, if an analyst were to set down characteristics he considers important but that participants and mediators in conflict situations never do consider important, they will almost invariably, if not always, be given zero weights. However, there could conceivably be a nuisance value in having such characteristics included in a table.
7. At this point, all that we need to know is that a property i is desirable for characteristic j; we do not need to know its relative importance ρ_{ji}, which is required in the next step.

8. In effect, we choose among potential candidates for the designation "ideal CMP" as if we were attaching a cost to the use of any p that has unnecessary properties. Nonetheless, certain problems in the use of this convention may arise, which we do not discuss since they are relatively minor compared to others we cannot adequately handle.

9. See Saaty and Khouja (1976) and pages 148–150 for one interesting rationale for the use of such numbers. Or, to achieve still more discrimination, the participants and the mediator may use one or more single-dimensional scaling techniques such as Thurstone scaling. See, for example, Baird and Noma (1978:chap 7).

10. Note that when a property i of a CMP is not needed to match an important characteristic j for a given conflict situation s, this means that the characteristics j' that property i does match (i.e., for which it is required) have zero weights for s (i.e., each $\overline{w}_{j'} = 0$) and hence by (9-1) $w_i = 0$.

11. A useful step might be to test the sensitivity of the ranking of CMPs along the index of inadequacy to changes in the $\overline{w}_j$ and the ρ_{ji}. Clearly it would be desirable to happen upon a conflict situation wherein the ranking of CMPs was invariant to the $\overline{w}_j$ and ρ_{ji} that different analysts and participants might propose.

12. Formally speaking, the problem here is to settle on an appropriate mapping θ from characteristics j to properties i.

13. We have just indicated that before participants choose a CMP to resolve the primary conflict, they must manage a sequence of preceding conflicts. In effect, one might claim that there are many stages involved in managing the entire conflict situation. At each stage there is an outcome o which is in part a function of the demands, proposals, or the like of the participants—which in our general framework can be viewed as the joint action a. At each stage, too, there is an environment z which largely consists of information, setting, and the like largely set by the mediator and analyst. If the conflict at any stage is managed, then the outcome o of that stage becomes part of the environmental input z to the outcome function at the next stage to be considered together with the joint action a at that stage. In this sense, we have a series of outcome functions: $o = f(a, z)$.

14. Again, we note that the above presentation is largely in conformity with traditional scientific method and rational thinking dominant in our Anglo-Saxon culture. But, with ideologically oriented participants, for example, religious fanatics, risk lovers, and revolutionary Marxists, the sequence of steps in our thinking process may be completely wrong. For situations involving these kinds of participants, the framework and sequence of though-stages may be totally different. Also, see Isard and C. Smith (1981:30–36).

10 NONQUANTITATIVE PROCEDURES FOR CONFLICT MANAGEMENT

10.1 INTRODUCTION

In this chapter, we break with the trend of development of the previous chapters. While quantitative approaches have considerable appeal because they can assign numbers to outcomes—sometimes very precise numbers—they very often fail to analyze strategic factors as a result of their preoccupation with description by numbers. They fail to take into account existing differences in ideology, perceptions, attitude, psychology, and the like. In fact, history suggests that qualitative approaches have been much more extensively used to manage conflicts than have quantitative approaches. This statement, however, should not be taken to imply that qualitative approaches are superior. It reflects the fact that adequate quantitative approaches were not available until recently. Moreover, the quantitative analyst can easily point to a record of dismal failure of qualitative approaches. But then this should not be taken to suggest that quantitative approaches can do better. In fact, they may do worse, especially if divorced from the relatively little bit of insight we have gained from the dismal record of qualitative approaches. So in this chapter we are motivated to explore, as best we can, what insights can be acquired from the accumulated wisdom of qualitative approaches, thereby to improve somewhat our quantitative approaches and temper the history of failures that the future undoubtedly will record for them. Hence, whatever we do can only be for the better.

Yet, we do not wish to spend an inordinate amount of time reviewing and evaluating the existing qualitative literature. Hence, we focus upon the writings of three major scholars, whose works we judge embody much of the accumulated wisdom of qualitative approaches. Readers might differ with our choice of scholars. Nevertheless, the accumulated wisdom that will be found in the writings of other major scholars is not likely to be much different.

In Section 10.2 we present the fundamental aspects of Burton's workshop interaction process emphasizing how a shift in focus from materialistic outcomes to both materialistic and nonmaterialistic can convert a conflict into a harmony situation. In Section 10.3, Kelman's workshop framework is discussed, with particular emphasis placed on those aspects which must be appropriately handled to insure a politically viable solution to a conflict. In Section 10.4, we present a number of the useful conflict management tools that have been suggested by Fisher. These tools include (1) the use of a legal balance sheet calculus in examining non-yesable propositions and formulating yesable propositions inclusive of credible threats and offers, (2) fractionation of a complex conflict into component parts, and (3) brainstorming sessions aimed at inventing new and innovative solutions when traditional avenues fail. In Section 10.5 we sketch one possible model of the learning aspects of a workshop interaction session through the use of dynamical systems analysis. Section 10.6 covers some concluding remarks.

10.2 BURTON'S WORKSHOP INTERACTION PROCESS: FROM ZERO-SUM TO POSITIVE-SUM GAMES, FROM MATERIAL NEEDS TO MATERIAL AND NONMATERIAL NEEDS

One of the best thought out and tested qualitative approaches to conflict management is Burton's problem-solving workshop, involving a reasonably well-defined interaction process among participants. In this approach, a mediator (or team of mediators) and a participant (or team of participants) representing each of the nations involved in a conflict are brought together in a workshop atmosphere and are invited to engage in face-to-face debate and discussion about their conflict situation. These discussions are informal and normally carried out in an academic setting in order to create conditions in which participants are willing to share their definitions of the conflict, their understanding of the factors lying behind its emergence, escalation and perpetuation, their perceptions of their own and their opponents' objectives and actions, and their assessments of alternative schemes or ways to resolve their conflict.

The mediator's role in this interaction process is that of initiating and structuring the participants' discussions. However, where appropriate, this role is supplemented by that of (1) translating one participant's contributions to the discussion into terms more likely to be understood by others and (2) feeding in information derived from the mediator's experience in handling other conflicts and from her knowledge of conflict theory.

Gradually, through the process of information production and exchange, the participants' views of the relevant characteristics of the conflict situation change, and their understanding of and appreciation for their opponents' point of view increase. These changes lead to altered preference structures and, in turn, may affect their ideas of what is feasible, necessary, and promising in the search for a solution to their conflict.

Of particular interest in Burton's framework are the four steps that he envisages taking place in a successful workshop. We formalize these steps so that they can be of more general application for workshops and other interaction processes that do not satisfy the specific characteristics considered necessary by Burton.

Step 1. Extension of Commodity Space to Include Noneconomic Goods. The first step involves the extension of the set of relevant goods and needs that participants associate with a conflict situation. Almost invariably, according to Burton, a conflict is perceived as involving primarily, if not exclusively, material goods (and resources). Participants fail to perceive that some, if not many, nonmaterial goods and resources are involved.

These nonmaterial goods are associated with certain universal human needs—needs which sociologists, sociobiologists, and others suggest must be satisfied if the individual behaving unit is to be a functioning and cooperative member of the larger society. Some examples of these goods and associated needs are:[1]

- c-respect, and the need to be respected (or recognized)
- c-security, and the need to have a sense of security

- c-participation, and the need to have identity
- c-power, and the need to exercise power (or control)
- c-sociality, and the need to have a sense of belonging
- c-skill, and the need to have an opportunity to be creative

These nonmaterial goods and their corresponding universal needs contrast with material goods and their associated materialistic needs such as:

- a luxurious home, and the need to live conspicuously
- a color television set, and the need to watch a football game in color
- a bottle of Coca-Cola, and the need to quench a compelling thirst

In any conflict situation, the possession of such material goods are often, according to Burton, not ends in themselves but rather the means by which to meet some more basic human needs—such as the need to survive, achieve, be secure, or be respected.

In effect, what Burton is arguing is that the set of goods, and their associated needs, upon which conflicting parties focus their attention must be extended to include not only economic goods where good 1 = wheat, good 2 = corn, . . . , good $\ell - 1$ = money, and good ℓ = labour (which are primarily traded and exchanged in economic markets, and are standardized in the sense that they have precise values in the form of prices), but also noneconomic (intangible) goods where good $\ell + 1$ = c-solidarity, good $\ell + 2$ = c-power, good $\ell + 3$ = c-respect, . . . , good ϕ = c-sanctions (which are not exchanged in formal markets, which are not well defined, and which at best have only implicit prices). This explicit recognition of the noneconomic (nonmaterial) as well as economic (material) aspects of the conflict is important, he claims, because it signifies that each participant's narrow goal (e.g., to maximize her own economic income, wealth, or the equivalent needs) should and can be replaced by a broader set of goals. That is, the set of goals should embody not only the need to have economic income, wealth, and the equivalent, but also the need to have identity, power, respect, security, and so forth. Further, in cases where the possession of a certain material good is not an end in itself, but rather a means toward an end (the end being the possession of a certain nonmaterial good), then acknowledgment of this fact can also lead to a recognition that alternative means (certain other non-material goods) can be employed to achieve that same end. This extension of the set of goods to include noneconomic goods thus represents one avenue through which the qualitative approach of Burton can be wedded with traditional quantitative social science approaches.

Step 2. Recognition that Welfare (Outcomes) is Dependent on the Extended Set of Commodities. The second step in Burton's framework is the recognition that welfare, in a sense the ultimate payoff that each behaving unit derives from the management (resolution) of the conflict, is dependent not only on the material (economic) goods, but also on the nonmaterial (noneconomic) goods that he receives.

Formally, each behaving unit's utility function becomes

$$u^J = u^J(b_1^J, b_2^J, \ldots, b_\ell^J, b_{\ell+1}^J, \ldots, b_\phi^J) \qquad J = A, \ldots, U \quad (10\text{-}1)$$

instead of

$$u^J = u^J(b_1^J, b_2^J, \ldots, b_\ell^J) \qquad\qquad J = A, \ldots, U \quad (10\text{-}2)$$

where $b_h^J(h = 1, 2, \ldots, \phi)$ is the allocation of good h that J receives from the management of the conflict.

This step is, in a sense, even more critical than the first. This is so because while a focus on outcomes measured in terms of material goods (resources) alone may lead to a view of the conflict as a zero-sum game, when the measurement of outcomes is extended to include nonmaterial goods (and their associated needs), then the zero-sum character of the game may disappear. This change comes about, according to Burton, because while the traditional economic goods (e.g., territory) are subject to scarcity—in the sense that what one behaving unit acquires, the other behaving unit loses—such is not the case for many noneconomic goods. Rather, it is a characteristic of at least a number of the latter goods that there is not a fixed amount available for consumption. More precisely, the amount of these goods available, given our social institutions, is not fixed by an upper bound as far as human beings can perceive.[2] Further, many of these non-economic goods display a characteristic that economists normally associate with public goods—that is, that the consumption of any one of these goods by one behaving unit does not reduce the amount available for consumption by other behaving units. Additionally,

Burton claims that some of these goods even have the property that the more that is consumed by behaving units as a whole, the more that becomes available for consumption by all—that is, up to a certain point, there exist positive externalities (agglomeration economies) associated with the consumption of these goods.

Because of these characteristics, it becomes possible to effect arrangements where in fact each party to the conflict can obtain more c-security, c-respect, c-rectitude, and other noneconomic commodities that are important to them, and therefore be better off—and in Burton's terms much better off—even though they must still divide up a fixed amount of territory and other economic goods. When this occurs, according to Burton, the zero-sum game disappears and a positive-sum game emerges. See Isard and C. Smith (1982b:87–88).

Step 3. Recognition that Welfare (Outcomes) to Participants Are Interdependent.   The third step in Burton's approach is the need for participants to perceive the interdependence of their utility outcomes. That is each must come to recognize that given their universal needs, he is better off the more satisfied other participants are with the outcome, *ceteris paribus.* For this to occur, the participants must become aware of, and sensitive to, each other's perceptions of the conflict situation and the outcomes likely to accrue to each from any joint action that might be adopted.

What Burton is in effect saying is that after a certain amount of debate and discussion in a workshop atmosphere, wherein participants come to recognize the interdependence of their utilities, the formal statement of each one's utility function given by (10-1) will be found to be inadequate. Each one's utility function should be rewritten as

$$u^J = u^J (u^A, \ldots, u^I, u^K, \ldots, u^U; b_1^J, b_2^J, \ldots, b_\phi^J) \qquad J = A, \ldots U \tag{10-3}$$

where within a certain range and appropriately defined limits

$$\frac{\partial u^J}{\partial u^L} > 0 \qquad J, L = A, \ldots, U \qquad J \neq L \tag{10-4}$$

Step 4. Reassessment of the Costs/Benefits of Alternative Joint Actions.   The fourth step in Burton's framework requires that participants adopt a benefit-cost approach in reevaluating the alternative joint actions available to them. In this reevaluation, they will now recognize that while there will surely be costs incurred (in terms of material goods foregone) when a concession is made, these costs should be contrasted with the benefits derived from the increase in (1) their c-security, c-respect, and other relevant noneconomic goods associated with the concession and (2) the utility of the participant(s) to whom the concession was made.

It is Burton's contention that once these four steps have been taken, the participants will automatically be able to resolve the conflict. This is so because the conflict has been transformed from a "problem" into a "puzzle" with the characteristic that while a specific solution may not be indicated beforehand, it is known that there is a solution and that the application of known theories or known sets of techniques is adequate for finding a solution.

In addition to the steps just outlined for transforming a zero-sum game into a positive-sum game, another important contribution that Burton makes derives from his recognition of the important role that attitudes and perceptions play in a conflict situation. The "conflict manager," he argues, should be concerned with the process by which these attitudes and perceptions are defined and redefined and with the means by which these changes can be accelerated. The workshop interaction process proposed by Burton is one means by which to bring about these changes. It creates conditions in which, as a result of greater communication between participants and appropriate activity by the mediator, new and more accurate information can be fed to participants, allowing them to select information they consider to be relevant and to be added to their stock of knowledge. With the right kind of increase in their stock of knowledge, Burton would argue that participants come to have ideas, perceptions, and attitudes that lead to joint actions that resolve rather than escalate the conflict.

As with any framework that might be proposed for resolving conflicts, there are weaknesses in Burton's workshop approach. One is that it may not always be beneficial to bring about an extension of the number of relevant goods or needs that participants might associate with a given conflict situation. Such may act to introduce more areas of disagreement rather than help solve the initial specific disagreements. This is particularly so when the new goods introduced are of the intangible noneconomic variety, because these goods (and their associated needs) may make it very difficult for a participant to assess the impacts of alternative joint actions. Some very simple guiding principles—such as equal improvements and equal concessions—become difficult to operationalize, while conflict management procedures relying on anything stronger than ordinal measurements are ruled out. In fact, this aspect of Burton's approach contrasts with the approach of Roger Fisher (to be discussed below), who argues that often the best strategy for resolving a conflict is that of "fractionation of the conflict." That is, Fisher suggests that frequently one should decompose the existing conflict into a number of smaller conflicts, and proceed to resolve them one by one, beginning with the more tangible ones.

Another weakness of Burton's approach is that it provides no way to relate the workshop process to the actual policy formation process. Even if a workshop process were successful in changing the attitudes and perceptions of each participant in the manner suggested in his four steps, the problem remains of transferring to the policy process such changes in attitudes and perceptions. Specifically, the problem is how to design and operate a workshop so as to ensure that the products of the workshop will be communicated to the relevant decisionmakers and thus have the potential to influence joint political action in the direction required for resolution of the conflict? This question is particularly pertinent when it is recognized that the very conditions that enhance the capacity of a workshop to produce changes in individual participants may be those conditions that reduce the likelihood that the participants (because of their changed attitudes and perceptions) will actually be able to influence the policy of the participants' national governments.

Perhaps the most serious weakness of Burton's approach is that, while he asserts that once a conflict is analyzed within his framework it can automatically be resolved, he does not discuss the specifics of how the participants do actually go about resolving their conflict. He seems to avoid the problem that there may be numerous solutions to the positive-sum game that evolves, and that the participating nations may not be in harmony with regard to which is the best of the compromise solutions. That is, while solutions can be found in which all participants gain compared with the existing situation, it is not likely that each of these solutions involve equal gains for all participants. In such an event, there may develop a conflict at another level—that is, a conflict over which of the available compromise procedures to adopt in moving from the existing situation to, say, the efficiency frontier.

10.3 KELMAN'S WORKSHOPS AND POLITICALLY VIABLE CONFLICT RESOLUTION

In many respects, Kelman's workshop approach resembles Burton's; however, there are important differences in emphasis. These differences arise from Kelman's attempt to overcome one of Burton's weaknesses—namely, inadequate attention to the problem of getting implemented the conflict-resolving ideas found acceptable by workshop participants. As already noted, the workshop process is by necessity interpersonal. Individuals learn from interaction within the workshop atmosphere and, as a result, experience changes in their attitudes, perceptions, and so forth. However, the workshop approach also implies an assumption that it is possible to bring about appropriate changes in joint political action by way of these changes in individual perceptions and attitudes. This is a strong assumption. The specific conditions for maximizing impact on individuals differ from those for maximizing impact on the system, and in many instances, they may in fact conflict with each other. Hence, Kelman advocates careful planning of all the basic elements of the workshop process to ensure that it can adequately serve what he considers to be its two objectives. These are: (1) to give participants the freedom, opportunity, and motivation to move away from strict adherence to official positions, and from attempts to justify the actions of their own side and score points by outdoing the other side in recitation of atrocities, and to encourage participants to absorb new information, explore new ideas, revise their attitudes, and engage in a process of creative problem solving; and (2) to increase the probability that the new information and ideas and the innovative proposals for conflict resolution that are generated can be effectively transferred to the policy formation process. See Isard and C. Smith (1982b:104–5).

From the very start, Kelman would suggest that the mediator select individuals to participate in the workshop having in mind the need to balance the contradictory requirements demanded by the two workshop objectives.[3] On the one hand, public officials directly involved with the conflict as part of their day-to-day activities would be in the best position to transfer new ideas to the policy-making process. On the other hand, unofficial participants are more likely to experience a change in their attitudes and perceptions since they are likely to be less constrained by public postures, more open to new information and insights, and more willing to explore new ideas. As a compromise, then, Kelman favors the selection of participants who engage in the workshop in their capacity as private citizens but who (1) have attitudes and perceptions representative of those held by an important interest group within their society and (2) have sufficient access to the decisionmaking process within this interest group that they will be able to feed their new attitudes and ideas into its policy-formulation process.[4]

Further, Kelman would suggest that the mediator attempt to create a workshop atmosphere, again having in mind the need to balance the contradictory requirements demanded by the two workshop objectives. For example, the creation of a novel atmosphere is required to overcome the standard practices (norms) that generally govern interactions among conflicting parties and to introduce practices that encourage them to consider the perspective of the other side and engage in a joint effort at creative problem solving. Change in participants is also facilitated by a setting insulated from outside distractions, pressures, and constraints. This insulation permits the development of a "cultural island" situation in which participants are encouraged to become more deeply immersed in the workshop interaction process and hence more willing to (1) question their previous assumptions, attitudes, and perceptions and (2) explore new ways of looking at the conflict. However, if the new ideas, attitudes, and perceptions generated by the workshop process are to be maintained by participants once they return to their respective societies (where the old norms, pressures, and constraints are dominant), then it is important that the participants' ideas, attitudes, and perceptions do not change too much during the workshop interaction process. Clearly, the workshop atmosphere would be too far removed from reality if a participant returns expressing points of view so deviant from the prevailing group or societal norms that his ideas are met with hostility and his proposed solutions (as workshop products) systematically rejected.

To replicate the outside environment more adequately within the workshop without interfering with the "novelty" and "cultural island" effects, Kelman proposes that each nation involved in the conflict be represented by a set of participants with a sufficiently wide range of viewpoints to reflect the different interests of its major interest groups. He recognizes that multiple rather than single representation for each nation does not per se guarantee that workshop outcomes will be more politically viable. Rather, such political viability depends upon (1) the extent to which participants to the workshop function as members of a national team or as individuals and (2) the manner in which intranational differences enter into the workshop interaction process.

On the one hand, change may occur more readily in workshops in which participants function as individuals rather than as team members. This is so since participants can deviate more readily from the official positions of their respective groups, and differences in points of view within each group can emerge more quickly, thus making available a wider range of ideas for discussion and problem solving. At the same time, however, such an arrangement may make the transfer of new attitudes more difficult. In particular, ideas developed and positions agreed to without participants' having first reached consensus within a national contingent are more vulnerable to attack and rejection by the respective nation's political leaders once participants return home. That is, while change is less likely to occur in workshops in which participants function as members of a national team, whatever changes do occur are more likely to survive beyond the workshop and enter the policy-making process.

Recognizing this dilemma, Kelman proposes that participants function as individuals during the main workshop interaction process, but that the mediator hold two separate intraparty sessions with the participants representing each national group. One would be prior to the workshop and another at the end or toward the end of the workshop. The purpose of the intraparty sessions prior to the main workshop is for members of each national group to meet one another and discuss internal disagreements without having to worry that such might weaken their united front in the main workshop interactions. The group can work out a plan of action to be adopted in the main workshop should any one member be perceived by the others as compromising too far in the direction of their opponent(s). Also, the mediator can both (1) accumulate information about each party's viewpoint of the conflict and of their opponent's, which may be helpful in suggesting topics to be raised for discussion within the main workshop and (2) begin to establish the norms of communication on which the main workshop will be based.

The function of the intraparty sessions held at the end of the main workshop is for each member of a national group to test out the acceptability of his new attitudes, perceptions, and ideas for conflict resolution in the presence of fellow nationals who have been through the same workshop experience. If among themselves these new ideas, attitudes, and perceptions are not acceptable, then they are even less likely to be acceptable within the larger society to which they are about to return.

In effect, what Kelman has done is to integrate his workshop interaction process more effectively into the real world conflict-resolution process. The preworkshop sessions serve as a link between the actual conflict situation and the main workshop interaction process. The inputs to these sessions are the ideas, perceptions, and attitudes derived directly from the actual conflict situation, while the output of these sessions serve as inputs into the main workshop. By creating the environment and setting the agenda for action within these initial sessions, the mediator can ensure that these inputs contribute to a more successful set of main workshop interactions.

During the main workshop interaction processes that follow, the mediator is responsible for (1) creating an environment that appropriately balances the requirements of realism on the one hand and novelty on the other and (2) setting an agenda for action in which participants focus first on the identification of the relevant characteristics of the conflict situation, second on the development of an awareness of and sensitivity to each others' attitudes and perceptions of the conflict situation, and finally on the identification of conflict resolution proposals acceptable to all participants.

The end-of-workshop sessions serve as a link between the main workshop interactions and the actual policy-formation process. The inputs to these sessions are the outputs of the main workshop process, and the outputs of these sessions serve as potential inputs into the policy-formation process. By creating a proper environment and setting a proper agenda in these final sessions, the mediator can increase the probability that their outputs will be transferred successfully to the actual policy-formation process.[5]

Although Kelman's approach represents a major extension of Burton's, it still has a number of weaknesses. Like Burton, he does not explicitly consider the higher level conflict over the choice of a conflict management procedure. He seems to adopt a satisficing approach. With him the main workshop interactions should come to an end once an idea (or set of ideas) for conflict resolution acceptable to all participants has been identified. He does not adequately recognize that the probability that a conflict management procedure will be implemented varies among conflict management procedures. Therefore, if he is concerned with maximizing the probability that the outputs of his workshop interaction process will contribute to the resolution of the conflict, then he should not be content with producing an "acceptable" or a "set of acceptable" conflict management procedures.

10.4 FISHER'S YESABLE PROPOSITIONS AND FRACTIONATION

Another significant attempt at bringing qualitative factors into conflict management procedures is that of Roger Fisher. His approach combines elements of those of Burton and Kelman as well as of the decisionmaking framework discussed in the early part of Chapter 3. He also employs selected properties of conflict management procedures presented in Chapters 3 through 8.

To present Fisher's analysis, we shall consider three cases and begin with a state of affairs—the result of a common joint action $a = (a^J, a^L)$—which is deemed unsatisfactory to participants J and L and wherein a mediator Z is present.

10.4.1 Case I: No Credible Threats and Offers

Against the background of the current situation, a proposition may be made by the mediator involving a change in actions by participants. In the first case we consider, assume that the proposition contains no credible threats or offers, and that it will be rejected by a participant if it does not yield a more desirable outcome to him (as he perceives it) than the current situation. It will be accepted if it yields a more desirable outcome (as he perceives it). In essence, we require three categories for comparing the new perceived outcomes with the current. They are:

- more desirable
- no difference
- less desirable

Where the focus is on utility we may, for comparative purposes, take the existing level of utility (satisfaction) derived from the current joint action a to be zero. That is, we set

$$u^J = 0 \qquad\qquad (10\text{--}5)$$

and

$$u^L = 0 \qquad\qquad (10\text{--}6)$$

Then for a proposition involving a change in the joint action, say from a to a', we can (loosely speaking) have for the new situation

$$u'^J, u'^L = \begin{cases} +1 \text{ more desirable} \\ 0 \text{ no difference (no change)} \\ -1 \text{ less desirable} \end{cases} \qquad (10\text{--}7)$$

Fisher would then define a *yesable proposition* in this kind of simplified situation as a joint action, a', that leads to a more desirable outcome (yields a utility of $+1$) for each participant.

Recall from Chapter 3 that utility u is a function of the outcome o. For example, for J, $u^J = u^J(o^J)$ where o^J relates only to the properties of the outcome o that are relevant to J. Further in Chapter 3, we assumed that all participants knew the relationship (i.e., the function f) that yielded the outcome o as a consequence of any joint action a (where $a = (a^J, a^L)$) and the realized state of the environment z. That is, each one knew

$$o = f(a,z) \qquad\qquad (10\text{--}8)$$

Since at the beginning of the mediation process characterized by an existing (or current) joint action a, the utility to both participants J and L is by definition $u^J = u^L = 0$, the task of the mediator Z is then to make a proposition a' which, as he perceives the total new situation, will be considered to be more desirable by both participants. Letting P^Z represent Z's perception, Z's task is to propose a proposition a' such that[a]

$$(1)\ P^Z(u'^J) = +1 \qquad\qquad (10\text{--}11)$$
$$(2)\ P^Z(u'^L) = +1 \qquad\qquad (10\text{--}12)$$

[a]Where u'^J is defined by

$$u'^J = u^J[P^J(f(a'))] \qquad\qquad (10\text{--}9)$$

and where u'^L is defined by

$$u'^L = u^L[P^L(f(a'))] \qquad\qquad (10\text{--}10)$$

Of course Z's perceptions in (10-11) and (10-12) may be wrong and J, L, or both may reject a'—that is, find that $u'^J \neq +1$, or $u'^L \neq +1$, or both. Then what Z has considered to be a "yesable" proposition turns out not to be a yesable proposition. This possibility suggests a third condition for a yesable proposition, a condition implicit in Fisher's writings as well as those of many others. It is that the level of satisfaction of the mediator himself—which depends on whether or not a proposition is yesable to all participants as he perceives it (that is, whether or not both $P^Z(u'^J)$ and $P^Z(u'^L)$ equal $+1$)—should also turn out to be higher as a result of his making proposition a'. That is, the mediator should receive a certain amount of own-respect, c-respect from the world, or other noneconomic commodities such as c-power or c-rectitude which leaves him in a more desirable state (from having put forth the proposition) than at the beginning of mediation. Hence, we should have

$$u'^Z = +1 \tag{10-13}$$

where

$$u'^Z = u^Z[P^Z(u'^J), P^Z(u'^L)] \tag{10-14}$$

At this point, exactly how does Fisher's mediator Z go about formulating a yesable proposition? First, the mediator puts down, *as he perceives it,* the important properties of the outcome of the choice (involving a change from the current situation) *as presently perceived by each participant.* This might be done after extensive discussion with each participant. This presently perceived choice is by definition a *non-yesable proposition,* for if it were yesable, it would have been adopted by each participant, and there would be no conflict.

More specifically, the mediator draws up a detailed balance sheet for all participants. For example, consider the situation on January 7, 1979 regarding the conflict between the Palestinian Leadership and the Government of Israel. Fisher (1979) describes it in Tables 10-1 and 10-2. In Table 10-1 for example, the Palestinian Leadership's presently perceived choice is formulated by Fisher to be: "Should we agree to the Israeli claim of sovereignty over East Jerusalem?"

On the left-hand side of the balance sheet there are listed the advantages (+) and disadvantages (−) to Palestinians if their leadership were to say "yes." For example, an advantage would be "We may get some local autonomy in East Jerusalem." A disadvantage

Table 10-1. Presently Perceived Choice: Palestinian Leadership.

Date of Draft:	*January 7, 1979*
Date of Choice:	*Current*
Party:	*Palestinian Leadership*
Question:	*Should we agree to the Israeli claim of sovereignty over East Jerusalem?*

If Yes	*If No*
(+) The Israelis will be pleasantly surprised.	(−) The Israelis won't be at all surprised.
(+) We may get some local autonomy in East Jerusalem.	(−) We may get some local autonomy anyway.
but:	*but:*
(−) We will be fiercely condemned as traitors by our people, and will lose our positions, prestige, and perhaps even our lives.	(+) Our people strongly back us.
(−) We destroy our unity, which is our chief strength.	(+) We maintain our unity.
(−) We give up our claim to rule ourselves.	(+) We stick to our goal of self-determination, which we will probably achieve sooner or later.
(−) We give up our claim to patronship over Haram-al-Sharif and the third holiest city in Islam.	(+) We maintain our claim to Al Ouds which we may get back.
(−) We resign ourselves to confiscation of our lands, Israeli police control, humiliating security checks, Israeli taxes, and interference in the education of our children.	(+) We continue to protest Israeli occupation and repression.
(−) Our Arab brothers condemn us to a man as traitors	(+) We have the strong backing of the whole Arab world.

Table 10-1. *(continued).*

If Yes	If No
(−) The whole world, including the U.S. is stunned.	(+) The whole world, including the U.S., supports our legitimate demands.
(−) The Israelis will still want more and may raise their demands seeing our concessions and weaknesses.	(+) We maintain a strong bargaining position.
	(+) We can always agree to this later if need be. Besides, time is on our side.

Source: Fisher (1979:53).

would be "We will be fiercely condemned as traitors by our people, and will lose our positions, prestige, and perhaps even our lives." Clearly, the disadvantages outweigh the advantages.

On the right-hand side of the balance sheet of Table 10-1, Fisher lists the advantages (+) and disadvantages (−) if the Palestinian leadership were to say "no" to the presently perceived choice. Clearly the advantages outweigh the disadvantages. Hence the Palestinian leadership is expected to say "no," and the presently perceived choice is thereby a non-yesable proposition.[6]

In a similar manner, Fisher would have the mediator construct a balance sheet of the advantages and disadvantages for the Government of Israel of her presently perceived choice, which is formulated as: "Should we agree to return East Jerusalem to Arab Sovereignty?" This is done in Table 10-2, where clearly the government of Israel is expected to say "no" (since on the left-hand side the negative outcome elements dominate and on the right-hand side the positive outcome elements dominate).

The task of the mediator now is to construct a "yesable proposition" (or target choice) as defined previously, to be put to the participants some weeks in the future. Fisher proposes a Plan X. He draws up balance sheets for the Palestinian leadership and the Government of Israel. See Tables 10-3 and 10-4, respectively. For each party, the question is "Should we agree to Plan X for East Jerusalem?" As the mediator perceives it, the "yes" response for each participant has

Table 10-2.   Presently Perceived Choice: Israeli Government.

Date of Draft:	*January 7, 1979*
Date of Choice:	*Current*
Party:	*Government of Israel*
Question:	*Should we agree to return East Jerusalem to Arab Sovereignty?*

If Yes	*If No*
(+) We may increase the chances for peace with the Arab States.	(–) We may delay peace with the states, but we won't get peace anyway with the Palestinians.
(+) The world including our ally the U.S. is pleasantly surprised.	(–) The world won't be at all surprised.
but:	*but:*
(–) We will be fiercely criticized by our constituency and condemned as traitors by many. We will be thrown out of office.	(+) We have the strong backing of our constituency.
(–) We weaken our bargaining position as the Arabs ask for more.	(+) We maintain a strong bargaining position.
(–) We don't know what we'll get in return.	(+) We won't have given up anything.
(–) Jerusalem will be divided again with barbed wire and walls.	(+) Jerusalem remains united.
(–) We will lose access to the Wailing Wall, the Old City, Jewish Quarter, the Mount of Olives, and the rest of East Jerusalem.	(+) We continue to have free and secure access to the Old City, and to all of Jerusalem.
(–) The security of West Jerusalem will be threatened by saboteurs and hostile soldiers.	(+) We maintain our security.

Table 10-2. *(continued).*

If Yes	If No
(−) Tens of thousands of Israelis will be expelled from their homes in Ramot, Ramot Eshkol etc. The new building ceases.	(+) The residents of the new quarters in East Jerusalem continue to live there and the building continues.
	(+) We can always decide later. Besides, time is on our side.

Source: Fisher (1979:52).

many more advantages than disadvantages given their perceptions, while the "no" response for each participant has many more disadvantages than advantages. This is evident from studying Tables 10–3 and 10–4. To Fisher, then, Plan X is a "yesable proposition."[7]

Further, recall Fisher's implicit assumption that the mediator himself is motivated to undertake his task. If he is successful, he receives satisfaction from own-respect or from the c-respect, c-prestige, or c-power, and perhaps even economic goods received from the world community at large or from the parts of the world community that are important to him. Therefore, for any Plan X that a mediator may be considering proposing, we may draw up a balance sheet, though it is of a somewhat different character than that for participants. We do so now, for it will help unravel some of the more complex conflict situations explored later. The question that faces the mediator is: "If I propose Plan X, (1) what are the probabilities that it will be adopted, and what advantages and disadvantages accrue to me if it is adopted and (2) what are the probabilities that it will not be adopted, and what are the subsequent advantages and disadvantages that accrue to me if it is not adopted?"

One simple type of balance sheet for the mediator is given in Table 10–5. The pluses and minuses on both sides of the balance sheet, together with the probabilities of Plan X being yesable to the participants, determines whether $u'^z = +1, 0$, or -1. If $u'^z \neq +1$, Plan X is not a "yesable proposition" to him. For example, it might not be acceptable, even with a low probability of rejection by one or more participants, if rejection would mean that the mediator would lose face or a tremendous amount of power, prestige, and so forth in the world community—a loss which he is not willing to risk.

Table 10-3.   Target Choice: Palestinian Leadership.

Date of Draft: *January 7, 1979*

Date of Choice: *Some weeks in the future*

Party: *Palestinian Leadership*

Question: *Should we agree to Plan X for East Jerusalem?*

If Yes		*If No*	
(+)	We rule ourselves in East Jerusalem for the first time in history.	(−)	We lose what will be the last chance for a long time to rule ourselves in East Jerusalem.
(+)	We are supported on the whole by our people.	(−)	New leaders, ready to accept Plan X, are emerging with popular support.
(+)	We regain patronship over the Haram-al-Sharif.	(−)	Israel retains control over Haram-al-Sharif.
(+)	There is no more confiscation of lands. Lands confiscated since 1967 are mostly returned. The rest are compensated at fair rates.	(−)	Our lands continue to be confiscated as we become increasingly an Arab island in a Jewish ocean.
(+)	We police and tax ourselves. We control our own schools.	(−)	We continue under Israeli occupation and Israeli control of taxes and education with no end in sight.
(+)	We are supported by most Arab countries, including Saudi Arabia and Egypt.		
(+)	Our security is guaranteed.	(−)	There will probably be a war in the near future in which our people will suffer greatly.
but:		*but:*	
(−)	There is still some opposition among our people.	(+)	We still have much support among our people.
(−)	Some Arab states criticize us.	(+)	We still have the support of many Arab states.

Source: Fisher (1979:55).

Table 10-4. Target Choice: Israeli Government.

Date of Draft:	*January 7, 1979*
Date of Choice:	*Some weeks in the future*
Party:	*Government of Israel*
Question:	*Should we agree to Plan X for East Jerusalem?*

If Yes	If No
(+) We sign a peace treaty with The Arab states and the Palestinians.	(–) We forego what may be the *last* chance of peace.
(+) The whole world, including the U.S., praises us.	(–) We are criticized by the whole world.
(+) We are supported on the whole by most of our constituency.	(–) We are criticized strongly at home.
(+) We continue to control the Wailing Wall and the Jewish Quarter.	
(+) Terrorism will cease.	(–) Terrorism will probably be stepped up. There will probably be war sometime in the near future.
(+) We will continue to enjoy free and secure access to the whole of Jerusalem.	
(+) Israelis can continue to live in any part of the city. Israelis in the new quarters in East Jerusalem will remain in their current living conditions.	
(+) Jerusalem will prosper with an increase in tourism and trade with the Arab countries.	(–) Jerusalem will continue to be in financial trouble.
but:	*but:*
(–) There is still considerable opposition, including many in our own party who call us traitors.	(+) We will have some domestic support.
(–) There is a chance that the arrangements will break down and Jerusalem will be divided again.	(+) We safeguard with our own forces a united Jerusalem, capital of Israel.

Source: Fisher (1979:54).

Table 10–5.   Mediator's Perceived Choice.

Date of Choice: *Some Date in the Future*

Party: *Mediator*

Question: *Is Plan X worth proposing?*

If Plan X is adopted	If Plan X is not adopted
(+) I become eligible for the Nobel Peace Prize (i.e., I gain much c-respect in the World Community).	(−) The world's evaluation of me as a wise man diminishes.
	(−) I may appear as a fool to a number of nations.
(+) As a citizen of the world community, I am more secure.	(−) My chances of future employment are reduced.
(+) I gain much own c-respect.	(− or +) nonadoption may worsen or improve relations between the parties and may impair or enhance the adoption of a new plan X'.
	(+) I gain some c-respect from having tried, and having taken an action other than "do nothing".
(−) My country's arm sales go down.	(+) I have learned something so that plan X' may be more successful (my stock of c-enlightenment has increased).
(−) Plan X is a piecemeal solution; it delays the realization of a drastic change in the world system which is required; it makes such realization more difficult.	(+) The parties have learned, as has the world at large. The world's stock of c-enlightenment has increased.

Formally speaking then, the conditions for a "yesable proposition" to be actually realized are:

$$
\begin{align}
&(1)\ P^Z(u'^J) = +1 \tag{10-15}\\
&(2)\ P^Z(u'^L) = +1\\
&(3)\ u'^J = +1\\
&(4)\ u'^L = +1\\
&(5)\ u'^Z = +1
\end{align}
$$

10.4.2 Case II: With Credible Threats and Offers

We now move to a somewhat more complicated but also more realistic case. Here the mediator has the opportunity to employ threats and offers in identifying a "yesable proposition." Such a situation, for example, might involve a U.N. mediator, who may be able to employ approval or disapproval of the U.N. General Assembly as an offer or threat, respectively, or perhaps the provision of additional or withdrawal of current financial assistance. Because of the set of offers and threats made by the mediator—which are most effective when they are both legitimate (in terms of both accepted law and precedent) and credible—each participant can no longer have the outcome of the current joint action a. Rather, offers and threats do or can change: (1) each participant's action space and/or (2) the function f relating actions to outcomes;[8] and thus force each participant to compare only two outcomes: (1) that of a' if both accept (here the outcome takes into account the offers and promises made, qualified by the probabilities that they will be carried out) and (2) that of a'' if both reject (here the outcome takes into account the threats made, qualified by the probabilities that they will be carried out).[9] The outcomes of the current situation will shortly become historical and can thus no longer provide the basis for the calculation of utility.

Following Fisher's approach, we arbitrarily set equal to zero both J's and L's utility for the situation that would eventuate were the proposition to turn out to be non-yesable and were, consequently, the joint action a'' (including threats) to be realized. That is:

$$
u''^J = 0
$$

and

$$u''^L = 0 \qquad (10\text{–}16)$$

where

$$u''^J = u^J[P^J(f(a''))]$$

and

$$u''^L = u^L[P^L(f(a''))] \qquad (10\text{–}17)$$

Then when J and L consider the utility they would receive were the proposition accepted by both and were, consequently, the joint action a' (including offers) to be realized, we obtain the utilities:

$$\text{u}'^J = u^J[P^J(f(a'))] \qquad (10\text{–}18)$$
$$\text{u}'^L = u^L[P^L(f(a'))] \qquad (10\text{–}19)$$

These utilities can be $+1$ (more desirable than u''^J or u''^L), 0 (no difference from u''^J or u''^L), or -1 (less desirable than u''^J or u''^L). Thus, when the mediator makes a proposition that *he* considers yesable, it must be that in his mind

$$(1)\ P^Z(u'^J) = +1 \qquad (10\text{–}20)$$
$$(2)\ P^Z(u'^L) = +1 \qquad (10\text{–}21)$$

and since the mediator's own welfare is involved, it must be that

$$(3)\ u'^Z = +1 \qquad (10\text{–}22)$$

This is so since $u^Z(f(a))$, the utility he derives from the current situation, the outcome of joint action a, is arbitrarily set equal to zero. That is, $u^Z(f(a)) = 0$, which indicates that the mediator too is not satisfied with the current situation and is searching for a more satisfactory situation for which u'^Z will be $+1$. In this case, u'^Z is no longer defined by (10–14) but rather becomes

$$u'^Z = u'^Z[P^Z(u'^J), P^Z(u'^L), \pi(a'')] \qquad (10\text{–}23)$$

where $\pi(a'')$ is the probability of a'' being realized because of rejection of a' by one or both participants. For $\text{u}'^Z = +1$, it must be that $P^Z(u'^J)$ and $P^Z(u'^L)$ be $+1$ *and* that the probability $\pi(a'')$ be sufficiently low for the mediator to risk making the proposition he perceives to be yesable to J and L.[10] For the yesable proposition to be actually realized, two additional conditions must be met. They are:

$$u'^J = +1 \qquad (10\text{-}24)$$

and

$$u'^L = +1 \qquad (10\text{-}25)$$

10.4.3 Case III: Leader-Follower Situation without Mediator

The third case, another that Fisher analyzes, is one where there is no mediator but where one participant, say J, acts as a leader, and a second, say L, as a follower. In effect, the leader assumes two roles: (1) that of a mediator extending offers and threats and (2) that of a participant engaged in conflict. Again we have an existing situation characterized by the joint action a, which leads to an outcome o, whose utility for the leader J we arbitrarily set at zero. That is

$$u^J = 0 \text{ for } u^J = u^J[P^J(f(a))] \qquad (10\text{-}26)$$

The leader is then motivated to search for a joint action a' that the follower will accept and which will yield a utility of $+1$ to the leader. On the other hand, the follower's current utility may be either satisfactory ($u^L = +1$) or not ($u^L \neq +1$). In searching for a joint action that will yield the follower a utility of $+1$, J considers propositions that embody both offers and threats. Accordingly, the current joint action a becomes historical as soon as J makes a proposition that he considers yesable; and the two relevant joint actions become a'', which ensues if L rejects J's proposition, and a' if L accepts. Accordingly, the conditions for a yesable proposition as perceived by J are

(1) $P^J(u'^L) = +1$ for $P^J(u''^L) = 0$ \qquad (10\text{-}27)

(2) $u'^J = +1$ for $u^J = 0^{11}$ \qquad (10\text{-}28)

where

$$u'^J = u^J[P^J(f(a')), P^J(u'^L), \pi(a'')], \qquad (10\text{-}29)$$

but for a yesable proposition it must be that

$$u'^J = u^J[P^J(f(a')), \pi(a'')|P^J(u'^L) = +1] = +1 \qquad (10\text{-}30)$$

The condition (10-30) is a combination of conditions (10-24) and (10-23) since J combines both a participant's role and a mediator's role. That is, for a proposition to be satisfactory to J it must first of all be such that $P^J(u'^L) = +1$—that is, J must perceive that it will be yesable to L. Moreover, it must be yesable to J. That is, his perception of the outcome for himself; namely, $u^J[P^J(f(a')), \pi(a'')]$ must be more desirable, namely $+1$, were the probability of rejection by L, $\pi(a'')$, equal to zero. But further, this condition should hold if $\pi(a'')$ is sufficiently small—which would be the case if J has not significantly misperceived L's perceptions. For the yesable proposition to be actually realized, one additional condition is

$$u'^L = +1 \qquad (10-31)$$

Fisher illustrates this type of situation starting with a proposition currently demanded by one participant but not acceptable to another. This situation motivates (or should motivate, according to Fisher) the former participant to become a leader (that is, both a mediator and a participant) and engage in a search for a yesable proposition. The particular situation examined by Fisher (1969b) is the one that faced the government of North Korea (L) in February 1968, after it had seized the U.S. Navy's electronic reconnaissance vessel *Pueblo* and its crew in waters off the coast of North Korea, and the U.S. government (J) was demanding the immediate return of the ship and the crew. To determine why this was not a yesable proposition to L, Fisher would have J construct the balance sheet in Table 10-6. On the left-hand side, J lists what he perceives to be the consequences that L perceives were she to say "yes" to the proposition "Return the ship and the crew." The first is "Almost no risk of military reprisal," perceived to be a positive outcome element. The second is "We admit the seizure was wrong," perceived to be a negative outcome element. And so forth, for three other negative outcome elements.

On the right-hand side, J lists what he perceives to be the consequences that L perceives were she to say "no" to the proposition "Return the ship and the crew." The first, "Some risk of military reprisal," is perceived to be a negative outcome element. The second, "We gain intelligence from the ship and crew," is perceived to be a positive outcome element. And so forth, for seven other positive outcome elements.

When J examines the table in toto and weighs the elements in the way he perceives L would do, he clearly sees that the demand "Re-

Table 10-6. North Korea's Choice Just after the Pueblo Was Seized.
("we" = North Korea)

If we return the ship and crew	If we keep the ship and crew
(+) Almost no risk of military reprisal.	(−) Some risk of military reprisal.
(−) We admit the seizure was wrong.	(+) We gain intelligence from ship and crew.
(−) We yield to U.S. military blackmail.	(+) We show U.S. to be power-less.
(−) We look incompetent.	(+) We divert U.S. from Viet-nam.
(−) We accept the legitimacy of spyboats.	(+) We support war against U.S.
	(+) We intimidate South Korea.
	(+) We tend to split South Korea from U.S.
	(+) We direct attention to U.S. spying.
	(+) We can always return ship and crew later.

Source: Fisher (1969:101).

turn the ship and crew" is not a yesable proposition to L. If L were to meet the demand and adopt the action, a^L, it involves, it would shift L's utility outcome from a base level of 0 to a level of − 1 (less satisfactory). Clearly, if J is to achieve a yesable proposition, he must change his current demand.

In general, J can change each of the three kinds of basic elements in a proposition for this type of situation:

1. the demand—that is, a change, for example, in the a^L components
2. the threat—that is, a change, for example, in the a^J components that would result if L did not meet the demand
3. the offer—that is, a change, for example, in the a^J components that would result if L did meet the demand.[12]

We illustrate one possible set of changes in the *Pueblo* example as follows:

PROGRAM: A POSSIBLE SCHEME DESIGNED TO INFLUENCE NORTH KOREA

Change the demand: Suggest that the crew be returned without prejudice to North Korea's position and that the disposition of the ship await a full settlement of the dispute.

Change the threat: Remove any threat of immediate military attack by words and by withdrawing U.S. naval ships from the area.

Identify the threat as being that if the dispute continues the U.S. is likely to embark on a long-term program of building up the military strength of South Korea.

Change the offer: Recognize the incident as one involving issues of fact and law with something to be said for each side.

Treat the dispute as one of many to be settled peacefully.

Play down urgency.

Indicate a willingness to apologize for any intrusion that did occur.

To examine whether this revised proposition is likely to be "yesable" to L, J constructs a new balance sheet. See Table 10–7. Examining both the right-hand side and the left-hand side and weighing the positive and negative elements on both sides in the manner he considers L would do, J concludes that L will say "yes" to this revised proposition.

The final step is J's examination of whether the proposition is yesable from his standpoint—that is, to check that the revisions made have not involved too great a concession to L. This he does by means of the balance sheet given in Table 10–8. In this table, we have listed Fisher's outcome elements to J (the United States) primarily as a participant. To these we have added three advantages and disadvantages that would accrue to the United States in its mediator role when it undertakes to be the leader. Specifically, we have added in italics three additional outcome elements to the left-hand side of balance sheet in Table 10–8 to suggest some of the types of outcomes that Fisher should have considered (and in many places in his writings implicitly does). Such is required to meet conditions (10–28) and (10–30), which we consider to be the relevant ones if a proposition is to be yesable for the leader. If upon examination of the balance sheet of Table 10–8, the proposition is not yesable to J, then he returns to the balance sheet of Table 10–6 to devise a revised program of change in the proposition to be put to L.

Table 10-7.   North Korea's Choice after Our Program. ("we" = North Korea)

If we return the crew		*If we keep the crew*	
(+)	No risk of military reprisal.	(−)	An increased risk of U.S.— South Korean build-up.
(+)	We look generous (men are being returned by agreement, not under threat).	(−)	Increased risk of close cooperation between U.S. and South Korea.
(+)	Our seizure has been partially vindicated.	(−)	We risk justifying increased U.S. overflights, etc.
(+)	We can keep the ship with some legitimacy.	(−)	We risk criticism from U.S.S.R., Poland, and neutrals.
(+)	We already have all the intelligence data we can get from the crew.		
(+)	U.S. accepts some responsibility.		
(+)	U.S. spyship provocations are less likely in the future.		
(−)	We may look soft.	(+)	We maintain our stance as a tough David standing up to Goliath.
(−)	We give up hostages which might be a future bargaining counter.	(+)	We can always return the crew later.

Source: Fisher (1969:104).

It is to be noted that Fisher also employs workshop procedures that have features resembling those of Burton and Kelman. He calls his workshops "brainstorming sessions" and suggests (1) a number of diagnostic tools that may be employed in initial stages, (2) a number of inventing and devising tools (mainly target balance sheets and yes-able propositions) that may be employed in intermediate stages, and (3) a number of marketing tools that may be employed in the later stages to help ensure that workshop (brainstorming session) products are at least considered by actual decisionmakers. See Fisher and Ury

Table 10-8. Our Choice: Should We Adopt the Suggested Program.
("we" = the U.S.)

If we follow the proposed program	If we do not
(+) There is a good chance the crew will be returned and the dispute settled peacefully.	(−) The crew will probably remain in North Korea indefinitely.
(+) If not, we will at least appear reasonable to many people.	(−) The dispute is likely to use up a good deal of time and effort
(+) *The world will respect us for our effort to avoid a military incident.*	(−) The dispute might flare up (but we can probably prevent that).
(+) *We would be looked upon not as a greedy self-interested big power, but as a responsible major nation.*	(−) Some domestic pressure will exist for the government to escalate the dispute.
(−) We may look soft to the world.	(+) We do not have to make any decisions now.
(−) We probably give up any chance of getting the ship back.	
(−) In substance, we let North Korea "get away with it."	(+) We can always do something later if we decide to.
(−) South Korea may get upset.	
(−) We will have to be more careful of our reconnaissance ships in the future.	
(−) *If it turns out that North Korea does not meet our revised demand, we will damage our reputation as a leader (and mediator) in the world community.*	

Source: Fisher (1969:105).

(1978) and Fisher (1979). In the above manner then, Fisher would develop yesable propositions that are particularly useful when it is not possible to quantify critical elements of an outcome.

10.4.4 The Fractionation Technique

Before concluding our presentation of Fisher's approach, we should make a few statements concerning his *fractionation* technique. See Fisher (1964) for further discussion. This technique essentially parallels the decomposition principle often employed in the social and natural sciences in order to deal with large complex problems for which solutions are not readily ascertainable, computable, or attainable for other reasons. Typically, the large complex problem is decomposed into a series of smaller problems where each is tractable, and where together they approximate as much as possible the large complex problem. In Chapters 3 through 8, the round-by-round procedures discussed represent one type of decomposition, where the notion of a solution to a problem achieved in one big step is replaced by the notion of a solution achieved through a series of small steps, one in each round. As noted previously, such decomposition, or fractionation to use Fisher's term, may be meaningful for a conservative "have" nation or other behaving unit since such decomposition may reduce risk for it when it perceives that it has much to lose and relatively little to gain from a "bad" compromise on a big issue.

Another relevant type of decomposition may be useful when the conflict situation involves actions covering many dimensions (issues). Then, by fractionating the problem, it becomes possible to move ahead in conflict resolution by allowing one participant to specify the level of the component of the joint action along one dimension of importance to him, while allowing the second participant to specify the level of the component along a second dimension of importance to him—desirably one that is related to the first in the eyes of participants. According to Fisher, this would constitute fractionation by *immediate physical issue* involved. Or, having in mind that the outcome may also be n-dimensional, we may employ Fisher's fractionation by *substance*. This involves the choice of a joint action that yields a level of outcome on one component of the outcome vector that is intensely desired by one participant, and at the same time a level of outcome on a second component that is intensely desired by a second participant—that is, *logrolling.* Or, where each participant embraces several interest groups or parties, we might have Fisher's fractionation by *interest groups or parties.* Here a sequence of rounds is considered where on each round one interest group in J and one interest group in L are each benefited to approximately the same extent. Or, Fisher's fractionation by *procedural precedent* may at times be useful to employ. Here, as with the GRIT approach, the mediator or participants start with relatively inessential, minor, or small issues (or changes in actions) on which participants can easily reach agreement. This builds up trust and establishes a precedent for conflict management and resolution. The participants then proceed step by step to increasingly more difficult issues (or changes in actions) until the entire conflict is resolved.

There can, of course, be other dimensions along which fractionation (decomposition, or disaggregation) can take place. For example, on the first round a procedure may be used that J most likes, and on the second round a procedure that L most likes may be used, and so forth. Moreover, at any one point in a conflict situation the mediator may suggest several simultaneous fractionations—such as by interest groups as well as by dimension of action, as well as for trust building purposes, and so forth. In essence, what Fisher and many others have suggested (often in less comprehensive and less systematic fashion) is the choice by the mediator of a sequence of yesable subpropositions that constantly shift directions, dimensions, and focus in order to manage as best as possible the total conflict. There are of course, as Fisher himself points out, disadvantages to this procedure. One might obtain a series of piecemeal solutions and leave the basic underlying conflict unresolved; or one might successfully treat a series of minor subconflicts but reach a point where no solution is possible on a difficult issue, which then negates all that has gone before and thus incurs a waste of time and resources. However, for long-stalemated situations, Fishers' fractionation approach is realistic and operational and can often work, or be judged to have the highest probability of working.

The above presents some of the main features of the Fisher approach as we perceive it. However, there are many other relevant aspects we should mention. One covers time-related factors included in Fisher's "when" category. For example, Fisher would recommend that given the myopic thinking of most political decisionmakers:

- the *demand* component of the proposition be made to look like a "fading opportunity"—that is, that the participants be made to feel a sense of urgency in making their decision regarding the proposition;
- the *offer* component of the proposition be so formulated that the beneficial consequences of saying "yes" accrue close to the point of time when the decision regarding the proposition is made;
- the *threat* component of the proposition be so formulated that the detrimental consequences of saying "no" do not immediately accrue, but at the same time do not accrue too far from the point of time when the decision regarding the proposition is made.

Fisher also suggests that the "who" aspects of a proposition be considered—that is, that the impacts of a proposition on the different sections (or interest groups or members) of a behaving unit be considered. For example, Fisher recommends that:

- the *offer* component of the proposition be so formulated that the beneficial consequences of saying "yes" accrue to those sections of the community from which the decisionmaker traditionally derives his main support; and that
- the *threat* component of the proposition be so formulated that the detrimental consequences of saying "no" accrue to those sections of the community from which the decisionmaker traditionally derives little if any support.

However, Fisher's approach is deficient in several major aspects. One is that it does not explicitly confront the problem of choice in the many situations where more than one yesable proposition may be possible.[13] In effect, Fisher does not take into account the efficiency criterion to which many economists, regional scientists, and applied mathematicians attribute first importance. Rather, Fisher's mediator (or leader) acts like a satisficer, being satisfied with and willing to stop his search at the first yesable proposition that may be identified; he does not search for the "best" yesable proposition. For a number of actual situations, this is a good procedure since the search for a best yesable proposition could well engender another type of conflict among participants over what is best. However, if any participant is an optimizer and desires a yesable proposition optimal for himself he may hold out for a proposition that has all pluses or even double pluses as suggested below. Hence, when there is more than one participant who is a dedicated optimizer, the Fisher procedure would run into difficulties and, in all likelihood, would be of little use.

A second shortcoming of Fisher's approach relates to his use of a simple three-category scale:

(+) for a significant advantage
(−) for a significant disadvantage
 (0) for everything else

In some conflict situations, certain advantages clearly dominate all other advantages, and likewise with disadvantages. Hence, there should be at least two more categories:

(+ +) for an overwhelmingly significant advantage
(− −) for an overwhelmingly significant disadvantage

On the other hand, why not add still other categories—for example, (+ + +) and (− − −)? If one were to do so, one would start to approach a Saaty-type scale discussed on pages 148–150 or even a set of cardinal weights. Posing the question of the appropriate number of categories (ranks) raises a fundamental problem of measurement that many social science disciplines confront, and have not adequately resolved. Hence, Fisher should not be too harshly criticized regarding the scale he employs. Notwithstanding, he has not fully exploited the possibilities for measurement. For example, he has not considered the possibilities for using ordinal rankings by participants, or from combining both qualitative and quantitative measures when the latter are available. Under these circumstances some of the discussion on multicriteria (attribute) analyses in pages 270–75 becomes relevant where Fisher's outcome properties are interpretable as criteria. We shall return to this point in Section 11.4.1, where we attempt to synthesize Fisher's contributions with others.

10.5 DYNAMICS OF LEARNING IN THE WORKSHOP APPROACH[14]

While it would not be useful to develop for the practitioner a rigorous formal mathematical model that may be said to characterize some of the dynamics involved in learning in the workshops of Burton and

Kelman, it is useful to state in this section some of the relations and principles that would be involved. This should facilitate synthesis of ideas and also encourage the effort of other scholars wishing to reformulate Burton and Kelman. We view learning as the building up of one or more stocks of relevant knowledge whereby a behaving unit is able to take "more informed" actions, make "more informed" proposals, and reach "more informed" decisions.

Consider a situation with several nations J, K, L, . . . , and a mediator Z. In a first case that we may examine, the role of the mediator is to provide as much relevant information as he can pertaining to the conflict situation. The participants are more or less passive in the sense that they do not produce and store information. Rather they receive information and act upon it at each time point. The basic question is then: What and how much information should be provided by the mediator? From a dynamical systems standpoint, the mediator may be conceived of as devoting his time, labor, and other inputs to producing information for the participants in the statements he may make, reports he may write, and visual displays he may present. In this sense, microeconomic theory suggests that he may employ his own labor and other inputs up to the point where the increasing marginal cost to him (say the increasing disutility of labor) comes to equal the decreasing value of the marginal product in terms of effective information produced by his labor.

While we know what the costs are, that is, the disutility of labor or the utility of leisure foregone—which of course only the mediator can measure—what is the value of the marginal product? At first glance, one might consider it to be the immediate significance of the information produced by the last unit of labor. In dynamical systems analysis, however, it is more. It is the significance of that information for not only the current period but for each point of time from the current period to the conclusion of the conflict resolution process. In this sense, the information produced by the last unit of labor is like a piece of capital, like an axe that continues to provide services from the time a forester finishes fashioning it to the time when he no longer requires it, at which time it may have some "scrap value." Thus, the relevant principle involves equating the marginal cost of producing that information, say the disutility of the marginal unit of labor, with the utility indirectly derived from the information produced over the period of time extending from the current point of time to the end of the conflict resolution process *plus* whatever significance that information may have for future use. But what is this utility to Z? In our simple context it may be viewed as satisfaction derived by the mediator from the c-respect and other noneconomic commodities that society bestows on him for producing the information that leads to conflict reduction. Since the bestowal of such c-respect and other noneconomic commodities may be received by the mediator at each point of time extending from the current to the end of the conflict resolution process, so will his derived satisfaction. Additionally, at the end of the process, there may be c-respect and other noneconomic commodities bestowed on the mediator for future or scrap value that the produced information may have, in which case the satisfaction is increased still more. In toto, then, the marginal cost of producing that information (say the disutility of the marginal unit of labor) is balanced against the cumulative utility (satisfaction) derived from that information produced, as has just been described.

Three basic factors governing the mediator's behavior may be depicted in Figure 10-1. There, at the top of the box at the left of the figure, the mediator inputs labor $y_{\ell h}^z$ to produce information y_h^z. This information goes to the conflict arena and changes the conflict situation. Information flows from this arena to the public (the social system) on change in the extent of the conflict at the current point of

Figure 10-1. Mediator Z: His Rationale for Information Production.

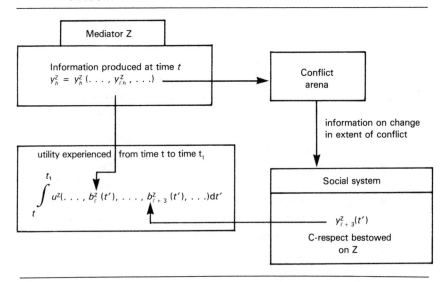

time and continues to do so until the end of the conflict mediation period (whether or not the conflict has been resolved). In accord with such change, the social system bestows c-respect and other noneconomic goods on the mediator, which he consumes as $b_{\ell+3}^{z}(t')$ at each point of time t' between the current time point t to the end of the period t_1. Such bestowal is indicated by the arrow from the social system box to the lower part of the mediator's box containing his utility function and recording the cumulation of utility over time. Balancing this flow is the flow within the mediator's box of the labor input $(y_{\ell h}^{z})$ to his utility function which affects the amount of leisure b_{ℓ}^{z} that he is able to enjoy and thereby causes a decrease of utility (disutility). Note, however, that this disutility is incurred only at the current time point t when the labor input is made.

A second case we may examine is where each participant J produces and accumulates information, and where the mediator is extremely passive (that is where he acts as a fictitious market participant and merely a channel through which information supplied by any participant is passed on to all others). Each participant in the workshop or other conflict management process is primarily motivated to maximize his utility (payoff). To do so he contributes his labor and other inputs in producing (on his own or during the discussion sessions) information about his view of the world, his preferences, expected outcomes from different proposals, and the like. In return, he expects to receive from the discussions and other interaction the basic commodity c-security. Hence, at any point of time he is motivated to produce information and engage in workshop activity and the like up to the point at which the disutility from the last unit of his labor input comes to equal the utility of the expected increase in c-security resulting from the statements and other enlightenment produced by his last unit of labor. In the simplest case, where the statements he produces do not constitute a stock of information, he follows the simple microeconomics condition of equating marginal disutility of his labor at any point of time t with the marginal utility at that time point from the increase in c-security that the marginal unit of labor indirectly produces at that time. If, however, the statements and proposals that are produced by that marginal unit of labor are significant as stock of information (that is, constitute capital), then his "marginal revenue equals marginal cost" condition is of the more complex form that characterizes Z's condition. In particular, if the information produced by that last unit of labor is in the eyes of the participant productive in managing conflict not only at the current point of time t but at each subsequent point of time, the utility in toto derived is the cumulation of the utility from the received c-security indirectly produced by that information (1) at time t and (2) at each subsequent point of time *plus* any future (scrap) value that information (as capital) may have at the end of the conflict resolution process. The participant balances this derived utility in toto against the disutility of the marginal unit of labor.

The basic factors governing participant J's behavior may be depicted in Figure 10-2. There, at the top of the box at the left of the figure, J inputs labor ($y_{\ell h}^{J}$) to produce information y_h^J. This information goes to the conflict arena and helps change (for the better) the conflict situation, not only at the current time t but at each subsequent point of time until time t_1, the end of the conflict period. Hence at each point of time t' during this period, J perceives that a certain amount of c-security $y_{\ell+13}^J(t')$ is produced from the resulting change in the extent of the conflict. This c-security then accrues to J and he derives satisfaction (utility) from the existence of (that is his consumption of) the corresponding amount $b_{\ell+13}^J(t')$ of c-security, as indicated by the arrows entering J's utility function from below. Balancing the cumulation of this utility from the current time point t to

Figure 10-2. Participant J: His Rationale for Information Production.

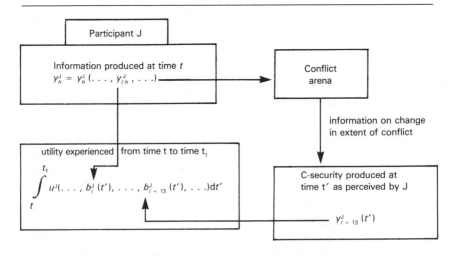

the end of the period t_1 is the disutility of the marginal unit of labor indicated by the arrow entering J's utility function from above. This disutility, however, is incurred only at the current time point t when the labor input is made.

The above two models are excessively simple. A more relevant model might involve the mediator not only in producing information but also in the role of coordinator. In such a role, he may then have control variables in addition to his own labor input. These might be the subsidies (incentives) and penalties (c-sanctions) that he might impose on the participants. Still more complex models would involve production of information by both participants and the mediator. They might also permit the information produced by any of the behaving units to affect the c-security received by any other participant at the current and subsequent points of time, as well as the c-respect bestowed upon the mediator.

We should also note the dynamics and learning that goes on in the Fisher brainstorming sessions where different propositions are explored as to whether or not they are yesable. If the first proposition put forth turns out to be yesable, then the workshop is over and the conflict is successfully coped with. If the first proposition is rejected, then another proposition is explored, and still another until a yesable one is identified. In essence, there is a learning process in Fisher. However, it is a somewhat different learning process than with Burton and Kelman. Generally, it does not have the gradual increase in information and/or increase in extent of concessions; nor does it have the gradual changes in demands, offers, and threats that one often associates with debate and discussion, especially when participants have positive attitudes. Rather, it is learning from a series of responses to a series of changes, usually significant ones, in demands, offers, and threats along one or more important dimensions of the conflict. Whereas the Burton and Kelman workshops may be modeled by differential equations (involving time as a basic variable), the Fisher brainstorming session needs to be modeled by a set of difference equations with time lags. In formulating such a model, however, the action spaces and functional form of the outcome function as well as the outcome vector change in time. Thus, the question arises whether or not one can say anything that is more than trivial about the necessary and sufficient conditions for reaching a stable solution, that is, a yesable proposition. To the extent that a difference equation model of Fisher can be made operational, with the use of data to yield specific relationships that may be said to approximate (replicate) those of the real world, to that extent the qualitative inputs of Fisher will later be able to be more fusable with a quantitative approach.

10.6 CONCLUDING REMARKS

In this chapter we have attempted to discuss in summary fashion some of the qualitative approaches to conflict management suggested by some of the leading scholars in this area. We have not attempted to present their approaches in a balanced fashion. Rather, we have emphasized those contributions central to their thinking that we perceive we can most easily combine with quantitative factors discussed in Chapters 3 through 8 in order to achieve a set of superior conflict management procedures. Several notions have been found to be most useful. One is that basic universal needs can be associated with most if not all conflicts and that, therefore, games that appear to be zero sum are in fact positive sum. Moreover, universal needs can be associated with noneconomic goods and also with concern for the next person's welfare. These goods and the welfare of others can be entered into a participant's utility function and therefore be considered when she selects a joint action (e.g., agreeing to a compromise solution) to maximize her utility.

The participants, environment, and agenda are all basic elements to workshop activity that may lead to ideas and outputs capable of generating a politically viable conflict resolution. Such resolution requires, according to Kelman, (1) *preworkshop* sessions to eliminate politically infeasible ideas, notions, and proposals, (2) *main workshop* sessions to engage in debate and discussion within a nonstandard environment to encourage creative and jointly acceptable proposals for compromise solutions, and (3) *end-of-workshop sessions* to repackage, when necessary, the workshop outputs in order that they can be understood by the different political leaders in the real world and thereby to facilitate their adoption.

Finally, while workshop and brainstorming sessions may be extremely valuable, a meaningful compromise solution must be a Fisher-type yesable proposition to all parties. That is, crudely speaking, it must be a proposition that each party perceives as having a predominance of advantages (pluses) when compared to disadvantages (minuses). Sometimes it may be necessary to fractionate the conflict and achieve a satisfactory resolution by component parts.

However, the qualitative approaches that have been discussed in this chapter need to be reformulated and developed further to be able to be synthesized with each other. Additionally they need to be still further reformulated and developed, as do the quantitative approaches discussed in Chapters 3 through 8, in order to move in the direction of an ideal synthesis. To this task we turn in Chapter 11.

APPENDIX TO CHAPTER 10
THE DELPHI TECHNIQUE[15]

10A.1 Basic Features of the Delphi Technique

Another qualitative approach that may be employed in conflict management and resolution is the Delphi technique. This technique is essentially a method for structuring a group communication process so that the process is effective in combining the knowledge and abilities of a diverse group of experts in the task of analyzing a complex problem. The term "expert" can be defined to include anyone who can contribute relevant inputs—academics, political leaders, business people, religious leaders, consumer advocates, and the like. The basic characteristics of the technique can be summarized as follows:

1. a structured, formal questionnaire for basic data collection and presentation is administered to participants by mail, in personal interviews, or at an iterative on-line computer terminal;
2. items to be included on the questionnaire may be decided upon by the analyst, the participants, or both;
3. the questionnaire is administered to participants over a sequence of rounds and is accompanied by a set of instructions specifying the nature of the responses required at each round;
4. participants respond to the items requiring quantitative data using the scale (nominal, ordinal, relative, etc.) specified—they may or may not respond to open-end verbal (qualitative) requests;
5. individual responses to items are kept anonymous for all iterations, and participants do not meet to discuss issues face to face;

6.   each iteration is accompanied by feedback in the form of a summary of the results of the previous round. This feedback usually involves a measure of central tendency, some measure of dispersion, or perhaps the entire frequency distribution of responses for items measured on a quantitative scale, and a summary of the "consensus" of opinion regarding items involving qualitative responses;

7.   where a participant's response on any item is highly divergent from the norm, and this response does not change from iteration to iteration despite a general convergence of opinion among remaining participants, then he may be asked by the analyst to provide written justification for his response on that item.

8.   this communication process continues until convergence of opinion, or "consensus," reaches a point of diminishing returns, as determined by the analyst.

10A.2 Possible Application of the Delphi Technique to Conflict Management

Although the Delphi technique as it was originally developed tended to deal with technical topics and seek a consensus among a fairly homogeneous group of experts, three possible areas of application to conflict management and resolution can be identified—Conventional Delphi, Goals Delphi, and Policy Delphi—each of which will be discussed in detail below.

10A.2.1 Conventional Delphi.   In this application, the emphasis is placed on obtaining a compromise (consensus of opinion) among participants on the joint action, development plan, or conflict management procedure that should be adopted in a given situation. First, a team of experts on the conflict situation is assembled. These experts would normally include representatives of the different interest groups involved in the conflict, as well as academics with a professional interest in the specifics of the conflict or in conflict resolution in general. Then iterative questionnaires focusing on the extent of (and/or reasons for) support and nonsupport of various joint actions, development plans, or conflict management procedures are administered to the individual participants in a manner protecting the anonymity of their responses. Feedback of results accompanies each iteration of the questionnaire, and iterations continue until a point of diminishing returns in convergence of opinion is reached. The final result is then the consensus of the experts on the acceptability of each joint action, development plan, or conflict management procedure included in the questionnaire. This usually takes the form of a written report by the Delphi investigator.

The most obvious problem with this application is that there is no guarantee that a convergence of opinion around (support for) a "unique" joint action will emerge. The technique does not contain any mechanism (except group pressure) for generating such convergence nor any means for establishing a give-and-take compromise process between iterations. In tough conflict situations, it may be extremely difficult for it to work. Also, even if the team of experts assembled by the Delphi investigator were to arrive at a "consensus" on the most acceptable joint action or conflict management procedure, the problem then arises of how to get it actually adopted.

10A.2.2 Goals Delphi.[16]   In this application, the emphasis is once again placed on obtaining a consensus among a team of experts. However, the focus is on developing some form of group goals consensus—that is, on identifying the goals (or objectives) that should be included in the social welfare function (objective function) and on establishing acceptable priorities (weights) to be placed on each of these goals (or objectives).

The first part of a Goals Delphi involves the generation of a mutually acceptable goals hierarchy and extends over a number of rounds during which the participants brainstorm relevant objectives for the problem area under investigation. When the analyst considers that the capacity of participants to suggest more objectives has been exhausted, they are each asked to group the objectives into a hierarchical structure (for example, via use of the categories high-priority, medium-priority, and low-priority). The analyst then prepares a composite of the participants' groupings (he may, for example, make use of cluster analysis or other multidimensional scaling techniques). This composite is then returned to participants as feedback, and they are each given an opportunity to revise their grouping of objectives in the light of this new information. A composite of the revised grouping is then prepared, and so the process continues until the analyst determines that a "group-accepted" goals hierarchy has been identified.

The second part of the Goals Delphi then includes the establishment of a set of weights for the goals identified in the first part and is also carried out over a number of rounds. Using a scaling technique (such as the Saaty scale discussed on pages 148–150) each participant assigns scores to each goal (i.e., to each cluster of objectives) and to each objective in terms of its contribution to the given goal. These scores are then analyzed and statistical information regarding the distribution of opinion is fed back to participants. They are asked to revise their weightings in the light of this information. Participants whose weight on an objective is at or nearby an extreme of the distribution may be asked to provide a written justification for this weight. The revised distributions are again analyzed, and the "reasons" are edited and returned to participants along with the statistical feedback before the next round of revisions takes place. This process continues until the analyst considers that convergence on a particular set of weights has been achieved or that further iterations would not be useful in bringing about a greater consensus of opinion on appropriate weights. When used in this manner, the Delphi technique can be interpreted as a variant of the recursive interaction procedure discussed on pages 256–263.

10A.2.3 Policy Delphi.[17]   In this application the emphasis is placed on the heuristic potential of the technique. That is, it is seen as an educational tool that can be used to explore the characteristics of a given conflict situation more thoroughly, leading to greater insight into the nature of the target problem and the policies that may be adopted to bring about its solution.

While the previous two applications aimed at achieving a group consensus on a particular topic, the Policy Delphi seeks to generate the strongest possible opposing view on the potential resolutions of major policy issue(s).

The procedure rests on the premise that those responsible for making actual decisions regarding a given conflict situation are not interested in having a group of outside experts generate the decisions for them, but rather in having an informed group: (1) ensure that all the options have been put on the table for consideration by them; (2) expose the differing positions taken on these options by interest groups involved in the conflict, as well as the principal arguments put forth to support these positions; and (3) document the likely impact on each interest group of adopting any particular option. Thus, a

Policy Delphi represents an alternative to the Fisher brainstorming sessions discussed on pages 359–361 as a method for correlating views on issues pertaining to a particular conflict situation, and for allowing participants representing such views the opportunity to react and assess their opponents' viewpoints without formally committing themselves (or the interest group they represent) to a particular course of action.

10A.3 An Evaluation of the Delphi Technique

A Delphi-type workshop can clearly serve a useful role in many conflict situations. This is particularly so when:

1. tensions among participants are so severe that the communication must be refereed by some third party and/or confidentiality insured;
2. a deadlock situation has developed and participants are unwilling to suggest avenues for escape before it is apparent that (the majority of) their opponents will be willing to go along with their idea; and
3. one of the participants to the conflict is a superpower or has an outspoken personality, and hence would tend to dominate a face-to-face exchange of opinion.

The Delphi technique also has a number of disadvantages. This is particularly so with the Conventional Delphi and Goals Delphi where an attempt is made to reach a group consensus on a highly sensitive issue. As Turoff (1970:94) points out:

It is possible . . . to observe two very different phenomena taking place. One is when the exercise starts with disagreement on a topic and ends with agreement. This can be very useful to those sponsoring the study if it does occur, but . . . is not a necessary result. Another process is to start with agreement on a topic and end with disagreement. In a sense this can be conceived as an education process taking place among the respondents who suddenly realize, as a result of the process, that the issue is not as clear-cut or simple as they thought.

Even in the case of the Policy Delphi, where an attempt is made to collect a wide range of opinions on possible solutions to a conflict, it is not clear that the Delphi communication process will be able to achieve this. For example, Sackmann (1975:71) asserts that, by discouraging an adversary process, a Delphi-type workshop may act to inhibit rather than encourage exploratory thinking. "The 'tyranny' of majority opinion may swamp that of the single maverick who may actually have better insights than the rest of the 'experts' who all agree with each other."

Finally, there are problems associated with the construction and execution of the questionnaire. For example, the analyst may find it difficult to avoid (1) excessive specification (imposing the analyst's views and preconceptions of the conflict on the respondents and not allowing adequately for the contribution of other perspectives) or (2) excessive vagueness (leading to ambiguous initial responses that may become less and less meaningful as the iteration process continues). Further, it may often prove difficult to identify appropriate techniques for summarizing and presenting the group response and ensuring common interpretations of the evaluation scales utilized in the exercise. These problems can be expected to be particularly severe when participants have different language and cultural systems or when qualitative rather than quantitative responses dominate the questionnaires.

In summary, the Delphi process cannot serve as a substitute for all other forms of communication in a conflict situation, however it may often provide a useful avenue for exchange of ideas among participants when a face-to-face meeting cannot be arranged or is felt to be premature.

NOTES

1. For one set of possible definitions of these goods, see Isard, T. Smith, et al. (1969:564–86).
2. Or, if there is an upper bound, then it is not exceeded by the capacities or desires of all behaving units to consume it. In the case for c-power, however, some political scientists argue that there is only a fixed amount available to be distributed among nations, interest groups, and individuals.
3. Kelman, however, does not explore the problem as deeply as one can. He does not consider what criteria should be set up for the selection of a mediator by participants and/or other individuals—particularly where the participants and/or other individuals may have different standpoints on what are relevant and important criteria.

4. At this point, we may ask the question: What motivates the participants to be involved? Clearly, the motivation of a participant can be presumed to occur in a number of different ways, one of which will be developed more fully on pages 367–369. Briefly stated, let each participant J be an average member of the interest group that he represents and be concerned solely with his self-interest. Therefore, as an average member of his interest group, he is motivated to see realized the c-security that could be achieved from a successful resolution of the conflict. Such makes him willing to provide time, effort, knowledge, and other inputs into the workshop activity. In effect he may be conceived to have an information production function that, together with other functions, relates the c-security he realizes to his labor and other inputs. He also has a utility function that relates his utility to the c-security realized (and consumed) and his labor and other inputs, which gives rise to disutility. He therefore is motivated to devote his time and effort (labor) in workshop activity up to the point where, as we shall fully discuss later, the disutility of additional time and effort (labor) starts to offset the estimated utility that might be derived from additional c-security.

5. We may finally ask what motivates the mediator to participate in the workshop interactions, a question that Burton and Kelman do not ask but which we consider relevant. As we will sketch more fully on pages 365–367, the mediator supplies (1) the input of his knowledge, (2) his labor inputs, and (3) diverse other inputs into a production process. This process yields new information, in terms of statements of new ideas and new suggestions that he proposes to participants during the workshop discussions. Since the mediator is a devoted individual, we can easily specify a "payoff" that he receives in terms of c-respect and the like that the world community and he himself (in the form of own c-respect) bestows on him should his efforts lead toward resolution of the conflict. Thus we may set up a utility function that relates his utility to (1) c-respect realized (and consumed) and (2) his labor inputs, which give rise to disutility. The mediator is therefore motivated to devote his time and effort (labor) in workshop activity up to the point where, as we shall fully discuss later, the disutility of additional time and effort (labor) required to achieve movement toward conflict resolution starts to offset the estimated utility that he would derive from additional c-respect.

6. In effect, Fisher's mediator identifies for a participant, say J, the outcome elements o_1^J, o_2^J, o_3^J, . . . that he perceives of importance to J and judges whether saying "yes" rather than "no" to a proposition involves a noticeable improvement (either a " + ", or nonpresence of a " – ") on each such element, or a noticeable deterioration (either a " – " or nonpresence of a " + ").

7.   Should the proposition perceived by the mediator to be yesable turn out to be rejected by one or more of the participants, then the mediator needs to revise his perceptions of what outcome elements are most important to participants. With these revised perceptions he may begin to devise another plan, say X', to be put to the participants.

8.   For example, one threat might be preclusion of access to a key waterway (e.g., the Suez Canal) essential to a nation's economy and its ability to function as a peacetime economy as well as a military power—thereby changing the nation's action space. An offer of know-how and trained personnel regarding a new technology to developing nations in conflict is an instance where the outcome function may be affected. Note that the threat (or offer) must not only be credible in the sense that it is within the technical capability of the political body (behaving unit) making it but also in that it is politically credible within that body.

Note that in allowing action spaces and outcome functions to be altered by propositions, Fisher's approach is superior to that of much traditional decisionmaking theory, which assumes that the action space of any participant is independent of the actions of others and that the outcome function remains unaffected by proposals. See Isard, T. Smith, et al. (1969:chaps. 5 and 6).

9.   Note that we do not consider the cases where one participant, say J, accepts and the other, say L, rejects. In many situations, one must do so. This, however, complicates the problem and forces the analyst, mediator, and each participant to consider four possible joint actions, namely a', a'', a''' (where J accepts and L rejects), and a'''' (where J rejects and L accepts). The reader may wish to pursue this more complicated analysis. It even may be that the participants' thinking goes beyond these four possible joint actions and takes on the character of policy options as in the Howard metagame approach (see Chapter 3, pages 42–48). This then leads to a set of possible joint actions and can lead to still more numerous and more complex joint policy options, and so forth. For most conflict situations of reality, consideration of only joint actions a' and a'' is sufficient. Hence, we restrict our analysis accordingly.

10. It can of course be the case that the mediator so wrongly perceives u'^J and u'^L that in fact his *realized* utility from what he perceives to be a yesable proposition is -1.

11. Here, as with the mediator discussed in the previous case, the side condition $u^J = u^J[P^J(f(a))] = 0$ indicates that J in his role as participant is not satisfied with the current situation. Therefore, since he can assume the role of mediator, he is motivated to propose a proposition that he judges will lead to an outcome that is more desirable to himself and that he perceives will be more desirable to L.

12.   Recall that a threat, offer, or combination of both by J can change the action space of L and also the outcome function f.

13.   It is interesting to raise the question of what is the optimal combination of demand, offer, and threat that L might make. For example, we might think of L making an offer of a development loan that can vary continuously and the threat of an increase in the price of oil or some other critical commodity that can also vary continuously. It is then pertinent to ask: "What combination of development loan and price of oil maximizes L's expected utility (ūlity) once L has taken into account the probabilities of yes and no by J to each possible combination?" Theoretically, one can employ a microeconomic approach and derive this optimal combination via first order and second order conditions.

14.   For further development of the ideas in this section, see Isard and C. Smith (1982f), where a model exploring the dynamics and learning in mediation and workshop interaction processes is presented.

15.   This appendix draws heavily from Linestone and Turoff (1975) and Sackmann (1975), to whom the reader is referred for further exposition.

16   Our discussion of the Goals Delphi relies heavily on Skutsch and Schofer (1973), to whom the reader is referred to for further details on this type of application.

17.   Our discussion of the Policy Delphi relies heavily on Turoff (1970) and Linestone and Turoff (1975), to whom the reader is referred for further details.

11 SYNTHESIS OF QUALITATIVE AND QUANTITATIVE APPROACHES

11.1 INTRODUCTION

The purpose of this chapter is to attempt to bring into one framework various types of conflict management procedures that may be applicable in an operational way to conflict situations. Our approach is to recognize that both qualitative and quantitative aspects are almost invariably present in any conflict situation. In an extreme case, qualitative aspects are at least present at the beginning and at the end. They are present at the beginning since participants must perceive that a conflict (i.e., a non-yesable proposition for each party) exists. They are present at the end, since whatever numbers characterize an acceptable compromise joint action must be able to be put into a balance sheet or equivalent form so that it does in effect become a yesable proposition or the like, as perceived by the leader or decision-maker and his constituency.

Quantitative aspects are present since almost invariably some of the characteristics of any given conflict situation can be described in quantitative terms, such as number of tanks, state of the economy (its GNP), and stocks of resources; also some of the outcome elements of any proposed compromise solution may be most effectively expressed using numbers, such as a division of territory, side payments and employment impact.

In Chapters 3 through 8 we systematically covered the quantitative CMPs that could each singly be employed in one or more conflict situations. In Chapter 10 we covered several qualitative approaches—Burton, Kelman, and Fisher—again, each to be singly employed in a conflict situation. In this chapter we examine different combinations of these techniques to be applied simultaneously (and thus frequently fused) or in sequential fashion.

In the next section we consider combinations of qualitative approaches covered in Chapter 10. In Section 11.3 we consider combinations of quantitative CMPs covered in Chapters 3 through 8. In Section 11.4 we consider (1) the combination and synthesis of quantitative CMPs with the qualitative Fisher approach, (2) the combination or fusion of quantitative CMPs with the qualitative Burton approach, and (3) the combination and synthesis of quantitative CMPs with the qualitative Kelman approach. Then we consider combinations and fusion that involve (1) a synthesis of more than one quantitative CMP and a single qualitative approach, (2) a combination of more than one qualitative approach with a single quantitative CMP, or (3) more than one qualitative with more than one quantitative approach. It would be exceedingly time consuming to consider all possible combinations and permutations. Hence, to present the comprehensive possibilities for synthesis, we develop a diagrammatic way of depicting the innumerable combinations that are possible.

11.2 FUSION OF QUALITATIVE APPROACHES

In the discussion of the several qualitative approaches presented in Chapter 10 it was clear that in many respects these approaches could be meaningfully combined. The most obvious avenues for synthesis arise because of the existence of some common or complementary elements within these approaches. However, we now examine more systematically the possibilities for useful combinations and fusion.

11.2.1 Burton and Kelman

The first combination that can be considered is that of the Burton and Kelman approaches. It can easily be effected since, although each approach involves different points of emphasis, both assemble participants for debate, discussion, and other forms of interaction within a workshop atmosphere. For example, a major point of emphasis in Kelman's approach is the identification in preworkshop sessions of constraints that each party feels it must impose on compromise solutions to be considered. Information regarding the nature of these constraints can serve as a valuable input to the workshop, whether this main workshop is of a Burton-type or Kelman-type. It can make workshop interactions more efficient by avoiding any focus on areas wherein nonfruitful debate and discussion might otherwise take place—either because such areas involve compromise solutions politically unacceptable to one or more participants or because such areas touch upon highly sensitive, emotionally charged issues on which participants are not prepared to engage in negotiations. As a result of a more effective structuring of the agenda for discussion, joint actions perceived by each party as involving positive outcomes can be more readily identified, and the search for a universal need (Burton's major point of emphasis) can be more easily pursued. However, it does not always follow that this would be the case. For example, a too sharply and/or too quickly focused agenda for workshop discussion may make it more difficult for participants to ease themselves into a positive attitude by preventing them from floundering around and discovering for themselves what makes sense and what does not. Of course, the discussions in the workshops and the evolving perception of the nature of interdependence may lead the participants to want to revise the bounds that they had originally set in preworkshop sessions. Accordingly, they may hold additional intranation mini-workshop sessions, in the Kelman style, for this purpose.

Once discussions in the workshop have successfully taken place and participants have come to identify universal needs and built up positive and (highly) cooperative attitudes, then according to Burton it becomes possible to reach an "obvious" compromise solution. With Kelman, however, there may still be the need to reach an explicit compromise solution in the main workshop and then proceed to an end-of-workshop session. In the latter, participants representing each nation meet separately to discuss how this "obvious" compromise solution may be packaged up for implementation by actual decisionmakers. In the above manner, then, a fusion of Kelman and Burton approaches can be achieved.

11.2.2 Fisher and Kelman

Kelman's workshop approach necessarily involves a third party. Thus, when we combine it with a Fisher *yesable proposition* approach it should be combined with a variant of the Fisher approach that also involves a third party. During the main workshop session, this third party may take a completely passive role and be present primarily to guide the discussions; or he may take on a more active role and set forth a plan for resolution of the conflict (involving a demand-offer-threat combination for each participant). In either case, the third party holds preworkshop sessions with each participant and identifies the constraints, at least for the first round of discussions, on the demand-offer-threat combination that might be proposed by himself or one of the participants. These constraints might be placed on the demands that can be made of a participant or on the nature of credible threats or offers that can be imposed.

For example, these constraints may rule out a proposition whose balance sheet for an opponent has a minus on one component and plusses on all others if the minus is on a component of overwhelming importance to the opponent and would say violate a basic principle of the dominant religion of his constituency. They may also place restrictions on certain kinds of threats that the third party (or participants themselves) judges may escalate the conflict, for example, by provoking immediate bombing by the opponent. Constraints, too, may place restrictions on certain kinds of offers, for example those that might be considered insulting to an opponent or whose acceptance would require what the opponent considers an unprincipled action on his part. Constraints can thus have strong filtering effects on proposable demand-offer-threat combinations.

Once the preworkshop activity has been conducted in the Kelman style, the participants might come together in workshop activity (as mentioned on page 359 and dubbed by Fisher, "brainstorming") whereby each can come to perceive better the interests and constraints of other participants and so forth. From such activity, yesable propositions may become evident and one may be successfully set forth and accepted. On the other hand, no yesable propositions may become evident. Or there may have resulted several rejections of propositions that did not involve credible threats. This experience might then suggest that a Kelman mini-workshop be conducted with each participating nation to allow reconsideration of the constraints imposed on acceptable demand-offer-threat combinations in the light of the insights gained during earlier debate, discussion, and interaction.

Alternatively, it may be that the Kelman approach is successfully employed not only during a preworkshop session but also during the main workshop activity. Then at the end-of-workshop session the participants may discuss not only how to tailor the particular compromise solution for acceptance by their political leaders but also how to transform the outcomes of the compromise solution into a balance sheet format for each participant and to devise a combination of credible threats and offers a la Fisher to be adopted in an effort to ensure adherence (give stability) to this compromise solution.

Yet, it may turn out that during the main workshop session neither the Kelman nor the Fisher approach leads to the emergence of a yesable proposition. The participants and the mediator may then decide, Fisher-style, to fractionate the conflict into a number of smaller conflicts. Each one of these smaller conflicts may then be returned to the Kelman preworkshop arena for the setting of constraints. Once these constraints have been set and the subsequent main workshop interaction embarked upon, the mediator may suggest a chronological sequence for consideration of the smaller conflicts. For example, he may suggest that discussions focus first on those smaller conflicts that, on the basis of his knowledge of the participants and the characteristics of the conflict situation, are more easily resolved. Working together toward the resolution of these initial conflicts may act to build up trust between and mutual security of participants, and thereby help ease the problem of managing the more difficult smaller conflicts. Also, the mediator may attempt to link together the resolution of these smaller conflicts when such linkage is meaningful to participants. For example, one or more participants may perceive these conflicts as either inextricably intertwined or view linkage as involving a form of legitimate or "principled" logrolling, enabling one participant to gain, say, a lion's share in one small conflict while the other gains the lion's share in a second. It should be noted that the resolution of any of these smaller conflicts may be achieved via a Fisher "yesable" proposition or by any other conflict management procedure.[1]

Still another scenario might develop in a situation where the Fisher and Kelman approaches are considered for joint use. To be specific, during the main workshop session, a number of sequences of proposition making might take place. For example, the mediator might propose a Plan X for joint adoption. One participant may not be prepared to accept Plan X, but propose that instead the group consider Plan X', involving a threat and offer by him. The mediator, in considering Plan X', decides whether he will now waive his previous offer and threat contained within Plan X. The other participant considers whether Plan X' is more yesable to him than Plan X. At this point, Plan X' may be preferred by all, and the workshop may come to an end with agreement reached on its adoption. On the other hand, Plan X' may be unacceptable to the other participant. However, the direction of change in Plan X incorporated in X' may suggest to the mediator a new Plan X", more likely to be acceptable to participants than the X'. The proposer must then be requested to waive his right to propose and carry out the threat embodied in X' and be willing to go along with Plan X" instead. This process could continue through Plan X''', X^{iv}, . . . , until Plan X*, which is acceptable to all, is proposed. In essence, a process of sequential amendments evolves, wherein at each point of amendment a participant relinquishes his right to exercise a previously made credible threat.

11.2.3 Fisher and Burton

Unlike Kelman, Burton does not suggest a preworkshop session. Rather, he goes directly into a main workshop interaction process, which has more structure and rationale than Fisher's brainstorming session. As discussed on page 359, the latter would merely bring individuals together to sort out ideas and hopefully to invent new ways of thinking and making proposals. On the other hand, Burton is vague about the actual formulation and implementation of joint proposals acceptable to participants—an area in which Fisher's yesable proposition approach is strong. Hence, a synthesis of the Burton and Fisher approaches can be fruitful. A first stage of a synthesized approach might involve, a la Burton:

1. the extension of the commodity space to include noneconomic commodities (universal needs);
2. recognition that the welfare (outcome) to any participant is dependent on this extended set of commodities;
3. recognition that welfare (outcomes) to participants are interdependent (this is a step that the Fisher approach also embraces); and
4. reassessment of the costs and benefits of alternative joint actions.

This last step is central to the Fisher approach in the sense that when a participant (or a mediator) sets forth a proposition, he has typically considered several possible propositions and selected one he perceives will be a yesable proposition for all concerned. This is particularly so for sophisticated participants and experienced mediators. However, recall that Fisher's approach does not involve a search for the optimal yesable proposition but only for a satisficing proposition.

While Burton would stop here, Fisher would go further. In particular, he would suggest the introduction of credible offers and credible threats that necessarily embody elements of implementation (after all, a threat or an offer can only be credible if it is put forth by a unit with implementation capability). This suggests that if a fused Burton-Fisher procedure is to be employed, those who engage in the workshop activity must be either the political leaders involved in the actual implementation of any proposition agreed to within the workshop or right-hand persons having the full confidence of these leaders and daily, if not hourly, contact with them.

Thus, while Burton directly changes the participants' perceptions of their utility functions by introducing new commodities and universal needs, Fisher directly changes the action space of participants and their outcome functions by introducing the possibility of credible offers and credible threats. So their approaches can be fused sequentially for certain kinds, albeit a highly limited number, of conflict situations wherein very influential persons have the time and inclination to assemble.

It is not always necessary that the application of the Burton approach precede that of Fisher. For example, we may imagine that a Fisher brainstorming session has been set up. While various ideas have been put forth and discussed at length, none have emerged that are likely to yield a yesable proposition. At this point, we may imagine that the political leaders or their right-hand men, confronting a high probability of warfare or the equivalent, might be willing to agree to a cooling-off period—a period during which a Burton workshop session might be held in which representatives of the different participants would have an opportunity to review the situation, perceive the needs of the different parties, and become better informed of their several interests in a leisurely setting more conducive to further understanding, eliminating misperceptions, and so forth. From such an interaction might come forth agreement on a compromise solution, which may be incorporated into a yesable proposition by one of the participants or the mediator.

There are a number of other ways that Fisher and Burton may intertwine. In reality, it often turns out that the Fisher phase comes first with a proposition involving a credible threat having been made by one participant and not accepted by his opponent. While in the process of carrying out the credible threat, or preparing to carry it out, the participant asks why what he thought would be a yesable proposition was not in fact a yesable proposition. He may in fact simulate, invite, or pursue a Burton workshop interaction process to discover the reasons for nonacceptance, involving perhaps his neglect of an outcome element relating to a hitherto nonexplicit universal need of the opponent. Such may then lead the participant to put forth a revised demand-offer-threat combination involving a relaxation of his previous threat. However, strictly speaking, this is inconsistent with the definition of a credible threat and the notion of the Fisher yesable proposition involving a credible threat. On the other hand, such is reality. This, then, suggests the important need to develop for our conflict management tool kit procedures that can capture key dynamic elements.

Moreover, note that the Fisher and Burton approaches cannot be fully pursued simultaneously as can the Kelman and Burton approaches. Since the Fisher approach can directly change the action space of participants (as when credible threats are involved), this negates an assumption implicit in the Burton framework—namely, that the joint action space remains unchanged while new commodities are introduced into their outcome space—that is, while universal needs come to be recognized. Thus, the full Fisher and Burton approaches can only be applied sequentially, though in several different ways—that is, with different sequences of their several basic elements.

11.2.4 Fisher, Burton, and Kelman

We may first consider a sequential synthesis of the Kelman, Burton, and Fisher approaches, since as pointed out earlier, Fisher's approach in full cannot be fused simultaneously with that of Burton. A reasonable and likely sequence would involve the Kelman and Burton approaches fused sequentially or simultaneously in a first stage (wherein the basic elements of the preworkshop, main workshop, and miniworkshop are captured) and Fisher's in a second stage. As indicated on pages 382–383, at the end of the first stage, participants would have had considerable interaction and would be fully aware of universal needs and constraints that must be heeded to yield a compromise solution that would be politically viable to participants. If the main workshop interaction was successful in reaching a compromise solution to which all participants are agreeable, a Kelman end-of-workshop session would be held to discuss implementation of this solution. It is at this stage that some aspects of Fisher's approach, in particular his use of a credible threat, may be grafted on to preclude nonadherence. That is, each participant may set forth a credible threat to be put into effect by his nation (constituency) should the other participant's nation defect from the compromise joint action agreed upon in the main workshop.

On the other hand, no compromise solution in the Kelman-Burton tradition may evolve during the main workshop interactions. At this point, one of the participants (or the mediator in his role as leader) might explore a number of propositions involving only demands and credible offers. Presumably, if one of these propositions is found yesable, and does not involve any credible threat, it could constitute a compromise solution to be actually suggested by the participants (behaving as representatives) to their respective political leaders for acceptance and implementation. On the other hand, no yesable proposition may arise because there was perhaps inadequate preworkshop preparation and appreciation by one or more participants of the full range of impacts, sensitivities, and perceptions of other participants; but in any case, at the end of this first main workshop, participants would be more cognizant of universal needs. The mediator may then introduce mini-workshops a la Kelman, wherein participants reexamine the constraints they insisted upon and come up with a more reasonable set. Subsequently, another main workshop interaction may be engaged in and, where necessary, additional rounds of mini-workshops and main workshops.

If after a series of such sessions no compromise solution emerges that is acceptable to all participants, we can imagine that the patience of one or more of the participants or of the mediator becomes exhausted. At that point, the possibility of credible threats as components of yesable propositions may be introduced. Extensive discussions and even additional mini-workshops again may take place. Eventually, however, we may imagine that either (1) a proposition (set forth by a participant or the mediator) is agreed to by all participants for acceptance by their leaders, or (2) none is found acceptable, in which case, on the advice of his respective representative, one or more leaders may, independently of the workshop, put forth a modified proposition inclusive of credible threats to his opponents. Possibly a counter-proposition may then be made by another participant as already discussed on pages 385–386. In fact, many patterns of actions and reactions may occur at this point, and the reader may develop many possible scenarios for himself. One that is particularly relevant would return the discussion to mini-workshops in a last-ditch effort to avoid an imminent outbreak of physical violence, with the directive to consider fractionation of the conflict. The particular fractionation to be considered may be specified in advance by the mediator where this is considered advantageous. Discussions may then proceed as discussed on pages 385–386.

A less likely and perhaps less reasonable sequence would involve the Fisher approach as part of the first stage. This could take place when the mediator recognizes at the start that there is no possibility of resolving an extremely complex conflict without fractionation. He therefore may call participants together for a pre-preworkshop session simply to reach some agreement on how to fractionate the conflict, or perhaps only to have them accept the principle of fractionation. Then, for each subconflict as perceived and defined by the mediator, participants might proceed with identification of constraints within a Kelman preworkshop session, move on to a main workshop session, and so on.

To sum up, we have suggested several ways to synthesize main elements in the Burton, Kelman, and Fisher approaches. Many syntheses are possible, and the practical mediator would select that combination that best fits the conflict situation on hand.

Conceivably, the combinations of approaches just discussed in the synthesis of qualitative procedures may lead to a yesable and implementable proposition. Yet, if many of the elements of the decision-making situation (e.g., the outcomes and actions) can be expressed in quantitative form, this may introduce more objectivity and reduce the participants' uncertainties about outcomes from alternative compromise solutions. Such additional information may in certain situations facilitate the reaching of a yesable and implementable proposition, with or without the involvement of credible threats. Hence we now should consider the introduction of the use of the quantitative CMPs into the workshop interaction. Their use in single fashion has already been discussed. However, before attempting to synthesize them with the qualitative approaches, we must first consider their possible use in combinations. To this question we turn in the next section.

11.3 FUSION OF QUANTITATIVE APPROACHES

A mere skimming of the contents of Chapters 3 through 8 indicates the almost infinite number of combinations of quantitative CMPs that might be considered. However, by focusing upon key notions and a few procedures of central importance, we are able to consolidate this almost infinite number into a limited number of *clusters of modules,* each of which can be considered as encompassing a large number of possible combinations.

11.3.1 Outcome/Action Compromise Clusters
(for situations where participants can only order their preferences (ordinal utility) and where a small (finite) number of joint actions is available)

The first cluster we shall consider will be the simplest. To do so, return to Table 3–2, wherein the numbers are used to indicate only order of preferences and where we have only a finite number of joint actions. On pages 32–36 we discussed the use of single-step action compromise or outcome compromise procedures, which we now may represent by the segment designated *a* in Figure 11–1.

One of the shortcomings of such procedures is that in many situations their solutions cannot be characterized as stable. We therefore might combine with either of these procedures a second procedure, such as Howard's metagame approach involving the notion of an inescapable sanction, which ensures that no participant finds it in his interest to defect from the solution reached in the outcome/action compromise procedure. We thus add to Figure 11–1 a segment *b* to obtain Figure 11–2.

Another major shortcoming of the outcome/action compromise procedure, even after being stabilized, is that the solution may not be efficient. We therefore may add a prespecified constraint that requires the stabilized compromise solution to fall within the efficiency set. We therefore add a segment *c* to Figure 11–2 to obtain Figure 11–3.

The efficiency constraint, however, is only one of several constraints that may be imposed. Others might include lower bounds— for example, requiring that the foreign aid program provided by the developed to the developing nations be of at least the level F (Food:

Figure 11-1.   An Outcome/Action Compromise Procedure.

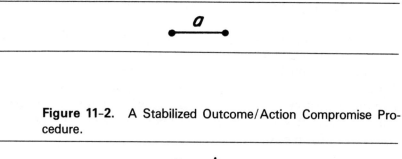

Figure 11-2.   A Stabilized Outcome/Action Compromise Procedure.

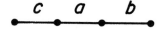

Figure 11-3.   An Efficiency Constrained Stabilized Outcome/Action Compromise Procedure.

Its Supply and Distribution), and that the level of control by developing nations of internal violence be of at least C_1 (Limited Control); or upper bounds—for example, requiring that the level of foreign aid provided by the developed to the developing nations not be more than IND (Industrial Development), and that the level of control of internal violence by developing nations not be more than that which corresponds to C_3 (Extensive Control). Hence in Figure 11-4 we allow for differently constrained outcome/action compromise procedures by substituting for segment c in Figure 11-3 the set of segments $c_1, c_2, c_3, \ldots$ where c_1 = an efficiency constraint; c_2 = a lower bound constraint on actions; c_3 = an upper bound constraint on actions; and so forth.[2] Also in Figure 11-4 we allow for the possibility of either an *action* compromise step, which we designate a_1, or an *outcome* compromise step, which we designate a_2.

Note that at the top of each segment of Figure 11-4 we designate the

Figure 11-4. A Cluster of Constrained Stabilized Outcome/
Action Compromise Procedures.

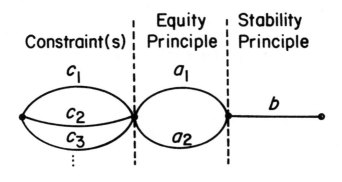

nature of the step involved, the first step in that figure being the choice
of the constraint to be imposed, the second step being the choice of the
equity principle to be adopted, the third step being the choice of a
stability principle if desired. From here on, the type of choice involved
at each step will be designated at the top of each figure.

Finally, we consider situations wherein participants like to approach
a compromise solution through a sequence of (typically small) steps.
Hence, we allow for a sequential outcome compromise or sequential
action compromise procedure by adding another segment, designated
d, to Figure 11-4 to derive Figure 11-5. The reader may refer to the
discussion on pages 37–39 to see how the d procedure can be added
on. Note that we may complicate Figure 11-5 by allowing participants to impose more than one constraint on the joint actions to be
considered, but such is not necessary since we view the segments c_1,
c_2, c_3 . . . each as pertaining to a single or a reasonable combination
of constraints.

As indicated on pages 32–39, there is no guarantee that an action
or outcome compromise procedure, sequential or not, will lead to a
unique solution. When such is the case for a given ordinal utility/
finite action situation, we may resort to other procedures—in particular, to the rank-oriented procedures discussed in Chapter 3.
Hence, for segments $d + a_1$, or $d + a_2$ in Figure 11-5, we may
substitute the principles:

Figure 11-5. A Cluster of Constrained Sequential Stabilized Outcome/Action Compromise Procedures.

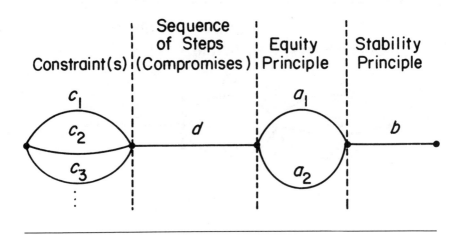

$a_1' = $ min the total of ranks;
$a_2' = $ max the total of rank improvements;
$a_3' = $ min the total of rank concessions;

and others discussed on pages 39–42. When a weighted rank procedure such as min the total of ranks (after weighting) is employed, an additional segment e may be required in order to arrive at a compromise set of weights. Hence, we derive Figure 11-6, where the weighting procedures that might be employed include

$e_1 = $ method of determining group priorities (Saaty);
$e_2 = $ recursive interaction;
$e_3 = $ simple averaging of proposed weights;

and others discussed on pages 190–192.

Observe that when the use of an action or outcome compromise procedure in the combination of Figure 11-5 does not lead to a unique solution, the rank-oriented procedures designated a_1', a_2', a_3', . . . may be inserted between the segment a_1 and b, or a_2 and b to obtain a unique solution. However, if participants find a rank-oriented procedure acceptable, they are likely to do so directly without compli-

Figure 11-6. A Cluster of Weighted Constrained Stabilized Rank-based Procedures.

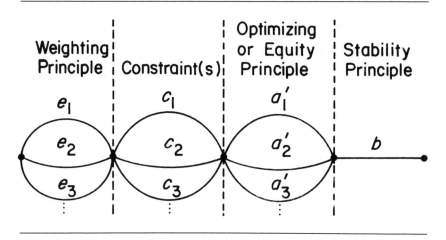

cating their interaction or negotiations with the segments $d + a_1$ or $d + a_2$. Hence we do not consider as generally feasible the more elaborate combination that adds a_1', a_2', a_3', . . . to Figure 11-5.

Finally, as a last resort, when none of the combinations represented in Figures 11-5 and 11-6 work, the mediator can add immediately before segment b a segment f representing a last-offer arbitration procedure. See pages 102-106 for discussion of this procedure.

11.3.2 Split-the-Difference Type Clusters (for situations where participants can only order their preferences (ordinal utility) and where continuous variation is possible in joint actions)

A second cluster of combinations centers around the core principle of (1) split-the-difference, designated g_1 in Figure 11-7 or (2) its substitute, alternating leader-follower principle, designated g_2, when it is possible to consider an even number of rounds and when participants are motivated to "split the difference" this way. As in Figure 11-5, a segment d can be added to permit a sequence of steps (compromises) involving successive application of such procedures, and the segment

Figure 11-7. A Cluster of Stabilized Sequential Split-the-Difference Type Procedures.

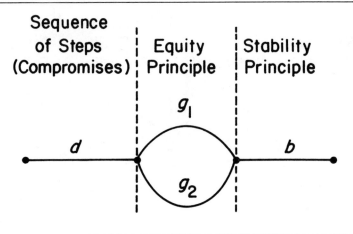

b can be added at the end to ensure stability of the final compromise joint action—that is, to preclude nonadherence. In Figure 11-7, the b segment is added to a situation characterized by a continuous joint action space. If the Howard metagame approach (first designed for a finite joint action space) is to be employed to assure stability, recall that each participant must commit himself to a credible inescapable sanction. This could be a commitment by a given participant to always shift the joint action (after any defection by his opponent from the agreed compromise solution) to his (the given participant's) best reply line (see Figure 4–5) or to some other prespecified threat-type of point.

Where participants have different needs, power, resource inputs, and so forth, simple unweighted averaging such as that involved in a split-the-difference procedure would not be appropriate. As discussed on pages 84–85, it may be necessary to employ a weighted average principle. Hence, to Figure 11–7 must be added weighting procedures depicted by segments e_1, e_2, e_3, . . . as designated above. This yields Figure 11–8.

To more sophisticated participants (especially when considerable uncertainty exists or when they are conservative), the use of simple sequential split-the-difference (weighted or unweighted) or alternating

Figure 11-8. A Cluster of Weighted Stabilized Sequential Split-the-Difference Type Procedures.

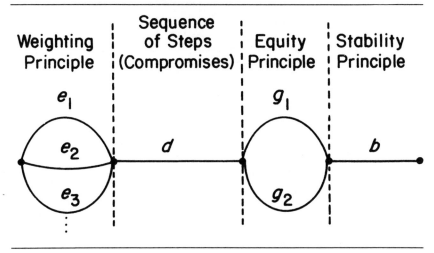

leader-follower procedures may not provide sufficient security against loss. Accordingly, a limited commitment property may be introduced as a constraint on each round. We have indicated this by introducing an h_1 segment between the e and d segments of Figure 11-8. See Figure 11-9. The property, limited commitment, however, may be insufficient. Another property, such as guaranteed improvement, may need to be added to the procedure thus far developed to yield the stretch h_2 rather than h_1. Even this extension may be insufficient to motivate participants to seek a compromise solution, say because of fear of being outwitted. Consequently, a veto power may be given to each participant, yielding stretch h_3 when combined with limited commitment and guaranteed improvement. When such is done, the sequences $e + h_3 + d + g_1$ and $e + h_3 + d + g_2$ correspond, respectively, to the split-the-difference and alternating leader-follower variants of the veto-incremax procedure discussed on pages 85–89 and 92–93.

While rationally minded, sophisticated participants may desire an outcome that is efficient, at the same time they may wish to avoid the infinite number of rounds strictly required to reach the efficiency frontier. After they have gone through two or more split-the-difference

Figure 11-9. A Cluster of Constrained Weighted Veto-Incremax Type Procedures with Stability Property

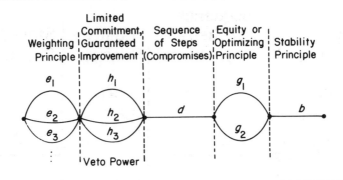

or alternating leader-follower rounds, they may opt to stop this sequential process and adopt a "last-resort" or "finishing-off" procedure such as

f_1 = equidistant improvement from a last reference (status quo) point in the joint action space

f_2 = achievement of minimum requirements (satisficing)

outlined on pages 74–75 and 206–207, respectively. These segments are inserted between g_1 and g_2 and b to obtain Figure 11–10. We have also allowed for the possibility that resource and other constraints may be required by adding a c segment. Figure 11–10 represents the basic frame for developing procedures applicable to situations involving ordinal utility and continuous action spaces. The reader is reminded that not all segments need be, nor should be, employed; and there may be a number of variations for each segment. One significant variation of the alternating leader-follower segment is the GRIT (Graduated and Reciprocated Initiatives in Tension-Reduction) procedure, discussed on pages 99–100. We can well imagine that at some point in a deadlock situation, as has happened many times in the past, one of the participants may make a unilateral concession or offer and initiate the GRIT process. Hence, within the g segment we can add the GRIT procedure, which may be designated g_3.

Figure 11-10.   A Cluster of Constrained Weighted Veto-Incremax Procedures with Finishing-Off and Stability Properties.

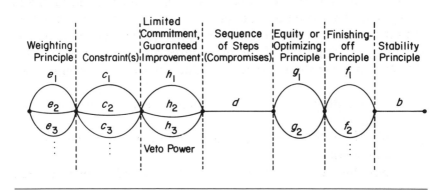

Another important variant of Figure 11–10 is possible when, for example, each participant controls an action with respect to one and only one objective, and where participants always find desirable an increase in the level of achievement of each objective. (See the discussion on pages 101–102.) Under these circumstances it is not necessary for participants to know the preference structures of others. Hence, within the g segment we can add a minimum information incremax procedure, which may be designated g_4.

11.3.3 Relative Improvement and Concession Clusters

A Finite Number of Joint Actions Available (for situations in which participants can state preferences in relative terms (relative utility)). In the previous two clusters, the core principles centered around fair changes in the joint action space (even when we discussed rank-oriented procedures which involve outcome compromises, the primary focus was still on choosing from among joint actions). In the third cluster of procedures, which we now discuss, the core principle directly centers around fair changes in the joint outcome (utility or objective achievement) space and only subsequently on the required joint actions.

When participants have relative utility functions, or think in terms of relative objective achievements, they can talk of comparable percentage changes when they have come to agree on relevant (0,0) and (1,1) points. They can therefore perform operations such as addition and subtraction on these percentage changes. Accordingly, they may be willing to adopt one of the procedures discussed on pages 131–147. We designate these k-type procedures where, for example,

k_1 = min the difference of percent improvements (weighted or unweighted);

k_2 = min the difference of percent concessions (weighted or unweighted);

k_3 = max the min percent improvement (weighted or unweighted); and

k_4 = min the max percent concession (weighted or unweighted).

$$\vdots$$

To the k segment they may want to add a b-type procedure to ensure a stable outcome and an e-type procedure to derive weights where necessary. We thus obtain a cluster of procedures as depicted in Figure 11–11. Since the combinations in this figure can result in inef-

Figure 11-11.   A Cluster of Weighted Stabilized Improvement/ Concession-based Procedures.

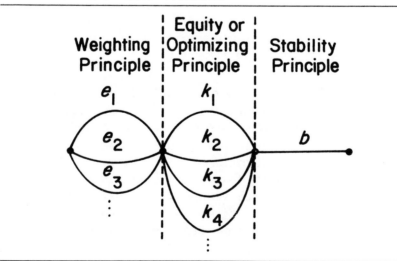

ficient outcomes, an unacceptably low level of improvement, or high level of concession for one or more participants, participants may want to include a c segment involving constraints such as

c_1 = efficiency;
c_2 = upper bounds on percent concessions;
c_3 = lower bounds on percent improvements;

and others discussed on pages 192–196. We thus obtain Figure 11–12.

Continuous Variation in Joint Actions Possible (where participants can state preferences in relative terms (relative utility)). Here the combinations are the same as in the previous part of this section, except that the k-type procedures in Figures 11–11 and 11–12 are replaced by ℓ-type where, for example,

ℓ_1 = max equal percent improvements (or weighted percent improvements);
ℓ_2 = min equal percent concessions (or weighted percent concessions); and

Figure 11-12.   A Cluster of Constrained Weighted Stabilized Improvement/Concession-based Procedures.

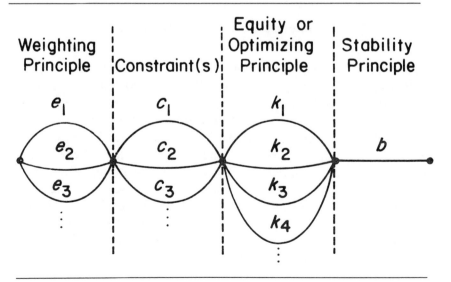

ℓ_3 = max total percent improvements (or weighted percent improvement).

These and other ℓ-type procedures are discussed on pages 155–160.

11.3.4 Absolute Improvement and Concession Clusters

A Finite Number of Joint Actions Available (where participants can state preferences in precise absolute terms (cardinal utility)).   Here the combinations are the same as in the first part of Section 11.3.3, except that the k-type procedures refer to absolute improvements or concessions instead of percent improvements or concessions[3] with appropriate restatement of constraints.

Continuous Variation in Joint Actions Possible (where participants can state preferences in precise absolute terms (cardinal utility)).   The combinations here are the same as those in the second part of Section 11.3.3, except that the ℓ-type procedures refer to absolute improvements or concessions instead of percent improvements or concessions[4] with appropriate restatement of constraints.

11.3.5 Efficiency Constrained Clusters

In certain situations, participants may focus on a particular property that is central in their thinking from the very start. Hence, it may be appropriate for a mediator or arbiter to be in a position to explore effectively all the combinations of procedures that are consistent with this property. For example, let participants consider efficiency to be of paramount importance. Accordingly we set c_1, the efficiency constraint, as the core segment in Figure 11–13. Assuming participants' most preferred joint actions do not coincide, a q segment representing procedures involving concession along the efficiency frontier must be added, as in Figure 11–14. The concession procedure that can be used depends upon the preference structure of participants or the type of measurement of objective achievements. Typical concession procedures are:

Figure 11-13.   An Efficiency Constraint.

q_1 = median efficient joint action principle;

q_2 = concession along the efficiency frontier principle; and

q_3 = Zeuthen concession (least to lose goes first) procedure, which requires utility or objective achievements to be statable in at least relative units. (See the discussion on pages 78–79, 76–77, and 160–162, respectively.)

Since several of these concession procedures do not yield a solution in a single round, a segment d is needed to allow for a sequence of steps (compromises). Also, since participants may be conservative in making concessions, a limited commitment property may be required on each round, as indicated by the addition of a segment h_1 in Figure 11-14. On the other hand, participants may not wish to engage in an excessively long sequence of compromise steps and may wish to add an f segment involving a last-resort or finishing-off type procedure. Finally, participants may wish to preclude nonadherence to the final outcome and hence add a segment b involving a stability-ensuring

Figure 11-14.   An Efficiency Constrained Cluster with Finishing-Off and Stability Properties.

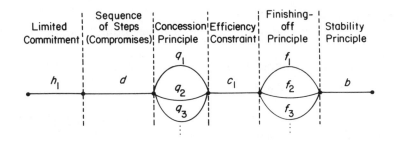

procedure. We thus obtain a cluster of procedures as depicted in Figure 11–14.

11.3.6 Multiobjective (Criteria) Oriented Clusters

In many situations, each of the several participants is concerned not with one objective but with several, and the central problem is to reconcile the different importances they attach to these objectives. Hence, it may be appropriate for the mediator to be in a position to explore all the combinations of procedures that are useful in this connection. Thus, we may organize the cluster figure differently. The core segment, designated n in Figure 11–15, now refers to the objective function with objective achievements as arguments. This function may relate to outcomes in the form of percent changes in objective achievements (when these can each be expressed only in terms of relative measurements) or absolute changes in objective achievements (when these can each be expressed in terms of cardinal measurements).

One first step that participants may find logical is to set down basic constraints to whatever program may be agreed to. These may include lower bounds (e.g., minimum food consumption per capita or minimum growth rates), upper bounds, efficiency, and so forth, which we have already designated by segments $c_1, c_2, c_3, \ldots$ respectively. To arrive at the binding magnitudes relating to these constraints, a procedure for resolving differences regarding binding magnitudes and/or the nature of the constraint function must be adopted. These procedures are indicated by segment m in Figure 11–15, where, for example:

$m_1 =$ recursive interaction;
$m_2 =$ simple averaging on proposed lower bounds, upper bounds, etc.;
$m_3 =$ last-offer arbitration on proposed lower bounds, upper bounds, etc.

These and other m type procedures are listed in Table 12–28 on p. 472.

A next step that participants may find logical is to attain agreement on a relevant objective function. This function may range from a simple total of ranks (perceived to be relevant by all participants) at one extreme, to a highly complicated function such as a translog at the other. First, participants need to establish the general form of the function and hence to adopt an r-type procedure where, for example:

r_1 = recursive interaction;

r_2 = last-offer arbitration on proposed objective functions;

r_3 = rank-oriented procedures on preference orderings of proposed objective functions.

Some similar r-type procedures are listed in Table 12–28.

Recall, however, that most political leaders will select some simple weighted average or like function of the objective achievements whether they are measured relatively, cardinally, or otherwise. Note also that we may need to include last-resort procedures in the r and m segments of Figure 11–15.

Once the form of the objective function is agreed upon, the participants need to adopt a procedure to determine the precise weights and values of other parameters. This is designated, as before, by the segment e in Figure 11–15.[5]

Finally, participants may wish to add on the end of the combination of procedures depicted in Figure 11–15 a segment b to achieve stability (i.e., preclude nonadherence to the compromise solution attained at the end of step n).

There are many other clusters that may be constructed to depict useful and practical combinations of the quantitative techniques, some of which the reader may wish to compose on his own.

Figure 11-15.   A Multiobjective (Criteria) Oriented Cluster.

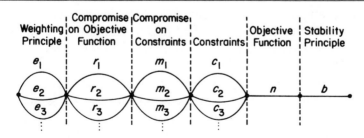

11.4 SYNTHESIS OF QUALITATIVE AND QUANTITATIVE PROCEDURES

Having treated the fusion of qualitative approaches in a conceptual manner in Section 11.2 and the fusion of quantitative approaches in a conceptual manner in Section 11.3, we are now ready to begin the overall fusion of qualitative and quantitative approaches. Again, we could do this in a conceptual manner. However, we feel that at this point in our presentation it is instructive to illustrate the fusion process with simple numerical examples. In order to do so effectively, we shall proceed in a step-by-step fashion. We shall first add the Fisher qualitative approach to the fused quantitative procedures, next the Burton approach, and then the Kelman approach. At the end we shall discuss and illustrate the overall fusion.

11.4.1 Fisher and Combinations of Quantitative Conflict Management Procedures

To begin, take the conflict situation depicted in Table 11-1. Along the left-hand tab we list a number of possible propositions (joint actions) designated α, β, γ, δ, ϵ, and θ. In Column 1 we list J's outcomes from each proposition for a situation where no threats or offers are made, and in Column 2, L's outcomes. As before, we use these outcomes sometimes to represent cardinal numbers, sometimes to depict relative values, and sometimes simply to indicate the order of preference of J and L, respectively.

Observe that the numbers in Columns 1 and 2 indicate that J most prefers proposition (joint action) θ and L most prefers proposition (joint action) α. Now imagine that all the quantitative-type CMPs in the clusters depicted in the previous section that are pertinent to the conflict situation have been considered by participants and found to be unacceptable by one or more. Or imagine that the participants' attitudes are so negative that they are not inclined to try any of the suggested CMPs.

To be more specific, suppose the outcomes of Table 11-1 have cardinal significance and that the mediator had suggested the use of the principle *min the total of absolute concessions*. This would have led to adoption of joint action θ, J's most preferred. However, such a joint action would have been unacceptable to L. Or, suppose the mediator had suggested the use of the principle *min the difference in absolute concessions*. This would have led to the adoption of joint action γ, involving a concession of 75 by J and only 48 by L. This could have been unacceptable to J since he would be making a concession almost twice as large as L's. Or, suppose the outcome elements of Table 11-1 have only ordinal significance and the mediator had proposed use of the principle *min the difference in rank concessions*. Again this would not have worked since there results a tie between γ and δ, with J preferring δ and L preferring γ. The mediator may have suggested different sets of weights and constraints and these, too, may have failed. For similar reasons, other concession procedures may not have worked. In such a situation then, the mediator may suggest to the more aggressive participant, say J, to try out a Fisher-type yesable proposition—that is, to combine a demand that a particular joint action be adopted with a reasonable threat or a generous offer. Alternatively, the more aggressive participant may have become frustrated with the mediator's pussyfooting and, taking matters in his own hands, put forth a combination of demand, offer, and threat a la Fisher.

To illustrate further, suppose there had been a strong rationale for using a CMP based on the principle *min the total of absolute unweighted concessions*. As already noted, this would lead to the choice of joint action θ, J's most preferred, but this is unacceptable to L. We now imagine that J takes the initiative without the intervention of a mediator. Several cases may develop. In the first simplified case, J makes a credible threat to be executed *if L does not accept J's most preferred plan θ*. This threat may be, for example, to close a strategic waterway (such as the Suez Canal) to the other's ships or to take over the local branch-plants owned and operated by the other's multinationals. If the threat is so credible that no discount factor applies, then we may imagine that in the minds of the participants the outcomes of the possible joint actions are changed to those indicated in Columns 3 and 4. In Column 3, the outcome to J associated with joint action θ remains unchanged at 230.[6] The outcomes of all other joint actions, however, must be diminished by the cost to J (say c) of carrying out the threat. In Column 4, the outcome to L of joint action θ remains unchanged, but the outcomes of all other joint actions are significantly reduced (say by 170) because they are now associated with the execution of the threat made by J. With the introduction of this credible threat, L's most preferred joint action becomes θ. Hence

Table 11-1. Outcomes with and without Credible Offers and Threats.

Joint Action or Proposition or Plan	Situations where no Threats or Offers are Made		Situation where J Makes a Threat if θ is Not Adopted		Situation where J Makes Offer if θ is Adopted		Situation where J Makes Both Offer if θ is Adopted and Threat if θ is Not Adopted	
	J	L	J	L	J	L	J	L
	(1)	(2)	(3)	(4)	(5)	(6)	(7)	(8)
α	60	216	$60-c$	$216-170$	60	216	$60-c$	$216-170$
β	130	192	$130-c$	$192-170$	130	192	$130-c$	$192-170$
γ	155	168	$155-c$	$168-170$	155	168	$155-c$	$168-170$
δ	190	136	$190-c$	$136-170$	190	136	$190-c$	$136-170$
ε	215	106	$215-c$	$106-170$	215	106	$215-c$	$106-170$
θ	230	98	230	98	$230-f$	$98+140$	$230-f$	$98+140$

both J and L agree that the joint action θ be adopted. Note in this first simplified case, the use of a credible threat by J resolves the conflict and makes θ a yesable proposition a la Fisher. Also note that to yield the above result, the numbers in Columns 3 and 4 need only indicate the order of preferences of J and L, respectively. The use of the number 170 to measure the negative effect on L if J executes the threat is arbitrary. We only require that a number (or set of numbers with the number being different for each joint action)[7] be employed that results in L identifying θ as her most preferred.

In a second simplified case, we may imagine that J's attitude is more positive. Rather than making a threat, J considers making an offer to L to induce L to accept joint action θ. This situation is illustrated with Columns 5 and 6 in Table 11-1. In Column 5, all outcomes to J are unchanged except that associated with plan θ. There, the outcome 230 is reduced by the cost to J of carrying out the offer, say f, where f is taken to be less than 15.[8] In Column 6, all outcomes to L are also unchanged except that associated with joint action θ, which now involves the offer. There, the outcome to L is now 98 plus the value to her of the offer, say 140, the total of which (namely 238) noticeably exceeds 216.[9] Note again that the introduction of the offer by J resolves the conflict in the sense that both now prefer the same joint action, namely θ. This joint action is again a yesable proposition from Fisher's standpoint, although for Fisher the numbers need only represent participants' ordinal preferences.

The next case is more realistic and more in keeping with Fisher's approach in that it includes a combination of demand, threat, and offer. In this case, the numbers in Columns 7 and 8 indicate outcomes to J and L, respectively, for the proposition that J makes—namely, a demand that joint action θ be adopted, an offer to help induce L to accept θ, and a threat to be executed should L not accept θ. In this more realistic case, the outcomes to J are reduced for all joint actions. His outcome from θ is reduced by the cost (say f) incurred by him in carrying out his offer, while his outcomes from all other joint actions are reduced by the cost (say c) incurred by him in executing his credible threat. See Column 7. Also, all outcomes to L are changed. Her outcome from θ is increased by the gain to her (say 140) from accepting J's offer, while her outcomes from all other joint actions are reduced by the estimated damage to her (say 170) as a result of J executing his credible threat. See Column 8. Once again, a conflict game is converted to a harmony game and the proposition—joint action θ

plus the associated offer and threat by J—becomes a yesable proposition since it succeeds in making θ most preferred by both J and L. Note that the use of a combination of offer and threat makes possible a greater flexibility in the yesable propositions that J might consider making. The two conditions that must be met are now: for J, $(230 - f)$ must exceed $(215 - c)$; and for L, $(98 + v)$ must exceed $(216 - d)$, where v is the value of the offer made to her by J and d is the cost to her of the execution of the threat made by J.[10]

Note that we have effectively changed L's value (ranking) of the possible joint actions by allowing J to be the more aggressive participant (e.g., the leader). In the situation where L too is aggressive, L might respond to J's proposition with a counter-proposition involving a combination of a demand, offer, and threat that could also constitute a yesable proposition were J to be passive (a follower rather than leader). However, of the two yesable propositions, J may prefer his, and L, hers. If the execution of each credible threat is deferred, new conflict then emerges over which of the two yesable propositions is to be adopted. Quite clearly, this process of yesable proposition and counter-yesable propositions may continue for a number of rounds. Such then becomes nonanalyzable. Hence, to be sure that the approach suggested above is effective, there may need to be restrictions placed on such an action and reaction process. For example, another principle—such as a toss of a coin to determine who shall be the leader—may be introduced.

There are numerous combinations of quantitative-type CMPs on which the Fisher qualitative-type approach can be grafted. To provide one more illustration, recall from the discussion on pages 391–405 that stability is a desirable property of a solution in a number of situations, and that several CMPs with a number of other desirable properties unfortunately yield solutions that lack stability. Suppose, for example, that one of the combinations of the cluster *Constrained Weighted Veto-Incremax Procedures with Finishing-off and Stability Properties,* depicted in Figure 11–10, were considered for adoption. Suppose participants desire to preclude nonadherence to the efficient solution reached, but that one of the participants finds the Howard metagame approach to ensure stability too complicated for acceptance. They may then agree to the following rule: "Once an efficient compromise joint action is reached, each participant sets down a credible threat to go into effect." These threats should be such that if any one were executed it would be so damaging to the other participant that he is not motivated to consider a unilateral change in action. Specifically, suppose in Figure 4–10 on p. 88 that the participants have employed an elaborate veto-incremax procedure and arrived at a solution s on the efficiency frontier, with outcomes of 155 for J and 168 for L. These are the outcomes associated with joint action γ in Columns 1 and 2 of Table 11–1.[11] To put a credible threat into effect at this stage may involve a change in the joint action space, making Figure 4–10 no longer relevant. J's credible threat might be to close a strategic waterway critical to the prosperity of L's economy—so critical that, however L adapted, she would be worse off than she was at the start of the conflict resolution process. L's credible threat might be to take over the branch-plants owned and operated by J's multinationals, which if executed would leave J much worse off than he was at the start. Moreover, it must be so that if both credible threats were executed simultaneously the outcomes to J and L would each be much worse than at the start.[12]

In the above sense, Fisher's use of a credible threat can effectively replace Howard's use of an inescapable sanction. However, the Fisher approach has additional merit. It can make a solution stable not only through the imposition of a credible threat involving an inescapable loss to the defector, but also through the imposition of a credible offer. For example, once an efficient solution s is reached, J may commit himself to make an offer to L of foreign aid on an annual basis of $10MM—an offer that would be immediately terminated should L defect even slightly from the efficient solution. Such an offer by J may also be combined with a credible threat. In this sense, Fisher's approach is broader than Howard's; however, one could extend Howard's approach to include both inescapable sanctions and guaranteed (credible) offers. Hence, in Figures 11–2 through 11–15, the b segment may be disaggregated to allow for a choice between

b_1 = Howard metagame approach (use of an inescapable sanction); and

b_2 = Fisher demand-offer-threat proposition approach.

Fisher's approach may be fused with one of the veto-incremax procedures of Figure 11.–10 in yet another way. At the end of each round, a guaranteed offer may be made by a mediator or interested third party to induce the participants to take the next step. For example, in the Iran-Iraq conflict of April 1982 the industrialized countries might get the two warring parties to take the first step toward resolution of their conflict through a guaranteed offer of $10MM aid to each, and then a second step by a guaranteed offer of $20MM aid to each, and so on to a solution where each is guaranteed an offer of $50MM aid.

In short, there are a number of different ways in which the Fisher approach can be grafted on to most, if not all, quantitative CMPs whether applied singly as discussed in Chapters 3 through 8 or in one of the combinations discussed on pages 391–405.

11.4.2 Burton and Combinations of Quantitative Conflict Management Procedures

We now proceed to graft the Burton approach onto a quantitative framework. To do so, recall that Burton's approach involves going beyond narrow (specific) objectives—like a low level of unemployment, a high level of environmental quality, and an extensive and diverse program of health services. It makes explicit broader (or more general) objectives—such as equal educational and employment opportunities, a high level of c-well-being, and long-run, soundly based security. By making explicit these more basic outcomes and the large weights that participants may want to attach to them, Burton in effect transforms participants' perceptions of the outcome elements associated with a given set of joint actions from a conflict game (such as that depicted in Table 11-2) to a harmony game (such as that depicted in Table 11-3) wherein each participant most prefers the same joint action.

To be more specific, consider the case of the two sets of nations J, the developed, and L, the developing. To keep the example simple, consider only six joint actions—namely those resulting from the following three possible direct actions of the developed nations J:

1.   AG (Financing Agricultural Development of the developing nations);
2.   IND (Financing Industrial and Agricultural Development of the developing nations); and
3.   INF (Financing Infrastructure, Industrial, and Agricultural Development of the developing nations)

Table 11-2.   Rankings Based on Selective Criteria.

Joint Action	J's Rankings		L's Rankings		Overall Ranking	
	Growth	Cost	Growth	Cost	J	L
	(1)	(2)	(3)	(4)	(5)	(6)
(INF, Much Control)	2	5^+	1	4^+	3	3
(IND, Much Control)	1	3^+	3	4^+	1	5
(AG, Much Control)	3	1^+	5	4^+	2	6
(INF, Little Control)	5	5^+	2	1^+	6	1
(IND, Little Control)	4	3^+	4	1^+	5	2
(AG, Little Control)	6	1^+	6	1^+	4	4

Table 11-3. Rankings Excluding and Including the Security Objective.

Joint Action	J's Rankings			L's Rankings			Overall Rankings			
							Excluding Security		Including Security	
	Growth	Cost	Security	Growth	Cost	Security	J	L	J	L
	(1)	(2)	(3)	(4)	(5)	(6)	(7)	(8)	(9)	(10)
(INF, Much Control)	2	5⁺	1	1	4⁺	1	3	3	1	1
(IND, Much Control)	1	3⁺	2	3	4⁺	2	1	5	2	3
(AG, Much Control)	3	1⁺	4	5	4⁺	4	2	6	3	5
(INF, Little Control)	5	5⁺	3	2	1⁺	3	6	1	4	2
(IND, Little Control)	4	3⁺	5	4	1⁺	5	5	2	5	4
(AG, Little Control)	6	1⁺	6	6	1⁺	6	4	4	6	6

and the following two possible direct actions of developing nations L involving the control of riots, civil war, assassinations, strikes, and demonstrations:

1.   much control; and
2.   little control.

These six joint actions are listed at the left-hand tab of both Tables 11-2 and 11-3.

The developed and developing nations each have a number of objectives. However, to simplify analysis, assume that each has only two objectives: (1) economic growth (GROWTH), and (2) avoidance of costs (COST). Now consider the ranking of the six joint actions for achieving each objective, first for J and then for L. In Column 1 of Table 11-2, the joint action (IND, Much Control) is perceived by J as contributing most to the GROWTH objective since it would result in growing markets in the developing countries and extensive and profitable trade with them. Thus (IND, Much Control) is given a rank of 1. The joint action (INF, Much Control) would also result in extensive trade, but in J's eyes would lead to such significant growth of developing nations that their industries would become competitive with industries in the developed nations and thus reduce the profits of the latter. Hence, (INF, Much Control) is given a rank of 2. Since J strongly prefers much control to little control for protecting its investments, the life of its nationals, and the like, (AG, Much Control) is given a rank of 3. Using similar arguments to the above, the other three programs are ranked by J as shown in Column 1.

In Column 2, the six joint actions are ranked by J in terms of their contribution to the COST objective. AG programs involve least cost and are each given a rank of 1^+.[13] INF programs are most costly and receive a rank of 5^+. IND programs are intermediate in cost and receive a rank of 3^+.[14]

Column 3 records L's ranking of the six joint actions regarding its GROWTH objective. An infrastructure program is viewed as contributing most to this objective. In addition, since more internal control is likely to result in more internal growth and development, other things being equal, (INF, Much Control) is ranked first, and (INF, Little Control) is ranked second for the same reason, and so forth.

With respect to the COST objective, the three programs involving little control involve the lesser cost for L and are given the rank 1^+, whereas the three programs involving much control involve greater costs and are given the rank of 4+.[15] See Column 4.

Given J's and L's rankings on each of their two objectives (and in a more general problem on each of their several objectives), J and L must each reach an overall ranking of the six joint actions. Since growth is more important than cost for J, (IND, Much Control) is ranked first while (AG, Much Control) is not; and the difference in costs between (AG, Much Control) and (INF, Much Control) is sufficiently large for the former to be ranked second and the latter third. And so forth. See Column 5.

In the case of L, (INF, Little Control) is obviously ranked first and (IND, Little Control) second. (INF, Much Control) is ranked third above (AG, Little Control), since the difference in cost is outweighed by the difference in growth. And so forth. See Column 6.

With J most preferring (IND, Much Control), which is very low on L's ranking, and L most preferring (INF, Little Control), which is at the bottom of J's ranking, we have sharp conflict. We now may imagine that at the suggestion of the mediator, J and L have tried all the procedures in the cluster *Outcome/Action Compromise Procedures* (whether or not sequential, constrained, or both) depicted in Figure 11–5 and also in the cluster *Rank-based Procedures* (whether or not weighted, constrained, stabilized, etc.) depicted in Figure 11–6 and have failed to find a mutually acceptable one.

At this point, the Burton approach may be found useful. We have discussed it thoroughly on pages 332–338. In effect, it introduces at least one more objective, a universal need, into the thinking of participants. We take this objective to be *mutual security* in the sense of absence of major war and belligerent threats. To make this explicit, we add two more columns to those of Table 11–2 to obtain Table 11–3, with J's security and L's security at the head of Columns 3 and 6, respectively, of the latter. After extensive interaction in a workshop setting, Burton would have made J and L fully aware of their common need for security. Such would now enter into their evaluations of the six joint actions. For example, in Column 3, J might rank (INF, Much Control) first in terms of contribution to his security objective, for that joint action removes any reason for L to engage in war or make belligerent threats since it leads to the highest standard of living in L, to the most effective attack on poverty in L, and also to maximizing L's dependence on peaceful economic interactions (trade). Following the same type of reasoning, J ranks (IND, Much Control) second. And so forth.

L might also come up with the same ranking as J. For example, since (INF, Much Control) removes the greatest amount of dissatisfaction among L's poverty-stricken population, this joint action may be viewed as contributing most to L's internal security and to reducing L's propensity to divert attention from internal problems by engaging in hostile acts directed at J and other nations. Hence, (INF, Much Control) is ranked first on security. And so forth. See Column 6.

With the objective security made explicit, the two participants must each reevaluate their preferences regarding the six joint actions. Since security is extremely important to both nations, each may give it a higher weight as an objective than either growth or cost. As a consequence, the joint action (INF, Much Control) now becomes most preferred by each, as indicated in Columns 9 and 10. In this way, the explicit consideration of a universal need converts a conflict game into a harmony game—that is, resolves the conflict.

As already indicated, we can consider in Table 11-3: many objectives for each participant; more than one universal need; a different number of joint actions; differences among participants in weights applied to objectives; different universal needs for the different participants; and so on. However, the manner for fusing the qualitative ideas of Burton with quantitative measures (and/or rankings) available for certain objectives remains unchanged, and can often result in a resolution of a conflict when the use of quantitative-type conflict management procedures in combination or singly cannot.

For this fusion to be useful, it is not necessary that Burton's approach yield a harmony game when added to a quantitative measure. For example, the explicit recognition of a universal need may cause the rankings of J and L to change in such a way that there is no joint action that each most prefers, but there may be a joint action that each comes to rank second. As a consequence, a one-step equi-rank concession procedure may be suggested as a useful compromise procedure. Moreover, participants may want to preclude nonadherence to the outcome from this equi-rank concession procedure. Hence, they may wish to add a b_1 or b_2 stretch to yield a figure such as Figure 11-16.

The above examples illustrate only a few of the many ways in which

Figure 11-16. *A Synthesis of Burton and Quantitative-type CMPs.*

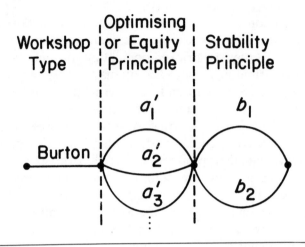

the Burton workshop procedure may be synthesized with quantitative-type conflict management procedures, singly or in combination.

11.4.3 Kelman and Combinations of Quantitative CMPs

We now consider avenues along which the qualitative aspects of Kelman's approach can be fused with the quantitative CMPs, singly or in combinations such as those discussed on pages 391–405. Recall that one of Kelman's major contributions is to structure debate, discussion, and interaction in such a way as to ensure that if a CMP or combination of CMPs is used to reach a solution within a workshop atmosphere, then that solution will be politically feasible. For example, preworkshop sessions with representatives of different interest groups from each nation are designed to help each nation distinguish the politically feasible from the politically infeasible compromise joint actions. Thereby, he ensures that, during the main workshop interactions, each nation suggests only those joint actions that are feasible for it. But also, such preworkshop sessions serve to inform the mediator of the boundary line between feasible and infeasible compromises for each party to the conflict. Given his knowledge of these constraints (boundaries), the mediator can then act to ensure that participants do not go off on tangents that may lead to escalation of hostility, emotional upsets, waste of time, and so forth, but rather stay within the bounds of discussion and interaction most likely to yield compromise solutions.[16]

To give a specific example of how Kelman's approach can be taken into account, go to Table 8–2, p. 274 where there are five objectives (criteria) and where plans α, β, γ, δ, and ϵ, and Z (the existing situation) are ranked by each of two participants, J and L. We see that plan α is ranked sixth by both participants and is considered worse than the existing situation Z. In all probability, this plan would not be proposed by either, and if it were brought up for discussion in any participant's preworkshop session, it would be rejected by them. The case of joint action β however, is somewhat different. For L, it is preferred to the existing situation Z, and hence might be discussed in L's preworkshop session and considered to be a joint action to be proposed for adoption during the main workshop discussions. However, for J, β is less preferred than the existing situation Z, and would thus be considered politically infeasible. It would be rejected by J during his preworkshop session, and the mediator would have come to know this. Hence, in the main workshop session, the mediator would guide the discussion so that only joint actions acceptable to both participants, namely γ, δ, and ϵ, and Z are proposed for adoption. By making explicit such constraints and bounds at the start, the preworkshop sessions act to define the restricted joint action space within which quantitative-type CMPs can be meaningfully employed. It is in this way, then, that Kelman's approach can be fused with the quantitative approaches treated previously. For example, Figure 11–5 can be extended to incorporate a Kelman workshop (or preworkshop) session to yield Figure 11–17.

Note that in an extreme case where the preworkshop sessions eliminate all but one joint action, and the same one, for both participants, there may be no need for the main workshop session. The only feasible joint action has already been identified, and the mediator need only inform the parties of its existence for the conflict to be resolved.

In another extreme case, the Kelman preworkshop session may reveal that there exists no joint action that is considered feasible by

Figure 11-17. A Synthesis of Kelman and Quantitative-type CMPs.

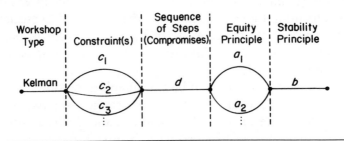

both participants—that is, the participants' sets of politically feasible joint actions do not intersect.[17] If this occurs, then the mediator knows that a main workshop session would be useless and that there must be a change in focus before proceeding further in the search for a compromise solution. Several possible means by which to change the focus have already been suggested—namely, recognizing the availability of joint actions not previously considered, using threats and offers a la Fisher, and identifying hitherto unrecognized needs a la Burton.

11.4.4 Fisher, Burton, and Kelman in Combination with Quantitative Conflict Management Procedures

Having now indicated how the approaches of Fisher, Burton, and Kelman can each be fused with quantitative CMPs whether singly or in combination, we now examine how all three can be applied together with quantitative CMPs in a single integrative framework. We can be very brief since we have already covered many of the linkages when we discussed different partial integrations.

A first step may be the application of the Burton approach, since his approach involves the addition of information in the form of outcome elements relating to previously ignored universal needs. See Figure 11-18. Once the additional information is incorporated into a table such as Table 11-3, we obtain a new set of rankings by the par-

Figure 11-18. A Synthesis of Burton, Kelman, Fisher, and Quantitative-type CMPs.

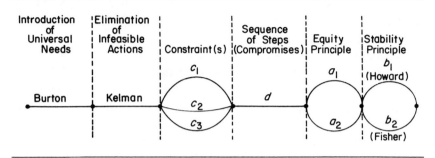

ticipants. Say the participants are J and L and that their rankings before and after the addition of information are as in Columns 1 and 2 and Columns 3 and 4, respectively, of Table 11-4. Note that after addition of information their most preferred joint actions are still not the same.

Table 11-4. A Conflict Situation with a Universal Need Considered.

Joint Action	Old Rankings Excluding Universal Need		New Rankings Including Universal Need	
	J (1)	L (2)	J (3)	L (4)
α	3	3	2	2
β	1	5	1	3
γ	2	6	3	5
δ	6	1	4	1
ϵ	5	2	5	4
Z	4	4	6	6

The second step may then be to eliminate politically infeasible joint actions a la Kelman. Again, see Figure 11-18. For example, the joint action Z may be eliminated because its score on one objective, say growth or security, is the lowest and unacceptable to either one or both parties.

Where conflict still exists, as evident in Columns 3 and 4 of Table 11-4, the third step may be to apply a single quantitative CMP or a combination of them together with constraints agreed upon beforehand to yield a compromise solution. For example, an outcome compromise procedure involving a one-step concession by each participant might be adopted, yielding joint action α as the compromise solution. See Figure 11-18. A final step may then be the addition of an inescapable sanction a la Howard or a credible threat a la Fisher to preclude nonadherence to the compromise solution.

To illustrate further, suppose that one participant, say J, is unwilling to agree to a one-step concession. He insists that when the ranks of the two participants for any given joint action are totaled, his most preferred joint action ranks higher than L's most preferred joint action, and that hence, his most preferred joint action should be adopted. He may also be unwilling to consider the use of any other single CMP or any combination of CMPs. At this point, a mediator may suggest that J search for a yesable proposition a la Fisher. He suggests to J that he (J) combine an offer and a threat with his demand that joint action β be adopted such that the resulting proposition is "yesable" to L. That is, the net effect of J's demand-offer-threat proposition would need to be such that L would rank the outcome from the combination of β and the offer above the outcomes of all other joint actions with the threat executed. If J's demand-offer-threat combination were found acceptable, then the resulting procedure would involve the sequential application of the Burton, Kelman, and Fisher approaches in a situation where no quantitative CMPs were found acceptable. An alternative would be for a mediator, for example, a U.N. secretary-general, to apply pressure on J to accept the compromise joint action α, which L is willing to accept. This pressure could take the form of either an offer or a credible threat (or a combination of the two) which in effect makes J prefer the outcome from α plus the offer to the outcome from β with the threat executed. The above demonstrates several step-by-step fusions of the several approaches. There are, however, many other possibilities of which we briefly note a few.

While it is desirable for the Burton step to precede the Kelman, it may be that the additional information required by Burton exceeds the limited information-processing capabilities of one or more participants. It may then be necessary to apply the Kelman step first to clear the way for nonconfusing and effective debate and discussion.[18] Once the set of joint actions is appropriately constrained, attention to and discussion of universal needs may be introduced a la Burton to resolve the conflict. If such does not produce a harmony game but merely narrows down the conflict, a next step may be to employ a combination of quantitative CMPs or a Fisher-type yesable proposition approach, or where necessary, both.

An alternative sequence might be set up that employs Fisher's approach first. Reexamine Table 11-2. Suppose L is the aggressor and examines propositions (i.e., combinations of demands, offers, and threats) that she considers would be yesable to J.[19] It may turn out that there are several combinations of demands, offers, and threats that L considers would be yesable to J and of approximately equal value to her. Or it may be that if she were informally to suggest to J several combinations of demands, offers, and threats and allow J to choose one of them, that this in itself would considerably reduce J's inclination to reject all her proposals. Suppose, for example, that L sets down three informal proposals for J's consideration. If J has a strong negative reaction to two of them, that leaves one which has not been rejected and which L may state formally as a demand-offer-threat combination for acceptance or rejection by J. If J rejects all three or refuses to respond to any, then L may randomly select the one to be advanced formally. Then all J can do is accept or reject the one that is chosen.

Alternatively, J may respond by saying that he cannot accept any of the three combinations set forth by L, but if L were willing to make his (J's) outcome under the third combination somewhat better, say by offering a tariff reduction of 3.0 rather than 2.5 percent, then he would accept this third proposition. The cost incurred by L in implementing this increased offer may be so great as to make the revised proposition no longer acceptable to L. At this point a mediator may suggest the use of a single CMP or combination of CMPs, such as split-the-difference, to reach a compromise combination of demands, offers, and threats. This then would represent a sequence in which the Fisher approach is the first step, and the use of a quantitative CMP like split-the-difference the second step. If the use of a CMP or combination of

CMPs did not result in a proposition acceptable to both, but only narrowed down the range of conflict, the introduction of a universal need a la Burton and constraints a la Kelman as a third step and a fourth step, respectively, might be undertaken. See Figure 11-19. This might then convert the reduced conflict situation into a harmony game. If not, then the final step may be the application of one of a rank-based CMP, perhaps including the use of constraints and weights. Again, see Figure 11-19.[20] Of course, other sequences are possible where the Fisher approach constitutes the first step.

As already noted, when the Fisher approach is adopted as the first step, an initial deadlock situation such as that described in Table 11-2 may stimulate both J and L to each simultaneously make a proposal involving a combination of a demand, offer, and threat. Clearly, as when two nations each threaten to invade the other if his demand is not met, a mediator may enter and, after pointing out the infeasibility of their joint demands, suggest the use of a simple or more complex CMP—for example, the application of a decremax procedure on their joint demands.[21] Alternatively, the mediator may get them to recognize explicitly (1) their mutual need for security, (2) that war does not necessarily contribute to security, and (3) that some joint action other than the one that would result from execution of their joint threats would result in outcomes much better for both. There of course may be more than one such alternative joint action, and the one which J most prefers may not be the one that L most prefers. In that situation, then, the use of a single CMP or a combination of them is called for to decide among these joint actions.[22]

Figure 11-19. Another Synthesis of Fisher, Burton, Kelman, and Quantitative-type CMPs.

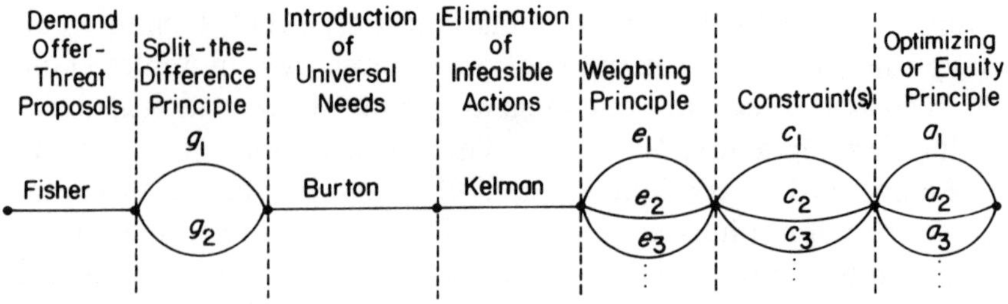

The above discussion illustrates a few sequences in which the Fisher, Burton, and Kelman approaches can be employed together with one or more of the quantitative CMPs singly or in combination. In essence, such sequencing involves putting Burton's universal needs into quantitative form, interpreting Kelman's approach largely as placing constraints on a quantitative model, and considering Fisher's yesable propositions as changing the joint action and/or joint outcome spaces of a quantitative model—even though the quantities involved need not go beyond rank numbers. Doing this achieves a good deal of synthesis. However, it can be argued that we have synthesized only parts of the Burton, Kelman, and Fisher approaches. Clearly, we have not effected such a fine synthesis that we can treat all qualitative and quantitative aspects of a conflict simultaneously to yield a net evaluation that then identifies the optimal management (compromise) procedure or path of procedures. Nonetheless, we feel that the discussion of this chapter does achieve a significant advance toward synthesis, and the reader can now construct on his own numerous combinations of procedures and pursue further the task of synthesis.

11.5 CONCLUDING REMARKS

In bringing this chapter to a close, we wish to stress again the considerable flexibility that is possible in constructing a procedure aimed at a target conflict situation. The procedure can be simple, somewhat involved, or complex depending on the needs of the situation and characteristics of participants. It can require only ordinal or relative preference structures when participants cannot attribute precise values to outcomes. It can take into account the personality characteristics of participants (conservative, bold, etc.), the constraints that a culture may impose, the different amounts of information available, and so forth.

In this synthesis of quantitative and qualitative procedures pursued in this chapter, our basic tool has been the cluster approach. This approach involves the construction of relevant combinations of quantitative procedures which then are to be augmented by qualitative approaches. Such augmentation can be pursued at different points in different ways within any cluster of quantitative approaches, as suggested by Figures 11–18 and 11–19. By this means we achieve critical elements of synthesis. While we have not presented in this chapter an adequate or thorough development of the possibilities for synthesis, nevertheless we have shown how one crude synthesis can be achieved. Further, our *mode* of synthesis as illustrated in Figures 11–18 and 11–19 represents only one possible mode and, as research proceeds, this mode is very likely to be found inefficient and inferior to some other mode. As noted in Chapter 1, many readers may find the beginnings at synthesis in this chapter of most use as a jumping-off point for more basic research, while many practitioners may from their experience quickly add new relevant elements and come up with greatly improved practical procedures. However, even with the successful conduct of much more basic research and the incorporation of insights from solid experience by practitioners, there is no guarantee that a practical procedure will be found for full resolution of any complex target conflict.

This chapter concludes the basic analysis in this book. However, for the busy practitioner, we present Chapter 12 to facilitate his use of the materials presented in this book, and in Chapters 13 through 15 we point up fruitful directions for future research.

NOTES

1. Other dimensions of fractionation can also be considered when combining the Fisher and Kelman approaches. For example, one type of fractionation suggested by Fisher is along a "participants" dimension. That is, there may not be just one decisionmaker representing a nation or interest group within a nation, but several. Some of these decisionmakers may be more liberal in their views and hence more suited to workshop interaction. This suggests that if a Kelman workshop interaction has come to a stalemate, with no new suggestions forthcoming, then shifting the segment of the leadership represented in the workshop away from the more conservative and toward the more liberal decisionmakers may open up the way for fresh discussions and suggestions—presumably more likely to lead to an acceptable compromise solution.

2. Technically speaking, we should add yet another segment to Figure 11–4 since the use of certain constraints (such as those involving lower and upper bounds) may require the adoption of an additional CMP in order for participants to reach agreement on appropriate binding magnitudes. To avoid further complication, we assume at

this point that such binding magnitudes are chosen as part of the selected constraints. At a later stage we will drop this assumption.

3. Of course, participants may still adopt percent improvement and/or concession-based procedures if they so desire. See pages 178–184 for a discussion of k-type procedures that may form the basis of the clusters in this category.

4. See the previous note, and refer to pages 222–228 for a discussion of ℓ-type procedures that may form the basis of the clusters in this category.

5. The procedures used to establish other parameters are taken to be the same as those used to establish weights. Also, once the form and precise parameters of the objective function have been agreed upon, participants may need to return to segment c to revise constraints and hence to engage in sequential recursive interaction. However, to avoid further complication of Figure 11–15, we do not add a d stretch to represent this sequence of steps.

6. There might be some dimunition (increase) of this payoff to J because the international community may frown (look favorably) upon the making of threats in this particular situation.

7. Similarly, in Column 3, c can be of a different order of magnitude for each joint action.

8. That is, less than $230 - 215$, since otherwise joint action θ would no longer be most preferred by J.

9. Again, the value of the offer to L is arbitrary provided that it exceeds $216 - 98 = 118$, and thus results in L identifying θ as her most preferred joint action.

10. More generally, when we recognize that c and d may vary among the joint actions, the conditions are: for J, the outcome to him of joint action θ less the cost to him of carrying out his offer to L (namely $230 - f$) must exceed the outcome to him from any other joint action less the cost to him of carrying out his threat should that joint action be adopted; and for L, the outcome to her of joint action θ plus the value to her of J's offer (namely $98 + v$) must exceed the outcome to her of any joint action less the cost to her of J's threat should that joint action be adopted.

Still more generally, should an initial CMP for which there exists a strong rationale lead participants to focus on a joint action other than θ, the above conditions remain appropriate when we substitute k ($k = \alpha, \beta \ldots$) for θ.

11. Recall that Figure 4–6 on p. 82, to which Figure 4–10 is related, involved smoothing out the outcome elements in Table 3–2 in order to derive the continuous joint action spaces of Figure 4–2. Thus, joint action γ might well correspond to a possible solution. Also, the reader will

note that we have used Table 3-2 to obtain the numbers in Columns 1 and 2 of Table 11-1.

12. A possible synthesis of a quantitative CMP and Fisher would occur when, after two warring tribes have inched their way to a solution—say in terms of using territory to which both have rights—the daughter of the chief of each tribe becomes a hostage of the other. Clearly, if each were to execute the threat to kill the other's daughter because the latter has defected, and the former follows suit, then they return to the initial state of war or conflict and are both worse off.

13. See Note 24 of Chapter 3 for the meaning of 1^+, 3^+, and 5^+.

14. It could be argued that a financial aid program by J costs less the higher the level of control that L provides. In this case, the ranks for (AG, Much Control) and (AG, Little Control) might become 1 and 2, respectively; the ranks for (IND, Much Control) and (IND, Little Control), 3 and 4, respectively; and the ranks for (INF, Much Control) and (INF, Little Control), 5 and 6, respectively.

15. It could be argued that it is less costly for L to achieve much control if J adopts an INF-based aid program rather than an IND- or AG-based aid program (since at least some infrastructure would be in place to help exercise control) and less costly with an IND-based program than with an AG-based program. In this case, the ranks in Column 4 would become 4, 5, 6, 1, 2, 3, reading from top to bottom.

16. As discussed on pages 341–342, his end-of-workshop sessions provide an additional check that these constraints were adhered to and a politically feasible compromise outcome identified.

17. Or where they do intersect, the overlap may be so small that none of the remaining joint actions would be considered a reasonable compromise joint action.

18. Also, certain joint actions may be technically infeasible (for example, all joint actions in Table 3-2 involving "Full Control" (C_4), since developing nations may not have the organization to effect such). These joint actions should be quickly eliminated, desirably before or at the start of the main workshop. Alternatively, a joint action may yield an outcome on one dimension that induces a psychological block in a participant's thinking and thus effectively eliminates the possibility of its acceptance by that participant. That joint action, too, should be eliminated at the start.

19. In one sense, when one of the participants makes a combination of demands, offers and threats a la Fisher he also is eliminating what he perceives to be politically unacceptable joint actions a la Kelman.

20. A still more involved version of the complex conflict management procedure depicted in Figure 11-19 would have several additional steps between the first step, namely the demand-offer-threat pro-

posals associated with the Fisher approach, and the second step, namely the use of a split-the-difference principle. These intermediate steps might, for example, comprise a veto-incremax procedure involving the determination of weights to be used to obtain a weighted average of demand-offer-threat proposals on each of a series of rounds wherein limited commitment, guaranteed improvement, and the veto power features are adopted on each round. Thus, between the Fisher and the g segments of Figure 11-19 would be added

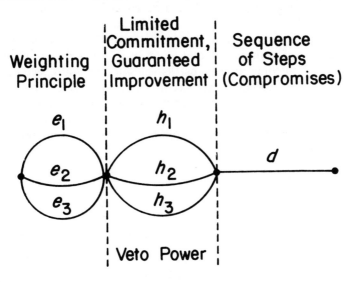

Further, a last step involving, for example, an inescapable sanction a la Howard, may be added to preclude nonadherence to the unique compromise solution that might finally be reached at the end of the a step. Thus, onto the end of the a segment of Figure 11-19 would be added

**Stability
Principle**

b

21.   If he so wishes, the mediator may construct new payoff tables building upon the minimally implied 4 by 4 payoff table when J and L each make a combination of a demand, offer, and threat. In this 4 by 4 table, the four actions of each party are: (1) "Yes" to the opponent's proposition, (2) "No" to the opponent's proposition, (3) the

participant's own demand and offer and (4) his execution of a threat. For this situation, however, only five joint actions are realizable: (1) J says "yes" and meets L's demand, and L carries out her offer; (2) J says "no," and L executes her threat; (3) L says "yes" and meets J's demand, and J carries out his offer; (4) L says "no," and J executes his threat; (5) both J and L say "no," and both execute their threats. Against the background of this payoff table, the mediator can then suggest to participants that they consider making alternative proposals involving reduced demands, reduced threats, and/or increased offers.

22. Still another variation might also have the mediator point up a number of joint actions that might be considered to result in an improved outcome for each participant but then allow each participant (perhaps in a Kelman-type preworkshop session) to eliminate whichever of these proposed joint actions they consider politically infeasible. Then a CMP or combination of CMPs might be applied to select a compromise joint action from among those remaining.

12 THE PRACTICAL APPLICATION OF CONFLICT MANAGEMENT PROCEDURES

12.1 INTRODUCTION

To bring to a close the development, analysis, and synthesis of conflict management procedures pursued in this book, we return to the issue of Chapter 2. That issue is how to identify in a quick and practical way those procedures that may be put to use in a given conflict situation by a knowledgeable third party. This third party may be a mediator, arbiter, concerned person, or the like;[1] sometimes, one or more of the participants themselves may take on the role of a third party. In addressing this issue again, we can now develop the argument in a manner more satisfactory to the analyst since we can use, where necessary, the technical materials developed in the manuscript subsequent to Chapter 2. We necessarily repeat some of the statements of Chapter 2 in order to keep the presentation in this chapter complete.

We speak of use by a knowledgeable third party. Clearly, to be able to determine which procedure may be best to try first, the third party must know a good deal about the conflict situation. Many characteristics of conflict situations that may be relevant have been listed in Tables 9-1, 9-2, and 9-3. The experienced third party knows what information is useful and has developed the necessary skills to acquire it when necessary. He may have secret or nonsecret discussions with each participant. Kelman-style, he may conduct preworkshop sessions with several representatives of each participating interest group or nation (see pages 339–343). Burton-style, he may hold workshops (see pages 332–338). Fisher-style, he may hold brainstorming sessions (see pages 359–361). He may, Saaty-style, gather together a set of experts (see pages 147–155), or employ the Delphi method (see pages 371–376) to get sound judgments. In any case, until the third party knows the forces driving participants (cultural, psychological, and the like), the issues involved, and other important dimensions of the conflict, he will not be in a position to make a wise choice of a conflict management procedure. We therefore assume that the third party initially has or knows how to go about acquiring the information that is requisite for the use of any procedure.

12.2 IDENTIFYING PROCEDURES FOR EACH GENERAL CATEGORY OF CONFLICT SITUATIONS: THE USE OF THE MASTER LIST AND SUBLISTS

First, in Table 12-1 we set down a master list of the basic conflict management procedures that have been discussed in previous chapters, including at the end several technical and presumably less practical procedures discussed in the appendixes of Chapters 5 and 8. This is the list from which we suggest selection of relevant procedures for use singly or in combination.

The next step is to eliminate the procedures that would not be useful for a given conflict situation. To do so, we pose four questions, each of which the third party must be able to answer. (We shall take up on pages 456–458 the case where the third party cannot answer all four.)

1.   How many joint actions (options, alternatives, plans, etc.) are possible, a *small* number (the finite case) or *many* (the continuous case)?[2]

True, there may be cases intermediate between a small number and many, but most cases do involve either a small or large number, and if they do not, the mediator will need to work out his own ways to identify one or more relevant procedures, perhaps finding it useful to follow a path similar to the one we are now treading. When the mediator answers this question, say the set of joint actions is a *small* number, then of the twenty-four tables indicated in Table 2–1 he can discard the twelve that apply to situations of many joint actions, and concentrate on the twelve that apply to situations with a small number.

2. What kinds of information do participants have concerning their preferences?

   (a) If they are concerned with their own welfare, internal satisfaction, or utility, can they only rank possible outcomes in order of preference (a case of *ordinal* preferences), or can they do more and state preferences in relative terms (e.g., state that outcome o_a is preferred twice as much as outcome o_b, a case of *relative* preferences), or can they do still more and attach precise numbers that indicate the value of different outcomes (e.g., $o_a = 100$, $o_b = 150$, etc., a case of *cardinal* preferences)?[3]

   (b) If they are concerned with objectives and the levels of their achievement, can outcomes regarding objectives only be ranked in order of level of achievement (a case of *ordinal* measurement), or can these outcomes be measured in relative terms (e.g., o_a represents twice the level of achievement of o_b, a case of *relative* measurement), or can they be measured precisely so that a definite number can be attached to the level of achievement on each objective (e.g., $o_a = 100$, $o_b = 150$ etc., a case of *cardinal* measurement)?

   When the mediator answers this question, he can, as we will discuss shortly, discard eight of the twelve tables and concentrate his attention on the remaining four—there being four for ordinal measurement, four for relative measurement, and four for cardinal measurement. His answer may be that participants can only *order* their preferences or measure objective achievements *ordinally.*

3. Are the participants concerned with *improvements* over their current position; or must they make *concessions* from stated (fixed) positions that differ, the position of each participant being that which he considers best out of self-interest or which he takes for some reason perceived to be valid?

Here, the mediator may not be able to answer the question. Also, it may be that he wants to retain flexibility and be able to have participants start either by conceding from infeasible positions or by improving from the existing. However, if the situation is clearly one or the other, say participants must make *concessions,* the mediator, in answering the question, discards two tables and retains two. Otherwise, he must retain all four.

4. Can the participants deal with procedures relating directly to the *outcomes* that participants will receive from any compromise solution, or will a direct focus on outcomes make it impossible for participants to reach agreement on a compromise? In the latter case, it becomes necessary to use procedures that focus on *actions* and only indirectly on the resulting outcomes. We have designated the former procedures *outcome-oriented* and the latter *action-oriented.*

Once again the mediator may not be able to answer the question. As we have already indicated, we shall take up on pages 456–458 the case where the mediator cannot answer all questions. However, suppose the mediator's reply is that participants can focus directly on *outcomes.* Then we are able to select one of the twenty-four tables to use. We reproduce here Table 2–1, which lists the twenty-four possible combinations of answers to these four questions. Each combination defines a general category of conflict situations, and in Column

Table 2-1.   General Categories of Conflict Situations.

Category	(1) Number of Options is	(2) Participants Can	(3) Participants Need to Focus On	(4) Participants Can Focus On	(5) Relevant Chapter 12 Table	(6) On Page Number
1	Small	Rank Outcomes	Improvement	Only Actions	12-2	441
2	"	"	"	Outcomes	12-3	442
3	"	"	Concession	Only Actions	12-4	443
4	"	"	"	Outcomes	12-5	444
5	"	Assign Relative Values	Improvement	Only Actions	12-6	445
6	"	"	"	Outcomes	12-7	446
7	"	"	Concession	Only Actions	12-8	447
8	"	"	"	Outcomes	12-9	448
9	"	Assign Precise Values	Improvement	Only Actions	12-10	449
10	"	"	"	Outcomes	12-11	450
11	"	"	Concession	Only Actions	12-12	452
12	"	"	"	Outcomes	12-13	453
13	Many	Rank Outcomes	Improvement	Only Actions	12-14	455
14	"	"	"	Outcomes	12-15	456
15	"	"	Concession	Only Actions	12-16	457
16	"	"	"	Outcomes	12-17	458
17	"	Assign Relative Values	Improvement	Only Actions	12-18	459
18	"	"	"	Outcomes	12-19	460
19	"	"	Concession	Only Actions	12-20	461
20	"	"	"	Outcomes	12-21	462
21	"	Assign Precise Values	Improvement	Only Actions	12-22	463
22	"	"	"	Outcomes	12-23	464
23	"	"	Concession	Only Actions	12-24	466
24	"	"	"	Outcomes	12-25	467

5 of Table 2–1 we note the table number in this chapter that lists the relevant conflict management procedures for that general category.

Suppose the answers to the four questions were: *A SMALL Number of Options, Participants Can RANK Outcomes in Order of Preference, Participants Need to Focus on IMPROVEMENT, Participants Can Focus on OUTCOMES.* Row 2 of Table 2–1 refers to that general category of conflict situations and indicates that Table 12–3 on page 442 is the appropriate table to which to refer. Table 12–3 shows that only twelve of the ninety-five less-technical procedures listed in the Master Table 12–1 are not eliminated. Clearly a third party can begin to consider as many as twelve for use. On the other hand, if the answers to the four questions indicated that the third party must consider the category: *MANY Options, Participants Can Assign PRECISE VALUES to Outcomes, Participants Need to Focus on IMPROVEMENT, and Participants Can Focus on OUT-COMES,* then there are twenty-five procedures available. Thus, the third party will definitely need to eliminate a number from consideration. See Table 12–23 on page 464.

12.3 EVALUATING RELEVANT PROCEDURES IN TERMS OF DESIRABLE AND UNDESIRABLE PROPERTIES

Our method for handling the problem of selecting an appropriate conflict management procedure enables the mediator quickly to eliminate a number of procedures falling in any category by testing whether they meet desirable properties. As already indicated on pages 10–11, one desirable property may be *preindeterminacy of outcomes.* In brief, this property helps avoid conflict among participants over which procedure to employ. This is so since when outcomes from the use of conflict management procedures are unable to be "predicted," then it is often possible to avoid the conflict situation that arises when one participant is able to determine that one procedure yields him a better outcome than a second procedure, but his opponent is also able to determine that the second procedure yields him (the opponent) a better outcome than the first procedure. Procedures whose outcome cannot be predetermined are shaded in the Master Table 12–1 and the twenty-four subsequent tables. In Table 12–3, we see that only four of the twelve procedures are shaded—that is, have a preindeterminate outcome. These four are preferable to the other procedures on that count.

Table 12-1. Procedures for Managing Conflicts over Outcomes Regarding Utility and/or Achievement of Objectives.

1. compromise over proposed actions, p. 34
2. a sequence of compromises over proposed actions, pp. 37–39
3. compromise over proposed outcomes, pp. 32–34
4. a sequence of compromises over proposed outcomes pp. 37–39
5. min total of ranks[a] (highest rank = 1), pp. 39–40, and 273–77 (weighted or unweighted)
6. min the difference in ranks, pp. 64 and 39–40 (weighted or unweighted)
7. max total of rank improvements[a], pp. 39–40 and 275–77 (weighted or unweighted)
8. min total of rank concessions[a], pp. 40–42 and 275–77 (weighted or unweighted)
9. max the min in rank improvements, pp. 64 and 39–40
10. min the max in rank concessions, pp. 64 and 40–42
11. min difference in rank improvement pp. 39–40 (weighted or unweighted)
12. max equal rank improvement, pp. 39–40 and 271–75 (weighted or unweighted)
13. min equal rank concession, pp. 40–42 and 271–75 (weighted or unweighted)
14. min difference in rank concession, pp. 40–42 (weighted or unweighted)
15. changing actions to "if . . . , then . . ." policies, pp. 42–48, 53–57
16. max good-cause payment, pp. 107–13 and 212–13
17. apportionment principles, pp. 114–19
18. min distance to the equidistant improvement line, pp. 74–75
19. min distance to the equidistant concession line, pp. 74–75
20. achievement of minimum requirements (satisficing), pp. 206–07
21. median efficient joint action, pp. 75 and 78–79
22. concession along efficiency frontier, pp. 76–77
23. split-the-difference, one-step, pp. 80–81 and 83–84
24. split-the-difference, a sequence of, pp. 80–83
25. weighted-average, one-step, pp. 84–85

Table 12-1. *(continued).*

---

26. weighted-average, a sequence of, pp. 84-85
27. leadership principle, pp. 96-97
28. aggressive follower principle, pp. 98-99
29. alternating leader-follower, pp. 92-93
30. GRIT (reciprocated tension-reducing actions, a sequence of), pp. 99-100
31. incremax (maximizing in each of a series of small improvement steps), with split-the-difference, pp. 85-88
32. incremax (weighted-average), pp. 88-89
33. incremax (alternating leader-follower), pp. 92-93
34. incremax (GRIT), pp. 99-100 and 124
35. decremax (maximizing in each of a series of small concession steps), with split-the-difference, pp. 89-92
36. decremax (weighted-average), pp. 89-92
37. decremax (alternating leader-follower), pp. 89-92
38. minimum information incremax, pp. 100-02
39. equidistant improvement in joint action space, pp. 74-75
40. equidistant concession in joint action space, pp. 74-75, 228-35
41. last-offer arbitration (with incentive to think of others), pp. 102-06
42. min difference in % improvements, pp. 131-38 and 141-46 (weighted or unweighted)
43. min difference in % concessions, pp. 135-38 (weighted or unweighted)
44. min difference in % goal achievements, pp. 173 and 146 (weighted or unweighted)
45. max the min % improvement, pp. 138-39 (weighted or unweighted)
46. min the max % concession, pp. 139-41 (weighted or unweighted)
47. max the total of % improvements[a], p. 141 (weighted or unweighted)
48. min the total of % concessions[a], pp. 141, 182 and 200 (weighted or unweighted)

Table 12-1.   *(continued)*

49. max total % goal achievement[a], pp. 146–47
     (weighted or unweighted)
50. min total of % goal shortfalls[a], pp. 173 and 146–47
     (weighted or unweighted)
51. min total penalty, pp. 181–82 and 197–200
52. max the max % improvement, p. 173
53. min the min % concession, p. 173
54. min deviation from average % improvement, pp. 243–44
55. min deviation from average % concession, pp. 243–44
56. max equal % improvement, pp. 155–56 and 224–25
     (weighted or unweighted)
57. min equal % concession, pp. 155–56
     (weighted or unweighted)
58. max equal % goal achievements, pp. 174 and 155
     (weighted or unweighted)
59. split-the-difference in outcome space, one-step, pp. 156–59
60. split-the-difference in outcome space, sequential, pp. 156–59   and
     238
61. weighted-average in outcome space, one-step, pp. 156–59
62. weighted-average in outcome space, sequential, pp. 156–59
63. alternating leader-follower in outcome space, pp. 159–60 and 238
64. GRIT in outcome space, p. 239
65. hierarchical programming, pp. 95–96 and 122–23
66. relaxed hierarchical programming, pp. 162–64
67. incremax in outcome space (split-the-difference), pp. 156–59   and
     238
68. incremax in outcome space (weighted-average), pp. 156–59
69. incremax in outcome space (alternating leader-follower),
     pp. 159–60 and 238
70. incremax in outcome space (GRIT), p. 239
71. decremax in outcome space (split-the-difference), pp. 156–59
72. decremax in outcome space (weighted-average), pp. 156–59
73. decremax in outcome space (alternating leader-follower)
     pp. 159–60

Table 12-1. *(continued)*

74. Zeuthen concession (least to lose goes first) pp. 160-62 and 240
75. method of determining group priorities (Saaty), pp. 147-55 and 165-68
76. max total utility[a], pp. 178-79, 190-97, 200-05, 222 (weighted or unweighted)
77. max total of objective achievements[a], pp. 190-97 (weighted or unweighted)
78. multiobjective programming with compromise weights, pp. 248-63
79. max total of absolute improvements[a], pp. 178-79 and 222-23 (weighted or unweighted)
80. min total of absolute concessions[a], pp. 181-2, 197-200 and 226-7 (weighted or unweighted)
81. max total of absolute goal achievement[a], p. 179 (weighted or unweighted)
82. min total of absolute goal shortfalls[a], pp. 214 and 181-82 (weighted or unweighted)
83. min difference of absolute improvements, pp. 179-80 (weighted or unweighted)
84. min difference of absolute concessions, pp. 182-83 (weighted or unweighted)
85. min difference in absolute goal achievements, p. 180 (weighted or unweighted)
86. max the min absolute improvement, p. 180 (weighted or unweighted)
87. min the max absolute concession, p. 183 (weighted or unweighted)
88. max the difference of absolute improvements, pp. 183-84
89. max the difference of absolute concessions, pp. 215 and 183-84
90. demand-revealing (no bluffing) method, pp. 184-88 and 239-40
91. max equal absolute improvements, pp. 224-25 (weighted or unweighted)
92. max equal goal achievements, p. 225 (weighted or unweighted)

Table 12-1. *(continued)*

93. min equal absolute concessions, pp. 227-28
     (weighted or unweighted)
94. min deviation from average absolute improvement, pp. 214, 179-80
95. min deviation from average absolute concession, pp. 215 and 182

Other more technical and presumably less practical procedures are

96. concordance-discordance method, pp. 279-84
97. min discrepancy from ideal (using rank correlation) pp. 284-85
98. max correspondence to underlying pattern of outcomes,
     p. 285
99. max total of ranks weighted by outcome "importance"
     pp. 285-86
100. max correspondence to outcomes weighted by relative impor-
     tance, p. 286
101. frequency above threshold value (using weighted ranks), pp. 286-7
102. equal role opportunities principle, pp. 169-70

---

[a]Side payments may be required. See Table 12-28, on p. 472.

  Techniques that have preindeterminate outcomes

  Techniques that may be high cost

  Techniques that require of a participant little or no information about
  other participants' preferences

When each participant has *little or no information about other participants' preferences* and cannot be informed about these preferences by the third party, then a second desirable property of conflict management procedures becomes obvious. This is that a procedure require of each participant little or no information about other participants' preferences. Procedures having this property are indicated with their names enclosed in a rectangle in the master table and subsequent tables.[4] In Table 12-3 only five of the twelve procedures are rectangularly blocked in, and of these, only three are both blocked in and shaded—that is, have both of the desirable properties thus far discussed.

A third property that may be employed to discriminate among conflict management procedures relates to cost. The use of some conflict

Table 12-2. A *SMALL* Number of Options, Participants Can *RANK* Outcomes in Order of Preference, Need to Focus on *IM-PROVEMENTS,* Can Focus Only on *ACTIONS* (Finite, Ordinal, Focus on Improvement, Action-Oriented).

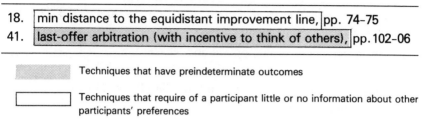

| 18. | min distance to the equidistant improvement line, | pp. 74-75 |
| 41. | last-offer arbitration (with incentive to think of others), | pp. 102-06 |

Techniques that have preindeterminate outcomes

Techniques that require of a participant little or no information about other participants' preferences

management procedures may involve the possibility of *high costs.* This may be so because they involve many rounds of debate, discussions, deliberations, negotiations, and the like, or because they involve much collection and processing of data at different times, or much shuttling back and forth, or many preworkshops, seminars. Those procedures that may be high cost are indicated in Table 12-1 and the subsequent twenty-four tables by an oval over the corresponding number.[5] In Table 12-3, only two of the twelve nontechnical procedures have an oval over their number, leaving ten that are very unlikely to be high cost. Of the latter, only three are blocked in, only three are shaded, and only two are both blocked in and shaded. These two are superior to all the others on one or more of the three counts already discussed. These two, then, should be initially considered for use—although the specifics of the conflict situation may immediately rule out these two and suggest reconsideration of some previously eliminated.

To illustrate our method further, take another category of conflict situations, namely that category where there are: *MANY Options, Participants Can Assign RELATIVE VALUES to Outcomes, Participants Need to Focus on CONCESSIONS, Participants Can Focus Only on ACTIONS.* The relevant procedures are listed in Table 12-20 on page 461. There are thirteen of them. Six of these thirteen are shaded—that is, their outcome is preindeterminate. Five of the thirteen are each blocked in by a rectangle—that is, are applicable when participants have little or no knowledge about other participants' preferences. Of these five, only two have an outcome that is preindeterminate, and one of these two has an oval over its

Table 12-3. A *SMALL* Number of Options, Participants Can *RANK* Outcomes in Order of Preference, Need to Focus on *IMPROVEMENTS,* Can Focus on *OUTCOMES* (Finite, Ordinal, Focus on Improvement, Outcome-Oriented).

---

5. min total of ranks[a] (highest rank = 1), pp. 39–40 and 273–77
    (weighted or unweighted)

6. min difference in ranks, pp. 64 and 39–40
    (weighted or unweighted)

7. max total of rank improvements[a], pp. 39–40 and 273–77
    (weighted or unweighted)

9. max the min in rank improvements, pp. 64 and 39–40

11. min difference in rank improvement, pp. 39–40
    (weighted or unweighted)

12. max equal rank improvement, pp. 39–40 and 271–75
    (weighted or unweighted)

15. changing actions to "if . . . , then . . ." policies, pp. 42–48, 53–57

16. max good-cause payment, pp. 107–13 and 212–13

17. apportionment principles, pp. 114–119

20. achievement of minimum requirements (satisficing), pp. 206–07

41. last-offer arbitration (with incentive to think of others), pp. 102–06

75. method of determining group priorities (Saaty), pp. 147–55, 165–8

---

[a]Side payments may be required. See Table 12-28, on p. 472

▨ Techniques that have preindeterminate outcomes

▢ Techniques that may be high cost

▭ Techniques that require of a participant little or no information about other participants' preferences

Other more technical and presumably less practical procedures are those in Table 12-1 numbered 98, 99, 100, 101, and 102.

number—that is, may be undesirable because its application may involve high costs.

In brief then, the three desirable properties thus far examined can quickly narrow down the procedures that a third party may initially wish to consider. However, to reiterate, it does not follow that he

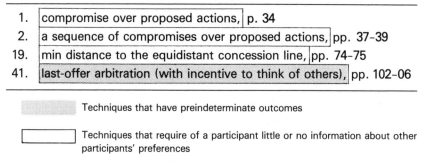

Table 12-4. A *SMALL* Number of Options, Participants Can *RANK* Outcomes in Order of Preference, Need to Focus on *CONCESSIONS,* Can Focus Only on *ACTIONS* (Finite, Ordinal, Focus on Concession, Action-Oriented).

1.	compromise over proposed actions,	p. 34
2.	a sequence of compromises over proposed actions,	pp. 37–39
19.	min distance to the equidistant concession line,	pp. 74–75
41.	last-offer arbitration (with incentive to think of others),	pp. 102–06

Techniques that have preindeterminate outcomes

Techniques that require of a participant little or no information about other participants' preferences

should use all or any of these properties to eliminate procedures since important specifics of his particular conflict situation may rule out a number of procedures immediately.

To help summarize the contents of Tables 12–2 through 12–25 we have constructed Table 12–26 on p. 468. We list at the left-hand part the twenty-four possible categories of conflict situations and the number of its corresponding table constructed from the Master Table 12–1. In Column 1, we record the number of nontechnical conflict management procedures that fall within each category (and its corresponding table). In the first category, *Finite, Ordinal, Improvement, Action,* this number is two; in the second category, *Finite, Ordinal, Improvement, Outcome,* it is twelve. As we go down Column 1, we see that the tenth category *Finite, Cardinal, Improvement, Outcome* has associated with it the largest number of procedures, namely twenty-six. In Column 2, we record for each of the twenty-four categories the number of conflict management procedures that are not eliminated when the preindeterminacy property is required. For example, in the first category, *Finite, Ordinal, Improvement, Action,* only one procedure is not eliminated. In the second category, *Finite, Ordinal, Improvement, Outcome,* only four procedures are not eliminated. And so forth.

Next, for each of the twenty-four categories we record in Column 3 the number of procedures that require little or no information by each participant about the preferences of other participants. For the

Table 12-5.   A *SMALL* Number of Options, Participants Can *RANK* Outcomes in Order of Preference, Need to Focus on *CONCESSIONS,* Can Focus on *OUTCOMES* (Finite, Ordinal, Focus on Concession, Outcome-Oriented).

3.	compromise over proposed outcomes, pp. 32–34
4.	a sequence of compromises over proposed outcomes, pp. 37–39
8.	min total of rank concessions[a], pp. 40–42 and 275–77 (weighted or unweighted)
10.	min the max in rank concessions, pp. 64 and 40–42
13.	min equal rank concession, pp. 40–42 and 271–75 (weighted or unweighted)
14.	min difference in rank concession, pp. 40–42 (weighted or unweighted)
16.	max good-cause payment, pp. 107–13 and 212–13
20.	achievement of minimum requirements (satisficing), pp. 206–07
41.	last-offer arbitration (with incentive to think of others), pp. 102–06

[a]Side payments may be required. See Table 12-28, on p. 472.

Techniques that have preindeterminate outcomes

Techniques that may be high cost

Techniques that require of a participant little or no information about other participants' preferences

Other more technical and presumably less practical procedures are those in Table 12-1 numbered 96 and 97.

first category, two require little or no information; for the second, five. And so forth.

In Column 4 of Table 12-26, we record the number of procedures whose outcome is preindeterminate and which at the same time require little or no information by each participant about the preferences of other participants. For the first category, the number is one. Going down Column 4, we see that the highest number for any category is five.

Finally, in Column 5 we exclude from the procedures counted in Column 4 those that may be high cost. Thus, going down Column 5, we see that no more than two remain in any category—the two

Table 12-6.   A *SMALL* Number of Options, Participants Can Assign *RELATIVE VALUES* to Outcomes, Need to Focus on *IM-PROVEMENTS,* Can Focus Only on *ACTIONS* (Finite, Relative, Focus on Improvement, Action-Oriented).

18.	min distance to the equidistant improvement line,	pp. 74–75
41.	last-offer arbitration (with incentive to think of others),	pp. 102–06

        Techniques that have preindeterminate outcomes

        Techniques that require of a participant little or no information about other participants' preferences

always being #20 *achievement of minimum requirements (satisficing)* and #41 *last-offer arbitration (with incentive to think of others).*

Actually, however, the method we have been following for narrowing down the set of relevant conflict management procedures is much too "mechanical" for use by a wise and practical third party—especially for categories of conflict situations that have a large number, such as category *Finite, Cardinal, Improvement, Outcome.* For many conflict situations, one or more of the three properties employed in deriving the numbers of Table 12-26 may be irrelevant, or very likely not of critical importance, and often much less important than other properties. Hence, we have constructed Table 12-27, on p. 469 which lists other properties that may be employed to discriminate among procedures.

As is clearly evident from our discussion in preceding chapters, it is often desirable that a procedure be *efficient*—that is, yield an efficient outcome—or be able to be constrained to be efficient. (Recall the definition of an efficient outcome from pages 71–72: An outcome is efficient if there is no other outcome possible that can make at least one participant better off without making any other participant worse off.)

We note in Table 12–27 that there are eight procedures that cannot meet this property. Therefore, if any of these eight are among those not already eliminated for a particular conflict situation, the third party may now wish to eliminate it. Also at this point, we may wish to discriminate among those that in and of themselves lead to an efficient outcome, and those that need to be constrained in order to ensure efficiency. The former may not only be more easily introduced

Table 12-7. A *SMALL* Number of Options, Participants Can Assign *RELATIVE VALUES* to Outcomes, Need to Focus on *IMPROVEMENTS,* Can Focus on *OUTCOMES* (Finite, Relative, Focus on Improvement, Outcome-Oriented).

15. changing actions to "if . . . , then . . ." policies, pp. 42–48, 53–57
16. max good-cause payment, pp. 107–13 and 212–13
17. apportionment principles, pp. 114–19
20. achievement of minimum requirements (satificing), pp. 206–07
41. last-offer arbitration (with incentive to think of others), pp. 102–06
42. min difference in % improvements, pp. 131–38 and 141–46 (weighted or unweighted)
44. min difference in % goal achievements, pp. 173 and 146 (weighted or unweighted)
45. max the min % improvement, pp. 138–39 (weighted or unweighted)
47. max the total of % improvements[a], p. 141 (weighted or unweighted)
49. max total % goal achievement[a], pp. 146–47 (weighted or unweighted)
52. max the max % improvement, p. 173
54. min deviation from average % improvement, pp. 243–44
75. method of determining group priorities (Saaty), pp. 147–55, 165–8

The third party may also wish to consider use of procedures:

5. min total of ranks[a] (highest rank = 1), (weighted or unweighted);
6. min the difference in ranks, (weighted or unweighted);
7. max total of rank improvements[a], (weighted or unweighted);
9. max the min in rank improvements;
11. min difference in rank improvement, (weighted or unweighted); and
12. max equal rank improvement, (weighted or unweighted).

However they are dominated by 49, 44, 47, 45, 42, and 42, respectively.

---

[a]Side payments may be required. See Table 12-28, on p. 472.

Table 12-7. *(continued)*

Techniques that have preindeterminate outcomes

Techniques that may be high cost

Techniques that require of a participant little or no information about other participants' preferences

Other more technical and presumably less practical procedures are those in Table 12-1 numbered 98, 99, 100, 101, and 102.

into the thinking of participants, but may involve less cost. Hence, in Table 12A-1, in the appendix to this chapter we list those procedures that may need to be constrained in order to yield efficient outcomes.

Proceeding still further, another desirable property of conflict management procedures is that their solution be stable—that is that they are able to eliminate any possibility of nonadherence to, failure to abide by, or defection from the compromise outcome that is reached from their application. This desirable property is referred to as *stability*. From Table 12-27, we see that there are no procedures with solutions that are not stable in and of themselves, or that cannot be constrained to yield a stable solution (for example, through the addition of an inescapable sanction a la Howard, or a credible threat a la Fisher). However, there is only one procedure that is stable in and of itself, namely #15 *changing actions to "if . . . , then . . ."*

Table 12-8. A *SMALL* Number of Options, Participants Can Assign *RELATIVE VALUES* to Outcomes, Need to Focus on *CONCESSIONS,* Can Focus Only on *ACTIONS* (Finite, Relative, Focus on Concession, Action-Oriented).

1.	compromise over proposed actions,	p. 34
2.	a sequence of compromises over proposed actions,	pp. 37-39
19.	min distance to the equidistant concession line,	pp. 74-75
41.	last-offer arbitration (with incentive to think of others),	pp. 102-06

Techniques that have preindeterminate outcomes

Techniques that require of a participant little or no information about other participants' preferences

Table 12-9. A *SMALL* Number of Options, Participants Can Assign *RELATIVE VALUES* to Outcomes, Need to Focus on *CONCESSIONS,* Can Focus on *OUTCOMES* (Finite, Relative, Focus on Concession, Outcome-Oriented).

---

3.   compromise over proposed outcomes, pp. 32–34

4.   a sequence of compromises over proposed outcomes, pp. 37–39

16.   max good-cause payment, pp. 107–13 and 212–13

20.   achievement of minimum requirements (satisficing), pp. 206–07

41.   last-offer arbitration (with incentive to think of others), pp. 102–06

43.   min difference in % concessions, pp. 137–38
     (weighted or unweighted)

46.   min the max % concession, pp. 139–41
     (weighted or unweighted)

48.   min the total of % concessions[a], pp. 141, 182 and 200
     (weighted or unweighted)

50.   min total of % goal shortfalls[a], pp. 173 and 146–47
     (weighted or unweighted)

51.   min total penalty, pp. 181–82, and 197–200

53.   min the min % concession, p. 173

55.   min deviation from average % concession, pp. 243–44

The third party may also wish to consider use of procedures:

8.   min total of rank concessions[a], (weighted or unweighted);

10.   min the max in rank concessions,

13.   min equal rank concession, (weighted or unweighted); and

14.   min difference in rank concession, (weighted or unweighted).

However, they are dominated by 48, 46, 43, and 43 respectively.

---

[a]Side payments may be required. See Table 12-28, on p. 472.

Techniques that have preindeterminate outcomes

Techniques that require of a participant little or no information about other participants' preferences

Other more technical and presumably less practical procedures are those in Table 12-1 numbered 96 and 97.

Table 12–10. A *SMALL* Number of Options, Participants Can Assign *PRECISE VALUES* to Outcomes, Need to Focus on *IM-PROVEMENTS,* Can Focus Only on *ACTIONS* (Finite, Cardinal, Focus on Improvement, Action-Oriented).

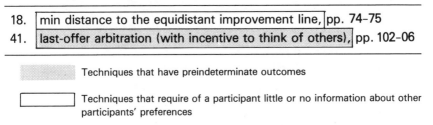

| 18. | min distance to the equidistant improvement line, | pp. 74–75 |
| 41. | last-offer arbitration (with incentive to think of others), | pp. 102–06 |

Techniques that have preindeterminate outcomes

Techniques that require of a participant little or no information about other participants' preferences

policies, since that already embodies the exercise of inescapable sanctions by participants.

Going beyond efficiency and stability, we note in Table 12–27 that another desirable property of a conflict management procedure is that when participants need to and can focus on improvement that the procedure *guarantee improvement.* From Table 12–27 we see that all conflict management techniques that permit an improvement focus and are sensible for use in the given situation can either in and of themselves guarantee improvement or be constrained to guarantee improvement. Those that need to be constrained to guarantee improvement are identified in Table 12A–2. The third party may wish to have this information since the imposition of a constraint can involve cost in time and effort, and represents another point at which agreement among participants needs to be reached.

Still another property may be found desirable. Recall from pages 86–88 that some participants may be conservative, cautious, and unwilling to take much risk; they only feel comfortable when conflict resolution proceeds by small steps, or when a maximum bound exists on the change in actions or outcomes to be permitted on each round. Hence, they may find desirable procedures wherein a participant will be required to make only a *limited commitment* to change on any given round. In Table 12–27 we list conflict management procedures that do not involve or cannot be constrained to involve limited commitment to change.[6] These may be eliminated from consideration by the third party should the given situation demand this.

Table 12-11. A *SMALL* Number of Options, Participants Can Assign *PRECISE VALUES* to Outcomes, Need to Focus on *IM-PROVEMENTS,* Can Focus on *OUTCOMES* (Finite, Cardinal, Focus on Improvement, Outcome-Oriented).

15.	changing actions to 'if . . . , then . . .' policies,	pp. 42–48, 53–57
16.	max good-cause payment, pp. 107–113 and 212–13	
17.	apportionment principles,	pp. 114–19
20.	achievement of minimum requirements (satisficing),	pp. 206–07
41.	last-offer arbitration (with incentive to think of others),	pp. 102–06
42.	min difference in % improvements, pp. 131–38 and 141–46 (weighted or unweighted)	
44.	min difference in % goal achievements, pp. 173 and 146 (weighted or unweighted)	
45.	max the min % improvement, pp. 138–39 (weighted or unweighted)	
47.	max the total of % improvements[a], p. 141 (weighted or unweighted)	
49.	max total % goal achievement,[a] pp. 146–47 (weighted or unweighted)	
52.	max the max % improvement, p. 173	
54.	min deviation from average % improvement, pp. 243–44	
65.	hierarchical programming,	pp. 95–96 and 122–123
66.	relaxed hierarchical programming,	pp. 162–64
75.	method of determining group priorities (Saaty),	pp. 147–55, 165–8
76.	max total utility[a], pp. 178–79, 190–97, 200–05 and 222 (weighted or unweighted)	
77.	max total of objective achievements[a],	pp. 190–97
	(weighted or unweighted)	
78.	multiobjective programming with compromise weights,	pp. 248–63
79.	max total of absolute improvements[a], pp. 79–80 and 222–23 (weighted or unweighted)	
81.	max total of absolute goal achievement[a], p. 179 (weighted or unweighted)	
83.	min difference of absolute improvements, pp. 179–80 (weighted or unweighted)	

Table 12-11. *(continued)*

---

85. min difference in absolute goal achievements, p. 180
    (weighted or unweighted)
86. max the min absolute improvement, p. 180
    (weighted or unweighted)
88. max the difference of absolute improvements, pp. 183-84
90. demand-revealing (no bluffing) method, pp. 184-88 and 239-40
94. min deviation from average absolute improvement, pp. 214, 179-80

The third party may also want to consider use of procedures:

5. min total of ranks[a] (highest rank = 1), (weighted or unweighted);
   pp. 39-40 and 273-77
6. min difference in ranks, (weighted or unweighted); p. 64
7. max total of rank improvements[a], (weighted or unweighted);
   pp. 39-40 and 275-77
9. max the min in rank improvements; p. 64
11. min difference in rank improvement, (weighted or unweighted);
    pp. 39-40 and
12. max equal rank improvement, (weighted or unweighted), pp. 39-40

However they are dominated by 76, 83, 79, 86, 83, and 83 respectively.

---

[a]Side payments may be required. See Table 12-28, on p. 472

Techniques that have preindeterminate outcomes

Techniques that may be high cost

Techniques that require of a participant little or no information about other participants' preferences

Other more technical and presumably less practical procedures are those in Table 12-1 numbered 98, 99, 100, 101, and 102.

Yet another factor for discriminating among procedures centers around whether or not a procedure yields a *unique solution.*[7] When a procedure is accepted for adoption by all participants and yields a unique solution, then no further problem exists.[8] But when it can

Table 12-12. A *SMALL* Number of Options, Participants Can Assign *PRECISE VALUES* to Outcomes, Need to Focus on *CONCESSIONS,* Can Focus Only on *ACTIONS* (Finite, Cardinal, Focus on Concession, Action-Oriented).

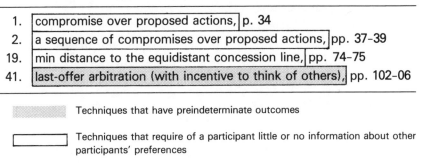

1.	compromise over proposed actions,	p. 34
2.	a sequence of compromises over proposed actions,	pp. 37–39
19.	min distance to the equidistant concession line,	pp. 74–75
41.	last-offer arbitration (with incentive to think of others),	pp. 102–06

Techniques that have preterminate outcomes

Techniques that require of a participant little or no information about other participants' preferences

yield one of several solutions, and this is known to participants, then there exists potential conflict, since participants' preferences over the possible solutions may differ. Hence procedures that have the undesirable property that they may not yield a unique solution, and thus may not terminate the conflict, are listed in Table 12–27.

We can proceed even further. Everything else being equal, it is generally agreed that procedures that provide a mechanism capable of *building up trust* are desirable. Such have "long run" types of benefits. They tend to reduce the probability of subsequent conflicts and to increase the stability of the compromise outcome. Moreover, they are psychologically appealing since they allow participants to move toward a compromise outcome in small steps initially while trust is at a low level; and they provide the hope for an increase in the size of the steps at later stages once trust has been established. Since trust tends to increase as does the number of times participants successfully interact, those procedures that involve a sequence of rounds tend also to provide potential for building trust. Yet, as already indicated, when a procedure involves a sequence of rounds, its use may involve high costs. As a result, our trust-building procedures are those that may be high cost except (as indicated in Table 12–27) for those high-cost procedures that do not involve much interaction by participants, namely (1) changing actions to "if . . . ,then . . ." policies; (2) method of determining group priorities (Saaty); (3)

Table 12-13.   A *SMALL* Number of Options, Participants Can Assign *PRECISE VALUES* to Outcomes, Need to Focus on *CONCESSIONS,* Can Focus on *OUTCOMES* (Finite, Cardinal, Focus on Concession, Outcome-Oriented).

---

3.   compromise over proposed outcomes, pp. 32–34

4.   a sequence of compromises over proposed outcomes, pp. 37–39

16.   max good-cause payment, pp. 107–13 and 212–13

20.   achievement of minimum requirements (satisficing), pp. 206–07

41.   last-offer arbitration (with incentive to think of others), pp. 102–06

43.   min difference in % concessions, pp. 137–38 (weighted or unweighted)

46.   min the max % concession, pp. 139–41 (weighted or unweighted)

48.   min the total of % concessions[a], pp. 142, 182 and 200 (weighted or unweighted)

50.   min total of % goal shortfalls[a], pp. 173 and 146–47 (weighted or unweighted)

51.   min total penalty, pp. 181–82 and 197–200

53.   min the min % concession, p. 173

55.   min deviation from average % concession, pp. 243–44

80.   min total of absolute concessions[a], pp. 181–82, 197–200 and 226–27 (weighted or unweighted)

82.   min total of absolute goal shortfalls[a], pp. 214 and 181–82 (weighted or unweighted)

84.   min difference of absolute concessions, pp. 182–83 (weighted or unweighted)

87.   min the max absolute concession, p. 183 (weighted or unweighted)

89.   max the difference of absolute concessions, pp. 215 and 183–84

95.   min deviation from average absolute concession, pp. 215 and 182

The third party may also wish to consider use of procedures:

8.   min total of rank concessions[a] (weighted or unweighted);

Table 12-13. *(continued)*

10. min the max in rank concessions;

13. min equal rank concession (weighted or unweighted); and

14. min difference in rank concession (weighted or unweighted).

However, they are dominated by 80, 87, 84, and 84 respectively.

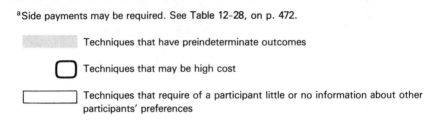

[a]Side payments may be required. See Table 12-28, on p. 472.

     Techniques that have preindeterminate outcomes

     Techniques that may be high cost

     Techniques that require of a participant little or no information about other participants' preferences

Other more technical and presumably less practical procedures are those in Table 12-1 numbered 96 and 97.

multiobjective programming with compromise weights; (4) demand-revealing (no bluffing) method, and (5) several highly technical procedures.

Recall from page 102 that for many diverse psychological reasons (insecurity, fear of being outwitted, etc.) it may often be desirable to allow participants the option to exercise a veto power at any of the intermediate steps or even at the final stage in the use of a conflict managment procedure. This power is rarely, if ever, explicitly embodied in a procedure per se and thus needs to be added on. However, because the specific characteristics of the conflict situation (including the participants) may be dominant in determining whether or not the addition of the veto power option is desirable, we have not attempted to list in Table 12–27 those procedures to which the veto power can or cannot be added.

Finally, we indicate in Table 12–27 a property that is frequently very important for procedures to have when full information regarding preferences does not exist. This is the *capability of eliminating bluffing.* Unfortunately, only three of our procedures have this property—namely, #16, max good-cause payment; #41, last-offer arbitra-

Table 12-14. *MANY* Options, Participants Can Only *RANK* Outcomes in Order of Preference, Need to Focus on *IM-PROVEMENTS,* Can Focus Only on *ACTIONS* (Continuous, Ordinal, Focus on Improvement, Action-Oriented).

(29.)	alternating leader-follower, pp. 92–93
(30.)	GRIT (reciprocated tension-reducing actions, a sequence of), pp. 99–100
(31.)	incremax (maximizing in each of a series of small improvement steps), with split-the-difference, pp. 85–88
(32.)	incremax (weighted-average), pp. 88–89
(33.)	incremax (alternating leader-follower), pp. 92–93
(34.)	incremax (GRIT), pp. 99–100 and 124
(38.)	minimum information incremax, pp. 100–02
39.	equidistant improvement in joint action space, pp. 74–75
41.	last-offer arbitration (with incentive to think of others), pp. 102–06

Techniques that have preindeterminate outcomes

Techniques that may be high cost

Techniques that require of a participant little or no information about other participants' preferences

tion (with incentive to think of others); and #90, demand-revealing (no bluffing) method.

12.4 DETERMINING WEIGHTS, CONSTRAINTS, BINDING MAGNITUDES OF CONSTRAINTS, AND SIDE PAYMENTS

We now have gone through the contents of Tables 12–1 to 12–27. However, many of these procedures may require weights on participants' utility outcomes, or on different objectives, or on other elements for a given conflict situation.[9] Hence, in Table 12–28 we have set down several of the more appealing or simpler ways in which

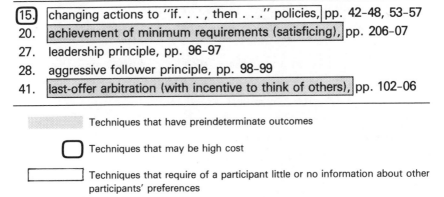

Table 12-15. *MANY* Options, Participants Can Only *RANK* Outcomes in Order of Preference, Need to Focus on *IM-PROVEMENTS,* Can Focus on *OUTCOMES* (Continuous, Ordinal, Focus on Improvement, Outcome-Oriented).

(15.)	changing actions to "if. . . , then . . ." policies,	pp. 42–48, 53–57
20.	achievement of minimum requirements (satisficing),	pp. 206–07
27.	leadership principle, pp. 96–97	
28.	aggressive follower principle, pp. 98–99	
41.	last-offer arbitration (with incentive to think of others),	pp. 102–06

- Techniques that have preindeterminate outcomes
- Techniques that may be high cost
- Techniques that require of a participant little or no information about other participants' preferences

these weights can be obtained. Additionally, the actions or outcomes of many procedures may need to be bounded (constrained). Hence, in Table 12–28 we list several of the more appealing or simpler ways in which participants may reach agreement on the binding magnitudes for these constraints.[10] Finally, a number of procedures, especially those that pertain to a "total" may need to allow for side payments. As indicated in the discussion on pages 275–278, it is extremely difficult to settle the problem of side payments, and there is little pertinent analysis in the literature. Nonetheless, we list in Table 12–28 some simple procedures that may be found useful.

12.5 PROBLEMS IN APPLYING THE METHOD AND AREAS OF NONAPPLICATION

At this point we should provide some guidance for the many situations where the third party cannot answer all four questions posed in pages 432–434. If he can answer only three, he then needs to work from more than one table. For example, if he cannot answer Question 1 on number of options (joint actions), he will need to work from (1) one relevant table of the twelve pertinent for situations in-

Table 12-16. *MANY* Options, Participants Can Only *RANK* Outcomes in Order of Preference, Need to Focus on *CONCESSIONS,* Can Focus Only on *ACTIONS* (Continuous, Ordinal, Focus on Concession, Action-Oriented).

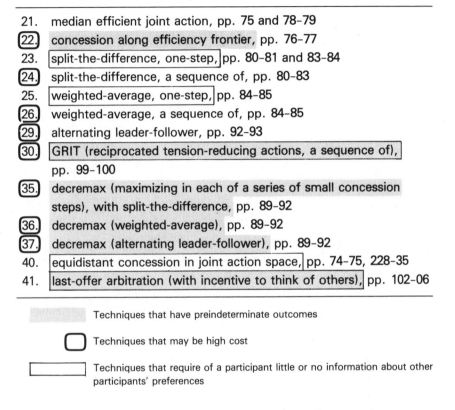

21.   median efficient joint action, pp. 75 and 78–79
22.   concession along efficiency frontier, pp. 76–77
23.   split-the-difference, one-step, pp. 80–81 and 83–84
24.   split-the-difference, a sequence of, pp. 80–83
25.   weighted-average, one-step, pp. 84–85
26.   weighted-average, a sequence of, pp. 84–85
29.   alternating leader-follower, pp. 92–93
30.   GRIT (reciprocated tension-reducing actions, a sequence of), pp. 99–100
35.   decremax (maximizing in each of a series of small concession steps), with split-the-difference, pp. 89–92
36.   decremax (weighted-average), pp. 89–92
37.   decremax (alternating leader-follower), pp. 89–92
40.   equidistant concession in joint action space, pp. 74–75, 228–35
41.   last-offer arbitration (with incentive to think of others), pp. 102–06

Techniques that have preindeterminate outcomes

Techniques that may be high cost

Techniques that require of a participant little or no information about other participants' preferences

volving a small number of options and (2) one relevant table of the twelve pertinent for situations involving many (continuous) options. If he cannot answer Question 2a or 2b on information relating to preferences, or to levels of objective achievements, respectively, he will need to work from (1) one relevant table of the eight concerned with participants who can only rank outcomes in order of preference (whether in terms of utility or objective achievements), (2) one relevant table of the eight concerned with participants who can assign relative values to outcomes, and (3) one relevant table of the eight concerned with participants who can assign precise values to outcomes. Frequently however, in the process of discussing the use of

Table 12-17. *MANY* Options, Participants Can Only *RANK* Outcomes in Order of Preference, Need to Focus on *CONCESSIONS,* Can Focus on *OUTCOMES* (Continuous, Ordinal, Focus on Concession, Outcome-Oriented).

41.	last-offer arbitration (with incentive to think of others)[a], pp. 102–06

[a]Since there is only one procedure in this outcome oriented category, the third party may wish also to consider the action-oriented procedures in Table 12-16 which are only indirectly oriented to outcome.

Techniques that have preindeterminate outcomes

Techniques that require of a participant little or no information about other participants' preferences

one or more procedures with participants the third party obtains additional information about the conflict situation, the preferences of participants, and their focuses, which enables him to answer the question that initially he could not. He then can concentrate on the list of only one table. Otherwise, he must proceed to eliminate procedures set down on more than one table on the basis of the desirable and undesirable properties already discussed, taking into account all special characteristics of the conflict situation.

A second major problem arises when participants are *asymmetric.* For example, consider again the four questions posed for the third party to answer. Regarding the number of possible options, one participant may perceive and be able to consider only a few, while a second participant may perceive and be able to consider many, possibly because the latter knows how to use a computer for programming analysis. Regarding information on preferences over outcomes (utility or objective achievements), one participant may be able only to rank outcomes in order of preference while another can attach precise values to outcomes. Moreover, one participant may be able to focus on outcomes, while the other cannot because of diverse psychological reasons. Still more, one participant may wish to focus on improvement from a current position, while the other may have fixed his thinking on some ''ideal'' and can only think of reasonable concessions from his ''ideal'' point. Or one participant may be cautious and not mind the high cost in time and effort involved in proceeding through a sequence of rounds with limited commitment on each

Table 12-18. *MANY* Options, Participants Can Assign *RELATIVE VALUES* to Outcomes, Need to Focus on *IM-PROVEMENTS,* Can Focus Only on *ACTIONS* (Continuous, Relative, Focus on Improvement, Action-Oriented).

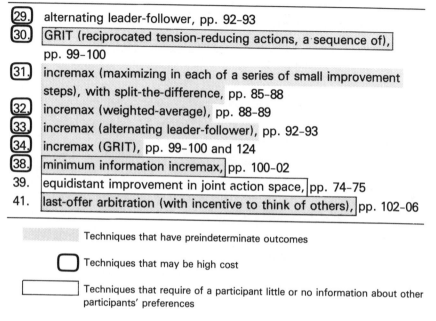

29.	alternating leader-follower, pp. 92–93
30.	GRIT (reciprocated tension-reducing actions, a sequence of), pp. 99–100
31.	incremax (maximizing in each of a series of small improvement steps), with split-the-difference, pp. 85–88
32.	incremax (weighted-average), pp. 88–89
33.	incremax (alternating leader-follower), pp. 92–93
34.	incremax (GRIT), pp. 99–100 and 124
38.	minimum information incremax, pp. 100–02
39.	equidistant improvement in joint action space, pp. 74–75
41.	last-offer arbitration (with incentive to think of others), pp. 102–06

▨ Techniques that have preindeterminate outcomes

⬜ Techniques that may be high cost

▭ Techniques that require of a participant little or no information about other participants' preferences

round, while the other is impatient, sensitive to cost, and wants to settle the conflict in one move. Or one participant may consider efficiency of predominant importance while another considers that property trivial. Likewise with stability, guaranteed improvement, veto power, and other (desirable or undesirable) properties. Or, if participants consider the same property of a procedure pertinent, they may attach different weights to it. In short, there are many possible asymmetries among participants, as has been discussed on pages 320–323.

In many important cases of asymmetry we are unable to suggest any way to proceed. But in others we can. For example, when participants have different amounts of information concerning their preferences for outcomes (utility or objective achievements), the third party can at least consider that category which requires no more information than the minimum amount that both participants have in common. This category would be one of the eight where par-

Table 12-19. *MANY* Options, Participants Can Assign *RELATIVE VALUES* to Outcomes, Need to Focus on *IM-PROVEMENTS,* Can Focus on *OUTCOMES* (Continuous, Relative, Focus on Improvement, Outcome-Oriented).

(15.)	changing actions to "if . . . , then . . ." policies,	pp. 42–48, 53–57
20.	achievement of minimum requirements (satisficing),	pp. 206–07
27.	leadership principle, pp. 96–97	
28.	aggressive follower principle, pp. 98–99	
41.	last-offer arbitration (with incentive to think of others),	pp. 102–06
47.	max the total of % improvements[a], p. 141 (weighted or unweighted)	
49.	max total % goal achievement[a], pp. 146–47 (weighted or unweighted)	
56.	max equal % improvement, pp. 155–56 and 224–25 (weighted or unweighted)	
58.	max equal % goal achievements, pp. 174 and 155 (weighted or unweighted)	
(63.)	alternating leader-follower in outcome space, pp. 159–160 and 238	
(64.)	GRIT in outcome space, p. 239	
(65.)	hierarchical programming, pp. 95–96 and 122–123	
(66.)	relaxed hierarchical programming, pp. 162–64	
(67.)	incremax in outcome space (split-the-difference), pp. 156–59 and 238	
(68.)	incremax in outcome space (weighted-average), pp. 156–59 and 238	
(69.)	incremax in outcome space (alternating leader-follower), p. 238	
(70.)	incremax in outcome space (GRIT), p. 239	

[a]Side payments may be required. See Table 12-28, on p. 472.

Techniques that have preindeterminate outcomes

Techniques that may be high cost

Techniques that require of a participant little or no information about other participants' preferences

Table 12-20. *MANY* Options, Participants Can Assign *RELATIVE VALUES* to Outcomes, Need to Focus on *CONCESSIONS*, Can Focus Only on *ACTIONS* (Continuous, Relative, Focus on Concession, Action-Oriented).

21.	median efficient joint action, pp. 75 and 78–79
(22.)	concession along efficiency frontier, pp. 76–77
23.	split-the-difference, one-step, pp. 80–81 and 83–84
(24.)	split-the-difference, a sequence of, pp. 80–83
25.	weighted-average, one-step, pp. 84–85
(26.)	weighted-average, a sequence of, pp. 84–85
(29.)	alternating leader-follower, pp. 92–93
(30.)	GRIT (reciprocated tension-reducing actions, a sequence of), pp. 99–100
(35.)	decremax (maximizing in each of a series of small concession steps), with split-the-difference, pp. 89–92
(36.)	decremax (weighted-average), pp. 89–92
(37.)	decremax (alternating leader-follower), pp. 89–92
40.	equidistant concession in joint action space, pp. 74–75 and 228–35
41.	last-offer arbitration (with incentive to think of others), pp. 102–06

Techniques that have preindeterminate outcomes

Techniques that may be high cost

Techniques that require of a participant little or no information about other participants' preferences

ticipants can only order their preferences when at least one of the participants can only do so, or one of the eight where participants can only state relative preferences when at least one of the participants can only do so (and where all other participants may be able to do more). However, caution is still required since it does not necessarily follow that the participants with the greater amount of knowledge will agree to use less than all the information they possess.

Or, when one or more participants can focus comfortably only on actions while another can focus on outcomes as well, the third party

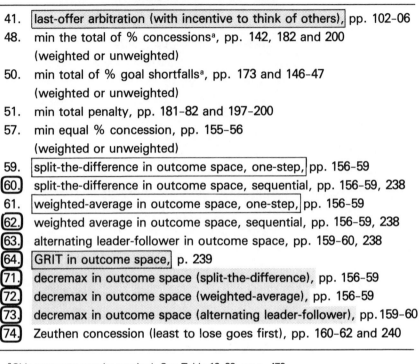

Table 12-21. *MANY* Options, Participants Can Assign *RELATIVE VALUES* to Outcomes, Need to Focus on *CONCESSIONS,* Can Focus on *OUTCOMES* (Continuous, Relative, Focus on Concession, Outcome-Oriented).

41. last-offer arbitration (with incentive to think of others), pp. 102–06
48. min the total of % concessions[a], pp. 142, 182 and 200 (weighted or unweighted)
50. min total of % goal shortfalls[a], pp. 173 and 146–47 (weighted or unweighted)
51. min total penalty, pp. 181–82 and 197–200
57. min equal % concession, pp. 155–56 (weighted or unweighted)
59. split-the-difference in outcome space, one-step, pp. 156–59
60. split-the-difference in outcome space, sequential, pp. 156–59, 238
61. weighted-average in outcome space, one-step, pp. 156–59
62. weighted average in outcome space, sequential, pp. 156–59, 238
63. alternating leader-follower in outcome space, pp. 159–60, 238
64. GRIT in outcome space, p. 239
71. decremax in outcome space (split-the-difference), pp. 156–59
72. decremax in outcome space (weighted-average), pp. 156–59
73. decremax in outcome space (alternating leader-follower), pp. 159–60
74. Zeuthen concession (least to lose goes first), pp. 160–62 and 240

[a]Side payments may be required. See Table 12-28, on p. 472.

Techniques that have preindeterminate outcomes

Techniques that may be high cost

Techniques that require of a participant little or no information about other participants' preferences

may suggest procedures where the focus is on actions. But again it does not follow that the participant(s) who can focus directly on outcomes will be willing to do otherwise; to do so might appear irrational to them. Or, when participants attach different weights to a relevant property, the third party may suggest they use a simple procedure to yield a compromise weight to be attached to that property

Table 12-22. *MANY* Options, Participants Can Assign *PRECISE VALUES* to Outcomes, Need to Focus on *IMPROVEMENTS,* Can Focus Only on *ACTIONS* (Continuous, Cardinal, Focus on Improvement, Action-Oriented).

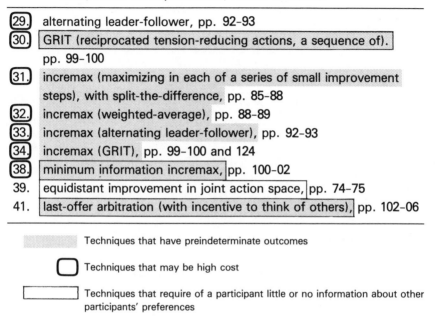

29.	alternating leader-follower, pp. 92–93
30.	GRIT (reciprocated tension-reducing actions, a sequence of). pp. 99–100
31.	incremax (maximizing in each of a series of small improvement steps), with split-the-difference, pp. 85–88
32.	incremax (weighted-average), pp. 88–89
33.	incremax (alternating leader-follower), pp. 92–93
34.	incremax (GRIT), pp. 99–100 and 124
38.	minimum information incremax, pp. 100–02
39.	equidistant improvement in joint action space, pp. 74–75
41.	last-offer arbitration (with incentive to think of others), pp. 102–06

Techniques that have preindeterminate outcomes

Techniques that may be high cost

Techniques that require of a participant little or no information about other participants' preferences

when selecting a compromise procedure to treat the main conflict. And so forth. Clearly the third party must be ingenious and inventive in overcoming the problem of asymmetry, just as he may need to be in suggesting a procedure for managing the main conflict.

12.6 OTHER ALTERNATIVES FOR THE THIRD PARTY WHEN FAILURE APPEARS IMMINENT

When agreement on the use of a conflict management procedure cannot be reached because of asymmetries discussed in the previous section, or because participants cannot come to agree even when asymmetries do not stand in the way, the third party may resort to other kinds of attacks on the problem. As discussed on pages 361–363, he

464   CONFLICT ANALYSIS

Table 12-23. *MANY* Options, Participants Can Assign *PRECISE VALUES* to Outcomes, Need to Focus on *IMPROVEMENTS,* Can Focus on *OUTCOMES* (Continuous, Cardinal, Focus on Improvement, Outcome-Oriented).

15.	changing actions to "if . . . , then . . ." policies,	pp. 42–48, 53–57
20.	achievement of minimum requirements (satisficing),	pp. 206–07
27.	leadership principle, pp. 96–97	
28.	aggressive follower principle, pp. 98–99	
41.	last-offer arbitration (with incentive to think of others),	pp. 102–06
47.	max the total of % improvements[a], p. 141 (weighted or unweighted)	
49.	max total % goal achievement[a], pp. 146–47 (weighted or unweighted)	
56.	max equal % improvement, pp. 155–56 and 224–25 (weighted or unweighted)	
58.	max equal % goal achievements, pp. 174 and 155 (weighted or unweighted)	
63.	alternating leader-follower in outcome space, pp. 159–60 and 238	
64.	GRIT in outcome space, p. 239	
65.	hierarchical programming, pp. 95–96 and 122–123	
66.	relaxed hierarchical programming, pp. 162–64	
67.	incremax in outcome space (split-the-difference), pp. 156–59, 238	
68.	incremax in outcome space (weighted-average), pp. 156–59	
69.	incremax in outcome space (alternating leader-follower), pp. 156–60, 238	
70.	incremax in outcome space (GRIT), p. 239	
76.	max total utility[a], pp. 178–79, 190–97, 202–05 and 222 (weighted or unweighted)	
77.	max total of objective achievements[a], pp. 190–97 (weighted or unweighted)	
78.	multiobjective programming with compromise weights, pp. 248–63	
79.	max total of absolute improvements[a], pp. 178–79, 222–23 (weighted or unweighted)	
81.	max total of absolute goal achievement[a], p. 179 (weighted or unweighted)	
90.	demand-revealing (no bluffing) method, pp. 184–88 and 239–40	

Table 12-23. *(continued)*

91.	max equal absolute improvements, pp. 224–25 (weighted or unweighted)
92.	max equal goal achievements, p. 225 (weighted or unweighted)

[a]Side payments may be required. See Table 12-28, on p. 472.

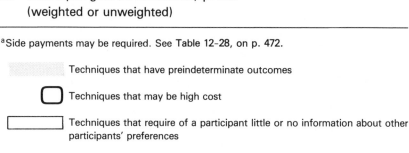

Techniques that have preindeterminate outcomes

Techniques that may be high cost

Techniques that require of a participant little or no information about other participants' preferences

may *fractionate the conflict.* That is, he may decompose the conflict into a number of subconflicts, each of a more manageable size, and set about resolving these smaller conflicts one by one. The easiest of these subconflicts may be taken up first so that participants can learn more about each other and about the use of conflict management procedures. Consequently, the more difficult subconflicts to be treated later may become easier to handle when it comes time to attempt to resolve them. It may also be desirable to link one subconflict to another in a logrolling manner where participants are agreeable to doing so, or to use other fractionation methods that Fisher has suggested.

If fractionation fails, there is of course the alternative of a return to a Burton-type workshop setting, Kelman-type preworkshop and workshop settings, Fisher-type inventive brainstorming sessions, or Delphi-type interaction and the like, as we have discussed in Chapters 10 and 11. This might be done either immediately or after a "cooling-off" period. Or, the third party may use a demand-offer-threat combination that he judges to be a "yesable" proposition for each participant and thus attempt to force the issue to a conclusion—at the risk of escalating the conflict if his demand-offer-threat combination does not turn out to be a yesable proposition to all participants. See pages 343–361 for relevant discussion.

Or, the third party may simply conclude that none of the procedures we have suggested can manage the conflict. Using whatever

Table 12-24. *MANY* Options, Participants Can Assign *PRECISE VALUES* to Outcomes, Need to Focus on *CONCESSIONS,* Can Focus Only on *ACTIONS* (Continuous, Cardinal, Focus on Concession, Action-Oriented).

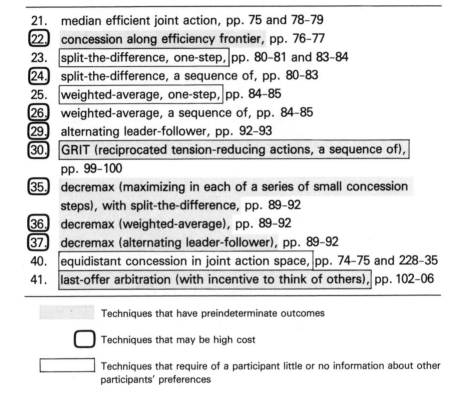

21. median efficient joint action, pp. 75 and 78–79
(22.) concession along efficiency frontier, pp. 76–77
23. split-the-difference, one-step, pp. 80–81 and 83–84
(24.) split-the-difference, a sequence of, pp. 80–83
25. weighted-average, one-step, pp. 84–85
(26.) weighted-average, a sequence of, pp. 84–85
(29.) alternating leader-follower, pp. 92–93
(30.) GRIT (reciprocated tension-reducing actions, a sequence of), pp. 99–100
(35.) decremax (maximizing in each of a series of small concession steps), with split-the-difference, pp. 89–92
(36.) decremax (weighted-average), pp. 89–92
(37.) decremax (alternating leader-follower), pp. 89–92
40. equidistant concession in joint action space, pp. 74–75 and 228–35
41. last-offer arbitration (with incentive to think of others), pp. 102–06

Techniques that have preindeterminate outcomes

Techniques that may be high cost

Techniques that require of a participant little or no information about other participants' preferences

insights he may have gained from our discussion of procedures for different conflict situations, he then may try to invent in an ad hoc manner a new procedure more suitably tailored to his conflict situation. He may be successful. However, he must recognize that there will be many, hopefully not the majority of, cases where all efforts will fail. Our knowledge of conflict and conflict management is too limited to expect more.[11]

12.7 CONCLUDING REMARKS

In this chapter we have tried to provide, on a basis more extensive than in Chapter 2, a method whereby the busy practitioner (third party)

Table 12-25. *MANY* Options, Participants Can Assign *PRECISE VALUES* to Outcomes, Need to Focus on *CONCESSIONS*, Can Focus on *OUTCOMES* (Continuous, Cardinal, Focus on Concession, Outcome-Oriented).

41.	last-offer arbitration (with incentive to think of others), pp. 102-06
48.	min the total of % concessions[a], pp. 142, 182 and 200 (weighted or unweighted)
50.	min total of % goal shortfalls[a], pp. 173 and 146-47 (weighted or unweighted)
51.	min total penalty, pp. 181-82, and 197-200
57.	min equal % concession, pp. 155-56 (weighted or unweighted)
59.	split-the-difference in outcome space, one-step, pp. 156-59
60.	split-the-difference in outcome space, sequential, pp. 156-59, 238
61.	weighted-average in outcome space, one-step, pp. 156-59
62.	weighted-average in outcome space, sequential, pp. 156-59, 238
63.	alternating leader-follower in outcome space, pp. 159-60, 238
64.	GRIT in outcome space, p. 239
71.	decremax in outcome space (split-the-difference), pp. 156-59
72.	decremax in outcome space (weighted-average), pp. 156-59
73.	decremax in outcome space (alternating leader-follower), pp. 159-60
74.	Zeuthen concession (least to lose goes first), pp. 160-62 and 240
80.	min total of absolute concessions[a], pp. 180-82, 197-200 and 226-27 (weighted or unweighted)
82.	min total of absolute goal shortfalls[a], pp. 214 and 181-82 (weighted or unweighted)
93.	max equal absolute concessions, pp. 227-28 (weighted or unweighted)

[a]Side payments may be required. See Table 12-28, on p. 472.

Techniques that have preindeterminate outcomes

Techniques that may be high cost

Techniques that require of a participant little or no information about other participants' preferences

Table 12-26. Number of Procedures with Selected Properties.

| | Categories | | | Relevant | | | Procedures | |
Table No.	Number of options	Preferences	Focus On:	Their Number[a] (1)	With Preindeterminacy (2)	With Little Information Required (3)	With Both the Preceding Properties (4)	And Excluding Those That May Be High Cost (5)
12.2	finite	ordinal	improvement action	2	1	2	1	1
12.3	"	"	" outcome	12	4	5	3	2
12.4	"	"	concession action	4	1	4	1	1
12.5	"	"	" outcome	9	3	2	2	2
12.6	"	relative	improvement action	2	1	2	1	1
12.7	"	"	" outcome	13	4	5	3	2
12.8	"	"	concession action	4	1	4	1	1
12.9	"	"	" outcome	12	3	2	2	2
12.10	"	cardinal	improvement action	2	1	2	1	1
12.11	"	"	" outcome	26	6	10	5	2
12.12	"	"	concession action	4	1	4	1	1
12.13	"	"	" outcome	18	3	2	2	2
12.14	continuous	ordinal	improvement action	9	7	4	3	1
12.15	"	"	" outcome	5	2	3	2	2
12.16	"	"	concession action	13	6	5	2	1
12.17	"	"	" outcome	1	1	1	1	1
12.18	"	relative	improvement action	9	7	4	3	1
12.19	"	"	" outcome	17	8	6	4	2
12.20	"	"	concession action	13	6	5	2	1
12.21	"	"	" outcome	15	5	4	2	1
12.22	"	cardinal	improvement action	9	7	4	3	1
12.23	"	"	" outcome	25	9	8	5	2
12.24	"	"	concession action	13	6	5	2	1
12.25	"	"	" outcome	18	5	4	2	1

[a]Excluding dominated and technical procedures.

Table 12-27.   Procedures with Selected Properties.

A. Procedures that are not or cannot be constrained to be *efficient*

Name:

23.   split-the-difference in action space, one-step, pp. 80–81, 83–84

25.   weighted-average in action space, one-step, pp. 84–85

27.   leadership principle, pp. 96–97

28.   aggressive follower principle, pp. 98–99

30.   GRIT (reciprocated tension-reducing actions, a sequence of), pp. 99–100

59.   split-the-difference in outcome space, one-step, pp. 156–159

61.   weighted average in outcome space, one-step, pp. 156–159

64.   GRIT in outcome space, p. 239

B. Procedures that are not stable or cannot be made *stable*

(none)

C. Procedures that are not or cannot be constrained to *guarantee improvement* (when the focus is on improvement)

(none)

D. Procedures that do not or cannot be constrained to involve *limited commitment*

Name:

15.   changing actions to "if . . . , then . . ." policies, pp. 42–48, 53–57

21.   median efficient joint action, pp. 75 and 78–79

23.   split-the-difference in action space, one-step, pp. 80–81, 83–84

25.   weighted-average in action space, one-step, pp. 84–85

27.   leadership principle, pp. 96–97

28.   aggressive follower principle, pp. 98–99

59.   split-the-difference in outcome space, one-step, pp. 156–159

61.   weighted average in outcome space, one-step, pp. 156–159

75.   method of determining group priorities (Saaty), pp. 147–155

90.   demand-revealing (no bluffing) method, pp. 184–88 and 239–40

Table 12-27. *(continued)*

98. max correspondence to underlying pattern of outcomes, p. 285
100. max correspondence to outcomes weighted by relative importance, p. 286
101. frequency above threshold value (using weighted ranks), pp. 286-7
102. equal role opportunities principle, pp. 169-70

E. Procedures that may not yield a *unique solution*

Name:

1. compromise over proposed actions, p. 34
2. a sequence of compromises over proposed actions, pp. 37-39
3. compromise over proposed outcomes, pp. 32-34
4. a sequence of compromises over proposed outcomes, pp. 37-39
15. changing actions to "if . . . , then . . ." policies, pp. 42-48, 53-57
20. achievement of minimum requirements (satisficing), pp. 206-07

F. Procedures that are or can be *trust building* (the same as high cost
except:

Name:

15. changing actions to "if . . . , then . . ." policies,
pp. 42-48 and 53-57
75. method of determining group priorities (Saaty),
pp. 147-55
78. multiobjective programming with compromise
weights, pp. 248-63
90. demand-revealing (no bluffing) method, pp. 184-88
96. concordance-discordance method, pp. 279-84
97. min discrepancy from ideal (using rank correlation),
pp. 284-85
98. max correspondence to underlying pattern of outcomes, p. 285
100. max correspondence to outcomes weighted by
relative importance, p. 286

Table 12-27. *(continued)*

G. Procedures that can *eliminate the effects of bluffing*

Name:

16. max good-cause payment, pp. 107-13 and 212-13
41. last-offer arbitration (with incentive to think of others), pp. 102-06
(90.) demand-revealing (no bluffing) method, pp. 184-88 and 239-40

Techniques that have preindeterminate outcomes

Techniques that may be high cost

Techniques that require of a participant little or no information about other participants' preferences

may obtain quick access to knowledge pertaining to conflict management procedures relevant to the conflict situation he confronts. We have shown how by answering four basic questions (or as many of the four as he can) he can quickly narrow down the list of ninety-five nontechnical procedures in Table 12-1 to a much smaller set given in one of the twenty-four tables (Tables 12-2 through 12-25). Which table he employs depends on the answers to the four questions. (If he cannot answer all four questions he needs to begin with more than one table, but in receiving responses of participants to the questions he may soon be able to identify the table of relevant procedures.) We of course assume that the third party is knowledgeable about the conflict situation. If not he must engage in private discussions, workshops, and other activity to acquire the requisite knowledge. He then proceeds to narrow down the relevant procedures in the relevant table through considering other properties of a procedure that are desirable or undesirable for his conflict situation. In this way, even though this table may contain a large number of procedures, for example twenty-six in the case of Table 12-11, he can quickly come to focus on a handful or less of procedures that are to be seriously considered.

At this point, the possible usefulness of this book comes to an end. Clearly, the specifics of a conflict situation are as important as the

Table 12-28.   Procedures for Determining Weights, Binding Magnitudes, and Side Payments.

Weights

a) simple averaging of proposed weights, p. 190

b) last-offer arbitration (with incentive to think of others) on proposed weights, pp. 102–06

c) equidistant concession on proposed weights, pp. 190, 228–35

d) method of determining group priorities (Saaty) pp. 147–55

e) recursive interaction, pp. 256–59

f) Delphi-type techniques, pp. 371–76

g) above subject to minimum requirements and other constraints, pp. 192–96 and 256–59

h) method of determining weights consistent with equal "social values" of participants' optimal strategies, pp. 211–12

Binding Magnitudes of Constraints

a) simple averaging of proposed binding magnitudes,

b) weighted averaging of proposed binding magnitudes, pp. 84–85

c) equidistant concession on proposed binding magnitudes, pp. 228–35

d) last-offer arbitration (with incentive to think of others) on proposed binding magnitudes, pp. 102–06

e) recursive interaction, pp. 259–63

f) method of determining group priorities (Saaty) pp. 147–55

g) max the lower bound or min the upper bound of proposed binding magnitudes, pp. 259–63

h) Delphi-type techniques, pp. 371–76

Side Payments[a]

a) simple averaging of proposed side payments,

b) weighted averaging by need, power or other criteria, pp. 84–85

c) last-offer arbitration (with incentive to think of others) on proposed side payment, pp. 102–06

d) recursive interaction, pp. 256–63

e) Delphi-type techniques, pp. 371–76

---

[a] Assuming only one participant makes payments.

Table 12-28. *(continued)*

Techniques that have preindeterminate outcomes

Techniques that may be high cost

Techniques that require of a participant little or no information about other participants' preferences

characteristics it may have in common with other conflict situations. These specifics must in large part govern the final choice of a procedure that the third party may wish to suggest to the participants.

Again we must reiterate that our framework is a static one. It fails to capture the dynamics of a conflict situation. It has also been constructed by persons who have been highly influenced by the scientific standards of a rationally oriented industrialized society and thus fails to cover many of the rationales that stem from other cultures, and hence procedures based on these rationales. It has other shortcomings, as noted in the next chapter. Nonetheless we feel that this framework can be of significant use for a number of important conflict situations.

NOTES

1. To repeat, we cannot of course hope to be able to suggest a workable procedure for every type of conflict situation. There are many that no known procedure can handle. There are others so special that a procedure must be precisely tailored for them. Thus, we only hope to be able to suggest one or more workable procedures for some important conflict situations.

2. For further comment on these two categories, see pages 67–69.

3. See pages 18–19 for discussion of these types of preferences.

4. However, if the participants have full confidence in the mediator, and are willing to accept his statement regarding the outcome of a procedure, then many of the procedures not blocked in rectangularly can be used when participants have little or no knowledge about other participants' preferences, provided the mediator knows much or comes to know much through interaction with participants.

Also the "little information" that may be required of participants can vary among these procedures. The specific requirements of each procedure are usually made explicit in a note to the discussion of that procedure in preceding chapters.

5. Where a procedure involves a sequence of rounds, we assume in general that it may be a high-cost procedure, although often the number of rounds may not be many and may be quickly gone through at little or moderate cost. Also, when a procedure requires extensive data (as in programming procedures), but where the data collection and processing has already been done, the use of the procedure may not involve high cost; yet we must classify it generally as a high-cost procedure.

6. Because it is difficult in the case of many procedures to determine whether a procedure involves in and of itself some form of limited commitment, we do not develop an appendix table on procedures that require constraints in order to involve limited commitment for participants.

7. Sometimes the "ties" problem is trivial and can easily be resolved by a toss of a coin or equivalent action. At other times, it is not trivial, as when a programming procedure yields an infinite number of solutions, each corresponding to a point on the edge of the feasibility set; a slight change in the program can yield a unique solution, but on the other hand could give rise to a major conflict since each of several slight changes may yield significantly different outcomes.

8. Except, perhaps, the need to make the solution stable; however, as discussed on page 47, this can be done by introducing inescapable sanctions a la Howard or credible threats a la Fisher.

9. When participants can state only ordinal utility functions, these weights may relate to distance concessions (or improvements). Also, when joint actions are ranked by individuals having ordinal utility functions, a different weight can be applied to each individual's ranks since ranks (unlike values attached to ordinal preference structures) are unique. When participants can state either relative or cardinal utility functions, however, these weights can relate as well to utility improvements (or concessions), percent or absolute, respectively. Participants' relative or cardinal utility functions need not be comparable to begin with because by agreeing on a set of weights they in effect make their utility functions comparable.

10. When participants focus on objective achievement when seeking a compromise joint action, constraints may relate to:

    1. percentage objective achievement improvements (or concessions) when objective achievements can be measured in relative units;

2.   percentage or absolute achievement improvements (or concessions) when objective achievements can be measured in cardinal units; and

3.   rank improvements (or concessions) in objective achievements when such achievements can be measured in ordinal units.

When participants focus on utility outcomes in seeking a compromise joint action, constraints may relate to:

1.   percentage utility improvements (or concessions) when they each have relative utility functions;

2.   percentage or absolute utility improvements (or concessions) when they each have cardinal utility functions; and

3.   rank improvements (or concessions) in utility outcomes when they each have ordinal utility functions.

When participants choose to focus only indirectly on outcomes, constraints may also relate to distances (either percentage or absolute) in the joint action space and other relevant elements.

11.   The analytic, technical reader will note that this chapter does not explicitly talk about syntheses of conflict managment procedures (whether qualitative or quantitative) as discussed in Chapter 11. This is purposely so since this chapter has been written for the practitioner. What is important to the practitioner is not whether scholars have or have not been successful in fusing ideas and approaches, but rather, what a given procedure can *do*. However, when we examine whether the procedures listed in the Master Table 12–1 have or can be constrained to have properties such as stability, efficiency, and guaranteed improvement, our discussion clearly implies the use of combinations of procedures. To illustrate, suppose a particular conflict situation falls in the category *Finite, Ordinal, Focus on Concession, Outcome-Oriented*. Suppose, too, that the participants are inclined to adopt procedure #8, min total of weighted rank concessions, but only if an upper bound on concessions (limited commitment) is set, and only if stability of the final outcome is ensured. This procedure with constraints regarding limited commitment and stability implies a variant of the weighted, constrained, stabilized, rank-based cluster as depicted in Figure 11–6 on page 395.

APPENDIX TO CHAPTER 12
SUPPLEMENTARY TABLES

Table 12A-1. Procedures that May Require Constraints to Be Efficient.

1.	compromise over proposed actions, p. 34
2.	a sequence of compromises over proposed actions, pp. 37–39
3.	compromise over proposed outcomes, pp. 32–34
4.	a sequence of compromises over proposed outcomes, pp. 37–39
6.	min the difference in ranks, pp. 64 and 39–40 (weighted or unweighted)
9.	max the min in rank improvements, pp. 64 and 39–40
10.	min the max in rank concessions, pp. 64 and 40–42
11.	min difference in rank improvement pp. 39–40 (weighted or unweighted)
12.	max equal rank improvement, pp. 39–40 and 271–75 (weighted or unweighted)
13.	min equal rank concession, pp. 40–42 and 271–75 (weighted or unweighted)
14.	min difference in rank concession, pp. 40–42 (weighted or unweighted)
15.	changing actions to "if . . . , then . . ." policies, pp. 42–48, 53–57
18.	min distance to the equidistant improvement line, pp. 74–75
19.	min distance to the equidistant concession line, pp. 74–75
20.	achievement of minimum requirements (satisficing) pp. 206–07
24.	split-the-difference, a sequence of, pp. 80–83
26.	weighted average, a sequence of, pp. 84–85
29.	alternating leader-follower, pp. 92–93
39.	equidistant improvement in joint action space, pp. 74–75
40.	equidistant concession in joint action space, pp. 74–75 and 228–35
41.	last-offer arbitration (with incentive to think of others) pp. 102–06
42.	min difference in % improvements, pp. 131–38 and 141–46 (weighted or unweighted)
43.	min difference in % concessions, pp. 137–38 (weighted or unweighted)

Table 12A-1. *(continued)*

44. min difference in % goal achievements, pp. 173 and 146
     (weighted or unweighted)
45. max the min % improvement, pp. 138-39
     (weighted or unweighted)
46. min the max % concession, pp. 139-41
     (weighted or unweighted)
51. min total penalty, pp. 181-182 and 197-200
52. max the max % improvement, p. 173
53. min the min % concession, p. 173
54. min deviation from average % improvement, pp. 243-44
55. min deviation from average % concession, pp. 243-44
60. split-the-difference in outcome space, sequential, pp. 156-59, 238
62. weighted average in outcome space, sequential, pp. 156-59, 238
63. alternating leader-follower in outcome space, pp. 159-60, 238
75. method of determining group priorities (Saaty), pp. 147-55
83. min difference of absolute improvements, pp. 179-80
     (weighted or unweighted)
84. min difference of absolute concessions, pp. 182-83
     (weighted or unweighted)
85. min difference in absolute goal achievements, p. 180
     (weighted or unweighted)
86. max the min absolute improvement, p. 180
     (weighted or unweighted)
87. min the max absolute concession, p. 183
     (weighted or unweighted)
88. max the difference of absolute improvements, pp. 183-84
89. max the difference of absolute concessions, pp. 215 and 183-84
94. min deviation from average absolute improvement, pp. 214, 179-80
95. min deviation from average absolute concession, pp. 215 and 182

Other more technical and presumably less practical procedures are:

97. min discrepancy from ideal (using rank correlation), pp. 284-85
98. max correspondence to underlying pattern of outcomes, p. 285

Table 12A-1. *(continued)*

---

(100) max correspondence to outcomes weighted by relative importance, p. 286

101. frequency above threshold value (using weighted ranks), pp. 286-7

▓▓▓▓▓▓▓▓ Techniques that have preindeterminate outcomes

◯ Techniques that may be high cost

[_____] Techniques that require of a participant little or no information about other
participants' preferences

Table 12A-2.   Procedures that Require Constraints to Guarantee
Improvement.

---

5. min total of ranks* (highest rank = 1), pp. 39-40 and 273-77
(weighted or unweighted)

6. min the difference in ranks, pp. 64 and 39-40
(weighted or unweighted)

7. max total of rank improvements*, pp. 39-40 and 275-77
(weighted or unweighted)

(15.) changing actions to "if . . . , then . . ." policies, pp. 42-48, 53-57

17. apportionment principles, pp. 114-19

20. achievement of minimum requirements (satisficing), pp. 206-07

47. max the total of % improvements*, p. 141
(weighted or unweighted)

49. max total % goal achievement*, pp. 146-47
(weighted or unweighted)

(75.) method of determining group priorities (Saaty), pp. 147-55

76. max total utility*, pp. 178-79, 190-97, 202-05, 222

77. max total of objective achievements*, pp. 190-97
(weighted or unweighted)

(78.) multiobjective programming with compromise weights, pp. 248-63

79. max total of absolute improvements*, pp. 178-79 and 222-23
(weighted or unweighted)

Table 12A-2.   *(continued)*

81.   max total of absolute goal achievement*, p. 179
(weighted or unweighted)

(90.)   demand-revealing (no bluffing) method, pp. 184–88 and 239–40

Other more technical and less practical procedures are:

(98.)   max correspondence to underlying pattern of outcomes, p. 285

99.   max total of ranks weighted by outcome "importance", pp. 285–6

(100)   max correspondence to outcomes weighted by relative importance, p. 286

101.   frequency above threshold value (using weighted ranks), pp. 286–7

*Side Payments may be required.

Techniques that have preindeterminate outcomes

Techniques that may be high cost

Techniques that require of a participant little or no information about other
participants' preferences

13 CONCLUDING REMARKS AND PROSPECT REGARDING PRACTICAL CONFLICT MANAGEMENT PROCEDURES

We now bring the basic part of this book to a close. While in our attempt at a systematic and comprehensive survey of existing conflict management procedures we have been able to refer to a fairly large number of procedures and while for the most part each can be used today for one or more different types of conflict situations, we still have far to go in developing more adequate procedures. We have consistently referred to the fact that the literature on and our construction of procedures fail to take into account the dynamics of a conflict situation and the process of its management. We have several times referred to learning by participants, to changes in their stock of knowledge, perceptions and misperceptions, aspirations, goals, objectives and targets, to changes in the social system environment, and to the appearance of threshold effects. We sorely need major research on these changes and their effects. True, for some conflict situations and their associated process of management, there may be only small or imperceptible changes, so that the dynamics of such may be ignored, particularly when other factors predominate. But, by and large, this is not the case for most conflicts of significance. Of course, there are important beginnings at the needed research. We can point to dynamical systems analysis, but such is really anemic dynamics. It presupposes no structural change, and in an adaptive deterministic fashion, charts out a time path toward an equilibrium state of affairs, or a set of prespecified terminal conditions, or the equivalent. But, for most major conflict situations the essence of their dynamics is structural change—in, for example, perceptions and misperceptions, objectives and targets, and the like. (For further discussion of these points, see pages 554–563.)

Catastrophe theory, as set forth by Thom (1974) and his followers, poses effectively the phenomena of threshold effects, sudden jumps in the progress of discussions and negotiations and major shifts in the participants' positions and attitudes. However, the behavioral interpretation of real-life catastrophes (in the Thom sense), whether we think of individual behavior or system behavior, is yet to be developed adequately for projection (or forecast) purposes. There have already been developed some bits of explanation on the system level, (see Isard and Liossatos (1979:317–26), (1978:139–41)[1], recent work by Allen (1981), Beaumont et al. (1981), and others[2]), but extremely little with regard to individual behavior.

There also exists evolutionary theory of a broad-ranging type relating to the formation of the survival-of-the-fittest and genetic self-interest hypotheses (Isard and C. Smith 1981)—but again, like long-run historical theories relating to the rise and decline of civilizations or population growth, these have little to contribute to our specific need with regard to the development of more adequate conflict management procedures.

Should there be further development in our understanding of the dynamics of conflict situations and the process of their management, it is highly likely that we will need to drop the notion of the use of a single procedure for the management of any nonsimple conflict. Rather, we will need to think in terms of a sequence of procedures. In Chapter 11, where we discuss the construction of a cluster of conflict management procedures for a given conflict situation, we at times implied a certain type of dynamics—that is, a set of stages in the process of conflict management wherein the "tailored" procedure is able to handle each stage as it comes up. But here we have something more in mind. As debate and discussion goes on, say in a main workshop, as a series of steps are taken, as a number of smaller issues are settled, as learning about perceptions, misperceptions, aspirations, objectives and targets occurs (whether one's own or the opponents'), the structure (basic properties) of the conflict situation also change, as already noted.[3] Hence, it follows that a conflict management procedure adequate at the start, say a very simple one, may no longer be adequate at an intermediate time when participants may have become more sophisticated. At that intermediate time, a recursive interaction or Howard approach may be the best procedure; and then a split-the-difference or some other less costly procedure may be appropriate at the last stage when only minor differences need to be ironed out. In effect, corresponding to the time path of structural change of a conflict situation should be a time path of the most appropriate conflict management procedure. That is, the time path of a particular conflict situation in the s-dimensional space of all possible conflict situations should map on to a time path of the ideal conflict management procedure in the p-dimensional space of all conflict management procedures. In practice, given our limited ability at working with a conceptual framework, the dynamics of a conflict situation can only be treated as shiftings over time of the categories in which a particular conflict situation falls. Accordingly, the corresponding time path of the ideal conflict management procedure reduces to a sequence of appropriate conflict management procedures. But what should be this sequence (shift pattern) of conflict management procedures? Should some kind of objective function control the pattern of shift—something that maximizes the welfare of society, or of the participants, or the mediator? Or should some satisficing criteria be employed? Or should there be some kind of index that would indicate when a shift should occur? Or should the determination of the shift pattern be left to the judgment of the mediator, or to the initiative of the participants?

The problem, however, goes even deeper. This is so because the choice of any conflict management procedure to be used at a point of time can alter the nature of the changing conflict situation—that is, affect its time path. Thus, there is a feedback effect which ideally should be captured.

Aside from the sorely needed developments in dynamics, we need to conduct much more research on how personality factors in a conflict situation can condition and influence the type of procedure applicable. Just as we were able to develop twenty-four different categories into which different target conflict situations might fall and at each of which different conflict management procedures might be aimed, we might be able to further categorize different conflict situations by combinations of personalities—learning versus nonlearning, aggressive versus passive, cooperative versus competitive, myopic versus nonmyopic. We have begun to spell out some of these in our discussion of conflict situation characteristics in Chapter 9. However, a more adequate introduction of personality type will lead to the specification of still more categories of conflict situations. For example, one might be *small, ordinal, focus on improvement, and focus on outcome, where participants are both aggressive leaders*; another might be the same except that *participants are both aggressive followers*; still another might be the same, except that *participants are cool, calculating and nonemotional*. While this more disaggregated classification may increase the difficulties and complexities of an analysis, at the same time it may lead to a better identification of one or more pertinent conflict management procedures.

The introduction of the personality factor points up another type of research need—namely, that on the cognitive aspects of decision-making, especially as it is associated with learning and changes in perceptions and related aspects during the discussion and interaction phases of a workshop-type activity, or a negotiation process. We need to pay more attention to such aspects as the sources of information of each participant; the credibility each attaches to information from each source; the filtering process each conducts; the limited set of beliefs, matters, and actions to which each attends; his expectations based on the past; and his memory and stock of supportive information to which his set of strategies is oriented. In short, all these factors must enter into the analysis of any conflict situation and the identification of the one or more relevant conflict management procedures.

Thus far, we have been assuming certain symmetries with regard to key variables in the process of conflict management. The consideration of the personality factor, however, immediately suggests the need for more research with regard to asymmetries. Certainly, asymmetries will typically exist among the personalities involved in any conflict. One participant may be aggressive, the other, a follower; one may be cool, the other highly emotional; one may be poorly informed, the other well informed; one may wish to focus on outcomes and the other only capable of thinking in terms of changes in actions; one may perceive the status quo as the relevant reference point and seek mutual improvements while the other sees it as the ideal point and so seek mutual concessions; one may be from an advanced industrialized culture and demand the use of sophisticated multiobjective programming while the other, being from a developing country, may mistrust such a technical procedure; one may be willing to engage in frank and open discussion during a workshop session while the other continually seeks to bluff and adopt other strategically oriented types of behavior.

Going beyond personality asymmetries, there typically exist differences in the resource base of participants (in their ability to hold out for a bigger share of the pie), in the pressures exerted by their constituencies, in their ability to break with tradition and custom (cultural or religious), in language systems and communication mechanisms, and in a host of other environmental characteristics.

Nonetheless, there is need for more fundamental research on the workshop itself—on the creation of more effective settings (environments); on the appropriate sequencing of stages (pre, main, post); on the transition from one focus (issue) to another; on the control of action and reaction processes, particularly with regard to credible offers, threats, and combinations of these; on how to further sensitize participants to the existence of universal needs and in general increase their receptivity to new information and their learning proclivities and capacities.

Moreover, there are many other less important places at which further research is required. First, there are situations wherein participants have interdependent utility functions. These functions were discussed in Chapter 6, pages 207–209 and also in Chapter 10, pages 332–336. However, we were unable to suggest which conflict management procedures could be meaningfully modified for application in these situations, nor point to any additional procedures specifically designed for these situations. This is an important area for research, for in reality many utility functions are interdependent. Second, much more basic research is required on multiobjective-multiparticipant and multicriteria-multiparticipant situations. Clearly, we need to explore a wider range of procedures to reach compromise solutions on weights, constraints, forms of objective functions, and other parameters.

It should be noted that by and large we have avoided treating situations involving stochastic elements wherein expected payoffs, expected utilities ($\overline{u}$lity), and other expected magnitudes are involved. We have done so because, as we have already noted (see pages 61, 287), the techniques currently available are much too sophisticated for practical use in the multiparticipant situations we treat in this book. Moreover, we have not looked into the possibilities of fuzzy set analysis (see pages 288–289), which is just developing. Again, we have not been able to see the practical applications of such an approach at this time, although there is much promise.

Another area wherein additional research must be conducted relates to the information variable as it affects behavior of participants and thus procedures that may be applicable to diverse conflict situations. We have already noted briefly (on page 24) that most frequently this variable is not treated explicitly because of its subjective nature as well as the many possible different states (imperfect and incomplete) that can obtain.

Clearly, we cannot close without again pointing up the urgent need to conduct intensive research on coalition analysis. (Recall that most of the discussion in the previous chapters relate to two-participant conflicts or, if more than two participants are involved, to situations where coalitions are not possible.) Currently, considerable research is being conducted on this subject in highly mathematical form by applied mathematicians, game theorists, operations researchers, mathematical economists, and the like. However, rigorous analyses involving the use of concepts such as the core, nucleolus, and fibre make such strong assumptions about participants and the conflict situation they confront that we are forced to acknowledge that such analyses currently have no more than an inkling of relevance to the real world. At the other extreme, the highly particularistic, historical case studies conducted by meticulous historians and political scientists provide little by way of general conclusions applicable to the problem at hand. What we need are some basic principles or ways to think about conditions influencing patterns of coalition formation among participants to a conflict. Without doubt, there are innumerable factors present in the formation, disruption, reformation, and seemingly unending cyclical and noncyclical aspects of coalition development and change. Yet, as with the innumerable factors referred to in the location study of an integrated iron and steel works (on pages 324–328), it should be possible to reduce them to a few basic ones whose interaction we then qualify in many different ways when we consider a whole range of nonbasic factors.

In particular, we should like to identify conditions governing the formation of stable coalition patterns with regard to different kinds of conflict situations. Assuming that a stable compromise solution is desirable, we should then like to tailor the construction of a conflict management procedure to increase the probability of reaching such a solution, while recognizing the realities of coalition formation and disruption.

While the past decades have not seen any major breakthrough in the development of coalition analysis, there are new, fruitful game-theoretic lines of research (Lucas 1982). Also, among social scientists, policy space analysis is developing that has great promise to unearth new insight (see Isard and C. Smith 1980). In particular, the wholesale transfer of knowledge from the traditional field of location theory has great potential for a major advance in coalition analysis. The parallel between agglomeration phenomena (in economics and regional science) and the formation of a coalition of political leaders with common agreed-upon positions on a set of issues is very striking. Hence, we would be remiss not to attempt to employ in coalition analysis the scientifically rigorous concepts of location theory as developed over the last century and a half. Likewise, the emergence of regionalism—the desire of ethnic-specific, cultural-specific, and other regions to break away from a national community earlier formed as a coalition (union) of states (provinces, etc.)—is much too like deglomeration forces (in economics and regional science) not to exploit deglomeration theory accumulated over many decades. See Isard and C. Smith (1982b:100–102).

In sum, we bring this book to a close recognizing the difficulties of further research on relevant conflict management procedures but at the same time noting a number of important lines of development that have considerable promise. There are also other lines involving long-run research of a more visionary character, which, for those who are interested, we present in the next two chapters.

NOTES

1. There, respectively, explanation has been in terms of how change in population numbers in a society causes abrupt change in the welfare of that society when the numbers reach a critical level or how change in attitude (e.g., anti-communism) can lead to an abrupt change in armaments expenditures once the attitude reaches a critical level.
2. See Kahn (1981). There, with population growth and expanding external demand abrupt spatial change in the internal urban structure takes place when critical densities are reached.
3. Thus, what we have in mind is different than the steps of preworkshop, main workshop, and end-of-workshop activities involved in the Kelman approach, which implicitly assume that the structure of the conflict situation has not changed significantly. Also, what we have in mind is basically different from other similar stage-type approaches where, for example, there is:

Stage 1. Education about the nature of the conflict situation, and where necessary the development of a common vocabulary, definitions and the like.

Stage 2. Familiarization with opponents' preferences, attitudes, objectives, targets, and points of view. Clarification of one's own.

Stage 3. Testing out different ideas, notions, and proposals for joint actions and policies.

Stage 4. Identifying specific proposals of significance and ironing out details essential for adoption and formalization of an agreement.

For a similar stage-type of approach, see Gentile (1981).

14 TOWARD A DEFINITION OF PEACE SCIENCE: PART I

14.1 INTRODUCTION

In this and the following chapter we shall make a first serious attempt at a full definition of the field of Peace Science.[1] In the past, we and others have variously defined the field as conflict theory and analysis, conflict management, and conflict resolution; or as embodying those efforts designed to cope with conflict and to establish world order or order within societies of different sizes and structures. We have frequently emphasized the field's cross-disciplinary character. We have claimed that it draws upon the existing concepts, tools, theories, models, and techniques of diverse fields—economics, mathematics, psychology, sociology, anthropology, political science, industrial relations, regional science, geography, biology, and law—and attempts to fuse the better elements of these. Nowhere, as far as we are aware, do we proceed further and detail concretely this fusion process and suggest a conceptual framework that embodies and explicates all the links among variables, approaches, and theories. We shall, however, attempt to do so in this and the next chapter.

We take the position that once fields become established and institutionalized they lose their flexibility. With time, they cumulatively, though never completely, lose ability to absorb new ideas and theories and move along drastically new directions. In contrast, a new field such as Peace Science, which has yet to find a definition, core, and boundaries acceptable to many scholars, is completely free to identify and embrace an optimal combination of concepts, tools, theories, models, and techniques. For at least a few years, until its scholars become widely recognized and acquire vested interests, it may redefine itself without constraint. It can draw upon the strong elements of existing fields while discarding sterile, excessively refined models, theories, and abstractions, and obsolete techniques and knowledge, thereby promising to achieve much in unifying and integrating social science and related knowledge.

In Section 14.2 we develop a broad conceptual framework for Peace Science and the general study of multination and other multiparticipant conflict. In each of the next three sections of this chapter and in the first section of Chapter 15 we detail a basic element of this framework. These elements are: the production subsystem (Section 14.3), the real interaction subsystem (Section 14.4), the decisionmaking subsystem (Section 14.5), and the cognitive interaction subsystem (Section 15.1). Then, in Sections 15.2 through 15.4 we discuss in turn the evolutionary character and structure of the social system, the role of information processes and possible frameworks for modeling the interrelations of the cognitive interaction and the real interaction subsystems.

14.2 A STEP-BY-STEP DEVELOPMENT OF A BROAD CONCEPTUAL FRAMEWORK

14.2.1 Begin with a Basic Production Subsystem with Simple Conflict among Two Participants over the Joint Action

In developing a definition of Peace Science we proceed in simple step-by-step fashion. A useful starting point is the basic classical notion of production. While we may envisage many behavioral units involved in a production process, it is convenient to limit ourselves to two at the start and to later generalize to n such units. Starting with an extremely simple case, imagine that at some decisionmaking point t in time a decisionmaking unit J chooses to provide some input a^J, and a decisionmaking unit L chooses to provide some input a^L, the joint input being $a = (a^J, a^L)$. Let z be the state of the environment existing at time t.[2] We then can imagine that the output y is given by a production function P as:

$$y = P(a,z) \qquad (14\text{-}1)$$

Such a production process is indicated in box form in Figure 14-1. There, too, we have indicated the payoff, satisfaction, or utility, u^J and u^L, that J and L, respectively, obtain from such production, where

$$u^K = u^K(y) \qquad K = J,L. \qquad (14\text{-}2)$$

Such for example, might result when a single output is produced—e.g., a work of art or a garden whose yield of services can be jointly consumed. Another type of outcome that may be realized is indicated in Figure 14-2, where the output $y = (y^J, y^L)$ is composed of two elements, y^J and y^L, which are the outputs going to J and L, respectively.

Conflict is of course implicit in Figures 14-1 and 14-2. Since utility functions in general differ among behaving units, we can easily visualize that of the possible y's there are differences among the units as to which is most desirable. If z and P are known, we may imagine that the most preferred joint action a^{J*} of J, which yields output y^{J*}

Figure 14-1.   Joint Action, Single Output, and Utility.

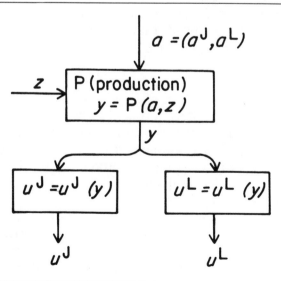

Figure 14-2. Joint Action, Separate Outputs, and Utility.

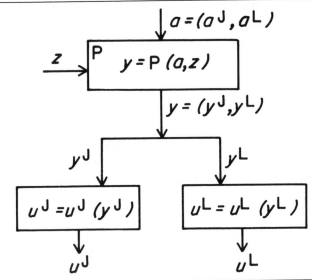

is different from the most preferred joint action a^{L^*} of L, which yields output y^{L^*}. That is, we may imagine with reference to Figure 14-1 that $u^J(y^{J^*}) > u^J(y^{L^*})$ and $u^L(y^{L^*}) > u^L(y^{J^*})$. This is indicated in Figure 14-3.[3] Hence, if J and L are both maximizers, there exists a conflict as to which action should be chosen. (For illustrative purposes we have introduced into Figure 14-3 a compromise action $\bar{a}$.) As shall become more apparent later, such conflict becomes more complex when:

1. the state of the environment is not known beforehand and only probabilities can be attached to the occurrence of the several possible states of the environment;
2. stochastic elements enter into the production relation; and
3. there are other behavioral units.

It suffices to indicate here that conflict between units (for example, nations J and L) is present from the start and its complexity tends to increase exponentially as additional factors are introduced.

Figure 14-3. Conflict Regarding Best Action and Action Compromise.

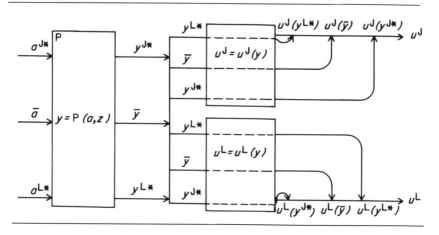

14.2.2 Add on the Decisionmaking Subsystem. Identify each Nation (Community) in a System as a Production Subsystem Plus a Decisionmaking Subsystem

Having focused on the production relation, we may now make a few elementary comments on the selection of the inputs a^J by J and a^L by L. Actually, a^J and a^L may be viewed as control inputs, orders, or commands. Each represents a decision. Hence, we may visualize a system S as indicated in Figure 14-4.[4] Alternatively, we may visualize J and L each as a subsystem (say a nation) represented by S^J and S^L, respectively. Each is composed of a decisionmaking unit C^K and a production unit P^K, K = J, L. Together P^J and P^L form the production subsystem P. See Figure 14-5.

To form a meaningful production subsystem P, we permit interdependence among the production units. There may be negative externalities (e.g., in the form of pollution from one unit which generally diminishes production of the other) or positive externalities (e.g., from trade in highly localized resources which generally increases output among production units who trade). We have indicated this by specifying in Figure 14-6 the interface inputs v^J and v^L (which enter into the production functions of J and L respectively) to reflect effects stemming from interaction and interdependence.

Figure 14-4.   A System of Decisionmaking Units and a Production Process.

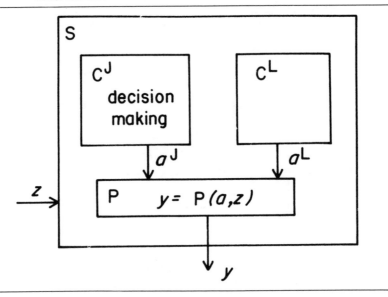

Figure 14-5.   A System Composed of Subsystems, Each Comprising a Decisionmaking Unit and a Production Unit.

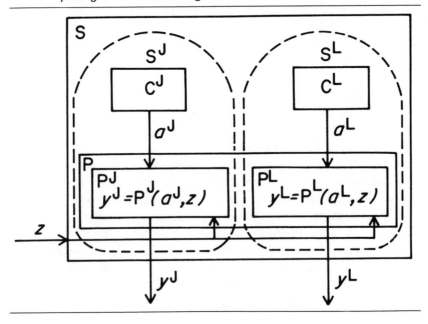

Figure 14-6. The System with Interface Inputs v^J and v^L and an Information Subsystem M.

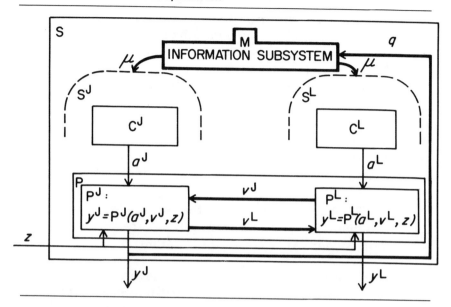

14.2.3 Add the Information Subsystem, Information Flows, and their Perception

Figure 14–6 explicitly recognizes that choice and decisionmaking within boxes C^J and C^L must be based upon information. It incorporates the *Information Subsystem* represented by box M, and information flows q on the outputs and inputs involved in the production processes P^J and P^L. These flows enter into the stock of information contained in the information subsystem and accumulate over time as "experience." Concomitantly, we have indicated information flows μ from the information subsystem box to the decisionmaking processes C^J and C^L. See also Figure 14–7.

It is widely recognized that the postulate of perfect information and of unrestricted information flow is unrealistic. We are aware of the many obstacles to the free flow of information, to an unimpeded storing of information, and to the reality that behaving units can only imperfectly perceive information. Moreover, because of different cultural backgrounds, language systems, experiences, and other factors, they do so in different ways. Hence, as was discussed with respect to the Fisher yesable proposition approach on pages 343–361 we need to add the factor of "limited perception," or the perception operator ρ^K, K = J,L in Figure 14–7. There, the perception factor converts every information flow into a more limited, biased flow. Thus z becomes $\bar{z}^J$ and $\bar{z}^L$, μ becomes $\bar{\mu}^J$ and $\bar{\mu}^L$,[5] and ν^J and ν^L become $\bar{\nu}^J$ and $\bar{\nu}^L$, respectively. Also in Figure 14–7 we have added information flows b^J and b^L regarding production experience that is received by the decisionmaking units C^J and C^L, respectively. These information flows may be complete or incomplete and may be filtered and/or transformed through perception and passed on as $\bar{b}^J$ and $\bar{b}^L$, respectively, to become available for inclusion in unmodified or modified form in the stock of the information subsystem.

14.2.4 Next, Make Explicit the Subsystem Coupling Function Regarding Real Interactions and System Filtering of Information

Two more important changes are effected in Figure 14–8. There we explicitly recognize that the system itself filters information (perceives only certain information as relevant and even distorts and transforms

Figure 14–7. The System, Information Flows, and Perceived Information.

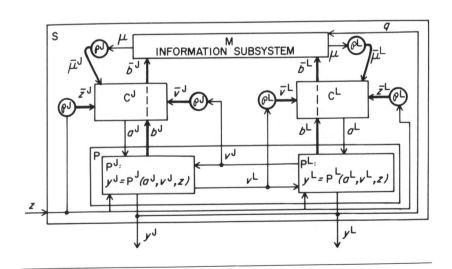

Figure 14-8.   The System, the Real Interaction Component R, and Filtering of Information.

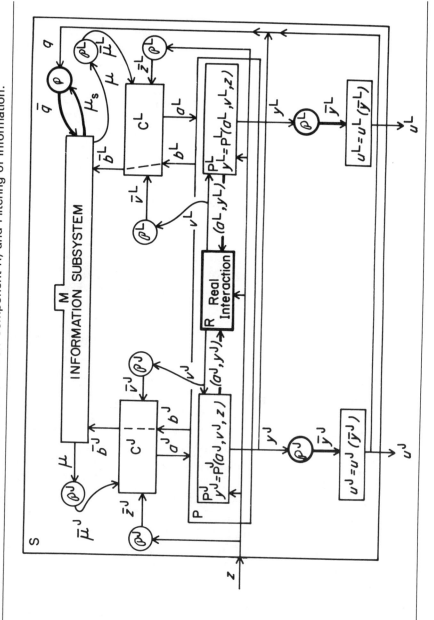

it), and does so from instructions generated by information that it has already stored. Thus we have a set of instructions μ_s going through the ρ operator to transform q into the flow $\bar{q}$ which is recorded and stored by the system. Also, bearing in mind that the system typically contains more than two nations or regions or organizations (each containing a decisionmaking unit and a production unit), we have added an R block. This block represents the subsystem coupling function whose arguments (dependent variables) are the inputs and outputs of each production unit. As "output," this function supplies each production unit K with the interface input v^K, K = J,L, . . . We have also indicated for J and L their perceptions of output $\bar{y}^J$ and $\bar{y}^L$ (as a transformation of actual output y^J and y^L) and changed their utility functions accordingly.

14.2.5 Finally, Introduce the Subsystem Coupling Function Regarding Cognitive Interaction and View the Framework as a Historic Process in Macrotime

We explicitly introduce in Figure 14–9 a cognitive subsystem C that embodies the decisionmaking units of each nation, region, or organization and also embodies a cognitive subsystem coupling function. In Peace Science, it is critically important to make explicit the full cognitive subsystem C. Here is where all the political bargaining, negotiation, coalition, and costrategic processes take place. Moreover, parallel to the subsystem coupling function R which primarily is based on real physical inputs and outputs and involves real physical interface inputs, and which has received most attention by traditional systems analysts, we must make explicit a cognitive subsystem coupling function I. Here, we have in mind the function that takes as inputs θ^K, K = J,L . . . covering both the information inputs to each decisionmaking unit K as that unit perceives them and its response (which may be in the form of threats, friendly statements, etc.). This function then returns to each decisionmaking unit C^K a systematic response v^K (a system output) which may be viewed as a cognitive interface input stemming from interaction at the cognitive level. The cognitive subsystem coupling function also receives (relies on) information μ from the information subsystem M and/or information d from the real interaction subsystem R on the nature and level of cur-

Figure 14-9. The System with the Cognitive Subsystem C, the Cognitive Interaction Component I, and History.

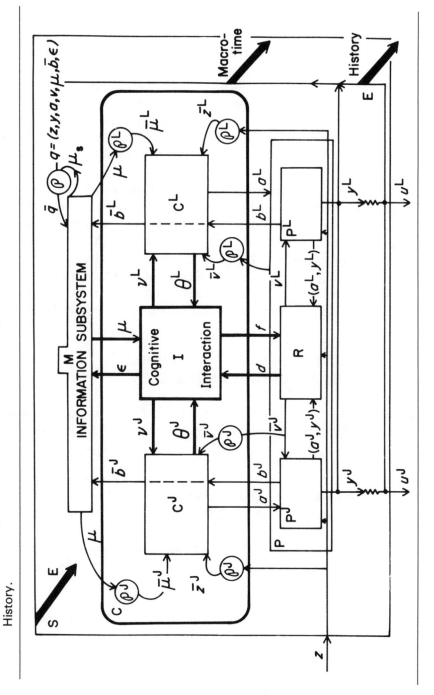

rent interaction (operation) at the real level. It then passes on information ϵ about deliberations, negotiations, and other cognitive interaction among the decisionmaking units to the information subsystem and also imposes commands or control inputs or chooses other actions f that directly affect the operation of the real interaction system.[6]

Additionally, in Figure 14-9 we have made explicit the reality of history, which we will later associate in part with *macrotime*.[7] Here we wish to keep constantly in mind evolutionary processes—involving both smooth and abrupt transitions in structure—and the influence of history, which are fundamental to the dynamics of conflict management.

In what follows we shall present detail on each box (subsystem) and its concrete relationship to others. After doing so, we shall conclude that the core of Peace Science comprises the area covered by topics included in, and relationships basic to, the three boxes: (1) the information subsystem M, (2) the cognitive interaction system I, and (3) the real interaction subsystem R. (These three boxes can be designated by the acronym MIR.) This core is unique to Peace Science and justifies its claim to existence as a separate social science discipline.

14.3 THE DETAIL OF THE P^K BOX, THE PRODUCTION SUBSYSTEM OF K

Having developed a broad conceptual framework, we now detail each block and the flows it generates and receives.[8] We begin with the P^K block, $K = J,L, \ldots$

14.3.1 Production Models: Economic and Ecologic Inputs and Outputs

As already indicated, we may generally state the production relation as:

$$y^K = P^K(a^K, v^K, z) \qquad K = J,L, \ldots \qquad (14\text{-}3)$$

where v^K represents diverse interface inputs, such as pollution in the form of SO_2, particulates, biological oxygen demand (BOD), or noise, that may flow into K's production arena and affect K's transformation possibilities; and where z refers to a state of the environment that relates to not only the physical properties such as climate and humidity, but also the social, political, and technological. Many specific production functions may be envisaged, such as the familiar Cobb-Douglas and the Leontief-type. However, it suffices to specify each possible production plan y^K in the production space Y^K as a vector, consisting of ℓ components where component y_h^K ($h = 1, \ldots, \ell$) is an output of a commodity when positive and an input when negative. These are indicated as economic goods in Figure 14-10, which is an enlargement of the P^K production box (K = J or L) of Figure 14-9.

When the P^K refers to a single organization, the specification of the selected input-output plan and the set of prices (which may be viewed as a set of interface inputs from the market system) yields the payoff (profit) to the organization. However, in Peace Science when we think of a nation or region, we think of many firms j, ($j = 1, \ldots, n$). Hence the total output or input of any commodity h is $\sum_j y_{hj}$ where y_{hj} is the output or input of the jth producer. From total outputs of all commodities we may derive Gross National Product (GNP), and Gross Regional Product (GRP) with which may be associated other macromagnitudes such as investment, consumption, and net exports. Hence, the Keynesian type of macroanalysis becomes relevant for studying the economy of the nation or region—and so do national and regional econometric models designed to examine implications of various policies, commands, and other actions summarized by the a^j input from the decisionmaking unit into the production process. This is also indicated in the upper part of Figure 14-10. Assuming the existence of a market economy within the nation as well as a world market to which the nation is connected by exports, imports, and flows of gold and currency (which are components of the interface input), these models together with others can determine prices, wages, profits, dividends, interest, and the like. There results a distribution of money income, real income, and welfare among individuals and relevant groups in the nation.

It is also useful to employ national and regional input-output analysis for both depicting the real physical flows among the economic sectors of a nation's system and for studying impacts of different types of decisionmaking and interface inputs upon that system. These features of input-output are well known. Equally important is the ability of input-output to take into account disturbances to the ecologic system stemming from real economic activity. Already there has been accumulated considerable information on the emissions by diverse

Figure 14-10.   The Real Production Box P^K

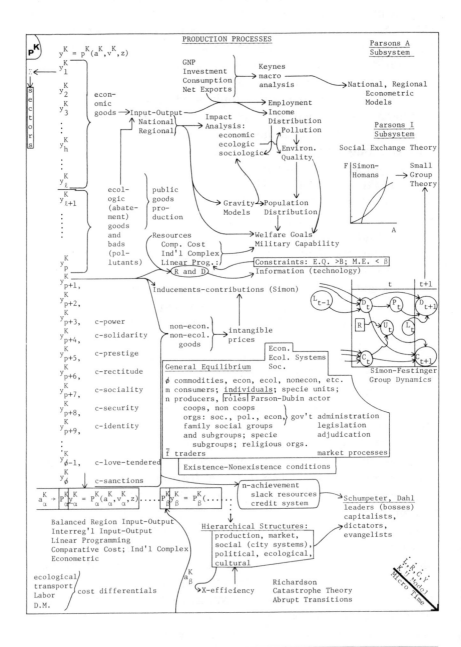

economic sectors of pollutants indicated as commodities $y_{\ell+1}, \ldots, y_p$ in Figure 14-10. Much of this information is usable in the form of constant production coefficients, within a properly designated range of levels of economic sector output. With these coefficients and their necessary adjustments, we can estimate emissions of various pollutants for different states of the economy. The emissions are in effect interface inputs into (disturbances to) the ecologic system which in large part determine environmental quality. Thus, input-output, together with other tools, permits analysis of diverse environmental impacts of the a^j inputs into the production system.[9]

14.3.2 Industry Location, Development, Programming and Policy

A very important factor in determining the relative economic power of any nation within the world system is its resource endowment. Given that endowment, it becomes pertinent to determine the types of basic industries that can locate and efficiently produce in that nation. The level of operation of these industries in a nation can be fruitfully derived with comparative cost analysis, industrial complex analysis, or both, in conjunction with other types of analyses that take into account political and social factors. These basic industry projections, when combined with an appropriately specified input-output or econometric model, can then suggest the economic strength of a nation in terms of production, investment, and thus its military capability and its ability to nurture research and development and thereby further such strengths.

Another tool, linear programming, employing much of the constant production coefficient approach of input-output can be fruitfully employed to maximize some objective of a national or regional economic system. This maximization is subject to resource (e.g., labor and capital) constraints and other constraints that may be set on the pollution of the environment, the inequality of income among classes of population, or on rates of unemployment among regions. More generally, linear programming is useful in establishing tradeoffs among different policies. Such tradeoffs may indicate how much improvement in environmental quality can be obtained for a given cutback in military expenditures, how much more low-income housing can be obtained for a reduction in highway construction, how much educational and cultural infrastructure is possible with an increase in business tax rates, and so forth.[10]

14.3.3 Noneconomic Commodities: Production and Exchange

The above discussion pertains primarily to tangible goods and economic services. However, many other goods, primarily nontangibles, are relevant. Using the symbol "c" to indicate the precise definition of a value or attribute as a commodity, we list at the left center of Figure 14-10 such noneconomic goods as c-power, c-solidarity, c-participation, c-well-being, c-rectitude, c-affection, c-sociality, c-skill, c-enlightenment, c-achievement, c-love-tendered, and c-sanctions. Further, we may add to this list commodities such as c-security and c-identity, which are particularly relevant for nations.

One classic noneconomic good which can only be produced and not exchanged among individuals and sectors is c-solidarity. As suggested by the early work of Lewin, Festinger, and others in group dynamics, individuals within a group can and do interact to produce solidarity, cohesiveness, or other commodities closely associated with c-solidarity. Among such are c-morale, c-sociality, and c-security. In one sense, much of the early work on group dynamics and of the Homans school, as mathematically formulated by Simon (see Isard, T. Smith, et al. 1969:chap. 15) and subsequently extended by Coleman (1964, 1979), Fararo (1973) and others, pertain to fundamental processes going on within the broad social production system.

Although operational frameworks and indices are yet to be devised to measure these goods and transactions in them, they must be made explicit within conceptual frameworks and theories—since the concept of noneconomic commodities enables us to bring into the production system the activities of diverse social and political groups that produce noneconomic goods and facilitate the exchange of them.

If one views economic production and economic market exchange as belonging to the Parsons A subsystem pertaining to the economy, one should then view social and political group activities designed to produce noneconomic goods and facilitate their exchange as belonging to the Parsons integrative I subsystem (see Parsons et al. 1961). Just as economic goods may be produced for export, so likewise can noneconomic goods. Just as economic goods may be internally exchanged in a market within a nation, so can noneconomic goods.

Just as we think of prices relating to economic goods, so may we do with respect to noneconomic goods. Difficulties arise here, however, because of our current inability to define precisely a unit of noneconomic good. Hence, prices for noneconomic goods are typically intangible. Finally, just as we may associate money income with the production of economic goods and the sale of labor and services of capital goods, we may also think of intangible (but effective) income associated with the production and exchange of noneconomic goods.

14.3.4 A General Equilibrium Framework

We have cited operational techniques to analyze the production of economic goods. Unfortunately, because noneconomic goods are not well defined or measurable, we do not have parallel operational techniques for treating their production. However, we can expand the restricted general economic equilibrium framework to incorporate economic, ecologic, and noneconomic goods and other aspects of the reality of the social system.[11]

Behavioral Units: Individuals, Organizations, Traders, and Governments.   In a general equilibrium framework succinctly sketched in the center of Figure 14–10 we may consider the list of economic, ecologic, and other noneconomic goods already mentioned. Associated with each is a tangible or intangible price established at a formal or informal market. Individuals and organizations come to these markets to exchange. We may think of m individual consumers and n producers in the nation. Some of the latter may be one-person units (e.g., a corner-grocery-store entrepreneur or a professional such as a private nurse). Others may be cooperative or noncooperative production organizations.

When we consider individuals, we can think of each in many roles:

1. as a one-person producer in isolation from society, producing for own and family consumption;
2. as a one-person producer in society, interacting with individuals outside his immediate family;
3. as a producer of c-love tendered through the giving of gifts to other individuals;
4. as an active participant in a noncooperative (such as a business firm);

5.   as a purchaser at the market of economic goods for own and family consumption and for gift giving;
6.   as a seller at the market of labor and of commodities he holds in stock;
7.   as a member of diverse cooperatives, small groups, religious organizations, and a constituent of diverse governments; and so forth.

For the individual, the performance of these various economic, social, and political roles involves conflicts for a number of reasons, including time, budget, and other constraints. (He has only a fixed amount of time to allocate to them and a limited money income to be spent on goods associated with them.) Within these constraints we may think of the individual as maximizing utility. He selects an action (which can have many components) and in so doing resolves the conflicts involved in the performance of his various roles.

With respect to production organizations, we may find it useful to think of two categories, although they cannot be sharply distinguished from one another. One category is largely competitive oriented, such as a competitive firm maximizing profits. We designate production organizations in this category as noncooperative, although frequently cooperation with consumers and laborers are involved in their operations. Often the noncooperative is a price-taking unit, having negligible influence upon prices. Given prices, it chooses a technically feasible production plan to maximize its effective income (wherein noneconomic commodities are weighted by intangible prices). A second category consists of cooperatives, such as a religious cult, wherein competitive activities are of lesser significance; there exist rules that specify in large part what every member is to contribute and receive. These rules simultaneously specify a large part of the cooperative's action—namely, its production plan. Its action space and the independent decisionmaking by its members are frequently highly restricted.

Active participants in a noncooperative are induced to contribute economic (e.g., labor) and noneconomic (e.g., c-respect) commodities to the noncooperative in order to receive from it economic (e.g., wages) and noneconomic (e.g., c-sociality) commodities. While most economic organizations tend to be noncooperative, many can be cooperative. Also, while many social groups, political clubs, families, kinship units, neighborhoods, and diverse communities are cooperatives, frequently they are noncooperatives in the sense that they are motivated to maximize effective income.

Organizations, just as individuals, may have many roles. In one role they may be required to maximize money profits. In another role, they may be required to contribute to community causes designed to promote local welfare, the inducement being receipt of c-respect or avoidance of negative c-sanctions. In still other roles, they may be required to help raise national morale and cohesiveness, minimize encroachments on individual liberties, maximize religious fervor, or enhance the standing of the national society with respect to other basic social and cultural values. These many roles can, however, be incorporated in the objective of maximizing effective income subject to specified constraints or embodied in the rules governing processes internal to cooperatives and their choice of a production plan.

In addition to individual consumers and production organizations, a general equilibrium framework embodies many traders (exporters and importers). The trader essentially chooses a plan covering the shipment from his location (nation) of many commodities to each of many destination points to maximize his gains from trade.

Administrative government units are distinct from political organizations (designed to produce c-power and related commodities) and from other cooperative and noncooperative production organizations. Such units are unique in that they not only produce goods and services in connection with diverse programs, but also, without the help of formal or informal markets, distribute goods and services to their constituents. (Some of these goods, such as medical services and welfare payments, are diminished when consumed by or allocated to a constituent. Others, such as police protection and environmental regulation, are not.) There exist many different types of administrative government units, general and program-specific; and each individual and nongovernment organization may be a constituent of a number of them. Each administrative government unit, subject to the tax moneys assigned to it by its appropriate legislative counterpart, seeks to allocate its resources among programs and distribute the goods and services of these programs to maximize the level of some index generally taken to measure constituency welfare—or to maximize some "welfare function" as defined and perceived by the top administrator and his associates.

Control Processes: Market (Economic and Noneconomic), Cooperative, and Legislative (Political).   In addition to the many and diverse behaving units in a society, there exist control processes. These processes regulate individual and group demands upon the system and resolve conflicting requirements and pressures. One is the familiar economic market mechanism. For example, where conditions of pure competition prevail, many individuals and noncooperatives enter the market to buy and sell commodities. No one individual or noncooperative is (or thinks it is) strong enough to influence any price. Each assumes that prices are independent of its own actions. Market equilibrium exists when the supply of and demand for a commodity are equated, or when there is an excess supply at zero price.

A second control process is the process that guides individuals in their active participation in noncooperatives. We conceive that there exists internal to each noncooperative a market (or submarket) to which individuals may bring commodities for exchange. As on the economic market, at the noncooperative market the value of the individual's contribution (supplies) must equal in exchange the value of commodities received (effective demand). For any economic commodity, the price at each noncooperative market is the same as at the economic market of the region. For noneconomic commodities, internal prices are set at the noncooperative market in accord with the forces of supply and demand at that market. Equilibrium at the noncooperative market for any noneconomic commodity exists when the demand for that commodity equals its supply or when excess supply exists at zero price. The organizational market price for a noneconomic commodity is an intangible price (that is, a price that cannot easily be stated in terms of a currency), which represents the money equivalent of a unit of that commodity in that market.

There are other basic processes within a society. Within cooperatives processes exist that establish and then carry out rules of operation and resolve conflicts among members. Also, within a society there are electoral processes. These can be incorporated within a general equilibrium framework.

The most important nonmarket processes are associated with political (particularly legislative) processes. We may hypothesize a body of representatives within each government unit. Each member of the body of representatives of the government unit represents the interests and desires of a subset of that unit's constituency. Usually, the representatives' constituencies are disjoint and collectively exhaust the unit's constituency.

At meetings of representatives, a political process is used to set the size and distribution of taxation and the allocation of tax revenues among competing programs. This may be through a competitive process similar to a "fictitious" market with an implicit price for tax money. If so, each representative would need to be responsible in the sense that whenever the implicit price of tax money rises (falls), he reduces (increases) the level of one or more programs he proposes, or increases (decreases) proposed tax rates, or both. Alternatively, the determination may be through a cooperative process wherein the rules for reaching a compromise proposal are prespecified, or it may be through some combination of cooperative and competitive processes.

The above general equilibruim framework is useful as a conceptual device. It is clearly nonoperational. To make it operational requires unrealistic assumptions. For example, input-output and linear programming require linear production and consumption functions, while comparative cost and industrial complex analyses ignore feedback effects from other sectors.

14.3.5 Macromodels of Social Group Production and Behavior

In treating noneconomic commodities, the above general equilibrium scheme emphasizes microbehavior. However, it is also useful to consider macro-type models, such as employed within group dynamics and similar approaches. Here, as indicated at the right in the center of Figure 14-10, we may think of such macrogroup variables as c-sociality or friendliness (F), activity (A), interaction, c-solidarity, or cohesiveness (C), pressure to achieve uniformity (U), pressure to communicate (P), perceived discrepancy of opinion and dissonance (D), and receptivity (L). Such macromodels can also be related to the microlevel of behavior. Or we can consider such macrovariables as orientation, heredity, and pressure to resolve conflicts, and consider steady states (defined in terms of these variables) in a macroframework. Into this framework we can introduce processes relating to learning, changing aspirations, and so forth.[12]

14.3.6 Emergence of Leaders

We also must consider processes in microtime (wherein system structure remains basically unchanged) that govern the emergence in the group or society of new leaders—economic entrepreneurs (capitalists), evangelists, political bosses, popular presidents, and dictators. These leaders may be of the Schumpeterian-type—i.e., individuals with high levels of need for achievement (designated n-achievement) who explore the terrain, identify slack resources, magnify the power of these slack resources via a credit system (economic, political, and social), and successfully produce large amounts of c-power. It is the possession of such c-power that categorizes them as leaders. In these processes, the emerging leaders frequently use an initial stock of information quite distinct from that possessed by other individuals. They invest heavily in acquiring new information to exploit the slack resources at their command and to induce others to align with them to generate agglomeration economies and externalities. Such new leaders may influence the production and consumption functions and other relationships within the production subsystem, P^K, of each K.

Processes by which leaders emerge are also paralleled by processes leading to time rate of change in macrovariables such as capital stock ($\dot{K}$), trade ($\dot{U}$), labor force ($\dot{L}$), environmental pollution ($\dot{R}$), consumption ($\dot{C}$), and production ($\dot{Y}$), within the nation. See the bottom right of Figure 14–10. At times, certain thresholds with respect to such variables are attained. Abrupt transitions in system structure may then result, and these are associated with change in macrotime.

14.3.7 The Hierarchical Structure of Regional Production within the National System

The production system P^K of nation K may encompass a whole set of subsystems, each subsystem being a region within the nation. Then our discussion of many nations within a world system can pertain to many regions α, β, . . . within a national system, and our discussion of a nation in a world system can pertain to a region in a national system. For example, take the production system of region α of nation K, represented by the P^K_α box at the lower right in Figure 14–10. Into this box comes an input a^K_α from the decisionmaking unit in that region. Next, for understanding regional production, we may employ regional econometric, regional demographic, regional input-output, comparative cost, industrial complex, and linear programming models. Also, there may be within the nation an R box with which (as shall be discussed later) may be associated interregional input-output, balanced regional input-output, interregional linear and nonlinear programming, and interregional comparative cost and industrial complex analysis. The latter are to be linked to ecological, transport, labor, decisionmaking, and other locational cost differentials among regions within nation K. Additionally, we can construct for each region a general equilibrium framework and macromodels pertaining to noneconomic goods, think of new regional leaders emerging, and so forth. Moreover, we can do the same for each subregion.

In short, we can model a decisionmaking system C^K and production system P^K for nation K as embracing a hierarchical structure of regions, subregions, localities, and so forth. Accordingly, all hierarchical theory and applied analysis pertains and can be utilized.[13]

14.4 THE DETAIL OF THE R BOX, THE REAL INTERACTION SUBSYSTEM

Having considered the internal characteristics of the production system P^K of each nation K (K = J, L, . . .), we take up certain external characteristics of these systems, in particular their interdependence. That is, we now must examine the R box. See Figure 14-11.

14.4.1 Different Kinds of Interface Inputs

As already indicated, the R box embodies systemic interrelations on the real level. This box generates the interface inputs feeding into P^K, the production system of each nation K. The environmental pollution that diffuses into nation K particularly from the part of the world surrounding nation K, can be one critical interface input (see the arrows to and from the left side of Figure 14-11). Such pollution interrelates the ecologic subsystem of K with that of the rest of the world. Migration into and out of nation K, determined by conditions both internal and external to the nation, is another interface input. Imports and exports from K as governed by the operation of the world's market and price system can be a third. With regard to noneconomic commodities, there may be exchanges involving flows of

Figure 14-11.   The Real Interaction Box R.

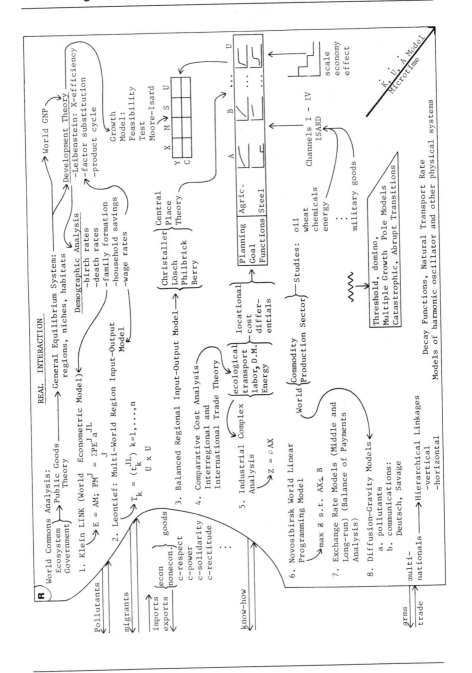

c-respect, as when a Nobel Prize is awarded to a constituent; or of c-power, as formerly associated with the stability of the post-World War II U.S. dollar; or of c-solidarity stemming from sharing value systems and ideology, for example, democratic processes or membership in an international organization such as World Health Organization; or of c-rectitude, as within the hierarchical structure of the Roman Catholic Church spread over many nations.

14.4.2 Econometric (LINK), Input-Output, Central Place Theory, and Linear Programming Methods of Analysis

As with the production subsystem of a nation, a number of operational techniques exist for examining and analyzing the interrelations among national production subsystems. One is the worldwide econometric model LINK, a macro-type model (Klein 1977). See Figure 14–11, upper left. This model ties together the ongoing major econometric models being used in each major country or region of the world. No attempt is made to construct at one research institution a standardized model to be applied to each country or region. Rather, the model assumes that each model-builder knows his own country (region) best. Each model-builder is free to design his model, save for equations like: (1) $E = AM$, which relates exports E of a country to every country's imports M via a matrix of constants A; and (2) $PM^K = \sum_L PE^K a^{KL}$, which ties K's import prices PM^K to export prices PE^K via a set of constants a^{KL} reflecting the relative amount of trade with each country L. In this way, a coherent system model is obtained having common import prices and consistent estimates of exports for world commodities. Then on the basis of past relationships the model can forecast exports, imports, GNP, and other basic magnitudes for each major nation such as Japan, France, Germany, the United Kingdom, the Soviet Union, Sweden, and the United States, and for world regions such as the Socialist economies of Eastern Europe (excluding the Soviet) and the developing countries of the world as an aggregate. System imports and exports are indicated in Figure 14–11.

Another technique that goes beyond strictly economic goods and encompasses critical ecologic goods (pollutants) is Leontief's (1977) multiworld region input-output model. Here, for major nations and regions of the world, basic economic sectors are identified with particular emphasis on those that are heavy polluters. The analyst can then project future levels of pollutant emissions in the several major nations and world regions. Once again, imports and exports of economic goods, pollutants, and other ecologic commodities serve as basic interface inputs; and the economy of each nation or world region K is linked to all others via the amount t_k^{JK} of commodity k ($k = 1, \ldots, \ell$) which K draws from a pool to which each nation J contributes.

A balanced world region input-output model has been conceived by Isard (Isard and Liossatos 1979:285–86). This model provides crude but early answers to the questions of national and regional impacts of world policies. It identifies a hierarchical structure of political authorities (world unit, nations, regions, and local areas) and corresponding commodities. *World* commodities have their production and consumption balanced on the *world level only*. *National* commodities have production and consumption balanced both at the *world and national levels*. *Regional* commodities have production and consumption balanced at the *world, national, and regional levels*. *Local* commodities have production and consumption balanced at *all levels*. Though any classification of this type must be blurred, typical world commodities would be nuclear fuel, wheat, oil, capital, and highly specialized labor skills. Typical national commodities might be national newspapers, books, and magazines. Typical regional commodities would be cement and the retail services of department stores. Typical local commodities would be shoe-repair services and corner-grocery retail services. While the balanced regional input-output model permits realization of tremendous savings in cost of information collection and processing, it oversimplifies decisionmaking processes and requires exceedingly strong assumptions such as uniformity of production and consumption behavior across nations and regions. These strong assumptions are the price of the quick and low-cost response to questions of policy impacts that can be dealt with by the model.

In its classification of commodities, the balanced regional input-output model draws upon, and indirectly contributes to, central place theory. See the center of Figure 14–11. Central place theory was initially developed by Christaller (1933) and Lösch (1940) and subsequently refined and widely disseminated by Berry (1967) and his associates. With respect to world organization, Philbrick (1973, 1980) has developed this analysis significantly. In this theory, the physical structure of society is depicted as a hierarchy of urban areas or central places. At the grass roots or lowest level of central places are individuals or family units spread over physical space. These individuals or families cluster in hamlets or neighborhoods to form the next-to-lowest order node (central place). In turn, sets of adjacent hamlets form the next higher node—a village or local government. Villages and local governments and their constituents are subservient to, but also support and sustain, towns and town governments—that is, nodes of a still higher order. In this way, successively higher order nodes—cities, primary urban centers, and metropolises—are formed. At the top of the pyramid is a single first-order node which a future world system capital would be. Society would be organized around this node which would simultaneously control and be controlled by all lower-order nodes and their constituents. The basic forces that lead to the spatial hierarchical organization of society are seen to be: (1) economies realized in producing and marketing commodities when scale of operation increases and (2) costs of transportation, communication, or other "frictions" involved in overcoming physical, ideological, or social distances. Thus, where scale economies are small and transport costs high, as in the production of bricks, production will be decentralized at many low-order nodes. Where scale economies are very large and transport and like costs are relatively low, as in the case of books or tractors, production will be concentrated at a relatively few points, each serving a very large market area and constituency. In the case of a world commodity, for example, reprocessed nuclear fuel, the tremendous scale economies in production (including costs of safeguards against diversion and protection from radiation hazards) suggest that there be only one or a relatively few production locations in the world, despite significant transport costs.

In terms of depicting real interaction in the world system, the approach of central place theory has basic limitations. It fails to take into account the uneven geographic distribution of resources, uneven topography, and uneven capability for transporting goods, people, and ideas, and the uneven distributions of populations and skills, that have developed in the world in part because of random factors. So while central place theory supplements the more mechanistic balanced regional and multiworld region input-output models and the macro-econometric LINK model by considering scale economies and transportation costs, it does not capture the implications of the uneven geographic distribution of resources. Here, locational analysis based primarily on locational cost differentials is desirable, as is embodied in comparative cost and industrial complex analysis.[14] We may think of transport cost differentials which have historically largely governed the location of the iron and steel industry, labor cost differentials which largely govern the geographical distribution of textile production, power cost differentials which largely govern the distribution of aluminum production, and decisionmaking cost differentials which largely govern the location of financial and central administrative headquarters of huge corporate entities. Finally, we must consider ecological cost differentials which are increasingly important; as the capacity of different regional environments to absorb pollutants (air, water, noise) become exhausted, ecologic costs rise sharply at these locations when compared to other locations in the world whose absorptive capacities are underutilized. In brief, locational cost differentials are instrumental in determining where certain key basic industries are distributed in the world and in determining the time pattern of change in such distribution. Such comparative cost and industrial complex analyses can be usefully complemented by intensive studies of particular basic economic sectors (such as energy and chemicals) and world commodities (such as oil, wheat, and steel). (For example, for energy see, among others, Haefele 1981.)

In thinking of interconnection among world regions and possible scenarios for the future of differentially developed regions, one might combine interregional linear programming (e.g., the Novosibirsk World Linear Programming Model)[15] with the above techniques and with a set of planning goal (target) functions, which may stem from the cognitive interaction box. Such could yield a single Moore-Isard type model.[16] This model considers explicitly commodity input requirements for capacity expansions. It can test the feasibility of a set of planning goal functions for each world region to identify inconsistencies and contradictions. It also can check the efficiency of a proposed world development path—where an efficient path has the property that no one world region can be made better off (for example, assigned a higher growth rate) without detriment to another.

Critical for the effective use of all the above models is the need to develop analysis pertaining to changes in exchange rates in the middle and long run. Such changes directly affect relative prices in all nations and their competitive ability in world markets, and thus, any middle and long-run projections of industrial and economic development. Acceptable exchange rate models for the middle and long run, with associated balance of payments analysis, are yet to be constructed.

14.4.3 Multiregion General Equilibrium Inclusive of the Ecologic Subsystem

All these models for the real interaction system are in their static formulation derivable from a general equilibrium system framework, noted at top center of Figure 14-11. When discussing the P^K production system of nation K, we sketched briefly a general equilibrium framework. Now, viewing a system of nations, we broaden this framework to incorporate many nations—each a political region. (We can also conceive of other exhaustive and nonoverlapping sets of regions.) This leads to the notion of an interregional general equilibrium system of U regions, each having m consumers, n producers, $\bar{f}$ traders (exporters and importers), and $\bar{e}$ government units of diverse types. We then can detail this structure in a fashion parallel to our discussion in Section 14.3.4. Here, however, the supply = demand equations in each political region (nation) dependent on large amounts of imports and exports become more critical, and so do balance of payments equations to account for movement of gold and currency. Moreover, behavioral equations that govern the choice of shipment plans by traders in each region become more complex because of the need to consider exchange rate fluctuations.

The extension of a general equilibrium system to many regions—political, cultural, or other—suggests that this system should be extended to cover the niches and habitats of diverse species as well as meaningful areas of the world's ecologic system. Conceptually, this extension involves many natural production activities in each region (such as phytoplankton, crustacea, and fish production). All these activities can be listed in a suitable order within a major section of an input-output table headed *Ecologic System*. The ecologic system might be grouped into two major categories, *Biotic* and *Abiotic*. Further, each of these can be disaggregated. For example, abiotic production activities can be listed as *climatic, geologic, physiographic, hydrologic,* and *soil*. Biotic can be disaggregated into *plants* and *animals*. Thus, natural wild strawberry production would fall under plants in biotic, and winter flounder would fall under animals. In such a table, we see exports of ecologic goods (pure water and pure air) from the ecologic system to the economic system, exports of economic bads (SO_2, B.O.D.) from the economic system to the ecologic system, and so forth. Accordingly, we have a table of four major blocks of cells. One refers to the economic system and contains intersector coefficients. A second refers to the ecologic system and contains interprocess coefficients. A third lists the input-output coefficients regarding ecologic commodities associated with the economic sectors. A fourth lists input-ouput coefficients regarding economic commodities associated with ecologic processes.[17]

Viewing the LINK model, diverse input-output and programming models, locational analyses (comparative costs and industrial complex), and central place theory against the background of the general interregional equilibrium framework just discussed affords one useful channel of synthesis for conducting world system analysis at the real production and interaction levels.[18]

14.4.4 Diffusion Processes, Multinationals, and World Public Goods

To analyze the spread of pollutants over physical space and to attack world environmental problems, we need diffusion models wherein nations are both behavioral and production units. See lower left of Figure 14–11. These diffusion models have much in common with the gravity-type models of regional science pertaining to the flows of economic goods, migrants, and commuting labor force among the regions or subareas of a "relatively" closed economy.[19]

We have very few operational models pertaining to the flow of noneconomic goods among national production subsystems. Deutsch and Savage (1960) have developed a gravity-type model relating to communications by international mail; and such a model can be extended to communication by telephone and other media (see Klaassen et al. 1972). Still much needs to be done here.

Multinational corporations play a key role in world interaction processes today. Because they have both production locations and administrative headquarters all over the world, they act to interconnect different parts of the global system. They diffuse and disseminate ideas, customs, technology, organizational forms, and management practices throughout the system as well as generate foreign currency flows and exports and imports of goods and bads, both economic and ecologic. They also play a strategic role in the arms trade, and indirectly exercise influence on arms races among and escalation of military expenditures within developing nations. Study of their functioning, especially covert, is essential.

Military expenditures within developing nations is in many cases a major impediment to their economic development. This assertion is closely related to the Leibenstein X-efficiency approach (see Leibenstein and Gentile 1979) which seriously questions the relevance of traditional economic analysis for understanding what transpires within developing countries in general. See the upper right of Figure 14–11. Selective rationality (reflecting limited perceptual and analytic capacities) rather than full rationality, personality factors, power drives, external pressures, and inertia are pervasive among individuals, households, firms, and other behaving units in such countries.

These elements seriously interfere with the operation of factor substitution and product cycle processes that traditional economic analysis would suggest. They generate markets that do not operate in accord with Western economic thought. Moreover, their influence upon demographic factors such as natural growth rates and the related phenomena of family formation, labor supply, wage rates, household savings, and the like are of critical importance. Further study of these relationships is essential for better understanding of how developing economies function and how their foreign policy decisions are reached.

While the R box pertains to nations in a world system, we can imagine within it an $\bar{R}$ box for the many regions within any given national system (when that nation's relations with the rest of the system are prespecified),[20] and within the $\bar{R}$ box (for a national system) an $\bar{\bar{R}}$ box for the subregions of any given region (when that region's relations with the rest of the national system are prespecified), and so on. In short, the pattern of real interaction that is relevant and to be analyzed depends upon the one or more levels in a hierarchical structure at which decisionmaking on an issue is of importance.

Additionally, the R box covers the production of world public goods. Here we may think of regulatory (advisory) activities of the International Atomic Energy Agency and perhaps in the future its operation of a nuclear fuel-reprocessing plant, or of a satellite weather report service provided via cooperative arrangements among organizations from many nations, or the exploration and management of ocean resources by a new U.N. unit. Appropriate analysis for such public goods production is sorely needed.

14.4.5 The Subsystem's Dynamics in Microtime, and Threshold (Takeoff) and Domino Effects

Finally, when we treat the real part of the world system, the subsystem P, and its R component we can take into account certain processes in *microtime*. These microtime processes are reflected in the simple $\dot{K}$ models of economists (Arrow and Kurtz 1970; Intriligator 1971) where $\dot{K}$ is the time rate of change of capital stock; or in the more complex $\{\dot{K}, \dot{U}\}$ and $\{\dot{K}, \dot{U}, \dot{A}\}$ models of regional scientists (Isard and Liossatos 1979:chaps. 6 and 14, respectively) where $\dot{U}$ is the time rate of change of flow of goods through a location and $\dot{A}$ is the time rate of change of accessibility of a given location to all other locations in the system. See the bottom right of Figure 14-11. However, such models, which parallel models of the harmonic oscillator, motion of a string, motion of a spring, electromagnetic waves, and other physical phenomena, and which involve decay functions and a natural transport rate, are not truly dynamic from a social science standpoint. They may indicate the path of adjustment given a perturbation in the economic system. Or they may indicate an optimal path of growth for reaching, at the end of a given period, certain targets that an economic system sets (assuming no structural change during that period). Or they may reflect an optimal economic investment path for a situation wherein a non-negligible, positive discount of future income (utility) is appropriate. However, in no case do they capture structural change in the system.

From an evolutionary, historic standpoint, such anemic dynamic models are only useful for short-run analysis. We know that practically every system is evolving, its structure constantly undergoing change. For analytical purposes, then, we currently find it useful to distinguish between macrotime wherein structure does change, and microtime wherein structure changes at most only negligibly. In effect, processes assumed in our analysis to occur only in microtime take place at one and only one point in macrotime. In general, history corresponds to macrotime (see the lower left of Figure 14-9), but our formal analysis of change in macrotime is woefully weak.

However, there is one point at which knowledge of macrotime processes is fruitfully developing. This is the area of multiple-growth phenomena and possibilities. Consistent with the framework of Thom's catastrophe theory (1974) and Prigogine's far-from-equilibrium analysis (1967), it is possible to replicate formally, and with a certain amount of rationale, spread effects of major discontinuous growth phenomena in a domino-like fashion. Once a primary region reaches the point where it can "take off," because certain thresholds have been achieved which makes possible new major agglomeration economies and externalities, a model can be constructed to indicate how other regions may experience sudden discontinuous growth due to the increases in demand for their exports in the first region, and so forth (Isard and Liossatios 1978a). A succession of "takeoffs" can then be realized, leading to a significant domino-type effect. Similarly, a model can be constructed to indicate how a big step disarmament by one or two big powers can lead to a succession of major declines in military expenditures among other lesser nations (Isard and Liossatos 1978).

14.5 THE DETAIL OF THE C^K BOX, THE DECISIONMAKING SUBSYSTEM OF K

Having treated the real production systems and interactions among them for a set of nations, we proceed to the decisionmaking subsystem C^K for each nation K, K = J, L. . . . See Figure 14–12.

14.5.1 Decisionmaking in Less Complicated Situations

Going back far enough in time, we may imagine that at some point in his development man reached a stage where he perceived consciously that he had more than one option for action in a given situation. Presumably thinking was involved and a decision was made to choose that action judged to lead to the better outcome. After further development, man perceived not only that there were two options, say: (1) wait for prey and (2) seek prey; but also that there was an environment, and that it might take one of two states: (1) rain and (2) shine. This would involve a still more complicated decision problem for him. After still more development, he recognized that in certain situations there are many options, many states of the environment, or both. As he perceived such complicated decision situations, he might have perceived other decision situations in which another behaving unit is present—a member of the opposite sex, for instance. Thus, we imagine him making very simple rules by which to reach deci-

Figure 14-12.   The Cognitive Decisionmaking Box C^K.

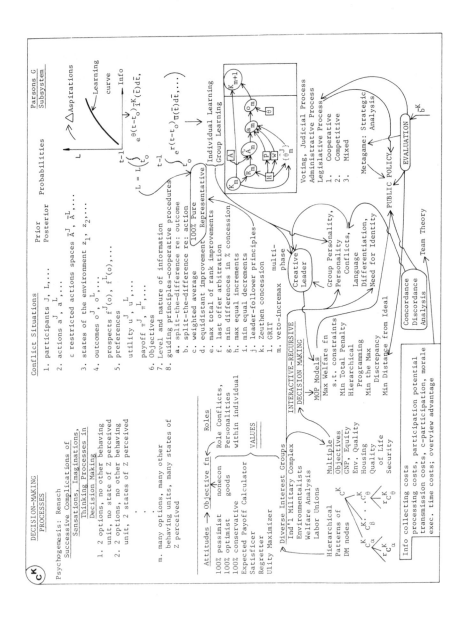

sions in the early stages of his existence, and more complicated rules in later stages. This ability to perceive (and generate) increasingly complex decision situations might be viewed, using Rensch's term, as "psychogenesis" (Rensch 1960) involving successive complications of sensations and imagination. See the upper right of Figure 14-12.

But the simple decision problems that primitive man confronted—such as two alternatives when he is not aware or cannot afford to be aware of the state of the environment—also occur today, often in very critical situations. For example, a prominent political figure may confront such a choice when he is suddenly faced with abduction. Wishing to stay alive, he has the choice of (1) letting himself be abducted, with a probability of subsequently being killed or (2) attempting to escape, with a probability of being shot in the attempt. This situation may require a split-second decision wherein the political figure has no time to take stock of the current state of the environment inclusive of the characteristics of his abductors.

A slightly more complicated decision might arise when (1) there are two possible states of the environment: a security force may or may not show up in time to save him from his abductors, and (2) the political figure has sufficient time to consider these two states—perhaps because of the time required for the abductors to break through the ring of his bodyguards. A still more complicated situation exists when the political figure realizes that he confronts a group led by an emotionally upset leader prepared to assassinate him. He (the political figure) then may consider the option of choosing a nonviolent approach to dissuade the leader and his group from killing him.

These situations may be generalized to involve many states of the environment, many behaving units each with a restricted action space, and many other factors such as perceptive ability, available information (both objective and subjective and its uncertain nature), propensity to take risk, the existence of threats, and so forth.

14.5.2 A Formal Statement of the Decision Problem

For a tremendously large number of individuals ranging from a primitive man type to a high political leader we may formally define a decision situation. This situation involves for the individual at a particular point in time and space a choice problem (with or without the presence of other behaving units) comprising, as discussed on pages 16–24, the following elements: actions and joint actions, state of the environment, outcomes (including prospects) and outcome functions, preferences and utility (payoff) functions, guiding principles, objectives and objective functions (inclusive of attitudes), and level and nature of information. See the top center of Figure 14–12. We do not consider it necessary to repeat these materials here.

14.5.3 Attitudes and Values as Basic Factors

Even in the very simplest decision situation it is clear that the *attitude* variable is a basic factor. See the left center of Figure 14–12. Let us say that the political leader knows from past experience or history that if he attempts to escape, the abductor will certainly shoot at him and that the probability of his being fatally shot is 50 percent. On the other hand, if he allows himself to be abducted, his expectation of death will depend upon his attitude. If he is a 100 percent optimist and believes that God is with him, he has zero expectation of death; thus he will not choose to attempt an escape. If he is an extreme pessimist and believes that the world is out to get him, he expects with almost 100 percent certainty that he will be killed by his abductors. Thus he will choose to attempt an escape. If he is neither of the above and believes in calculating probabilities on the basis of "objective" information and other factors, he may instantly evaluate the situation and determine a probability of being killed by his abductors were he to choose not to escape. If this probability is below 0.5, then, as an expected payoff (utility) maximizer, he will not attempt to escape. If it is above that figure, he will choose to attempt to escape. Other attitudes have been examined in connection with the discussion of objectives on pages 20–24 and on pages 206–207.

In addition to the attitudinal factor, the values of the decision-maker can also be critical. For example, in addition to the value attached to survival, there may be in the leader's culture a significant value attached to courage and fearlessness in threatening situations. Thus, on the one hand, he may calculate the value of the cowardly action "attempt to escape" as 0.5 times the value of life. On the other hand, if there is a 40 percent chance of surviving if he allows himself to be abducted but also a large amount of c-respect accorded to him by his society for being fearless, he calculates the value of the action ''do not attempt to escape'' as 0.4 times the value of both life and the c-respect that he would receive.

At this point we observe that the utility or payoff function, which records the values that the political leader assigns to each of his actions, includes not only the economic commodities normally associated with it by economists and psychologists, but also noneconomic commodities. The latter are extremely important when we consider the several roles of the political leader. In his role as a consumer he may maximize utility from consumption of economic goods. However, as already indicated, he may receive certain noneconomic goods such as c-respect and c-sociality as a member of a social circle. He may receive c-prestige and c-rectitude as a member of a religious organization. He may receive c-affection as a member of a family and kinship unit, and most significant for many political leaders, he may receive c-power as a member of his political party and system. Hence, when seeking to understand and influence his behavior, we must include all these goods as arguments in his utility function. See the discussion on pages 332–338.

14.5.4 Conflicts Internal to the Decisionmaker

In the traditional consumption theory of economics, the individual is subject to a budget constraint. Additionally, within society, the individual is subject to a labor constraint. He needs to allocate his daily twenty-four hours to sleep, leisure, and diverse activities. Clearly, conflict arises in the allocation of his marginal hours. These hours can be spent in earning more income to consume more goods, or with the family to produce and receive more c-affection, or with a political organization to produce and receive more c-power. Such conflict is internal to the individual and is resolved once he can state his preferences unambiguously. He then may choose the action, consistent with his guiding principles, that optimizes his utility. Such conflict resolution, however, is not as simple as appears at first blush since guiding principles, too, can be either relaxed or strengthened, and thereby affect the production and receipt of economic and noneconomic goods. Moreover, additional constraints imposed on his actions by all elements of his environment may leave few alternatives in his restricted action space that are perceived as feasible (noncontradictory).

At this point we should recognize the existence of different personalities within the individual. He may be aggressive and impersonal when as an economic entrepreneur he is a profit maximizer. He may be warm and friendly within a family situation. He may be passive and a follower within a church organization. He may be cool, tense, impersonal, and a "rational" expected-payoff calculator in political decision situations, yet emotional and "irrational" in crisis conditions. As a political leader he may be a regretter. The possession of several such personalities may intensify the internal conflicts the individual confronts.

14.5.5 Conflicts among Several Participants in a Decisionmaking Process and Cooperative Procedures

Having touched upon some conflicts within an individual as a single participant in the decisionmaking unit C^K of nation K, we now examine conflicts among individuals within that unit. As noted, typically many behaving units are involved in a decision situation. Frequently, we have a game-type situation where the payoff or utility one participant receives depends upon the action taken by the other. This point is implicit in Figure 14–3. In these interdependent decision situations guiding principles or other elements involving cooperative approaches can be employed.

We have extensively discussed these principles and approaches in connection with the conflict management procedures developed in Chapters 3 through 8 and 10 and 11. Some of these are listed in the center of Figure 14–12. They are split-the-difference regarding outcomes, split-the-difference regarding actions, weighted average, equidistant improvement, max total of rank improvements, last offer arbitration, min difference in percent concession, max equal increments, min equal decrements, leader-follower principles, Zeuthen concession, GRIT, and veto-incremax. Moreover, as noted toward the left bottom of Figure 14–12, when we treat the formulation of public policy (within a nation), an extremely important area for understanding multination conflicts, typically several conflicting and noncommensurable objectives are involved. Such may be maximizing growth of GNP; minimizing discrepancies in per capita income; improvement of environmental quality, housing, and the general quality of life; and military security. Typically there exist several different interest groups: the industrial-military complex; the environmentalists; economists concerned with inflation, unemployment, and welfare; labor unions; and others, each with representatives in the decision-making body. In general, each of these different groups has different preferences with respect to the possible programs of a national government. In general, each finds a different set of policies optimal. Thus, conflict exists. In such a situation, recursive-interactive programming may be introduced by which, during a series of successive steps, additional information is introduced to arrive at a compromise or satisficing solution. Here multiobjective programing (MOP) models, as discussed in earlier chapters, can often be effectively used. For example, welfare may be maximized, subject to constraints; total penalty may be minimized; hierarchical programming may be pursued; the min of the max discrepancy may be identified; or the distance from a technically infeasible ideal point may be minimized.

We could discuss a number of other techniques—such as concordance-discordance analysis—that have been used or have significant potential. However, for the moment we have indicated sufficiently the nature and variety of the approaches that are currently being explored. (See Table 12-1.) In our discussion of the I box on pages 537–538 we return to this subject.

In addition, solutions to conflict situations on specific issues may be reached by majority voting procedures, or on several issues at a time by majority voting procedures wherein logrolling (vote trading by representatives) is practiced. There are also judicial, administrative, and legislative processes that involve conflict management. All these are too well known to be discussed here.

14.5.6 Individual Learning Processes

Finally, as already mentioned several times, while these various procedures are pursued, especially those that involve several rounds or plays, learning may take place. See the right side of Figure 14-12. Learning is a process in the cognitive system that parallels in part dynamics in the real production system. There exist many learning models. One type of model might be an analytic model that projects the behavior of an individual (or group) in a sequential decision situation. It is posited that the individual behaves rationally and employs logical deduction in identifying and taking an optimal action at each point, given the situation as he perceives and knows it. In contrast are the adaptive models, deterministic and stochastic. These characterize the individual's play-by-play choice behavior as a process whose transition from state to state is governed by some underlying behavioral mechanism. Adaptive models involve a much less elaborate set of assumptions about the individual's behavior than do rational-type analytic models. Adaptive models assume only that there exist certain discernible patterns in the individual's choices from play to play which tend to reveal some "structural" behavior, be it rational or otherwise. The problem is to discover that part of the individual's behavior which remains invariant from play to play and thereby to reveal as much as possible the underlying structure of this behavior.

Hence, while the analytic and adaptive models differ with respect to the kind of choice behavior postulated, each focuses on certain time-invariant aspects of the individual's decision behavior—whether "rational decision policies" or simple "decision mechanisms."

To be specific, consider a simple adaptive learning model of the Bush-Mosteller variety (see Isard, T. Smith, et al. 1969:chap. 15) involving a stochastic behavioral mechanism based on response reinforcement. If the individual's action space is defined to consist of two actions, a_1 and a_2, and if the choice of one of these actions, say a_1, on any play t leads to a reward for the individual, then it is posited that the probability of his choosing a_1 on the next play will be reinforced. Further, it is posited that such reinforcement is subject to a certain diminishing intensity, which tends to reduce successive reinforcements gradually to zero, thereby producing some limiting value $\lambda_1 (0 \leq \lambda_1 \leq 1)$ which the probability of choosing a_1 approaches asymptotically as $t \to \infty$.

In addition to reinforcement, there should be in an individual's learning model a factor relating to continual change in the individual's stock of information, inclusive of experience. For example, we may consider his stock at any moment to be the accumulation of bits of information $\bar{i}(t)$ and $\bar{u}(t)$ that he and the groups to which he belongs have respectively garnered over time, properly discounted or, in the case of certain pieces of information, upcounted. But the learning process is much more complex. It may be a function of the order in time in which the individual's actions and events in his environment occur, of the socialization process to which he was exposed, and of the "scripts," "schema" and "packages" to which he was subjected as a result of being associated with diverse groups.[21]

14.5.7 Group and Macro-Micro Learning Processes

Not only individuals learn; groups do as well. Usually group learning takes place simultaneously with learning by individuals in the group. Such then requires a more complex model. For example, consider a situation in which a policy of a political party is to be determined. Let the determination of this policy involve a series of rounds of deliberations and discussions over a number of months, and let these deliberations and discussions involve negligible costs to the political party. The policy may relate to the level of military expenditures. Security may be viewed as the output of such expenditures. To be specific, we may imagine that there is a particular function Θ to be estimated which links national security to the level of military expenditures. If the party members were fully aware of this outcome function Θ, presumably they could settle on a final policy statement. But the individual members are not fully informed of Θ. We then can imagine that the individual members $K = J, L, \ldots$ attempt to estimate this outcome function on each round, $\hat{\Theta}^K_m$ being K's estimate on any round m. See the diagram at the center of the right-hand side of Figure 14–12.

Assume that each member must estimate the "best" level of military expenditures—that is, the level that in his mind would yield maximum security. In the individual's mind, every other level yields less security, the difference from maximum security increasing with difference between that level and the estimated individual's "best" level. Now let each member K in the initial round of discussion propose the level he considers best as the optimal course of action for the group. The leader of the group, responsible for constructing on any move a set or agenda of relevant alternatives (namely, the restricted action space $\widetilde{A}_m$ as a subset of the unrestricted action space A), may decide that the largest proposal for military expenditure should not exceed the smallest by more than \$15 billion. (Again, see the diagram at the center of the right-hand side of Figure 14–12.) Such then establishes the maximum spread among alternatives, which constitutes a control variable for the political leader. In locating this spread of alternatives within the action space A to represent the thinking of the various members and reflect the "orientation" R of the party, he may choose as the center point a weighted average of the member's proposals. Once the agenda, that is, the restricted action space $\widetilde{A}_m$, is established and made known, each member makes a proposal within that restricted action space—a proposal reflecting what he thinks is best for the party. We then may imagine that there exists a cooperative procedure (based upon past cultural and other inheritance H) that applies a decision weight to the proposal of each member and accordingly established the party policy a_m for that round as a weighted average.

That party policy is then adopted which, given the actual but unknown function Θ, generates some level of security o_m in the real world. This experience represents an addition to the stock of knowledge K_m. Each member of the political party observes this outcome. Depending on his attitude, state of knowledge, and perceptive ability, this outcome may lead him to change his estimate $\hat{\Theta}_m^\kappa$ of the true outcome function and alter his estimate of the best policy; and thus lead to a new round of decisionmaking. This feedback of information completes the decision cycle. Such feedback becomes a basic piece of information that allows each individual to learn. It reinforces or fails to reinforce his first estimate of the best level of military expenditures and leads him in a second round to choose from the restricted action space perhaps another level of military expenditures as best. Similarly, such feedback allows the leader to learn, and may lead him on the second round to change not only the maximum spread of levels of military expenditures for debate and discussion, but also the central position of the spread. Another weighted average of the members' proposals is obtained that identifies the party's policy on the second round. Such change in the average represents group learning. It leads to a new level of realized security, which then leads to a third round of proposals, and so forth.

Models have been developed that do allow the individuals and the group to learn and that finally converge to an equilibrium position for each individual as well as the group (Isard, T. Smith, et al. 1969: 802–10). Such models also are realistic in terms of individual learning and allow learning by a leader who is guided by more than simple weighted averages. They also can involve the coordinative use of new information.

Simultaneous learning by the group and its members comes to influence (1) the group's orientation and its personality, a basic factor in national decisionmaking and (2) the type of guiding principles and cooperative procedures that may be feasible to propose to that group for use. At the same time, such learning, combined with knowledge of different actions being proposed and procedures employed to resolve differences among group members, changes (increases or relaxes) pressures to achieve group uniformity and in particular to eliminate language and sociocultural differences. However, when the size of a national body and the level of its hierarchical structure and number of decisionmaking nodes increase, so does impersonality and, in turn, the need for language differentiation and cultural diversity. This need, which can become critical, in part reflects the need for identity by individuals and often leads to the formation of small groups, institutions, and diverse organizations as well as to ethnic group accentuation. Increase in language differentiation and cultural diversity, however, implies preservation of particularistic values associated with identity and greater differences of opinion on specific issues. Such tends to increase the potential for conflict, resulting from the different interpretations of words, sets of words, and patterns of argument and reasoning that develop (see Gale and Gale 1977). Consequently, the degree of allowable language differentation and cultural diversity is a function of experience, accumulation of knowledge, the need for identity, and the survival objective of the larger body.

At this point, we recognize that the qualities of a leader can vary significantly. There are those leaders—the 100 percent pure representatives—who function to serve the members of a group or its constituents and undertake simply to carry out the members' wishes. They cover the more routine, efficient administrators associated with a bureaucracy. At the other extreme are leaders who take as their mission the maximization of the welfare of the members of the group (constituency), including themselves. They are often motivated to move in new and even drastically new directions if such is consistent with optimization. They justify such steps, particularly when only minimal debate and discussion is possible, on the basis of their access to more as well as a different set of information. These leaders are *creative* decisionmakers, and for them the learning process is much more critical than for the members of the group.

14.5.8 Hierarchical Structure of Decisionmaking and Informational Processes

The hierarchical structure of decisionmaking is of course an essential feature of reality. As a decisionmaking body increases in size (in part reflecting increase in complexity of economic structure, the urban system, and transportation and communications phenomena, and thus in the complexity of decisionmaking itself) basic components must be decentralized. This in turn leads to a hierarchical pattern of decisionmaking nodes. See the lower left of Figure 14–12. The particulars of the hierarchical pattern that emerges are dependent upon: (1) *information collection costs* (costs of collection by local nodes tend to be lower in general because of greater local visibility), (2) *information processing costs* (these tend to be lower at the top node because of scale economies, but also higher if slack resources are available at the local nodes), (3) *information transmission costs* (as in graph theory, these increase with distance or number of connections between originating and terminating nodes), (4) *executive-time decision costs* (these tend to be lower at the top node despite higher wages there because of fewer personnel involved, but also higher at the top node if slack resources are available at local nodes), (5) *overview advantage* (this results from lower likelihood of error, in general, at the top node), (6) *c-participation and morale* (which reflect the actual participation of a population on average in decisionmaking and the effect on its productivity), and (7) many other factors largely associated with the production and exchange of noneconomic commodities. (See Isard, T. Smith, et al. 1969:chap. 3). We recognize the existence and importance of *hierarchical structures* in economic organizations (such as multinationals) which cover many national territorial units; and that such hierarchical structures cut across world societies differently than hierarchical structures in political organizations (such as the NATO and Warsaw Pact blocs of nations) or sociocultural organizations (such as the Roman Catholic Church and the Women's International League for Peace and Freedom).

Note that team theory may be viewed as a specific type of theory of hierarchical organization. Team theory pertains to situations where all participants in the organization share a common goal—such as win a war, survive, be the leading power, maximize profits, or come out first in competition. In such theory, the aim is to allocate resources to the nodes, collect and process information at the different nodes, and transmit it among nodes, so as to achieve that common goal (see Marschak and Radner 1971).

14.5.9 Policy Evaluation

Finally, it should be born in mind that the public policy that derives from all these ongoing processes covered in the C^K box and involving individuals, groups, and their conflicts, is subject to reevaluation. Commands, orders, or inputs are passed down to the production system. Outcomes are realized given the state of environment that occurs. Information b^K about such outcomes is transmitted back to the decisionmaking unit and interpreted in terms of the perceptions of that unit. As in the group learning process, such information then provides the basis for *evaluation* of public policy and for its change. All this in turn suggests a sequence over time of commands, orders, and specified inputs. Such a sequence represents phenomena in both microtime and macrotime and will be discussed more extensively in connection with the I box on pages 554–555. Also we should keep in mind that all processes and activity within the C^K system is part of the larger Parson's G subsystem (see Parsons et al. 1961).

Policy evaluation takes place not only at the national level but also at the system level, particularly within the cognitive interaction I box. We turn to the discussion of the processes that take place in this box in the first section of the next chapter.

NOTES

1. This chapter draws heavily on Isard (1979, 1980).
2. We take $a^J \epsilon A^J$ and $a^L \epsilon A^L$ where A^J and A^L are the prespecified choice (action) spaces of J and L, respectively. We take $z \epsilon Z$ where Z is the set of possible states of the environment.
3. Or we might imagine that where $y = (y^J, y^L)$, as in Figure 14-2, $u^J(^J y^{J*}) > u^J(^J y^{L*})$ and $u^L(^L y^{L*}) > u^L(^L y^{J*})$, where for example, $^J y^{L*}$ and $^L y^{L*}$ are the outcomes to J and L respectively, when L's most preferred outcome is realized.
4. To keep this and many other figures as simple as possible, we omit the utility boxes of Figures 14-1 and 14-2. Also, bear in mind that a^J and a^L coming out of the C^J and C^L boxes respectively are *control* inputs (commands) while the a, a^J, and a^L within the production functions $P(a, z)$, $P^J(a^J, z)$, and $P^L(a^L, z)$ are the commodity inputs that correspond to these control inputs. Similarly, with respect to the state of the environment z and the interface inputs v^J and v^L to be discussed.
5. It may also be the case that the system itself restricts the information that is passed on to each behaving unit so that J and L receive incomplete information μ^J and μ^L, respectively, which in turn are perceived as $\bar{\mu}^J$ and $\bar{\mu}^L$.
6. We recognize of course that the two-way classification of interactions as *real and cognitive* is questionable in many ways. Also we must

allow for *commands* and *feedback information* to flow directly between the cognitive interaction I box and the production units P^J and P^L—as, for example, the command of an International Olympic Committee regarding the use of drugs by members of each national team or the International Whaling Committee regarding the inputs (killings) of whales in the whaling industry of each nation. To avoid complicating Figure 14-9 we take all such commands and feedback information to flow through the decisionmaking units C^J and C^L.

7.   The general relationships depicted by Figure 14-9 and discussed in this section are restated as mathematical mappings and functions in Isard (1979a).

8.   When the reader becomes impatient or cannot see potential applications, he should proceed to pages 570–573.

9.   See Isard (1975:360–69) for further discussion of the manner in which the input-output model can be extended to generate estimates of pollutant emissions.

10.   See Isard et al. (1960:chaps. 8–12) for detailed discussion of the techniques noted in this section.

11.   See Isard, T. Smith, et al. (1969:chaps. 13 and 14) for a detailed presentation of this expanded general equilibrium framework.

12.   See Isard, T. Smith, et al. (1969:chap. 15) for some preliminary investigations into this area of research.

13.   See Pattee (1973) for an overview of this type of analysis.

14.   See Isard (1975) for a general overview of this type of analysis.

15.   See Granberg and Rubinshtein (1979) for details on the structure of this model.

16.   See Isard et al. (1960:715–18) and Isard, T. Smith, et al. (1969:989–91) for details on the structure of this model.

17.   See Isard et al. (1972) for an example of such a table and for a more detailed discussion of the usefulness of the input-output approach as a means for integrating analyses of economic and ecologic processes.

18.   For further details, see Isard and C. Smith (1982c).

19.   See Isard et al. (1975) for examples of such diffusion models.

20.   For an operational one see Isard and Anselin (1982) and Isard and C. Smith (1982).

21.   See Nisbet and Ross (1980) and Gamson (1982) for definitions of these terms.

15 TOWARD A DEFINITION OF PEACE SCIENCE: PART II

15.1 THE DETAIL OF THE I BOX, THE COGNITIVE INTERACTION SUBSYSTEM

In this chapter, we continue the discussion of Chapter 14. We now turn to the details of interaction at the cognitive level among the U participants, say nations, in a closed system. There are many approaches to the study of the cognitive interaction subsystem covered by the I box. See Figure 15-1. Each has certain strong elements but each is incomplete. Typically, analysis of the cognitive interaction subsystem (I box) fails to take into account adequately the concomitant processes in the real interaction subsystem (R box) and consequently, the interface between the two. In fact, some scholars would insist that interaction of the processes within these two subsystems are so inextricably linked that only one overall subsystem (box) is relevant. However, we consider it desirable at this stage of development of Peace Science to keep the two types of subsystems and their internal processes and interactions distinct. A unique contribution of Peace Science will be to specify and examine the interface between the two types of interactions and subsystems.

535

Figure 15-1. The Cognitive Interaction Box I.

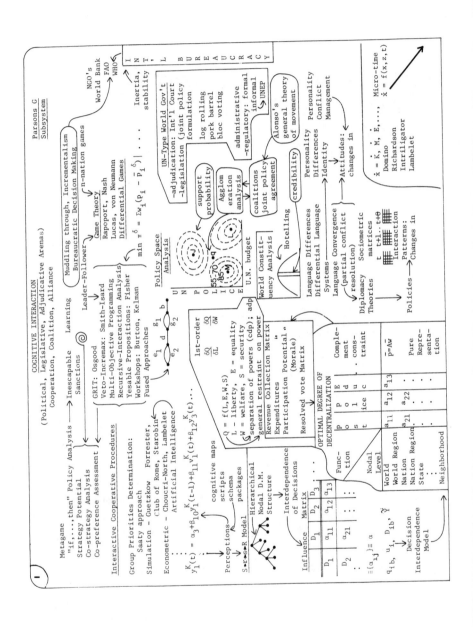

15.1.1 Conflict Management Procedures and Some Traditional Approaches

To begin, we mention some of the techniques relevant for coping with conflicts among nations or other behavioral units discussed in earlier chapters, but not all of which were listed in the center of Figure 14–12. As indicated at the top of Figure 15-1, these include: meta-game analysis (changing actions to "if, . . . , then" policies), the Saaty approach (method of determining group priorities), GRIT (reciprocated tension-reducing actions, a sequence of), veto-incremax, multiobjective programming with compromise weights, recursive interaction procedures, Fisher's yesable proposition approach, Burton's and Kelman's workshop approaches, and numerous approaches fusing quantitative and qualitative elements. In addition, as already mentioned on pages 486–487, game theoretic approaches, such as those associated with von Neumann and Morgenstern (1953), Nash (1953), Rapoport, (1967), Shapley (1950), Lucas (1982), and Brams and Wittman (1980) as well as the new thrusts within differential game analysis provide insights on strategic behavior, especially of sophisticated political leaders and others who have access to teams of experts. The contributions of these approaches have been extensively treated in the international relations and associated literature; we shall not discuss them here. Nor for the same reason shall we discuss the several factors, approaches, or analyses listed toward the bottom right and at the center right of Figure 15-1—namely, diplomacy (balance of power) theories, problems of conflict arising from personality differences. Nor shall we futher discuss the importance of differential language systems to achieve identity for members of a group or society and related studies. Also, we shall not discuss the familiar traditional analyses of legislative, administrative, adjudicative, and regulatory processes that occur within a United Nations or any other type of world government. Nor shall we discuss the role of units such as the World Bank, Food and Agriculture Organization, World Health Organization, United Nations Environmental Programme, or NGOs (nongovernmental organizations); nor the many important but by now well known simulation models, such as those by Guetzkow (1963), Starobin (1976), Choucri et al. (1976), and others. Rather, we now wish to discuss newer and less familiar types of analyses. In particular we wish to consider the macroeconometric-type analyses concerned with understanding past behavior of nation systems to provide insights for forecasting future behavior.

(Such analyses draw heavily upon econometric techniques used in studying the real interaction processes covered by the R box.) In these analyses we find proper emphasis on cognitive variables (or their proxies) pertinent for the cognitive interaction subsystem covered in the I box.

15.1.2 Econometric Modeling of Multination Conflict

As noted in Figure 15-1, an application of econometric-type analyses to multination systems is by Choucri and North (1975).[1] These scholars address the long range causes of international conflict, and in so doing they examine some key issues and difficulties encountered in using econometric analyses to project international relations. The roots of warfare, they contend, can be found in the basic attitudes and characteristics of nations, the most critical variables being population, resources, technology, and response propensities in pressure situations. Within a nation, a combination of population growth and developing technology places rapidly increasing demands upon resources, often resulting in internally generated pressures. As Choucri (1973: 17) states:

> The greater this pressure, the higher will be the likelihood of extending national activities outside territorial boundaries. We have termed this tendency to extend behavior outside national boundaries *lateral pressure.* To the extent that two or more countries with high capability and high pressure tendency (and high lateral pressure) extend their interests and psycho-political borders outward, there is a strong probability that eventually the two opposing spheres of interest will intersect. The more intense the intersection, the greater will the likelihood be that competition will assume military proportions. When this happens, we may expect competition to be transformed into conflict and perhaps an arms race or cold war. At a more general level of abstraction, provocation will be the final act that can be viewed as the stimulus for large-scale conflict or violence. But an act will be considered provocation only in a situation which has already been characterized by high lateral pressure, intersections among spheres of influence, armament tensions and competitions, and an increasing level of prevailing conflict.

> Major wars, we have argued, often emerge through a two-step process: in terms of internally generated pressure (which can be traced to population dynamics, resource needs and constraints, and technological development) and in terms of reciprocal comparison, rivalry, and conflict, on

a number of salient capability and behavior dimensions. Each process tends to be closely related to the other, and each, to a surprising degree, can be accounted for by relatively nonmanipulable variables (or variables that are controllable only at high costs). And it is these variables, we hypothesize, that provide the long range roots of conflict and warfare.

We depict the Choucri-North model in Figure 15-2, using in part the symbols of Figure 14-9. It consists of a system of five equations for simultaneous estimation. Each equation pertains to a dependent variable in one of the boxes sketched in the center of Figure 15-2 and includes independent variables relating to the state of the environment and interface inputs (from the rest of the system) and lagged dependent variables. For example, a typical equation might be:

$$y_1^K(t) = \alpha_3 + \beta_{10}y_1^K(t-1) + \beta_{11}\,v_1^K(t) + \beta_{12}\,y_3^K(t) + \beta_{14}[z_2^K(t) \cdot z_3^K(t)] + \mu_3(t) \tag{15-1}$$

where

$y_1^K(t)$ = military expenditures in nation K in year t;

$y_1^K(t-1)$ = military expenditures in nation K in year $t-1$;

$v_1^K(t)$ = military expenditures in nation K's nonallies in year t;

$y_3^K(t)$ = a scaled variable (from 1 to 30) denoting intensity of intersections among nation K's spheres of influence in year t;

$z_2^K(t)$ = population of nation K in time t;

$z_3^K(t)$ = national income of nation K (in standardized form) at time t;

$\mu_3(t)$ = an error or disturbance term at time t; and

$\alpha_3, \beta_{10}, \beta_{11}, \beta_{12}, \beta_{14}$ are parameters to be estimated.

The virtues and limitations of the Choucri-North model have been discussed in the standard political science literature. Here we wish to establish its cognitive character. While such variables as population, income, and military expenditures pertain to analyses covered by the R box (the real interaction subsystem), the variable intensity of intersections does not. Further, the parameters β_{10}, β_{11}, β_{12}, and β_{14} reflect perceptions and other highly subjective elements and not simple technical and market relations. They embody the cognitive maps (Axelrod 1976), scripts, and schema (Nisbitt and Ross 1980), packages (Gamson 1982), data stories (Bennett 1981), and other concepts and frameworks that cognitive psychologists and related social scientists have recently been developing. These parameters in essence sum-

Figure 15-2. The Choucri-North Model of International Violence.

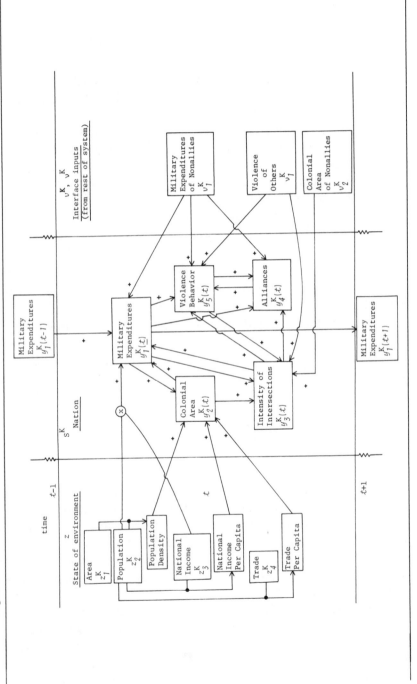

marize the outcome (in terms of an average *net* response coefficient) of the numerous rounds of action and reactions involved in the thought processes and statements of the leaders of a given nation. The response coefficients β_{10}, β_{11}, β_{12}, and β_{14} parallel coefficients of an inverse matrix of a Leontief input-output system in the sense that they capture direct and indirect effects; but they do not reflect technical engineering requirements for production. Rather, they reflect psychological responses over a series of rounds. Further, within each round they reflect the outcome of deliberations of the head of a state in communication (often indirect and subtle) with his advisers and agents, and his constituents in general. Such deliberations aim to achieve an optimal strategic response (considering all possible direct and indirect repercussions). The response is often to some perceived threat by another nation, or it represents steps directed toward certain widely shared and explicit goals, such as survival of country. Military expenditures, arms trade, investment, and colonial expansion are in every case the accumulation and aggregation of the effects of decisions made by individual human beings acting singly and in groups of diverse size and type.

One cannot claim that cognitive variables do not enter into the R or the P^K boxes. We do know, for example, that a household's consumption may partly depend on its perception of the consumption of a neighboring household (a "keeping-up-with-the Jones" effect), but such consumption behavior is typically not of a complex round-by-round or sequence-of-rounds character. If there are feedbacks, they usually do not escalate to a break point. We also know that price wars among business firms can lead to break points like bankruptcy in the real production system, but such break points are not a regular occurrence in models of the real interaction system (R box). In brief, while cognitive processes do enter into the models of the real production and the real interaction systems, they do so to a much smaller extent than in models of the cognitive and cognitive interaction systems. In the former models, they rarely lead to dominant escalation effects. In the latter, they may often do so. The major escalations arising from the basic decision processes of political leaders generate such outcomes as war, terrorism, revolution, colonial expansion races, and so forth.

15.1.3 Decision Interdependence and an Hierarchical Structure of Decisionmaking Nodes

A basic aspect of the cognitive interaction system relates to the complex interdependence of policies and other decisions. One of the many useful frameworks for depicting such interdependence portrays the decisionmaking structure of a nation or a system of nations as an hierarchically organized set of decision nodes. See the left center of Figure 15-1. At the top is the node at which some of the most important and complex decisions are made. In these first-order decisions, very large scale economies are realized from the use of the finest decisionmaking minds and facilities. As already indicated on pages 531–532 in another connection, to the top node must come information from many if not every node in the system—some information being raw information that is collected, other information being processed either at the node of collection or at a node along the way to the top. The economies realizable at the top node may outweigh all the costs involved in the transmission of (1) information to that node and (2) information about the decision reached at that node to other nodes in the system. Many times, however, the decisions to be made at the top are prescribed by law, custom, and other factors.

Next there are second-order nodes, each with a tributary area containing lower-level nodes. Again, law, custom, and efficiency (in terms of scale economies, transmissions costs, etc.) may dictate the set of decision areas in which decisions are to be made at each second-order node. Again, information selected from many if not all nodes in each tributary area is transmitted to the relevant second-order node; and information on the decision reached at that node is passed on to several or all nodes in the tributary area. And so on down to the nth order decision nodes (the village, neighborhood, or family unit) and n^{th} order decisions.

In brief, we may conceive a population fairly evenly distributed over physical space subject to influence by all kinds of decisions. Imposed on this space is a set of decisionmaking nodes. See Figure 15-3 for a more detailed sketch of a hierarchical decision-node structure. This set of nodes in part parallels a system of central places. Instead of commodities flowing, as in a central place system, we have information flowing. Instead of constraints on economic activities imposed by production functions, as in a central place system, we have constraints on decisionmaking activities imposed by law, custom, information processing, and transmission functions. In other respects, we find parallels between a central place system and a hierarchical decision-node structure.[2] There are a number of major flaws in the central place and Lösch type of theory. One is its failure to take account of the interdependence of economic activities. So too, the hierarchical

Figure 15-3. A Hierarchical Decision-Node Structure within a System.

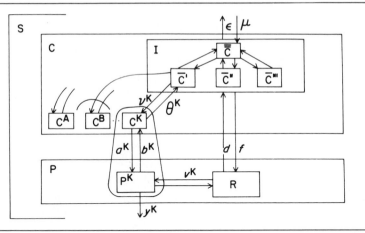

decision-node structure already depicted does not take into account the interdependence of decisionmaking activities and of decisions. We now wish to do so.

15.1.4 Decision Interdependence and a Leontief-type Matrix of Influence Coefficients

For the moment, concentrate on interdependence at a single node, say the top node. There, one type of decision activity may relate to military expenditures, decision area D_1; another to the level of a foreign aid program, decision area D_2; a third to the level of a low-income housing program, decision area D_3; . . . ; and the last to the level of research and development activities, decision area D_n. These decisionmaking activities may be listed in order along the rows and columns of a matrix in checkerboard Leontief fashion, as indicated at the left lower center of Figure 15-1. In each cell of the matrix is a coefficient indicating the influence of an average-type decision in one area on an average-type decision in another. For example, the coefficient α_{21} in Row 2 Column 1 (which can take both positive and negative values) might indicate the influence of one unit (one million dollars) of military expenditures (of an average character) upon the level of typical foreign aid (in million dollar units). With the use of these coefficients, we can begin to model in an operational manner the effects of a decision in one area upon the decision in another. The decision set in each area may consist of a finite number of possible decisions or be continuous. The interdependence may be significant for only 3, 4, or 5 rounds, or for many more. In the latter case, the use of an inverse may be appropriate provided the α_{ij} do not change from round to round; but they may change, in which case only a round-by-round approach is valid. Further, with the use of a balanced region input-output framework, the interdependence that exists at any node may be extended so that decisions at any one node (say a U.N. node or the capital of a major power) can influence and be influenced by decisions at many other nodes (where the different nodes may have different rules for reaching a decision in any given decision area). These decisions would include those on level of production in each economic sector (see Isard, T. Smith, et al. 1969:93–105). As a consequence, a critically important decision area (such as environmental management) that involves the coordination of numerous decisions at many global, national, regional, and local nodes comes to influence all kinds of decisions at most (if not all) nodes.

15.1.5 Decision Interdependence and Decentralization of Functions by Nodes

The interdependence of decisions among all nodes relates to another key question: that of the proper degree of decentralization of governmental and other functions among nodes. To examine this question, imagine a matrix whose rows refer to a set of n relevant levels of decisionmaking nodes and whose columns refer to m specific functions. See the table at the bottom to the left of Figure 15–1. The rows may refer to world, world region, nation, national region, state (provincial, prefecture), metropolis, local (county, township), and neighborhood levels. The columns may refer to postal services, fire protection, police (international, national, state, and local), education, research training, environmental management, and other functions. There are several different ways in which the cells of this matrix may be filled in. One is to list in each column the percentage distribution by type node of total world expenditures on the particular function listed at the head of the column. Such an expenditure matrix (designated A) is a useful descriptive device. Another way is to list in each column the percentage distribution by type node of the revenues collected to perform the function at the head of the column, thereby yielding a revenue collection matrix $\overline{A}$. Still a third way is to develop an administrative (engineering-type) efficiency matrix $\overline{\overline{A}}$ to understand better the actual and potential performance of the real interaction and production systems covered by the R and P^K (K = J,L, . . .) boxes. Here, in each column an analyst lists the percentage distribution of expenditures by type node that corresponds to the most efficient performance of that function for society as a whole, when viewed from a strictly narrow administrative and engineering standpoint that ignores externalities.

A fourth type of matrix, which captures more of the political process and cognitive interaction, depicts potential political participation. It presents estimates of *community participation potential* regarding a given function when that function is distributed in different ways among the several levels of nodes (see Isard, and T. Smith, et al. 1969:chap. 3). This matrix may be supplemented by a matrix estimating at each node the amount of local debate and discussion (or the associated potential for community morale) that might be anticipated with different degrees of spatial decentralization regarding a particular function.

15.1.6 The Compromise Authority-Allocation Matrix: Problems in Attainment

With these several types of matrices plus information on (1) current and likely future technology, (2) changes in tastes, (3) social trends, and so forth, every representative in a group can be asked to develop (propose) an *authority-allocation* matrix. In this matrix he indicates an allocation of authority (or control) over each function by type node in accord with what he considers best from the standpoint of the constituency of the node or level of node he represents. Such authority might be associated with expenditures, revenue collection, efficiency, community participation potential, or some combination of these factors and thus be only a qualitative measure of some notion of general power to govern or control.

To assist each representative in arriving at this type of matrix, an analyst might develop for him other sets of numbers. He might post-multiply the expenditures matrix A of order *nxm* by a column vector of weights $w = (w_1, \ldots, w_m)$, indicating the percentage distribution of world expenditures among functions, to obtain the column vector $p = Aw$, having n components, each of which gives the percent of total world expenditures for all functions as a whole associated with the corresponding level of node. He might also postmultiply the revenue collection matrix $\bar{A}$ by a column vector of weights $\bar{w} = (\bar{w}_1, \ldots, \bar{w}_m)$, indicating the percentage distribution of world revenues among functions, to obtain $\bar{p} = \bar{A}\bar{w}$, each component of which gives the percent of total world revenues collected for all functions as a whole associated with the corresponding level of node. Finally, he might postmultiply the efficiency matrix $\bar{\bar{A}}$ by the appropriate set of weights $\bar{\bar{w}} = (\bar{\bar{w}}_1, \ldots, \bar{\bar{w}}_m)$, indicating the percentage distribution of world expenditures among functions, to obtain $\bar{\bar{p}} = \bar{\bar{A}}\bar{\bar{w}}$, each component of which gives the percent of total world expenditures for all functions as a whole that would be associated with the corresponding level of node were there efficient performance of each function, narrowly defined so as to exclude externalities. The resulting p, $\bar{p}$, $\bar{\bar{p}}$ vectors may then help the representative construct his own matrix allocating authority for each function by type node.

After each participant has developed his own authority-allocation matrix, the differences among them must be resolved, perhaps through recursive interactive procedures. As discussed on pages 256–263, the several participants may be asked to make concessions in order to reach, perhaps after several rounds of interaction, a compromise matrix acceptable to all. In doing so, side payments and logrolling may be required.

There are many problems in attempting to develop such a compromise matrix. First, reconsider the expenditures matrix. Money spent in the performance of any two functions may not have been done so with the same efficiency. Adjustments of expenditure data to a standard efficiency level would then be required. Moreover, dollars of expenditures are not a good proxy for a proper allocation of power. This is clear when we compare the very small expenditures on the judiciary with the very large expenditures on administrative functions, for example, highway construction. What is required is a set of weights to take into account adequately the concept of separation of power and other critical qualitative elements, which are extremely important for the operations at any given node, world, national or regional.

Separation of power also relates to the division of power among the different levels of nodes—at times called the *areal division of power.* Such division pertains to the problem of imposing general restraints on power at any level of node to avoid undue concentration at that level. Because externalities are involved, such restraints on power are determined not only by the number of functions, either in whole or part, assigned to each level of node, but also by the particular cluster or complex of functions so assigned. At the same time, at each node within any given level there must be a proper complement of functions with sufficient diversity to insure the realization of a minimum amount and quality of local debate and discussion and potentially a minimum amount of morale and c-solidarity. This complement can be expected to vary among nodes, at least among nodes on different levels.

With full, partial, or even no recognition of these problems, we can thus imagine a group of political leaders representing different nations considering the particular task of the proper allocation of a number of important functions, in whole or part, to new or existing world organizations. Such organizations may be located at the different world nodes—for example, United Nations Environmental Programme at Nairobi, the International Atomic Energy Agency at Vienna, and the International Court of Justice at The Hague. Much cognitive interaction among the leaders may take place on a recursive basis. Such ultimately determines, say, the amount of national sovereignty each leader proposes to yield regarding each function— e.g., the control of terrorism. Of course, in the give and take of recursive interaction, the personality of each leader comes to be involved and may generate obstacles to the attainment of a compromise authority-allocation matrix, and in fact come to affect what is attained. Desirably, the structure implied by a compromise matrix should not only be implementable but should also incorporate sufficient flexibility in the exercise of power to allow international control units effectively to adjust for changes in technology, social processes, and so forth.

15.1.7 Allocation of Authority and the Basic Values: Liberty, Equality, Welfare, and Security

Involved in the problem of a proper allocation of authority among decisionmaking nodes (world, national, regional, etc.) are the basic values of *liberty, equality, welfare, and security.* See the center of Figure

15-1. These in a very broad sense determine the quality of a world society. The first three were the primary concerns of the seventeenth eighteenth, and nineteenth centuries, respectively. The last is a major concern of the twentieth century. We may think of a quality of world society Q given by the function

$$Q = f(L,E,W,S) \tag{15-2}$$

where L = liberty, E = equality, W = welfare, and S = security, all appropriately measured. The question is how to maximize the quality of world society subject to constraints such as limited resources, existing technology, and biological requirements. We may imagine first-order conditions defined in terms of resource costs—i.e., amounts of resources needed to produce a unit of each of these grand values, provided such resource costs can be roughly established. We might then proceed to consider tradeoff functions among these grand variables, and conduct stability analysis of the type found in a number of macromodels. Or we might replace the above grand values L, E, W, and S by variables more easily measured. Here, we may consider legislative, adjudicative, and administrative powers at different levels of disaggregation, as already discussed, with restraints imposed on concentration of power at any node or level of node; allowable discrepancies among nodes in per capita income and access to education, health, and other infrastructure facilities; and so forth. While any approach that examines such grand values is nonoperational, political leaders in the international arena do consciously consider them. Although we cannot specify the tradeoff functions implicitly employed by political leaders, they are nonetheless there (as in the case of civil rights today), no matter how fuzzily perceived. They are there when leaders consider yielding liberty and national sovereignty to a world node. They are there when with regard to particular issues they express willingness to accept partial national subjugation to a world unit to obtain gains that might accrue from (1) more effective regulation of the environment, terrorism, and the like; (2) larger amounts of funds for development assistance; or (3) the larger amount of security obtainable from more effective control of fissionable materials and nuclear weapons. All such analysis, which clearly involves cognitive interaction, is relevant to Peace Science, especially that involving the yielding of national sovereignty to world nodes and the establishment of a proper hierarchical system of nodes with a proper distribution of power and authority among them.

15.1.8 Multination Interaction in Policy Space

Some of the above analysis may be viewed by the several national leaders as the problem of selecting an optimal location in multidimensional policy space. See the two-dimensional diagram in the center and to the right of Figure 15-1. Also refer to Figures 7-4 and 7-7 and the discussion related to them on pages 228-235. Each leader perceives a number of well-defined policy issues. With regard to each issue, each leader may perceive a set of well-defined policies. Further, he may assume that each member of his constituency has a well-defined preference structure over all possible joint policies. (Where there are n policy issues, a joint policy is a point or location in the n-dimensional policy space and represents a combination of policies, one on each issue.) Given the preference structures of his constituents, the leader can associate a level of expected support with each point within the space and then propose that joint policy which maximizes his expected support. In the two-dimension diagram in Figure 15-1, we have indicated such joint policies for leaders J, L, and M. We have also drawn around these joint policies isosupport level curves, indicating the locus of joint policies of a given leader that generates a given fraction of total support from his constituency. For M, we have specifically indicated the isosupport level curves that correspond to locuses of positions generating support from .85, .70, and .55 of his constituents. It is expected that when each of several leaders proposes his best joint policy in a number of important international situations, there will be inconsistency and nonagreement on a number of issues. For example, there may result inconsistent proposals among national leaders regarding the size of a U.N. budget, or a U.N. Police Force. As time passes, the level of constituent support for a leader espousing a given joint policy diminishes if that policy does not lead to agreement on a critical issue, such as a U.N. budget. Thus, each leader confronts two levels of support for his joint policy, depending on whether or not that joint policy is consistent with the joint policies proposed by leaders of other nations. The differences in these two levels of support may in fact become large enough with time so as to motivate leaders to agglomerate at a single location in policy space, say at point q—in essence, to agree on the size of a U.N. budget and other issues. At this stage, much if not all agglomeration analysis of traditional location theory becomes relevant.

As indicated in previous chapters, there are other situations in the international arena where interdependence of outcomes exists and generates cognitive interaction. For example, in an arms race, each leader's level of support depends not only on the joint policy he chooses (including the size of military expenditures) but also on policies independently chosen by leaders of other nations—for example, their levels of military expenditures. This then often motivates leaders to employ some cooperative procedure (split-the-difference, veto-incremax, etc.) so that each sets values for his control variables consistent with his and every other leader reaching a common position. For each leader, such a position might in the middle or long run correspond to greater support from his constituency compared to what he would have received under narrow-minded, self-interested optimization.

Agglomeration analysis in policy space pertaining to the attainment of agreement on a common joint policy is closely allied with coalition analysis—both the simple type developed by Gamson (1961a, 1961b, 1962, 1964) and the more complex type developed by Isard, T. Smith, et al. (1969). These two kinds of analyses are also related to questions of (1) unification of states into larger political bodies, and the reverse, namely, the splitting up of nations and blocs into smaller independent political units and bodies; and (2) centralization and decentralization of functions and activities already discussed on pages 531–532. They are also related to the familiar Hotelling analysis of competition among U participants for a market or constituency distributed along a line or in a 2-dimensional or n-dimensional policy space—for it is against the background of the actual or expected outcome of such competition that the gains from the agglomeration or coalition formation can be identified or estimated. See Isard, T. Smith, et al. (1969, Chap. 9).

In parallel fashion, various voting procedures that may be employed to determine joint policies can be viewed as a form of agglomeration analysis—since a vote to adopt a common policy position is an agreement by a winning coalition to locate at a given point (such as point q in Figure 15–1) in the relevant policy space.

Agglomeration and coalition formation are exceedingly complex processes—since agglomeration and coalitions can form at a number of levels—and thus the relative advantages and disadvantages of each level as well as its implementability must be considered. Specifically, one level can be the all-participant coalition, which would involve the agreement by all nations to some form of world government. Another level currently exists with respect to the NATO and Warsaw Pact blocs. Still another level is the common market level, and so on. And to be realistic, such agglomeration and coalition formation must allow for behavioral units to migrate out of an existing coalition (agglomeration) into another one, existing or new. Here, Alonso's general theory of movement promises to have considerable application (see Anselin and Isard 1979). Also, in our analysis we may employ concepts such as minimal winning coalitions, disruptive coalitions, coalitions in the core, nucleolus, parity-norm, strategic potential, n-times adjusted critical isodapanes (Isard 1977) and solution sets.

15.1.9 World Constituency and Credibility

Other important situations arise when the constituencies of the relevant leaders are interdependent (up to this point we have been assuming them to be independent). As is well known, there exists a world constituency for whose support the United States, the U.S.S.R., and other major powers compete. Accordingly, when any major power attempts to maximize its support from this constituency subject to certain constraints, there develop sequences of actions and reactions by the several major powers. Some of these sequences lead to stable, short-run equilibrium positions. However, when such positions are highly inefficient, as in the Prisoner's Dilemma game, the participants may be motivated to cooperate to arrive at more efficient outcomes. For example, in the past the involvement of the United States and the U.S.S.R. in the Middle East, Asia, Africa, and Latin America has often been tempered by their concern for support from the nonaligned part of the world constituency and, for example in the 1970s, by their desire to minimize support given by the nonaligned constituency to Mainland China (Isard and T. Smith 1971).

To illustrate, take the two-dimensional policy space of Figure 15–4. For each of the nonaligned world constituents, plot as a point the most preferred combination of level of policy B and level of policy C. We would normally expect to obtain an irregular distribution of points. To facilitate analysis, however, assume the resulting distribution is fairly dense and symmetric within the circle around the center $\bar{a}$. (The analysis remains unaffected for reasonably asymmetric distributions.) Also, assume that the probability of support for any major power by a nonaligned constituent falls off regularly, and in the same way for all constituents, with distance of the major power's

Figure 15-4.   A Distribution of and Specific Joint Policies in a Two-Dimensional Policy Space.

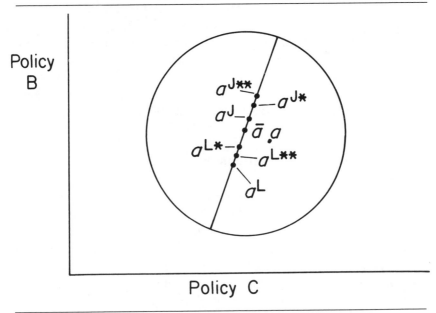

Policy B

Policy C

proposed combination in policy space from his (the constituent's) most desired combination. (The analysis remains unaffected when this is reasonably relaxed.) Further, assume that if a nonaligned world constituent supports a major power, he supports that major power whose proposed combination is closest to that most preferred by the constituent.

Imagine one major power chooses the position given by point a^J. Then the other major power's optimal position a^L, given a^J, will lie on the diameter through $\bar{a}$ and a^J on the side of $\bar{a}$ opposite a^J. If shortsighted, self-interested reactions are taken wherein each major power attempts to maximize the support given him by the world constituency, an inefficient set of equilibrium positions (a^{J*}, a^{L*}) may arise. We then can imagine that each power is motivated to enter into cooperative procedures to obtain a more efficient outcome, possibly a Pareto efficient outcome, and one which might correspond to positions a^{J**} and a^{L**} for J and L, respectively.

Still assuming only two major powers, we next recognize that there is a certain amount of fuzziness in the international arena. Big powers may make proposals and state intentions regarding policies in order to woo the nonaligned world constituency, and these proposals and statements might correspond to the points already indicated on Figure 15-4. But in reality the actions these powers take may deviate from their proposals and statements of intentions—because of random factors on the international scene (unexpected developments and events) or because the international scene is so complex that a nation cannot foresee the operation of at least several different constraints. Both of these reasons for deviation may be well appreciated by the world constituents. But there is a third reason for deviation, namely self-interest. Recognizing that it can always fall back on the excuse of inability to unravel the complexity of the situation, the play of random factors, unexpected events, and so on, a big power may purposely deviate. But such deviation cannot be too great nor for too long a time before a big power loses credibility in the eyes of the nonaligned world community. So, credibility, too, is a factor influencing the range of feasible joint policies that a big power may consider in seeking support from nonaligned world constituents—a factor whose nature and impact are yet to be adequately researched.

There are many other concepts, tools, theories, techniques, and models that might be introduced into the cognitive interaction box I. The analysis of changing attitudes over time may be related to changing patterns of interaction among the relevant leaders or groups in the international or any other community. Sociometric-type matrices may be employed and used for longitudinal analysis where one allows for entry and exit of participants into the arena being studied (Isard, et al. 1977). The role of international bureaucracy and both its governmental decisionmaking and inertia must be examined. Clearly, while we have enumerated some of the main elements within the I box for understanding cognitive interaction, requiring years of further research, there are still others to be explicated and investigated. We now turn to another critical area of research in Peace Science for further creative synthesis of ideas.

15.2 THE EVOLUTIONARY CHARACTER AND STRUCTURE OF THE SOCIAL SYSTEM

Thus far we have been pursuing static or comparative statics analysis. We have ignored the fact that the structure of most, if not all, systems changes over time. True, if the change is extremely slow, it may in many circumstances be neglected. But in Peace Science, it would not be realistic to assume extremely slow change or static conditions at all times. We must explicitly confront the factor of change, smooth or abrupt.

15.2.1 Dynamical Systems Analysis in Microtime for Adaptive Self-Stabilization

Turn to Figure 14–9 on p. 499. There, input z from the environment directly affects the production subsystem of each nation, region, and community. Also, when perceived as $\bar{z}^K$ by decisionmaking unit K, (K = J, L, . . .), it influences the orders and commands that K makes. The input z is depicted as exogeneous to the system, although at times one may claim that the environment is not exogenous—after all, man has a major nuclear bomb capability which he can employ to cause major disturbance of his environment.

Following evolutionary theory, we view change in the environment as one cause of change in the social system through time. Let the state of the environment change (by a major amount) to z' which is ultimately perceived by K as $\bar{z}^K$. This implies a new command vector a^K and a new production vector y^K and in turn, though only in part successively, new vectors, $v^{K'}$, $\bar{v}^{K'}$, d', f', $b^{K'}$, $\bar{b}^{K'}$, $q^{K'}$, $\bar{q}^{K'}$ ϵ', μ', μ'_s, $\bar{\mu}^{K'}$, $\nu^{K'}$, $\theta^{K'}$, $u^{K'}$. But only in macro- (long-run) time[3] can these new vectors, as adaptations to environmental pressures or opportunities, be viewed as "equilibrium" responses. In micro- (short-run) time, a number of, if not many or all, first responses to a z' (including initial perceptions of it by behaving units) are very likely to fall short of being equilibrium responses—that is, to involve a stochastic or disturbance element. This in turn generates responses that are nonequilibrium. This is so because not only are the first responses likely to be nonequilibrium, but also succeeding responses are likely to be nonequilibrium responses to the previous responses even if some of the latter were equilibrium ones. In helping to depict this process, a dynamical systems model, involving responses in microtime to perturbations of the system for given parameters (strictly speaking, parameters that change only in macrotime) can be very useful. It can be used in an auxiliary fashion to specify "laws of change" for a system moving in microtime toward a stable equilibrium position. It has, in this regard, been extensively employed in the analysis of investment processes by economists.

To illustrate, let the vector x be the state of the system, $\dot{x}$ being its time rate of change. In its simplest form, a dynamical system may be portrayed as

$$\dot{x} = f(x, z, t,) \tag{15-3}$$

where t is time. An equilibrium position, a position leading to no change in state, which is sometimes designated a critical point or steady state, is defined by $\dot{x} = 0$ and is a solution to $0 = f(x, z, t)$. Thus as z, the state of the environment, changes in macrotime, so in general should x^*, the equilibrium position of the system. But in the short run there may be perturbations represented by the vector δx_0 at time t_0 in the equilibrium response following a change in z. A new meaningful state will then evolve if the system is such that the successive responses in the short run are properly dampened[4], and in particular if asymptotical stability obtains—that is, if for any trajectory $x = v(t, x_0, t_0)$ which passes through x_0 at t_0, we have

$$x = v(t, x_0, t_0) \rightarrow x^* \text{ as } t \rightarrow \infty \tag{15-4}$$

See Figure 15-5. There, corresponding to the vectors δx_0 at time t_0, δx_1 at time t_1, . . . , and δx_n ($\rightarrow 0$) at t_n, we make explicit the deviation from equilibrium commands δa_1^J, . . . , δa_n^J of J, and, δa_1^L, . . . , δa_n^L of L and the associated deviations in interface inputs and system outputs when a perturbation is limited to be δa_0^J. A dynamic systems approach is fruitful for Peace Science and other social sciences in understanding a number of adaptive processes of a self-regulating character. It is especially helpful for understanding a system's stability conditions for each of the many states of the environment realizable when the environment is taken to change gradually. It helps thereby to understand sudden abrupt changes (cases of instability) in the response of the system to some nonmajor change of the environment. Such study, of course, has been of central interest to evolutionary theorists who have posed the problem of abrupt system change from a diversity of standpoints.

15.2.2 Long-run Nonformal Evolutionary Theory

There, of course, have been the evolutionary theorists like Huxley (1969), Teilhard (1969), Waddington (1961), and Needham (1943) who look broadly at processes in macrotime. Many see social evolution

Figure 15-5.   A System with Asymptotic Stability Reacting to a Perturbation δa_0^J.

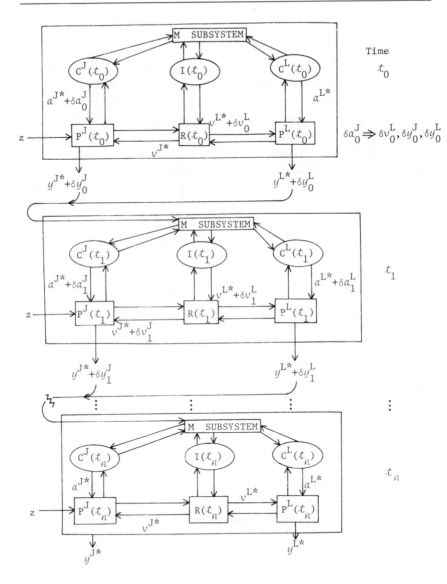

where δa_n^J, δa_n^L, δy_n^J, . . . $\to 0$ as $n \to \infty$

as the development over time of increasingly complex hierarchical organizations of behaving units, with increasing specialization, diversity, interdependence, and intricacy of design and linkages, direct and indirect. For example, Huxley (1969), in summarizing Teilhard's thesis of the *progressive psycho-social evolution* of man, associates with evolution the concept of complexification. It is the increasingly elaborate organization over time of inorganic and organic matter, extending from subatomic units to atoms, to molecules (inorganic and organic), to cells, to multicellular units, to cephalized metazoa with brains, to early man, and finally to a multicultural society. Such complexification, however, has not been random; rather, with increase in knowledge and communication, and with migration, interbreeding, and cultural diffusion in general, it has and continues to move toward a *convergent integration* of all living and nonliving matter.

Elsewhere, Isard and Kaniss (1978) have summarized various contributions to evolutionary theory as they relate to structure, control, and language hierarchies and to world organization. They have discussed:

1. van Bertanlanffy's (1952), Sorokin's (1962), and Jantsch's (1975) ideas on *immanence*—that is, on the intrinsic properties of systems to evolve increasingly complex structures and the self-directing aspects of systems that incorporate mutations into their activities.

2. Layzer's (1975) related ideas on hierarchic construction. Layzer suggests that genetic variation is not a strictly random process but rather, a process in which natural selection regulates recombination and mutation rates to increase the amplitude of variation in the initial phases of an adaptation and gradually restricts the amount of variation once a fitness peak is reached. Restriction of variation at one level leads to high-amplitude variation at the next higher level, the formation of higher levels being an inherent property of living systems.

3. Simon's (1973) and Laszlo's (1972) views that the most efficient and rapid way to form a new higher level of hierarchy is from stable intermediate units or subsystems (wherein each subsystem retains some of its stabilized properties in the higher level structure while yielding to constraints on others), and that natural selection favors this way.

4. Bronowski's (1970) ideas on the hidden stratified stabilities in nature, wherein the stable units of matter that compose one layer are the raw material for random encounters that will produce higher configurations, some of which will chance to be stable.

5. Prigogine's (1967) notion of "order through fluctuation" whereby over time the entropy of a given structure or level in an open system becomes so great that random perturbations cause a relatively sharp and sudden increase in fluctuations of the system as it responds to the perturbations, leading to disequilibrium behavior which in time can drive the system to higher levels of organization.

6. Dahrendorf's (1959) views that there are two critical requirements of a theory of change: (a) the construction of a model of a functionally integrated structure and (b) the discovery of certain forces that lead to a modification of the structural model.

7. Whyte's (1965) ideas on coordinative constraints wherein a successful mutation represents a change from one solution of the coordinative conditions to another which proves to be more efficient in the external competitive process. These ideas are consistent with Pattee's (1973) principle of statistical closure.

Recently, fresh ideas have been generated by the new field of sociobiology. Based on his long career in observing the characteristics of different ant and animal societies, Wilson (1975) develops the case for the evolution of cooperative traits and mechanisms (associated with the existence and behavior of 'altruists') rather than purely competitive and aggressive traits. (See also Layzer 1981.) Like Mayr (1963) and other biologists, he considers internal aggression as costly to these species in that it requires the use of resources that could be devoted to other survival-related purposes. Conflict-resolution mechanisms tend to evolve that allow species to avoid these costs whether they are direct or indirect.

A more recent contribution by Gould (1977) sets forth ideas divergent from the notion of progressive and increasing complexification of social organization. Most evolution theorists concentrate solely on "forward" moves in the development process. With Gould, "backward" moves to avoid dead ends are also critically important. As with other evolutionary theorists, Gould recognizes the dangers of overspecialization and that such can lead to extinction of species—as has been the case with cities and industrial sectors in the human system. Gould, however, also recognizes the existence of *heterchrony,* namely, changes in the rate of development and time of appearance of characteristics already present in ancestors. Specifically, he speaks of *hypermorphosis,* namely, acceleration of development stages, which allows a species to arrive at the ancestor's final stage earlier and add a new final stage or characteristics to change or counteract the characteristics becoming obsolete. This is the familiar process of increasing complexity which evolutionary theorists typically point to. But Gould also speaks of *paedomorphosis,* namely, retardation of development stages, which allows a species to avoid the dead end, the overspecialization that has become obsolete, by eliminating the final stages of development at which the overspecialization appears. The new adult of the species will be characterized by the *juvenile* traits of the ancestor and will in general be less specialized and less differentiated. It will have returned to a more generalized form or set of activities. But with time, from this form, it may probe entirely new, perhaps revolutionary, directions for adaptation along unexplored channels and ultimately move along a new direction, especially one suitable for the changed environmental conditions. So, too, some claim, for the human species and evolution of its social, political and economic units. Also see Isard and C. Smith (1981:48–56).

15.2.3 Formal Models of Abrupt Change and Transition

The thinking of evolutionary theorists concerned with species development through time suggests that two types of formal models are required. One should depict gradual change in an established direction; the other should depict abrupt change involving either a basically new direction, a sudden jump to another level or structure of organization, or other noncontinuous transition. The dynamical system model outlined on pages 554–555 and involving the equation $\dot{x} = f(x, z, t)$ can treat both gradual change in the environment z and other parameters for which t is an index, as well as random perturbations that give rise to adaptive, self-regulating responses in the system. It breaks down, however, when thresholds are reached or to use Thom's (1974) characterization, when the catastrophe set is reached.

To illustrate the latter point, consider a system for which the law of change (equation of motion) is:

$$\dot{x} = -x^3 + \alpha x + \beta \qquad (15\text{-}5)$$

For any given positive value for α, the equilibrium solution x^* (defined by $\dot{x} = 0$) is a function of β and is given by an S-shaped curve as in Figure 15-6. As fully discussed in Isard and Liossatos (1978, 1979: 316–26) with specific reference to big-step disarmament and domino effects, we may take welfare, security, or some other element as a function of the state x of the system. As the value of the coefficient β changes from low to high values, we see how the equilibrium value of x increases from $h'\, b'$ to $g'\, d'$ to $0c'$. However, note that when $\beta = g'$ there are two equilibrium values for x, namely $g'd'$ and ag'. Moreover at every value of β greater than g' but less than g, there are three equilibrium values for x. For example for $\beta = j$, the three values are $e'j$, jf, and je. It has been speculated that as β reaches the

Figure 15-6.   Variation of Equilibrium States x with β for a Fixed Positive Value for α.

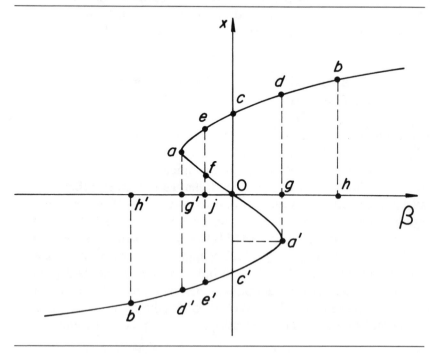

value g' and then passes it, the probability that the equilibrium state will jump from the lower branch to the upper branch increases as the value of β grows. The increase may be quite small until β comes close to the zero value, and then sharply increase and approach unity quickly for values of β somewhat greater than zero. It reaches unity at values for β greater than g for which only one equilibrium can exist. Moreover, it has been shown that the equilibrium states corresponding to points along the stretch aa' are highly unstable.

Whatever the speculation, it is clear that a jump or threshold effect in a system's state must occur for any situation depictable by Figure 15–6 as β increases from negative to positive values; and it can be claimed that at least several important types of situations are depictable by Figure 15–6 or some other member of the Thom family of curves. Hence we need a theory of abrupt transition. We know that in the study of matter, the abrupt transition from liquid to a gaseous state, for which the above figure serves as a good model, can theoretically take place anywhere within the stretch after d' and up to and including a' (Callen 1960). Experimentally, however, it has been shown to begin at c' and reach completion beyond c'.

Here we may quote Callen (1960:162–63) where he refers to a thermodynamic system involving the macrovariables volume, pressure, and temperature. (In this quote we replace his notation by the notation on our Figure 15–6. Words in italics are our own.)[5]

If the reader will permit us the luxury of an anthropomorphic terminology, we may now inquire about the manner in which the system, slowly brought to the state c', becomes aware of the existence and attractiveness of the competing state c. We may well visualize that the system at c', faced with the unpleasant result of an increasing Gibbs [*decreasing welfare*] function if it ventures to alter its state slightly, returns from this slight exploratory excursion to the locally preferable state c'. How then is it to learn that far removed at c is an [*equally attractive state*]? To answer this question, we must appeal to the perspective afforded by statistical mechanics. According to statistical mechanics, the microstate of a system in equilibrium is not static, but the system perpetually undergoes rapid fluctuations. It is by means of these fluctuations that the system probes and explores to discover the state with the *maximum* value of the appropriate potential (welfare). To be specific, with reference to our particular system brought to the state c', the system is not quiescent on the microscopic scale, but rather there are local fluctuations in density from point to point, the average density being that corresponding to the point c'. Of course, small fluctuations in density are most probable and large fluctuations, such as that required to take a small portion of the system to the state c, are very rare indeed. So the system may sit for a very long time at c', until eventually a large spontaneous fluctuation occurs, taking a small portion of the system to c. This fluctuation, unlike others, does not decay, for the portion of the system brought to c finds its new state equally satisfactory to its initial state. Such a stabilized fluctuated portion of the system then becomes a nucleus for the growth of the second phase. The study of the formation and growth of such phase nuclei is an important branch of modern kinetic theory.

In most practical instances a system brought to the state c' does not have to wait for the eventual appearance of a spontaneous fluctuation to take it to c, for artificial fluctuations are often induced by outside mechanisms.

In parallel fashion, we conceive the microstate of a social system in equilibrium to be not static but perpetually undergoing rapid fluctuations. Its numerous firms, consumers, traders, organizations, governments, and planners are not average-type behaving units. Rather the behaving units in any class differ greatly among themselves and from units in every other class; and as a consequence, they can differ greatly in their intensity and extent of interactions with other units and the environment. Thus, some of any class are always exploring, most frequently in small ways. Before the system comes to c' in macrotime, these explorations, even the occasional large ones, all regress to the equilibrium state. They do, too, when the system is at c', except for the very large fluctuations. If the system sits for a long enough time at c', eventually there will occur large spontaneous explorations by one or more units, especially under the stimulus of random shocks from the external environment. Reacting to these shocks, one or more behaving units may jump to c. Since the situation at c is just as good as at c', especially if several units have arrived at c at approximately the same time, those reaching c remain there and form the nucleus for growth of numbers at c.

This kind of interpretation, however, is not satisfactory. In physics one resorts to statistical mechanics to derive a fuller explanation of transition phenomena. This suggests that we ought to employ probabilistic concepts and a stochastic model of the social system when more than one attractor is present. One model that does encompass both deterministic and probabilistic behavior focuses on the most probable value of x, the state of the system (Isard and Liossatos 1979:326–40). At any time t it assumes that there exists a probability distribution of states that we may hypothesize to be sharply peaked around the state of maximum probability which is the mean. Hence, the relevant equation of motion is one that pertains to the mean, because such an equation of motion is (1) a good approximation to the equation of motion governing the state in a purely deterministic model and (2) has the advantage of being more "realistic" since it is embedded in a stochastic process. However, this model can only be considered to be a first probe into what is required.

15.3 SOME NOTES ON THE M BOX: SEARCH FOR NEW INFORMATION AND THE ROLE OF INFORMATIONAL PROCESSES

The dynamical systems approach and some of the abrupt transition models implicitly assume that the system *with its existing stock of knowledge* can reach an equilibrium solution when the environment changes from z to z'. They posit that the system requires no new knowledge. Yet, in many situations a change in the environment may involve entirely new phenomena. The social system (and its behaving units) may not be able to derive from its current stock of knowledge (the M subsystem) information about how to cope with these new environmental phenomena. It may need to search for new strategies—that is, accumulate new information and innovate—because the old strategies are no longer working. Before it can do so, however, it needs to generate a search process.

How is this search process initiated and the new information generated? According to Kaniss (1978), who views the adaptation of any system to a basic change in the environment as an *informational* process, this process always goes on (and speeds up at appropriate times) via the decentralization of information-acquisition responsibilities among the system's microunits. Such decentralization economizes on the use of resources and/or time in the realization of information needed to adapt (and survive).

Specifically, when a system needs to change its state—that is, discard information specifying obsolete elements, procedures, and activities while combining nonobsolete information with new information to specify new elements, procedures, and activities—it relies for this on information competition among its heterogenous microunits. These units perform different roles in the "macrofunctioning" of the system. They face different incentives for the collection (or conservation) of information. (These incentives exist all the time, though they may be miniscule at times when the system is well adapted to the environment, and significant when the system is maladapted; hence, search for information is constantly going on.) Those microunits that have achieved success, typically the highly specialized, highly developed ones, have *incentives to conserve existing information stocks*—stocks that pertain to *past* patterns of activity. The less successful microunits, typically the less-specialized, less-developed units, have *incentives to collect new information* on new activities and forms of specialization; their expected benefits from new information tend to be relatively large and their costs relatively low. When a macrosystem begins to decline in efficiency of performance due to maladaptation (reflecting the increasing obsolescence of the activity patterns of its more successful, highly specialized units), resources will begin to flow from the highly developed microunits and their associated elements to the *less*-successful, less-developed microunits, so that nonobsolete information can be combined with new information in the pursuit of new adaptive directions. This takes place because "expected" rates of return on resources are higher when employed by the latter units. Kaniss (1978) argues further that the highly specialized microunits, because of their incentives for information conservation (i.e., for nonchange), typically cannot initiate an adaptive transformation. Rather, the less developed microunits can (and do) do so, often in less-developed sectors of the system. Later this transformation spreads and engages other units at other locations throughout the system. Competition from the less-developed microunits and sectors forces disinvestment in obsolete patterns and information in highly developed microunits and sectors since these latter increasingly decline in profitability. This allows the system effectively to change adaptive directions and perform new specialized functions.[6]

The above approach is basic to understanding the overall functioning of a social system. However, it must be supplemented by other approaches to provide a full understanding of the system—especially of the several specific roles of its information M subsystem. Moreover, the emphasis of this approach on processes within the M box as well as flows going in and out of it (see Figure 14-9) must be supplemented by study at the cognitive level of the important flows into and out of the C^K and I boxes. The latter flows are primarily perceptions of information stemming from the M box, and the current environment, actions, and outcomes, as well as commands and actions. In the C^K and I boxes is where previous policy and strategy is evaluated on the basis of experience. Here is where negotiations, bargaining, and compromise take place. True, as with the workshop approaches of Burton and Kelman (see pages 332-343), cognitive and cognitive interaction processes may be viewed as another set of information collection, processing, and transmission activities. But we consider these informational activities of a specialized type, not of the general type that, for example, Kaniss (1978) discusses. The former are oriented to a particular conflict situation and intricately intertwined with psychological factors; the latter are in turn related to (1) physiological (genetic) traits of the decisionmakers and leaders who are interacting, often under pressure, and (2) the socialization (education, cultural, ethical) processes to which they have been exposed and which largely determine their attitudes, objectives, and other characteristics.[7]

At this point, it is useful to sketch some of Master's (1975) thinking. According to him, at any point of time the stock of information that a system possesses can be usefully disaggregated for analytical purposes into three or perhaps four component stocks. As is widely recognized, the gene pool can be conceptualized as a system of information storage, processing, and transmission. Hence, one stock that is currently uncontrolled by man but might not remain so is contained within the gene pool of the total system population. This stock establishes the reaction ranges within which cultural processes can operate to institute values, norms, roles, and the like, to which individual behavior must conform. In microtime (the immediate short run and the middle run), such constraints do not change significantly, so their causative role can be ignored.

Cultural information forms a second stock. It develops from the previous complex interactions of individuals, organizations, cultural institutions, and the gene pool. This stock is *potentially* available to all decisionmaker(s) at the point of time when a decision is made. However, because information is accumulated by different cultures, much of the stock of information over all cultures is not accessible to all individuals or groups in the world. Not only are there language barriers to impede the spread of information and differences in the ways information is coded, stored, and retrieved, but there are also knowledge barriers in the sense that there does not exist complete knowledge about the availability of such information—e.g., a tribe in the Andes may not know of the availability of information elsewhere in the world. A third stock of information is that possessed by the individual, much of which consists of experience and is not easily transferable in a precise (objective) form to other individuals and groups.

It is perhaps useful to construct a figure, namely Figure 15-7, to indicate the role such stocks play in the information subsystem M. Here we follow Masters (1975). The top nonbold box pertains to a species or a system population as a whole. Within this population, every sociocultural unit, indicated by the middle nonbold box, is contained (as indicated by the arrows going from the top to the middle

Figure 15-7. Interrelations between Information Stocks at the Biological, Cultural, and Individual Levels.

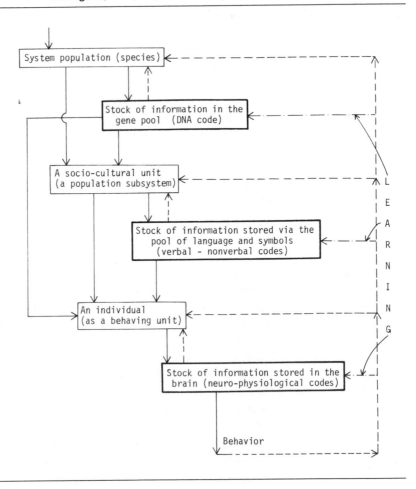

nonbold box in Figure 15-7). Next, within some culture, every individual behaving unit (excluding hermits and the like), indicated by the bottom nonbold box, is contained.

Each of these three levels has its own information stock as indicated by the three bold boxes in Figure 15-7. Associated with the system population is a gene pool (and the corresponding DNA code). This information stock places constraints (reaction ranges) on every sociocultural unit within the system population. Associated with each sociocultural unit is a pool of language and symbols (and the corresponding verbal-nonverbal codes). This information stock (already reflecting the constraints of the gene pool on the given cultural unit) places another set of constraints on each individual member of that unit. Finally, associated with the individual is the pool of knowledge stored in his brain (on the basis of neuro-physiological codes). This information stock—already reflecting the constraints of both the gene pool on the culture and the language and symbols system on his accumulated experience—gives rise to his behavior, including nonaction.

Figure 15-7 also depicts feedback effects via dashed arrows. The gene pool partially controls the characteristics of any future population; language and symbols at any point of time come to influence further development of any sociocultural unit; and finally, an individual's pool of knowledge at any point of time also comes to influence his characteristics. In addition, behavior of the individual comes to influence (1) the system population, (2) the sociocultural unit, and (3) the individual himself, since his behavior determines whether or not he survives as a member of the system's population, as a member of a particular cultural unit, and as an individual. His behavior also influences the three stocks of information in the system via the learning process. See the dot-dash lines in Figure 15-7.

Although there is agreement among scholars that behavior and acquired traits of an individual (or set of individuals) cannot influence directly the gene pool, it has become increasingly recognized that acquired traits and modifications of the behavior of an individual (or set of individuals) that improve chances of survival and reproduction can increase the probability of genetic mutations or recombination "fixing" the adaptive trait. Through this indirect mechanism, known as the "Baldwin Effect," the gene pool (stock of information) changes and in this sense the species "learns." At the sociocultural level, the feedback of the individual's behavior leads to change in the stock of knowledge stored via the pool of language and symbols as well as leading to change in that pool—the latter constituting social learning. This feedback is also indicated in Figures 14–7 and 14–8 by the information flow q to the information in subsystem M. Lastly, there is feedback of the individual's behavior on his stock of knowledge which constitutes the basic input for individual learning. This feedback also is indicated in Figure 14–7 and 14–8 by the information flow b^J to the cognitive unit C^J.

15.4 POSSIBLE FRAMEWORKS FOR MODELING THE INTERACTIONS OF THE COGNITIVE INTERACTION AND REAL INTERACTION SUBSYSTEMS

15.4.1 Toward a Broad Conceptual Framework

From a conceptual standpoint, Pattee (1977, 1978a, 1979a, 1979b) has begun to sketch specific ways in which the linkages d and f between the cognitive interaction and real interaction subsystems in Figure 14–9 can be modeled. One way is to explicitly categorize processes as rate-dependent (the real interaction processes) and rate-independent (the cognitive interaction processes). As already noted, the real interaction processes in the R box, as well as those in the production boxes P^K (K = J, L, . . .), can be described by equations of motion and, in general, by dynamical systems analyses; such has already been done on an extensive basis. In contrast, the cognitive interaction processes in the I box, as well as those in the decisionmaking boxes C^K (K = J, L, . . .), cannot be so described. Rather, they must be described by another general compact form of analysis which is yet to be developed, although there exist voluminous writings on these processes. Such analysis would embrace the numerous specific and highly partial relationships that have been studied and found to be valid. Clearly, continued research on cooperative and hybrid cooperative-competitive procedures and multilateral negotiation techniques is a direction required to help fill this void.

More important is the need to link and integrate the two sets of processes. A model needs to be designed whereby (1) inputs (commands, orders, information) from the cognitive interaction subsystem enter into the real interaction subsystem and (2) inputs of information about the operation of the real interaction subsystem continuously feed into the cognitive interaction subsystem for constant policy evaluation at the system level. (Of course, the production P^K and the decisionmaking C^K subsystems are inextricably enmeshed in these processes.) Obviously, a model that provides such linkages cannot be deterministic, for if it were, it would lead to infinite regress, as Rosen (1970) and Pattee (1977) have indicated. Rate-independent processes in ordinal time[8] are involved. As a step in the right direction, a stochastic model wherein only the mean or expected value of magnitudes is determined might be suggested. See, once again, Isard and Liossatos (1979:326–40). But such a model, while more realistic than existing ones in certain respects, would not capture the explicit interplay of rate-dependent and rate-independent processes. Moreover, we know little about the underlying probability distributions of the magnitudes, and thus must assume them—e.g., that they are Gaussian—if the system they depict is to have stability and other desirable properties.

A much more fruitful direction would be to recognize, as Pattee (1977) clearly has, that there are two distinct modes of operation within any social system and organism: the dynamic (real production and real interaction) deterministic mode and the linguistic (decisionmaking and cognitive interaction) mode. Each requires a separate type of analysis. Each provides a constant flow of inputs to the other. Each operates parallel to the other through time and space. Each must be constrained by the other so that the two work in complementary fashion—a requirement if the single living (behavioral) system to which they pertain is to survive. That is, they must operate consistently for the system's survival. Thus their models must be analytically complementary, though not synthesizable into one. Further, complementarity implies: (1) the need for measurement and for subjective decisions on what to measure and how; (2) the consequent shaping of the deterministic model to be employed for understanding the workings of the production and real interaction subsystems; (3) the subjective determination of initial (or terminal) conditions for this model; and (4) the need to develop a language system (to write, read, and interpret information and messages and to formulate social policy and exercise control inputs) while being at the same time influenced by the outputs and very operation of the deterministic part of the system. Explicit, too, must be the flexibility inherent within the linguistic mode (there is none in the deterministic mode). This allows the society or living organism to survive in a changing environment by being able to adapt to it, frequently by new hierarchic construction.

15.4.2 Toward a Comprehensive
Practical Framework

The Pattee framework and others like it are highly conceptual and provide little effective knowledge for policy formation and social decisionmaking today. Fortunately, with the use of certain strong assumptions—in particular those that characterize economic and regional science models—it is possible to move in the direction of operationalizing the linkage already emphasized in the Pattee framework and in Figure 14-9. To do so, consider the model depicted in Figure 15-8 which elsewhere has been developed and designated an integrated multinational model (see Isard and C. Smith 1982c).[9] In this figure, we indicate in four bold elliptical boxes around the central I circle four different approaches to analyze the P production subsystem of the world, inclusive of the P^K ($K = J, L, \ldots$) and R components. These are: (1) the Leontief World Input-Ouput Model, (2) the LINK (Econometric) Model; (3) the Novosibirsk World Programming Model, and (4) an Industrial Location, Interregional Trade, Comparative Cost-Industrial Complex Model. These have been discussed respectively on pages 511–516; they are presented in fuller detail in Isard and C. Smith (1982c). They are each operational and can be employed to make projections of magnitudes (such as gross product, consumption, and exports) useful for decisionmaking at the world, world-region, and national levels.

First, consider the connection of the I box with the first R box, namely the R_3 box representing the Leontief World Input-Output Model. We have already sketched on pages 256–257 three possible scenarios developed by Leontief (1977), each presumably most preferred by one of three different groups of nations. We have also suggested relevant CMPs (i.e., inputs based on flows from the I box). In Figure 15-8 we suggest that GRIT, action-outcome compromise and min-max percent concession, under appropriate conditions, are several procedures that might be employed by participants in conflict over the final demand targets to be employed in the model.

A second significant connection indicated in Figure 15-8 links the I box with another R box, namely the R_1 box representing the LINK (Econometric) Model. The most important components of this connection would relate to military expenditures, arms trade, and foreign aid. The LINK model should have behavioral equations pertaining to these magnitudes, since its basic structure involves behavioral equations

Figure 15-8.   Linkages between I and R Boxes.

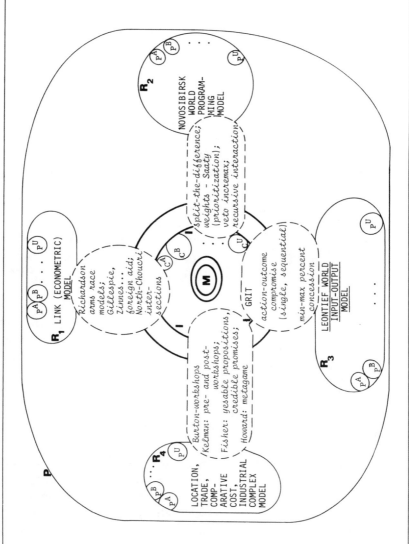

relating to the economic production subsystem P and its markets. The former behavioral equations would pertain to propensities (tendencies) arising in the I box. Their inclusion would act to modify at least some of the economic magnitudes currently projected via behavioral equations in the R_1 box. These magnitudes might be investment, GNP, or consumption.

For example, one behavioral equation to be added might be as follows:

$$\Delta ME^J(t) = \alpha \, (ME^L(t-1) - ME^J(t-1))^\gamma + \beta ME^J(t-1) + \dots$$

where ME^J and ME^L are military expenditures in countries J and L, respectively. Thus we have the change $\Delta ME^J(t)$ in J's military expenditures at any point of time related via parameters α, β (representing propensities, reaction tendencies, fatigue, etc.) to (1) the difference in military expenditures in L and J in the previous period qualified by some factor γ, (2) the level of J's military expenditure in the previous period, and (3) one or more other factors.

In Figure 15–8 we suggest that findings on Richardson arms race models (Lambelet et al. 1979) and the approaches of Gillespie et al. (1975) and Choucri and North (1975) might be employed to establish effective linkage.

A third significant connection in Figure 15–8 links the I box to still a third R box, namely the R_2 box representing the Novosibirsk World Programming Model. Here, as has been briefly discussed on page 516, we have a basic linear programming model. Into this model we can feed key inputs from the I box. Such could relate to the objective function, in particular, the form of the function, the objectives to be included, the weights to be attached to each objective, and other elements discussed on pages 248–263. Agreement on these issues might be achieved employing a split-the-difference procedure, weights derived via a Saaty procedure to determine priorities, a veto-incremax approach, or some recursive interaction process. Or agreement might be reached from the use of a fused procedure discussed on pages 404–405. Still more, the world programming model might be extended to embody dynamic input-output relations in an Isard-Moore model (see Isard et al. 1960:716–17).

Still another linkage from the I box to the fourth R box, namely the R_4 box, is possible using the Fisher-Burton-Kelman qualitative approaches to conflict management, either singly or in combination, and perhaps fused with one or more quantitative approaches (see Chapters 10 and 11). Suppose we take seriously the proposal for a New Economic Order, wherein the developing nations seek mutually to stimulate each other's economic development through an ambitious program of joint cooperative actions aimed at significantly increased trade among themselves. They then would need to identify several industrial complexes to be constructed according to a realistic time schedule and consistent with the expected availability over time of investment capital (from household savings, highly industrialized countries, etc.). The several complexes identified through differential cost and revenue analysis might be steel, petrochemicals, and university research and development activities. However, since the realization of major scale economies would require one and only one location for each of these three complexes among the several (generally more than three) nations participating, a first question would be: Which nation gets which complex (if any)? A second question would be: Which complex is first developed, which second, and which third? To make acceptable a plan that might call for a petrochemical complex to be the first constructed say in nation J, credible promises (a la Fisher) to other nations would need to be made. These promises would differ among the nations and would need to be related to the investment capital each nation provides for the petrochemicals complex as well as being related to the nature of investment (if any) planned at a later time to take place in each nation.

As indicated in Figure 15-8, other conflict management procedures—the Howard metagame approach, for instance—might also be employed to effect the connection between the I box and this particular R box.

Finally, note that the models in the four boxes, R_1, R_2, R_3, and R_4 in Figure 15-8 can be effectively fused from a conceptual standpoint—and already there are indications that such fusion can be made operational. It thus follows that all the conflict management approaches and connections found applicable for any one of the models in these four boxes may be found applicable to a fused model for the R box—as well as other procedures, singly and in combination, which have been discussed in Chapters 3 through 11. In this manner a more flexible set of more comprehensive linkages for operational use can be achieved.

15.5 CONCLUDING REMARKS

We now wish to bring to a close the discussion of the field of Peace Science. We have defined it as a field that covers a *new combination* of (1) subject matter and (2) associated concepts, theories, techniques, and tools. The core compromises the interconnections (linkages) of three basic components of any social system: (1) the information component M, (2) the cognitive interaction component I, and (3) the real interaction component R—the MIR array. This core, which we have represented on Figure 14-9 as a vertical array of boxes and their linkages, can be claimed to be unique and in fact orthogonal to the focuses of most if not all other social sciences. The cores of these other social sciences tend to embrace subjects and materials that are contained in one of the horizontal arrays of boxes and linkages in Figure 14-9. We do not wish to imply that the focus of Peace Science never goes beyond the subjects covered in the MIR array. It does jut out here and there, at times significantly. Nor do we wish to imply that the cores of other social sciences do not vertically jut out, at times very significantly. They all do.

Much remains to be developed in the field of Peace Science. As yet we have not detailed the materials that are and should be contained in the M box. That detailing awaits future work by scholars in the field. Undoubtedly, however, the information component will be found to be relatively less developed than other components we have discussed. Additionally, we need to specify more concretely the critical interconnections (linkages) between the M and I components. This area, too, needs to be researched in depth, both from a conceptual and an operational standpoint.

Turning to the I box, we find that much further study is required. In particular, the findings in the several cognitive sciences regarding group "scripts," "schema," and "packages" need to be incorporated to account for group behavior and the constraints the group places on individual behavior. Likewise, the notion of history as data must be more fully developed and eventually embodied in models.

Moreover, much conceptual thinking is still required on the linkages of the I and R components. The ideas that stem from Pattee's thinking represent just one possible beginning. Many more need to be explored and vigorously scrutinized for validity. Fortunately, however, with regard to *operational* linkage, we can definitely point to a solid basis for a beginning. We can effectively fuse world economic (production-type) models with a number of the quantitative and qualitative conflict management procedures discussed in Chapters 3 through 12.

Hence, we can conclude that the field of Peace Science is more than a haphazard assemblage of different concepts, ideas, theories, tools, and techniques concerned with conflict analysis, management, and resolution. It has structure and a clear operational axis that has been not only identified but is being implemented. Yet at the same time the field should be viewed as extremely variable and flexible. In particular, definition should be left open because, as stated earlier, it is highly desirable for it to incorporate *at its very core and beginning stages* of development the kind of dynamics that would be contained in an evolutionary (history) box (and which for lack of dimensions we have indicated by the E arrow in Figure 14–9). As already noted, dynamic elements should be embedded at the start in most topics and processes associated with them which are discussed in the M, I, and R boxes. This should be done in more fundamental ways than the anemic dynamics that dynamical systems analysis allows. If such were to be accomplished, then it could be said that Peace Science is orthogonal to other social sciences in still another dimension—namely, in its treatment of dynamics. Even more important, if such were accomplished, it would represent a qualitative jump in the ability of social sciences to understand and replicate reality as well as project it.

NOTES

1. The Choucri-North study is a natural outgrowth of earlier studies by North and his colleagues, for example, North, Brody, and Holsti (1964). In this study, the conflict model is of a stimulus response (S-r-s-R) variety.

2. While the decisionmaking structure may be hierarchical, real production takes place at locations in physical space and real interactions occur between such locations. In the pure physical sense, there is no hierarchical structure. However, the delineation of regions, subregions, and subsubregions in physical space (and thus social accounting by regions, subregions, etc.) should for an efficient system conform to the hierarchical pattern of nodes in the decisionmaking structure. Specifically, the slicing of the P (production) box of the overall system S into smaller production boxes must give meaning to the pattern of commands and orders handed down by the nodes of highest order, the nodes of next-to-highest order, and so forth.

3. See Isard and Liossatos (1979:13) for a distinction between macro-
    and microtime.

4. The new state of the system cannot be considered meaningful if a ran-
    dom disturbance gives rise to explosive reactions. The system may,
    however, be considered meaningful, at least to some extent, if the re-
    sulting instability is not excessive.

5. In this quote, the words in italics "equally attractive state" replaces
    his "even more attractive," which we believe is more appropriate in
    the context of our discussion.

6. For a full presentation of these ideas see Kaniss (1978). Also see Bon-
    ner in Pattee (1973), Arbib (1972), Levins in Pattee (1973), Schum-
    peter (1950), and Usher (1954).

7. At the production level, too, informational processes occur but they
    are of still less general significance. What goes on there is largely
    physical. Physical inputs like labor, ore, fuel, and interface inputs
    (such as particulate and SO_2 concentrations) determine outputs that are
    largely physical; and trade by and large involves the movement of
    physical goods. Yet, even here we cannot in our analysis avoid the
    order or command as information flows. Nor can we avoid the evalua-
    tion aspect based on information flows on outcomes and involving the
    calculation of GNP, profits, and other magnitudes to indicate how well
    the production subsystem is doing. Such evaluation is part of a con-
    stant testing by those in control—the successful. It corresponds to
    "development" testing in the "small" by the "haves." So it is a key in-
    formational process.

8. See Isard and Liossatos (1979:chap. 1) for a discussion of this con-
    cept of time.

9. See also Isard and Anselin (1982) and Isard and C. Smith (1982),
    from which this paper drew many of its ideas. Further relevant discus-
    sion is in Isard and C. Smith (1982a:45–64).

REFERENCES

Ackoff, R.L. 1962. *Scientific Method: Optimizing Applied Research Decision.* New York: Wiley.

Alexander, J.M. 1976. "A Study of Conflict in Northern Ireland: An Application of Metagame Theory." *Journal of Peace Science* 2, no. 1:113–34.

Allen, P.M. 1981. "Self-Organization in Human Systems." In *Essays in Societal Systems Dynamics and Transportation: Report of the Third Annual Workshop in Urban and Regional Systems Analysis,* edited by D. Kahn. Washington, D.C.: U.S. Dept. of Transportation, Research and Special Programs Administration.

Anselin, L. and W. Isard. 1979. "On Alonso's General Theory of Movement." *Man, Environment, Space and Time* 1, no. 1:52–63.

Arbib, M. 1972. *The Metaphorical Brain.* New York: Wiley.

Arrow, K. 1963. *Social Choice and Individual Values.* New York: Wiley.

Arrow, K.J., and M. Kurz. 1970. *Public Investment, the Rate of Return, and Optimal Fiscal Policy.* Baltimore, Md.: Johns Hopkins Press.

Axelrod, R., ed. 1976. *Structure of Decision: The Cognitive Maps of Political Elites.* Princeton, N.J.: Princeton University Press.

Baird, J.C., and E. Noma. 1978. *Fundamentals of Scaling and Psychophysics.* New York: Wiley.

Balinski, M.L., and H.P. Young. 1974. "A New Method for Congressional Apportionment." In *Proceedings of the National Academy of Science of the USA* 71:4602–6.

Balinski, M.L., and H.P. Young. 1975a. "The Quota Method of Apportionment." *The American Mathematical Monthly* 82:701–30.

577

Balinski, M.L., and H.P. Young. 1975b. "On Huntington Methods of Apportionment." *SIAM Journal of Applied Mathematics C* 33:701–30.

Balinski, M.L., and H.P. Young. 1977. "Apportionment Schemes and the Quota Method." *American Mathematical Monthly* 84:450–55.

Balinski, M.L., and H.P. Young. 1979. "Quotatone Apportionment Methods." *Mathematics of Operations Research* 4:31–48.

Beaumont J.; M. Clarke; P. Keys; H. Williams; and A. Wilson. 1981. "The Dynamical Analysis of Urban Systems: An Overview of Ongoing Work at Leeds." In *Essays in Societal Systems Dynamics and Transportation: Report of the Third Annual Workshop in Urban and Regional Systems Analysis*, edited by D. Kahn. Washington, D.C.: U.S. Dept. of Transportation Research and Special Programs Administration.

Bennett, J.P. 1981. "Data Stories." Paper presented at North American Conference of Peace Science Society (International), Philadelphia, Pa., November 9–11.

Bergson, A. 1976. "Social Choice and Welfare Economics under Representative Government." *Journal of Public Economics* 6:171–90.

Berry, B.L. 1967. *Geography of Market Centers and Retail Distribution* Englewood Cliffs, N.J.: Prentice Hall.

von Bertanlanffy, L. 1952. *The Problem of Life*. New York: Wiley.

Birkhoff, G. 1976. "House Monotone Apportionment Schemes." In *Proceedings of the National Academy of Sciences of the USA* 73: 684–86.

Bishop, R.L. 1960. "Duopoly: Collusion or Warfare." *The American Economic Review* 50, no. 5:932–61.

Bishop, R.L. 1963. "Game Theoretic Analysis of Bargaining." *Quarterly Journal of Economics* 77, no. 4:559–602.

Blair, P.D. 1979. *Multiobjective Regional Energy Planning*. Boston, Mass.: Martinus Nijhoff.

Bonner, J. 1973. "Hierarchical Control Programs in Biological Development." In *Hierarchy Theory: The Challenge of Complex Systems*, edited by H. Pattee, pp. 49–70. New York: Braziller.

Boulding, K.E. 1962. *Conflict and Defense*. New York: Harper and Row.

Boyce, D.E.; A. Fahri; and R. Weischedel. 1974. *Optimal Subset Selection: Multiple Regression, Interdependence and Optimal Network Algorithms*. Berlin: Springer-Verlag.

Bradley, S.P.; A.C. Hax; and T.L. Magnanti. 1977. *Applied Mathematical Programming*. Reading, Mass.: Addison-Wesley.

Brams, S. 1977. "Deception in 2x2 Games." *Journal of Peace Science* 2, no. 2:171–203.

Brams, S. 1980. *Biblical Games: Strategic Analysis of Stories in the Old Testament*. Cambridge, Mass.: MIT Press.

Brams, S., and D. Wittman. 1980. "Non-Myopic Equilibria." Paper presented at First International Congress of Art and Science, Cambridge, Mass., June 6–23.

Bronowski, J. 1970. "New Concepts in the Evolution of Complexity: Stratified Stability and Unbounded Plans." *Zygon* 5:18–35.

Burton, J.W. 1969. *Conflict and Communication: The Use of Controlled Communication in International Relations.* London, Macmillan.

Burton, J.W. 1972. "Resolution and Conflict." *International Studies Quarterly* 16, no. 1:5–30.

Burton, J.W. 1979. *Deviance, Terrorism and War.* New York: St. Martin's Press.

Butler, D. 1970. "Topics in the Theory of Fair Division." Unpublished Master's thesis, Cornell University.

Callen, H.B. 1960. *Thermodynamics.* New York: Wiley.

Choucri, N. 1973. "Applications of Econometric Analysis to Forecasting in International Relations." *Papers of the Peace Science Society (International)* 21:15–39.

Choucri, N., and R. North. 1975. *Nations in Conflict: National Growth and International Violence.* San Francisco: W.H. Freeman.

Choucri, N.; D. Ross; and D.L. Meadows. 1976. "Toward a Forecasting Model of Energy Politics: International Perspectives." *Journal of Peace Science* 2, no. 1:97–111.

Christaller, W. 1933. *Die zentralen Orte in Suddeutschland.* Translation by C. Baskin. 1966. *The Central Places of Southern Germany.* Englewood Cliffs, N.J.: Prentice Hall.

Cohen, S.P.; H.C. Kelman; F.D. Miller; and B.L. Smith. 1977. "Evolving Intergroup Techniques for Conflict Resolution: An Israeli-Palestinian Pilot Workshop." *Journal of Social Issues* 33, no. 1:165–88.

Cohon, J.L. 1978. *Multiobjective Programming and Planning.* New York: Academic Press.

Coleman, J.S. 1964. *Introduction to Mathematical Sociology.* New York: Free Press.

Coleman, J.S. 1979. "A Theory of Revolt within an Authority Structure." *Papers of the Peace Science Society (International)* 28:15–25.

Dahrendorf, R. 1959. *Class and Class Conflict in Industrial Society.* Stanford, Calif.: Stanford University Press.

Delft, A. van, and P. Nijkamp. 1977. *Multi-criteria Analysis and Regional Decision-Making.* The Hague: Martinus Nijhoff.

Deutsch, K.W. and I.R. Savage. 1960. "An Import-Export Model" *Econometrica* 28:551–72.

Domanski, R. 1981. "The Problem of Joint Description and Optimization of Transport and Urban Systems." Paper presented at the Fourth International Transport Conference, Tokyo, Japan, August 12–14.

Doob, L.W., ed. 1970. *Resolving Conflict in East Africa: The Fermeda Workshop.* New Haven, Conn.: Yale University Press.

Doob, L.W. 1974. "A Cyprus Workshop: An Exercise in Intervention Methodology." *The Journal of Social Psychology* 94:161–78.

Doob, L.W., and W.J. Foltz. 1973. "The Belfast Workshop: An Application of Group Techniques to a Destructive Conflict." *Journal of Conflict Resolution* 17:489–512.

Dubins, L.E. 1977. "Group Decision Devices." *American Mathematical Monthly* 84:350–56.

Dubins, L.E., and E.H. Spanier. 1961. "How to Cut a Cake Fairly." *American Mathematical Monthly* 68:1–17.

Englebrecht-Wiggans, R. 1977. "On the Fair and Efficient Allocation of Indivisible Commodities." *Technical Report*, no. 356. Cornell University: School of Operations Research and Industrial Engineering.

Farber, H.S. 1980. "An Analysis of Final Offer Arbitration." *The Journal of Conflict Resolution* 24, no. 4:683–705.

Fararo, T.J. 1973. *Mathematical Sociology.* New York: Wiley.

Fishburn, P.C. 1970. *Utility Theory for Decision Making.* New York: Wiley.

Fisher, R. 1964. "Fractionating Conflict." In *International Conflict and Behavioural Science*, edited by R. Fisher, pp. 91–109. New York: Basic Books.

Fisher, R. 1969a. "Effective Influence of Decisions in an International Setting." *Papers of the Peace Science Society (International)* 12:103–8.

Fisher, R. 1969b. *International Conflict for Beginners.* New York: Harper and Row.

Fisher, R. 1972. *Dear Israels, Dear Arabs: A Working Approach to Peace.* New York: Harper and Row.

Fisher, R. 1978. *Points of Choice.* New York: Oxford University Press.

Fisher, R. 1979. "Coping with International Conflict." Unpublished Manuscript.

Fisher, R., and W. Ury. 1978. *International Mediation: A Working Guide.* New York: International Peace Academy.

Fisher, R., and W. Ury. 1981. *Getting to Yes.* Boston, Mass.: Houghton Mifflin.

Gale, S., and B. Gale. 1977. "Language and Conflict: Towards a Semiotic Theory of Harmonia Mundi." *Journal of Peace Science* 2, no. 2:215–30.

Gamson, A. 1961a. "A Theory of Coalition Formation." *American Sociological Review* 26, no. 3:373–82.

Gamson, A. 1961b. "An Experimental Test of a Theory of Coalition Formation." *American Sociological Review* 26, no. 4:565–73.

Gamson, A. 1962. "Coalition Formation at Presidential Nominating Convention." *The American Journal of Sociology* 68, no. 2:157–71.

Gamson, A. 1964. "Experimental Studies on Coalition Formation." *Advances in Experimental Social Psychology*, vol. I: 81–110. New York: Academic Press.

Gamson, A. 1982. "The Political Culture of Arab-Israeli Conflict." *Conflict Management and Peace Science* 5, no. 2:79–93.

Gentile, R. 1981. "Stages in Negotiation—A Conceptual Structure and Some Empirical Results from SALT 1." Unpublished Ph.D. dissertation, University of Pennsylvania.

Gillespie, J.V.; D.A. Zinnes; and G.S. Tahim. 1975. "Foreign Military Assistance and the Armaments Race: A Differential Game Model with Control." *Papers of the Peace Science Society (International)* 25:35–51.

Glugiewicz, E., and W. Isard. In press. "Conflict Analysis in Regional Science." *Regional Science and Economic Development* 1, no. 1.

Gould, S.J. 1977. *Ontogeny and Phylogeny*. Cambridge, Mass.: Harvard University Press.

Granberg, A.G., and Rubinshtein. 1979. "Some Lines of Development of the United Nations Global Input Output Model." Novosibirsk: Institute of Economics and Organization of Industrial Production, Siberian Branch of the U.S.S.R. Academy of Sciences.

Granberg, D. 1980. "Structural Conditions which make GRIT a Feasible and Effective Strategy for Peace." Paper presented at the First International Congress of Art and Science, Cambridge, Mass., June 6–23.

Guetzkow, H.S. 1963. *Simulation in International Relations*. Englewood Cliffs, N.J.: Prentice Hall.

Haefele, W. 1981. *Energy in a Finite World: A Global Systems Analysis*. Cambridge, Mass.: Ballinger Publishing Company.

Haimes, Y.Y.; W.A. Hall; and H.T. Freedman. 1975. *Multiple Objective Optimization in Water Resources Systems*. Amsterdam: Elsevier.

Hill, M., and C. Lomovasky. 1980. "A Minimal Requirement Approach to Plan Evaluation in Participatory Planning." Paper presented at the First International Congress of Art and Science, Cambridge, Mass., June 6–23.

Houthakker, H.S., and M. Kennedy. 1978. "Long-range Energy Perspectives." In *Energy Options and Conservation*, edited by R.E. Mallakh and D.E. Mallakh. Boulder, Colo.: International Research Center for Energy and Economic Development.

Howard, N. 1968. "Metagame Analysis of Vietnam Policy." *Papers of the Peace Science Society (International)* 10:126–42.

Howard, N. 1971. *Paradoxes of Rationality: Theory of Metagames and Political Behaviour*. Cambridge, Mass.: MIT Press.

Howard, N. 1971a. "The Arab-Israeli Conflict: A Metagame Analysis." *Papers of the Peace Science Society (International)* 19:35–60.

Howard, N. 1973. "A Computer System for Foreign Policy Decision-Making." *Journal of Peace Science* 1, no. 1:61–68.

Howard, N. 1975. "Examples of a Dynamic Theory of Games." *Papers of the Peace Science Society (International)* 24:1–28.

Huxley, J. 1969. "Introduction." In *The Phenomenon of Man* by P. Teilard de Chardin, pp. 11–28. New York: Harper and Row.

Hwang, C.L., and A.S.M. Masud. 1979. *Multi-objective Decision-Making-Methods and Applications.* Berlin: Springer-Verlag.

Hwang, C.L., and K. Yoon. 1981. *Multiple Attribute Decision Making.* Berlin: Springer-Verlag.

Intriligator, M.D. 1971. *Mathematical Optimization and Economic Theory.* Englewood Cliffs, N.J.: Prentice Hall.

Isard, W. 1948. "Some Locational Factors in the Iron and Steel Industry Since the Early Nineteenth Century." *Journal of Political Economy* 56:203–17.

Isard, W.; D.F. Bramhall; G.A.P. Carrothers; J.H. Cumberland; L.N. Moses; D.O. Price; and E.W. Schooler. *Methods of Regional Analysis: An Introduction to Regional Science.* Cambridge, Mass.: MIT Press.

Isard, W. 1967. "Location Games: With Applications to Classic Location Problems." *Papers of the Regional Science Association* 19:45–80.

Isard, W. 1968. "Veto-Incremax Procedure: Potential for Vietnam Conflict Resolution." *Papers of the Peace Science Society (International)* 10:148–62.

Isard, W.; K.E. Bassett; C.L. Choguill; J.G. Furtado; R.M. Izumita; J. Kissen; R.H. Seyfarth; and R. Tatlock. 1972. *Economic-Ecologic Analysis for Regional Development.* New York: Free Press.

Isard, W. 1975. *Introduction to Regional Science.* Englewood Cliffs, N.J.: Prentice Hall.

Isard, W. 1977. "Location Theory, Agglomeration and the Pattern of World Trade." In *The International Allocation of Economic Activity,* edited by B. Ohlin, pp. 159–77. London, Macmillan.

Isard, W. 1979. "Desirable Properties of Social Decision Procedures and Social Rationality." Paper presented at Regional Science Conference, Karlsruhe, West Germany, February 2–3.

Isard, W. 1979. "A Definition of Peace Science, the Queen of the Social Sciences, Part I." *Journal of Peace Science* 4, no. 1:1–47.

Isard, W. 1980. "A Definition of Peace Science, the Queen of the Social Sciences, Part II." *Journal of Peace Science* 4, no. 2:97–132.

Isard, W., and L. Anselin. 1982. "Integration of Multi-Regional Models for Policy Analysis." *Environment and Planning A* 14:359–76.

Isard, W., and W.M. Capron. 1949. "The Future Locational Pattern of Iron and Steel Production in the United States." *Journal of Political Economy* 57:118–33.

Isard, W., and J.N. Cumberland. 1950. "New England as a Possible Location for an Integrated Iron and Steel Works." *Economic Geography* 26:245-59.

Isard, W., and P. Kaniss. 1976. "A Note on the Joint Use of GRIT and Veto-Incremax Procedures." In *Frontiers in Social Thought*, edited by M. Pfaff, pp. 307-18. Amsterdam: North Holland.

Isard, W., and P. Kaniss. 1978. "Structure, Control and Language Hierarchies and World Organization." *Journal of Peace Science* 3, no. 1:63-91.

Isard, W., and R.E. Kuenne. 1953. "The Impact of Steel upon the Greater New York-Philadelphia Industrial Region: A Study in Agglomeration Projection." *The Review of Economics and Statistics* 35:289-301.

Isard, W., and P. Liossatos. 1978. "A Formal Model of Big Step Disarmament and Domino Effects." *Journal of Peace Science* 3, no. 2:131-46.

Isard, W., and P. Liossatos. 1978a. "A Simplistic Multiple Growth Pole Model." *Papers of the Regional Science Association* 41:7-13.

Isard, W., and P. Liossatos. 1979. *Spatial Dynamics and Optimal Space-time Development*. New York: North Holland.

Isard, W., and C. Smith. 1980. "Elementary Locational Analysis in Policy Space." *Papers of the Regional Science Association* 45:17-44.

Isard, W., and C. Smith. 1980a. "Matching Conflict Situations and Conflict Management Procedures." *Conflict Management and Peace Science* 5, no. 1:1-25.

Isard, W., and C. Smith. 1981. "The World System: Its Structure, Behavior and Analysis—Summary Article I, Towards an Integration of General Approaches." *Man, Environment, Space and Time* 1, no. 2:21-58.

Isard, W., and C. Smith. 1982. "Incorporation of Conflict and Policy Analysis in an Integrated Multiregion Model." Forthcoming in a book on the Umea conference, June 1981.

Isard, W., and C. Smith. 1982a. "The World System: Summary Article II Toward an Integration of Partial, Sectoral Analyses." *Man, Environment, Space and Time* 2, no. 1:42-82.

Isard, W., and C. Smith. 1982b. "The World System: Summary Article III Toward an Integration of Approaches to Conflict Analysis and Resolution." *Man, Environment, Space and Time* 2, no. 1:83-119.

Isard, W., and C. Smith. 1982c. "Linked Integrated Multiregion Models at the International Level." *Papers of the Regional Science Association* 50.

Isard, W., and C. Smith, 1982d. "Toward a More Scientific Approach to Conflict Management in Transportation and Other Areas." Forthcoming in a book on the Tokyo, August 1981 conference.

Isard W., and C. Smith. 1982e. "Managing Conflicts among Border and Other Impacted Regions." Forthcoming in a book on the Guanajuato, July 1981 conference.

Isard, W., and C. Smith. 1982f. "A Dynamical Systems Approach to Learning Processes in Conflict Mediation and Interaction." In *International and Regional Conflict,* edited by W. Isard and Y.M. Nagao, Cambridge, Mass.: Ballinger.

Isard, W., and T. Smith. 1966. "On the Resolution of Conflicts among Regions of a System." *Papers of the Regional Science Association* 17:19–46.

Isard, W., and T. Smith. 1967. "Coalition Location Games: Paper 3." *Papers of the Regional Science Association* 20:95–107.

Isard, W., and T. Smith. 1967a. "On Social Decision Procedures for Conflict Situations." *Papers of the Peace Science Society (International)* 8:1–29.

Isard, W.; T. Smith; P. Isard; T.H. Tung; and M. Dacey. 1969. *General Theory: Social, Political, Economic and Regional.* Cambridge, Mass.: MIT Press.

Isard, W., and T. Smith. 1970. "On Political Conflict Resolution in Policy Spaces." *Papers of the Peace Science Society (International)* 15:129–145.

Isard, W., and T. Smith. 1971. "The Major Power Confrontation in the Middle East: Some Analysis of Short-Run, Middle-Run, and Long-Run Considerations." *Papers of the Peace Science Society (International)* 15:31–50.

Isard, W.; F. Cesario; and T. Reiner. 1975. *Marginal Pollution Analysis for Long Range Forecasts.* Regional Science Dissertation and Monograph Series, no. 4. Ithaca, New York: Program in Urban and Regional Studies, Cornell University.

Isard, W.; T. Reiner; and R. van Zele. 1977. *Socio-economic Analysis of Energy Facilities, with Particular Reference to Hartsville (Tennessee) Impact Area.* Report for the Regional and Urban Studies Section, Oak Ridge National Laboratory, Oak Ridge, Tenn.

Jantsch, E. 1975. *Design for Evolution.* New York: Braziller.

Kahn, D. 1981. *Essays in Societal Systems Dynamics and Transportation: Report of the Third Annual Workshop in Urban and Regional Systems Analysis.* Report No. DOT-TSC-RSPA-81-3. Washington, D.C.: U.S. Dept. of Transportation, Research and Special Programs Administration.

Kaniss, P. 1978. *Evolutionary Change in Hierarchical Systems: A General Theory.* Regional Science Dissertation and Monograph Series, no. 9. Ithaca, New York: Program on Urban and Regional Studies, Cornell University.

Keeney, R., and H. Raiffa. 1976. *Decisions with Multiple Objectives: Preferences and Value Tradeoffs.* New York: Wiley.

Kelman, H.C. 1972. "The Problem Solving Workshop in Conflict Resolution." In *Communication and International Conflict,* edited by R.L. Merritt, pp. 168–204. Urbana: University of Illinois Press.

Kelman, H.C. 1978. "Israelis and Palestinians: Psychological Prerequisites for Mutual Acceptance." *International Security* 3:162–86.

Kelman, H.C. 1979. "An International Approach to Conflict Resolution and its Application to Israeli-Palestinian Relations." *International Interactions* 6, no. 2:99–122.

Kelman, H.C., and S.P. Cohen. 1976. "The Problem Solving Workshop: A Social Psychological Contribution to the Resolution of International Conflicts." *Journal of Peace Research* 13:79–90.

Klaassen, L.H.; S. Wagenaar; and A. van der Weg. 1972. "Measuring Psychological Distance between the Flemings and Walloons." *Papers of the Regional Science Association* 29:45–62.

Klein, L.R. 1977. *Project LINK.* Athens: Center for Planning and Economic Research.

Kuhn, A. 1963. *The Study of Society: A Unified Approach.* Homewood, Ill.: Richard D. Irwin and Dorsey Press.

Kuhn, H.W. 1967. "On Games of Fair Division." In *Essays in Mathematical Economics: In Honour of Oskar Morgenstern,* edited by M. Shubik, pp. 29–37. Princeton, N.J.: Princeton University Press.

Lambelet, J.; U. Luterbacher; and P. Allan. 1979. "Dynamics of Arms Races: Mutual Stimulation vs. Self-Stimulation." *Journal of Peace Science* 4, no. 1, 49–66.

Lasswell, H.D., and A. Kaplan. 1950. *Power and Society, A Framework for Political Inquiry.* New Haven, Conn.: Yale University Press.

Laszlo, E. 1972. *Introduction to Systems Philosophy.* New York: Gordon and Breach.

Layzer, D. 1975. "Genetic Variability and Biological Innovation." Unpublished Manuscript, Harvard University.

Layzer, D. 1981. "Is Man a Peaceable Animal?" *Man, Environment, Space and Time* 1, no. 2:88–96.

Leibenstein, H., and R. Gentile. 1979. "Microeconomics, X-efficiency Theory and Policy." *Man, Environment, Space and Time* 1, no. 1:1–26.

Levins, R. 1973. "The Limits of Complexity." In *Hierarchy Theory: The Challenge of Complex Systems,* edited by H. Pattee, pp. 109–27. New York: Braziller.

Leontief, W.W. 1980. "The Future of the World Economy." *Scientific American* 243, no. 3:207–30.

Leontief, W.W., et al. 1977. *The Future of the World Economy, A United Nations Study.* New York: Oxford University Press.

Lichfield, N.; P. Kettle; and M. Whitbread. 1975. *Evaluation in the Planning Process*. Oxford: Pergamon Press.

Lindskold, S. 1980. "GRIT: Evidence, Implications for Trust, and Prospects for Use." Paper presented at the First International Congress of Art and Science, Cambridge, Mass., June 6–23.

Lindskold, S., and M.G. Collins. 1978. "Inducing Cooperation by Groups and Individuals: Applying Osgood's GRIT strategy." *Journal of Conflict Resolution* 22:679–90.

Linstone, H.A., and M. Turoff, eds. 1975. *The Delphi Method: Techniques and Applications*. London: Addison-Wesley.

Little, I.M.D. 1952. "Social Choice and Individual Values." *Journal of Public Economy* 60:422–32.

Lösch A. 1940. *Die raumliche Ordnung der Wirtschaft*. Translation by Woglom, W.H., and G. Stopler. 1954. *The Economics of Location* New Haven, Conn.: Yale University Press.

Loucks, D. 1977. "An Application of Interactive Multiobjective Water Resources Planning." *Interfaces* 8:70.

Lucas, W.F. 1978. "The Apportionment Problem." *Technical Report*, No. 388. Cornell University: School of Operations Research and Industrial Engineering.

Lucas, W.F., ed. 1982. *Lectures on Game Theory*. American Mathematical Society Monograph.

Luce, R.D., and H. Raiffa. 1957. *Games and Decisions*. New York: Wiley.

March, J.G., and H.A. Simon. 1958. *Organizations*. New York: Wiley.

Marschak, J., and R. Radner. 1971. *Economic Theory of Teams*. New Haven, Conn.: Yale University Press.

Masters, R.D. 1975. "Politics as a Biological Phenomenon." *Social Science Information* 14, no. 2:7–63.

Mayr, E., 1963. *Animal Species and Evolution*. Cambridge, Mass.: Harvard University Press.

McClelland, D.C. 1961. *The Achieving Society*. Princeton, N.J.: Van Nostrand.

Nash, J.F. 1953. "Two-person Co-operative Games." *Econometrica* 21:128–40.

Needham, J. 1943. *Time: The Refreshing River*. New York: Macmillan.

von Neumann, J., and O. Morgenstern. 1953. *Theory of Games and Economic Behaviour*. Princeton, N.J.: Princeton University Press.

Nijkamp, P. 1977. *Theory and Application of Environmental Economics*. Amsterdam: North Holland.

Nijkamp, P.; P. Rietveld, J. Spronk; W. van Veenendaal; and H. Voogd. 1979. *Multi-dimensional Spatial Data and Decision Analysis*. New York: Wiley.

Nisbett, R., and L. Ross. 1980. *Human Inference: Strategies and Shortcomings of Social Judgement*. Englewood Cliffs, N.J.: Prentice Hall.

North, R.; R. Brody; and O. Holsti. 1964. "Some Emperical Data on Conflict Spiral." *Papers of the Peace Science Society (International)* 1:1–14.

Osgood, C.E. 1966. *Perspectives in Foreign Policy*. Palo Alto, Calif.: Pacific Books.

Osgood, C.E. 1979. "GRIT for MBFR: A Proposal for Unfreezing Force-Level Postures in Europe." *Peace Research Reviews* 8, no. 2:77–92.

Paelinck, J.H.P. 1976. "Qualitative Multiple-criteria Analysis, Environmental Protection, and Multiregional Development." *Papers of the Regional Science Association* 36:59–74.

Parsons T., et al. 1961. *Theories of Society* vols. I and II. Glencoe, Ill.: Free Press.

Pattee, H. ed. 1973. *Hierarchy Theory: The Challenge of Complex Systems*. New York: Braziller.

Pattee, H. 1977. "Dynamic and Linguistic Modes of Complex Systems." *International Journal of General Systems* 3:259–66.

Pattee, H. 1978a. "The Complementarity Principle and the Origin of Macromolecular Information." *Biosystems* 11:217–26.

Pattee, H. 1979a. "The Complementarity Principle in Biological and Social Structures." *Journal of Social and Biological Structures* 1:191–200.

Pattee, H. 1979b. "Complementarity Versus Reduction as Explanation of Biological Complexity." *American Journal of Physiology* 236:no. 5: R241–46.

Philbrick, A.K. 1973. "Present and Future Spatial Structure of International Organization." *Papers of the Peace Science Society (International)* 21:65–72.

Philbrick, A.K. 1980. "Hierarchical Nodality in Geographical Time-Space." Paper presented at First International Congress of Art and Science, Cambridge, Mass., June 6–23.

Philbrick, A.K., and R.H. Brown. 1972. "Cosmos and International Hierarchies of Function." *Papers of the Peace Science Society (International)* 19:61–90.

Pill, J. 1971. "The Delphi Method: Substance, Context, A Critique and Annotated Bibliography." *Socio-Economic Planning Sciences* 5:57–71.

Prigogine, I. 1967. *Introduction to Thermodynamics of Irreversible Processes.* New York: Wiley, Interscience.

Rapoport, A., ed. 1974. *Game Theory as a Theory of Conflict Resolution*. Ann Arbor, Mich.: University of Michigan Press.

Rapoport, A. 1967. *Fights, Games and Debates*. Ann Arbor, Mich.: University of Michigan Press.

Rapoport, A., and A.M. Chammah. 1965. *Prisoner's Dilemma: A Study in Conflict and Cooperation*. Ann Arbor, Mich.: University of Michigan Press.

Rawls, J. 1971. *Theory of Justice*. Cambridge, Mass.: Harvard University Press.

Reinhold, R. 1980. "Science Unit Revises Study on Radiation's Cancer Risk." *New York Times*, 30 July:A12.

Rensch, B. 1960. *Evolution above the Species Level*. New York: Columbia University Press.

Rietveld, P. 1980. *Multi-Objective Decision Methods and Regional Planning*. Amsterdam: North Holland.

Rosen, R. 1970. *Dynamical System Theory in Biology: Stability Theory and its Applications*. New York: Wiley.

Saaty, T.L. 1979. "The U.S.-OPEC Energy Conflict—The Payoff Matrix by the Analytic Hierarchy Process." *International Journal of Game Theory* 8, no. 4:225–34.

Saaty, T.L. 1981. *Analytic Hierarchy Process: Planning, Priority Setting, Resource Allocation*. New York: McGraw Hill.

Saaty, T.L., and J.M. Alexander. 1977. "The Forward and Backward Processes of Conflict Analysis." *Behavioral Science* 22:87–98.

Saaty, T.L., and J.M. Alexander. 1977a. "Stability Analysis of the Forward-Backward Process: Northern Ireland Case Study." *Behavioral Science* 22:375–82.

Saaty, T.L., and M.W. Khouja. 1976. "A Measure of World Influence." *Journal of Peace Science* 2, no. 1:31–48.

Sackmann, H. 1975. *Delphi Critique: Expert Opinion, Forecasting and Group Process*. Lexington, Mass.: Lexington Books.

Samuelson, P.A. 1965. *Foundations of Economic Analysis*. New York: Atheneum.

Schelling, T.C. 1963. *The Strategy of Conflict*. New York: Oxford University Press.

Scholter, A., and G. Schwödiauer. 1980. "Economics and the Theory of Games: A Survey." *Journal of Economic Literature* 18:479–527.

Schumpeter, J. 1934. *The Theory of Economic Development*. Cambridge, Mass.: Harvard University Press.

Sen, A.K. 1970. *Collective Choice and Social Welfare*. London: Holden-Day.

Shapely, L.S. 1950. "A Value for N-Person Games." In *Contributions to the Theory of Games II, Annals of Mathematical Studies, 24*, edited by H.W. Kuhn and A.W. Tucker, pp. 307–17. Princeton, N.J.: Princeton University Press.

Simon, H.A. 1955. "A Behavioral Model of Rational Choice." *Quarterly Journal of Economics* 69, no. 1:99–114.

Simon, H.A. 1957. *Models of Man*. New York: Wiley.

Simon, H. 1973. "The Organization of Complex Systems." In *Hierarchy Theory: The Challenge of Complex Systems*, edited by H. Pattee, pp. 1–27. New York: Braziller.

Singer, E. 1962. "Extension of the Classical Rule of Divide and Choose." *Southern Economic Journal* 28:391–94.

Skutsch, M., and J.L. Schofer. 1973. "Goals-Delphi for Urban Planning: Concepts in Their Design." *Socio-Economic Planning Sciences* 7:305–13.

Sorokin, P. 1962. *Social and Cultural Dynamics*. New York: American Book Company.

Starobin, L. 1976. "Our Changing Evolution: Strategies for 1980." Unpublished Ph.D. dissertation, University of Pennsylvania.

Starr, M.K., and M. Zeleny. eds. 1977. *Multiple Criteria Decision Making*. New York: North Holland.

Steinhaus, H. 1948. "The Problem of Fair Division." *Econometrica* 16:101–4.

Stern, J.L.; C.M. Rehemus; J.J. Loewenberg; H. Kasper; and B.D. Dennis. 1975. *Final Offer Arbitration*. Lexington, Mass.: Heath.

Tarbell, D.S., and T.L. Saaty. 1980. "The Conflict in South Africa: Directed or Chaotic." *Journal of Peace Science* 4, no. 2:151–68.

Teilhard de Chardin, P. 1969. *The Phenomenon of Man*. New York: Harper and Row.

Thom, R. 1974. *Structural Stability and Morphogenesis*. New York: Benjamin.

Turoff, M. 1970. "The Design of a Policy Delphi." *Technological Forecasting and Social Change* 2, no. 2:149–71.

Usher, P. 1964. *A History of Mechanical Invention*. New York: McGraw.

Varian, H. 1978. *Microeconomic Analysis*. New York: Norton.

Vickrey, W. 1961. "Counterspeculation, Auctions, and Competitive Sealed Tenders." *Journal of Finance* 16:8–37.

Vickrey, W. 1978. "Demand Revealing Procedures and International Disputes." *Papers of the Peace Science Society (International)* 28:97–104.

Waddington, C. 1961. *The Ethical Animal*. New York: Atheneum.

Walton, R.D. 1970. "A Problem Solving Workshop on Border Conflicts in East Africa." *Journal of Applied Behavioral Science* 6, no. 4:453–89.

Waelbroeck, J.L., ed. 1976. *The Models of Project LINK*. New York: North Holland.

Whyte, L.L. 1965. *Internal Factors in Evolution*. New York: Braziller.

Wilson, E.O. 1975. *Sociobiology: The New Synthesis*. Cambridge, Mass.: Harvard University Press.

Zeuthen, F. 1930. *Problems of Monopoly and Economic Welfare*. London: G. Routledge and Sons.

AUTHOR INDEX

591

SUBJECT INDEX

ABOUT THE AUTHORS

Walter Isard is professor of economics at Cornell University. He received his Ph.D in economics from Harvard University and has subsequently been awarded honorary doctorates from Poznan Academy of Economics (Poland), Erasmus University of Rotterdam (Netherlands), University of Karlsruhe (West Germany), Umea University (Sweden), and University of Illinois. Dr. Isard has been active in peace research for many years and was a founding member of the Peace Science Society (International). He has authored or co-authored numerous articles and books, including *Methods of Regional Analysis* (MIT Press, 1960), *General Theory: Social, Political, Economic and Regional* (MIT Press, 1969), and *Spatial Dynamics and Optimal Space-Time Development* (North Holland, 1979).

Christine Smith has just completed her Ph.D. studies at Cornell University. She received her earlier education at University of Queensland (Australia), and will return to take up a research position there. Over the past three years she has co-authored a number of articles with Dr. Isard.